Corporate Law

Christopher C. Nicholls
of the Ontario Bar

Purdy Crawford Chair in Business Law
Faculty of Law
Dalhousie University

2005
EMOND MONTGOMERY PUBLICATIONS LIMITED
TORONTO, CANADA

Printed in Canada.

Edited, designed, and typeset by WordsWorth Communications, Toronto.

We acknowledge the financial support of the Government of Canada through the Book Publishing Industry Development Program (BPIDP) for our publishing activities.

Library and Archives Canada Cataloguing in Publication

Nicholls, Christopher C.
    Corporate law / Christopher C. Nicholls

ISBN 1-55239-119-1

    1. Corporation Law—Canada.   I. Title.

KE1389.N52 2004   346.71'066   C2004-907108-4
KF1415.ZA2N52 2004

Preface

Academic books about corporate law must tread a fine line. The business corporation has real work to do. It is no sterile laboratory specimen. And vibrant "living" institutions simply won't stand still long enough to be probed and tugged at by the curious.

Among practitioners there is considerable doubt about whether academic corporate law books are of much use. A volume of general "off-the-shelf" doctrinal research is welcome enough. That sort of book can come in rather handy—in the stressful moments before a hastily convened client meeting, say, or when in search of a convenient springboard for more detailed client research. But the further published sources begin to stray from case summaries and annotations, the less interest they hold for the busy corporate practitioner. Theoretical discussions about corporate law are, in particular, apt to strike no-nonsense solicitors as silly, unhelpful, and very far removed from the "real world" in which the business corporation was always intended to operate.

But there is a further consideration. Though it has become trite and even tiresome to say so, Canadian university law faculties must not only function as schools of professional training but must also strive to remain true to the broader educational and research goals of the modern university.

With all that in mind, let me suggest where this text might fit. Its primary purpose is to introduce the basic topics that are usually thought to comprise the law of business corporations in Canada. The approach is chiefly doctrinal, but it also touches here and there on the principal academic discussions that have been advanced about the subject. The goal is to provide the reader—a reader who is assumed to be new to the study of corporate law and has not much in the way of practical business experience—with some understanding about what the study of corporate law entails, and how the academic discussions of the topic relate to the doctrinal considerations.

While this text is meant to introduce readers to much of the traditional "learning" about corporate law, it is not, however, meant to leave the traditions unexamined or unchallenged. Albert Einstein is said to have described common sense as merely that collection of prejudices acquired by age 18. To the cynical, the common law may seem to comprise that collection of prejudices laid down in the minds of judges when they were in law school. If there is any truth to this observation, I hasten to add, it should be understood as a critical commentary on the nature of legal education and not on the nature of judges. To simplify and synthesize the massive collection of the learning that has gone before us requires a cunning use of shortcuts and summaries, consolidations, abstracts, and even summaries of summaries. Not all of the material available for this purpose is of uniform quality. One would hardly expect that it could be. Still, it should surprise no one that once small errors have crept into the body of received knowledge, they tend to stay. Over time, what were once shunned as pesky vermin become welcomed as familiar pets, and through reassuring repetition, we easily mistake for independent verification what is simply yet another echo.

"Conceptual conservatism" is the very grand name that is apparently used by behavioural economists to describe that unavoidable human tendency to hold fast to ideas first learned and still understood, and to stubbornly resist letting them go, even in the face of incontrovertible evidence disproving them.[1] It is a cognitive bias that goes some way to explaining a few of the peculiarities one observes in the development of the common law. Some celebrated "leading" cases become authorities for "rules" that were as likely to have originated in the minds of early textbook writers as in the words of the judges themselves. And once firmly associated with those propositions for which their styles of cause have become virtual synonyms, these seminal decisions are elevated to a stature approaching Holy Writ. From such intimidating heights these authorities remain almost immune from any serious critical revisiting.

This is not all to the bad. The fact that a well-worn legal principle cannot, perhaps, actually be teased from the text of an eponymous judicial decision is hardly fatal. A sensible idea might just as well be given one name as another. Or as a leading English jurist has so recently put it, a reasonable principle ought to be followed "whatever the legitimacy of its descent."[2] So, although I have mentioned a few interesting discrepancies of this sort in this book, I have tried not to waste much time crowing over them.

In any event, this volume is really only a sampler. It is intended to be introductory and as non-technical as possible. For a comprehensive recitation of all of the recent Canadian corporate law cases, statutory developments, and theoretical research, the reader must turn elsewhere. The aim of this book is to provide a detailed but still rough sketch, not a completed portrait.

A short word about the title of this book. A little over 10 years ago, Roberta Romano of the Yale Law School published a wonderful little collection of her papers in a volume entitled *The Genius of American Corporate Law*.[3] I toyed briefly with the idea of Canadianizing this title, and calling my book something like, *The Above-Average Intelligence of Canadian Corporate Law*. I was, however, led to understand that such a title would be regarded as too eccentric in some quarters, and yet, in others, to be suggestive (at least by Canadian standards) of rather dangerous elitism. So I have settled on the current title, which I am afraid is neither imaginative nor inspiring.

---

1   M. Nissani and D.M. Hoefler-Nissani, "Experimental Studies of Belief-Dependence of Observations and of Resistance to Conceptual Change" (1992), 9 *Cognition and Instruction* 97-111.

2   *Johnson v. Gore Wood & Co.*, [2001] 1 All ER 481, at 499 (HL) per Lord Bingham.

3   The "genius" identified by Professor Romano, by the way, was said to lie in the "federalist organization" of American corporate law—in other words, in the corporate charter competition that is said to have done so much to influence American corporate law, and to have placed the unlikely state of Delaware in the centre of the US public incorporation map.

It has become customary to thank people in the preface to a book like this. As one gets older, the list of one's intellectual debts grows longer, and so writing a preface becomes more difficult than ensuring compliance with the *Bulk Sales Act*.

This book was written over a period of about two years and in four cities: Halifax, Toronto, Cambridge (England), and Orillia (Ontario). I sketched out the basic framework for the book while teaching Business Associations at Dalhousie University, where I joined the faculty in 1997 after labouring in the corporate law trenches of Bay Street and Bermuda long enough to understand how important to our profession law schools are. The casebook from which I taught this course at Dalhousie was originally compiled by Les O'Brien and Dawn Russell. I have no doubt that much of the organization of this book was very importantly influenced by those materials. The fall of 2002, I spent in Toronto, teaching Business Organizations at the University of Toronto Law School, and working as a consultant in the Corporate Finance and Mergers and Acquisitions Practice Group at McCarthy Tétrault. This was a perfect marriage of academic and private practice influences. I am very grateful to Dean Ron Daniels at U of T as well as the many other members of the U of T faculty who were such wonderful hosts during my brief sojourn there, in particular Tony Duggan, Colleen Flood, Michael Trebilcock and, of course, Jacob Ziegel. At McCarthys, I was thankful for the support and help of many friends old and new, most especially Rene Sorrell, Michael Barrack, Brian Graves, Shea Small, David Tenant, and Bill Richardson.

The manuscript for this book was at last completed while I was on sabbatical leave during the 2003-4 academic year. I spent that year as a visitor at the University of Cambridge Faculty of Law's Centre for Corporate and Commercial Law. While at Cambridge, I benefited very much from the support of many remarkable faculty members. I should, in particular, mention here Brian Cheffins and Len Sealy, as well as Eilis Ferran, John Armour, and John Tiley. At Dalhousie, my thanks go to the "usual suspects": Dean Dawn Russell for her continued commitment to ensure that Dalhousie Law School's business law program is, and continues to be, second to none in Canada; and my business law colleagues at the law school, particularly Keith Evans and Michael Deturbide. I must also say a particular word of thanks to the staff of the Dalhousie Law Library. They are a treasured resource of Dalhousie Law School for whom I continue to be exceedingly grateful. Thanks, too, to Emond Montgomery, especially to Peggy Buchan, and to Paula Pike and Cindy Fujimoto of WordsWorth Communications for their excellent work on the manuscript.

To all of these people I offer my warmest and sincerest thanks. But my final words of appreciation I offer to my family: my children, Robbie, Diana, and Tori, and most especially my wife, Andrea. I am never sure I have fully and fairly expressed my gratitude to her for all that she makes possible for me. It is a great and humbling gift. And I am deeply grateful.

C.C.N.
Cambridge, England
April 2004

Table of Contents

Chapter One   Introduction to the Law and Legal Theory of Business Corporations

Chapter Two   The Mechanics of Incorporation

Chapter Four   Private Corporations

Chapter Five   Promoters' Cases and Pre-incorporation Contracts

Chapter Six Contracting Authority, Corporate Seals, and Ultra Vires

Chapter Seven Piercing or Lifting the Corporate Veil

Chapter Eight Criminal and Tortious Liability of Corporations

Chapter Nine   The Basic Structure of the Modern Business Corporation

Chapter Ten   "Best Interests of the Corporation": Shareholder Voice and Directors' Duties

Chapter Eleven   Interested Directors' Contracts, Corporate Opportunities, and Directors' and Officers' Personal Liability

Chapter Twelve   Financing the Corporation

Chapter Thirteen   Corporate Statutory Remedies: Derivative Actions and Oppression Remedies

Chapter Fourteen Corporate Statutory Remedies: Dissent and Appraisal Rights, Compliance Orders, "Winding-Up" Orders, and Investigation Orders

Frequently Cited Statutes and Regulations

Federal

Canada Business Corporations Act (CBCA), RSC 1985, c. C-44.

Canada Business Corporations Regulations, 2001 (SOR/2001-512).

Provincial

Business Corporations Act (BC), SBC 2002, c. 57.

Companies Act (NS), RSNS 1989, c.81.

Companies Act (PEI), RSPEI 1988, c. C-14.

The Corporations Act (Man.), CCSM, c. C225.

Corporations Act (NL), RSNL 1990, c. C-36.

Business Corporations Act (Alta.), RSA 2000, c. B-9.

The Business Corporations Act (Sask.), RSS 1978, c. B-10.

Business Corporations Act (Ont.), RSO 1990, c. B.16.

Business Corporations Act (NB), RSNB 1981, c. B-9.1.

Business Corporations Act (NWT), SNWT 1996, c. 19.

International

Companies Act, 1985 (UK).

CHAPTER ONE

Introduction to the Law and Legal Theory of Business Corporations

CORPORATE LAW

"Corporation law is a pretty pedestrian thing." So declared the Dickerson committee in its seminal 1971 review of Canadian corporate law.[1] Once a subject has been declared "pedestrian" (especially by such eminent commentators), its reputation for glamour lies almost hopelessly beyond repair. But there is consolation. However unglamorous, corporate law continues to have considerable practical importance.

The corporation has become the dominant form of business organization in Canada and in many other industrial countries, too. The rising worldwide importance of the corporation as an economic phenomenon has not gone unnoticed, nor has the impressive size of leading multinational enterprises. The implications of corporate growth for the law governing corporations have drawn the attention of learned commentators. As long ago as 1932, Adolf Berle and Gardiner Means wrote:

> The rise of the modern corporation has brought a concentration of economic power which can compete on equal terms with the modern state—economic power versus political power, each strong in its own field. The state seeks in some aspects to regulate the corporation, while the corporation, steadily becoming more powerful, makes every effort to avoid such regulation. Where its own interests are concerned, it even attempts to dominate the state. The future may see the economic organism, now typified by the corporation, not only on an equal plane with the state, but possibly even superseding it as the dominant form of social organization. The law of corporations, accordingly, might well be considered as a potential constitutional law for the new economic state, while business practice is increasingly assuming the aspect of economic statesmanship.[2]

The corporation's imposing economic significance explains why it attracts so much attention and scrutiny from the press, politicians, professors, and protestors. But is the

---

1   Robert W.V. Dickerson et al., *Proposals for a New Business Corporations Law for Canada*, vol. I, Commentary (Ottawa: Information Canada, 1971), at 2 (Dickerson committee).

2   Adolf A. Berle and Gardiner C. Means, *The Modern Corporation and Private Property* (New York: Macmillan, 1939), at 357.

law of the corporation of any great interest? Is it truly becoming the "constitutional law for the new economic state"? Let us hope not. Nevertheless, I believe corporate law is of considerable interest. The animating concepts and foundational principles of corporate law, despite the dismissive comments of Mr. Dickerson's committee, comprise an intellectually challenging as well as a practically important body of knowledge.

WHAT IS A CORPORATION?

The word "corporation" is best viewed as a demarcation of genus rather than of species. There are for-profit, non-profit, ecclesiastical, and charitable corporations. Universities are corporations and so, too, it is generally agreed, is the English monarch.[3] All of these entities share the fundamental trait that they may for many useful purposes be conceived of as artificial legal "persons." (This observation is true even of the English monarchy though not, of course, of any individual English king or queen.) Each of these entities is thought to possess, in the eyes of the law, a personality (or perhaps a "personhood") that is separate and distinct from the human beings who serve as the entity's office holders, directors, employees, or other agents.

There is nothing about the word "corporation" that necessarily implies an organization that is seeking to earn profits. Yet, when socially conscious protestors lament the perceived "corporatization" of our public institutions, it is unlikely that they are complaining that the world has fallen too much under the corrupting influence of the sort of corporations that run large charities or own Buckingham Palace. In the lexicon of the popular press and the foot soldiers of the anti-globalization movement, "corporation" has become a synonym for that one particular species of body corporate that exists to earn profits: the *business* corporation.[4]

This popular modern tendency to associate the word "corporation" almost exclusively with profit-making entities obscures an important fact. The "corporation" is a concept that may be (and historically invariably was) understood quite apart from the profit-making commercial enterprises that are operated in corporate form today. The formative years for English and Canadian business corporations occurred during the 19th century. Those years witnessed what might be called the "corporatization" of the business com-

---

3   That the English sovereign is a corporation sole has been generally recognized for many years. However, it is worth noting that the great English legal scholar F.W. Maitland, one of the most articulate advocates of the so-called realist view of the corporation, raised some doubt as to the pedigree of this characterization. Referring to the writings of Lord Coke, to whose work he suggests the conception of the corporation sole was in no small part due, Maitland wrote, "Coke knew two corporations sole that were not ecclesiastical. ... They were a strange pair: the king and the chamberlain of the city of London." See F.W. Maitland, "The Corporation Sole" (1900), 16 *Law Quarterly Review* 335, at 340.

4   Indeed, it might be said that it is the large business corporation that is the particular target of many progressive critics and protestors. Consider, for example, the recent book by Professor Joel Bakan, *The Corporation: The Pathological Pursuit of Profit and Power* (Toronto: Viking, 2004). Professor Bakan explains in his introduction, at page 3 that, "[t]hroughout the book I use the word 'corporation' to describe the large Anglo-American publicly traded business corporation, as opposed to small incorporated businesses, or small and large not-for-profit or privately owned ones."

pany: the development and gradual acceptance of the idea that an incorporated *business* company could fully exhibit the same defining features as other (not-for-profit) corporate bodies of much older vintage.

What, precisely, is a corporation—for-profit or otherwise? The corporation is an abstract concept. One cannot touch a corporation, photograph it, or draw a picture of it. We "see" a corporation only through the effects it has on the world in which it operates. A business corporation may manufacture goods by the warehouse-full, purchase impressive office towers, and employ thousands of people. Yet not the warehouses, nor the offices, nor even the employees—however high their corporate rank—are the corporation itself.[5] The precise nature of such an artificial legal entity may be difficult to define (other than in the sort of functional, legal terms that are the subject of most of the remaining chapters of this book). But it is still possible to develop a general intuitive sense of what a corporation is because it shares some of the features of other non-incorporated associations that are likely to be familiar to most people.

Consider the operation of a small club organized by a group of people with a common interest. Imagine, for example, that a number of avid teacup collectors fortunate enough to live in the charming East Anglian Village of Girton decide to form a new club to promote the interests and advantages of teacup collecting. They choose a name: the Girton Teacup Collectors Club. And they soon set about to organize themselves.

The club members may decide that, to carry on their activities, they will need some money. So it is agreed that every club member must pay a small initiation fee upon joining. Modest annual membership dues will also be levied to cover current expenses. Once the club has money in its coffers, prudence will demand that some rules be put in place setting out just who will have the authority to make spending decisions on behalf of the club, who will be authorized to make withdrawals from the club's bank account, draw cheques, and so on. If the club has only a very few members, all of whom like and trust one another, decisions about these sorts of things can probably be reached by consensus. But, if the club becomes very large, achieving consensus on every issue may no longer be possible. Apart from anything else, it may not always be feasible for every member to attend every meeting. Requiring unanimous agreement on all club decisions might be tantamount to ensuring that no important decisions could ever again be taken. So, as the club grows in size, some formal voting and approval structures will need to be put in place.

The club's voting rules need not be complex. Perhaps it will be agreed that, as long as a majority of the members favours taking some action, the club will take that action. Or perhaps some sorts of decisions will seem much more important to the club's future than others. For these weightier matters, instead of a simple majority, the consent of some larger proportion of the members will be needed: two-thirds, say. Once the club's voting and spending rules have been settled, no doubt someone will suggest that they ought to be written down and kept in a special book somewhere, to prevent future bickering over what precisely has already been agreed to. Rules of this kind might then become the basis

---

5   In chapter 8, the actions of some corporate directors or officers are sometimes identified as those of the corporation for purposes of criminal or tort liability. But this sort of attribution is a far cry from saying that a corporation is nothing more than its officers and directors.

of the new club's constitution. Collectors planning to join the club in future could then be shown a copy of this constitution so that they might have a clear idea of just what they are getting into.

Now suppose that some time has passed. The Girton Teacup Collectors Club has grown very large. Its members number in the dozens. Its treasury overflows with thousands of dollars (or, since Girton is in England, thousands of pounds). It is no longer practical to hold a vote on each and every administrative decision that the club must make. The time has come to elect club officers who will take on the responsibility of managing the affairs of the club. The members will thus delegate a certain amount of decision-making authority to these club officers; but "major" decisions (whatever they may be) will still need to be ratified or approved by all the members at a general meeting, in accordance with the voting thresholds mentioned earlier.

It is next decided that such a thriving club needs a regular meeting place, or club-house. A small building on High Street is purchased to be the club's headquarters. Perhaps a few modest pieces of furniture and other comforts are acquired to furnish the new space. As new members join the club, they are, naturally, permitted to use the new clubhouse—even though no part of their membership dues was actually used to buy it. Conversely, as old members move away, quit the club, and stop paying their annual dues, they are no longer entitled to use the clubhouse, even though the membership dues they paid in the past had helped to purchase it.

This much is clear to everyone: the clubhouse somehow belongs to the club itself, and not to those men and women who happened to be members of the club at the time the building was purchased. But what precisely does it mean to say that the "club" owns the building? What is "the club"? What evidence of the club's "existence" could be shown to a bank or a government authority? At best, a copy of the club's written constitution might be produced. But that piece of paper is no more the club itself than the *Constitution Act, 1867* is the nation of Canada. In a limited sense, the constitution "defines" the club; the club is the particular organization operated in accordance with this particular written constitution. But from a more practical perspective, the club is no more or less than the aggregate of its individual members, whoever they might be, from time to time.

A business corporation has many organizational features in common with the Girton Teacup Collectors Club. A business corporation is formed when people[6] with a common goal come together and take steps to formalize their association. (Unlike the typical club, of course, the business corporation's goal is linked to carrying on for-profit activities, and the method for forming the business corporation is specifically prescribed by statute.) But just as a club typically settles on a suitable name, chooses officers, and eventually crafts a written constitution, so too the organizers of a business corporation select a name by which it will be identified, choose directors, and take steps to formalize a number of important matters in its constitutional documents. In the case of Canadian business

---

6   It has been possible for many years in Canada for a single person to incorporate a business and thus obtain, among other things, the benefit of limited liability. The implications of such single-shareholder corporations are discussed later in this book. It is also possible for corporations to, themselves, create additional corporations.

corporations, there are typically two such documents, neither one of which is typically called a "constitution" or even a "charter."[7] Instead, in most Canadian jurisdictions, these two documents are known as: (1) the articles of incorporation[8] and (2) the bylaws.[9] The reason that the corporate constitution is, in effect, parcelled up into two separate documents like this (usually referred to collectively by lawyers as the corporation's "constating documents"[10]) appears to be a holdover from a practice that developed before the first general incorporation statutes were enacted in the 19th century.[11]

Although the business corporation may be created in a more formal way than the club, once formed, it has, just as our imaginary club does, a kind of separate existence all its own. In fact, the separate existence of a corporation is formally recognized in law in a way that the existence of a club or other unincorporated organization is not. A corporation can own property in its own name; it can enter into contracts; and it can sue, and be sued, too. It is, for legal purposes, a single, distinct entity. Yet as a practical matter, there are living, breathing people behind this entity. There will be regular meetings when those people are asked to vote on matters relating to the governing of the corporation; and so this separate distinct "entity" is also, paradoxically, a kind of collective, rather like the club. Many of the tensions and uncertainties that arise in the law of business corporations are linked to this curious entity/collective dualism.

COMPANIES, CORPORATIONS, AND BODIES CORPORATE

The words "company," "corporation," and "body corporate" are used interchangeably by many people. Detailing pedantic disputes over the meaning and use of the words "company" and "corporation" is hardly the most interesting way to introduce the study of this area of law. But the words are so often encountered that newcomers to the field are frequently curious to know whether there is any essential difference between a "company" and a "corporation" and, if so, what that difference is.

---

7   The *Companies Act* (PEI), s. 4, does refer to the grant of a charter, by letters patent, to create a corporation. The *Business Corporations Act* (BC) also defines the word "charter" to include a corporation's articles, notice of articles or memorandum, regulations, bylaws or agreement or deed of settlement, and other similar records in the case of corporations formed under "an Act, statute, ordinance, letters patent, certificate, declaration or other equivalent instrument or provision of law" (s. 1(1), definition of "charter").

8   In Nova Scotia, the equivalent document is called the "memorandum of association"; in Prince Edward Island, "letters patent." In British Columbia, for corporations incorporated under the new *Business Corporations Act,* the equivalent document is now referred to as a "notice of articles." (*Business Corporations Act* (BC), ss. 10 and 11.)

9   In British Columbia and Nova Scotia, the equivalent document is known as the "articles of association."

10 In *Duha Printers (Western) Ltd. v. The Queen,* [1998] 1 SCR 795, the Supreme Court of Canada refers to the articles and bylaws of a corporation as its constating documents, and holds as well that a unanimous shareholder agreement (discussed further in chapter 4) has a status comparable to that of the constating documents. Indeed, at one point in the judgment, the court states that a unanimous shareholder agreement is a constating document, at least for the purpose of determining *de jure* control of the corporation.

11 Paul L. Davies, *Gower & Davies: Principles of Modern Company Law,* 7th ed. (London: Sweet & Maxwell, 2003), at 57.

Attempting to define either term with precision is not a new problem. Writing in 1910, Frank Evans complained that "[i]f it is difficult accurately to define a corporation, it is almost impossible to give a clear and correct definition of a company."[12] Both terms are in common use today, although, when describing incorporated businesses, the term "company" is much preferred in the United Kingdom, while the term "corporation" is more often used in North America. If, for example, one were to study the law of business corporations in the law faculty of a British university, one would most likely do so in a course called "company law." L.C.B. Gower suggests that this differing terminology arises from the fact that

> the modern English business corporation has evolved from the unincorporated partnership, based on mutual agreement, rather than from the corporation, based on a grant from the state, and owes more to partnership principles than to rules based on corporate personality. Thus we in England still do not talk about business corporations or about corporation law, but about companies and company law.[13]

The term "company law" is occasionally used to describe courses offered by Canadian common law schools, too.[14] To some, this term is thought to be a more accurate course title than "corporate law." The word "company," to them, signals a for-profit corporation[15] in a way that the generic term "corporation" may not. This makes the word appropriate for the law school course title because courses of this kind, on either side of the Atlantic, do tend to deal almost entirely with the law of for-profit enterprises.

This association of the word "company" with for-profit corporations is not, however, universal. In the minds of some, the word "company" does not imply a for-profit venture. What's more, historically, use of the word "company" was not confined to the designation of *incorporated* enterprises at all.[16] Instead, the word was regularly used to describe a kind of *unincorporated* partnership enterprise. Indeed, in many modern business corporations statutes in Canada and elsewhere, the word "company" has been thought ambiguous,

---

12   Frank Evans, "What Is a Company?" (1910), 26 *Law Quarterly Review* 259, at 260. Evans also cites language from *Smith v. Anderson*, [1879] 15 Ch. D 247, in which it was suggested (at 261) that a company is distinguished from an ordinary partnership by virtue of the fact that the membership of a company is constantly changing (whereas a partnership is a contract between specific individuals). Evans also cites a later case for the proposition that a company is an association larger than a firm, and in which share interests are transferable without unanimous consent. That same case made clear that a company could be incorporated or unincorporated. Ibid., at 263, quoting *Stanley Tennant v. Stanley*, [1906] 1 Ch. 131.

13   L.C.B. Gower, "Some Contrasts Between British and American Corporation Law" (1956), 69 *Harvard Law Review* 1369, at 1371-72.

14   See infra footnote 30.

15   See, e.g., Davies, supra footnote 11, at 3: "in common parlance the word 'company' is normally reserved for those associated for economic purposes, *i.e.* to carry on a business for gain."

16   Indeed, as Davies notes, citing *Re Stanley*, [1906] 1 Ch. 131, at 134, "company has no strict legal meaning." Ibid. John Howard has written that the term "company" was said to refer to a kind of partnership, with common stock and transferable interests, but not a separate legal person. See John L. Howard, "The Proposals for a New Business Corporations Act for Canada: Concepts and Policies" in *Special Lectures of the Law Society of Upper Canada 1972* (Toronto: Richard de Boo, 1972), 17, at 31.

or perhaps old-fashioned, and has been deliberately replaced with the word "corporation." But, in some contexts, especially when dealing with certain historical sources, it is still quite important to distinguish between the term "company" and the term "business corporation."

Pursuing this question further is a rather barren exercise. For most practical purposes, in Canada, the history of the words "company" and "corporation" has been forgotten, and any precise differences in their meanings obscured. The two terms may be used interchangeably today without catastrophic consequences. Some Canadian corporate statutes are called "companies"[17] acts, others "corporations"[18] or "business corporations" acts,[19] but all provide for the incorporation of entities with virtually identical fundamental attributes.

As for the term "body corporate," it, too, is a synonym for corporation. However, in many Canadian corporate statutes, the phrase "body corporate" serves a somewhat more specific purpose. It is the term that is used whenever the drafters intend to refer to an entity *incorporated under any statute in any jurisdiction*, whereas use of the word "corporation" in such a statute is limited to those bodies incorporated under that one, particular statute. So, for example, in the *Canada Business Corporations Act* (CBCA), whenever the word "corporation" is used, it refers to a corporation incorporated under the CBCA itself. When the phrase "body corporate" is used, however, it refers to any incorporated entity whether incorporated under the CBCA, the corporate legislation of any of Canada's provinces or territories, the Delaware *General Corporation Law*, or any other such statute in any other jurisdiction.

Alas, this usage convention is not uniform throughout the country. For example, under the BC *Business Corporations Act*, the word "company" is used to refer to enterprises incorporated under the BC Act itself or a "former *Companies Act*" (a defined term referring to nine former BC corporate statutes stretching back to the 19th century) that has not ceased to be a company.[20] The word "corporation" in the BC Act is used to refer to entities incorporated under any statute whatsoever.[21] The Nova Scotia *Companies Act* uses only the word "company" to refer to Nova Scotia corporations, and makes no mention of corporations from other jurisdictions. The Prince Edward Island *Companies Act* defines "company" to mean a PEI incorporated company, and uses the term "body corporate" sometimes when referring specifically to entities incorporated under statutes other than Prince Edward Island's statute[22] and sometimes evidently using the term to mean incorporated entities under any statute (including PEI's).[23] In at least one section of the PEI statute, a different phrase altogether is used: "corporation incorporated under the

17   For example, *Companies Act* (NS); *Companies Act* (PEI).

18   For example, *The Corporations Act* (Man.); *Corporations Act* (NL).

19   For example, *Canada Business Corporations Act* (Can.); *Business Corporations Act* (Alta.); *The Business Corporations Act* (Sask.); *Business Corporations Act* (Ont.); *Business Corporations Act* (NB).

20   *Business Corporations Act* (BC), s. 1(1), definition of "company."

21   Ibid., s. 1(1). Technically, the definition of "corporation" excludes municipalities and corporations sole. The BC Act also makes use of the term "foreign corporation" to refer, essentially, to corporations other than those incorporated under BC law.

22   See, e.g., *Companies Act* (PEI), ss. 85 and 86.

23   Ibid., ss. 1.1 and 69.

laws of Canada or any province thereof."[24] The Saskatchewan *Business Corporations Act* is a little trickier. For most parts of the statute, it uses the words "corporation"[25] and "body corporate"[26] as they are used in the CBCA. But in parts II and III of the legislation, the word "corporation" refers to *any* incorporated entity, whether incorporated under the Saskatchewan statute or otherwise.[27]

In any event, in this book, the terms "corporation," "body corporate," and, occasionally, "company" will be used interchangeably unless the context otherwise indicates.

BUSINESS CORPORATIONS

It is the for-profit business corporation that is the usual focus of Canadian and US law school courses in business associations,[28] business organizations,[29] and company law[30] (as well as in courses titled corporations[31]); and it is the business corporation that is the principal focus of this book. Contrary to the cynical views of some law students, this curricular emphasis is not the product of some insidious Bay Street (or even Wall Street) plot to lure pliant, young recruits into the service of the wealthy pinstripe-suited elites. Rather, it reflects the incontrovertible importance that the business corporation has assumed in Canada and other modern industrial societies, and the concomitant need to understand how our legal system, past and present, has dealt, and should deal, with this economically and socially important phenomenon.

A BRIEF HISTORY OF THE BUSINESS CORPORATION

The business corporation has a long history, even if not a particularly inspired one. Its ancient roots may be traced to forms of business organization that existed in classical antiquity and developed throughout the Middle Ages and the Renaissance.[32] However, the principal features of the modern Canadian business corporation (if not necessarily our corporate statutes) may be traced to two somewhat more recent English forms of busi-

---

24   Ibid., s. 12(2).

25   *The Business Corporations Act* (Sask.), s. 2(1)(j).

26   Ibid., s. 2(1)(g).

27   For the most part, parts II and III deal with routine administrative matters such as filing public records, and so on. But at least one section, s. 267, deals with the requirement to include the corporate name on invoices, etc., a requirement that, in most other Canadian corporate statutes, applies only to corporations incorporated in that particular jurisdiction.

28   See, e.g., University of Victoria, University of Calgary, Osgoode Hall Law School (York University), University of Windsor, Queen's University, McGill University, and Dalhousie University.

29   See, e.g., University of Saskatchewan, University of Toronto, University of Ottawa, and University of New Brunswick.

30   See, e.g., University of Alberta and University of Western Ontario.

31   See e.g., the University of British Columbia.

32   Jonathon Barron Baskin and Paul J. Miranti Jr., *A History of Corporate Finance* (Cambridge: Cambridge University Press, 1997), at 37ff.

ness organization: (1) "regulated companies" and (2) joint stock companies, of which those formed by "deed of settlement" were especially influential. Gower has asserted that company law, "of all branches of the law is perhaps the one least readily understood except in relation to its historical development."[33] He is undoubtedly correct in his assessment; but for a complete recounting of that history, the reader is well advised to consult one of the many excellent surveys of the history of the corporate form, including that found in early editions of Gower's book.[34] All that will be noted here is how the practical needs of business gradually influenced the legal attributes of the corporation.

Regulated Companies

One of the earliest British ancestors of the business corporation was the regulated company. The regulated company, a form of enterprise that arose in 13th century England,[35] was a corporation formed by the grant of a charter from the Crown. The original impetus for incorporation appeared to be tied to the need for a legal entity that could be the grantee and repository of monopoly trading rights on behalf of merchants. In fact, the notion that there is some necessary link between incorporation and the grant of some kind of trading monopoly appears to have become quite strongly entrenched; and, as Berle has suggested, it may have been this early association of the granting of a state "privilege" with the establishment of a corporation that led to the still common (but now mistaken) view that the conferring of incorporated status is *itself* a valuable state privilege, rather than a mere convenience for business people and government alike.[36]

---

33   L.C.B. Gower, *Gower's Principles of Modern Company Law*, 5th ed. (London: Sweet & Maxwell, 1992), at 19.

34   The most recent edition of *Gower*, supra footnote 11, no longer includes a significant discussion on the history of the corporation. Paul Davies, the current author, points out in his preface that his decision to replace this material with "a more functional introduction" was in fact made on the suggestion of the late Professor Gower. Much of the historical discussion here owes a significant debt to Gower's fifth edition, supra footnote 33, chapters 2 and 3, as well as to the sources upon which Gower principally relied, as cited at page 19 of his work.

35   Baskin and Miranti, supra footnote 32, at 58.

36   Adolf A. Berle, *Studies in the Law of Corporation Finance* (Chicago: Callaghan & Company, 1928), at 11. The confusion between the grant of corporate charter and the grant of exclusive trading privileges is seen in a number of leading writers of the past. In *Leviathan*, for example, Thomas Hobbes explains that:

> The end of [merchants] incorporating is to make their gain the greater, which is done in two ways: by sole buying and sole selling, both at home and abroad. So that to grant to a company of merchants to be a corporation or body politic is to grant them a double monopoly, whereof one is to be sole buyers, another to be sole sellers. For when there is a company incorporate for any particular foreign country, they only export the commodities vendible in that country, which is sole buying at home and sole selling at abroad.

See Thomas Hobbes, *Leviathan*, Richard Tuck, ed. (Cambridge: Cambridge University Press, 1996).

Adam Smith makes a very similar (if less critical) observation in *Wealth of Nations*:

> When a company of merchants undertake, at their own risk and expense, to establish a new trade with some remote and barbarous nation, it may not be unreasonable to incorporate them into a

As Gower explains, regulated companies did not carry on business themselves.[37] That was not originally their point. It was the individual members of these companies, either acting alone or in partnership or association with one another, who carried on business, taking advantage of the monopoly rights that had been granted to the umbrella organization (that is, the regulated company). This concept can perhaps be illustrated by way of a somewhat imperfect modern analogy. The Law Society of Upper Canada is the corporation[38] that today governs the legal profession in the province of Ontario. In effect, the Law Society has a monopoly on lawyers' services in the province. Of course, the Law Society does not, itself, carry on the practice of law. But, in order to become eligible to practise law, and call oneself a lawyer in Ontario, one must become a member of the Law Society. The Law Society determines who will be permitted to become its members and it is these members, either as sole practitioners, or by forming partnerships among themselves, who take advantage of the functional monopoly that has been entrusted to the Law Society.

One does not, needless to say, expect that the Law Society, itself, will form a law firm and begin legal practice on its own. However, some of the regulated companies did begin to operate with their own joint stock. Members of a company were at first permitted (but not obliged) to participate; but eventually, in the case of some leading companies, participation in the company's joint stock became a requirement of membership. This evolution from umbrella organization to operating company occurred sometime during the 17th century. The East India Company's development is the classic and perhaps earliest example of this process. As Gower explains,[39] the East India Company, which was granted a monopoly over trade with the Indies, originally operated as a kind of hybrid. That is, the company had a joint stock to which members could, if they wished, subscribe. But if members preferred instead to carry on trade privately (taking advantage of the monopoly privilege the company enjoyed), they could certainly do that. Gradually, the company's own joint stock supplanted the individual members' trading. By 1692, members were not at all permitted to trade privately.[40]

Joint Stock Company

The term "joint stock company," Gower tells us, was actually coined to distinguish one type of company (a firm formed to carry on private trade to profit its members) from

---

joint stock company, and to grant them, in case of their success, a monopoly of the trade for a certain number of years. It is the easiest and most natural way in which the state can recompense them for hazarding a dangerous and expensive experiment, of which the public is afterwards to reap the benefit.

See Adam Smith, *Wealth of Nations*, Book V, Ch. 1, Pt. III (Amherst, NY: Prometheus Books, 1991), at 480-81. Hunt thus notes that "the idea that a company was synonymous, or at least coextensive, with monopoly persisted well into the nineteenth century." Hunt, infra footnote 44, at 17.

37   Supra footnote 33, at 21.

38   *Law Society Act*, RSO 1990, c. L.8, s. 2(2).

39   Supra footnote 33, at 21.

40   Ibid.

another type of company (the "regulated company" in the original sense of an umbrella organization to which trading monopolies were granted).[41] Joint stock companies were not, originally, corporations (although, in the mid-19th century, legislation was passed permitting them to incorporate). They were, instead, more like partnerships. What distinguished a joint stock company from an ordinary partnership was that members would contribute capital to a common fund that would then be managed on behalf of the members by a small management group, usually known as "governors," but according to Formoy, the term "director" came into common use at the end of the 17th century, in place of the term "assistant," another designated office in many joint stock companies.[42] A member's interest in a joint stock company could be bought and sold—rather like shares in a modern corporation—and indeed the shares of many joint stock companies, including very speculative ventures, were regularly bought and sold.[43] Thus, when one reads of the mania of share speculation in England that culminated in the infamous South Sea Bubble in 1720, it should be remembered that while some of the shares being bought and sold at that time were shares of companies that had royal or government charters (some in good standing, some not), others were probably shares of unincorporated joint stock companies, rather than of business corporations as we know them today. The earliest English general incorporation statute, the *Joint Stock Companies Act* of 1844, represented, as Hunt notes, the first time the distinction between ordinary partnerships and joint stock companies received legislative recognition.[44] It might be noted that the term "joint stock company," although it has generally been eliminated from most modern corporate statutes, is still occasionally used by commentators to refer to business corporations, and survives in other forms, as well. For example, in Nova Scotia, the long title of the *Companies Act* is *An Act Respecting Joint Stock Companies*, and the government office that administers incorporations in that province is still referred to as the Registrar of Joint Stock Companies.

The South Sea Bubble

An account of the development of corporate law would not be complete without some mention of the South Sea Bubble. In the early years of the 18th century, the South Sea Company was formed in England and was granted a monopoly over trade with South America. The South Sea Company had an ambitious plan: to raise money from investors to retire the English national debt. The South Sea Company floated its shares, and did indeed raise significant sums from investors. Unfortunately, the price of the South Sea Company's shares plummeted in 1720. Many investors lost the greater part of their

---

41   Ibid.

42   Ronald Ralph Formoy, *The Historical Foundations of Modern Company Law* (London: Sweet & Maxwell, 1923), at 21.

43   Formoy indicates that "before the end of the seventeenth century there was an open and highly organised market at London in stock and shares." Ibid., at 9.

44   Bishop Carleton Hunt, *The Development of the Business Corporation in England 1800-1867* (Cambridge, MA: Harvard University Press, 1936), at 89.

investment. The price collapse was linked to revelations of scandal and what would today be branded illegal insider trading.[45]

From a corporate law perspective, the significance of the South Sea Company debacle is that it is associated with the passage of an unfortunate piece of English legislation referred to today as the *Bubble Act* of 1720.[46] This Act was passed, not in response to any perceived or anticipated problems with the South Sea Company (those problems had not arisen at the time of its passage). Rather, it was enacted in response to an apparent proliferation of speculative joint stock company share sale schemes being touted by far "less reputable" organizations. It has been argued that the promoters of the South Sea Company actually lobbied for this legislation, with the hope of eliminating unwanted competition for the promotion of stock.[47] And it has been further suggested that, if that was the Act's goal, it was apparently a success. The demand for stock soon outstripped the now reduced supply, helping to drive the South Sea Company's shares still higher in what must surely have been the most dreadful example of the unintended adverse consequences of misconceived legislation. In any event, what the Act purported to do was to challenge the legality of companies that had not been incorporated either by an act of Parliament or by the Crown. The language of the statute was, however, fraught with ambiguity. In particular, as discussed further in chapter 3, it included a sort of "grandfathering provision" that permitted (without really defining) the continued operation of some pre-existing unincorporated business associations.

Deed of Settlement Companies

So-called deed of settlement companies were a type of joint stock company that used the law of trusts to facilitate the pooling of capital and the division of share interests. The property of these unincorporated companies was held by trustees, and the corporate business was conducted by directors.[48] Formoy has suggested that the deeds of settlement were "really the forerunner of the articles of association of a modern company."[49]

Companies and the Corporate Law Intersect

What should be noticed from even this very simple historical sketch, is that the trading companies that developed in England were not necessarily corporations. The implications of "incorporation" may not, prior to the mid-19th century, have been fully recog-

---

45   For a colourful account of the South Sea Bubble, see Charles Mackay, *Extraordinary Popular Delusions and the Madness of Crowds* (London: Richard Bentley, 1841), reprinted with a foreword by Andrew Tobias (New York: Harmony Books, 1980), at 46-88.

46   31 6 Geo. 1, c. 18.

47   Formoy, supra footnote 42, at 28, notes that the "South Sea Company, knowing the importance of keeping up the price of their stock, and imagining that the fall of their stock was due to the traffic of these bubbles, obtained under the Act a *scire facias* against three companies by name."

48   L.S. Sealy, *Cases and Materials in Company Law*, 7th ed. (London: Butterworths, 2001), at 1-2.

49   Formoy, supra footnote 42, at 41.

nized anyway, and business people did not appear to be clamouring for formal incorporated status before that period.

Of course, some companies *were* incorporated, but incorporation was not readily available. There were only two ways for a company to become incorporated: by royal charter (companies incorporated in this way are sometimes called common law companies, evidently because the common law was the basis of the Crown's authority to incorporate), and, later, by special act of Parliament (that is, a specific act incorporating a specific company.) Needless to say, neither of these avenues of incorporation would likely be open to the small business entrepreneur or, indeed, to anyone without political ties.[50]

By the early 19th century, new pressures began to build for formalizing English company law. As Hunt notes, in the early 19th century the line between joint stock companies and true corporations was already beginning to blur, a development that pressed the need for corporate legislative reform:

> The new quasi-corporate company was ... one of the main lines of advance towards freedom of incorporation. ... [I]t had begun to establish itself between the old common-law partnership, on the one hand, and the corporation, strictly speaking, on the other. Unable to arrest, Parliament was eventualy able to regulate this vehicle for the attraction and employment of the capital of investors who took no active part in management; and, still later, "by a sort of legislative hocus-pocus," as McCulloch put it, "such associations were to be metamorphosed into corporations."[51]

There were, thus, a series of initiatives leading, at last, to the passage of the first so-called general incorporation statute in England—the *Joint Stock Companies Registration and Regulation Act* of 1844 (generally referred to today as the *Joint Stock Companies Act* of 1844). This Act made it possible for companies to incorporate without having to obtain a charter from the Crown or their own, tailor-made, act of Parliament.[52] But the 1844 Act was not a great success. It called for a somewhat cumbersome incorporation procedure, and, as discussed further in chapter 3, it did not provide limited liability to shareholders. Although limited liability does not appear to have been an overriding concern in earlier times, by the mid-19th century, its importance to business people had become well recognized.

Pressure began to build in England for an easily available form of business organization that would offer investors limited liability. Some of these pressures came from abroad. In France, it was possible to carry on business through a société en commandite. This is a form of business organization that survives today, and that was replicated in the United States, the United Kingdom, and English Canada as the "limited partnership." (Indeed, the English phrase "limited partnership" is today rendered into French as "société en commandite.")

---

50 Hunt notes, for example, that in 1855 the *Circular to Bankers* had argued against any governmental discretion over the granting of corporate charters because "the liberty to associate for purposes of trade is undoubtedly a fundamental principle in the civil rights of nations." Supra footnote 44, at 123.

51 Ibid., at 29.

52 According to Wegenast, the basis for this statute was early American state incorporation statutes. See F.W. Wegenast, *The Law of Canadian Companies*, reprinted with an introduction by Margaret P. Hyndman (Toronto: Carswell, 1979), at 20.

The société en commandite (and, indeed, the modern limited partnership) is a business organization characterized by two classes of participants: those who operate and manage the business (known as general partners in Canadian limited partnership law)[53] and other, mainly passive, investors who contribute money in exchange for a future share in the profits of the limited partnership's business, but with no expectation (and indeed, typically, no legal right) to take an active part in control or management of the business. (Under Canadian limited partnership law, these investors are known as "limited partners."[54])

The société en commandite was in wide use on the continent by the mid-19th century and had been adopted as well in a number of American states and in Ireland;[55] but there was no comparable business vehicle in England. Indeed, an unsuccessful attempt had been made in 1818 to bring the limited partnerhsip to England.[56] A significant "lobbying" effort was undertaken to try to persuade Parliament to enact similar legislation that would allow for the creation of English limited partnerships. Through a curious (and fascinating) sequence of events,[57] this lobbying effort culminated not in the immediate enactment of limited partnership law, but rather in the granting, in 1855, of "limited liability" to shareholders of companies incorporated under the *Joint Stock Companies Act*. Limited liability is discussed in some detail in chapter 3. Suffice it to say here that the grant of limited liability to shareholders made the corporation an ideal vehicle for pooling the funds of passive investors to carry on business enterprises of significant scale.[58]

No attempt will be made in this text to chronicle the development of general corporate legislation in England or in Canada. The Canadian story in particular is complex because early Canadian corporate legislation in different provinces borrowed variously from both English and American sources while at the same time evidently pioneering a distinctly Canadian method of corporation. Wegenast provides an outstanding canvass of the development of the earliest Canadian corporate statutes.[59] In a more recent historical study, Risk has suggested that the earliest Ontario (or Upper Canadian) statutes in 1860 and 1864 were more heavily influenced by American than by English models. (The earliest

---

53   See, e.g., *Limited Partnerships Act* (Ont.), RSO 1990, c. L.16.

54   See, e.g., ibid., s. 9.

55   Formoy, supra footnote 42, at 44.

56   Hunt, supra footnote 44, at 52.

57   See, e.g., Paddy Ireland, "The Triumph of the Corporate Legal Form, 1856-1914," in John Adams, ed., *Essays for Clive Schmitthoff* (Abingdon, UK: Oxon Professional Books, 1983), 29, at 32ff. See also Hunt, supra footnote 44, at 116ff.

58   England did, eventually, enact limited partnership legislation as well, but not for some 50 years later. By the time the *Limited Partnership Act* was introduced, many commentators thought it was redundant—that is, the corporation was an eminently superior business vehicle and the limited partnership had little of value to offer. See, e.g., Francis Beaufort Palmer, *The Companies Act, 1907 and The Limited Partnerships Act, 1907 With Explanatory Notes* (London: Steven and Sons Limited, 1908), at 71: "It is said and not without some reason that the Limited Partnerships Act, 1907 falls very far short of a workable scheme, and that the facilities afforded by it compare unfavourably with those afforded by the Companies Acts, 1867 to 1907." What those early commentators could not have anticipated was that income tax laws would one day make the limited partnership an extremely useful vehicle.

59   Supra footnote 52.

American general incorporation statutes preceded the English *Joint Stock Companies Act of 1844* by a number of years.[60]) A further discussion of the varying models of incorporation statute is found in chapter 2.

INCORPORATION IN CANADA: THE CONSTITUTIONAL QUESTION

In Canada, the federal and provincial governments have virtually concurrent legislative authority in the field of business incorporation. Every province and territory has its own incorporation statute, and there is a federal incorporation statute as well.

This unusual state of affairs gives rise to two questions, one legal and the other practical. First, how is it that both the federal and the provincial governments have constitutional authority to legislate with respect to incorporation? Second, on a practical level, on what basis would a business person decide to incorporate his or her business under one of Canada's corporate statutes rather than another? The latter question is discussed in chapter 2.

The provinces' constitutional authority for enacting corporate legislation is found in s. 92(11) of the *Constitution Act, 1867*, which gives to the provinces the authority to make laws in relation to "The Incorporation of Companies with Provincial Objects." This might suggest that provincially incorporated corporations are somehow limited to carrying on business within their province of incorporation. This is not so. In *Bonanza Creek Gold Mining Company, Ltd. v. R*,[61] the Privy Council imposed a limitation on the *legislature* as to what powers and rights it could grant to a provincial corporation, but imposed no limits on the capacity of such a corporation to accept powers and rights to carry on business beyond the province's boundaries. Put more simply, although a provincial legislature cannot, obviously, give provincial corporations the right to carry on business in another jurisdiction (any more than it can give individual citizens of its province such rights), it can, by legislation, permit the creation of corporations that have the capacity to carry on business anywhere. Of course, to carry on business in any particular jurisdiction, the corporation will need to be permitted to do so, lawfully, in that jurisdiction. That limitation, however, is true of individuals as well. Significantly, however, a corporation carries the internal corporate law of its incorporating jurisdiction with it whenever it ventures abroad.[62]

---

60 R.C.B. Risk, "The Nineteenth-Century Foundations of the Business Corporation in Ontario" (1973), *University of Toronto Law Journal* 270, at 278. Risk suggests that the earliest US general incorporation statute was a Massachusetts law from 1799 and that a New York law from 1811 may have been particularly influential in Canada.

61 [1916] 1 AC 566 (PC).

62 See, e.g., J.G. Castel and Janet Walker, *Canadian Conflict of Laws*, 5th ed. (Toronto: Butterworths, 2004), at 30-31:

> [T]he law of the state, province or territory under which a corporation has been incorporated or organized determines whether it has come into existence, its corporate powers and capacity to enter into any legal transaction, the persons entitled to act on its behalf including the extent of their liability for the corporation's debts and the rights of its shareholders.

There is no express mention in the *Constitution Act, 1867* of the federal government's power to make laws in relation to the incorporation of companies. However, in *Parsons v. Citizens Insurance Co. of Canada*,[63] the Privy Council held that the federal government had such an authority under its residual power.

Thus, today, there is in force a federal incorporation statute (the *Canada Business Corporations Act* (CBCA)), as well as corporate statutes in every Canadian province and territory. Moreover, although, theoretically only a federally incorporated corporation may carry on business throughout Canada as of right, as a practical matter, this distinction has come to mean very little. Provincially incorporated companies, through mutually beneficial reciprocal arrangements, can, and do, carry on business throughout the country. The practical question of why one might choose to incorporate under one Canadian corporation statute rather than another is addressed in chapter 2.

CORPORATE LAW SCHOLARSHIP

Corporate law scholarship, indeed legal scholarship in general, tends, very broadly speaking, to be bifurcated into the doctrinal and the theoretical.[64] Doctrinal approaches still tend to dominate Canadian corporate law scholarship.[65] Canadian law journals and leading textbooks unpack the cases ancient and modern through which the well-established principles and the contestable nuances of Canadian corporate law have been defined and developed. They also review and critique the legislation that has sometimes codified, sometimes contradicted, and occasionally confused the principles developed in these cases. The predominantly doctrinal focus of Canadian corporate law scholarship contrasts markedly to the academic writing on corporate law found in the United States, where theoretical perspectives cloy the pages of law journals and help pad the tenure applications of ambitious young scholars (especially those whose natural abilities have not been sullied by prolonged exposure to real-life legal practice).

In particular, the leading theoretical approach to the study of corporate law—law and economics—has had a pervasive (if not always beloved) influence not only on legal writing[66] but also on the teaching of corporate law at leading US law schools. To be sure, some of Canada's well-known law and economics scholars have made significant contributions, from time to time, in the corporate law arena. But there does not appear to be (so

---

63   (1881), 7 App. Cas. 96 (PC).

64   The seminal Arthurs report on legal education actually identified seven basic methodologies pursued in Canadian law schools: doctrinal, historical, theoretical, comparative (Canadian), comparative (transnational), interdisciplinary (empirical), and interdisciplinary (non-empirical). See *Law and Learning*, Report to the Social Sciences and Humanities Research Council of Canada by the Consultative Group on Research and Education in Law (Ottawa: SSHRC, 1983), at 77.

65   See, e.g., Kathleen A. Lahey and Sarah W. Salter, "Corporate Law in Legal Theory and Legal Scholarship: From Classicism to Feminism" (1985), 23 *Osgoode Hall Law Journal* 543, at 557, in which the authors assert that Canadian corporate law scholarship "is overwhelmingly doctrinal."

66   One leading corporate law scholar, for example, has suggested that the economic approach to corporate law "has predominated in the literature for the past two decades (at least in the US)." See Brian R. Cheffins, "The Trajectory of (Corporate Law) Scholarship" (2004), 63 *Cambridge Law Journal* 456, at 502.

far, at any rate) a critical mass of Canadian corporate law scholarship in the US law and economics tradition.

This book will frequently refer to the law and economics approach to the study of corporate law for two reasons. First, no serious modern study of corporate law would be complete without some introduction to law and economics. Second, the economic approach to corporate law has done much to invigorate the study of the topic and enliven dreary principles with provocative, entertaining, and, at times, insightful arguments.

The doctrinal approach to the study of corporate law is reflected in, and perhaps reinforced by, the method of teaching corporate law adopted in Canadian law schools. Most corporate law teachers generally use some variant of the "case method," and the case method, by its very premises, may foster a doctrinal orientation to the subject. Members of the practising bar generally prefer a doctrinal approach to the study of corporate law; and at several Canadian law schools, practising lawyers—rather than full-time academic lawyers—have been recruited to teach the basic business organizations/business associations course.

But academic freedom and intellectual curiosity have together worked to ensure that the modern law school curriculum is no longer the mere servant of the perceived short-term needs of the practising bar. What's more, the influence of US scholarship has increased in Canada. Each year, more and more young academics return from pursuing LLM studies at leading US universities to take up academic postings at Canadian law schools. And so, although doctrinal study of corporate law cases and statutory provisions is still probably the norm in Canadian law schools, attention to secondary literature on the subject is growing, to the delight of the scholars, at least, although sometimes to the chagrin of the practitioners.

Three principal issues might be said to lie at the heart of most theoretical corporate law scholarship, at least in North America. These three issues do not occupy watertight compartments; there is considerable overlap between and among them. For simplicity sake, however, these three topics may be identified and briefly described as follows:

- corporate personality,
- theory and purpose of the "firm," and
- the function of corporate law.

Corporate Personality

"Realist," "Fiction," and "Concessionist" Theories of the Corporate Entity

More than 50 years have passed since H.L.A. Hart recorded that "the juristic controversy over the nature of the corporate personality is dead."[67] That "juristic controversy" surrounds the theoretical implications of the notion that the corporation is a separate legal entity. The doctrinal implications of this notion are discussed in some

---

67   H.L.A. Hart, "Definition and Theory in Jurisprudence" (1954), 70 *Law Quarterly Review* 37, at 49. See also Cheffins, supra footnote 66, at 479: "By 1930 the dialogue had largely run its course, with the general consensus being that a corporation was an important legal form which was more than a mere contractual aggregation but which could not truly be equated with a natural person."

detail in chapter 3. However, at a theoretical level, debate among legal academics over the separate legal entity principle early in the 20th century centred on two (or perhaps three) broadly competing theories of the corporate form. Despite Hart's pronouncement, the legacy of that scholarship still occasionally informs academic discussions of corporate law today. These competing theories of the corporate form are the realist theory, on the one hand, and the "fiction theory" (and its close cousin, "concession theory"), on the other hand.

The realists contend that the corporation, in common with any collective body, necessarily has a kind of personality of its own that is the product of neither legislative nor judicial action. (For a simple illustration of this idea, one might review the Girton Teacup Collectors Club example presented earlier in this chapter.) Adolf Berle has credited A.V. Dicey with the observation that

> [i]t is a fact which has received far too little notice from English lawyers that, whenever men act in concert for a common purpose, they tend to create a body which, from no fiction of law, but from the very nature of things, differs from the individuals of whom it is constituted.[68]

Dicey's observation is the *locus classicus* of the realist position,[69] the intellectual roots of which are frequently traced to German theorist Otto Gierke.[70] In English scholarship, the idea is especially associated with the work of Cambridge legal scholar F.W. Maitland,[71] who translated Gierke's work into English. Defenders of the realist view can invoke many analogies and metaphors to illuminate their central thesis that the corporation should not be understood merely as some abstract, artificial creation of the law (or the sovereign), but rather as the simple recognition of a reality familiar to all of us: when people come together in a group, the group takes on a kind of collective life of its own. An audience sitting in a theatre may collectively laugh at some foolish joke in a play or a film that not one individual member of that audience would find amusing if he or she were watching the performance alone. A jury might collectively arrive at a verdict that not one member of the jury, acting individually, would have settled on, and so on. According to this view, the corporate "entity" was not created by law, but was merely recognized and perhaps

---

68   A.V. Dicey, quoted by Adolf A. Berle Jr., *Studies in the Law of Corporation Finance* (Chicago: Callaghan & Company, 1928), at 4.

69   John Dewey, writing in 1926, claimed that "[a]lmost every English writer, beginning with Maitland, who has written on behalf of the doctrine of the 'real personality' of corporate bodies, has felt obliged to quote" Dicey's statement. John Dewey, "The Historic Background of Corporate Legal Personality" (1926), 35 Yale *Law Journal* 655, at 673.

70   Otto Gierke, *Political Theories of the Middle Age*, translated, with an introduction by Frederic William Maitland (Cambridge: Cambridge University Press, 1987).

71   See, e.g., Maitland, supra footnote 3. H.L.A. Hart, however, has challenged (or at least qualified) this conventional characterization of Maitland's views. As Hart put it, "I do not understand why [Maitland] is called a Realist or thought to have accepted the doctrine of Gierke that he expounded, for though he was certain that fiction and collective-name theories 'denatured the facts,' he left the matter with a final question to which he then saw no answer. ... Such was Maitland's question: When [a hypothetical sovereign state] Nusquamia owes you money who owes you this?" Hart, supra footnote 67, at 51.

formalized by the law. That separate "entity" (if it may quite sensibly be described as such) would, in all key respects, have existed without judicial or legislative action.

The fiction theorists, however, contend that a corporation is a legal fiction, existing only "in contemplation of law,"[72] and as their close cousins, the concessionists[73] would have it, is dependent on a state (or royal) concession. Without such a concession, they say, corporations never did, and never could, exist. In his famous *Commentaries*, Blackstone staked out an early version of the concessionist position. He asserted that the corporate form, which he claimed to be of Roman origin, was distinguished in England from the civil law corporation for which, he said, "it does not appear that the prince's consent was necessary." No such ontological argument applied to the English corporation, says Blackstone, for in England, "the king's consent is absolutely necessary to the erection of any corporation, either impliedly or expressly given."[74] Blackstone also made a key observation about the corporation elsewhere in the *Commentaries* where he described the corporation as a franchise, in a passage cited many years later by two of the opinions delivered in the landmark 1819 US Supreme Court case *Dartmouth v. Woodward*.[75]

The historical accuracy of Blackstone's account of the origin of the English corporation has not gone unchallenged. More than 70 years ago, for example, Adolf Berle contended that, contrary to Blackstone's assertion, corporations existed in England before any corporate charters were ever granted by state authority, and that such corporations "were sued in common name, had a common seal, held property, contracted obligations and so on."[76] To be sure, Berle was certainly not referring to trading or business corporations; but recall that Blackstone's sweeping statement did not purport to draw any distinction between commercial and non-commercial corporations.

Berle traced what he regarded as the mistaken view that corporations were creations of the Crown or of the state to a bald and unsupported assertion in Coke's commentary on Littleton.[77] The gaffe, he says, was then perpetuated by Robert Brody. Of Brody, Berle derisively writes this:

---

72 See *Dartmouth College v. Woodward*, 17 US 518 (1819), at 636.

73 Dewey long ago noted that concession theory "while often confused with the 'fiction' theory, had a different origin, and testifies to quite a different situation of conflict of interests." Supra footnote 69, at 666. He went on to explain:

   [T]here is nothing essentially in common between the fiction and concession theories, although they both aimed toward the same general consequence, as far as limitation of power of corporate bodies is concerned. The fiction theory is ultimately a philosophical theory that the corporate body is but a name, a thing of the intellect; the concession theory may be indifferent as to the question of the reality of a corporate body; what it *must* insist upon is that its legal power is derived. [Ibid., at 667.]

   The distinction Dewey described is, however, frequently blurred by modern scholars.

74 William Blackstone, *Commentaries on the Laws of England*, vol. 1, chap. 18 (published as a facsimile edition with an introduction by Stanley N. Katz (Chicago: University of Chicago Press, 1979), at 460.

75 Supra footnote 72. Blackstone is quoted by Washington J, at 663, and by Story J, at 701. The quoted passage is from Blackstone, supra footnote 74, vol. 2, chap. 3, at 37.

76 Berle, supra footnote 36, at 7.

77 Ibid., at 9.

Himself the king's physician and no lawyer, but keeper of the records of the Tower of London. His history was bad and his logic worse. … He attributed every corporate exist-ence in England to a royal concession … though, as a matter of history, corporations existed first.[78]

It is the concessionist position that often seems much the more intuitively obvious (and perhaps attractive) to many novice corporate law students. Indeed, the realist view is often regarded with some astonishment and even resentment by those learning about it for the first time. "How can this be?" they object. "Corporations are obviously created by the state. After all, they may be formed only if there is specific legislation authorizing their formation. They enjoy the unique privilege of limited liability, a privilege that is clearly a creation of statute, which no body of persons can presume to bestow on themselves in the absence of such accommodating legislation. How, then," they may rail (perhaps with increasing exasperation), "can anyone be so ignorant of these fundamental facts? How can anyone seriously suggest that the corporation is other than a mere creation of statute?"

The realist view is not, however, quite so easily dismissed as that. Of course it is true, today in Canada, that the establishment of new corporations is authorized by specific pieces of enabling legislation. But this is not the end of the matter. Recall that almost every Canadian business corporation statute today is what has been called a "registration-style" act.[79] Such a statute provides for incorporation essentially as a matter of right (provided various administrative requirements are satisfied) rather than as a privilege, which may be bestowed only at the discretion of the state.

However, even setting to one side the form of modern Canadian corporate legislation, there is a second and more fundamental issue. The mere existence of legislation that mandates legal formalities in respect to some matter does not prove state authorship of that matter. All parents of children born in the province of Ontario must, for example, register those births with the government.[80] The government subsequently issues a birth certificate; but needless to say, the government does not, thereby, create the child. Issuing a birth certificate is a routine administrative action, a formal recognition of a pre-existing reality. So, too, say the realists, is the issuance of a certificate of incorporation. As Berle has stated, in disputing a reference in Kent's *Commentaries*[81] describing the corporation itself as a "franchise,"

> as a matter of history, corporations existed first, and if they wished to exercise govern-mental power, then asked for a franchise, but they could exist without the franchise and a considerable number had existed thus for several centuries.[82]

---

78   Ibid., at 11. This confusion between the grant of a corporate charter and the grant of exclusive trading privileges in connection with a corporate charter is seen elsewhere. One encounters it, for example, in Thomas Hobbes's description of corporations in *Leviathan*, supra footnote 36.

79   See discussion in chapter 2. The exception is the Prince Edward Island *Companies Act*, which provides for incorporation by letters patent and so preserves, at least in theory, a discretion to refuse incorporation.

80   *Vital Statistics Act*, RSO 1990, c. V.4, s. 9(2).

81   James Kent, *Commentaries on American Law* (Boston: Little, Brown, 1873).

82   Berle, supra footnote 36, at 11. This text immediately follows the passage accompanying note 78, supra.

Reasoning of this sort rarely moves the concessionists. They insist that it is facile, and that it too carelessly ignores the critical distinction between mere partnerships, on the one hand, and true corporations, on the other. Perhaps it is true, they may concede, to assert that business *partnerships* are inevitable. Perhaps partnerships may well pre-exist state action. But a partnership is very different from a corporation—a fact that the slow evolution of general incorporation legislation only too plainly evidences. Ordinary partners, among other things, do not enjoy limited liability, except in the case of those special types of partnerships for which special legislation has been enacted.[83] Limited liability is a privilege universally enjoyed by the shareholders of corporations, and it is a privilege that exists only because there is specific legislation that has created it. All this talk of juries, audiences, and birth certificates simply misses the mark as far as corporations are concerned.

This rejoinder may, however, overstate the uniqueness of the corporate form, and in particular the extent to which the availability of limited liability has come to define the business corporation. Investors can (and, evidently, historically did) effectively (albeit imperfectly) limit their liability contractually or otherwise.[84] Moreover, as discussed in chapter 3, it appears that, in the United Kingdom at any rate, transferability of share interests, rather than limited liability of shareholders, was originally considered to be the key attribute of investment vehicles appropriate for the pursuit of larger business enterprises.[85]

If the concessionists (or perhaps the fiction theorists) hold something of a "trump card," it is probably this: in the real-life, workaday experience of the Canadian corporate

---

83   These special types of partnerships in Canada include limited partnerships (see, e.g., *Limited Partnerships Act*, supra footnote 53) and, more recently, limited liability partnerships (see, e.g., *Partnerships Act*, RSO 1990 c. P.5, s. 44.1). In the United States, there is an additional form, the limited liability limited partnership. (See, e.g., s. 17-214 Delaware revised *Uniform Limited Partnership Act*.)

84   This is an argument often associated today with law and economics scholars. See, e.g., Frank H. Easterbrook and Daniel R. Fischel, *The Economic Structure of Corporate Law* (Cambridge, MA: Harvard University Press, 1991), at 41. However, the argument certainly pre-dates the modern law and economics movement. For example, writing in 1932, Berle and Means sought to debunk the notion that the concepts of separate legal entity and limited liability constitute valuable state-granted privileges:

> More accurately, the associates are granted a legal convenience in that they may use the courts without writing the name of every shareholder into their papers. The reverse process—that of liability to be sued under a single name—is manifestly not advantageous to them, but is rather a measure of fairness to their opponents. "Limited liability" again need not be assumed as a state-granted privilege. A clause could be put in every contract by which the apposite party limited his right of recovery to the common fund: the incorporation act may fairly be construed as legislating into all corporate contracts an implied clause to that effect. The only real question turns on non-commercial liabilities—such as liability for negligent injury by a corporate agent—a liability which, however, is in large measure within the control of the state anyhow. It would be quite as fair to assume that a corporation act operated as a limitation of the plaintiff's right to recover as to claim the limitation as a "privilege" for the defendant. Admiralty, bankruptcy and other divisions of law furnish illustrations of limitations on the right of recovery which legal scholars have never felt it necessary to justify by theories of grants of "privilege" to the ship or the bankrupt.

> See Berle and Means, supra footnote 2, at 128, note 2.

85   As Hansmann and Kraakman have recently contended, it may be that historically the corporation was important not because it shielded shareholders from the corporation's creditors, but rather because it shielded the assets of the business from the shareholders' creditors. See Henry Hansmann and Reinier Kraakman, "The Essential Role of Organizational Law" (2000), 110 *Yale Law Journal* 387.

lawyer, the realist view seems to have very little significance. Gower asserts (revealingly, in a footnote only) that

> legal personality, in the sense of the capacity to be the subject of legal rights and duties, is necessarily the creation of law whether conferred upon a single human being or a group and the Realist and other theories are of no direct concern to the lawyer (as opposed to the political scientist) except in so far as they have influenced the judges in the development of the law.[86]

Here in Canada, Ziegel et al. have similarly suggested that

> [w]hatever the merits of the various theories, it seems fairly clear that modern Canadian business corporations legislation has embraced the fiction theory.[87]

And so they have. Whether this was merely an act of legislative usurpation is a question to which no answer will be attempted here.[88]

However, still open for debate is the question whether explicit legislation is necessary to create a separate organizational entity. One notes that, in 2002, the Supreme Court of Canada, in *Berry v. Pulley*,[89] acknowledged that trade unions—lacking any explicit legislative basis on which to claim the status of "separate legal entities"[90]—nevertheless, through the development over time of duties and powers,

> have become recognized as entities which possess a legal personality with respect to their labour relations role. This status not only allows a union member to bring suit against his or her union directly, but also enables the union to enter into contracts of membership with each of its members.[91]

Indeed, the court in *Berry v. Pulley* endorsed a similar conclusion reached by the Supreme Court in 1960 in *International Brotherhood of Teamsters v. Therien*,[92] and a subsequent and more general statement of the concept embodied in the language of Estey J from his judgment in *International Longshoremen's Association*.[93] There, Estey J concluded that,

---

86   Gower, supra footnote 33, at 4, note 7. This note is preserved in the current edition. See also Davies, supra footnote 11, at 4, note 5).

87   Jacob S. Ziegel et al., *Cases and Materials on Partnerships and Canadian Business Corporations*, 3rd ed. (Toronto: Carswell, 1994), at 139.

88   One does note that Frederick Pollock boldly asserted in 1911 that "[t]he time has come, I think, to ask whether any English Court ever officially or semi-officially adopted [the fiction theory], and I make bold to answer in the negative." Frederick Pollock, "Theory of Corporations in Common Law" (1911), 27 *Law Quarterly Review* 219, at 235. Whether any Canadian corporate scholar would presume to make a similar bold claim is unclear.

89   [2002] 2 SCR 493.

90   The court did note, at para. 43, that language in the BC *Labour Relations Code* refers to trade unions as legal entities for the purposes of that statute, and it also referred to various provisions in other Canadian provincial labour relations statutes. However, the union in question in *Berry v. Pulley* was subject to the *Canada Labour Code*.

91   *Berry v. Pulley*, supra footnote 89, at para. 3.

92   [1960] SCR 265.

93   [1979] 1 SCR 120.

"regardless of the status of trade unions under statutory law, '[i]t would take the clearest possible language' to show that legislatures did *not* wish to establish the bargaining agent as a legal entity for labour relations purposes."[94]

Having concluded that a trade union contracts with its members as a separate entity, the Supreme Court in *Berry v. Pulley* went on to accord to the members of such unions— again without the aid of any express legislative enactment—the "privilege" of limited liability:

> [S]ince the union itself is the contracting party, the liability of the union is limited to the assets of the union and cannot extend to its members personally.[95]

The court was quick to warn against extending its reasoning too carelessly to other forms of unincorporated associations.[96] It is only logical to infer, the court stresses, that it is trade unions to which the legislature intended to grant the status of legal entity.[97] And to be sure, the court's reasoning resonates with the concessionist notion that this is a "status" that is within the power of the legislature to confer or withhold.

Still, the implication of the result reached in this case is clear: it was *not* an explicit act of the legislature that granted to the union the status of a separate legal entity, and it was certainly no legislative provision that conferred on the union's members the benefits of limited liability. Rather, the link to the legislature was, at most, an inference drawn from a realistic assessment of the way in which unions must operate.[98] Further, the court seems to suggest that a legislature would be able to effectively reverse this inference only through the use of the clearest of language. In other words, the onus is on the legislature to *undo* by express legislation the entity status that has emerged through association. Trade unions have thus achieved, in respect of their labour relations role, the status of separate legal entities, and their members have acquired the "privilege" of limited liability, all in the absence of express statutory language conferring either of these attributes.[99]

It is not uncommon for ideological disputes to masquerade as competing views of history. As Dewey recognized almost eight decades ago, the concept of the corporation as a separate legal entity—and thus the realist/fiction/concessionist issue—is not merely an artifact of legal history about which disinterested scholars engage in intellectually honest

---

94   *Berry v. Pulley*, supra footnote 89, at para. 45 (emphasis added).

95   Ibid., at para. 48.

96   Ibid., at para. 51.

97   Ibid., at para. 51.

98   See especially, ibid., at para. 50.

99   The fact that organizations such as trade unions acquire a kind of corporate-like separate personality, notwithstanding that they are not, technically, corporations, has long been recognized. F.W. Maitland, writing at the turn of the 20th century, recounted the following story: "Lately in the House of Commons the Prime Minister [Arthur James Balfour] spoke of trade unions as corporations. Perhaps, for he is an accomplished debater, he anticipated an interruption. At any rate, a distinguished lawyer on the Opposition benches interrupted him with 'The trade unions are not corporations.' 'I know that,' retorted Mr. Balfour, 'I am talking English, not law.'" See F.W. Maitland, "Moral Personality and Legal Personality" in *The Collected Papers of Frederic William Maitland*, vol. III (Cambridge: Cambridge University Press, 1911), 304, at 305.

debate with the common aim of discerning an objective truth. The issue has a political dimension to it.[100] Broadly speaking, those who are wary of corporate power and view increased government regulation as generally benevolent and benign, are likely to support the concessionist view. Those who are wary of government regulation and have greater faith in the markets, tend to embrace the realists' position.

There are broader political dimensions to the debate over the nature of the corporate personality, too, and those are discussed in the next section.

Reification and Personalizing of the Corporation

Some commentators have bemoaned the tendency of courts and others to use the notion of the corporation as a separate legal entity to needlessly, and misleadingly, "reify" the corporation—that is, to treat the corporation as a "thing" and therefore ignore the reality of the corporation as a mere convention by which human beings organize their business affairs.

Related to this complaint is the oft-heard lament that, by characterizing corporations as "persons," the courts have opened the door to a perfidious assertion of corporate rights—including constitutional rights—a development that has, in the minds of the most ardent anti-business activists, potentially elevated the corporation above the individual citizen. Although proponents of the latter claim appear to ignore the fact that the most fundamental right of citizenship—the right to vote—is not one enjoyed by any Canadian corporate body, their general complaint about the effects of conferring "personhood" upon corporations—especially business corporations—follows an intellectual tradition that is worthy of further mention.

Horwitz has argued that the debate over the nature of the legal entity in the late 19th century reflected "a crisis of legitimacy in liberal individualism arising from the recent emergence of powerful collective institutions."[101] If the individual were the proper focus of all political inquiry, in other words, the realists' conception of the corporate entity as having real existence—absent some artificial legal status—posed a serious theoretical threat. As Horwitz puts it, "[i]n their emphasis on corporate 'personality,' early natural entity adherents attempted simply to capitalize on the language of natural rights individualism by portraying the corporation as just another right-bearing person."[102] Harry Glasbeek has also explored and exposed this apparent paradox—namely, that the central wealth-generating vehicle in a society that glorifies individualism is, in fact, a collective; to preserve the ideals of liberalism, this collective must, therefore, be characterized as an individual.[103] As Glasbeek has put it,

---

100 Dewey, supra footnote 69, at 664ff.

101 Morton J. Horwitz, "Santa Clara Revisited: The Development of Corporate Theory" (1986), 88 *West Virginia Law Review* 173.

102 Ibid., at 221.

103 See, e.g., Harry J. Glasbeek, *Wealth by Stealth* (Toronto: Between the Lines, 2002), at 80: "[I]f the corporation can be made to appear as a market actor, just as if it were an individual flesh and blood human being, all will be hunky-dory in market-capitalism land."

[s]overeign *individuals*, taking risks while they optimize their own resources, are at the core of our political and legal liberalism and of our market-based economic principles. The corporation is a fly in the ointment because, by functional definition, it is a *collective* ... . It is only by virtue of a great legal sleight of hand that we are able to treat the corporation as *a separate legal person*, that is, as *an individual*. This permits us, at least abstractly, to say that the corporation is not a living contradiction in our legal, political and economic spheres.[104]

The fact that business corporations might enjoy constitutional protections appears to be of especial concern to some. In the United States, the application of the *Bill of Rights* to corporations began with the celebrated 1886 US Supreme Court decision in *Santa Clara Co. v. Southern Pacific Railroad*.[105] Critics of the *Santa Clara* decision have frequently been quite troubled by the supposedly cavalier way in which the justices in that case asserted that corporations ought to enjoy the protection of the equal rights provisions of the 14th Amendment to the US Constitution—an amendment known to have been enacted to end the evil of slavery, not to assist commercial enterprises. Morton Horwitz, however, in a carefully researched study of the *Santa Clara* decision,[106] found that the argument before the Supreme Court was not, in fact, based upon the "personhood" of the corporation at all. On the contrary, it was essentially a plea to the court to *disregard* the corporate entity. Horwitz cites the brief of the corporation's counsel in the case who argued that the Constitution must apply to corporations principally because

statutes violating their prohibitions in dealing with corporations must necessarily infringe upon the rights of natural persons. In applying and enforcing these constitutional guaranties, *corporations cannot be separated from the natural persons who compose them.*[107]

In other words, Horwitz emphasizes that *Santa Clara* had nothing to do with recognizing corporations as persons possessing the same rights as individuals; rather, it recognized that, in some contexts, corporations must be treated as an aggregate of individuals lest the individuals associated in a corporation forfeit the freedoms that they would otherwise enjoy.

In Canada, as a formalistic matter, Hogg and others have suggested that where the *Canadian Charter of Rights and Freedoms* purports to enshrine the particular right of any "person," such a right ought to be enjoyed by corporations as well as by individuals because corporations are, as a matter of law, persons. Hogg goes on to note that, unless at least some of the Charter's provisions are understood to protect the rights of corporate persons, Canadian freedoms may be seriously eroded. He offers by way of example the right to freedom of speech, which, if not enjoyed by corporations through which virtually

---

104 Harry J. Glasbeek, Comments on "The Limits of Limited Liability" in *The Future of Corporation Law: Issues and Perspectives*, Papers Presented at the Queen's Annual Business Law Symposium 1997 (Toronto: Carswell, 1999), 30, at 34. Note, however, that it is the neo-classical law and economics scholars today who actually downplay the notion of the corporation as a separate legal entity.

105 118 US 394 (1886).

106 Horwitz, supra footnote 101.

107 Extract from brief of John Norton Pomeroy, citing Argument for Defendant, *San Mateo v. Southern Pac. R.R. Co.*, 116 U.S. 138 (1882), cited in Horwitz, ibid., at 177. (Horwitz states that emphasis appears in original.)

all of Canada's newspapers and other media are operated, would be of little practical significance.[108] The Supreme Court of Canada has provided some guidance on the question of when a corporation will or will not be able to invoke the protections of the Charter, holding variously, for example, that s. 2(b) of the Charter does indeed protect corporations[109] and that s. 8 might also be asserted by a corporation;[110] but that the s. 7 right to security of the person cannot be enjoyed by such an artificial person.[111] Ultimately, however, the question of how or whether provisions of the Charter apply to corporations is a matter of constitutional law and not a matter of corporate law, so no more will be said about the subject here.

Theory and Purpose of the "Firm"

Introduction

So accustomed have most of us become to the existence and operation of organized business enterprises that we rarely pause to consider what combination of interests and incentives might have led to the development of the very peculiar legal fiction known as the business corporation. We know a good deal about the historical events that led to the enactment of modern corporate statutes. A few of those events have been touched on earlier in this chapter. But, for the underlying logic of the corporate form, we must look beyond historical records to the insights provided by legal and economic theorists. At one time, neoclassical economic theory had very little to say about the corporation that was of interest to legal scholars. The corporation (or, more generically, "the firm"), as Hart puts it, was "treated as a perfectly efficient 'black box,' inside which everything operates perfectly smoothly and everybody does what they are told."[112] However, economists have subsequently developed two economic approaches to the theory of the corporation that have had significant impact on legal thought: transaction cost theory and agency theory.

Transaction Cost Theory

Transaction cost theory is usually traced back to the work of Nobel economics laureate Ronald Coase.[113] Coase is best known to students of the law for his seminal paper, "The Problem of Social Cost,"[114] in which he explained what would come to be known as the

---

108 Peter W. Hogg, *Constitutional Law of Canada*, 4th ed. (Toronto: Carswell, 1997).

109 *Irwin Toy Ltd. v. Quebec (A-G)*, [1989] 1 SCR 927.

110 *Thompson Newspapers Ltd. v. Canada (Director of Investigation and Research, Restrictive Trade Practices Division)*, [1990] 1 SCR 425.

111 Supra footnote 109.

112 Oliver Hart, *Firms, Contracts, and Financial Structure* (Oxford: Clarendon Press, 1995), at 17.

113 Coase received the Bank of Sweden Prize in Economic Sciences in Memory of Alfred Nobel in 1991, "for his discovery and clarification of the significance of transaction costs and property rights for the institutional structure and functioning of the economy." See online at http://www.nobel.se/economics/laureates/1991/index.html.

114 Ronald H. Coase, "The Problem of Social Cost" (1960), 3 *Journal of Law and Economics* 1.

"Coase Theorem," and so, in the view of at least one famous law and economics proponent, helped launch the "new" law and economics movement.[115]

Years earlier, in 1937, Coase wrote a short but influential paper, "The Nature of the Firm."[116] In that paper, he identified a curious puzzle. In market economies, he noted, economists assume that the price mechanism (in other words, market-based transactions) drives the economic system. Yet, in those same economies, organized firms (including corporations) undeniably play a pivotal role. This seems paradoxical because firms appear to be organized precisely to avoid operation of the price mechanism in intrafirm dealings, in favour of a kind of central command system. Should we not be surprised, in other words, to find that such organizations designed to avoid market-based transactions *internally*, nevertheless play a critical role within economies that are supposedly based upon faith in the operation and efficiency of markets? What can explain this apparent contradiction?

The answer, Coase suggested, is that firms are organized to allocate resources without recourse to any price mechanism whenever it is difficult to determine the prices at which internal firm resources are best allocated and where the contracting costs involved are high. Coase's argument is anchored in his functional definition of the firm:

> A firm, therefore, consists of the system of relationships which comes into existence when the direction of resources is dependent on an entrepreneur.[117]

From Coase's definition of the firm follows his important conclusion that firms will continue to grow in size until they reach the point at which the cost of performing one additional transaction within the firm is equal to the cost of undertaking that same transaction in the market (or equal to the cost of having a second firm undertake that transaction instead).

Coase's argument, needless to say, is not a theory of corporations, as such. It pertains to the "firm" as an economic unit. But Coase's economic analysis of the business firm has had an immeasurable influence on modern economic analyses of the corporation, an intellectual debt acknowledged, for example, by two leading figures in the corporate law and economics community, Frank Easterbrook and Daniel Fischel, in their widely read 1991 text, *The Economic Structure of Corporate Law*.[118] Transaction cost theories are associated with a number of economists today, including, Oliver Williamson.[119]

Agency Theory

The second principal economic approach to the firm is agency theory. Agency theory has had a profound impact on corporate legal scholarship in the United States, and indeed has been influential in the teaching of corporate law at many leading US law schools as well.[120]

---

115   Richard A. Posner, *Economic Analysis of Law*, 6th ed. (New York: Aspen, 2003), at 23.

116   Ronald H. Coase, "The Nature of the Firm" (1937), 4 *Economica* 386.

117   Ibid., at 393.

118   Easterbrook and Fischel, supra footnote 84, at 355.

119   See, e.g., Oliver E. Williamson, *The Economic Institutions of Capitalism* (New York: Free Press, 1985).

120   For example, in the description of the course in business organizations offered at the Yale Law School, it is stated that "[b]ecause the key problem for corporate law is one of agency relations—how to align

Agency theory also addresses a paradox. In the simple neoclassical economic model, the business firm is assumed to be attempting to maximize its profits, because maximizing profits is in the firm's own interests. There is, however, a problem with this model. Why do we assume that a firm will necessarily be run so as to advance the firm's own interests? To say that neoclassical economics assumes that everyone rationally acts in his or her own self-interest is not a satisfactory answer. Firms, after all, can act only through human managers. Should we not assume, then, that the human beings who actually make the firm's decisions will act in their *own* self-interest, rather than in the interests of the firms they manage?[121]

Of course, there is no conflict between personal interests and firm interests if the firm's managers and the firm's owners are the same people. But what if the firm is owned by one person (or one group of people), yet is run by others? Will each manager not be tempted— that is, acting in his or her own interest—to divert value that would otherwise belong to the firm to himself or herself? Is that not, in fact, precisely what an economic model predicated on the assumption of the universal pursuit of rational self-interest predicts?

This theoretical divergence of owners' and managers' interests was translated into a practical critique of large American corporations in one of the most influential works on corporate law ever written: Adolf A. Berle and Gardiner C. Means's 1932 book, *The Modern Corporation and Private Property*.[122]

Berle (a lawyer) and Means (an economist) examined the development of American corporations over the 50-year period beginning in 1880, and concluded that owner-run businesses had been supplanted by businesses "owned" by large groups of widely dispersed public investors. This resulted, they declared, in a "separation of ownership and control."[123] The implication of this separation was that the interests of managers and shareholders might well diverge, but shareholders—strangers to one another, often separated by great distances, and each, perhaps, holding a financial stake too small to justify taking serious action to call managers to account—were not well positioned to prevent managers from shirking or, worse still, from raiding the proverbial corporate till.

A possible answer to the problem posed by Berle and Means was provided by agency costs theory. Michael Jensen and William Meckling wrote the seminal paper on this topic

---

management's incentives with shareholders' interests—the course will examine how legal rules, markets and institutional arrangements mitigate, or magnify, the central problem." Bulletin of Yale University, Yale Law School, 2002-2003, page 52. Available online at http://www.yale.edu/bulletin/pdffiles/law2002.pdf.

121 Consider, for example, Adam Smith's classic observation that "[i]t is not from the benevolence of the butcher, the brewer or the baker, that we expect our dinner, but from their regard to their own interest. We address ourselves not to their humanity but to their self-love, and never talk to them of our own necessities but of their advantages." Adam Smith, *Wealth of Nations*, book I, chap. 2 (Amherst, NY: Prometheus Books, 1991), at 20.

122 Berle and Means, supra footnote 2.

123 Berle and Means attempted to document the significance of the separation of ownership and control, but they were not the first to identify the phenomenon at least in the abstract. Thorstein Veblen, the economist perhaps best known today as the person who coined the phrase "conspicuous consumption," also noted this phenomenon in his 1904 book, *The Theory of Business Enterprise* (New York: Scribner, 1904): "This method of capitalization, therefore, effects a somewhat thoroughgoing separation between the management and the ownership of the industrial equipment." (I am grateful to Brian Cheffins for directing me to Veblen on this issue.)

in 1976.[124] Agency theory takes its name from its central animating concept—that is, an attempt to understand the nature of an economic relationship in which one person (an agent) enjoys significant control over the assets of another person (the principal) who has the residual economic interest in those assets. In the case of a corporation, it is the managers (that is, the officers and directors) who are the "agents" and the shareholders who are the principals. Of course, corporate directors and officers are not shareholders' agents in the legal sense—they cannot bind shareholders contractually, for example. The terms "agent" and "principal" are thus used by Jensen and Meckling in an economic sense, not as legal terms of art.

Jensen and Meckling acknowledge that if the managers of a firm are not entitled to keep all of its profits (because they are not also the firm's owners), they might well have an incentive not to act in the best interests of the firm. They might simply shirk, for example, because hard work is quite disagreeable, while relaxation is pleasant. Or they might use the firm's resources for their own benefit, for example, by providing themselves with opulent perquisites.

Naturally, Jensen and Meckling note, the people who are interested in maximizing the firm's profits (that is, the shareholders, in the case of a business corporation) would be aware of these management temptations. They would want to keep their managers honest; so they would use a number of strategies to monitor the managers' actions and try to align the managers' interests with their own (through cleverly designed profit-sharing schemes, for example). But, strategies like this come at a cost. Jensen and Meckling label these costs, "monitoring costs."

Now, the managers might well have good reason to want to prove to the shareholders that they, the managers, can be trusted to work hard and not to take unfair advantage of their position. They might want to do this because, for example, they are aware of what might happen if they don't. The cost to the shareholders of continually monitoring the managers might soon become so burdensome for the shareholders that the profitability and even the viability of the firm might be placed in jeopardy. But how can managers credibly convince the shareholders of their integrity? They might offer voluntarily to prepare detailed financial accounts to be reviewed by the shareholders and scrutinized by an independent auditor. These sorts of measures, though, also impose costs (either in dollar terms, or in terms of the managers' forgone leisure). The costs incurred by managers to convince shareholders that they are loyal, Jensen and Meckling call "bonding costs."

Ultimately, however, the costs incurred by monitoring and bonding will not entirely eliminate the risk that non-owner managers will underperform or divert firm resources. The remaining costs created by the agent/principal relationship are referred to as "residual loss" by Jensen and Meckling. But they, and other writers after them (many of whom share a concern that governments might think it appropriate to try to use heavy-handed legislation to reduce agency costs), argue that there are a number of market forces that might well ensure that residual losses are kept to a minimum.

For example, product markets restrain managerial opportunism. If managers run their firms inefficiently, the price of the products or services produced by their firms will rise

---

124 Michael Jensen and William Meckling, "Theory of the Firm: Managerial Behavior, Agency Costs and Ownership Structure" (1976), 3 *Journal of Financial Economics* 305.

relative to those of their competitors. Profits will fall. Investors will be difficult (or more expensive) to find and so, eventually, the firm might simply be pushed out of business, leaving the managers out of work. Realizing this might happen, managers should be expected to have strong incentives to do their best to run their firms efficiently. Furthermore, labour markets, including the market for corporate executives, constrain managerial wrongdoing. Managers who acquire a reputation for destroying value will not only endanger their current jobs, but will jeopardize the likelihood of their obtaining future jobs. Finally, the market for corporate control[125] will constrain managerial opportunism. If managers shirk their duties or destroy firm value, the market price for their corporation's shares will fall. This fall in share prices might entice a rival firm to launch a bid to acquire the shares and take control of the firm, knowing that, by firing the existing incompetent managers, the firm's assets can be used more profitably. Aware that allowing the firm's price to fall could tempt such a bidder to seek control in this way, managers should be motivated to perform their jobs wisely and well.

The Firm as a "Nexus of Contracts"

The notion of the corporation as a distinct legal person dominates the reasoning of Canadian judicial decisions. However, in the law and economics literature, the corporation is regularly conceived of as a "nexus of contracts." This theory of the firm, and indeed the phrase "nexus of contracts" itself, is particularly associated with two influential academic articles: the first by Alchian and Demsetz[126] and the second by Jensen and Meckling,[127] although the prominence of the idea today in legal scholarship also owes much to the work of Easterbrook and Fischel.[128]

Alchian and Demsetz argue that the distinction between ordinary market transactions and "transactions" that take place within firms may not be as great as Coase's vision of the firm assumed. Put more simply, in Coase's view, firms exist because market transactions are sometimes more costly than intrafirm transactions. Firms work because employees follow orders, whereas markets work because contractors can freely negotiate prices. Alchian and Demsetz disagree. They assert that the firm

> has no fiat, no authority, no disciplinary action any different in the slightest degree from ordinary market contracting between any two people. ... To speak of managing, directing, or assigning workers to various tasks is a deceptive way of noting that the employer continually is involved in renegotiation of contracts on terms that must be acceptable to both parties.[129]

---

125 The seminal paper on this subject is Henry Manne, "Mergers and the Market for Corporate Control" (1965), 3 *Journal of Political Economy* 110.

126 A. Alchian and H. Demsetz, "Production, Information Costs, and Economic Organization" (1972), 62(5) *American Economic Review* 777.

127 Supra footnote 124.

128 Supra footnote 84. In the United Kingdom, the leading law and economics study of corporate (or company) law is Brian R. Cheffins, *Company Law: Theory, Structure, and Operation* (Oxford: Clarendon Press, 1997).

129 Supra footnote 126, at 777-78.

Jensen and Meckling take this idea one step further. Alchian and Demsetz principally looked at the firm in terms of the employer/employee relationship. Jensen and Meckling recharacterize the firm entirely in functional, rather than in institutional terms. It is not simply the employer/employee relationship that can be modelled in contractual terms, they argue. The firm itself is nothing but a "nexus for a set of contracting relationships among individuals,"[130] a kind of meeting place for the contractual (or contractual-like) relationships that exist between all of the participants whose resources combine in the corporate enterprise—the employees, the suppliers, the creditors, the customers, and so on. The nexus of contracts view, in other words, denies altogether the significance of the corporation as a separate entity. It contends that a corporation is not really a thing at all.[131]

If the firm can be so deconstructed into an elaborate network of contracts, what are the principal subjects of negotiation that characterize such contracts? William Klein[132] identifies four basic elements that are the subject of negotiation in all of these firm-defining or constitutive "contracts":

1. allocation of risk,

2. allocation of return (or profits),

3. allocation of control, and

4. duration of the relationship.

The "nexus of contracts" view offers a much more complex conception of the corporation than suggested by the early Berle and Means critique. The problem identified by Berle and Means was a simple two-sided tug of war: managers on one side and owners (shareholders) on the other. But the importance of the shareholders within the corporation's management structure is much diminished if the corporation is more accurately conceived as a focal point for a complex network of relationships involving multiple participants—shareholders and managers, certainly, but also creditors, employees, suppliers, customers, and so on. In fact, in the nexus of contracts model, shareholders are not conceived of as "owners" at all. The concept of ownership is not relevant because the corporation is not a thing to be owned. Thus, shareholders are, instead, cast as the holders of the residual economic interest in the corporation—they stand at the end of the corporate value line. All other fixed claimants—creditors, employees, and so on—must have their claims paid in full before the shareholders receive any return at all. But, if the corporation generates sufficient wealth to satisfy all of its other fixed claimants, the holders of the residual economic interest are entitled to the surplus—an entitlement that offers potentially unlimited upside. Managers, on this view, are charged with the obligation to maximize the interest of the holders of the residual economic interest because if there is any value created for them, then, by definition, all other corporate claimants will also be remunerated in full. All corporate participants (or "stakeholders" or "constituents") will accordingly be made better off. However, as discussed further

---

130 Supra footnote 124, at 311.

131 Ibid.

132 William A. Klein, "The Modern Business Organization: Bargaining Under Constraints" (1982), 91 *Yale Law Journal* 1521.

below, this "shareholder primacy" implication has been challenged on the basis of social democratic norms, as in the team production corporate law model of Blair and Stout,[133] and on the grounds that a superior alternative economic model of the firm exists.

Function of Corporate Law

The nexus of contracts model stresses the constructive power of the markets, and minimizes the impact and importance of formal legal rules.[134] It is assumed that most of the matters that are dealt with in corporate statutes can, in fact, be achieved by the parties themselves through private agreement, at least in the absence of transaction costs.[135] Corporate law should, according to this view, be crafted to achieve for the participants the result for which they would have bargained privately had they been able to do so without cost.

Recently, scholars have challenged the notion that corporate law is not a significant part of the corporate value-creation equation. Hansmann and Kraakman, for example, argue that corporate law is essential to permit "asset partitioning."[136] By this term they mean not only the traditional protection offered by limited liability, but also the protection that the corporate structure provides each investor from the adverse consequences of liabilities incurred by other investors. Indeed the latter type of partitioning is particularly significant.[137] Although limited liability might be achieved—albeit at significant cost— by private contracting, they argue, affirmative asset partitioning (or entity shielding) can be accomplished only through organizational law.

To similar effect is Margaret Blair's recent suggestion[138] that the corporate structure facilitates investment in long-lived, firm-specific assets that would not otherwise be possible.

Charter Competition and the Delaware Phenomenon

One particular subject of scholarly interest in the United States involves investigation into the supposed competition among states (there is no federal US corporate law) to

---

133 Margaret M. Blair and Lynn A. Stout, "A Team Production Theory of Corporate Law" (1999), 85 *Virginia Law Review* 247.

134 The model has been strongly criticized. See, e.g., Robert C. Clark, "Agency Costs Versus Fiduciary Duties," in John W. Pratt and Richard Zeckhauser, eds., *Principals and Agents: The Structure of Business* (Boston: Harvard Business School Press, 1985), 55.

135 See, e.g., Bernard S. Black, "Is Corporate Law Trivial?: A Political and Economic Analysis" (1990), 84 *Northwestern University Law Review* 542.

136 Hansmann and Kraakman, supra footnote 85.

137 In this they are no doubt correct. It is interesting to note that Gower mentioned this aspect of the historical evolution of companies some years ago (although he did not dub it "asset partitioning"). Speaking of the special-act companies of the late 17th century, he noted, "although [the fact that an individual would not be liable for the company's debts] was recognized, [the corporation] appears at first to have been valued mainly because it avoided the risk of the company's property being seized in payment of the members' separate debts." Gower, supra footnote 33, at 23.

138 Margaret Blair, "Locking in Capital: What Corporate Law Achieved for Business Organizers in the Nineteenth Century" (2003), 51 *UCLA Law Review* 387.

attract incorporations. The advantage to a state of attracting incorporators from other states may include, among other things, state fees and taxation revenues that might be raised from these corporations as well as the money that will flow into the state as local lawyers and other service providers are hired to facilitate the incorporation and the ongoing administration of these corporations.

Note that state competition for corporate charters has nothing to do with attempting to lure a corporation's actual business operations to the state. Entrepreneurs who only ever intend to carry on business in California, for example, may still, if they wish, incorporate their business in Nevada, or New York, or Hawaii for that matter. Incorporation in a state does not require one to carry on any business in that state.

Early in the 20th century, many US corporations chose to incorporate (or reincorporate) in New Jersey, in part because New Jersey's flexible corporate law allowed one corporation to hold shares in another. New Jersey's stronghold on such incorporations was broken in 1913 when a number of statutes were passed that made New Jersey's corporate law unattractive, especially for larger firms.[139] Delaware soon became, and remains to this day, the undisputed American champion in the competition to attract incorporations from out of state. Indeed, some commentators have suggested that the competition is over.

What explains Delaware's success? First, note that Delaware does *not* attract a significant number of private corporations. Evidently, neither Delaware nor any other US state is the obvious favourite of smaller corporations. However, large, public corporations tend to favour Delaware.

The Delaware phenomenon has generated a vast body of academic literature—both theoretical and empirical. Much of that literature builds on the basic question raised in two articles published in the 1970s. The first, by William Cary,[140] argues that if states compete in trying to attract incorporations, the standards of corporate legislation will deteriorate. It is managers, not shareholders, who choose where to incorporate (or reincorporate), and managers will choose the state that most favours them, at the expense of the shareholders. In this "race to the bottom," shareholders will surely be the losers.

But, if it is true that one state's corporate legislation (say, Delaware's) favours managers at the expense of shareholders, won't shareholders also be able to figure that out? No one will invest in corporations incorporated in value-destroying states. Thus, if one state is attracting more incorporations than another, it must be because that state's legislation is *more* attractive to investors. There is no race to the bottom; there is a race to the top. It is not surprising that the race-to-the-top thesis, first propounded by Ralph K. Winter,[141] has

---

139 For a discussion of why and how New Jersey amended its laws, see William E. Kirk III, "A Case Study in Legislative Opportunism: How Delaware Used the Federal-State System to Attain Corporate Pre-Eminence" (1984), 10 *Journal of Corporate Law* 233.

140 William L. Cary, "Federalism and Corporate Law: Reflections upon Delaware" (1974), 83 *Yale Law Journal* 663.

141 Ralph K. Winter, "State Law, Shareholder Protection, and the Theory of the Corporation" (1977), 6 *Journal of Legal Studies* 251.

found many supporters in the law and economics community.[142] Moreover, there is some empirical evidence that incorporating in Delaware actually does increase a firm's value.[143]

When law students first hear of the Delaware phenomenon they are often left scratching their heads. "Why don't other states simply pass a corporate statute exactly like Delaware's?" they ask. "Then Delaware would no longer have any advantage." But, the matter is not that simple. Although having a flexible statute such as Delaware's may be a necessary condition for attracting public corporations, it is clearly not a sufficient condition. It has been suggested that it is not simply the substance of Delaware's corporate law that creates Delaware's advantage. Delaware's edge also derives from the highly specialized and respected Delaware Chancery Court as well as the significant body of judicial precedent that has now developed in Delaware. That jurisprudence cannot be transplanted to another state with the simple stroke of a legislative drafter's pen. Moreover, as Kahan and Kamar have recently argued, it is unclear that other states actually have a reason to try to compete with Delaware now.[144]

In any event, research into the Delaware phenomenon is fascinating and quite illuminating, but far too voluminous even to attempt to summarize here.

What is intriguing from the Canadian perspective is whether there is any similar competitive federalism at work in the Canadian corporate law arena. In Canada, there does not appear to have been anything quite like the Delaware phenomenon (notwithstanding the occasional attempts by members of certain provincial bars to claim such "status" for their local statute). Indeed, it is noteworthy that one of the express purposes of the CBCA was to push Canadian corporate law in the opposite direction—to encourage legislative uniformity, rather than diversity. Section 4 of the CBCA explicitly states that one of the goals of the Act is "to advance the cause of uniformity of business corporation law in Canada."[145]

The topic has generated some academic literature, notably papers by Ron Daniels[146] and by Jeffrey MacIntosh and Douglas Cumming,[147] as well as practitioners' perspectives.[148] The issue has, however, not attracted the same sort of attention in Canada that it has

---

142 Roberta Romano of Yale Law School has been an especially vigorous proponent of the salutary benefits of competitive federalism, and has argued that similar benefits could be realized in the securities law field if states were allowed to compete to regulate securities issuers. See Roberta Romano, "Empowering Investors: A Market Approach to Securities Regulation" (1998), 107 *Yale Law Journal* 2359.

143 Robert Daines, "Does Delaware Law Improve Firm Value?" (2001), 62 *Journal of Financial Economics* 525.

144 Marcel Kahan and Ehud Kamar, "The Myth of State Competition in Corporate Law" (2002), 55 *Stanford Law Review* 679.

145 Canada's corporate statutes are not, however, altogether uniform. There are a number of differences, in some cases quite fundamental, in others, rather technical in nature. A number of these specific differences are discussed in chapter 2.

146 Ronald J. Daniels, "Should Provinces Compete: The Case for a Competitive Corporate Law Market" (1991), 36 *McGill Law Journal* 130.

147 Jeffrey MacIntosh and Douglas Cumming, *The Role of Interjurisdictional Competition in Shaping Corporate Law: A Second Look*, Working Paper WPS-49 (Toronto: Law and Economics Association, 1996).

148 See, e.g., Wayne D. Gray, "Corporations as Winners Under CBCA Reform" (2003), 39 *Canadian Business Law Journal* 4.

attracted south of the border. It is possible that there are even simpler economic and geographic explanations for the failure of any Canadian "Delaware-like" jurisdiction to emerge. Even in the United States, where the pool of very large public corporations is vast, it appears that the economic benefits of seeking to attract a significant number of incorporations are only material for a very small state and that, indeed, there does not appear to be sufficient bounty to be shared by more than one such small state. In Canada, where there are far fewer large public corporations that would be able (or willing) to pay large franchise taxes, it may well be that there is simply no real economic incentive for even the smallest provinces to expend significant resources in an effort to attract a disproportionate share of incorporations. Moreover, Delaware— though a small state—is reasonably close (as was New Jersey)—to the major US financial centre, New York City. In Canada, those provinces with a population as small as, or smaller than, Delaware's, tend to be the most far removed from Canada's financial heartland. Needless to say, however, a more considered view of this question would require empirical study.

Corporate Governance

Corporate governance has become especially topical following the widely publicized series of US corporate scandals that began with a significant earnings restatement by Enron Corporation in October 2001 (followed by that company's bankruptcy some two months later). The subject had been important to corporate lawyers for years before that; but the scandals led to renewed popular interest in what had previously been considered a fairly specialized field.

The notorious corporate scandals that prompted recent reform initiatives principally involved two types of misconduct: the wrongful diversion by corporate managers of corporate assets (and the related failure of outside auditors and perhaps outside directors to detect or deter this diversion), and the misrepresentation of corporate financial results. Many of these misrepresentations may have been motivated by obvious and immediate pecuniary self-interest (such as the desire to inflate stock prices long enough to make the exercise of executive stock options profitable). It is also possible, though, that some misrepresentations arose as the unintended byproduct of the somewhat complicated incentives at play when managers' desire to enhance their credibility as value-producing managers tempts them to shore up their corporation's sagging share prices in times of financial adversity.

In the heightened scrutiny to which public corporations were subject after the recent cluster of firm-shaking mistakes, a host of other sorts of misadventures were also revealed. These included allegations of unlawful insider trading, disturbing conflicts of interest involving firm auditors and others, questionable securities sales and "sell side"[149] equity analysts' research practices, and woeful directorial inattentiveness. The boardroom failings, in other words, appeared to involve breaches of both traditional branches of corporate directors' duties: the duty of care, diligence, and skill, and the duty to act honestly and in good faith, with a view to the best interests of the corporation.

---

149 That is, analysts employed by securities firms selling securities, rather than analysts employed by institutional investors ("buy side").

The modern corporate governance question is also linked to broader questions about the role of the business corporation itself. Put simply, what, precisely, does it means to insist that corporate directors and officers act "in the best interests of the corporation?" Does this phrase mean, for all practical purposes, "best interests of the shareholders"? If so, how are the best interests of widely dispersed, highly diverse shareholders to be divined?

And if it is, in any event, mistaken to equate the best interests of the corporation solely with the shareholders' interests, the inquiry becomes more complex still. Who, besides the shareholders, are deserving of the corporate directors' fealty? Employees? Suppliers? Creditors? Customers? Government? The natural environment? The local community? All people at all times everywhere?

This question has recently reached the Supreme Court of Canada,[150] and was alluded to very briefly earlier in this chapter in the discussion of competing theories of the firm. The subject is taken up again in chapter 10. But the reader is warned that a complete and even-handed treatment of this topic—in view of the extensive academic literature that has been developed on the subject—would require book-length treatment in and of itself.

Finally, one of the most intriguing developments in modern corporate law scholarship has come in the area of international comparative corporate governance. Much of this scholarship originated in the United States, and was in no small part intended not to produce a global unifying theory of corporate law, but rather to provide insights into specific features of American corporate governance, and possible hints for reform of US institutions. However, the subject has now captured the imaginations of many scholars both inside and outside the United States.

Scholars have attempted, among other things, to account for the differing patterns of corporate share ownership observed in different jurisdictions. Why is it that large public corporations in the United States tend to be very widely held, while public corporations in other major industrial countries such as Germany and Japan (sometimes called "blockholder systems"[151]) tend to have dominant shareholders?

Influential papers by such scholars as La Porta et al.[152] have maintained that a link may be drawn between a country's legal protections for minority shareholders and patterns of share ownership within that country. Specifically, in those systems where minority shareholders enjoy fewer legal protections, share ownership will tend to be less widely dispersed.[153] "Market systems," such as those of the United States and the United

---

150 *Peoples Department Stores Inc. v. Wise*, 2004 SCC 68. The implications of this decision are discussed in chapter 10.

151 See, e.g., William W. Bratton and Joseph A. McCahery, "Comparative Corporate Governance and the Theory of the Firm: The Case Against Global Cross Reference" (1999), 38 *Columbia Journal of Transnational Law* 213, at 218.

152 See, e.g., Rafael La Porta, Florencio Lopez-de-Silanes, Andrei Shleifer, and Robert Vishny, "Investor Protection and Corporate Governance" (2000), 58 *Journal of Financial Economics* 3; and see also Rafael La Porta, Florencio Lopez-de-Silanes, and Andrei Shleifer, "Corporate Ownership Around the World" (1999), 54 *Journal of Finance* 471 and "Legal Determinants of External Finance" (1997), 52 *Journal of Finance* 1131.

153 For a survey of some of this literature, see Christopher C. Nicholls, "Governance, Mergers and Acquisitions, and Global Capital Markets" in Janis Sarra, ed., *Corporate Governance in Global Capital Markets* (Vancouver: UBC Press, 2003), at 85.

Kingdom, according to this theory, offer the strongest protections to minority shareholders, while civil law countries, in particular, may offer the weakest shareholder protections.[154] Other intriguing links have been drawn by Mark Roe between national political systems and aspects of corporate governance;[155] and most recently an ambitious attempt has been undertaken by Kraakman et al. to define those fundamental aspects of corporate law that might be regarded as universal.[156] Much has been written, too, about the possibility that, over time, market pressures on diverse governance systems internationally may lead to systemic convergence—at least (or perhaps at most) to "functional convergence."[157] Indeed, as one writer has (not approvingly) observed, "[t]oday the academy has become much enamored with the notion of 'global' convergence in corporate governance."[158]

This comparative corporate law scholarship represents an important step in understanding the corporation, and, more particularly, in assessing the relationship between the corporation as an economic phenomenon and the legal rules and institutions that both define and support the corporation as a legal phenomenon. Most of this text, however, will focus more narrowly on Canadian corporate law, leaving significant comparative considerations to be explored elsewhere.

154 La Porta et al., supra footnote 152.

155 See, e.g., Mark J. Roe, *Political Determinants of Corporate Governance: Political Context, Corporate Impact* (New York: Oxford University Press, 2003). See also Roe's influential earlier work, *Strong Managers, Weak Owners: The Political Roots of American Corporate Finance* (Princeton: Princeton University Press, 1994).

156 Reinier R. Kraakman et al., *The Anatomy of Corporate Law: A Comparative and Functional Approach* (Oxford: Oxford University Press, 2004).

157 John C. Coffee Jr., "The Future as History: The Prospects for Global Convergence in Corporate Governance and Its Implications" (1999), 93 *Northwestern University Law Review* 641, at 650; for a stronger convergence thesis, see Henry Hansmann and Reinier Kraakman, "The End of History for Corporate Law" (2001), 89 *Georgetown Law Journal* 439. Some commentators argue, however, that there may be good reason to doubt whether the forces of international convergence will prevail. See, e.g., Lucian A. Bebchuk and Mark J. Roe, "A Theory of Path Dependence in Corporate Ownership and Governance" (1999), 52 *Stanford Law Review* 127; Bratton and McCahery, supra footnote 151; and Douglas M. Branson, "The Very Uncertain Prospect of 'Global' Convergence" (2001), 34 *Cornell International Law Journal* 321, at 325: "There is no massive 'global' convergence in corporate governance."

158 Branson, ibid., at 323.

CHAPTER TWO

The Mechanics of Incorporation

CHOICE OF INCORPORATING JURISDICTION

As seen in chapter 1, once business people have decided to incorporate, they have further choices to make. They may choose to incorporate under any one of Canada's provincial or territorial corporate statutes (regardless of where they actually intend to carry on business); or they may choose, instead, to incorporate under the federal corporate statute, the *Canada Business Corporations Act* (CBCA). On what basis would a business person choose to incorporate under the statute of one jurisdiction rather than another?

The answer to this question is not a simple one. In the United States, as discussed in chapter 1 under the heading "Charter Competition and the Delaware Phenomenon," it is clear that the state of Delaware has attracted a wildly disproportionate number of incorporations of large, public corporations. It seems equally clear, however, that no single Canadian province can realistically claim to be the "Delaware of Canada" (although, on at least one measure—attracting a disproportionate number of public corporations—the federal CBCA has enjoyed some Delaware-like success; and, as discussed in chapter 3, a unique type of corporation available as an option under Nova Scotia's *Companies Act*—the unlimited (liability) company—has recently been found to be especially useful for certain cross-border ventures from a US tax perspective).

Legal practitioners are well aware of the sometimes technical variations among corporate statutes that might, in some circumstances, and for some companies, tend to make one jurisdiction more desirable than another.[1] This chapter begins at the most abstract level, by surveying the three different "models" of corporate statute in Canada, before turning to some of the more specific statutory differences that have been identified from time to time.

Types of Canadian Business Corporation Statutes

There are three basic theories or models of incorporation statutes, and examples of all three may be found among Canada's federal and provincial incorporation statutes.

---

1   For a canvass of many of these considerations, see Wayne D. Gray and Casey W. Halladay, *Guide to CBCA Reform: Analysis and Precedents* (Toronto: Carswell, 2002), at 73-77.

Memorandum[2] and Articles of Association

This is the model of corporate law that characterizes the UK *Companies Act*, and the Canadian corporate statutes that were originally based on the UK model (namely, the BC *Business Corporations Act* and the Nova Scotia *Companies Act*). This model has two fundamental characteristics. First, it is premised on the theory that the corporation's constating documents constitute a *contract* between the members. This contractual orientation is made explicit in the statutes.[3] Second, these statutes provide for incorporation by "registration," which means that they permit a corporation to be formed as of right by those incorporators who have complied with the statutory provisions and paid the necessary fees. There is no discretion, in other words, granted to any government official to refuse to incorporate a company as long as all of the statutory requirements have been satisfied.

Letters Patent

Incorporation by letters patent, pursuant to a general incorporation statute, is the model of corporate law that, according to Wegenast,[4] was a uniquely Canadian invention, but that today survives only in the *Companies Act* of Prince Edward Island. In a letters patent jurisdiction, the corporate constitution does not constitute a contract between the members. It is embodied in "letters patent" granted to the incorporators. Moreover, what the government has power to "grant," it also has power (at least theoretically) to withhold. Thus, the government retains the discretion to refuse to issue letters patent to applicants, although whether this discretion would ever be exercised today is unclear.

Articles of Incorporation/"Division of Powers"

This third model of corporate law, essentially derived from the US approach, is now the most common in the common law provinces of Canada. It is the basis for the corporate law statutes of Alberta, Saskatchewan, Manitoba, Ontario, New Brunswick, and New-

---

2   When British Columbia recently enacted a new corporate statute, the legislature replaced the concept of "memorandum" with a so-called notice of articles. However, the underlying contractual theory of incorporation from the BC *Company Act* was retained.

3   See, e.g., *Companies Act* (UK), s. 14; *Business Corporations Act* (BC), s. 19(3); and *Companies Act* (NS), s. 24(1).

4   F.W. Wegenast, *The Law of Canadian Companies*, reprinted with an introduction by Margaret P. Hyndman (Toronto: Carswell, 1979), at 22. Corporations had certainly been granted letters patent in the United Kingdom as well, but not pursuant to a general statute akin to the UK *Companies Act*. Wegenast does not suggest how Canadian legislatures happened upon this idea. One possibility is that the idea was an extension of a concept found in two English statutes that pre-dated passage of the first English general incorporation statute in 1844. These two "trading companies" acts (4 & 5 Wm. IV, c. 94 and 1 Vic., c. 73) empowered the King and the Queen, respectively, to grant letters patent to any company of persons, and to provide to those companies certain corporation-like privileges. Of course, it is clear that neither of these English statutes (the second, it should be mentioned, repealed and replaced the first) provided for the creation of corporations. To the contrary, the purpose of the legislation seemed, in fact, to be to extend certain useful trading privileges to unincorporated companies. The language used in the 1834 statute, for instance, states that "it would be expedient to confer upon such Associations, or some of them, *some of the Privileges of and incident to Corporations created by Royal Charters*" (emphasis added).

foundland, as well as the federal corporate statute, the CBCA. Under what Professor Bruce Welling has usefully called a "division of powers" statute, the corporation's constating documents are not, as in a memorandum jurisdiction, contractual in nature. It is, generally speaking, the statute itself that defines a number of key roles for the directors and shareholders (subject, however, to the ability of the shareholders to enter into a special statutorily recognized agreement known as a unanimous shareholder agreement).[5] However, as in the memorandum jurisdictions, the division of power statutes also provide for incorporation by registration. That is, as long as the incorporators comply with the statutory requirements, incorporation is of right.[6]

Is there any enduring practical significance to these differing models of incorporation? One notes that some Canadian jurisdictions that once had statutes based on the letters patent or memorandum model subsequently abandoned those models in favour of the more "modern" CBCA-style approach. Others did not.

If one model is "superior," would we not expect all jurisdictions to adopt it? Perhaps in those jurisdictions that have not yet adopted the CBCA-style model, the explanation is simple legislative inertia. Corporate legislation is rarely a top priority for members of provincial legislatures. Promising to modernize a province's corporate law is not likely to win a campaigning politician many votes. Moreover, the influence of those with a vested interest in the status quo cannot be ignored. Lawyers, for example, who have developed local expertise in an antiquated statute may not be eager for their legislature to replace it with a new version,[7] no matter how objectively "superior" it might be. (It was no comfort for unemployed buggy whip manufacturers to be told that cars were more efficient than horses.) Alternatively, national legislative uniformity may be seen as rather pointless. If Canada were to have 14 totally identical corporate statutes, surely 13 of these statutes would be largely unnecessary.

It is difficult to find compelling, practical arguments that prove that one *model* of incorporation statute is inherently superior or inferior to another. Needless to say, for certain specific business transactions, one particular Canadian corporate statute may, indeed, be preferable to another; but the advantage in such cases will typically be linked to the presence or absence of a specific statutory provision, not to the underlying theoretical model upon which the statute as a whole is based. Thus, for example, the Nova Scotia unlimited (liability) company is

---

5   See Bruce Welling, *Corporate Law in Canada*, 2nd ed. (Toronto: Butterworths, 1991), at 55ff. The significance of the unanimous shareholder agreement is discussed further in chapter 4.

6   It has been suggested that recent changes to the CBCA represent a move away from this concept because s. 8(2) of the CBCA states that "the Director may refuse to issue a certificate of incorporation" if the notice of registered office or the notice of directors filed with the articles "indicates that the corporation, if it came into existence, would not be in compliance with this Act." However, it seems more reasonable to say that the recent changes have clarified rather than abrogated incorporators' rights. The Director must surely, after all, have had the discretion to refuse incorporation in cases where the necessary statutory requirements for incorporation had not been fully complied with.

7   Neither legislative inertia nor a vested interest in the status quo explains the recent BC experience. British Columbia recently undertook an extensive revision of its corporate statute, leading to the recent enactment of the *Business Corporations Act*. But, it was nevertheless decided that the new statute ought to remain a memorandum/articles of association "style" statute, though, as a technical matter, the "memorandum" has been replaced by a document known as "notice of articles."

an option in Nova Scotia that has attracted hundreds of new incorporations from American-based incorporators. As it happens, Nova Scotia's *Companies Act* is memorandum-style legislation. But a CBCA-style or letters patent statute could easily be amended to provide incorporators with the option to create unlimited liability companies too.

Accordingly, from a practical perspective, it appears that specific technical differences between Canada's various corporate statutes are of far greater significance to prospective incorporators than the underlying philosophy of the statute in which these various provisions appear. The following section discusses these sorts of statutory differences.

Some Purported Advantages of Particular
Canadian Corporate Statutes

Practitioners are well aware of the various peculiarities of each of Canada's many corporate statutes. Given the right set of circumstances, any one of these distinct features might well prove advantageous or disadvantageous to a prospective incorporator. Among the most frequently cited differences are the following:

- Federal incorporation is sometimes said to offer certain advantages for corporations that wish to carry on business nationally because such corporations are entitled to use their name nationally, and to carry on their business throughout the country.[8] (As mentioned earlier, this advantage may now be more theoretical than real.[9])
- Some jurisdictions permit corporations to issue par value shares, while others do not.
- Some jurisdictions permit corporations (rather than only individuals) to be directors of other corporations, but most do not.
- Some jurisdictions place restrictions on where meetings may be held, and others do not.
- Some jurisdictions place restrictions on where the corporation's registered office may be located, and others do not.
- Some jurisdictions have less onerous director liability provisions than other jurisdictions.
- Some corporate statutes require that corporations have a certain number of Canadian residents on their boards of directors. Others have more lenient residency requirements. Some have no residency requirement at all. Statutes of this latter sort may be especially attractive to foreign owners wishing to set up a Canadian corporation. As explained in chapter 4, however, the practical effect of resident Canadian director requirements can often be overcome through the use of a unanimous shareholder agreement.
- Some have rules restricting intercorporate share ownership. Others are more flexible on this matter.
- At one time, most Canadian corporate statutes had formal rules restricting the provision of financial assistance by corporations to shareholders, directors, officers,

---

8   CBCA, s. 15(2).

9   But see Gray and Halladay, supra footnote 1, at 74, where they argue that the right of a federal corporation to use a name nationally "without the necessity of a trade mark registration" may still have value.

employees, or to any person in connection with the purchase of the corporation's shares. A few jurisdictions did not have such rules, making those jurisdictions attractive for corporations planning certain types of transactions. Recently, however, most Canadian jurisdictions have taken steps to remove or substantially reduce the effect of their financial assistance rules.

• One Canadian jurisdiction (Nova Scotia) permits the incorporation of unlimited (liability) companies—a vehicle that offers certain US tax advantages.

There are other commonly heard but rather irrational explanations for favouring one jurisdiction over another. For example, at one time, it was suggested that it was more "prestigious" to incorporate under the CBCA than under one of the provincial statutes. Given that incorporation under the CBCA is by mere registration (meaning that everyone who correctly fills in the forms and pays the fees is entitled, as of right, to receive a certificate of incorporation), it is not clear what the source of this "prestige" was thought to be. Indeed, there is only one jurisdiction in Canada where incorporation is *not* as of right—Prince Edward Island. Yet, one rarely hears it suggested that PEI is Canada's most prestigious incorporation jurisdiction; in fact, according to one recent study, Prince Edward Island's "share" of new Canadian incorporations in the April 1, 2001 to March 31, 2002 period was actually slightly less than one might have predicted given the province's percentage of Canadian GDP.[10] If the CBCA's mandatory governance rules were more onerous than those of the provincial statutes, perhaps a compelling argument for "prestige" could be made out. But any suggestioin that the CBCA regime is inherently superior is highly contestable. Further, "prestige," in any event, is likely to be of greatest importance to publicly traded corporations. Such corporations will be subject to additional requirements imposed by securities legislation and, if their shares trade on a securities exchange (such as the Toronto Stock Exchange or the New York Stock Exchange), to the more demanding listing rules of the exchange as well. Of course, it may be that the perceived prestige of federal incorporation arises merely as the result of misinformation, especially, perhaps, in foreign jurisdictions where Canadian corporations wish to pursue business opportunities (and may have some interest in perpetuating the myth that CBCA incorporation is especially prestigious).

In any event, for small, private corporations (which comprise the overwhelming majority of corporations in Canada),[11] it is unlikely that these sorts of technical distinctions are of much significance. One suspects that most smaller businesses in Canada elect to incorporate under the statute of the province in which the incorporators live and intend to work, and small corporations in any province or territory are no doubt well served by their local legislation.[12]

---

10 See Wayne D. Gray, "Corporations as Winners Under CBCA Reform" (2003), 39 *Canadian Business Law Journal* 4, at 33.

11 Gray reports that in the April 1, 2001 to March 31, 2002 period, 144,527 new corporations were incorporated in Canada. But, there are only about 4,000 Canadian corporations with publicly traded shares in total.

12 Gray and Halladay, for example, assert that purely local businesses will generally choose to incorporate under their local provincial statute. Supra footnote 1, at 76.

THE PRACTICALITIES OF INCORPORATION UNDER THE CBCA

Some of the academic literature on corporate law is heady stuff, which is regularly punctu-
ated with references to "transaction cost economics," "incomplete contracts," and "agency
theory." Sadly, the average corporate lawyer in private practice is rarely fortunate enough
to find clients willing to pay high hourly rates for densely footnoted scholarly expositions
on such theoretical ruminations. The practical and the theoretical worlds of corporate law
do, however, occasionally intersect. The detailed practical statutory requirements for
incorporation, in particular, can help to illuminate how the abstract concept of a corporation as a separate legal entity is translated into a real-life working phenomenon.

The incorporation mechanics are somewhat different for each Canadian corporate
statute. For simple illustrative purposes, though, it will be convenient to focus on the one
general incorporation statute in force in every province and territory of Canada: the
CBCA. Incorporators of a CBCA corporation (or, more often, their lawyers) begin the
incorporation process by drafting the articles of incorporation for their planned corporation. For the simplest corporations (those, in particular, that have no complicated classes
of shares to deal with), this exercise largely consists of filling in the boxes of a standardized form, "Form 1,"[13] obtained from Corporations Canada (the branch of Industry
Canada charged with administering the CBCA). (The exercise is very different when
complex share conditions are involved. These require the drafting expertise of experienced lawyers, and can run on for many pages.)

The current version of Form 1 requires incorporators to provide a number of specific
details about their proposed corporation: the name of the corporation, the jurisdiction
where the office is to be situated, classes and number of shares, share conditions,
restrictions on share transfers, number of directors, restrictions (if any) on kind of
business, and the identities of the incorporators.

The Name of the Corporation

There are five points to note about the corporate name:[14] (1) legal element, (2) business
name or style, (3) rules governing choice of corporate name, (4) name search, and
(5) numbered companies.

Legal Element

Every CBCA corporation's name must include, among other things, a "legal element"—
that is, a word such as Limited, Incorporated, Corporation, or an abbreviated form such
as Ltd., Inc., or Corp.[15] (or the French language version of any of these words). The

---

13   Until 2001, Form 1 could be found in the regulations enacted under the CBCA. However, in order to
     provide increased flexibility, the CBCA was amended in 2001 to permit the director appointed under the
     Act to determine the required forms. Thus, s. 6(1) of the CBCA provides that "articles of incorporation
     shall follow the form that the Director fixes" and must include the specified information discussed below.

14   See CBCA, s. 6(1)(a).

15   Ibid., s. 10(1).

conventional explanation for this requirement is that it is intended to signal to those dealing with the corporation that they are doing business with a limited liability entity.[16] Wegenast once disputed, for somewhat technical reasons, whether such a tag was ever properly attached to Canadian corporations, but his objections are obviously moot given the explicit statutory requirement today that such an element must form part of the name of every Canadian business corporation. The traditional explanation of the legal element requirement was premised on the idea that corporate status was somehow suspect; it detracted from the stature or credibility of a business. Creditors, it is said, must be put on warning that they are dealing with a (dodgy) limited liability corporation, not a (forthright, respectable) partnership or sole proprietorship in which the owners stand fully behind their business obligations. The "cautionary suffix," as the legal element is sometimes called, was to be, as the Dickerson committee put it, "a red flag warning the public of the dangers which they ran if they had dealings with limited liability corporations."[17] Paradoxically, however, it is also commonly suggested that, in fact, incorporation confers some measure of *enhanced* prestige on businesses—making creditors and investors more eager, not less eager, to do business![18] Moreover, the Dickerson committee, in recommending that any corporation be entitled to choose as the legal element of its name, the word "incorporated" as well as the older term, "limited," noted that "the corporation has become such a commonplace form of organization that the need for this warning device seems much less compelling."[19] It was, indeed, for this reason that the Dickerson committee thought it would be unnecessary and unduly burdensome to force a corporation that had originally been incorporated under another statute that did not impose this requirement to be forced to change its name to include a cautionary suffix if such a company were continued under the CBCA.[20] Accordingly, the committee recommended that there be authority to waive the requirement that a CBCA corporation's name include a legal element in those circumstances, and the Director's authority to grant such a waiver is now found at s. 10(2). Thus, today it is not entirely clear whether the use of a suffix such as "limited" is truly a burden, a benefit, or simply a quaint vestige of history.

Business Name or Style

The corporate name that appears in the articles need not be the only name under which the corporation carries on its business. It is possible for a corporation to carry on business not only under its own proper corporate name, but also under a "business name or style."[21] So, for example, a corporation with an uninspiring corporate name such as

---

16   See, e.g., Robert W.V. Dickerson et al., *Proposals for a New Business Corporations Law for Canada*, vol. I, Commentary (Ottawa: Information Canada, 1971), at para. 57 (Dickerson committee). This use of the term "limited," according to Gower, Lord Bramwell claims to have invented. See L.C.B. Gower, *Gower's Principles of Modern Company Law*, 5th ed. (London: Sweet & Maxwell, 1992), at 46.

17   Dickerson committee, supra footnote 16, at para. 57.

18   See, e.g., Edward Manson, "One Man Companies" (1895), 11 *Law Quarterly Review* 185.

19   Dickerson committee, supra footnote 16, at para. 57.

20   Ibid., at para. 58.

21   CBCA, s. 10(6).

Restaurant Holding Company Inc. might choose to operate the restaurant it was created to run under a somewhat snappier moniker, such as "Fred's Fancy Fine Foods." Notice that this business style contains no legal element, such as Limited or Inc. Indeed, such a non-corporate name is not permitted to include such a legal element.[22] "Fred's Fancy Fine Foods" would be the name that customers would read on the restaurant's sign, and would, indeed, be the only name by which the public would likely know the business. When corporations use such business names or styles, they are often said to be "carrying on business" or "doing business as" the chosen name. These phrases are commonly abbreviated to "c.o.b." and "d.b.a.," respectively. Thus, for certain legal purposes, this hypothetical restaurant might be identified as "Restaurant Holding Company Inc. c.o.b. Fred's Fancy Fine Foods." Alternatively, the fact that Fred's Fancy Fine Foods is merely a business name and not the legal name of the corporation itself might be indicated by writing, "Fred's Fancy Fine Foods, a division of Restaurant Holding Company Inc."

The CBCA explicitly permits the use by a corporation of such a non-corporate business name or style,[23] provided that the full corporate name is always set out "in all contracts, invoices, negotiable instruments and orders for goods or services issued or made by or on behalf of the corporation."[24]

To ensure that members of the public are able to determine readily the identity of corporations carrying on business using such business names or styles, provincial legislation typically requires that any corporation operating in the province under such a business name must record that name in a government registry that is accessible to the public.[25] It is sometimes argued that if a corporation fails to identify itself by its full corporate name when required by statute to do so, the appropriate consequence may be the forfeiture of its limited liability.[26] (Indeed, under the BC *Business Corporations Act*,

---

22   Ibid.

23   Ibid., s. 10(6).

24   Ibid., s. 10(5). Similar language is found in provincial corporate statutes, but with some noteworthy variations. For example, the Nova Scotia *Companies Act* also includes an older requirement that the corporate name be "painted or affixed" outside every place at which the corporation carries on business. See *Companies Act* (NS), s. 80(1).

25   See, e.g., *Business Names Act* (Ont.), RSO 1990, c. B.17, s. 2(1). If a corporation operating under a business name or style does not register that name or style pursuant to this statute, the corporation "is not capable of maintaining a proceeding in a court in Ontario in connection with that business except with leave of the court" (s. 7(1)). Leave is to be granted so long as the court is satisfied that "(a) the failure to register was inadvertent; (b) there is no evidence that the public has been deceived or misled; and (c) at the time of the application to the court, the person is not in contravention of this Act or the regulations" (s. 7(2)). Although this test is normally not an onerous one, in the recent case of *DC Foods (2001) Inc. v. Planway Poultry Inc.*, [2004] OJ no. 3327 (QL) (SCJ), Glithero J was not satisfied that the failure to register was inadvertent, nor that there was no evidence that the public had not been deceived. As a result, leave to maintain an action was not granted.

26   See, e.g., *City Press Inc. v. Green (c.o.b. B & G Print & Litho)*, [1996] OJ no. 1823 (QL) (Gen. Div.). The Ontario Court of Appeal has indicated, however, that failure to comply with s. 10(5) of the Ontario *Business Corporations Act* (which is substantially identical to s. 10(5) of the CBCA) "does not create automatic personal liability." See *Truster v. Tri-Lux Homes Ltd.* (1998), 18 RPR (3d) 1, at 6 (Ont. CA). However, the court also recognized that, depending on the facts, personal liability could follow because

it is expressly provided that if an officer or director knowingly permits the company not to use its name as required, that individual becomes personally liable to indemnify a purchaser, supplier, or company securityholder who has been misled by the failure.[27] There is a similar, though more limited, provision in the Nova Scotia *Companies Act*.[28]) In fact, an Ontario court recently held that a lawyer was liable for failure to advise a client with respect to the proper use of a corporate name and that the consequences of not using the corporate name properly could include personal liability for the client.[29] The rationale underlying the imposition of personal liability in such cases appears to run as follows: Third parties must be properly alerted to the fact that they are dealing with limited liability entities, so that they may carefully consider whether or not they are prepared to risk doing business with such entities. It is, therefore, not appropriate to extend to the members of these entities the privilege of limited liability in relation to any debts that have been incurred in dealings with parties who were not properly informed that they were dealing with a limited liability enterprise. Though this logic has superficial appeal, it is far from unassailable. First, it should not be forgotten that limited liability is available to corporations (or, more accurately, to their shareholders) not only in respect of the claims of voluntary creditors (such as banks and other lenders), but also in respect of claims of involuntary creditors, such as tort claimants. Surely tort claimants never choose to "deal with" the entities that injure them, incorporated or otherwise. However, we do not, for that reason only, demand that the privilege of limited liability should be forgone in the case of tort claims against corporations. Furthermore, business corporations are not the only organizations whose members enjoy limited liability; other limited liability vehicles—such as certain non-profit corporations and, in at least some jurisdictions,

---

"if one expects to benefit from [the protection of incorporation] then others must, at a minimum, be informed in a reasonable manner that they are dealing with a corporation and not an individual." Ibid., at 7. As an earlier court had put it, "the matter is one of holding out and not of an automatic statutory liability." *Watfield International Enterprises Inc. v. 655293 Ontario Ltd.* (1995), 21 BLR (2d) 158, at 163 (Ont. Gen. Div.). In *Watfield*, although the plaintiff had been misled as to *which* corporation it was dealing with, the court found that the plaintiff was aware that it was dealing with an incorporated entity, and not with the individual defendants. Thus, the individual defendants were held not to be personally liable. A related class of cases turns on the consequences of failing to inform a creditor that a business formerly operated as a sole proprietorship has been conveyed to a corporation. It has been suggested that, to avoid liability under such circumstances the former sole proprietor must provide adequate notice to third parties. See, e.g., *Emco Ltd. (c.o.b. Emco Supply) v. Nault* (1997), 36 BLR (2d) 142 (Man. QB). Creditors entering into oral, rather than written, contracts with a corporation would not benefit from the protections supposedly conferred by the Act's requirement that the corporation's full name appear on such documents as corporate contracts. See, e.g., *Clow Darling Ltd. v. 101393 Ontario Inc.*, [1997] OJ no. 3655 (QL) (Gen. Div.)

27 See *Business Corporations Act* (BC), s. 158. For a recent case in which individuals were found personally liable under the predecessor section of the BC *Company Act* (s. 106(3)), see *Race-Way Construction & Management Ltd. v. Barker-Taylor*, 2003 BCCA 163.

28 *Companies Act* (NS), s. 80(6). This provision does not extend to the failure to include the corporate name in a corporate contract, but does call both for a fine or for personal liability for a director, manager, or officer where the name is omitted from a "bill of exchange, promissory note, cheque or order for money or goods."

29 See *Turi v. Swanick* (2002), 61 OR (3d) 369 (SCJ).

limited partnerships—are under no similar obligation to include in their names any legal element signalling to prospective creditors the limited liability status that the law confers on their members or limited partners. Yet, creditors of such entities are not, for that reason, entitled to argue that limited liability ought not to be enjoyed by members of non-profit corporations or by limited partners.

Rules Governing the Choice of Corporate Name

The CBCA,[30] and the regulations made under the CBCA,[31] set out a number of specific rules that circumscribe the range of permissible corporate names. The general principle is stated in the Act: a corporation may not have a name that is reserved for another corporation or "that is, as prescribed, prohibited or deceptively misdescriptive."[32] "Prescribed" of course means (as in other Canadian statutes) prescribed by regulation. The CBCA regulations include a detailed set of corporate naming rules. Generally speaking, these rules are intended to prohibit a corporation from adopting a name that will mislead the public in some way (for example, by falsely suggesting that the corporation has some official status or is associated with or sponsored by some professional organization or other institution—including certain regulated institutions—or by giving a false impression about the nature, method of production, or place of origin of the corporation's goods or services); or that will confuse the public (for example, by being indistinct or confusingly similar to the name of another corporation, or to a trademark or trade name).

Name Search

Unless incorporating under a designating number, as discussed below, incorporators must submit a NUANS name search report relating to their proposed corporate name at the time they submit their articles of incorporation. This search must be dated not more than 90 days prior to the date on which the articles are submitted. NUANS stands for "newly upgraded automated name search"[33] and refers to a name search system and corporate name database owned and maintained by Industry Canada. Computerized searches of proposed corporate names may be conducted through this database to determine whether a proposed name is similar to a name already in use. These searches, in most Canadian jurisdictions, were traditionally conducted for incorporators or their lawyers on a fee-for-services basis by private name search firms (or "NUANS search houses"). Such firms are still widely used, but the federal government now also allows incorporators to perform searches directly[34] for a modest fee ($20). Although the NUANS system is owned by the federal government, NUANS searches—appropriately weighted for the regions in which they are conducted—are also typically required in connection with provincial incorporations.

---

30   CBCA, s. 12.

31   *Canada Business Corporations Regulations, 2001*, ss. 17-34.

32   CBCA, s. 12(1).

33   See http://www.nuans.com/nuansinfo_en/faq.htm#system.

34   See NUANS Direct Access Project Web site at http://www.gol-ged.gc.ca/pathfinder-expl/summaries-sommaires/2/101-20-NUANS-PS_e.asp.

Numbered Companies

When a corporation is formed, the incorporators may decide that, instead of trying to devise a distinct corporate name (an exercise that has become increasingly difficult as the number of Canadian corporations continues to grow), they will simply set up their corporation with a designating number name. To use popular jargon, they will incorporate a "numbered company." A CBCA numbered company's name has three parts: the designating number (which is assigned to the company by the CBCA Director); the word "Canada"; and, finally, a legal element (that is, "limited," "incorporated," or "corporation," depending on the preference of the incorporator).[35] When an incorporator wishes to incorporate under a designating number, rather than a name, he or she requests the Director to assign a number to the corporation. (In any event, for filing purposes, all corporations are assigned a number by the Director. The only difference, in the case of numbered companies, is that this number is used not only for the Director's internal records purposes, but also as part of the corporation's official legal name.) Thus, if the number assigned by the Director to our hypothetical corporation is 999999, the corporation's complete legal name will then become, for example, "999999 Canada Limited." That is the name that will appear on the corporation's seal (if it chooses to adopt one) and that is the name that will be required to appear on the corporation's contracts, invoices, and so on.[36] Of course, such a numbered company can also choose to carry on business under an adopted business name or style, in the same way that any other corporation may choose to do. (In other words, "Fred's Fancy Fine Foods" can be adopted as the business name or style of 999999 Canada Limited, just as it can become the business name or style of Restaurant Holding Company Inc.) The chief advantages of incorporating a company using a designating number rather than a name are these. First, it can speed up the incorporation process slightly because the incorporators will not need to take the time to try to craft a distinctive name.[37] Second, it is slightly less expensive because is it not necessary to obtain a NUANS name search when one incorporates a numbered company. (This option represents a very modest cost savings, because it is now possible to obtain a NUANS search for as little as $20.)

Law firms across Canada routinely incorporate "shelf companies" so as to have corporations immediately available for their clients' future use. These shelf companies are invariably incorporated as numbered companies. Large, public corporations that routinely incorporate many single-purpose or limited-purpose subsidiaries (that will typically have no direct dealings with the public) also find it convenient to incorporate these companies under a designating number rather than going through the tedious and unnecessary process of trying to coin new, distinctive corporate names. Occasionally, investigative news stories in the popular media suggest that there is something suspicious about the use of numbered companies. Reporters sometimes imply that numbered companies

---

35   CBCA, s. 11(2).

36   Ibid., s. 10(5).

37   This was the principal benefit identified by the Dickerson committee when it first recommended that the federal corporation statute permit incorporation with a designating number. See Dickerson committee, supra footnote 16, at para. 63.

are the preferred business vehicle of disreputable characters seeking, perhaps, to conceal their identities or their true (nefarious) intentions. Such inferences are unjustified and, in fact, betray a lack of understanding of the Canadian incorporation process. First, recall that no name chosen for a corporation by its incorporators needs to have any connection whatsoever with the names of the incorporators themselves. In fact, it is manifest that there is nothing more (or less) anonymous or transparent about a distinctive, coined corporate name such as "Blaxtext Corporation Canada Limited," than there is about a numbered company name such as "999999 Canada Limited." Furthermore, the publicly filed and publicly available information about every company—whether incorporated with a name or a designating number—is identical in every respect (except in the case of that tiny fraction of Canadian corporations that have sold securities to the public and are therefore subject to the more extensive public disclosure regime applicable to such companies under provincial securities laws).[38] Incorporators publicly reveal neither more nor less information about themselves regardless of whether they choose to incorporate under a designating number or under a traditional number-free name. It may be that the news writers who have convinced themselves that there is something suspect about numbered companies have confused the concept of numbered companies with the quite distinct concept of numbered bank accounts. It is well known that numbered bank accounts permitted in some offshore banking jurisdictions are intended to preserve the anonymity of the account holders, and so are thought to be especially useful to those who have good reason to keep their financial activities far from the disinfecting light of day. A numbered company, however, has nothing in common with a numbered bank account.

The Jurisdiction Where the Registered Office Is Situated

Following amendments to the CBCA in 2001, the articles themselves now need only specify the province or territory (and not, as in the past, the "place" within a province) in which the corporation's office will be located.[39] However, the full address of the corporation's registered office must also be provided in a separate notice filed along with the articles.[40] The address of the registered office must be available not only to the Director—for the purposes of delivering notices pursuant to the CBCA—but also to the general public so that, among other things, members of the public (including, for example, creditors of the corporation or victims of torts committed by the corporation) can readily determine an address for service. The registered office address need not be an address at which the corporation carries on its business. It is not uncommon for small, private corporations to designate as their registered office the address of their solicitor so that any administrative notices that the corporation might receive from time to time may be dealt with expedi-

---

38 For a detailed discussion of these rules, see Jeffrey G. MacIntosh and Christopher C. Nicholls, *Securities Law* (Toronto: Irwin, 2002), at 253ff.

39 CBCA, s. 6(1)(b). Although s. 6(1)(b) refers on its face only to "the province in Canada," s. 35(1) of the federal *Interpretation Act*, RSC 1985, c. I-21, states that, in every Act of Parliament, " 'province' … includes Yukon, the Northwest Territories and Nunavut."

40 Ibid., ss. 7 and 19(2); Form 3, "Notice of Registered Office or Notice of Change of Address of Registered Office."

tiously. The registered office may be changed by a simple director's resolution[41] to any other address within the province or territory that was specified in the articles (followed by the filing, within 15 days, of a notice of change of address of registered office).[42] However, if the corporation wishes to change the province or territory in which its registered office is located, this will require an amendment to its articles.[43] Such an amendment can be made only by special resolution of the shareholders[44] (that is, a resolution passed by at least two-thirds of the votes cast at a shareholders' meeting, or authorized by a unanimous written resolution of the shareholders).[45] It might be noted, however, that a CBCA corporation is permitted to have its registered office in any province or territory in Canada. Typically, corporations incorporated under one of the provincial corporate statutes are obliged to have their registered office within the province of incorporation.[46]

Shares of the Corporation

Classes and Maximum Number of Shares

Corporate share capital is discussed in some detail in chapter 12. In this chapter, only one general point will be noted. At one time, it was customary for corporate statutes to require a corporation to fix specifically the total number of shares that the corporation was authorized to issue in its constating document (that is, in the case of a CBCA corporation, the articles of incorporation).[47] In many jurisdictions throughout the Commonwealth, a clause of this sort is still required. Corporations in those jurisdictions are dissuaded from setting the amount of authorized share capital too high because often fees or taxes are calculated based on the authorized capital as stated in the articles (that is, the total dollar amount of capital—divided into shares—that the corporation is *permitted* to issue), rather than on its issued capital (that is, the number of shares the corporation has *actually issued*).

Requiring corporations to specify their total authorized capital at the time of incorporation may create problems. For one thing, a corporation might well underestimate how many shares it will need to sell to raise sufficient capital throughout its entire corporate existence. Thus, at some future point, the corporation might well discover that it has, in effect, "run out" of available shares to issue, just at a time when it needs to raise money by selling additional equity. This problem is not insoluble; the corporation's articles can always be amended to increase its authorized capital. However, amending the articles requires shareholder approval, and to obtain shareholder approval it is necessary to obtain a unanimous written shareholder resolution or to convene a shareholder meeting. Calling a shareholder meeting—at least in the case of a large, public corporation—is a

---

41   CBCA, s. 19(3).

42   Ibid., s. 19(4).

43   Ibid., s. 173(1)(b).

44   Ibid., s. 173(1).

45   Ibid., s. 2(1), definition of "special resolution."

46   See, e.g., *Business Corporations Act* (Ont.), s. 14.

47   CBCA, s. 6(1)(c).

cumbersome, time-consuming, and somewhat expensive process. Needless to say, this cumbersome procedure may result in lost opportunities and inefficiencies.

Now that the CBCA no longer requires corporations to specify the maximum number of shares that it is authorized to issue, CBCA corporations typically take full advantage of this flexibility. They generally choose, in other words, to place no upper limit whatsoever on the number of shares they may issue. A typical provision to this effect in a corporation's articles might read: "The Corporation is authorized to issue an unlimited number of [common/preferred] shares."

Share Conditions

If there are two or more classes of shares, the share conditions are to be set out in the corporation's articles. If a class of shares may be issued in one or more series, the articles must set out the authority of the directors to fix the number of shares of each series and to determine the specific series conditions.[48] Item 3 of Form 1 does not explicitly state on its face the need to include share conditions. However, the statute itself is clear on this point and the instructions for completing Form 1 produced by the CBCA Director do refer to the need to include share conditions in the articles.[49]

Note that the requirement to include share conditions technically applies only "if there are two or more classes of shares." The reason for this limitation is that, if a corporation has only one class of shares, the Act mandates that all shares in that class are equal in every respect, and have full voting rights, as well as the right to receive dividends if and when declared and to receive the remaining property of the corporation when it is wound up or dissolved.[50] It is unlikely, however, that most legal practitioners would omit share conditions in a corporation's articles, even where the corporation has only a single class of shares.

The topic of share conditions is, once again, dealt with in greater detail in chapter 12. Briefly put, share conditions typically deal with the following share rights:

1. the right of shareholders to vote their shares, in particular when elections are held to choose members of the corporation's board of directors;

2. the right of the shareholders to receive dividends if and when they are declared by the corporation (that is, distributions of cash or property from the corporation while it is an ongoing business);

3. the right of shareholders to receive distributions of the remaining property of the corporation when the corporation has been wound up or dissolved, although only after all of the corporation's creditors have been paid in full; and

4. other (sometimes complex and sophisticated) rights relating to attributes of the shares aimed at satisfying investor preferences and the issuing corporation's financing needs, such as redemption, retraction, exchange, or conversion rights.

---

48   Ibid., ss. 6(1)(c)(i) and (ii).

49   Indeed, the instructions do not make clear that the CBCA only requires share conditions to be included if there is more than one class of shares.

50   CBCA, s. 24(3).

Restrictions on Share Transfers or Ownership

The articles of incorporation are required to set out any restrictions on share transfers or ownership.[51] If the shares of a corporation are publicly traded (for example, on a securities exchange such as the Toronto Stock Exchange), the corporation's articles will not include any restrictions on share ownership or transfer. (Stock exchanges will typically not permit corporations to list their shares if their articles contain such restrictions.) However, restriction on share transfers will often be included in the articles of what are generally referred to as private corporations or private companies (although, as explained in chapter 4, neither of these terms is actually used in the CBCA). In the case of such private companies, the articles might, for example, state that shares may not be transferred by a shareholder without the prior written consent of a majority of the directors or perhaps of a majority of the shareholders. There have traditionally been at least two reasons for including such transfer restrictions. First, small, private corporations—in which the shareholders are also the managers of the business—typically wish to impose restrictions on the transfer of shares so that shareholders are not, in effect, forced into business with people they would not necessarily have chosen as business associates. Second, at one time, it was very important that a share transfer restriction was included in the articles of every private corporation. Such a restriction was one of three specified provisions that a "private company" (as defined, at one time, for purposes of most provincial securities statutes) was required to have in its constating documents. It was important for such corporations to qualify as "private companies" for provincial securities law purposes because private companies enjoyed an exemption from the requirement to produce a long, detailed disclosure document known as a prospectus when it sold its shares or other securities. Although private companies did not, by definition, sell their shares or other securities to the public, they did, nevertheless, often sell securities to the family members of the promoters and perhaps to small numbers of other "non-public" purchasers. To ensure the legality of these sales, it was important that an appropriate exemption from provincial securities law prospectus requirements could be identified, of which the "private company" exemption was the most obvious. The provincial private placement rules have changed significantly in the past few years. The availability of prospectus exemptions has become somewhat more sophisticated. The "private company" exemption, as such, no longer operates the way it once did.[52] However, the presence of share transfer restrictions is still an important feature of modern "private issuer" and "closely held issuer" prospectus exemptions.

Number of Directors

The articles of incorporation are required to set out the minimum and maximum number of directors.[53] A corporation is not required to fix the precise size of its board of directors at the time of filing its articles of incorporation, except in one case that is not relevant at

---

51   Ibid., s. 6(1)(d).

52   For a discussion of this subject, see MacIntosh and Nicholls, supra footnote 38, at 179ff.

53   CBCA, s. 6(1)(e).

this point.[54] It may, instead, provide for a flexible board, specifying only two things: the minimum number of directors that the corporation must always have on its board, and the maximum number of directors that the corporation's board must not, at any time, exceed. The minimum number cannot be smaller than one.[55] In other words, every CBCA corporation must always have at least one director. Indeed, if the corporation is a distributing corporation (that is, a corporation that has sold its securities to the public),[56] it must, at all times, have at least three directors.[57] At the time the articles of incorporation are filed, a second short notice document must be filed along with the articles, naming the people who are to be the first directors of the corporation.[58] The directors named in this "Notice of Directors" remain in office until the first annual meeting of shareholders.[59] The requirement to name initial directors is important because, without initial directors, no one is authorized to issue the initial shares of the corporation or to undertake the initial steps essential to organize the corporation.[60] Of course, no one can be forced to become, or to remain, a director against his or her will. Therefore, one might ask, what is the consequence to a corporation if its directors all resign and no replacements can be found? Clearly, the corporation would be in breach of the statute. In theory, this could expose the corporation to prosecution under the Act and might even force its dissolution. But it is highly unlikely, as a practical matter, that the CBCA Director would initiate any action of this kind unless a complaint about the matter had been received. It is equally unlikely, under most circumstances, that shareholders of a corporation would press vigorously to have their corporation fined or dissolved.

Business Restrictions

The articles of incorporation are required to set out any restrictions on the business the corporation may carry on.[61] As discussed further in chapter 6, at one time, corporations were required to include in their articles the specific "objects" for which the corporation was incorporated. So fundamental were such objects considered to be, that early English incorporation statutes provided that a corporation's objects, as specified at the time of its incorporation, could never later be changed, even with the unanimous consent of the shareholders.

The CBCA no longer requires a corporation to include in its articles a statement of corporate objects. However, the incorporators, at the time the corporation's articles are

---

54 The size of the board does need to be fixed when a corporation has adopted "cumulative voting." Cumulative voting is explained further in chapter 12.

55 CBCA, s. 102(2).

56 "Distributing corporation" is defined in CBCA, s. 2(1) and *Canada Business Corporations Regulations, 2001*, s. 2(1). The concept is discussed in chapter 8.

57 Ibid.

58 CBCA, ss. 7 and 106(1); Form 6, "Notice of Directors, Notice of Change of Directors or Notice of Change of Address of Present Director."

59 CBCA, s. 106(2).

60 Ibid., s. 104(1).

61 Ibid., s. 6(1)(f).

prepared, may voluntarily include restrictions on the corporation's business in the articles. The instances in which incorporators may wish to impose such restrictions are rare. Most incorporators, preferring to take full advantage of the maximum flexibility provided by the CBCA, simply state in the articles that "there are no restrictions" on the corporation's business.

Needless to say, the fact that a corporation may be incorporated without any restrictions whatsoever placed on the scope of its business, means that an examination of a corporation's articles may tell the reader nothing whatsoever about the nature of the business that a corporation is carrying on. That consequence was precisely what the Dickerson committee intended.[62] The drafters of the CBCA regarded this as "a positive advance."[63] The practice of drafting broad, all-encompassing corporate objects clauses had become commonplace by the time of the Dickerson committee report. Thus, the drafters noted, readers of a corporation's constitution would likely be deceiving themselves if they thought that the objects that appeared there actually confined the corporation to any particular line of business. Accordingly, in the Dickerson committee's view, it was far better to make explicit in the articles the operational flexibility that corporations, in fact, already enjoyed, such that "anyone reading articles of incorporation will immediately realize that they cannot be relied upon for information as to the business actually being carried on by the corporation, and that further inquiries will have to be made."[64]

Other Provisions

Traditionally, the most common "other provisions" typically included in the articles of a private corporation have been those provisions that enabled the corporation, under certain provincial securities laws, to be eligible for "private company" or similar exemptions, as discussed under "Restrictions on Share Transfers or Ownership," above. As mentioned, relatively recent changes in so-called private placement (or exempt distribution) rules under provincial securities laws have diminished somewhat the critical importance of including private company provisions in a corporation's constating documents themselves. This issue is discussed further in chapter 4.

Incorporators

The term "incorporators" refers to the persons who initiate the incorporation process, and sign (and file) the articles of incorporation. In some jurisdictions, the incorporators are required to become the corporation's first shareholders, a practice that reflects the historical concept that the purpose of incorporation was, in effect, to "constitute the incorporators as a corporation." The CBCA, however, does not require incorporators of a CBCA corporation to become shareholders, directors, or officers.

---

62   Dickerson committee, supra footnote 16, at para. 81.

63   Ibid.

64   Ibid.

An incorporator may be an individual or another corporation (whether incorporated under the CBCA or in some other jurisdiction). However, no individual is eligible to incorporate a CBCA corporation if he or she

1. is less than 18 years of age,

2. is of unsound mind and has been found as such by a court in Canada or elsewhere, or

3. has the status of bankrupt.

Relationships between holding corporations and subsidiary corporations are so common today that it may seem surprising to learn that, historically, the idea of one corporation incorporating or even owning shares in another was highly controversial. The fact that a corporation from another jurisdiction is permitted to incorporate a CBCA corporation does, however, raise an interesting issue. Can a CBCA corporation lawfully be incorporated by a body corporate that has been incorporated in a jurisdiction where, for example, there are no restrictions on corporations being formed by individuals regardless of their age or status as bankrupt? Put more simply, if a Canadian bankrupt or minor were to incorporate a corporation in a foreign jurisdiction where they were allowed to do so, could that foreign corporation then lawfully incorporate a CBCA corporation, even though the foreign corporation's sole shareholder would not have been permitted to incorporate under the CBCA in his or her personal capacity?

What does seem clear is that it is not permissible for partnerships or limited partnerships to incorporate corporations under the CBCA, since these organizations are neither "individuals" nor "corporations" as those terms are defined by the CBCA.

COST

Incorporation is not a free government service. Incorporators must pay a fee to incorporate, and may incur fees for a NUANS name search as well, unless they have chosen to incorporate under a designating number rather than a name. The fees vary from jurisdiction to jurisdiction, but they are generally quite modest in every Canadian jurisdiction. For example, the fee that must be paid at the time articles of incorporation are filed to incorporate a CBCA corporation is $250 (reduced to $200 if the filing is made online). A more significant cost of incorporation will likely be legal fees if the incorporators choose to have their incorporation documents prepared by lawyers. There is certainly no legal requirement that lawyers be involved in incorporating a CBCA corporation (although in some jurisdictions in the world, the involvement of legal counsel is mandatory). Many non-lawyers maintain that involving a lawyer in a routine incorporation is both unnecessary and unduly expensive. Most lawyers, not surprisingly, take the opposite position. Even for the simplest incorporation, legal fees are not likely to be less than several hundred dollars. For example, at the time of writing, a Toronto law firm posts on its Web site that its flat fee for a basic incorporation (not including government filing fees) is $399.

Sadly, the fees and costs do not end with the receipt of the certificate of incorporation. A corporation needs to be maintained, annual reports need to be filed, and so on. Again, none of these matters, individually, is unduly expensive, but collectively they can be burdensome at least to the smallest of businesses.

SUMMARY AND CONCLUSION

This chapter surveyed a number of the practical matters to which one must attend when a corporation is incorporated. The incorporation process for a CBCA corporation has been used as a ready example, although the mechanics are similar when creating corporations under Canadian provincial and territorial corporate statutes as well. As one reviews the somewhat more abstract and theoretical discussions about corporate law elsewhere in this book, it may be useful to remember how, in practical terms, this metaphysical abstraction comes into existence, and how the parameters of that existence, for commercial purposes, are embodied in documents endowed with significance by means of legislative enactment and bureaucratic process.

CHAPTER THREE

Fundamental Characteristics of the Modern Canadian Business Corporation

INTRODUCTION

Any seasoned business lawyer can compile a lengthy list of corporate characteristics. If the list prepared by one such lawyer were closely compared to a list drafted by another, one would no doubt notice a few differences. But there would be many more similarities. In fact, the following six fundamental features of every Canadian business corporation would be most likely to appear on every list:[1]

- operated for profit,
- separate legal entity,
- limited liability,
- perpetual existence,
- transferability of share interests, and
- centralized management.

OPERATED FOR PROFIT

The first attribute—that a business corporation is operated for the purpose of making a profit—is definitional.[2] A profit motive distinguishes the *business* corporation from other incorporated entities such as non-profit corporations and societies, incorporated

---

1   Prior to changes made to US tax law in 1996, the US Internal Revenue Service used a six-factor test, very similar to this list, to determine whether a business enterprise should be treated as a "corporation" for US tax purposes. Two of these factors are common to all for-profit associations, and so the test came to be known as the "four-factor" test—those four factors being: centralized management, continuity of existence, limited liability, and transferability of interests. See Treas. reg. 301.7701-2(a)(1). See also David A. Skeel Jr., "Corporate Anatomy Lessons" (2004), 113 *Yale Law Journal* 1519, at 1525, listing the "traditional five-factor description of the corporation," at note 13.

2   See, e.g., Roberta Romano, *The Genius of American Corporate Law* (Washington: The AEI Press, 1993), at 2: "Corporate law presumes that firms should be managed for shareholders', and not managers', interests when those interests conflict. Profit maximization (in a world where cash flows are uncertain, this is equivalent to maximizing equity share prices) is the goal."

municipalities, universities, and so on. The for-profit mission of business corporations is not a goal explicitly stated in or mandated by Canadian business corporation statutes. It was, however, clearly understood to be the basis on which companies registered under early English companies legislation were operated,[3] and remains an implicit and defining feature of the business corporation.[4]

Of course, to say that a business corporation is invariably a for-profit enterprise does *not* necessarily imply that the corporation's *exclusive* goal is to maximize corporate profits. Indeed, an extensive body of financial economic and governance literature has developed around the question of precisely what the duties of corporate managers are, and how those duties are to be carried out. It would not at all be inconsistent with a profit-making mandate, for example, to argue that the ultimate end of business corporation managers is

1. *to maximize shareholder value* (an end to which pursuing corporate profits is the well-understood means);

2. *to maximize enterprise value*; or

3. *to optimize shareholder value in light of the competing (or, ideally, complementary) need to recognize the interests of other non-shareholder stakeholders or constituents.*

In other words, one might distinguish between ultimate corporate goals (the "ends") and the corporate profit-making objective (the "means"). How one defines the ultimate corporate goal, of course, may well influence the interpretation of the profit-making objective as well. In fact, differing views on the corporation's ultimate corporate goal might even affect how the term "profit" is properly to be defined. About lofty questions of "ultimate corporate ends" reasonable people (including reasonable judges) may well

---

3   Section 4 of the *Companies Act, 1862*, 25 & 26 Vict., c. 89, provided that companies, associations, or partnerships with more than 20 members (or 10, in the case of banks) were required to be registered under the Act (unless formed under some other act of Parliament or letters patent) if "formed ... for the Purpose of carrying on any other Business that has for its Object the Acquisition of Gain by the Company, Association, or Partnership, or by the individual Members thereof."

4   In *Anderson Logging Co. v. The King*, [1925] SCR 45, at 56, Duff J stated:

The sole *raison d'être* of a public company is to have a business and to carry it on. If the transaction in question belongs to a class of profit making operations contemplated by the memorandum of association, *prima facie*, at all events, the profit derived from it is a profit derived from the business of the company.

This passage was later cited with approval by the Supreme Court of Canada in *Canadian Marconi v. R*, [1986] 2 SCR 522, at para. 9. At one time, it was common for business corporations and not-for-profit corporations to be incorporated in Canada under the same statutes, albeit pursuant to separate sections, and in some cases separate parts of such statutes. This is still true in some jurisdictions. Today, however, in some jurisdictions, the incorporation of business corporations and not-for-profit corporations is provided for by separate statutes. So, for example, the federal *Canada Business Corporations Act* is the statute under which a business corporation may be incorporated federally, while the *Canada Corporations Act*, RSC 1970, c. C-32—the statute that at one time provided for the incorporation of both for-profit and not-for-profit entities—is the statute under which federal not-for-profit corporations may be formed today.

differ. The Supreme Court of Canada has recently shed some light on this issue in *Peoples Department Stores Inc. v. Wise*,[5] a decision discussed further in chapter 10. But on the chief means for achieving those ends there is consensus: the carrying on of for-profit ventures—in one way or another—is invariably the means by which the business corporation pursues whatever may be its ultimate enterprise goal, and is invariably what distinguishes the business corporation from other important corporations such as charities, universities, incorporated municipalities, and other not-for-profit corporate bodies.

The pursuit of profit is not unique to the business corporation. It is an organizational characteristic that the business corporation shares in common with the partnership form.[6] But the context within which the business corporation pursues financial gain differs significantly from that in which partnerships operate. The profits of a partnership are truly the profits of the partners. The profits of a corporation, by contrast, are *not* properly considered the profits of its shareholders. At the same time, the shareholders must not be viewed as mere bystanders whose claim to corporate profit distributions, in the form of dividends, is no different from the hopeful pleas of panhandlers.[7] The nature of the financial claims of a corporation's shareholders is nuanced and important. The question of the shareholder/corporation relationship is taken up further in chapters 9 and 10.

Two final notes about the use of the word "business" in the phrase "business corporation." Although only a for-profit entity may properly be incorporated under business corporation legislation (such as the *Canada Business Corporations Act* (CBCA) and its provincial counterparts), such corporations need not carry on *active* business enterprises. They may be—and indeed frequently are—mere holding corporations that exist to hold the shares of other corporations. Second, unlike a general partnership, which, by definition, does not exist unless and until a business venture is carried on in common, a business corporation may be incorporated and validly exist *before* it undertakes any activities. So it is that law firms across Canada routinely incorporate an inventory of so-called shelf companies—corporations that are incorporated generally with a number name, and typically issue a single share in exchange for nominal consideration (perhaps $1) to a lawyer, paralegal, law clerk, or legal assistant who works for the firm and who has responsibility for maintaining such shelf companies. The purpose of incorporating shelf companies is to have them available on a moment's notice for clients, especially clients who need corporations to complete a business transaction.

---

5   2004 SCC 68.

6   Canadian provincial partnership statutes typically define partnership as "the relation that subsists between persons carrying on a business in common with a view to profit." (See, e.g., *Partnerships Act* (Ont.), RSO 1990, c. P.5, s. 2.)

7   Professor Welling, by contrast, has suggested that corporate dividends should be considered as no more than "corporate gifts," no different from any other form of corporate charity or "giveaways." See Bruce L. Welling, *Corporate Law in Canada: The Governing Principles*, 2nd ed. (Toronto: Butterworths, 1991), at 645 and 662.

SEPARATE LEGAL ENTITY

There is surely no proposition of corporate law more firmly ingrained in the minds of Canadian lawyers than this: a corporation is a separate legal entity, a distinct legal person. A corporation is separate and distinct from the human beings who serve as its officers, its directors, its employees, and its agents. Perhaps most critically, a corporation is separate and distinct from those men and women who own its shares—its shareholders or stockholders[8] or, as some corporate statutes call them, its members.[9] That a corporation is such a distinct legal person is recognized for purposes of Canadian legislation by the federal *Interpretation Act*[10] and its provincial counterparts.[11] (It is worth noting, however, that the word "person," whenever it appears in a Canadian statute, does not invariably include a corporation. The statute's definition section must always be checked on this point.[12])

Of course, every action that this distinct artificial person performs must be carried into effect by natural persons—that is, by human beings. The implications of this latter, rather obvious, observation account for much corporate law jurisprudence.

The separate legal entity doctrine has proved an especially useful workhorse. It has not only buttressed the reasoning of innumerable corporate law judicial decisions, but has also helped to sustain the careers of many legal academics.

However notoriously well known the separate legal entity principle may be, there are at least two important reservations about it that are useful to keep in mind. First, perhaps surprisingly, the legitimacy of the origins of the "separate legal entity" doctrine has been disputed. Second, the "doctrine" itself is, after all, merely a metaphor, not a description of observed physical phenomena. As Cardozo famously noted in *Berkey v. Third Ave. Ry. Co.*:[13]

---

8   The term "stockholder" is rarely used in Canada. It is common in the United States where its meaning, for all practical purposes, is equivalent to the Canadian term "shareholder." In the United Kingdom, there is a technical distinction between shares and stock, still preserved in the UK *Companies Act*, but which a leading English corporate law text criticizes as "merely a source of confusion." See Paul L. Davies, *Gower & Davies: Principles of Modern Company Law*, 7th ed. (London: Sweet & Maxwell, 2003), at 627.

9   The term "members" is still used in the Nova Scotia *Companies Act*, but is there specifically equated—in the case of a company limited by shares—with the term "shareholders." (See *Companies Act* (NS), First Schedule, Table A, reg. 1(2)(e).) Although the Table A regulations are not mandatory, they constitute a "default" set of articles of association. They are deemed to be a company's articles of association unless the members effectively opt out of them in whole or in part. (See *Companies Act* (NS), s. 21.)

10   *Interpretation Act* (Can.), RSC 1985, c. I-21, s. 35(1).

11   *Interpretation Act* (Alta.), RSA 1980, c. I-7, as am., s. 25(1)(p); *Interpretation Act* (BC), RSBC 1996, c. 238, s. 29; *Interpretation Act* (Man.), CCSM c. 180, s. 17 Sched.; *Interpretation Act* (NB), RSNB 1973, c. I-13, s. 38; *Interpretation Act* (NL), RSNL 1990, c. I-19, s. 27(1)(t); *Interpretation Act* (Ont.), RSO 1990, c. I.11, s. 29(1); *Interpretation Act* (PEI), RSPEI 1988, c. I-8, s. 26(o.1); *Interpretation Act* (Que.), RSQ 1977, c. I-16, s. 61(16) (defining "persons" to include "natural or legal persons"); *The Interpretation Act, 1995* (Sask.), SS 1995, c. I-11.2, s. 27(1).

12   Students of securities regulation, for example, are often surprised to discover that the word "person" in the Ontario *Securities Act* does *not* include incorporated entities. (Whenever that statute refers to an incorporated entity, the word used is "company.") See *Securities Act*, RSO 1990, c. S.5, s. 1(1).

13   155 NE 58 (NYCA 1926).

Metaphors in law are to be narrowly watched, for starting as devices to liberate thought, they end often by enslaving it.[14]

Doctrinal Evolution of the Separate Legal Entity Principle

The theoretical ruminations surrounding the concept of the corporation's legal personality canvassed briefly in chapter 1 will not be repeated here. Instead, this chapter will focus on the conventional Anglo-Canadian legal formulation of the corporation as a separate legal entity and the implications of that doctrine as they are usually articulated by the courts. The abiding legal principles in these cases are sometimes elusive. One key to unlocking this sometimes dissatisfying jurisprudence lies in a recognition of the extent to which the modern business corporation—alone among bodies corporate—has a second non-corporate ancestor: the partnership. The business corporation is not strictly defined (at least in the way that other non-business corporations are) in terms of the property it must conserve or the narrowly defined objects it exists to pursue. Indeed modern Canadian corporate law statutes do not typically require a business corporation to state its objects.[15] Rather, the corporation is expected—like its partnership ancestor—to make profits, by whatever lawful means the managers think expedient.

Of course, a partnership is generally regarded in law as a collective of its partners, not a separate entity. That legacy has also informed the development of corporate law. At many of those very points along the historical road that the business corporation was being more strongly recognized as an organic "one" (rather than as merely an aggregate or collective), it was, paradoxically, also identified as a vehicle effectively "owned" by its shareholders, and its profits, as indirectly belonging to its shareholders. Viewed this way, the early business corporation in some ways resembled a large partnership with multiple dormant or "sleeping" partners. The modern insistence in some quarters that business corporations must be defined either as pure corporations, on the one hand, or not "real" corporations at all, on the other, may therefore mislead. It is based on an overly simplistic dichotomy that gives insufficient weight to the fact that the law (and business practice) have found it both reasonable and useful to treat the business corporation as a distinct single entity in some contexts, and yet as a kind of shareholder collective in others. This duality of nature sometimes strikes its critics as incoherent or irrational. It is neither. It is precisely this dual nature that may go some way to account for the enduring success of the business corporation as a form of commercial enterprise. And it defies neither logic nor the laws of nature to allow for such duality of nature.[16]

---

14   Ibid., at 61.

15   The *Companies Act* (PEI), s. 6(c) does require applicants for letters patent to state the purpose for which the corporation is to be formed.

16   Melvin Eisenberg, for example, in arguing that a corporation has a "dual nature" consisting "in one aspect of reciprocal arrangements" and "in another [of] a bureaucratic hierarchy," has pointed out that in modern quantum theory, light can accurately be characterized as both a wave and a particle phenomenon. See Melvin A. Eisenberg, "The Conception That the Corporation Is a Nexus of Contracts, and the Dual Nature of the Firm," [1999] *Journal of Corporation Law* 819, at 829. One need not have recourse to anything as erudite as quantum physics, however, to recognize that it is not at all illogical to say that,

No attempt will be made here to trace rigorously the origins of the doctrine of separate legal entity back to its earliest historical roots. It will be noted only that joint stock companies, an important English predecessor of the modern business corporation, were regularly referred to as a type of partnership even after the passage of legislation conferring on them the status of bodies corporate. As Grantham and Rickett note, the application of partnership legal principles to corporations was common in the 19th century, a fact particularly well illustrated, as they observe, by the title of Lindley's important 1860 text, *Treatise on the Law of Partnership, Including Its Application to Companies.*[17] By the end of that century, companies (the term used in the seminal English corporate statutes of 1856[18] and 1862[19]) were no longer being described as partnerships. Not only

---

in many instances, a thing can be described in two different (and apparently contradictory) ways simultaneously. Is a 30-year-old man young or old? Does "logic" not demand that he be only one or the other? Certainly not. We fully recognize that the answer to the question depends entirely on the context in which it is asked. A 30-year-old man is very young, for example, to be winning a Nobel prize; but he is very old to be attending primary school. Indeed, the suggestion that a question such as this could ever be answered without an understanding of the context in which it was asked would strike most of us as rather absurd. Likewise, when one asks, "is a corporation a separate legal entity or isn't it?" logic by no means demands that there must be one, immutable answer in all contexts. Instead, it behooves us to ask, "in what specific context is the question asked?" A wag might retort that while one may have two different answers to the question "is a 30-year-old man young?," there is only one correct answer to the question, "is this *particular* man 30 years old or isn't he?" In other words, while some adjectives allow for contextual interpretation, certain factual statements do not. If the question of a corporation's status as a separate legal entity is a question of that sort, then it would indeed be illogical for the law to give contradictory answers. But surely no conclusion of law is ever as incontrovertible as the kind of facts that are defined as a matter of convention. (That is, there is no sense in disputing a person's age in years, provided we are all agreed on the conventions to be used when we measure things like years. Properly understood, these questions really involve tautologies: is 30 years (that is, the measure of this man's age) equal to 30 years (that is, as that measure of age is conventionally defined)? The proposition that a corporation is a separate legal entity involves no such definitional circularity. It is thus far more akin to the question of whether a 30-year-old man is young, than to the question whether a particular man is or is not 30 years old. H.L.A. Hart recognized the extent to which the "theories of the corporate form" were, in effect, deceptions of language:

> [I]f we characterize adequately the distinctive manner in which expressions for corporate bodies are used in a legal system then there is no residual question of the form "What is a corporation?" There only *seems* to be one if we insist on a form of definition or elucidation which is inappropriate. Theories of the traditional form can only give a distorted account of the meaning of expressions for corporate bodies because they all, in spite of their mutual hostility, make the common assumption that these expressions must stand for or describe something, and then give separate and incompatible accounts of its peculiarity as a complex or recondite or a fictitious entity; whereas the peculiarity lies not here but in the distinctive characteristics of expressions used in the enunciation and application of rules.

See H.L.A. Hart, "Definition and Theory in Jurisprudence" (1954), 70 *Law Quarterly Review* 37, at 55.

17   Ross Grantham and Charles Rickett, "The Bootmaker's Legacy to Company Law Doctrine," in Charles E.F. Rickett and Ross B. Grantham, eds., *Corporate Personality in the 20th Century* (Oxford: Hart Publishing, 1998), 1, at 2, note 8.

18   *The Joint Stock Companies Act, 1856*, 19 & 20 Vict., c. 47.

19   *Companies Act, 1862*, supra footnote 3.

was the business corporation recognized as a separate legal entity, but the courts were eventually prepared to carry the separate entity principle to its logical (if not necessarily desirable) conclusion.

The above gallop through history brings the reader to the case of *Salomon v. A. Salomon & Co., Ltd.*,[20] a 19th century decision of the English House of Lords, which, for several generations of English and Canadian lawyers, has been heralded as the definitive authority on the matter of the business corporation as a separate legal entity, and a "true" corporation.

Salomon's Case

For English and Canadian lawyers, the separate legal entity principle is ineluctably linked with the 1896 House of Lords decision in *Salomon v. A. Salomon & Co., Ltd.*[21] The case is often regarded as the only proper starting point for the study of corporate law in England and in Canada. For several reasons, however, it seems unlikely that *Salomon's* case did more than confirm what was already well understood by the late 19th century legal profession to be the law on the point of the business corporation's distinct legal identity. The case did, however, represent a breakthrough for *de facto* sole-shareholder corporations, at a time when such corporations were not (technically) permitted by the governing general incorporation statute.

I have sometimes facetiously described *Salomon's* case as the *King Lear* of the corporate law canon. An aging father, moved to share his business "kingdom" with his somewhat covetous (or at least impatient) children,[22] conceives an orderly succession plan. Unlike the foolish Lear, however, Aron Salomon shrewdly retained the reins of power. His scheme involved the transfer of the assets of the boot-making business he had founded and had for many years conducted as a sole proprietorship to a new company duly incorporated at his direction under the English *Companies Act, 1862*. Of this new company, called A. Salomon & Company, Limited, Aron Salomon was to be the largest, single shareholder. But two important features of this otherwise straightforward transaction would come to enrage Salomon's creditors and challenge the jurists of England's highest courts.

First, the *Companies Act* required every corporation to have at least seven shareholders.[23] Although Salomon's company was in technical compliance with this requirement, it was clear that none of the seven members except Aron Salomon himself had any real economic stake in the company, as the shareholdings of the company readily reveal. The seven shareholders were Aron Salomon, his wife, and his five adult children. Yet of the 20,007 shares issued by A. Salomon & Company, Limited, Aron Salomon held 20,001 outright; and there were suggestions that even the remaining six shares ostensibly owned by his spouse and offspring were actually held by them merely as trustees or nominees on Aron Salomon's behalf.

---

20   [1897] AC 22 (HL).

21   Ibid.

22   Said Mr. Salomon of these children, we are told, "they troubled me all the while." Ibid., at 48.

23   *Companies Act, 1862*, supra footnote 3, s. 6.

More curious still were the sale terms for the boot business arrived at between Aron Salomon (as seller) and this new company (which, of course, he fully controlled) as purchaser. The fair value of the transferred business assets was reckoned by the court to be just £10,000. Yet, the value placed on the assets for purposes of the sale from Aron Salomon to the new corporate entity was in excess of £39,000, an amount famously described by Lord Macnaghten as

> a sum which represented the sanguine expectations of a fond owner rather than anything that can be called a businesslike or reasonable estimate of value.[24]

Had Mr. Salomon received from the purchasing company only common shares in exchange for these transferred assets, this overvaluation would likely have escaped serious scrutiny. Although the sale would have inflated the corporation's balance sheet, potentially to the detriment of lenders who may have advanced funds in reliance on the figures appearing in the company's accounts, it would not, at least, have deprived the creditors of the right to seize whatever assets the company might still be found to possess on liquidation. But in fact, £10,000 of the purchase price paid by the company to its founder came in the form of a corporate debenture (that is, a corporate I.O.U., secured by a charge over the assets of the business). That made all the difference. When the company eventually was forced into liquidation, the corporation's indebtedness to the holder of this debenture ranked ahead of all of the other debts owing to the company's unsecured creditors. Mr. Salomon, in other words, had managed to engineer a scheme by which he had secured a claim over all the assets of his business, a claim ranking prior to the business's other outside creditors. And, note the amount of this prior claim: £10,000— an amount representing virtually the entire original value of the business's assets.[25]

Law students are most familiar with the House of Lords' decision in *Salomon's* case, a decision generally sympathetic to the supposed plight of the "pauper" Salomon, and supportive of the legitimacy of the transactions briefly described above. But it is illuminating to consider the rather different light in which the matter was viewed at trial and in the English Court of Appeal. In these courts, Aron Salomon was roundly condemned. Salomon's actions were, in the words of Lindley LJ in the Court of Appeal, "a device to defraud creditors."[26]

That the Law Lords should have so readily accepted the innocence (or at least the acceptability) of Salomon's scheme, commenting at one point that he had been "dealt with somewhat hardly"[27] is curious enough. That they should thereupon have permitted

---

24   Supra footnote 20, at 49.

25   The facts were actually slightly more complex than this summary suggests. Mr. Salomon had, sometime before the liquidation, borrowed £5,000 from Edmund Broderip and, to secure repayment of the loan, had transferred legal title in the debentures to Broderip. Broderip, in fact, became the registered owner of the debentures on the company's books; but, like all secured creditors, Broderip's interest in the debentures only extended to the amount of the debt he was owed. Aron Salomon remained the beneficial owner of the debentures, and so was entitled to any remaining value after the debt owing to Broderip had been satisfied.

26   *Broderip v. Salomon*, [1895] 2 Ch. 323, at 339 (CA).

27   Supra footnote 20, at 47 (per Lord Macnaghten).

the seniority of Salomon's debenture to prevail over the interests of the unsecured creditors is still more troubling. The legal key to this particular outcome lies in Lord Macnaghten's observation that "[a]ny member of a company, acting in good faith, is as much entitled to take and hold the company's debentures as any outside creditor."[28] And although *Salomon's* case has certainly garnered its fair share of praise, both at the time it was decided and subsequently, more than one voice has echoed Kahn-Freund's celebrated description of the judgment as a "calamitous decision."[29]

Salomon's case is often said to form the basis for the modern view that a business corporation is a separate legal entity. It is regularly cited, too, as the first case to recognize the legitimacy of the sole-shareholder corporation.[30] However, while the judgment certainly affirms the first proposition,[31] it by no means originated it. And as for the second proposition, it is worthwhile noting that that issue (as a strict question of law, admittedly, rather than as a practical matter) was not before the court in *Salomon's* case.[32]

That companies created under the *Companies Act, 1862* constituted true corporations and separate legal entities required no judicial fiat from the House of Lords or any other court. Section 18 of the statute was unambiguous on the point:

> Upon the Registration of the Memorandum of Association, and of the Articles of Association in Cases where Articles of Association are required by this Act or by the Desire of the Parties to be registered, the Registrar shall certify under his Hand that the Company is incorporated, and in the Case of a Limited Company that the Company is limited: The Subscribers of the Memorandum, together with such other Persons as may from Time to Time become Members of the Company, *shall thereupon be a Body Corporate by the Name contained in the Memorandum of Association, capable forthwith of exercising all the Functions of an incorporated Company.*[33]

---

28 Ibid., at 52.

29 O. Kahn-Freund, "Some Reflections on Company Law Reform" (1944), 7 *Modern Law Review* 54, at 54. A contemporary note on *Salomon's* case suggested that the House of Lords' decision "would have been impossible thirty or even twenty years ago. When the founders of company legislation spoke of seven or more persons being 'associated,' they meant such an association as, without the help of the statute, would have made those persons members of an ordinary partnership. And where the materials for a real partnership do not exist, there it would not have occurred to any equity lawyer to see the materials for a company." See (1897), 13 *Law Quarterly Review* 6, at 7.

30 See, e.g., Jacob S. Ziegel et al., *Cases and Materials on Partnerships and Canadian Business Corporations*, 3rd ed., vol. 1 (Toronto: Carswell, 1994), at 137.

31 See, e.g., supra footnote 20, at 51: "The company attains maturity on its birth. ... The company is at law a different person altogether from the subscribers to the memorandum" (per Lord Macnaghten). Also, at 42: "It is to be observed that both Courts treated the company as a legal entity distinct from Salomon and the then members who composed it, and therefore as a validly constituted corporation. ... It is not another name for the same person; the company is *ex hypothesi* a distinct legal person" (per Lord Herschell).

32 That is, Salomon's company did, as a technical matter, have the required seven shareholders, notwithstanding that the economic interest of those shareholders other than Aron Salomon himself was insignificant. One hastens to note that this fact was clearly understood by Ziegel et al., who refer—quite accurately—to the fact that *Salomon's* case vindicated the use of "*de facto* one person [corporations]." See supra footnote 30, at 138.

33 *Companies Act, 1862*, supra note 3, s. 18 (emphasis added).

Nor does it seem likely that the English legal profession was in much doubt as to how these words ought to be interpreted. An English corporate text written some 20 years before the House of Lords decision in *Salomon*, for example, declares as an apparently non-contentious fact that

> The first object of the [1862] Act was to incorporate all companies formed under its provisions, or, in other words, *to consider the company as an individual* having a distinctive name, and capable of suing and being sued, and of contracting in such name. ... [T]he members of the company have a distinct existence from the company itself, and actions may be brought by the company against individual members, and by individual members against the company.[34]

Nor is this the only reference to such a proposition that pre-dates *Salomon's* case.[35] Indeed, Professor Sealy has noted that the doctrine had been recognized by the courts at least as early as the 17th century.[36]

There appears to have been popular awareness of the new concept before *Salomon*, as well, though by no means popular approval. In fact, while dull corporate statutes might not be expected to inspire the creation of light entertainment, the principle of limited liability endorsed by the 1862 Act actually found its way into not one but two contemporary light operas by Gilbert[37] and Sullivan: *The Gondoliers*, first performed in 1889, and the lesser-known play, *Utopia, Limited*, first performed in 1893. In neither was the principle portrayed in very flattering terms.[38] In both, however, there is a fairly clear articulation of the precise implications of incorporation (and limited liability) for trading enterprises.

As for the position of sole-shareholder or "one-man" companies, as they were sometimes called at the time, it is easy to see why *Salomon's* case has become associated with

---

34   Sir Henry Thring, *The Law and Practice of Joint-Stock and Other Public Companies* (London: Stevens & Sons, 1875), at 17.

35   Francis Beaufort Palmer produced a 36-page, one-shilling pamphlet in 1877 in which he extolled the advantages of transforming a business into a limited company. Among those advantages, he explained, was this:

> In contemplation of law a partnership is a mere association of individuals, but a company is a *person* distinct from its members. This being so a company is free from many inconveniences which are incident to a partnership.

Francis Beaufort Palmer, *Private Companies: Or How to Convert Your Business into a Private Company, and the Benefit of So Doing*, 2nd ed. (London: Stevens & Sons, 1878), at 12. See also text accompanying notes 49 and 50, infra.

36   L.S. Sealy, *Cases and Materials in Company Law*, 7th ed. (London: Butterworths, 2001), at 56, note 13, citing *Edmunds v. Brown and Tillard* (1668), 1 Lev. 237 and noting also *Foss v. Harbottle* (1843), 67 ER 189 (Ch. D.).

37   W.S. Gilbert, it may be recalled, was, for four years, a practising barrister. See Hesketh Pearson, *Gilbert: His Life and Strife* (London: Methuen, 1957), at 19.

38   In *The Gondoliers*, the Duke of Plaza-Toro, finding himself "in straitened circumstances" but with considerable "social influence," proposes the formation of "a Company, to be called the Duke of Plaza-Toro, Limited" on whose board of directors he will serve as a member. (*Gondoliers*, Act I, line 326, p. 881.) The Duke's daughter, Casilda, is mortified by the prospect: "But it's so undignified—it's so degrading! A Grandee of Spain turned into a public company? Such a thing was never heard of!" (*Gondoliers*, Act I, lines 334-335, p. 881.)

their vindication. Aron Salomon was, for all practical purposes, the only shareholder of A. Salomon & Company, Limited. Holding 20,001 of the 20,007 issued shares, he had virtually the entire residual economic interest in the enterprise. Indeed, as was pointed out earlier, there were suggestions that even the six shares nominally held in the names of other members of his family were beneficially owned by him as well. The headnote of the case that appears in the English Reports includes the phrase "one-man company" in the catchlines, and reference to "one-man companies" does appear in the speech of Lord Macnaghten, where his lordship dubs the phrase "a taking nickname," but one which "does not help one much in the way of argument."[39] There is, moreover, discussion of the

---

Satire of the limited company is especially essential to the plot of *Utopia, Limited*, as the title suggests. The play is set in the mythical land of Utopia, where the daughter of the ruler, King Paramount, has just returned from taking a degree at Girton College (Cambridge) and brings with her the promise of anglicizing the land of Utopia. Utopia's remarkable system of government—"Despotism tempered by dynamite"—essentially involves conferring on a monarch absolute power, but then, to assure the power is not abused, placing the monarch under the watchful eye of two "wise men." (*Utopia, Limited*, Act I, line 80, p. 979.) At the first sign of despotic indiscretion, these wise men are constitutionally mandated to authorize a third—the "Public Exploder"—to blow up the King with dynamite, and then to rule in his place. The two wise men, well aware of the power over the king their rather unique constitutional responsibilities afford them, exploit that power shamelessly by subjecting the King to a series of petty humiliations. The King's Girton-educated daughter, Zara, seeks to free her father from the hold of the wise men by transforming Utopia into a state modelled on English institutions. To that end, she has brought from England six "flowers of progress"—six men, each of whom personifies one of the six "principal causes that have tended to make England the powerful, happy, and blameless country" that it is reputed to be. (*Utopia, Limited*, Act I, lines 1048-1049, p. 1025.) One of the six is a company promoter named Mr. Goldbury:

> A Company Promoter this, with special education,
>
> Which teaches what Contango means and also Backwardation—
>
> To speculators he supplies a grand financial leaven,
>
> Time was when *two* were company—but now it must be seven. (*Utopia, Limited*, Act I, lines 1143-1146, p. 1031.)

The final line is an unmistakable reference to the requirement in the then current English corporate statute that seven incorporators (and shareholders) were required to form a limited company. Goldbury's delightful song, spoofing incorporation under the 1862 Act, and casting satiric scorn on the ready availability of limited liability it afforded to company promoters is as clear and as witty a denunciation of the concept as critics of the concept could hope to find. So taken is King Paramount with the wonders of incorporation that he resolves to become the world's first incorporated sovereign.

Mr. Goldbury goes further still. Zara reports that "Mr. Goldbury, who, discarding the exploded theory that some strange magic lies in the number Seven, has applied the Limited Liability principle to individuals, and every man, woman, and child is now a Company Limited with liability restricted to the amount of his declared Capital! There is not a christened baby in Utopia who has not already issued his little Prospectus!" (*Utopia, Limited*, Act II, lines 61-65, p. 1045.) When once King Paramount has converted his kingdom to a limited company, the threats of his two sadistic wise men to blow him up if he defies them are deflected. Says the King to the sabre-rattling wise men: "You may *wind* up a Limited Company, You cannot conveniently *blow* it up!" (*Utopia, Limited*, Act II, lines 298-299, p. 1059.)

(All references in this footnote are from: *The Complete Annotated Gilbert and Sullivan*, Ian Bradley, ed. (Oxford: Oxford University Press, 1996).)

39   Supra footnote 20, at 53.

economic reality of A. Salomon & Company, Limited as a sole-shareholder company, particularly in the judgment of Lord Herschell.[40]

A contemporary note on the case suggests that "[i]ts real significance is that it interprets the policy of the Companies Act to sanction an individual trading with limited liability";[41] and more recently, both Gower[42] and Sealy[43] have attached great weight to this aspect of the decision. However, recall that the legislation under which Salomon's company had been formed did not permit a company to be incorporated with only one shareholder (or indeed, with fewer than seven shareholders);[44] and Salomon's company was in technical compliance with that provision—there were seven shareholders, notwithstanding the economically insignificant interests held by six of them.

The issue considered by the court, therefore, was whether mere formal compliance with this requirement was enough to satisfy the statute and so ensure the integrity of the corporate body formed under it. The issue before the House of Lords, in other words, was whether A. Salomon & Company, Limited had ever been validly incorporated at all. There was no real doubt that, if found to be validly incorporated, the corporation would constitute a separate legal entity. That point, as suggested above, had surely been settled years before *Salomon*. Lord Halsbury declares that it is the most important, and perhaps the sole, question raised by the case to determine whether the corporation has been validly constituted in accordance with the governing legislation.[45] Another way of framing the question, perhaps, is that the House of Lords was asked to confirm that the 1862 Act did not simply confer corporate status on a pre-existing joint stock company, in the way that its predecessor, the 1844 *Joint Stock Companies Act*,[46] had done. Rather, a corporation could be validly formed under the 1862 Act without a genuine economic partnership ever having existed.

It is evident from certain statements in the judgments that Aron Salomon was by no means the first English entrepreneur to enlist subscribers with no genuine economic interest in the corporation to serve as "ciphers" or "placeholders" to satisfy the seven-subscriber statutory minimum.[47] In fact, following the 1895 judgment of the Court of Appeal in *Salomon* (which, unlike the later decision of the House of Lords, suggested

---

40   See, e.g., ibid., at 44.

41   Note in (1897), 13 *Law Quarterly Review* 6.

42   L.C.B. Gower, *Gower's Principles of Modern Company Law*, 5th ed. (London: Sweet & Maxwell, 1992), at 48-49. The current edition of this work also refers to the fact that the case "finally [established] the legality of the 'one-man' company (long before EC law required this)." See Davies, supra footnote 8, at 29.

43   L.S. Sealy, supra note 36, at 56, note 13: "The true significance of *Salomon's* case in its more immediate context is that it confirmed the legitimacy of the 'private' company and paved the way for its recognition by statute in 1907." On the latter point, see chapter 4, infra.

44   The *Companies Act, 1862*, supra footnote 3, ss. 6 and 8.

45   Supra footnote 20, at 20 (per Lord Halsbury LC). Mr. Goldbury appears to have had the jump on the House of Lords. See footnote 38, supra.

46   7 & 8 Vict., c. 110.

47   Supra footnote 20. Indeed, recall the one-shilling guide published by Francis Beaufort Palmer in 1877, as referred to earlier, supra footnote 35.

that all seven shareholders must have a real economic interest in a validly constituted company), a critical comment on that decision asserted that,

> out of the thousands of private companies which have been formed in the last quarter of a century under the Companies Acts, it may be doubted if there are 10 per cent. which will satisfy the new test [i.e., that all seven shareholders be bona fide traders].[48]

In fact, Francis Palmer had, almost two decades before the House of Lords decision, published a pamphlet[49] on incorporating private corporations that dealt very specifically with the way in which a sole proprietorship might be incorporated with "the aid of a few friends"[50] who would agree to take the requisite shares necessary to comply with the seven-shareholder statutory requirement, a requirement that Palmer regarded as "rather irrational."

That the House of Lords was prepared to give effect to form over economic substance in determining that Salomon's company complied with the statutory requirements, must surely have been regarded as important, especially in view of a sometimes overlooked provision of the *Companies Act, 1862*: s. 48. That section explicitly stated that the consequence of *knowingly* being a member of a company with fewer than the statutorily mandated seven shareholders for a period of six months was that a member would become liable for "the Payment of the whole Debts of the Company contracted during such Time."[51] Of course, Aron Salomon had neither ignored nor overtly flaunted the seven-subscriber legislative requirement. His company had complied with the requirement—in form, at any rate. Section 79 of the Act (also unmentioned by the House of Lords) did provide that a company "may be wound up by the Court" if it had fewer than seven members,[52] but did not

---

48   Note (1895), 11 *Law Quarterly Review* 212.

49   Palmer, supra footnote 35. This pamphlet appears to have been fairly well known in late 19th century English business circles. It is referred to, for example, in an 1895 article on single-shareholder companies by Edward Manson as "Mr. Palmer's little book." See Edward Manson, "One Man Companies" (1895), 11 *Law Quarterly Review* 185, at 186. Indeed, Palmer's one-shilling pamphlet could have been in a number of respects a blueprint for Mr. Salomon's undertaking. For example, Palmer notes that "[i]f, in any case, it is determined to borrow money on debentures, it is usual in a company to offer the debentures to the shareholders in the first place." (Palmer, supra footnote 35, at 27.) Furthermore, he explains, that "[a] company has the capacity of contracting with its shareholders and of suing and being sued on such contracts. ... So if a shareholder lends money to the company, he can sue for it just as if he were not a shareholder." (Ibid., at 13.)

50   Ibid., at 21. He went on to note that "[t]he services of extra subscribers are generally obtained without difficulty. ... In private companies the extra subscribers are very commonly relations or clerks of the owner or owners of the business." Ibid., at 21.

51   *Companies Act, 1862*, supra footnote 3, s. 48.

52   Ibid., s. 79(3). At least one of the Law Lords left open the possibility, however, of a proceeding being brought to prove that a company had no effective existence in cases where a certificate of incorporation had been obtained notwithstanding a failure to comply with the minimum shareholder requirements. Supra note 20, at 30 (per Lord Halsbury). Even this possibility could be open to dispute, though, for as another judge (Lord Davey) noted, "it is not certain that s. 18, making the certificate of the registrar conclusive evidence that all the requisitions of the Act in respect of registration had been complied with, would be an answer" to the hypothetical argument that the company, lacking seven shareholders, did not in law exist. Ibid., at 55.

suggest that this particular deficiency would result in a *de facto* revocation or annulment of a corporate charter.

Perhaps the principal contribution of *Salomon's* case is not, as it were, the novelty of the tune, but rather the volume at which it was played. It neither introduced the doctrine that a corporation is a separate legal entity (since the relevant legislation had done that more than three decades earlier) nor explicitly endorsed the legitimacy of the single-shareholder corporation (since Salomon's company had the statutorily mandated seven members).[53] Rather, it served as an authoritative and robust declaration of the separate legal entity principle. Unlike the trial judge and the judges in the Court of Appeal, the Law Lords were unwilling to treat Mr. Salomon as the mere alter ego of his incorporated business, even under circumstances that might seem to some to weigh heavily in favour of a decision against Mr. Salomon.[54] After the House of Lords' ruling in *Salomon*, creditors would surely be minded to pay close attention to words such as "limited" or "inc." whenever they appeared in the name of a business debtor. The House of Lords had given clear warning (if not early enough warning for A. Salomon & Company, Limited's creditors) that courts could not be expected to step in after the fact to save careless creditors from their own lack of diligence in dealing with incorporated entities.

A few unsettling questions arise from *Salomon's* case. First, not all creditors are equally positioned to perform the due diligence investigations necessary to ensure that an apparently solvent debtor has not shielded himself behind or within an empty incorporated shell. Of course, had *Salomon's* case unfolded in most Canadian jurisdictions today, the existence of the security interest created by the corporation's debenture would have had to be registered under the appropriate provincial *Personal Property Security Act* (PPSA) before it would be effective against a trustee in bankruptcy or other secured creditors with perfected interests.[55] But it is unlikely that PPSA registration is of practical significance to small, trade creditors since they are unlikely to perform searches of the PPSA registry before each and every delivery of goods or services.

As a more general matter, private corporations, as discussed further in chapter 4, are not required to make public disclosure of their financial information. Although large, institutional lenders (such as banks) certainly can, and do, obtain this sort of information from private corporate borrowers, smaller creditors—especially trade creditors who supply ongoing goods and services to a business without demanding immediate cash payment—rarely have the means, the resources, or the bargaining leverage to demand, examine, or assess the financial information of their corporate customers. At least one

---

53   A contemporary note at the time, in fact, raised the possibility that in a future case, there might still be "room ... for the argument that there is no real association and nothing capable of registration," suggesting that "perhaps the One-Man Company is not quite safe after all." Supra footnote 41, at 7.

54   Lord Halsbury's judgment very much hints at this when he contends that "the truth is that the learned judges [i.e., the trial judge and those on the Court of Appeal] have never allowed in their own minds the proposition that the company has a real existence. They have been struck by what they have considered the inexpediency of permitting one man to be in influence and authority over the whole company; and, assuming that such a thing could not have been intended by the Legislature, they have sought various grounds upon which they might insert into the Act some prohibition of such a result." Supra footnote 20, at 33-34.

55   See, e.g., *Personal Property Security Act* (Ont.), RSO 1990, c. P.10, s. 20(1).

commentator, it is true, has dismissed such considerations as irrelevant, asserting that small creditors must know what to expect when they deal with incorporated debtors.[56] However, his reasoning on this point suffers from a certain circularity. To say that creditors ought to know what to expect when they deal with a corporation is surely not, without more, a proper basis on which a court ought to determine that one particular outcome, rather than another, is *the* outcome that ought to be the one "expected." Put another way, why should creditors "expect" that courts will not protect their interests until the issue has been definitively ruled on?

Recall, in particular, the specific issue before the court in *Salomon*. The issue was not whether the unpaid creditors of a particular corporation could, as a matter of course, seek compensation from the shareholders of that same corporation. The issue was whether an individual who was (effectively) the sole shareholder of a corporation could gain a *priority* over all of the corporation's unsecured creditors in the way that Mr. Salomon had sought to do. How could one say that the outcome in *Salomon's* case ought to have been "expected" by creditors until the House of Lords had conclusively decided the matter? What would the creditors have "expected" after the rulings of the trial court and the Court of Appeal, both of which went against Mr. Salomon? Labelling the outcome of the House of Lords decision as "expected" can hardly, therefore, be said to justify the reasoning in the case.

The robustness of the separate legal entity principle after *Salomon* is evident in many subsequent cases, of which one of the most frequently "anthologized" is the decision of the Privy Council in *Lee v. Lee's Air Farming Ltd.*[57] This case involved a company with a single shareholder, Mr. Lee, who was also the company's sole director, officer, manager, and employee. The company was in the business of aerial top-dressing, and Mr. Lee, a pilot, was killed while flying an aircraft on company business. An issue arose as to whether his widow was entitled to compensation under New Zealand workers' compensation legislation. If, at the time of his death, her deceased husband was properly characterized as a "worker" (that is, an employee) of the company, Lee's Air Farming Ltd., the benefits would be forthcoming. But if, as a matter of law, he could not be characterized as an employee—on the ground that one cannot be an employee of one's self—then no benefits would be payable.

The Privy Council held that Mr. Lee had, indeed, been an employee of the corporate entity. They invoked *Salomon* in support of the proposition that an incorporated company was legally distinct from the individual human beings who performed actions on its behalf, even in the case of one-person companies. Lord Morris said that "the deceased was in some contractual relationship with the company. That relationship came about

---

56   See David Goddard, "Corporate Personality—Limited Recourse and Its Limits" in Grantham and Rickett, supra footnote 17, 11, at 22: "The decision to give credit is a deliberate choice to assume the risks of bad debts in order to increase the levels of business. In most cases, the decision is not moreover to give credit to a particular company or person but rather to give credit to all customers, or to certain classes of customer. The issue then becomes one of assessing the long run risk of dealing on credit terms with the relevant class of customers—reinforcing the irrelevance of debate as to whether it is practical or realistic to investigate the affairs of each individual debtor."

57   [1961] AC 12 (PC).

because the deceased as one legal person was willing to work for and make a contract with the company which was another legal entity."[58] It was, therefore, in the court's view, "a logical consequence of the decision in *Salomon's* case that one person may function in dual capacities."[59]

Many other examples could be offered to illustrate the now non-contentious proposition that, absent exceptional circumstances (many of which are discussed further in chapter 7), a corporation is a separate legal entity, distinct from its shareholders.

Separate Legal Entity and Limited Liability

The twin corporate doctrines of separate legal entity and limited liability have, over time, become so closely linked that many modern commentators have come to consider them as merely two sides of the same coin. Naturally, according to this eminently logical view, shareholders ought not to be liable for the debts or obligations of a corporation just as I ought not to be liable for the debts or obligations of my next-door neighbour (or any other distinct, different person). Yet, although the link between incorporation and limited liability appears to be a logical one, the two concepts were certainly de-coupled in the earliest English general incorporation statutes. The *Joint Stock Companies Act* of 1844[60] did not in fact grant limited liability to a corporation's shareholders. Indeed, it expressly disclaimed any such limitation.[61] Perhaps, as some have suggested, this was simply because the 1844 statute had not yet clearly defined joint stock companies as real corporations. Thus, for example, one reads in a 19th century Canadian text on joint stock companies that a joint stock company, even if incorporated, is nevertheless not a "perfect corporation."[62] On this theory, the idea that a business corporation (as we would now call it) might constitute a separate legal entity had not yet been fully developed; so, naturally, the idea that limited liability was an inevitable consequence of incorporation was also less apparent before the definitive decision in *Salomon's* case.

Hunt, citing *Elve v. Boyton*, asserts that "under common law, limited liability was an inseparable incident of incorporation."[63] Wegenast certainly regarded limited liability as a necessary consequence of distinct corporate personality. In his seminal text on Canadian corporate law, he declared that "[a] full-fledged corporation being in law a different person from its members, it follows that the debts and obligations of the corporation are not those of its members, unless so made by statutory enactment."[64] He cites the early

---

58   Ibid., at 25.

59   Ibid., at 26.

60   Supra footnote 46.

61   Ibid., ss. 25 and 45.

62   Charles Henry Stephens, *The Law and Practice of Joint Stock Companies* (Toronto: Carswell & Co., 1881), at 52.

63   Bishop Carleton Hunt, *The Development of the Business Corporation in England 1800-1867* (Cambridge, MA: Harvard University Press, 1936), at 41.

64   F.W. Wegenast, *The Law of Canadian Companies* (Toronto: Carswell, 1979) (reprint from original 1931 edition), at 5.

English House of Lords decision in *Oakes v. Turquand*[65] as authority for this proposi-tion. That case, decided under the English *Companies Act, 1862*, concerned the poten-tial liability of a shareholder to pay amounts remaining unpaid[66] on his shares for the benefit of the company's unpaid creditors on a winding up of that company. Put more simply, the creditors sought to have the shareholder pay more money into the company so that there would be more money available to satisfy the company's debts. The shareholder sought to be relieved from making such payments on the basis that he had been deceived by the company's fraudulent prospectus into agreeing to purchase shares in the first place.

There were three judgments delivered in *Oakes v. Turquand*. It is not entirely certain on which of these judgments Wegenast was purporting to rely. Lord Chelmsford does touch on the link between limited liability and separate corporate personality. He refers, for example, to a portion of the judgment of Lord Cairns in *The Reese River Mining Company, Ex Parte J. Smith*.[67] There, Lord Cairns drew the link between limited liability and separate legal personality, albeit in a slightly different way—namely, that to achieve limited liability for shareholders, the incorporated entity had to become the party with whom all creditors contracted.[68] Lord Chelmsford affirms, too, that shareholders do not contract with the corporation's creditors; only the corporation does that. So, if sharehold-ers are to have any liability to the creditors "it is a statutable liability."[69]

In Lord Colonsay's judgment, however, there is little to suggest that limited liability and separate legal personality of the business corporation are inextricably linked. Indeed, referring to the statutory requirement that corporations maintain a register of sharehold-ers, he says that "it is plain from the reason of the thing that no credit would otherwise be given to the abstraction of a company" but for such disclosure.[70] In other words, it appears from Lord Colonsay's reasoning that he actually conceived there to be a link—not a separation—between the identities of the individual shareholders and the corpora-tion itself. Lord Colonsay's judgment is replete with references to the fact that a company incorporated under the 1862 Act is not a "perfect corporation,"[71] but rather a "quasi-corporation."[72] It would be a mistake, he maintains, to regard such enterprises

> as unqualified corporations, and in no respect as partnerships. ... I think it would be contrary to the tendency and scope of all the statutes to hold that these companies are

---

65   *In re Overend, Gurney & Co.; Oakes v. Turquand* (1867), LR 2 HL 325.

66   The shares, in other words, had been issued on a "partly paid" basis. The shareholder had paid part of the originally agreed price in cash, and the remainder was to be paid at some later date on demand (or call) for payment made by the issuing company. Most Canadian corporate statutes today forbid the issuance of shares on an unpaid or partly paid basis. See, e.g., CBCA, s. 24, and the discussion in chapter 12.

67   Law Rep. 2 Eq. 264.

68   Supra footnote 65, at 346.

69   Ibid., at 350.

70   Ibid., at 376.

71   Ibid., at 374.

72   Ibid.

stripped of all the characteristics of mercantile partnerships, and clothed with all the attributes of perfect corporations, without qualification.[73]

But again, perhaps it is the judgment of Lord Cranworth upon which Wegenast has primarily relied. Lord Cranworth does emphasize the notion that

the direct remedy of a creditor is solely against the incorporated company. He has no dealing with any individual shareholder, and if he is driven to bring an action to enforce any right he may have acquired, he must sue the company, and not any of the members of whom it is composed.[74]

Yet even in articulating this proposition, Lord Cranworth is careful to distinguish between what he calls a "mere common law corporation," on the one hand, and "a company formed under the statutes of 1862," on the other.[75] It is telling, too, that in the very first paragraph of his judgment, Lord Cranworth equates joint stock companies with partnerships, notwithstanding that it is clear from the context of his remarks that the "joint stock companies" to which he is referring are companies incorporated under the *Companies Act, 1862*.[76]

In Lord Cranworth's analysis of the *Companies Act, 1862*, he does not seem to suggest that the mere fact of incorporation necessarily or *ex hypothesi* implies limited liability. Indeed, to the contrary, much of his judgment is based on a fairly close reading of provisions in the 1862 Act that operate to confer limited liability on members of a limited company—provisions that would presumably be superfluous if the very act of incorporation itself implied limited liability. It should, moreover, be recalled that at the time the 1862 Act was enacted, incorporators were required to elect between three different types of incorporation, and one of them, the unlimited company, did not confer limited liability on its members at all.[77]

In any event, even apart from the early legislative de-coupling of the concepts of separate legal entity and limited liability, there are other useful reasons to consider these two concepts separately. The distinctness or separateness of persons does not, without more, necessarily eliminate the possibility that one person will be held accountable for the actions of another. After all, notions of vicarious liability and thus transferred (or at least shared) liability have long been a part of our law. The indisputable separateness of individual human beings has not made it impossible for the law to hold one person liable, under certain circumstances, for the acts of another. Agents can certainly expose their principals to liability, a proposition that might at first glance seem quite at odds with the concept of individual responsibility. That an agent (or "servant") can thus be

---

73   Ibid., at 376-77.

74   Ibid., at 357.

75   Ibid., at 358.

76   "It is of the utmost importance that persons dealing with joint stock companies should be in no doubt as to who are the persons to whom they are entitled to look as liable to perform the obligations and pay the debts of the *partnership*." Ibid., at 357 (emphasis added).

77   Such an election is still a feature of one Canadian corporation statute. (See the Nova Scotia *Companies Act*, s. 9.)

regarded as a virtual appendage of her or his principal is a paradox, as others have recognized, that seems not to have very much troubled great liberal thinkers[78] and which is today sometimes rationalized as one of the signs of the law's enhancement of economic efficiency.[79]

The absolute sovereignty of the individual, in other words, is not an inviolable principle of our legal system. Thus, the mere crystallization of the concept of the corporation as a separate legal entity need not necessarily have led to the conclusion that corporate shareholders must enjoy the protection of limited liability. The law, for example, might instead have conceived the corporation, in appropriate circumstances, to be a kind of agent for its shareholders. The agency argument was, of course, put forward in the *Salomon* case itself (ultimately without success), and is still the expressed basis for some judgments in which the corporate "veil" is lifted or pierced, as discussed in chapter 7. The point offered here is only that it is a mistake to argue that the separate legal entity principle is simply limited liability by another name. Whether, and under what circumstances, corporate shareholders should enjoy limited liability are questions engaging distinct policy considerations. It is to those considerations that we now turn.

LIMITED LIABILITY

The most important practical consequence of incorporation in the eyes of most Canadian legal practitioners is the proposition that the liability of corporate shareholders for the debts and other obligations of the corporation is strictly limited to the amount, if any, remaining unpaid on their shares.[80] In fact, in most modern Canadian jurisdictions where corporate shares must be paid for in full before they may even be validly issued,[81] the expression "limited liability" has become something of a misnomer. The principle might be more aptly expressed as "shareholder immunity," a phrase that in fact appears in a heading to the CBCA statutory provision that deals with the matter.[82]

In 1926, the *Economist*, in a passage quoted by Bishop Hunt, suggested that "the economic historian of the future ... may assign to the nameless inventor of limited liability, as applied to trading corporations, a place of honor with Watt and Stephenson,

---

78 One notes, for example, that John Locke asserted that the basis for property rights is that an individual is entitled to "the Labour of his body." Yet, somehow the labour of a servant does not give property rights to the servant, but to the servant's employer: "the Turfs my Servant has cut ... become my Property." John Locke, *Two Treatises of Government* (Cambridge: Cambridge University Press, 1960), chap. 5, para. 28, at 330.

79 Frank H. Easterbrook and Daniel R. Fischel, *The Economic Structure of Corporate Law* (Cambridge, MA: Harvard University Press, 1991).

80 This statement is true, at least, for corporations that offer limited liability to their participants. In the case of professional service corporations, or unlimited companies, the principal practical advantages arise from income tax considerations that are beyond the scope of this book.

81 See, e.g., CBCA, s. 25(3).

82 CBCA, s. 45. It goes without saying that this marginal note, as the *Interpretation Act* makes clear, "forms no part of the enactment, but [is] inserted for convenience of reference only." *Interpretation Act* (Canada), supra footnote 10, s. 14.

and other pioneers of the Industrial Revolution."[83] However, as critical as the concept seems today, it appears that limited liability was not originally considered a fundamental attribute of the business corporation. This observation may at first seem surprising, but appears to be borne out by a review of the development of business corporation law.

Limited liability, according to Gower, was not a practical concern for members of the earliest companies—that is, prior to the passage of general incorporation statutes in England in the mid-19th century. Company membership was in continual flux, he notes, meaning that members could not readily be identified by prospective plaintiffs in any event, making the formal recognition of limited liability largely superfluous.[84] However, as the need to attract passive investment capital for large-scale enterprise grew, the English business community clamoured for an investment vehicle that would offer providers of capital the same advantages of limited liability already available in France and other European jurisdictions where limited partnerships (or their equivalents) could be established. It was the demand by the English business community for new limited partnership legislation that led instead—or, as matters eventually unfolded, as well[85]—to the establishment of a limited liability regime for the shareholders of business corporations.[86]

Economic Explanation for Limited Liability

The justification for limited liability is somewhat more elusive than a superficial consideration of the topic might first suggest. Most business people, if asked to explain the rationale for statutorily enshrined limited liability for corporate shareholders, would probably answer that such protection is necessary to encourage risk taking. But such an answer is, at best, incomplete. If it were true, for example, that limited liability was essential to encourage business risk taking, then one might expect to observe an undersupply of those products or services produced or delivered by organizations that are forbidden by law to operate through limited liability vehicles. Casual observation seems to belie this notion. For example, the practice of law in most Canadian jurisdictions could not, until very recently, be carried on in corporate form (or through any other form of limited liability organization);[87] and even in those jurisdictions that today permit the incorporation of legal practices, individual professionals typically remain exposed to unlimited personal professional liability.[88] But, it is rarely suggested that the unavailability

---

83   *Economist*, December 18, 1926, cited in Hunt, supra footnote 63, at 116.

84   Paul L. Davies, *Gower's Principles of Modern Company Law*, 6th ed. (London: Sweet & Maxwell, 1997), at 32.

85   Eventually, Parliament enacted legislation providing for the creation of limited partnerships. Such legislation also exists in Canadian jurisdictions today. See, e.g., *Limited Partnership Act*, RSO 1990, c. L.16.

86   For a detailed description of the events that culminated in the enactment of the *Limited Liability Act*, 18 & 19 Vict., c. 133, see Davies, supra footnote 84, at 40ff.

87   Now, of course, many Canadian jurisdictions permit law firms to operate as "limited liability partnerships," a form of partnership that does not insulate professionals from the consequences of their own negligence, but limits their exposure to liability arising from the acts of their partners. See, e.g., *Partnerships Act* (Ont.), RSO 1990, c. P.5, ss. 10(2)-(4) and 44.1-44.4.

88   See, e.g., *Business Corporations Act* (Ont.), RSO 1990, c. B.16, s. 3.4.

of limited liability has left Canada with a chronic undersupply of lawyers; indeed, it is more frequently argued that, if anything, there may be an oversupply of legal practitioners.

Moreover, if business entrepreneurs were truly so easily cowed by financial risk as this justification for limited liability suggests, one would predict that few, if any, businesses would be operated in Canada as sole proprietorships given the ease and fairly low expense associated with establishing sole-shareholder corporations. It appears, however, that the number of new sole proprietorships typically outstrips the number of new incorporations in any given year. Business owners are, indeed, prepared to assume personal risk.

Much of the lobbying in recent years for expanded rights of incorporation, in fact, appears to be linked more to a desire by incorporators to achieve favourable income tax consequences than to avoid personal liability. Furthermore, even if the encouragement of risk taking were an *explanation* for conferring limited liability on corporate shareholders, it would not, without more, constitute an adequate *justification* for doing so. There would also need to be sound reasons to believe that limited liability was necessary not simply to encourage *more* risk taking but to ensure an optimal level of risk taking. Put simply, too much risk taking is surely just as bad as too little—especially when limited liability permits some or all of the burdens of that risk taking to be shifted away from the risk takers themselves.

This latter concern may be described, more formally, as a moral hazard problem. Moral hazard is a term used to refer to the tendency of people to engage in riskier behaviour than they would otherwise when they are aware that the adverse consequences of their risky behaviour will be borne by someone other than themselves. It is a phenomenon often associated with insurance underwriting: people who have purchased theft insurance, insurers fear, may tend to be more careless in guarding their property against theft than they would be if they, and not their insurance company, bore the risk of paying to replace any property that might be stolen from them. Shareholder limited liability creates a similar moral hazard problem because the risk of business failure is not borne in full by shareholders. A portion of the risk is shifted to others, in particular, to creditors of the failed corporation. The moral hazard arising from limited liability could, theoretically, result in inefficiently high levels of risk taking in the economic system as a whole. It is by no means true that the more risk taking there is, the better. Thus, the rationale for limited liability requires a more subtle explanation than is offered by the pat response that it encourages risk taking.

Other explanations have been offered. Baskin and Miranti,[89] for example, have noted that, historically, limited liability was linked not to entrepreneurial risk taking as such, but rather to a perceived need, in the 19th century, to amass larger pools of capital to engage in large-scale enterprise, such as railway construction. Implicit in this sort of explanation is that the case for limited liability is strongest in the context of large, publicly traded corporations, but rather weaker in the context of private corporations, especially sole-shareholder corporations.

---

89   Jonathon Barron Baskin and Paul J. Miranti Jr., *A History of Corporate Finance* (Cambridge: Cambridge University Press, 1997), at 139.

Other commentators have advanced more ambitious economic rationales. In an influential 1980 paper,[90] Halpern, Trebilcock, and Turnbull offer an economic explanation for corporate limited liability. Their analysis considers corporate limited liability from an insurance perspective. Because the effect of shareholder limited liability is to shift risk from shareholders to creditors, they argue, limited liability is functionally equivalent to shareholder liability insurance. Accordingly, in their view, the central economic question is whether corporate limited liability is the most efficient way of providing this kind of insurance.

Their argument may be briefly summarized as follows. One can imagine an alternative model to limited liability. If corporate shareholders are not shielded from the debts and obligations of the corporations in which they have invested, they would be required (in order to safeguard assets they do not intend to expose to the risk of the business) to obtain insurance for the risk of such loss from third-party insurers. The key question for the authors is, therefore, which of these two regimes—third-party insurance or shareholder limited liability—would be more efficient? Halpern et al.'s analysis suggests that, in an unlimited liability regime (where shareholders obtain third-party insurance), information costs would generally be higher than in a limited shareholder liability regime. Their reasoning runs as follows. If shareholders are personally liable for the debts and obligations of a corporation, then anyone extending credit to the business operated by that corporation would surely base his or her credit assessment not only on the creditworthiness of the corporate entity itself, but also on the creditworthiness of all of that corporation's shareholders. Such an assessment would involve significant information costs in the first instance. But if shareholders also wish to insure against the risk of business loss (and shareholders with significant assets surely would want to do so), then any insurance company providing such insurance would also incur significant information costs as it attempts to price such insurance.

Moreover, they argue, without limited liability, organized capital markets would operate in difficult-to-predict ways (if, in fact, they could operate at all). Each outstanding share of the same company would potentially have a different value depending on the wealth of the individual holder of that share. In other words, if the corporation became insolvent, a wealthy shareholder would be at greater risk of having his or her assets seized to pay the corporation's creditors than a less wealthy shareholder. Thus, the value of a corporate share would vary inversely with the wealth of the owner of that share.

Creditors, too, they note, would have higher information costs in a world of unlimited liability. They would need to investigate not only the creditworthiness of the business entity to which they are advancing funds, but also the creditworthiness of the individual shareholders of that business—both at the time of the initial advance of funds, and from time to time while any loan amounts remain outstanding.[91] The authors acknowledge that these information costs could to a significant extent be shifted from creditors to those companies providing insurance to shareholders, but they argue that "[i]t is unlikely that

---

90   Paul Halpern, Michael Trebilcock, and Stuart Turnbull, "An Economic Analysis of Limited Liability in Corporation Law" (1980), 30 *University of Toronto Law Journal* 117.

91   See also on this point, the "asset partitioning" view of the firm advanced by Henry Hansmann and Reinier Kraakman, "The Essential Role of Organizational Law" (2000), 110 *Yale Law Journal* 387.

insurance companies are more efficient than creditors in obtaining and evaluating information of both a start-up and ongoing nature."[92]

Finally, on their analysis, shareholders themselves would incur greater costs. They would continually need to monitor not only the performance of the firm in which they hold shares, but also the identity and financial health of all other shareholders. After all, the probability that any one shareholder would be financially affected by the failure of the firm would be directly related not only to the probability of the firm's failure, but also to the ability of his or her fellow shareholders to shoulder any unsatisfied firm liabilities in the event of such failure.

A strict unlimited liability rule could also militate against efficient portfolio diversification, they point out. An investor's risk of insolvency would increase (not decrease) with each additional investment he or she makes in another unlimited liability enterprise. And, while the authors recognize that this effect could be solved if shareholder liability were based on a concept of proportionate liability—rather than strictly unlimited liability—they note that a proportionate liability regime would have adverse effects on investment values.[93]

Halpern et al. note that their argument is most compelling in the case of claims of a corporation's voluntary creditors (for example, lenders, trade creditors, and employees). It is less compelling in the case of claims of involuntary creditors (for example, tort claimants). In fact, the authors suggest that in many instances, a rule of unlimited liability would be more efficient in the case of involuntary creditors.

This latter idea was developed by Hansmann and Kraakman. In a well-known 1991 paper, they propose a scheme for imposing proportionate liability upon shareholders for corporate torts.[94] Hansmann and Kraakman's proposal often appeals to those who are concerned about a dissipation of incentives to monitor corporate wrongdoing and, indeed, it is a carefully reasoned and thoughtful argument. A full critique of Hansmann and Kraakman's work is well beyond the scope of this discussion. However, one or two observations will be offered here. First, it should be emphasized—as Hansmann and Kraakman readily recognize[95]—that the only sort of tort claim that would expose shareholders to personal liability under the Hansmann/Kraakman scheme would be a "firm-ending" claim: that is, a liability so large that the corporation's own resources would not be sufficient to satisfy it. In the case of large, public corporations, such claims would be exceedingly rare, of course. Hansmann and Kraakman, however (writing in 1991), assert that there is some reason to believe that the risk of such claims is likely to increase in the future.[96] Nevertheless, at present, it seems fair to suggest that their "solution" is intended to address a tiny fraction of corporate tort claims. Their proposal, in other words, may be

---

92   Halpern et al., supra footnote 90, at 135.

93   For a discussion of a scheme of proportionate shareholder liability for corporate torts, see Henry Hansmann and Reinier Kraakman, "Toward Unlimited Shareholder Liability for Corporate Torts" (1991), 100 *Yale Law Journal* 1879.

94   Ibid.

95   Ibid.

96   Ibid., at 1895.

fairly said to take aim at the proverbial crack "an inch wide but a mile deep." Further-more, the imposition of personal liability on shareholders of public companies—the shares of which change hands on equity exchanges daily—seems highly impractical. The authors acknowledge the problems associated with attempting to impose liability on a large, fluid group of shareholders—not only in terms of determining which shareholders should be held liable for torts, but also in terms of effectively enforcing judgments against shareholders even after they have been identified. However, they rather seriously underestimate, and so downplay, the realities of these practical problems—problems that frankly would almost surely overwhelm any putative benefits that such a scheme might offer in terms of compelling firms to fully internalize the risks of their corporate activi-ties. Finally, it is interesting to note that around the turn of the 20th century, corporate shareholders in most US states were in fact exposed to a certain kind of proportionate (albeit capped) "double liability."[97] But this regime, tellingly, has not evidently with-stood the test of time. Accordingly, the Hansmann and Kraakman proposal, while a useful stimulus of law school classroom and academic conference discussion, is of doubtful practical utility.

Still, the economic rationale for limited liability seems to be most persuasive in the case of large, publicly traded corporations, rather doubtful in the case of most small, private corporations, and all but non-existent in the case of sole-shareholder companies. It may be that limited liability for sole shareholder companies can be justified on the basis of what Hansmann and Kraakman have elsewhere described as "asset partition-ing."[98] Their argument, simply put, is that single-shareholder corporations facilitate business financing by permitting a business owner to finance his or her business entirely on the basis of specified business assets, rather than personal assets. A detailed critique of this well-known thesis will not be attempted here. Note, however, that a sole proprietor (that is, the sole owner of an unincorporated business) could certainly finance on the basis of specified assets as well by way of a non-recourse secured lending transaction.

A second concern raised by Hansmann and Kraakman is that personal creditors of an individual operating an unincorporated business could compel a liquidation of that business on failure by the owner to satisfy personal (as opposed to business) debts. As a practical matter, however, that possibility is equally a concern in the case of an incorporated entity, because a shareholder's creditors could, of course, seize the shares of a sole-shareholder corporation, and then—as shareholder—compel liquidation of the corporation.

In short, the economic justifications for extending limited liability to a corporation's shareholders seem somewhat unpersuasive in the case of sole-shareholder corporations. However, the popular, if somewhat sentimental, image of the "small-business person" persists. And so, for the foreseeable future, any serious reconsideration of the propriety or economic sense of permitting sole-shareholder corporations is sure to remain a politi-cal non-starter.

---

97 Morton J. Horwitz, "Santa Clara Revisited: The Development of Corporate Theory" (1986), 88 *West Virginia Law Review* 173.

98 Indeed, Hansmann and Kraakman have argued that opposition to the existence of sole-shareholder business corporations "stems from a failure to appreciate this important asset partitioning functioning of the corporate form." See Henry Hansmann and Reinier Kraakman, supra footnote 91, at 405.

Unlimited (Liability) Companies

A discussion of limited liability in Canada would not be complete without some mention of the increasingly popular "unlimited liability company." Nova Scotia is the only jurisdiction in Canada where it is possible to incorporate "unlimited companies"—that is, corporations that expose their shareholders to the debts and other obligations of the company to an unlimited degree.[99] The fact that the statute includes such a provision might seem peculiar enough to the uninitiated; but what is more remarkable is that more than two thousand unlimited companies have been incorporated in Nova Scotia within the past decade[100]—many affiliated with some of the largest and most well-known American corporations.

The concept of unlimited companies that appears in the Nova Scotia *Companies Act* was taken from and modelled on the English *Companies Act*.[101] It is not entirely clear why the English *Companies Act, 1862* originally included this provision, but at least three explanations are possible. First, the unlimited company may have provided a more efficient regime for voluntary windup.[102] Second, the unlimited company might have been an attractive alternative to a general partnership (for those business people who, for whatever reason, could not or did not wish to incorporate a limited company) because the unlimited company offers somewhat greater protection from member liability than the traditional partnership.[103] Finally, it is also possible that in 1862, when limited liability for registered companies was still a relatively novel concept, there was some wariness of the new corporate form within the business community. Accordingly, legislators may have sought to provide business people with the option of signalling their integrity by retaining unlimited liability and thus forgoing the "shady" advantages offered by the limited liability shield. In the early days of limited liability, for example, companies to whom this new benefit was not available were known to trumpet the advantages of dealing with an enterprise whose members could be held liable for the firm's

---

99   *Companies Act* (NS), s. 9(c). Since this section was written, on March 9, 2005, Bill 16, the *Business Corporations Amendment Act, 2005*, received first reading in the Alberta legislature. If enacted, this bill would introduce the unlimited liability corporation to Alberta's *Business Corporations Act*. Available online at http://www.assembly.ab.ca/adr/adr_template.aspx?type=bills_bill&selectbill=016.

100 Wayne Gray reports that, as of May 9, 2002, there were 2,430 existing Nova Scotia unlimited companies. In 2001, 626 new unlimited companies were formed; in 2002, 647 such companies were formed. Wayne D. Gray, "Corporations as Winners Under CBCA Reforms" (2003), 39 *Canadian Business Law Journal* 4, at 23, note 124. Virtually all of these 2,430 companies have been incorporated since 1996. See Christopher C. Nicholls, *Nova Scotia Unlimited (Liability) Companies* (unpublished monograph, on file with author).

101 The Nova Scotia *Companies Act* was originally enacted in 1900, based on the English *Companies Act, 1862*, together with amendments to that statute as of that time. See Wegenast, supra footnote 64, at 24. Unlimited companies may still be formed in England. See *Companies Act, 1985*, UK 1985, c. 6, s. 3(1)(f).The relative rarity of such companies was referred to by Ground J in *National Bank of Canada v. Clifford Chance* (1996), 30 OR (3d) 746 (Gen. Div.).

102 See Francis Beaufort Palmer, *Company Law*, 2nd ed. (London: Stevens & Sons, 1898), at 251.

103 For example, members of an unlimited company were liable for the debts of a company only on a windup. As long as the company was a going concern, shareholders could not be sued personally (as partners in a general partnership could be). As well, a member of an unlimited company who had ceased to be a member at least one year before the company was wound up, was free from liability altogether. A

obligations.[104] And evidently, even in England today the use of the unlimited company is thought to have such signalling advantages, especially in certain industries.[105]

PERPETUAL EXISTENCE

Blackstone suggests that it is perpetual existence that defines the corporation, and that is the corporate form's very raison d'être.[106] It is easy enough to understand this view when one recalls the early association of the corporate form with not-for-profit institutions such as churches and the English monarchy. Perpetual existence can also be a very valuable attribute of a business corporation, since in the case of large enterprises it facilitates long-term investment in long-lived enterprises.[107]

In the case of small, closely held corporations, perpetual existence makes certain types of tax-efficient estate planning strategies possible. Consider, for example, one of the most well-known estate planning techniques—the so-called estate freeze. In Canada, since the abolition of estate taxes, the most onerous tax obligation faced by the beneficiaries of a significant estate is the capital gains tax that must typically be paid on the accrued gains of a wealthy deceased taxpayer's estate. The taxpayer's death triggers a so-called deemed disposition of the taxpayer's assets; and to the extent that the fair market value of those assets is greater than the assets' cost (or, more technically, the assets' adjusted cost base), the excess is taxable at capital gains rates. Although "rollover" provisions may enable beneficiaries to defer paying tax on such accrued but unrealized capital gains, often no such rollover relief is available. An estate freeze tempers the effect of capital gains taxes that will be payable on a taxpayer's death by effectively stopping the capital gains accrual clock from running at a moment of the testator's choosing. In other words, the purpose of an estate freeze is to lock in the value of the taxpayer's estate as of the day the freeze is undertaken so that any future appreciation in value accrues to the individuals who will be the beneficiaries of the taxpayer's estate. A simple estate freeze is accomplished by incorporating a new holding corporation to which the shares of the taxpayer's personal holding corporation are transferred. Although transferring assets to a corporation usually constitutes a disposition that will attract capital gains tax, the

---

member of an unlimited company was also not liable for any debts contracted after he had ceased to be a member. No past member was liable for contribution unless a court found that existing members were unable to satisfy their required contributions. See *Companies Act, 1862*, supra footnote 3.

104   Gower, citing Dubois, refers specifically to the unincorporated Phoenix Assurance Company making just such a claim of superiority to its competitor, Royal Exchange Assurance. Gower, 5th ed., supra footnote 42, at 33.

105   Ibid., at 266. In the most recent edition of that text, the author suggests that "the unlimited company may be attractive for those shareholders who are willing to stand behind their company and for whom the advantages of privacy or flexibility of capital structure are important." See Davies, supra footnote 8, at 16.

106   William Blackstone, *Commentaries on the Laws of England*, vol. 1, chap. 18. (Published in facsimile edition with an introduction by Stanley N. Katz (Chicago: University of Chicago Press, 1979), at 455.)

107   Margaret Blair has recently maintained that the development of the corporation is best understood as a method of locking in capital to encourage long-term investment in firm-specific assets. See Margaret Blair, "Locking in Capital: What Corporate Law Achieved for Business Organizers in the Nineteenth Century" (2003), 51 *UCLA Law Review* 387.

Income Tax Act[108] permits transfers of assets to a corporation in exchange for shares of that corporation to be made on a tax-deferred (that is, rollover) basis. The taxpayer's interest in this new corporation typically takes the form of redeemable,[109] retractable,[110] "high-low" (that is, high market value, low adjusted cost base for tax purposes) preferred shares with a redemption (and retraction) value equal to the fair market value of the corporation's assets. The taxpayer's intended beneficiaries (generally her or his children) are issued common shares in the same corporation. Because redeemable, retractable preferred shares—with no residual right to participate in the earnings or assets of the issuing corporation—do not increase in value as the value of the issuing corporation increases,[111] all future increases in the underlying value of the corporation will now effectively accrue to the holders of the common shares—that is, the taxpayer's beneficiaries, not the taxpayer. Because capital gains in Canada are taxed only when realized, this accretion in value will not be taxed in the hands of the taxpayer's beneficiaries until they choose to sell or otherwise dispose of the shares they own. When the taxpayer eventually dies, his or her estate will be liable to pay tax on all capital gains that accrued before the date of the estate freeze, but any subsequent appreciation in value will now be represented by an increase in the value of the common shares, which will be held not by the deceased taxpayer's estate, but directly by his or her beneficiaries.

Although perpetual existence thus continues to be one of the key advantages incorporation may offer, it is surely not quite the defining attribute of the business corporation that Blackstone's comment suggests. Early English statutes permitted the incorporation of corporations with limited "lives," and in some jurisdictions today (although not in Canada), corporate legislation specifically allows for the creation of "limited duration companies."[112]

Of course, the fact that corporations do not die does not mean that their existence can never be brought to an end. Corporations can certainly be wound up or dissolved and thereupon cease to exist. The significance of "perpetual existence" as a corporate attribute is that it is *possible* (though not necessarily inevitable) that the corporation's existence will continue indefinitely.

---

108 *Income Tax Act*, RSC 1985, c. 1 (5th Supp.), s. 85.

109 That is, shares that may be purchased (redeemed) by the issuing corporation at any time for a price specified in the share conditions.

110 That is, shares that the shareholder may require the corporation to redeem at any time at a price specified in the share conditions.

111 If shares have no residual rights to receive dividends, no residual rights to receive property of the corporation on a windup, and may be redeemed by the issuing corporation at any time at a fixed dollar amount, the fair market value of those shares can never rise above that fixed dollar amount. This is true even if the shares entitle the holder to a regular, fixed dividend. Usually, shares paying a fixed dividend will rise in value if market interest rates fall. But if the shares are redeemable at any times at a fixed dollar amount by the issuing corporation, any potential buyer will recognize that the shares can be repurchased at any time, and so will not be prepared to pay a premium based on the assumption that the shares will remain outstanding and, therefore, the (above market) dividend will continue to be paid.

112 See, e.g., the Companies Law of the Cayman Islands, Part VIII. The principal advantage of the limited duration company appears to be that it may, like the Nova Scotia unlimited company, be treated as a corporation for most purposes, but as a partnership for certain other (chiefly US tax) purposes.

TRANSFERABILITY OF SHARE INTERESTS

The transferability of share interests from one holder to another is an exceedingly important feature of the modern business corporation. In fact, in no small way, free transferability of share interests underlies some of the greatest strengths and the greatest weaknesses of the modern capitalist system.

To understand the basis for this bold statement, it is helpful to try to imagine a world in which investors cannot readily convey their equity stakes in a business enterprise to others. Equity interests that are difficult to convey do exist in our world now. A general partnership interest, for example, is more difficult to buy and sell than a corporate share. A partnership is defined in terms of the relationship between the partners, and in the absence of agreement between the partners to the contrary, no one may be admitted as a partner without the agreement of all existing partners.[113] A mere assignee of a partnership interest (that is, one who has not become a partner in accordance with the terms of the partnership agreement), may become entitled to receive the assigning partner's share of partnership profits, but is not otherwise entitled to enjoy the usual rights of partnership.[114] So, although one might contractually agree to assign one's share of a partnership's profits to a third party, such an assignment can involve a complicated realigning of property interests, with considerable residual uncertainty as to the assignor's and the assignee's respective rights.

For entrepreneurs who have business plans that require significant amounts of capital to be raised from outside investors, transfer restraints and uncertainties of this sort are problematic. Even if an entrepreneur seeking cash can assure prospective investors that their liability will be limited, it may nonetheless be difficult to coax them to advance the necessary funds without a reasonable prospect that they may exit from the investment if they choose within a reasonable period of time. It might sometimes be possible to provide such an exit to investors by permitting them simply to withdraw their capital from the business at some point in the future. But allowing investors to take back their funds may be highly undesirable from the perspective of the business and its other investors. As Hansmann and Kraakman have noted, if each investor had the right to withdraw his or her capital from the business at any time, there would be a danger that some investors might act opportunistically by threatening to withdraw capital at a time when the business is cash-strapped. The other investors would then be forced to pay more than the withdrawn interests were actually worth so as to ensure the survival of the business. Or, again, one investor's personal financial circumstances might compel him or her to seek withdrawal of his other investment for reasons wholly unrelated to the business, but potentially at a time when such a capital withdrawal would be especially damaging to the business.[115] Facilitating the ready transferability of share interests, therefore, makes it possible for a market to develop in which shares can be bought and

---

113 See, e.g., *Partnerships Act* (Ont.), supra footnote 6, s. 24(7).

114 Ibid., s. 31(1).

115 It is precisely concerns of this sort that are identified by Hansmann and Kraakman as explaining the crucial significance of the corporate form as a means of what they call "affirmative" and "defensive" asset partitioning. See Hansmann and Kraakman, supra footnote 91.

sold and thus affords investors an exit mechanism that does not threaten the ongoing viability of the corporation's business.

Historically, the free transferability of shares had great legal significance. The infamous *Bubble Act* of 1720[116] rendered the operation of certain kinds of unincorporated companies illegal. According to Gower, it was companies with freely transferable shares that were, for a time, thought to be those at risk of prosecution under this statute.[117] Accordingly, unincorporated joint stock companies, to avoid running afoul of the legislation, thought it necessary to place some kind of constraint on the free transferability of their shares. Indeed, it is possible that for members of the business community during the *Bubble Act* era (roughly from 1720 to 1825), legal reforms that would provide for free share transferability were regarded as more fundamental for the health and survival of a business enterprise than the provision of limited liability. This was so, Gower says, because companies with a large number of fluctuating members could, as a practical matter, insulate their members from any serious risk of liability in any event. Thus, "unlimited liability, though a danger to the risk-taker, was often a snare and a delusion rather than a protection to the public and no handicap at all to the dishonest promoter."[118]

The transferability of corporate shares raises a number of intriguing issues. These issues all turn, in one way or another, on the elusive legal character of the share itself, and are discussed further in chapter 12.

CENTRALIZED MANAGEMENT

Robert Clark asserts that "[t]he single most important fact of corporate law is that managerial power is legally *centralized*."[119] Indeed, a recent decision of the Delaware Chancery Court refers to the "director-centred nature" of Delaware corporate law, noting that "[i]t is through this centralized management that stockholder wealth is largely created, or so much thinking goes."[120] Perhaps the simplest way to conceive of the significance of centralized management as a key corporate attribute is to compare the well-defined corporate organizational structure with the much more loosely defined governance rules of alternative forms of business enterprise such as partnerships. In a business corporation, as discussed at greater length in chapters 9 and 10, shareholders—in their capacity as shareholders—take no active part in the day-to-day management of the corporation. Instead, their primary role is to elect members to the corporation's board of directors. It is that body, rather than the shareholders, that is charged with managing the business of the corporation or, especially in the case of larger corporations, with supervising the management of the corporation. By contrast, in a partnership, other than a

---

116 6 Geo. 1, c. 18.

117 Davies, supra footnote 84, at 29.

118 Ibid., at 32.

119 Robert Charles Clark, *Corporate Law* (New York: Aspen Publishers, 1986), at 21 (emphasis in original).

120 *Hollinger v. Hollinger International Inc.*, CA no. 543-N (Del. Ch. Ct. 2004), at 59 (per Vice-Chancellor Strine). Vice-Chancellor Strine cited in support of this statement Stephen M. Bainbridge, "Director Primacy in Corporate Takeovers: Preliminary Reflections" (2002), 55 *Stanford Law Review* 791.

limited partnership, each partner is presumed to have a right to take part in the management of the business.[121] There is no necessary separation between the role of a business's
equity investors and that of its managers. This separation between investment and management (or, as it is commonly described, between ownership and control)[122] may have
been particularly useful in the formation of large, complex corporations, which called for
the expertise of specialist professional managers.

Remember, however, that the significance of centralized management as a corporate
characteristic is not entirely unique to the corporation. After all, partnerships may, if the
partners so choose, be structured in order that management power is effectively conferred
on an executive body not dissimilar from the corporate board of directors. Nor is it
impossible for corporations—small, privately held corporations, at any rate—to opt out
of the conventional corporate management structure in favour of some other kind of
more direct shareholder democracy.[123] Nevertheless, the conventional centralized management structure is, for business corporations, the default rule, as a matter of law, and
the norm, as a matter of business practice. Moreover, the conventions of the corporate
management structure are clearly defined and well understood, and so facilitate, among
other things, a dynamic and well-functioning securities market. Simply put, the purchaser
of a common or ordinary share of a Canadian public company may base his or her
investment decision primarily on financial considerations. It is not usually necessary for
him or her to investigate the possible effects of widely divergent governance structures,
because the fundamental management organs of all public corporations are, in most
essential respects, the same. Of course, the conventions of the corporate centralized
management structure do raise important legal and economic issues, in particular issues
arising from the potential divergence of the interests of managers and investors. Those
issues have become especially salient in the wake of the high-profile governance failures
of 2001 and 2002. These matters are discussed further in chapters 9 and 10.

CONCLUSION

A careful review of this chapter will reveal that, at one time or another, each one of the
six fundamental corporate characteristics has been considered by one or more observers
to be the single most important feature of the business corporation. No doubt the fact that
all these characteristics are found in a single business vehicle helps account for the
singular success of the modern business corporation and its enduring popularity. Yet, as is
true of so many things, a business corporation's greatest strengths are also, on occasion,

---

121 See, e.g., *Partnerships Act* (Ont.), supra footnote 6, s. 24(5). This presumption is made subject to the
express or implied agreement among the partners.

122 The phenomenon of the growing separation of ownership and control in American public corporations
was famously identified and studied by Berle and Means in their seminal 1932 work. See Adolf A. Berle
and Gardiner C. Means, *The Modern Corporation and Private Property* (New York: Macmillan, 1939).
For a brief outline of Berle and Means' thesis, see chapter 1.

123 See, for example, CBCA, s. 146, which provides that shareholders may enter into a unanimous shareholder agreement that restricts, in whole or in part, the power of the corporation's directors. The
unanimous shareholder agreement is discussed in chapter 4.

its greatest weaknesses. In the chapters that follow, the implications of each of these corporate attributes, and the challenging legal issues they raise, will be explored in greater detail.

CHAPTER FOUR

Private Corporations

INTRODUCTION

In the lexicon of social democrats and free-trade protesters, the word "corporation" has come to be associated with "big business." This association is neither new nor entirely without some historical justification. At least one academic commentator has suggested that there may be a link between the development of the modern legal conception of the corporation, and apologies for the growth of very large businesses, especially in the period beginning after the First World War.[1]

Certainly the corporate form does facilitate the accumulation of pools of capital that would be too large for even the wealthiest of individuals and families to purchase with their personal assets. Defying the logic of Adam Smith (who saw little future for corporations in all but a handful of industries),[2] these modern corporate behemoths and leviathans appear to have provided the opportunity for wealthy capitalists to lever already large fortunes to achieve economic control over enterprises of almost incomprehensible size. Their growth is surely one of the most important economic phenomena of the past century.

Of the economic, social, and political implications of such corporate giantism, no more will be said here. From the necessarily more narrow and pragmatic lawyer's perspective, it is of principal importance to offer this gentle reminder. Although large public corporations are certainly the most visible manifestations of the corporate form, they are not the most common. Most Canadian corporations are actually small enterprises with few shareholders.

Corporations that have never sold their shares or other securities to the public are often referred to as "private," "closely held," or "close" corporations—all terms that are discussed in more detail below. To be sure, not all of these ostensibly "small," private corporations are running corner grocery stores and video shops. Many are merely sub-sidiaries of (much larger) corporate entities[3]—their corporate "parents"—and have been

---

1   Morton J. Horwitz, "Santa Clara Revisited: The Development of Corporate Theory" (1986), 88 *West Virginia Law Review* 173.

2   Adam Smith, *Wealth of Nations*, book V, chap. 1 (Amherst, NY: Prometheus Books, 1991), at 482.

3   That one corporation is permitted to incorporate another is typically permitted expressly by Canadian corporate statutes. See, e.g., *Canada Business Corporations Act* (CBCA), s. 5(2).

established to accommodate some specific corporate transaction, to hold particular corporate assets, or to fulfill some other tax or operational purpose.

But a considerable number of private corporations are not merely the instruments of big business. They are the vehicles of closely held, often family owned, businesses. They have been incorporated to gain the corporate benefits of limited liability, estate planning, and often certain favourable income tax treatment.

THE DISTINCTION BETWEEN PRIVATE
AND PUBLIC COMPANIES

Commentators and business people have long recognized the absurdity of purporting to treat alike, for corporate law purposes, widely held billion-dollar, multinational businesses, on the one hand, and small, family owned corner stores, on the other. Accordingly, corporate legislation, in Canada and elsewhere, occasionally distinguishes between public and private corporations for various purposes.[4] Historically, one of the most important legal consequences of such a distinction related to the different rules to which corporations of each sort were subject concerning public disclosure of financial statements: public corporations were required to make such disclosure; private corporations were not.[5] Recognizing that some private corporations are in truth, however, merely part of larger corporate enterprises, the special exemption from such public filing requirements was frequently denied to these offspring of public corporations. So, for example, company legislation in the United Kingdom once categorized private companies as either "exempt" (that is, exempt from the requirement to file financial information) or "non-exempt." And although this same terminology was not adopted in Canada, Canadian corporate statutes in the past have also drawn distinctions between private corporations based on the aggregate size of those corporations when considered together with their affiliates.[6]

Times have changed. The requirement to file financial and other information publicly has increasingly come within the ambit of Canadian securities regulation, rather than corporate law; so the need for corporate statutes to draw distinctions between corporations for this particular purpose has diminished.[7] In the meantime, business practice and investor concerns have brought to light other policy reasons to differentiate between widely held (that is, public) and closely held (or private) corporations.

---

4   The terms "public" and "private" corporation have also occasionally been used to distinguish between public sector (i.e., government) and private sector entities. This book, however, is concerned only with business corporations operating within the private sector, and so the discussion in this chapter is limited to the distinction between those private sector firms that are, nevertheless, categorized as either public or private corporations.

5   For a succinct summary of the historical distinctions between private and public companies in English law, see *Report of the Committee on Company Law Amendment* (London: Her Majesty's Stationery Office, 1945) ("Cohen committee report"), at para. 49, p. 26.

6   See, e.g., (old) CBCA, RSC 1985, c. C.44, s. 160.

7   The distinction is not, however, wholly irrelevant in Canada. See, e.g., CBCA, supra note 3, s. 160.

This chapter considers the distinguishing features of public and private corporations, and the corporate law framework within which they operate in Canada.

Private and Public Companies: Early English and Canadian Origins

The legal distinction between "private" and "public" companies has an interesting and illuminating history. Gower notes, for example, that in the 18th century, unincorporated companies were often referred to as "private" companies, while the term "public" companies was reserved for incorporated business entities.[8] This distinction was significant at the time because the infamous *Bubble Act* of 1720 had made it illegal for certain kinds of unincorporated companies to operate. The *Bubble Act* was rather ambiguous, however, on the question of *which* unincorporated companies would be considered illegal. Evidently, the view emerged that one of the key features characterizing the illegal sort of unincorporated company was free transferability of such a company's shares.[9] Promoters of unincorporated businesses were wary of prosecution under the Act, and so took care to ensure that shares of the firms they were promoting were subject to transfer restrictions.[10]

Thus, the earliest use of the public company/private company distinction in English law was closely connected to the free transferability of shares, a distinction that survives to this day in Canadian securities laws.

As explained in chapter 1, English and Canadian corporate statutes in the 19th century began to regularize and formalize corporate law. The earliest English corporate law statutes had no particular reason to draw any distinction between public and private companies because they really were not concerned with private companies. They were primarily aimed only at larger public-type companies in any event—namely, companies with a minimum number of members (more than 25 in the 1844 legislation)[11] or companies with freely transferable shares. Smaller business enterprises would not, in those days, have been incorporated. Indeed, when the privilege of shareholder limited liability was first introduced in 1855, enjoyment of that privilege was made conditional, among other things, on companies having a certain minimum size.[12] The subject had been debated in England, and the "dangers" of extending limited liability to small partnerships was specifically adverted to.[13]

---

8   L.C.B. Gower, *Gower's Principles of Modern Company Law*, 5th ed. (London: Sweet & Maxwell, 1992), at 30, note 49.

9   "Shares" in this sense would mean shares in the joint stock, effectively an interest in partnership profits, because the unincorporated companies of this period were, as a matter of law, partnerships.

10   Gower, supra footnote 8, at 30.

11   7 & 8 Vict., c. 110, s. 2.

12   18 & 19 Vict., c. 133, s. 1(4).

13   See, e.g., Paddy Ireland, "The Triumph of the Company Legal Form, 1856-1914," in John Adams, ed., *Essays for Clive Schmitthoff* (Abingdon, UK: Professional Books, 1983), 29, at 33, recounting the concerns raised by Lord Grey that the proposed *Limited Liability Act* might make it possible for companies with as few as three members to enjoy limited liability, and the confident response that such a view was a "mistake" because "the minimum number of persons who could do so was 25," a numerical threshold that was also inserted into the bill.

Gradually, however, through a process that began with the *Companies Act, 1862*,[14] and culminated in *Salomon's* case[15] in 1896, it became clear that the full benefits of incorporation—including the benefits of limited liability—were available even to corporations with but a single beneficial shareholder.[16]

At this critical point in its history, corporate law could readily have moved in either of two directions. Legislators might have decided to clamp down on *Salomon*-type sole-shareholder companies, and so restore the registered corporation to its original intended purpose: to provide a means for larger enterprises to be formed in order to pool capital from passive investors for large-scale indivisible enterprise. Many would argue that this would have been a sensible approach. Kahn-Freund, for example, wrote in 1944 that "it is open to doubt whether there is a case for the continued existence of private companies."[17] He did not mean by this that there would be any lack of demand for such vehicles on the part of entrepreneurs. Rather, his point was that such vehicles could be justified only in the rarest circumstances because, for the most part, they were something of an abuse of the corporate form.

However, corporate law took a second path. Rather than seeking to reverse the House of Lords' decision in *Salomon*, legislators essentially institutionalized it (without immediately permitting, however—at least explicitly—incorporation by a single owner).[18] And so, the first legislative distinction between "public" and "private" companies appeared in the English corporate statute in 1907.[19] Indeed, the origin of the term "private company" that now appears in many Canadian securities law statutes (and one Canadian corporate statute) may be traced to that English legislation, the English *Companies Act, 1907*.[20] The phrase was defined in s. 37 of that statute in this way:

"private company" means a company which by its articles—

    (a) Restricts the right to transfer its shares; and

    (b) Limits the number of its members (exclusive of persons who are in the employment of the company) to fifty; and

    (c) Prohibits any invitation to the public to subscribe for any shares or debentures of the company.[21]

---

14   25 & 26 Vict., c. 89.

15   *Salomon v. A. Salomon & Co., Ltd.*, [1897] AC 22 (HL). *Salomon's* case is discussed in detail in chapter 3.

16   Although, for many years, the formal requirement for a larger number of registered shareholders persisted.

17   O. Kahn-Freund, "Some Reflections on Company Law Reform" (1944), 7 *Modern Law Review* 54, at 58.

18   The explicit statutory recognition of single-shareholder companies was slow to come. However, Canadian corporate statutes now typically permit incorporation by a single incorporator. (See, e.g., CBCA, s. 5(1).)

19   As Ziegel et al. note, this statutory change followed the recommendations of the Loreburn committee. See Jacob S. Ziegel et al., *Cases and Materials on Partnerships and Canadian Business Corporations*, 3rd ed., vol. 1 (Toronto: Carswell, 1994), at 123.

20   7 Edw. VII, c. 50.

21   Ibid., at s. 37(1).

Private companies were permitted to have as few as two members;[22] but although the statute was passed some 10 years after the House of Lords landmark decision in *Salomon's* case,[23] single-shareholder companies were not expressly provided for.

The significance of the new private company definition was summarized in a contemporary annotated version of the 1907 statute:

> A private company enjoys all the privileges and is exempt from many of the obligations imposed on public companies; it need not file a statement in lieu of prospectus ... ; it can commence business as soon as it is incorporated ... ; and the restrictions on the appointment of directors and allotment of shares do not apply to it ... . It need not include in its annual summary a statement in the form of a balance sheet ... ; it need not file or forward to its members the report required by Section 12 of the Act of 1900 to be forwarded to every member at least seven days before the statutory meeting ... ; nor need it give to its preference shareholders and debenture holders the same right of inspecting and receiving the balance sheets and reports as are possessed by the ordinary shareholders.[24]

Ziegel et al. report that this public/private distinction was emulated by the drafters of Ontario's corporation law in 1912, and thereafter by Canada's federal statute and most other provincial corporate statutes as well.[25] Writing in 1931, Wegenast notes that "the sole purpose of the distinction [between public and private companies] is to relieve private companies from the necessity of filing either a prospectus or a 'notice in lieu of prospectus.' "[26]

The link between the requirement to file a prospectus and a company's characterization as either "public" or "private" underlies the inclusion of "private company" as a defined term in many Canadian provincial securities law statutes. The Ontario *Securities Act*, for example, includes a definition of private company that clearly shows its English ancestry:

> "private company" means a company in whose constating document,
>   (a) the right to transfer its shares is restricted,
>   (b) the number of its shareholders, exclusive of persons who are in its employment and exclusive of persons who, having been formerly in the employment of the company, were, while in that employment, and have continued after termination of that employment to be, shareholders of the company, is limited to not more than fifty, two or more persons who are the joint registered owners of one or more shares being counted as one shareholder,
>   (c) any invitation to the public to subscribe for its securities is prohibited;[27]

This definition was originally included in the legislation to support specific exemptions from the registration and prospectus requirements otherwise imposed by the statute upon a corporation (or other issuer of shares or other securities) when it sells (or, more

---

22   Ibid., at s. 37(4).

23   Supra footnote 15.

24   D.G. Hemmant, *The Companies Act, 1907 Annotated* (London: Jordan & Sons, 1908), at 61.

25   Ziegel et al., supra footnote 19, at 253.

26   F.W. Wegenast, *The Law of Canadian Companies*, reprinted with an introduction by Margaret P. Hyndman (Toronto: Carswell, 1979), at 12.

27   *Securities Act*, RSO 1990, c. S.5, s. 1(1), definition of "private company."

technically, "trades" and "distributes") any of its securities. Trades and distributions of the securities of private companies, as defined in the provision reproduced above, were, at one time, exempt from the registration and prospectus requirements, respectively. In other words, such companies were permitted to raise money by selling their securities to a modest number of people—all of whom were connected to the company in some way—without having to incur fees to registered securities dealers, and without having to undertake the expensive and time-consuming process of complying with the statutory procedures that accompany a public offering of securities.[28]

Companies that did not satisfy the "private company" definition enjoyed no such exemption; so, unless some alternative exemption from the registration and prospectus rules were available to them, these companies would be required to produce a prospectus each time they sold shares or other securities.

Recent changes to securities law in Ontario have now made the private company definition something of a dead letter in that province.[29] Elsewhere in Canada, for securities law purposes, the similar term "private issuer"[30] has supplanted the term "private company" in importance. The term "private company" is still found in the PEI *Companies Act*,[31] and companies incorporated under that statute must indicate in their application for letters patent whether the company to be incorporated is to be a private company. However, the corporate statute itself does not otherwise appear to deal significantly with private companies.

In the United Kingdom, private companies can be readily distinguished from public companies by the nature of the legal element (or cautionary suffix) in their corporate name. All public companies must include "public limited company" or "Plc" in their corporate names, while the names of private companies must include the word "limited"

---

28   The exemption from the registration requirement (that is, the requirement that the seller itself be, or that the sale be conducted through, a securities professional who is registered with—that is, licensed by—securities regulatory authorities) was found in s. 35(2)10 of the Act. The corresponding exemption from the prospectus requirement (that is, the requirement that, when securities are distributed, the seller must prepare, clear with regulators, and deliver to purchasers a detailed disclosure document called a prospectus) was found in s. 73(1)(a). Although these provisions have not been formally repealed as of the date of writing, they have been effectively nullified by new Ontario private placement rules that came into effect in November 2001. These new rules, among other things, eliminated the "private company" exemption in Ontario, and created a new "closely held issuer" exemption. For a detailed discussion of the newer rules, see Jeffrey G. MacIntosh and Christopher C. Nicholls, *Securities Law* (Toronto: Irwin, 2002), at chap. 7.

29   Ibid., at 188ff.

30   See Multilateral Instrument 45-103, available online at http://www.albertasecurities.com/. At the date of writing, it is understood that securities regulators in most Canadian provinces (including Ontario) are preparing a new multilateral instrument (MI) that will replace OSC Rule 45-501 in Ontario, NB Rule 45-501 in New Brunswick, and MI 45-103 in those provinces that had previously adopted MI 45-103. This new multilateral instrument is expected to include the term "private issuer" and to define this term using a definition that is substantially similar to the one that now appears in MI 45-103, s. 1.1. Since the foregoing was written, the Canadian Securities Administrators, in December 2004, did, indeed, publish for comment this new proposed instrument: National Instrument 45-106. See (2004), 27 *Ontario Securities Commission Bulletin* (Supp. 3), 1.

31   *Companies Act* (PEI), s. 1(e).

or "ltd."[32] No such distinction is made in Canada, where all corporations—public or private—may use the same suffixes, as chosen by the incorporators from those permitted by the incorporating statute.

CANADIAN REFORMS

When the Dickerson committee undertook its comprehensive review of the federal corporate statute in 1971, it specifically eschewed the "traditional private–public corporation dichotomy."[33] Instead, as the committee explained,

> we have defined "corporation" in different ways in different parts of the Draft Act where it seemed necessary or desirable to create a distinction. Corporations are therefore distinguished on functional rather than on doctrinal grounds.[34]

Thus, for example, statutory requirements concerning the minimum number of a corporation's directors and the obligation of a corporation's management to solicit proxies in connection with a shareholder meeting differed depending on the numbers of the corporation's shareholders or on the question of whether the corporation had ever issued securities to the public (some of which were still outstanding in the hands of more than one shareholder).

That same approach is found in the current version of the *Canada Business Corporations Act* (CBCA) as well. But, although the CBCA still contains no definition of, or references to, "private companies," it has, since November 2001, formally classified certain corporations as "distributing corporations."[35] This statutorily defined term denotes what many practitioners would describe informally as "public companies," or what are known for most provincial securities law purposes as "reporting issuers."[36]

Distributing corporations are subject to a number of additional requirements under the CBCA, discussed more fully in the section entitled "The Public Corporation," below. With the express adoption of this general "distributing corporation" definition,[37] the

---

32   See Paul L. Davies, *Gower & Davies: Principles of Modern Company Law*, 7th ed. (London: Sweet & Maxwell, 2003), at 14.

33   Robert W.V. Dickerson et al., *Proposals for a New Business Corporations Law for Canada*, vol. I, Commentary (Ottawa: Information Canada, 1971), at 10 (Dickerson committee).

34   Ibid., at para. 36.

35   CBCA, s. 2(1); *Canada Business Corporation Regulations, 2001*, SOR/2001-512, s. 2. See also footnote 37, infra.

36   The concept of "reporting issuer," at the date of writing, is used in the securities legislation of every Canadian province except Prince Edward Island. It refers to an issuer of securities (usually a corporation) that is subject to the ongoing public disclosure obligations of provincial securities laws. For a further discussion of the term "reporting issuer," see MacIntosh and Nicholls, supra footnote 28, at 254ff. British Columbia has recently passed new securities legislation, not yet in force at the date of writing, in which the term "public issuer" replaces the term "reporting issuer."

37   In earlier versions of the CBCA, a definition of "distributing corporation" did appear, but for the limited purposes of part XI of the Act. In addition, in several sections of the CBCA where the drafters wished to impose special obligations on corporations with publicly held securities, because the Act did not specifically include "distributing corporation" as a defined term, the sections would, instead, repeat in full the following lengthy and awkward verbal formulation: "a corporation, any of the issued securities of which

federal statute has now come full circle. Early corporate statutes included only a definition of "private company"; all other corporations were considered public corporations by default. The modern CBCA now includes only a definition of "distributing corporation"; all other corporations are, in effect, private companies, by default.[38]

The Ontario *Business Corporations Act* provides a similar taxonomy, but adopts the term "offering corporation"[39] rather than "distributing corporation," to describe corporations that have issued their securities publicly. The new British Columbia *Business Corporations Act* uses the term "public company" to mean a "reporting issuer" for Canadian securities law purposes, a company with securities registered under the US *Securities Exchange Act of 1934*, or a company with securities that trade on an exchange or are reported through a quotation and trade reporting system.[40] The term "distributing corporation" is also found in the Alberta *Business Corporations Act*,[41] *The Business Corporations Act* (Saskatchewan),[42] and the Newfoundland and Labrador *Corporations Act*.[43] The *Corporations Act* (Manitoba) uses the cumbersome phrase formerly found in the CBCA (discussed further below). The New Brunswick *Business Corporations Act* occasionally refers to corporations that have "shares listed on a prescribed stock exchange."[44] The term "public company" is used in the PEI *Companies Act*.[45]

One final note on corporation taxonomy. The CBCA does include a special definition of "personal body corporate."[46] A personal body corporate is, essentially, an individual or family holding company. However, the use of this definition in the CBCA is very narrow. It is included only for the purposes of the proportionate liability provisions, discussed in chapter 12.

THE PUBLIC CORPORATION

The "Public"

The phrase "public corporation" is not a legal term of art in Canada.[47] It does not today appear in Canadian corporate statutes (although, as noted above, the term "public company" is used in the corporate statutes of British Columbia and Prince Edward Island).

---

are or were part of a distribution to the public and remain outstanding and are held by more than one person." See, e.g., (old) CBCA, s. 102(2).

38   This development parallels a similar earlier development in the United Kingdom where "public company" became the defined term, and "private company" the default category. See Ziegel et al., supra footnote 19, at 253.

39   *Business Corporations Act* (Ont.), RSO 1990, c. B.16, ss. 1(1) and (6).

40   *Business Corporations Act* (BC), s. 1(1).

41   *Business Corporations Act* (Alta.), s. 1(p).

42   *The Business Corporations Act* (Sask.), s. 2(1)(o).

43   *Corporations Act* (NL), s. 2(m).

44   See, e.g., *Business Corporations Act* (NB), s. 60(3).

45   *Companies Act* (PEI), s. 1(f).

46   CBCA, s. 237.5(2).

47   As indicated above, however, the term has been specifically defined in corporate statutes in other jurisdictions, including the United Kingdom.

However, it is a term popularly used to refer to corporations that have sold securities (especially equity shares) to members of the public and that have their shares (or other securities) listed for trading on a stock exchange such as the Toronto Stock Exchange or the TSX Venture Exchange. The meaning of the "public" in this context has been considered by the courts in a number of cases.[48] These cases have arisen primarily in a securities law context.

The legal definition of the "public" has been an important concept in the administration of Canadian securities law for two reasons, both related to the availability of exemptions from the statutory requirement that an issuer of shares or other securities produce, file with regulators, and deliver to purchasers a detailed disclosure document— a prospectus—in connection with the sale of any such securities.

First, at one time, the fundamental securities law obligation to produce and deliver a prospectus was triggered whenever an issuer (usually a corporation) distributed securities "to the public." Recent securities law reforms in Ontario and several other Canadian jurisdictions have replaced the concept of distribution "to the public" with the broader concept of "distribution," an all-encompassing term that is a foundational component of the securities law "closed system."[49] Thus, the fine distinctions that were once important in determining whether a sale of securities had been made "to the public" have become less important in these closed-system jurisdictions.

However, there is a second reason that the meaning of the "public" has been significant for securities law purposes. As mentioned earlier, certain Canadian securities statutes have long provided a special exemption from the requirement to prepare and file a prospectus in connection with the sale of securities by any issuer that is a "private company" or, more recently, a "private issuer." To qualify for this exemption (and so be relieved from the time-consuming and expensive prospectus obligation), an issuer must satisfy a number of prescribed tests. Traditionally, one of those tests stipulated that the issuer must not invite the "public" to subscribe for its securities.[50] Recently, the prospectus exemptions have been revised in a number of Canadian jurisdictions, and the private company exemption no longer has the significance, particularly in Ontario, that it once did.[51] Nevertheless, in many Canadian jurisdictions, it appears that the notion of offering securities to the public will continue to be relevant for assessing the availability of the private-issuer prospectus exemption.[52] It is beyond the scope of this book, however, to canvass the case law that has developed around the concept of the "public" for securities law purposes.

---

48 See, e.g., *R v. Piepgrass* (1959), 23 DLR (2d) 220 (Alta. CA); *R v. McKillop*, [1972] 1 OR 164 (Prov. Ct.).

49 See, e.g., *Securities Act* (Ont.), supra footnote 27, s. 1(1), definition of "distribution"; see also, MacIntosh and Nicholls, supra footnote 28, at 59-61.

50 See, e.g., *Securities Act* (Ont.), supra footnote 27.

51 For a discussion of the prospectus exemptions in Ontario that have supplanted the "private company" and "private issuer" exemptions, see MacIntosh and Nicholls, supra footnote 28, at 188-90. But note also the pending developments referred to in footnote 30, supra.

52 See, e.g., Multilateral Instrument 45-103, s. 1.1, definition of "private issuer," and s. 2.1(1)(k). See also proposed National Instrument 45-106, supra footnote 30, s. 1.1, definition of "private issuer," and s. 2.4(1)(k). See also proposed National Instrument 45-106, supra footnote 30, s. 1.1, definition of "private issuer," and s. 2.4(1)(k).

"Distributing Corporation"

The CBCA now uses the phrase "distributing corporation" to refer to those (usually larger) corporations with public shareholders—that is, investors who are not necessarily related in any way to the founders of the business, and who may buy and sell shares of the corporation in anonymous transactions through the facilities of securities exchanges such as the Toronto Stock Exchange. The significance of the definition is that the application of certain provisions of the CBCA, discussed further below, turns on whether a corporation is a distributing corporation.

The CBCA's definition of "distributing corporation" is as follows:

> (a) a corporation that is a "reporting issuer" under [the securities statutes of Ontario, Quebec, Nova Scotia, Manitoba, British Columbia, Saskatchewan, Alberta, or Newfoundland]; or
>
> (b) in the case of a corporation that is not a "reporting issuer" referred to in paragraph (a), a corporation
>
> > (i) that has filed a prospectus or registration statement under provincial legislation or under the laws of a jurisdiction outside Canada;
> >
> > (ii) any of the securities of which are listed and posted for trading on a stock exchange in or outside Canada, or
> >
> > (iii) that is involved in, formed for, resulting from or continued after an amalgamation, a reorganization, an arrangement or a statutory procedure, if one of the participating bodies corporate is a corporation to which subparagraph (i) or (ii) applies.
>
> (2) A corporation that is subject to an exemption under provincial securities legislation, or to an order of the relevant provincial securities regulator that provides that the corporation is not a "reporting issuer" or "distributing corporation" for the purposes of the applicable legislation, is not a "distributing corporation" for the purpose of the definition of that expression in subsection (1).[53]

The CBCA also provides for the Director under the CBCA to exempt corporations, on an individual or class basis, from the definition.[54]

One of the most significant aspects of this new definition is that it attempts to integrate the federal corporate statute with the concept of "reporting issuer" used in most provincial securities laws, so as to avoid vexing inconsistencies. Reporting issuers— precisely the companies that would be popularly described as "public companies"—are typically subject to the full panoply of provincial securities regulation from which non-reporting issuers are generally exempt.[55]

---

53   CBCA Regulations, supra footnote 35, ss. 2(1) and (2).

54   CBCA, ss. 2(6) and (7).

55   For a discussion of the concept of "reporting issuer" and the securities law implications of the term, see MacIntosh and Nicholls, supra footnote 28, at 254 ff. Paradoxically, the Ontario *Business Corporations Act*, which uses the term "offering corporation" rather than "distributing corporation," adopts a definition for the phrase "offering corporation" that does *not* incorporate by reference the definition of "reporting issuer" found in Ontario's own provincial securities statute. However, functionally the Ontario definition is equivalent to the CBCA's concept of a "distributing corporation." (*Business Corporations Act* (Ont.), s. 1(1).)

The Significance of the CBCA's "Distributing Corporation" Definition

For the most part, the CBCA's requirements are the same for both distributing corporations and other corporations. In a few key areas, however, distributing corporations are subject to different (usually additional) statutory obligations. Those differences are surveyed in this section.

Board of Directors' Requirements

First, the CBCA's board of directors' requirements differ depending on whether or not a corporation is a distributing corporation. A distributing corporation must have at least three directors, at least two of whom are neither officers nor employees of the corporation or any of its affiliates.[56]

Non-distributing corporations need only have one director, if they so choose,[57] although they may, of course, have more directors if they wish. Requiring small, private companies to have more than one director is unnecessary and, in the case of sole-shareholder companies—which are now expressly sanctioned by the CBCA[58]—would be particularly ludicrous. Indeed, it has been occasionally proposed that, in the case of closely held corporations whose shareholders have assumed the powers and responsibilities of the corporation's directors by way of unanimous shareholder agreement (discussed further below), the statute ought perhaps to dispense altogether with the formal requirement that every corporation appoint at least one director. This suggestion has not yet, however, found favour with the legislators.

The requirement that at least two of a distributing corporation's directors not be members of the corporate management team represents an attempt to deal, at least to some extent, with the persistent corporate governance problem that arises when corporate managers—whose interests do not necessarily always coincide with those of the corporation's shareholders—control the board. This issue—a classic example of the agency problem discussed in chapter 1—has become a particularly hot topic following the legal and regulatory reforms promulgated in response to the wave of US corporate accounting scandals in 2001 and 2002. These governance matters are dealt with in more detail in chapters 9 and 10.

Public Filing of Financial Statements

One of the more traditional "public–private" company distinctions relating to the public filing of financial statements, also has a current parallel in the CBCA. Distributing corporations are required under the CBCA to file their annual financial statements with the Director.[59] Non-distributing corporations have no such obligation.

---

56   CBCA, s. 102(2).

57   Ibid.

58   Ibid., s. 5(1).

59   Ibid., s. 160.

Access to Corporate Records

The rules relating to access to corporate records are also slightly different for distributing corporations. Certain records of any CBCA corporation are available for inspection by that corporation's shareholders and creditors, as well as by their personal representatives and the CBCA Director.[60] If the corporation is a distributing corporation, however, most of these records are more generally available to be examined by any other person as well.[61]

It is important, in the case of corporations whose securities are publicly traded, that prospective investors have access to these corporate records. Moreover, access to the share register in particular is important to firms considering a proxy contest or takeover bid of the corporation in cases where the corporation's directors or officers oppose such action.[62]

Requirement to Appoint an Auditor

Furthermore, a distributing corporation is required to appoint an auditor.[63] Other CBCA corporations may, by shareholder resolution, decide not to appoint an auditor.[64] The rationale for this distinction is clear. The primary function of the auditor is to review the corporation's financial statements in order to assist the shareholders, collectively, in their "task of overseeing management."[65] The separation of management and share ownership that characterizes distributing corporations rarely poses a practical problem in private, closely held corporations where the principal shareholders also typically serve as directors and officers. Accordingly, where the shareholders themselves see no need for the appointment of an auditor, there is no compelling reason for the law to put such a corporation to the needless expense of having an external audit performed.

Note that the CBCA does not, however, simply exempt non-distributing corporations from an audit requirement. The drafters were clearly mindful of the fact that not all closely held corporations are alike. In some cases, not all shareholders of a private corporation will also be members of its board of directors. Accordingly, in order for a resolution dispensing with an auditor to be effective, that resolution must receive the

---

60   The records that are available for examination are: the corporation's articles and bylaws (including all amendments); any unanimous shareholder agreements; shareholders' resolutions and any minutes of shareholders' meetings; the notices of directors and of change of directors' or directors' addresses, filed by the corporation with the CBCA Director; and the securities register (which records the names and addresses of each of the corporation's shareholders and other securityholders, the number of securities held by each, and details of any securities transfers). (CBCA, s. 20(1).) As well, following amendments to the CBCA enacted in 2001, shareholders are also entitled to examine *those portions (but only those portions) of* minutes of meetings of directors or committees of directors that contain disclosures of directors' or officers' interests in a material contract or material transaction with the corporation. (CBCA s. 120(6.1).)

61   Ibid., s. 21(1).

62   The relationship between the takeover bid rules in provincial securities laws, and the access to the share register provided for under corporate legislation is discussed in Christopher C. Nicholls, *Corporate Finance and Canadian Law* (Toronto: Carswell, 2000), at 358.

63   CBCA, s. 162(1).

64   Ibid., s. 163.

65   *Hercules Management Ltd. v. Ernst & Young*, [1997] 2 SCR 165, at 205.

consent not merely of a simple majority of the corporation's shareholders, but the consent of *all* of the corporation's shareholders, including those whose shares do not normally entitle them to vote.[66] Moreover, even when such a unanimous shareholder resolution has been passed, it remains valid only until the next annual shareholder meeting.[67]

Audit Committee

Closely related to the requirement to appoint an external auditor, is the statutory requirement for a distributing corporation to appoint an audit committee[68]—that is, a committee of the board of directors that has special duties with respect to the review of the company's financial statements prior to their approval by the board,[69] and that acts as a liaison between the board of directors and the corporation's outside auditors. A majority of the members of the audit committee must be independent—that is, they must be neither officers nor employees of the corporation.[70] The hoped-for independence of the audit committee is thought to provide an additional check on the audit process. Auditing firms have—as recent US accounting scandals have revealed—often seemed to be beholden to corporate management who may well have been involved in their selection and who also are in a position to award lucrative consulting contracts to the same accounting firms appointed as the firm's auditors. In their desire to accommodate those who pay their fees, auditors may well have been tempted—consciously or unconsciously—to act not as vigilant protectors of the shareholders' interests, but rather as cooperative "team players."

Recent statutory and regulatory reforms—most notably the US *Sarbanes-Oxley Act of 2002*[71] and the US Securities and Exchange Commission rules promulgated pursuant to that legislation and, in Canada, Multilateral Instrument 52-110, an initiative of Canada's securities regulators, which requires most reporting issuers (with limited exceptions) to establish an audit committee and includes rules as to the composition and responsibilities of such committees[72]—have addressed these issues specifically in a way that goes well beyond the modest requirements in the CBCA.

---

66 CBCA, s. 163(3).

67 Ibid., s. 163(2).

68 Ibid., s. 171(1). The drafting of s. 171(1) is somewhat unfortunate. It purports to impose the audit committee requirement upon "a corporation described in subsection 102(2)." The cross-reference is intended to limit the application of s. 171 to those distributing corporations, "any of the issued securities of which remain outstanding and are held by more than one person." However, it might have been preferable to repeat this language in s. 171 because, of course, s. 102(2) does not refer only to such corporations, but, in fact, specifies requirements for all CBCA corporations before describing the special requirements that apply to this class of distributing corporations.

69 Ibid., s. 171(3).

70 Ibid., s. 171(1).

71 Pub. L. no. 107-204.

72 (2004), 27 OSCB 3252. For a general discussion of the role of national and multilateral instruments within the framework of Canadian securities regulation, see MacIntosh and Nicholls, supra footnote 28, at 83-84.

Calling of Shareholder Meetings

The CBCA's procedures governing the calling of shareholder meetings distinguish between distributing and non-distributing corporations. Corporations must normally provide at least 21 days' notice for the calling of shareholder meetings.[73] However, corporations that are not distributing corporations are permitted to provide in their articles or bylaws for shorter periods of notice.[74]

Compulsory Acquisition Rules

A provision was recently added to the CBCA's "compulsory acquisition" rules, and this provision also turns on the distinction between distributing and non-distributing corporations. The compulsory acquisition rules provide a method by which a person who holds most of the shares of a CBCA corporation may lawfully acquire all of the remaining shares from the minority shareholders, even if those minority shareholders do not actually wish to sell their shares. Such an extraordinary provision is, not surprisingly, subject to many specific conditions, and must be pursued strictly in accordance with a host of protective statutory rules.

First, the compulsory acquisition provisions are available only to a person who has just completed a successful takeover bid for the shares of the corporation. The bid must have been accepted by at least 90 percent of the holders of the corporation's shares (excluding the shares originally held by the person making the bid). The compulsory acquisition provisions then permit the bidder, if it wishes, to acquire the remaining shares from holders who did not accept the bid.[75] The price to be paid for these remaining shares must either be the bid price or, at the election of these shareholders, "fair value" as determined by the court.[76] There is a time limit imposed on a bidder who wishes to take advantage of this section. The bidder must act within 60 days of termination of the takeover bid, and, in any event, not more than 180 days from the commencement of the bid.

It may seem peculiar that the CBCA would permit majority shareholders to force minority shareholders to sell their shares in these circumstances. But this statutory provision is thought to offer a reasonable compromise between two important goals: safeguarding the legitimate interests of the minority shareholders, and recognizing the practical and administrative difficulties of being compelled to operate a business corporation as a public company when virtually all of the corporation's shares are in the hands of a single owner.

The purpose of the compulsory acquisition provision is thus to allow bidders whose offer to purchase a corporation's shares has enjoyed an overwhelming level of acceptance to acquire all of the remaining shares of that corporation as well, so that it will no longer be obliged to continue to observe many needless and expensive public company formalities. Those formalities would include, for example, the requirement to convene regular

---

73   CBCA, s. 135(1); CBCA Regulations, s. 44.

74   CBCA, s. 135(1.1)

75   Ibid., s. 206(3).

76   Ibid., s. 206(3)(c).

formal annual meetings, to prepare information circulars and solicit proxies in respect of such meetings, and to satisfy ongoing securities law public reporting requirements. The cost of these measures would be largely wasted if they were incurred only to accommodate the interests of a small number of shareholders whose voting rights could not, in any event, have an impact on corporate decisions, and whose economic interest in the corporation would be minimal. The compulsory acquisition rules also prevent holders of small numbers of shares from behaving opportunistically by seeking to extract unfairly high prices for their shares from prospective bidders, and thus deterring the launching of good-faith bids in the first place.[77]

Prior to amendments to the CBCA in 2001, the compulsory acquisition provisions gave to bidders, and only to bidders, the option of deciding whether they wished to acquire those shares remaining in the hands of the minority holders after completing a successful takeover bid for 90 percent or more of the corporation's outstanding shares. However, shareholders who have chosen not to tender to a takeover bid that later proves to be successful may also have an interest in having their shares subsequently acquired by the successful bidder. When a public corporation has a majority shareholder holding 90 percent or more of the outstanding shares, the remaining minority shares will trade in a very thin market. It will be difficult, in other words, for such minority shareholders to liquidate their interest at a time of their choosing, at a price that is not subject to a sharp, minority-interest discount.

Moreover, if a public corporation's shares had been widely held prior to the completion of a successful takeover bid, for a variety of other reasons, the value of the remaining minority shares may very well fall once the bid is completed. Among other things, the market may recognize the possibility for such a large majority shareholder to reap so-called private benefits of control. As Gilson and Gordon have put it, "[n]on-controlling shareholders will prefer the presence of a controlling shareholder so long as the benefits from reduction in managerial agency costs are greater than the costs of private benefits of control."[78] In other words, it might be feared that value will—perhaps in rather subtle and clandestine ways—find its way from the corporation into the hands of the majority shareholder, and so not be fully reflected in the share price of the corporation's minority shares. The garnering of such benefits may involve actions falling well short of the kind of breach of fiduciary duty that could be remedied by launching a derivative action or application for an oppression remedy, as discussed in chapter 13. Nevertheless, the risk of such value diversion could well lead to erosion of share value from the small shareholders' perspective.

Recognizing that the position of a minority shareholder can often involve much "unpleasantness,"[79] some corporate statutes—including the Ontario *Business Corporations*

---

77   For a further discussion of the rationale underlying compulsory acquisition provisions and the related issue of amalgamation squeeze-outs and other "going-private transactions," see MacIntosh and Nicholls, supra footnote 28, at 333ff.

78   Ronald J. Gilson and Jeffrey N. Gordon, "Controlling Controlling Shareholders" (2003), 152 *University of Pennsylvania Law Review* 785, at 785-86.

79   See *Re Jury Gold Mines Dev. Co.*, [1928] 4 DLR 735, at 736 (CA): "He is a minority shareholder and must endure the unpleasantness incident to that situation."

Act[80] and, following recent 2001 amendments, the CBCA—now give minority shareholders the right to force the successful takeover bidder to acquire their shares within a
specified time following the bid and at the bid price (or, in the case of the Ontario
Business Corporations Act at a price offered by the bidder or at "fair value").[81] Needless
to say, this provision applies only when the target corporation is a distributing corporation (CBCA)[82] or an offering corporation (Ontario *Business Corporations Act*).[83]

Going-Private and Squeeze-Out Transactions

Closely related to these mandatory acquisition rules are the new CBCA provisions
regulating "going-private transactions" and "squeeze-out transactions." These terms both
refer to corporate transactions that result in the elimination of minority shareholders'
equity interests, without such shareholders' consent. The difference between the two is
this. "Going-private transaction" is the term used when the transaction undertaken involves a distributing corporation.[84] "Squeeze-out transaction" is the term used when the
transaction undertaken involves a corporation that is not a distributing corporation.[85]

The inclusion in the CBCA of these concepts represents the culmination of a long
legal evolution. A going-private or squeeze-out transaction might be initiated by a majority shareholder for precisely the same reason that such a shareholder might wish to make
the sort of post-takeover bid compulsory acquisition described earlier—namely, to acquire
100 percent ownership of the corporation and so, in the case of public companies, to end
the ongoing requirement to hold annual meetings, solicit proxies, and so on.

In many cases the majority shareholder will not be able to satisfy the conditions of the
90 percent compulsory acquisition provisions. Accordingly, a practice developed in
Canada by which majority shareholders who wished to "take the corporation private"
would attempt to force out minority shareholders by the strategic use of other provisions
of corporate law—especially statutory amalgamation provisions. Here was how the trick
was done. Under the CBCA, and many other Canadian corporate statutes, when two
companies amalgamate, the shareholders of each of the predecessor (amalgamating)
corporations usually give up their old shares, and receive in return shares in the new
amalgamated corporation. But, if the amalgamation agreement between the amalgamating corporations permits it, shareholders can be given different consideration for their old
shares. In other words, on amalgamation, the amalgamation agreement can specify that
the minority shareholders of one of the amalgamating corporations will not receive
equity shares in the new amalgamated corporation at all, but instead will be given cash or
redeemable securities and so will cease to have any equity interest in the surviving

80   *Business Corporations Act* (Ont.), s. 189.

81   See, e.g., CBCA, s. 206.1; *Business Corporations Act* (Ont.), s. 189(4).

82   Ibid., s. 205.1(1).

83   *Business Corporations Act* (Ont.), s.187(1).

84   CBCA, s. 2(1), definition of "going-private transaction," and CBCA Regulations, s. 3(1).

85   CBCA, s. 2(1), definition of "squeeze-out transaction."

corporation. The minority shareholders, who are threatened with losing their equity interest in this way, might well object. But as long as the controlling shareholder holds at least two-thirds of the shares of each amalgamating corporation, their objections will be to no avail. The amalgamation agreement does not need to be approved unanimously. It is enough if it is approved by a vote of at least two-thirds of the shareholders of each of the amalgamating corporations. Such "squeeze-out" amalgamations were thus seen as a useful and expedient alternative to the more restrictive compulsory acquisition rules.

At one time, the courts cast doubt on the propriety of this sort of going-private transaction.[86] In the case of CBCA companies, it was noted, for example, going-private transactions of this type seemed to represent attempts to do an "end run" around the 90 percent compulsory acquisition provision. Allowing an end run like this would lead to an anomaly. The rules surrounding the "compulsory acquisition provisions" that applied when a shareholder had acquired at least 90 percent of a corporation's shares were deliberately crafted to be quite restrictive. How odd it would be to permit *less successful* bidders, holding considerably less than 90 percent of a corporation's shares, to achieve the same outcome but with fewer protections for minority shareholders.

In the meantime, provincial securities regulators and legislators began to take increasing interest in going-private transactions. In Ontario, for example, public companies were permitted to complete going-private transactions, provided they complied with a series of specific rules, intended to ensure that minority shareholders were not being unfairly exploited by the majority shareholders who had orchestrated these manoeuvres.[87] Over time, it was recognized that there were, on balance, many advantages to permitting going-private transactions, provided that they were completed in accordance with an appropriately protective provincial regime. That approach is now formally recognized by the CBCA, and is discussed further in chapter 14.[88]

There are also special rules that apply when a distributing corporation has undertaken a bid to repurchase all of its own outstanding shares of a single class from its shareholders, then subsequently seeks to acquire the remaining shares from any shareholders who initially declined to accept the offer. Once again, these rules apply only where the repurchase offer has been made by a distributing corporation.[89]

---

86   See, e.g., *Alexander v. Westeel-Rosco Ltd.* (1978), 22 OR (2d) 211 (HCJ); *Carlton Realty Co. Ltd. v. Maple Leaf Mills* (1978), 22 OR (2d) 198 (HCJ).

87   Originally, the approach of the Ontario Securities Commission was embodied in OSC Policy 9.1. That policy was subsequently replaced by OSC Rule 61-501 (2000), 23 OSCB 2679. Rule 61-501 was materially amended effective June 29, 2004 (2004), 27 OSCB 5975.

88   See CBCA, s. 193: "A corporation may carry out a going-private transaction. However, if there are any applicable provincial securities laws, a corporation may not carry out a going-private transaction unless the corporation complies with those laws." CBCA s. 194, which refers to squeeze-out transactions, does not make reference to compliance with provincial laws because provincial measures such as OSC Rule 61-501 only apply to reporting issuers (or "distributing corporations" as they are called under the CBCA). Recall that "squeeze-out transactions" are transactions involving corporations that are not distributing corporations.

89   CBCA, s. 206(7.1)

Proxy Solicitation

Perhaps one of the most important distinctions between distributing and non-distributing corporations arises in the context of proxy solicitation. This is an area, though, where the functional approach of the Dickerson committee still survives in the CBCA, such that larger, non-distributing corporations are subject to many of the same requirements as distributing corporations.

The subject of proxy solicitation is dealt with in more detail in chapter 9. For present purposes, it is sufficient simply to say that, in order to protect the voting rights of shareholders who may not be able to attend a shareholder meeting in person, the CBCA permits shareholders to exercise their vote by proxy. It is a common requirement of provincial securities legislation that the management of "reporting issuers" (that is, public corporations) solicit proxies in connection with shareholder meetings.[90] In other words, managers must inform shareholders of their right to vote by proxy, and provide them with the necessary form of proxy.

This is an area, however, where corporate laws and securities laws intersect. Many Canadian corporate statutes also include mandatory management proxy solicitation rules. Often, these rules apply only to offering or distributing corporations.[91] The CBCA, however, includes mandatory proxy solicitation rules that apply not only to distributing corporations, but also to non-distributing corporations with more than 50 shareholders.[92] (Prior to amendments made in 2001, the CBCA rule was even more widely cast, and applied to corporations with as few as 15 shareholders, a threshold that still applies in the Saskatchewan[93] and Alberta[94] corporate statutes.)

The requirement for private corporations to solicit proxies seems to be of rather doubtful utility, but it has been suggested that it may be necessary to protect the interests of minority shareholders of larger, private corporations. In any event, for smaller, private corporations, shareholder meetings are typically far less formal affairs than those of public corporations. In fact, it is not uncommon for private companies to dispense with formal meetings altogether and transact business, as expressly permitted by law, by way of signed, written resolutions.[95]

Trust Indentures

Part VIII of the CBCA, which deals with rules relating to trust indentures,[96] is also limited to distributing corporations—or to companies in the process of becoming distrib-

---

90 See, e.g., *Securities Act* (Ont.), supra footnote 27, s. 85. For a discussion of the Ontario *Securities Act* proxy rules, see MacIntosh and Nicholls, supra footnote 28, at 262ff.

91 See, e.g., *Business Corporations Act* (Ont.), s. 111; *Corporations Act* (NL), s. 250; *The Corporations Act* (Man.), ss. 143(1) and (2) (the Manitoba Act includes a further limitation: the provision does not apply to a corporation with fewer than 15 shareholders).

92 CBCA, ss. 149(1) and (2).

93 *The Business Corporations Act* (Sask.), ss. 143(1) and (2).

94 *Business Corporations Act* (Alta.), ss. 149(1) and (2).

95 See, e.g., CBCA, s. 142.

96 These rules are canvassed in chapter 12.

uting corporations. However, as explained further below, the term "distributing corporation" does not actually appear in part VIII.

Trust indentures are agreements entered into between a trustee (typically a trust company) and a corporation that intends to issue debt securities, such as bonds or debentures, to the public. Trust indentures are discussed further in chapter 12. Briefly put, however, the trust indenture contains all of the terms and conditions of the debt—rather like a loan agreement—and establishes that it is the role of the trustee to monitor the issuing corporation's performance of its obligations. In the event of default, it is the trustee that initiates the necessary enforcement actions.[97] The independence and vigilance of the indenture trustee are critical to the efficacy of the trust indenture mechanism. Accordingly, the CBCA—and other provincial corporate statutes[98]—includes certain mandatory procedures aimed at reducing conflicts of interest and enhancing the effective monitoring of a corporate borrower's compliance with the terms of the trust indenture when a public offering of debt securities is undertaken.

The regulation of trust indentures, then, is primarily aimed at protecting smaller debt investors who have no effective way of monitoring the corporations in which they have invested. However, part VIII of the CBCA is not, as a technical matter, limited in its application to "distributing corporations," as defined by the CBCA. The trust indenture provisions in the Act pre-dated the addition of the defined term "distributing corporation" in 2001; but it is not simply this legislative history that accounts for part VIII's unique qualifying language. Elsewhere in the CBCA, the concept of "distributing corporation" is used in contexts where the drafters wish to impose appropriate ongoing requirements on companies whose shares are currently being traded on public markets. Much of the focus of part VIII is on requirements surrounding the initial issuance of debt securities to the public. In other words, part VIII regulates actions that could be taken by an issuer that is not yet a distributing corporation, but is in the midst of completing a public offering of its securities and so is about to become a distributing corporation. Accordingly, in order to achieve their legislative objective, it is crucial that the trust indenture provisions apply not only to corporations that have already distributed securities to the public in the past, but also to issuers that are distributing such securities to the public for the very first time.

Thus, the limiting language found in s. 82(2) provides that part VIII of the CBCA applies to "a trust indenture if the debt obligations issued or to be issued under the trust indenture are part of a distribution to the public." A distribution to the public could normally be effected in accordance with provincial securities laws only if the issuing corporation duly filed and delivered a prospectus, and thus became a "reporting issuer" (or equivalent) in any one of the Canadian provinces. Recall that the CBCA regulations deem any entity that is a "reporting issuer" in any of those provinces where that term is

---

97   The relationship between the indenture trustee and the corporation is, however, somewhat complicated, and certain practical difficulties can arise when a trustee undertakes enforcement action. For additional discussion of this point, see Mark R. Gillen and Faye Woodman, eds., *The Law of Trusts: A Contextual Approach* (Toronto: Emond Montgomery, 2000), at 665-73.

98   *Business Corporations Act* (Alta.), part 7, div. 1; *The Business Corporations Act* (Sask.), part I, div. VII; *The Corporations Act* (Man.), part VII; *Business Corporations Act* (Ont.), part V; and *Corporations Act* (NL), part VII.

statutorily defined,[99] or that has filed a prospectus under provincial legislation, to be a distributing corporation.[100]

Stated Capital Rules for Open-End Mutual Funds

Finally, in the interest of completeness, one notes a further technical CBCA provision applicable to distributing corporations. In the case of distributing corporations that are open-end mutual funds, the CBCA allows a special exception from the statutory rules relating to stated capital. Some of the implications of the stated capital rules are canvassed in chapter 12.[101]

CLOSELY HELD CORPORATIONS AND
SHAREHOLDER AGREEMENTS

The corporate form is increasingly used by small-business owners. As noted earlier in this chapter, small, non-public corporations were defined statutorily as "private corporations." Although the term "private corporation" is still commonly heard, on the recommendation of the Dickerson committee, the definition of "private company" was excised from the federal corporate statute.

There are a host of other names that are used to describe especially small corporations with relatively few shareholders—most or all of whom are also corporate directors or managers. Two of the most common labels are "close corporations" and "closely held corporations." Neither of these terms has any precise legal meaning in Canada; but the terms are, nevertheless, frequently used in practice to indicate a subset of non-distributing (or non-offering) corporations (or, perhaps, non-reporting issuers) that, from the perspective of their principals, very much resemble partnerships. In fact, such corporations have often been described as "incorporated partnerships."[102]

Of course, the business relationship between entrepreneurs who have chosen to carry on their business in partnership form is typically governed by their partnership agreement. Similarly, some or all of the shareholders of a close corporation may wish to provide by way of private agreement for various matters relating to the voting of their shares or the conduct of the business and affairs of their corporation. Such shareholder contracts or shareholder agreements have long been used by the shareholders of small, private companies and, as discussed below, have been explicitly recognized by modern corporate statutes.

In fact, the CBCA and some provincial corporate statutes have provided for a special sort of shareholder agreement—the "unanimous shareholder agreement"—pursuant to

---

99   The eight provinces are Ontario, Quebec, Nova Scotia, Manitoba, British Columbia, Saskatchewan, Alberta, and Newfoundland. See CBCA Regulations, s. 2(1) and Sched. 1.

100 CBCA Regulations, s. 2(1). CBCA, s. 2(1), definition of "distributing corporation."

101 Ibid., s. 26(12).

102 This phrase is mentioned, for example, by the Supreme Court of Canada in *Duha Printers (Western) Ltd. v. Canada*, [1998] 1 SCR 795, at 828.

which shareholders may privately contract to assume management control in a way that would not necessarily have been permitted at common law. The unanimous shareholder agreement is a device by which closely held corporations can—for all practical purposes—enjoy the benefits of incorporation together with the flexibility of partnership. Indeed, when the Dickerson committee proposed that the CBCA permit such unanimous shareholder agreements, it explained that such an agreement was intended to permit a closely held corporation "to operate, in effect, as a partnership with limited liability."[103] Elsewhere in the committee's report, the drafters indicate that under the CBCA's new unanimous shareholder agreement provisions, "close corporations are ... equated with incorporated partnerships."[104]

Shareholder Agreements at Common Law

To appreciate the significance of the concept of the unanimous shareholder agreement as it exists today in the CBCA and in a number of provincial corporate statutes, it is useful to briefly survey the law governing ordinary shareholder agreements as it had developed prior to the Dickerson committee's report.

Perhaps the three most fundamental provisions of most shareholder agreements are (1) those that provide for the way in which the shares will be voted in certain circumstances. Such provisions, for example, might ensure that each shareholder is to be represented on the board of directors or have a right to participate in the corporation's decision making; (2) those that impose restrictions or conditions on each shareholder's right to transfer his or her shares;[105] and (3) those that deal with the often-related issue of how the shareholders may "exit" from the corporation, either because the relationship between the shareholders has deteriorated, or because one shareholder wishes to liquidate his or her investment.

At common law, shareholders could lawfully agree to pool their votes, either by way of a voting trust, or by way of shareholder agreement, and these agreements could be specifically enforced.[106] In the case of a voting trust, authority to vote the shares in accordance with the instructions of the shareholders would be granted to a trustee. The principal advantage of a voting trust was that it minimized the likelihood of "defection" by one or more shareholders who were parties to a voting agreement. In other words, by conferring legal title in the shares on a trustee who then became bound to vote them in accordance with the trust, the trust arrangement made it practically impossible for a shareholder who might subsequently change his or her mind from attempting to vote his or her shares in some other way.

---

103 Dickerson committee, supra footnote 33, at para. 38.

104 Ibid., at para. 486.

105 There is a considerable body of law on the effect of share transfer restrictions and, importantly, the legal effect of a purported transfer of shares made in contravention of such restrictions. See, e.g., *Peat Marwick Ltd. v. Goldfarb* (1983), 40 OR (2d) 330 (CA).

106 See, e.g., *Greenwell v. Porter*, [1902] Ch. 530; *Motherwell v. Schoof*, [1949] 4 DLR 812 (Alta. SC); *Ringuet v. Bergeron*, [1960] SCR 672. See also the Dickerson committee's discussion, supra footnote 33, at para. 298ff.

Such shareholder agreements, although generally lawful, were subject to an important limitation: they could not fetter the discretion of a corporation's directors. In other words, if a shareholder of a corporation was also a member of the corporation's board of directors, any provision in a shareholder agreement that purported to govern how that person must decide certain matters, when acting in his or her capacity *as a director*, would not be lawful. Such void provisions could, however, be severed from an otherwise enforceable agreement. This distinction between valid and invalid purposes was delineated in the early case of *Motherwell v. Schoof*,[107] a decision to which the Dickerson committee specifically referred.[108]

The Supreme Court of Canada also endorsed this view of the law in *Ringuet v. Bergeron*,[109] a decision that illustrates just how elusive this theoretical distinction between agreeing as shareholder, and agreeing as director can prove to be in practice. *Ringuet* concerned the enforceability of a shareholder agreement entered into in 1949 between the respondent (Bergeron) and the appellants. The agreement provided, among other things, that the parties would exercise their votes to ensure that they were each elected to the board of directors, and to ensure that they were appointed to the respective offices specified in the agreement. Thus, according to the agreement, the respondent was always to hold the offices of secretary-treasurer and assistant general manager of the corporation. The agreement provided for a rather onerous penalty provision in the event that any party violated these terms. The enforceability of these penalty provisions, though an interesting subject, is not relevant to the corporate law issues raised by the decision.

Judson J, writing for the majority, endorsed *in principle* the view that had been articulated in the dissenting opinion of the lower court: "[w]hile majority shareholders may agree to vote their shares for certain purposes, they cannot by this agreement tie the hands of directors and compel them to exercise the power of management of the company in a particular way."[110] Mr. Justice Judson did not believe, however, that the agreement in question violated this principle because, he found, it purported only to govern the conduct of the signatories at shareholder meetings, rather than in their capacities as directors:

> It is no more than an agreement among shareholders owning or proposing to own the majority of the issued shares of a company to unite upon a course of policy or action and upon the officers whom they will elect. There is nothing illegal or contrary to public order in an agreement for achieving these purposes. Shareholders have the right to combine their interests and voting powers to secure such control of a company and to ensure that the company will be managed by certain persons in a certain manner. This is a well-known, normal and legal contract and one which is frequently encountered in current practice and it makes no difference whether the objects sought are to be achieved by means of an agreement such as this or a voting trust. Such an arrangement is not prohibited either by law, by good morals or public order.[111]

---

107   Supra footnote 106.

108   Supra footnote 33, at para. 299.

109   Supra footnote 106.

110   Ibid., at 683.

111   Ibid., at 684.

Fauteux J, in dissent, disagreed on this critical factual point. He found that the agreement did, indeed, purport to govern actions to be taken by the parties in their capacity as corporate directors and, as such, ought not to be permitted.

The final outcome in *Ringuet*, as a matter of policy, has much to commend it. There are few compelling reasons to prevent shareholders in a private company from agreeing among themselves how they wish to order their business affairs. There is little to be said for striking down such agreements subject to extreme situations where the relief of the statutory oppression remedy, discussed in chapter 13, may be appropriate. But however one may welcome the outcome of the case, the reasoning on which it was based is not altogether satisfying. It appears, for example, that one of the key provisions of the shareholder agreement that was found to have been wrongfully dishonoured required that the plaintiff be elected as the corporation's secretary-treasurer and assistant general manager. Yet the appointment of such offices is not normally within the purview of a corporation's shareholders. It is the corporation's directors that appoint officers.[112] Accordingly, it is not entirely clear that the matters on which the shareholders of the corporation had agreed to act in unity were, in fact, matters coming within the traditional ambit of shareholder powers.

Was it reasonable, as a general matter, for the courts to frown on agreements that purported to fetter director discretion? Easterbrook and Fischel, commenting on a parallel development in the United States, represented by the 1934 decision *McQuade v. Stoneham*,[113] criticized what they condemned as the court's "mechanical" (and inappropriate) application of public company principles to the governance of close corporations.[114] Recall that Easterbrook and Fischel are proponents of the "contractarian" model of the corporation—the concept that the corporation is merely a nexus of contracts, for which the primary role of incorporation statutes is to enable, rather than to mandate or regulate. In publicly traded corporations, on this view, there are a host of matters in respect of which the members cannot conveniently (or costlessly) enter into explicit contracts; accordingly, the law must provide an appropriate default position. But in the case of close corporations, the barriers to private contracting are few. On this view, then, it would be inappropriate to allow the default rules (rules that are needed only when it is impossible to enter into explicit contracts) to trump such explicit contracts. Thus, Easterbrook and Fischel confidently and happily declare *McQuade* a "fossil."[115]

Unanimous Shareholder Agreements

In Canada, it might be more accurate to describe cases such as *Ringuet v. Bergeron* as antiques, rather than fossils. As will be seen, however, modern unanimous shareholder agreement provisions in Canadian corporate statutes now do away with the sometimes

---

112 See, e.g., CBCA, s. 121(a). This provision is subject to the articles and the bylaws and any *unanimous* shareholder agreement (as defined in the CBCA), but not to shareholder agreements generally.

113 263 NY 323 (1934).

114 Frank H. Easterbrook and Daniel Fischel, *The Economic Structure of Corporate Law* (Cambridge, MA: Harvard University Press, 1991), at 234-35.

115 Ibid., at 235.

murky distinction between valid agreements to exercise shareholder voting power and invalid fettering of director discretion.

The Dickerson committee recommended the inclusion in the CBCA of a statutory provision that would expressly permit all shareholders to enter into a "unanimous shareholder agreement," and in such agreement to restrict in whole or in part the directors' powers. The committee included such a statutory provision to effectively reverse the "unnecessarily rigid"[116] effect of judicial decisions that held that even where the shareholders acted unanimously, a shareholder agreement could not operate to fetter director discretion. (It was assumed that the parties to these agreements were both shareholders and directors.)[117]

However, the statutory language originally proposed by the Dickerson committee differed somewhat from the wording actually adopted by Parliament. The committee's proposed provision read, in part, as follows:

> An otherwise lawful agreement among all the shareholders of a corporation ... is valid, notwithstanding that the agreement restricts in whole or in part the *discretion or* powers of the directors to manage the business and affairs of the corporation.[118]

When the CBCA was finally enacted, in addition to specifying that such an agreement must be in writing, the drafters chose to omit the phrase "discretion or." Thus, what appeared to be among the most critical reasons for proposing this provision in the first place was not explicitly addressed by the statutory language. This technical deficiency prevailed for more than a quarter century. It was at last corrected in 2001, and s. 146 of the current version of the CBCA now explicitly confers power on a corporation's shareholders to fetter directors' discretion by way of a unanimous shareholder agreement.[119]

A unanimous shareholder agreement, as defined in the CBCA, is quite different from an ordinary shareholder agreement. In fact, even if a shareholder agreement is signed by all of a corporation's shareholders, that agreement is not necessarily a unanimous shareholder agreement within the meaning of the statute. This is so because the definition of unanimous shareholder agreement, in s. 2(1), refers to "an agreement described in subsection 146(1) or a declaration of a shareholder described in subsection 146(2)." To come

---

116 Supra footnote 33, at para. 299.

117 In fact, Dickerson himself would later describe as "not realistic" the suggestion that shareholders would assume the powers of the directors by way of a unanimous shareholder agreement but then proceed to elect a board of directors comprising other individuals who would have no duties. Robert W.V. Dickerson, *The Canada Business Corporations Act: Implications for Management and the Accountant* (Hamilton, ON: Society of Management Accountants of Canada, 1978), at 59.

118 Dickerson et al., *Proposals for a New Business Corporations Law for Canada*, vol. II, Draft Canada Business Corporations Act (Ottawa: Information Canada, 1971), at para. 11.14(2), p. 90 (emphasis added).

119 CBCA, s. 146(6). One small note of caution here. In some jurisdictions, it is possible for professionals (such as lawyers and accountants) to incorporate their professional practices. Typically, special rules apply to such professional corporations intended to ensure that only professionals—who are typically regulated directly or indirectly by specific legislation relating to their professions—are members of such corporations. Accordingly, in such professional agreements, voting agreements or shareholder agreements (including unanimous shareholder agreements) that would have the effect of giving to non-professionals membership or voting rights are void. (See, e.g., Ontario *Business Corporations Act*, ss. 3.2(4) and (5).)

within the meaning of either of these subsections, an agreement[120] (or a resolution signed by a sole shareholder)[121] must be one

> that restricts, in whole or in part, the powers of the directors to manage, or supervise the management of, the business and affairs of the corporation.

It may be very important to determine whether a particular agreement is or is not a unanimous shareholder agreement as defined. Only a statutorily defined unanimous shareholder agreement can have the effect of shifting what would otherwise be directors' liabilities onto the shareholders who are parties to such an agreement.[122] This is why it is not uncommon for agreements to which all shareholders are parties to contain a provision expressly declaring that such agreements are *not* unanimous shareholder agreements within the meaning of the legislation.

Moreover, a unanimous shareholder agreement has greater corporate constitutional significance than an ordinary shareholder agreement. The Supreme Court of Canada in *Duha Printers (Western) Ltd. v. Canada*[123] equated such agreements with a corporation's constating documents—ranking on a par, in other words, with the corporation's articles and bylaws. Directors and officers are statutorily obliged to comply with a unanimous shareholder agreement.[124] Compliance with a unanimous shareholder agreement may be enforced, not only through a conventional breach of contract claim, but by way of a statutory compliance order, as in the case of a breach of the corporation's articles.[125] A unanimous shareholder agreement may impose additional shareholder voting thresholds (beyond those required by the CBCA itself);[126] it may require the directors to place additional information before the annual meeting,[127] limit the directors' power to manage the corporation's affairs,[128] and, specifically (among other things), limit the directors' authority under the statute to issue shares,[129] authorize the corporation to borrow money,[130] deal with corporate bylaws,[131] appoint officers,[132] and determine director, officer, and employee remuneration.[133]

Its constitutional significance is reinforced by the fact that a unanimous shareholder agreement, unlike an ordinary shareholder agreement, can become binding on shareholders

---

120 CBCA, s. 146(1).

121 Ibid., s. 146(2).

122 Ibid., s. 146(5).

123 [1998] 1 SCR 795.

124 CBCA, s. 122(2).

125 Ibid., s. 247. See also the discussion of remedies in chapter 14.

126 Ibid., s. 6(3).

127 Ibid., s. 155.

128 Ibid., s. 102.

129 Ibid., s. 25.

130 Ibid., s. 189.

131 Ibid., s. 103.

132 Ibid., s. 121.

133 Ibid., s. 125.

who were not among the original signatories. The CBCA provides that "a purchaser or transferee of shares subject to a unanimous shareholder agreement is deemed to be a party to the agreement."[134] Such a provision could work considerable unfairness on a transferee of shares who was not aware that a unanimous shareholder agreement existed at the time that he or she acquired the shares. To relieve against this unfairness, the Act provides that if a purchaser or transferee was not made aware that the shares he or she was acquiring were subject to a unanimous shareholder agreement, either by a legend placed on the share certificates[135] themselves, or otherwise, he or she may rescind the transaction by which he or she acquired the shares within 30 days of becoming aware of the existence of the agreement.[136]

Note that the CBCA states that a transferee *and a purchaser* of shares will be bound by the terms of a unanimous shareholder agreement. Some other Canadian corporate statutes, including the Ontario *Business Corporations Act*, refer only to transferees.[137] This difference is not trivial. The addition of the word "purchaser" to the CBCA provision in 2001 was intended to ensure that subscribers of new shares from the corporate treasury as well as transferees of previously issued shares would equally be bound by the provisions of a unanimous shareholder agreement.

In *Sportscope Television Network Ltd. v. Shaw Communications Inc.*,[138] a shareholder of a corporation incorporated under the Ontario *Business Corporations Act* who had acquired its shares in the corporation by converting a previously issued debenture and as the result of an amalgamation was held not to be bound by a unanimous shareholder agreement because it was not a "transferee" of the shares. *Sportscope* would presumably have been decided differently under the current CBCA provision.

Although the CBCA's unanimous shareholder agreement provisions are rarely litigated, a number of theoretical questions have arisen surrounding the concept of such an agreement. For instance, it has occasionally been asked whether a unanimous shareholder agreement could, by its terms, provide for subsequent amendments to be effected with less-than-unanimous approval. If so, would this not potentially undermine the policy rationale on which such agreements are based? In some jurisdictions, this issue is dealt with expressly by statute. For example, under the Alberta *Business Corporations Act*, a unanimous shareholder agreement cannot be amended except with the written consent of all shareholders at the effective date of the agreement.[139] In contrast, the Ontario *Business Corporations Act* states that a unanimous shareholder agreement may indeed provide that "any amendment ... may be effected in the manner specified therein,"[140] clearly anticipating the possibility of amendments by less-than-unanimous consent.

134   Ibid., s. 146(3).

135   Ibid., s. 49(8).

136   Ibid., s. 146(4).

137   *Business Corporations Act* (Ont.), s. 108(4).

138   (1999), 46 BLR (2d) 87 (Ont. Gen. Div.).

139   *Business Corporations Act* (Alta.), s. 146(8).

140   *Business Corporations Act* (Ont.), s. 108(6)(a).

Where a statute is silent on the issue, however, on what basis can it be said that shareholders—who have been expressly permitted to enter into such contracts—ought to be disallowed from contracting with respect to such a conventional matter as a contractual amending procedure? Although the courts have not provided definitive guidance on this matter, it is interesting to note the early views of Robert Dickerson, who chaired the committee upon whose recommendations the unanimous shareholder agreement provision was introduced into the federal incorporation statute. Dickerson suggested that "[p]resumably ... the original agreement could itself provide for amendment by fewer than all the parties."[141]

A second issue raised by unanimous shareholder agreements is their impact on the role of corporate directors. It is problematic that a corporation must always have at least one director, even in cases where the directors may have no power to act, owing to the existence of a comprehensive unanimous shareholder agreement that strips their powers away. Dickerson noted that his committee would in fact have preferred that no directors be required in such a case, but "this idea ran aground on the shoals of nationalism. The rule ... requiring every corporation to have a majority of 'resident Canadians' on its board of directors was thought to be more important."[142] This statement suggests that the drafters were especially concerned about corporations incorporated by foreign nationals. The presence on the board of foreign-controlled corporations of totally powerless resident Canadian directors would seem to offer cold comfort to fervent Canadian nationalists. Indeed, it has long been recognized that the CBCA's resident Canadian director requirements are rather easily circumvented in the case of CBCA corporations incorporated as subsidiaries of foreign corporations. Such corporations need only execute unanimous shareholder agreements, then appoint to their boards Canadian nominees who are no more than placeholders. It is clear, however, that the residency requirement is of political importance, not practical importance. A 1996 Industry Canada discussion paper canvassed this issue in some detail. This paper noted that any attempt to eliminate corporate directors would likely be "quite controversial, as it would represent a departure from convention and tradition."[143]

The above discussion has focused upon the unanimous shareholder agreement provisions found in the CBCA. Similar provisions are found in many other Canadian statutes as well. However, there are two other flexible variations of unanimous shareholder agreement legislation in place in Alberta and British Columbia.

First, under the Alberta *Business Corporations Act*, there is no requirement that an agreement restrict the directors' powers in some ways in order to constitute a unanimous shareholder agreement within the meaning of the Act—although, of course, the agreement may have this effect.[144]

Second, under the Alberta statute, a unanimous shareholder agreement may *exclude* all (but not less than all) of the special rules applicable to unanimous shareholder agreements.[145]

---

141 Dickerson, supra footnote 117, at 58.

142 Ibid., at 59.

143 Industry Canada discussion paper (1996), at para. 117.

144 *Business Corporations Act* (Alta.), s. 146(1).

145 Ibid., s. 146(9).

Third, the Alberta statute provides that a unanimous shareholder agreement may be binding not only on transferees of existing shares, but also on new shareholders to whom the corporation has issued shares directly. This provision, like the similar language added to the CBCA in 2001, is aimed at addressing the sort of issue raised in *Sportscope v. Shaw*, discussed above.

Fourth, the rights of a shareholder who has acquired shares without knowledge of the existence of the unanimous shareholder agreement are unique. As discussed above, under the CBCA, a purchaser or transferee of shares without knowledge of a unanimous shareholder agreement may rescind the transaction by which he or she became a shareholder within 30 days of becoming aware of the agreement.[146] Under the Ontario Act, a purchaser who had no knowledge of the unanimous shareholder agreement is not bound by it, unless reference to the agreement had been noted conspicuously on the transferred share certificate.[147] Under the Alberta *Business Corporations Act*, however, purchasers of newly issued shares and transferees of previously issued shares are given slightly different remedies in the event that they have acquired their shares without knowledge that they are subject to a unanimous shareholder agreement. A purchaser of new shares from the corporation—provided he or she was not an existing shareholder—may rescind the purchase by giving notice within a "reasonable time" after becoming aware of the existence of the unanimous shareholder agreement.[148] A transferee of shares, on the other hand, may, within 30 days of acquiring actual knowledge of the existence of the agreement, send a notice of objection to the corporation, and demand that the corporation purchase the shares at fair value.[149] If the transferee had paid more than fair value for the shares, he or she then has the right to recover the difference from the transferor.[150]

The approach toward unanimous shareholder agreements found in the BC *Business Corporations Act* has other distinct features. First, the BC Act does not explicitly refer to unanimous shareholder agreements at all, but instead provides a functional equivalent. Section 137 of the statute states that "the articles of a company may transfer, in whole or in part, the powers of the directors to manage or supervise the management of the business and affairs of the company."[151] Such a provision may be included in the articles at the time of incorporation (or, equivalently, when the company is "recognized" under the Act)[152] or may be added later if so authorized by special resolution.[153] Unlike the unanimous shareholder agreement provisions of the CBCA and other similar legislation, the BC Act allows for powers of management to be transferred not only to a corporation's

146 CBCA, s. 146(4).

147 *Business Corporations Act* (Ont.), s. 108(5) and s. 56(3).

148 *Business Corporations Act* (Alta.), s. 146(2).

149 Ibid., ss. 146(4) and (5).

150 Ibid., s. 146(6).

151 *Business Corporations Act* (BC), s. 137(1).

152 The concept of "recognition" is used in s. 3 of the BC statute to refer not only to incorporation, but also to other means by which a body corporate might become subject to the Act, including by way of amalgamation, continuation, or conversion.

153 *Business Corporations Act* (BC), s. 137(1).

shareholders, but also to any other person or persons. Any such transferee acquires the rights, powers, duties, and liabilities of the directors "whether arising under the [*Business Corporations Act*] or otherwise"[154] to the extent of the transfer, and the directors, in turn, are relieved of such rights, duties, powers, and liabilities.[155]

STATUTORY RECOGNITION OF CLOSELY HELD CORPORATIONS: THE DELAWARE EXAMPLE

It has occasionally been suggested that it might be advantageous for Canadian law to give formal statutory recognition and even greater operational flexibility to small corporations with few shareholders (the prototypical "incorporated partnerships").

Many jurisdictions have enacted specialized "close corporation" legislation. One example of such a close corporation regime is the corporate law of Delaware. Delaware's *General Corporation Law* devotes a special subchapter to those entities that it defines as "close corporations."[156] (The US Model Business Corporations Act also contains special provisions for such close corporations.)[157]

A "close corporation" is defined by the Delaware statute to mean

> a corporation organized under this chapter whose certificate of incorporation contains the provisions required by §102 [the section of the statute dealing generally with the formal requirements for certificates of incorporation] and, in addition, provides that:
>
> (1) All of the corporation's issued stock of all classes, exclusive of treasury shares, shall be represented by certificates and shall be held of record by not more than a specified number of persons, not exceeding 30; and
>
> (2) All of the issued stock of all classes shall be subject to 1 or more of the restrictions on transfer permitted by §202 of this title; and
>
> (3) The corporation shall make no offering of any of its stock of any class which would constitute a "public offering" within the meaning of the United States Securities Act of 1933.[158]

The parallels between this definition and the traditional definition of "private company" in English company law and "private issuer" in Canadian securities law are clear. However, the Delaware statute does not use this definition merely to distinguish close corporations from public corporations for purposes of public filing rules or proxy solicitation requirements. Instead, it provides for a separate close corporation regime, which allows such smaller entities to operate truly as "incorporated partnerships," arguably with flexibility even greater than that available to CBCA corporations subject to comprehensive unanimous shareholder agreements.

---

154   Ibid., s. 137(2)(a).

155   Ibid., s. 137(2)(b).

156   8 Delaware Code, subchapter XIV.

157   Commentators have suggested that the US model ought not to be adopted in Canada. See, e.g., Brian R. Cheffins, "U.S. Close Corporation Legislation: A Model Canada Should Not Follow" (1989), 35 *McGill Law Journal* 160.

158   Supra footnote 156, s. 342(a).

For example, the Delaware legislation provides that shareholder agreements that restrict the powers of the corporation's directors may validly be entered into by a mere majority of the corporation's shareholders[159] (rather than by all of the shareholders, as required under the CBCA). Moreover, a Delaware close corporation may dispense with a board of directors altogether, and be managed directly by its shareholders, if its certificate of incorporation so provides.[160] Indeed, the statute specifically permits the shareholders of a close corporation to provide by written agreement for the corporation to be operated as a partnership:

> No written agreement among stockholders of a close corporation, nor any provision of the certificate of incorporation or of the bylaws of the corporation, which agreement or provision relates to any phase of the affairs of such corporation, including but not limited to the management of its business or declaration and payment of dividends or other division of profits or the election of directors or officers or the employment of stockholders by the corporation or the arbitration of disputes, shall be invalid on the ground that it is an attempt by the parties to the agreement or by the stockholders of the corporation to treat the corporation as if it were a partnership or to arrange relations among the stockholders or between the stockholders and the corporation in a manner that would be appropriate only among partners.[161]

Finally, the Delaware statute provides that the certificate of incorporation of a close corporation can give to any one or more stockholders the right to have the corporation dissolved, or to have the corporation dissolved upon the occurrence of some specific event[162]—provisions that would make a corporation share many attributes of a partnership or joint venture.

Currently, the nearest thing to a statutory definition of close corporations in the CBCA is found in the CBCA concept of "personal body corporate" in s. 237.5(2). "Personal body corporate" is defined as

> a body corporate that is not actively engaged in any financial, commercial or industrial business and that is controlled by an individual or a group of individuals, each member of which is connected by blood relationship, adoption or marriage or by cohabiting with another member in a conjugal relationship.

This definition was added to the CBCA in 2001 for a very limited purpose. As explained in greater detail in chapter 10, the 2001 amendments to the CBCA included the concept of modified proportionate liability in the case of financial losses for which more than one defendant is responsible.[163] Despite the introduction of proportionate liability,

---

159 Ibid., s. 350.

160 Ibid., s. 351. Note that, in such a case, the shareholders are deemed to be the directors of the corporation for purposes of the statute, and are subject to liability as directors.

161 Ibid., s. 354.

162 Ibid., s. 355.

163 CBCA, s. 237.1, definition of "financial loss," and s. 237.3. This new regime is properly described as one of *modified* proportionate liability because in cases where damages awarded against a co-defendant are uncollectible, a defendant may be required to pay damages above those representing his or her proportionate share. (See CBCA, ss. 237.3(3) and (4).)

however, certain classes of plaintiffs are to continue to be entitled to recover damages from responsible defendants on a joint-and-several basis. Defendants, in such cases, will not enjoy the protection that proportionate liability would otherwise provide.

Thus, *individual* (as opposed to incorporated) plaintiffs, for example, will enjoy the right to recover from defendants on a joint-and-several basis. But this right is also extended to any plaintiff that is a "personal body corporate" if the value of any such plaintiff's financial interest in the corporation was not more than $20,000.[164]

CONCLUSION

Private, closely held corporations are the norm in Canada. Large, publicly traded corporations, are very much the exception. The law that has developed to accommodate the desire of entrepreneurs to operate "incorporated partnerships" reveals an ongoing attempt to balance traditional corporate law principles with practical small-business realities. What is not a significant concern for such enterprises, however, is the agency problem that is a perpetual challenge for large, public corporations. That subject will be examined in some detail in chapters 10 and 11.

---

164   CBCA, s. 237.5(1)(b); CBCA Regulations 2001, s. 95.

CHAPTER FIVE

Promoters' Cases and Pre-incorporation Contracts

INTRODUCTION

Because a corporation is a legal person distinct from the human beings that sponsor or promote its creation, two types of legal issues frequently arise around the time of a corporation's formation. The first issue involves a unique conflict-of-interest problem. It occurs when the founder of a new corporation (usually referred to by the courts as the "promoter"[1]) makes a contract with the very corporation he or she is organizing. Consider this simple example. Suppose a promoter establishes a new corporation, ABC Corp., then seeks to sell a factory that he owns to ABC Corp. The promoter's understandable desire to obtain the highest possible price for himself will inevitably conflict with the corporation's interest in paying the lowest possible price. If the promoter is also in a position to make decisions for the corporation, he can ensure that ABC Corp. will agree to pay whatever price he chooses to set. Should the law be concerned with this sort of conflict?

The second legal issue arises when the promoter[2] has just begun the process of setting up a corporation—he has planned to create a new corporation, but the necessary paperwork has not been filed, so the corporation does not yet exist. Difficulties can arise when the promoter in this situation attempts to enter into contracts with third parties *on behalf of* the yet-to-be formed corporation. If those contracts are not honoured, how should the law sort the matter out? Who can sue whom?

Cases of the first sort that involve conflicts between the promoter and the corporation itself are often referred to as "promoters' cases." Cases of the second sort that involve promoters' disputes with third parties are usually called "pre-incorporation contracts cases."

---

1   As Lord Blackburn observed in *Erlanger v. New Sombrero Phosphate Company*, [1877-78] 3 AC 1218 (HL), at 1268: "Throughout the *Companies Act*, 1862 ... , the word 'promoter' is not anywhere used. It is, however, a short and convenient way of designating those who set in motion the machinery by which the Act enables them to create an incorporated company."

2   The recently passed BC *Business Corporations Act*, SBC 2002, c. 57, s. 20(1) refers to such a person as a "facilitator."

PROMOTERS' CASES

Framing the Issue

Corporations do not spring forth spontaneously like weeds in a garden. They are deliberately created by entrepreneurs to perform specific business tasks. The individuals who undertake to form a business corporation have come to be known as "promoters"—a name, as some have noted, not always associated with the most esteemable practices.[3] When a promoter first decides to incorporate a company, he or she may intend, as well, that this new company will eventually purchase from the promoter some assets for use in its new business. Often, the very reason for choosing to incorporate in the first place is to transform what was an unincorporated business (a sole proprietorship or a partnership) into an incorporated entity, and so benefit from enjoying limited liability, perhaps some income tax advantages, and so on.

We often speak informally of a sole proprietor "incorporating his or her existing business." But as a legal matter, the process involves two distinct steps. First, the corporation must be incorporated—that is, the articles (or, perhaps, the memorandum) filed with the appropriate government office, initial directors named, and so on. Then, once formed, the corporation will need to act through its duly appointed officers to acquire the assets and undertaking of the business. The sole proprietor's business, in other words, is not simply endowed mystically with corporate status; rather, the sole proprietor must legally convey the assets of the business from himself or herself to the new corporate entity. This conveyance might take the form of a contribution of capital—that is, the sole proprietor might transfer the assets and undertakings of the business to the corporation in exchange for shares of the new corporation. In Canada, the transfer of such business assets in exchange for the issuance of shares is the usual way in which previously unincorporated businesses are incorporated, because, in such cases, the *Income Tax Act* explicitly allows for a capital gains "rollover." In other words, the transferor is allowed to avoid the immediate payment of tax on any capital gains that have accrued on the business assets. How does the promoter arrive at the price at which he or she will sell these assets to the new corporation? Does the price, in fact, matter? After all, if the new corporation is never going to have any investors other than the promoter, who will care if the price the corporation agrees to pay is too high? (Recall from chapter 3 that this very point was made by Lord Macnaghten in *Salomon's* case.)

But what if the corporation has other shareholders or creditors? If an overvaluation leads to an inflated balance sheet, creditors of the corporation might well be deceived if they were to advance money to the corporation on the basis of the presumed accuracy of the stated values that appeared on the corporation's financial statements. And, if shares in the new corporation are to be sold to other shareholders, the investment decision of those shareholders will surely be based on the presumed value of the assets owned by the corporation. If the corporation has grossly overpaid for the assets, the shareholders will have been induced to invest on unfair terms. It is precisely this concern that animates what are sometimes called "promoters cases."

---

3   See, e.g., Paul L. Davies, *Gower & Davies: Principles of Modern Company Law*, 7th ed. (London: Sweet & Maxwell, 2003), at 90.

So, for example, in *Erlanger v. New Sombrero Phosphate Co.*,[4] the defendants purchased for £55,000 a leasehold interest in the island of Sombrero in the West Indies—an island on which phosphate of lime was mined. This sale was arranged on August 30, 1871, although for technical reasons not relevant here, it could not formally be completed until sometime later.

The defendants then initiated the incorporation of a corporation. This new corporation agreed to purchase the leasehold interest from the defendants for £110,000—that is, for twice the price that the defendants paid for it. The purchase contract between the defendants and the corporation was dated September 20, 1871, less than a month after the original purchase. Had the value of the leasehold interest really doubled in just three weeks, or was something else afoot here?

The initial directors of the new corporation, appointed at the time of its incorporation, included a majority of individuals who were "friendly" to the promoters. It was this friendly board that approved the purchase contract on the part of the corporation. The corporation raised the money to fund the purchase by issuing shares. The new shareholders who were enticed to invest were not informed about this rather remarkable increase in the island's value. They were not the only ones left in the dark. Evidently, the minority of the corporation's directors who were genuinely independent of the promoters had not been told, when they approved the purchase contract, that the leasehold interest the corporation was buying for £110,000 had been acquired just three weeks earlier for half this amount.

The company fell on hard times a year later. A new board of directors was appointed. Under its new management, the corporation brought an action against the promoters seeking, among other remedies, to have the contract by which the island interest had been originally sold to the corporation set aside. The case was argued all the way to the House of Lords. The Law Lords held that the contract should indeed be set aside. The judgments delivered included a number of sternly worded passages. Consider the words of Lord Cairns, for example. He did question whether, on the specific facts of this case, the company had sought its remedy on a sufficiently timely basis. And he did concur with the general proposition that a promoter was certainly not absolutely barred by law from ever selling property to a corporation that he or she had incorporated. However, he also said:

> If he [i.e., the promoter] does [sell property to a corporation in such a case] he is bound to take care that he sells it to the company through the medium of a board of directors who can and do exercise an independent and intelligent judgment on the transaction.[5]

Lord O'Hagan put the matter this way. Yes, the law certainly might permit promoters to seek to sell their property to the corporation they created, but such a sale

> involved obligations of a very serious kind. It required, in its exercise, the utmost good faith, the completest truthfulness, and a careful regard to the protection of the future shareholders.[6]

---

4   Supra footnote 1.

5   Ibid., at 1236.

6   Ibid., at 1255.

The promoters had not discharged the considerable obligations to which their planned resale of the contract had thus subjected them—obligations that a number of the Law Lords characterized as fiduciary in nature.[7] The contract, accordingly, was held to be voidable. It lacked, again to use Lord Cairns's words, "the exercise upon it of the intelligent judgment of an independent executive."[8]

The reasoning in the promoters' cases is based on a simple proposition: it is unjust for promoters to use their effective control over a corporation to exploit that corporation for their own private gain. In this sense, these cases share some features in common with those that involve interested directors' contracts, and the wrongful seizing by officers and directors of corporate opportunities. Cases raising these issues are discussed in chapter 11. Indeed, when promoters are also directors of the purchasing corporation at the time of such a disputed acquisition, the sale contract is the prototypical "interested directors'" contract.

But the precise legal basis for most promoters' cases is somewhat different from those involving self-interested directors. The difference arises from the way in which the courts have articulated the nature of the relationship between the promoter and the not-yet-created corporation. In *Erlanger*, for example, a key distinction is drawn between two different types of cases: (1) those in which a promoter acquires property always intending, from the moment of acquisition, to resell the property to a corporation that the promoter will help establish; and (2) those in which the promoter acquires property without any intention, at least initially, of re-selling this property to a corporation, and only later decides to form a corporation and to sell the property to that corporation. The distinction between these two types of cases appears to affect, among other things, the scope of remedies available to the aggrieved parties.

If a promoter has profited from his sale to a corporation of property that it was always his intention to "flip" in this way, he might be liable to account for that profit. But if the promoter's initial acquisition and subsequent disposition to the corporation of property are not linked in this way, it may be that the only remedy available to the corporation is to have the contract declared void.[9] The promoters' cases establish that the promoter has a fiduciary obligation to the company that he or she forms. The law needs to impose such an obligation to ensure that the corporation is not, in effect, exploited by the promoter at a time when the promoter has complete control over the corporation's decision-making machinery. In the case of sole-shareholder corporations, the risk of exploitation is immaterial. Indeed, in the case of most private, closely held corporations, the risk of exploita-

---

7   See, e.g., Lord Gordon's judgment, ibid., at 1284; Lord Cairns's judgment, ibid., at 1236; Lord O'Hagan's judgment, ibid., at 1255; and Lord Blackburn's judgment, ibid., at 1269. The fact that the promoter stands in a fiduciary relationship to the new company has long been recognized. See, e.g., F.W. Wegenast, *The Law of Canadian Companies* (Toronto: Carswell, 1979), at 743 and the authorities referred to at note 16 therein.

8   Supra footnote 1, at 1239.

9   See, e.g., the judgment of Lord Blackburn in *Erlanger*, supra footnote 1, at 1267. Eilis Ferran has, however, noted that care must be taken to distinguish between: (1) recovery of the difference between the price paid by the promoter and the price paid by the corporation (which has been disallowed); and (2) recovery of the difference between the price paid by the corporation and the fair market value of the property (which ought to be allowed). Professor Ferran also suggests that the restriction of remedies in the older promoters' cases appears to be out of step with more recent judicial treatment of faithless fiduciaries. See Eilis Ferran, *Company Law and Corporate Finance* (Oxford: Oxford University Press, 1999), at 172.

tion is likely minimal. However, for corporations issuing securities to the public, the risk is very real. But how is one to characterize the relationship between today's promoters and tomorrow's (prospective) shareholders? In one of the seminal promoters' cases, *Gluckstein v. Barnes*,[10] the House of Lords placed some emphasis on the nature of this relationship, dubbing the future shareholders of the planned company the so-called coming constituents.[11] In that case, Lord Robertson described the relationship between the promoters and the soon-to-be formed company in this way:

> [T]he company had been so far organised that its executive was provisionally appointed. ... [I]n the present instance the company, even in this, its inchoate stage, was identifiable through its executive. I hold that from the moment this step was taken the coming directors stood in a fiduciary relation to the company whose interests were to be in their sole hands.[12]

Such fiduciary obligations do not make it impossible for the promoter to enter into valid contracts with the corporation. Legitimate concerns about the possibility that a promoter might foist an unfair contract on a corporation that he or she has undertaken to form must not lead to an impractical counsel of perfection. For example, no one would seriously suggest that a promoter ought not to be able to charge to the company the various costs incurred in its incorporation, notwithstanding the admittedly peculiar notion that, by so doing, the corporation is asked to pay expenses that, by definition, it never could have incurred or authorized. Similarly, the conventional contract rule that "past consideration is no consideration"[13] might stand in the way of a promoter receiving shares of a corporation in exchange for services undertaken on its behalf prior to incorporation,[14] but the rigidities of the "past consideration" rule have been largely obviated in Canada by express statutory provisions that do allow a corporation to issue shares in consideration of past services,[15] and the specific issue of incorporation and organization expenses may also now be found in statute. For example, s. 25(4) of the CBCA states that,

> (4) In determining whether property or past services are the fair equivalent of a money consideration, the directors may take into account reasonable charges and expenses of organization and reorganization and payments for property and past services reasonably expected to benefit the corporation.

But if sales by promoters are not to be prohibited outright, then under what circumstances ought they to be allowed? How literally, for example, should *Erlanger*'s prescription of an independent board be taken? Davies and Gower have pointed out that it surely cannot be the case that the law actually requires that *any* sale of property by promoters to the corporation that they have helped create must be approved by an independent board of directors. As they correctly note, "an entirely independent board would be impossible

10   [1900] AC 240 (HL).

11   Ibid., at 257 (per Lord Robertson).

12   Ibid., at 257.

13   See, e.g., G.H.L. Fridman, *The Law of Contract*, 4th ed. (Toronto: Carswell, 1999), at 118.

14   See Davies, supra footnote 3, at 98, note 59.

15   See, e.g., CBCA, s. 25(3).

in the case of most private and many public companies."[16] So, it is not necessarily approval by an independent board that is required for such a sale. What is necessary, is that the promoters ensure that full disclosure has been made of all the material facts, in particular to third-party investors. As Wegenast has put it, "[The promoters] may make profits but they must not be secret."[17]

The risk of non-disclosure will be greatest in those cases where the corporation has public investors—that is, investors who are strangers to the promoters. Public investors may well have been induced to purchase shares in the corporation in the first place on the basis that the corporation owned valuable assets. In other words, they may well have been relying on the presumed value of the assets that were sold to the corporation by the promoters. Not surprisingly, the legislative response to promoters' contracts has focused on such public companies, and has tried to address the dangers of these sales by requiring independent valuations and mandating full disclosure. In Britain, s. 104 of the *Companies Act* requires independent valuation and shareholder approval for certain significant sales of assets to a public corporation by a subscriber to the company's memorandum.[18] Similar requirements apply to transfers of assets to companies "re-registered" as public companies (as opposed to companies originally formed as public companies).[19]

In Canada, the sale of shares of public companies is now, for the most part, regulated by securities laws rather than by corporate statutes. Protections may be found in the rules promulgated by provincial legislatures and Canadian securities regulators governing the preparation of prospectuses—that is, the detailed public disclosure documents that corporations are obliged to prepare, deliver to prospective securities purchasers, and file with securities regulators when they offer their securities to the public.[20]

Canadian securities laws all generally address the problem posed by a promoter's sale of property to a corporation that later seeks to raise money from public investors in much the same way. These laws are intended to protect investors by ensuring that they have all the facts before they buy securities. In other words, if promoters have sold property to a corporation that later offers its securities to the public, the details of that sale must be fully disclosed.

Although the principle is straightforward, the securities rules needed to implement this principle are quite detailed and technical. To illustrate, some of the relevant provisions from Ontario's securities rules are set out below.

First, the Ontario *Securities Act* offers a rather technical definition of the term "promoter":

---

16   Davies, supra footnote 3, at 92.

17   Wegenast, supra footnote 7, at 745.

18   Specifically, if the subscriber, within two years of the date on which the company has been issued its trading certificate under s. 117 of the *Companies Act*, seeks to transfer non-cash assets to the company equal to one-tenth or more of the company's nominal share capital, the assets must be independently valued, and the agreement must be approved by the shareholders. *Companies Act, 1985* (UK), s. 104.

19   Ibid., s. 103.

20   For a detailed discussion of the public offering process, see Jeffrey G. MacIntosh and Christopher C. Nicholls, *Securities Law* (Toronto: Irwin Law, 2002), at 139ff.

"promoter" means,

(a) a person or company who, acting alone or in conjunction with one or more other persons, companies or a combination thereof, directly or indirectly, takes the initiative in founding, organizing or substantially reorganizing the business of an issuer, or

(b) a person or company who, in connection with the founding, organizing or substantial reorganizing of the business of an issuer, directly or indirectly, receives in consideration of services or property, or both services and property, 10 per cent or more of any class of securities of the issuer or 10 per cent or more of the proceeds from the sale of any class of securities of a particular issue, but a person or company who receives such securities or proceeds either solely as underwriting commissions or solely in consideration of property shall not be deemed a promoter within the meaning of this definition if such person or company does not otherwise take part in founding, organizing, or substantially reorganizing the business;[21]

This defined term then feeds into a specific prospectus disclosure requirement. The "general prospectus form" that is used by corporations when they offer securities to the public in Ontario for the first time is mandated by the Ontario Securities Commission. It has a somewhat cumbersome and bureaucratic-sounding designation: Form 41-501F1.[22] Item 21 of Form 41-501F1 deals with a promoter's sale of property to the corporation. It requires a prospectus issued by the corporation when it distributes its securities to make the following disclosure:

For a person or company who is, or has been within two years immediately preceding the date of the prospectus or *pro forma* prospectus, a promoter of the issuer or a subsidiary of the issuer state ...

(c) the nature and amount of anything of value, including money, property, contracts, options or rights of any kind received or to be received by the promoter directly or indirectly from the issuer or from a subsidiary of the issuer, and the nature and amount of any assets, services or other consideration therefor received or to be received by the issuer or a subsidiary of the issuer; and

(d) for an asset acquired within the two years of the date of the preliminary prospectus or *pro forma* prospectus or thereafter, or to be acquired, by the issuer or by a subsidiary of the issuer from a promoter

(i) the consideration paid or to be paid for the asset and the method by which the consideration has been or will be determined

(ii) the person or company making the determination referred to in subparagraph (i) and the person or company's relationship with the issuer, the promoter, or an associate or affiliate of the issuer or of the promoter, and

(iii) the date that the asset was acquired by the promoter and the cost of the asset to the promoter.

The mischief addressed in the promoters' cases is certainly greatest in the context of public corporations, and so it is that securities law rules such as these—rather than

---

21   *Securities Act* (Ont.), RSO 1990, c. S.5, s. 1(1).

22   Ontario Securities Commission Rule 41-501 (2002), 23 OSCB (Supp.) 835.

traditional corporate law—have become the primary means of addressing the problem. Little more, therefore, needs to be said about the subject here. However, before leaving the topic to turn to the issue of pre-incorporation contracts, one additional point deserves mention. Occasionally, the analysis in the promoters' cases is not dissimilar from the approach taken to the corporate opportunities cases discussed in chapter 11. The promoters are regarded as trustees for the as-yet-unformed corporation, such that the property they acquire is, in equity, the corporation's (once it is formed), subject, needless to say, to payment by the corporation of the price. One of the most intriguing aspects of this approach is the fact that, as Davies[23] has observed, if a promoter can, indeed, be a trustee for a not-yet-formed company, it is odd that this same theory did not avail in the pre-incorporation contract context, with which the next section deals.

PRE-INCORPORATION CONTRACTS

Framing the Issue

It happens with surprising frequency. A business person wants to incorporate a new corporation to undertake some particular business venture. Before the incorporation process is complete—perhaps before it has even really begun—urgent action is required. The promoter needs to enter into some contract on behalf of the new business. Perhaps some goods that the soon-to-be formed corporation will eventually need can be purchased at an especially attractive "fire sale" price. Perhaps arrangements for some critical business service must be made well in advance of some rapidly approaching deadline; but the promoter's lawyers have not yet filed the articles of incorporation.

For these or any number of other reasons, a promoter may find herself in a fix. She does not want the corporation she is forming to lose out on a valuable opportunity; but that corporation does not yet exist, and so cannot enter into the necessary contracts itself. In such circumstances, the promoter may feel constrained to attempt to contract on behalf of the newly planned (but not-yet-formed) corporation. The promoter in such a case naturally hopes to avoid incurring any kind of personal liability. She might, therefore, try to signal her intention to act solely as a kind of agent for the unformed corporate entity. Perhaps she will recite somewhere in the contract that she is signing "on behalf of a corporation to be incorporated" or "in trust for a corporation to be incorporated" or language to similar effect.

As is so often the case in the practical world of business, where the signatories to such a contract each honour their respective commitments—as they usually do—no thought will ever be given to the esoteric legal question of how an artificial person that did not actually exist when the contract was signed could possibly be held legally bound by the terms of such an agreement. But in those relatively rare cases when things go awry and one party or the other defaults, this theoretical question takes on important legal significance.

This problem of "pre-incorporation contracts" has now been explicitly addressed in the CBCA and in a number of other Canadian corporate statutes. Those statutory

---

23   See Davies, supra footnote 3, at 93, note 22.

approaches are discussed later. But to understand the context in which these legislative provisions were enacted, it is important to consider how the common law originally dealt with the matter. It was the weakness and uncertainty in the common law to which Parliament and provincial legislatures intended to respond. However, those legislative responses led to some troubling judicial interpretations, and then to a second round of legislation.

The pre-incorporation contract problem represents a very useful illustration of the interplay between the common law and the statutory regulation of corporations. Consideration of the pre-incorporation contract problem also compels us to think very carefully about the legal meaning of the corporation as a separate legal entity.

For these reasons, the pre-incorporation contract issue is considered in greater detail than most other topics in this book.

The Common Law Position

The common law approach to pre-incorporation contracts may be conveniently analyzed by first distinguishing between two particular types of pre-incorporation contract cases:

- those involving contracts entered into when both contracting parties are fully aware that no corporation has yet been incorporated ("type 1" cases); and
- those involving contracts entered into when at least one (and usually both) of the parties mistakenly believes that a non-existent corporation is, in fact, in existence at the time the contract was entered into ("type 2" cases).[24]

This convenient distinction is offered for the purpose of organizing the following discussion. However, the courts have not consistently made any such distinction. Indeed, no distinction of this sort at all was drawn in the seminal pre-incorporation contract case, *Kelner v. Baxter*[25]—a decision that might now be characterized as a classic type 1 case.

At least one jurist, referring to *Kelner*, has warned:

> Some statements in textbooks and in judgments that abbreviate the effect of that decision can be at least misleading, unless they be read with the facts well in mind.[26]

Taking that sober caveat to heart, the facts in *Kelner v. Baxter* were these. The plaintiff, Kelner, had entered into a contract to sell £900 of wine to be used in a hotel business. The

---

24 Type 2 cases might be further subdivided into those cases in which the promoter (but not the third-party contractor) is aware the corporation does not yet exist, and those in which both the promoter and the third-party contractor mistakenly believe that the corporation exists. Such a distinction was drawn by Ziegel et al. in their influential casebook, *Cases and Materials on Partnership and Canadian Business Corporations*, 3rd ed., vol. 1 (Toronto: Carswell, 1994), at 270, and is suggested in some other sources as well. At least one recent Ontario case has attached significance to this distinction. (See *1080409 Ontario Limited v. Hunter* (2000), 50 OR (3d) 145, at para. 33 (SCJ).) But, the court in that case appeared to be attempting to circumvent problems that had been created by the Divisional Court's analysis in *Westcom v. MacIsaac*, a case that has subsequently been, at least for practical purposes, even if not formally, overruled by the Ontario Court of Appeal.

25 (1866-67), 2 LRCP 174.

26 *Black v. Smallwood* (1966), 117 CLR 52 (Aust. HC), per Windeyer J.

contract specified a particular date on which payment for the wine was to be made. The wine was duly delivered by the plaintiff, but no payment was made by the specified date. The plaintiff sued the individuals who had signed the contract on behalf of the hotel. But the wrinkle was this: the contract had been signed not simply by the individual defendants in their own personal capacities. These words of qualification were written after their signatures: "on behalf of the proposed Gravesend Royal Alexandra Hotel Company, Limited."[27] This company the parties did eventually intend to incorporate (and did subsequently incorporate), but the company did not exist on the day the contract for the purchase of the wine was entered into.

The defendants argued that because they had not purported to enter into the purchase contract in their personal capacities, they could not be held personally liable for a purported breach of that contract. The liability, they argued, was solely that of the corporation, a corporation that had in fact become insolvent by the time the action was commenced.

The court disagreed, and held that the individual defendants were obliged to pay for the wine out of their own pockets. They could not avoid this personal liability by hiding behind the corporation in the name of which they had purported to act when they signed the sales contract, because no such corporation existed at the time of signing.

The outcome of the case is clear enough—the individual defendants were held liable. What has been debated for almost a hundred years since the decision was rendered, however, is the precise legal basis for the court's ruling. Perhaps the most straightforward reading of the decision is this. The individual defendants were held liable because it was clear that all signing parties—the defendants as well as the plaintiff—had intended the contract to be legally enforceable. The seller, after all, had delivered the wine. No one thought he was making a gift of the bottles; he was expecting to be paid. Imposing personal liability on the individual defendants was the only way in which such a contract—undoubtedly intended to be enforceable—could in fact be enforced, because as a matter of law, a corporation that did not exist at the time a contract was entered into could never become liable under that contract. There was simply no theory of law that allowed for enforceability against the corporation in such a case. Agency law would not prevail: an agent cannot act for a non-existent principal. Nor would it even be possible for a corporation subsequently to ratify (or to adopt) a pre-incorporation contract previously entered into on its behalf. As a matter of law, a party can only ratify a contract into which it could have legally entered in the first place. Because a non-existent person cannot validly make a contract, the corporation could not have entered into the pre-incorporation contract on the date it was made, and therefore could not validly ratify it on some later date either.[28] So, there were only two alternatives: either this pre-incorporation contract

27   Len Sealy has noted a small discrepancy between two reported versions of *Kelner v. Baxter*. The summary of the facts in the report of the case at [1867] NS vol. 31, at 95 includes the word "proposed," whereas in a different reporter, (1866-67), 2 LRCP 174, the word "proposed" is omitted. However, in the judgments themselves, as reported, the language recited includes the word "proposed" in both. (See (1866-67), 2 LRCP 174, at 182 and the same language in NS vol. 36, at 97.) See L.S. Sealy, *Cases and Materials in Company Law*, 7th ed. (London: Butterworths, 2001), at 27.

28   As to whether trust law might have solved the problem, see Davies, supra footnote 3.

was a nullity, or it was enforceable against the individual defendants who had signed it. Because the parties to the contract had clearly not intended that it be a nullity—they had meant for it to be enforceable against *someone*—they must have intended it to be personally binding on the individual signatories.

This interpretation of *Kelner v. Baxter* can certainly be supported by statements found in the various judgments rendered by the court in that case. In later decisions, however, courts appeared to suggest that the question of a promoter's personal liability turns on formalistic considerations—that is, on matters relating to the form of the signature that had been affixed to the contract. Mention of these formal elements can be found in the *Kelner v. Baxter* judgments as well, but it was really from later cases that the view gradually emerged that a promoter's liability might be determined in whole or in part by the form of signature adopted by the promoter.[29] Gower not only seemed to regard such formalistic considerations as fundamental to the common law of pre-incorporation contracts,[30] but even went so far as to argue that modern suggestions to the contrary represent a kind of revisionist legal history. This new view, he said, is the result of changes in the courts' "perception of the common law in this area,"[31] triggered by the addition of s. 36C to the English *Companies Act*, which is discussed further below.

Two cases in particular are often cited in support of the notion that the form of signature adopted by the promoter is determinative: the English Court of Appeal's judgment in *Newborne v. Sensolid (Great Britain) Ltd.*,[32] and the decision of the High Court of Australia in *Black v. Smallwood*.[33]

Newborne v. Sensolid was a type 2 pre-incorporation contract case—that is, one in which the parties to the relevant contract were under the mistaken belief that the corporation existed at the time the contract was signed. In *Newborne*, however, when the true facts were revealed (that is, when it was discovered that the contracting corporation did not exist), the promoter did not seek to escape personal liability under the pre-incorporation contract. Instead, he sought to retain the benefit of the contract in his personal capacity.

---

29   Lord Denning also attributed the notion that the form of signature was critical to interpretations of three later pre-incorporation contract cases—*Hollman v. Pullin*, [1884] Cab. & Ell. 254; *Newborne v. Sensolid (Great Britain) Ltd.*, [1954] 1 QB 45 (CA); and *Black v. Smallwood*, supra footnote 26: "Those three cases seem to suggest that there is a distinction to be drawn according to the way in which an agent signs a contract." *Phonogram Ltd. v. Lane*, [1982] 1 QB 938, at 943.

30   "[P]rior to the European Communities Act 1972 the legal position of the promoter and the other party seemed to depend on the terminology employed. If the contract was entered into by the promoter and signed by him 'for and on behalf of XY Co. Ltd' then, according to the early case of *Kelner v. Baxter*, the promoter would be personally liable. But if, as is much more likely, the promoter signed the proposed name of the company, adding his own to authenticate it ... then, according to *Newborne v. Sensolid (Great Britain) Ltd.*, there was no contract at all." Paul L. Davies, *Gower's Principles of Modern Company Law*, 6th ed. (London: Sweet & Maxwell, 1997), at 141 (footnotes omitted).

31   Ibid., at 142. Gower cites, specifically, the judgment of Oliver LJ in *Phonogram Ltd. v. Lane*, supra footnote 29.

32   *Newborne*, supra footnote 29.

33   Supra footnote 26.

The plaintiff (the promoter) had signed a contract for the sale to the defendant of a quantity of tinned ham. The plaintiff purported to sign that sale contract not in his individual capacity, but as agent (or perhaps more accurately, as signing officer) for a corporation. Because the form of signature used by the promoter in *Newborne* is thought to be of special importance, it is reproduced:

> "Yours faithfully, Leopold Newborne (London) Ld." [The promoter's signature then appeared beneath the corporate name.]

When the defendant refused to accept delivery of the ham, the seller "corporation" sued. But it was discovered that the corporation in whose name the promoter, Newborne, had signed the contract did not, in fact, exist. Thus facing the possibility of being non-suited, Newborne—relying on *Kelner v. Baxter*—argued that as a promoter he was not only personally bound by the burdens of this pre-incorporation contract (as in *Kelner*) but was surely entitled to claim its benefits as well.

The Court of Appeal disagreed. In their reasons, the judges drew a careful distinction between the facts in *Newborne* and the situation that had obtained in *Kelner v. Baxter*. The crucial distinction, according to the court, was that in *Newborne* it was the supposed company—and only the company—that had purported to contract. Because this company did not, in fact, exist, the contract was a nullity. These facts differed materially from the situation in *Kelner*, they argued. In that earlier case it was not the (non-existent) company itself that had purported to contract; rather it had been the individual promoters who had signed, albeit purporting to act, as the letter of agreement in *Kelner* made clear, *on behalf of* the (non-existent) company.

This was a narrow distinction to be sure: *Newborne* was said to be an example of a non-existent corporation's own purported action; *Kelner*, an example of the actions of individuals taken *on behalf of* a non-existent corporation. But it was this distinction that was thereafter seized on by some lawyers and judges to argue that the form of the promoter's signature as it appeared on the contract made all the difference. Was the contract executed by the as-yet-unformed corporation itself—with the promoter's signa-ture simply purporting to evidence the corporate signature (as in *Newborne*)? Or was there, instead, some verbal formula used (as in *Kelner*) to signal that the signature was actually the promoter's own—perhaps qualified by some language claiming (with no legal effect, as it turned out) that the promoter was purporting to act as "agent" or perhaps "trustee" for a corporate principal or beneficiary?[34] In the former case, the promoter would be neither subject to the burdens nor entitled to the benefits of the contract. In the latter case, the contract would be the promoter's, and only the promoter's, own. He could sue to enforce it, or be sued under it.

The significance of the form of promoter's signature is often said to explain the Australian case of *Black v. Smallwood*[35] as well. As will be seen below, however, in some respects *Black v. Smallwood* represents a bridge between the formalistic analysis of some older English cases, and the intentions-based test that has emerged in at least some Canadian courts.

---

34 Gower, for example, shared this interpretation. See supra footnote 30.

35 Supra footnote 26.

The disputed contract in *Black v. Smallwood* was a land sale agreement. The purported purchaser under that agreement was Western Suburbs Holdings Pty. Ltd. All the parties to the contract believed that this corporation existed. They were wrong. The corporation had never been formed.

The court applied *Newborne v. Sensolid* and held that the defendants (who had signed as directors of the non-existent corporation) could not be held personally liable under the contract. Was this conclusion based on the form of the signature? Perhaps. Support for the formalistic view of the law can certainly be found in the judgment of Barwick CJ, and Kitto, Taylor, and Owen JJ.[36] However there are also suggestions in that same judgment and in the concurring judgment of Windeyer J, of a different rationale, one that extends beyond technical wording differences. Windeyer J, in fact, seems to disparage the quibbling over such formal considerations as "the progeny by miscegenation of early technical rules relating to the form of the execution of deeds."[37] He suggests that subjective intention, not merely intention inferred from the form of signature used, might well be the key to understanding the common law authorities. Windeyer states, for example:

[In *Kelner v. Baxter*] when the goods were bought it was well known to all concerned that the company had not yet been formed. ... Here, instead of both parties knowing that the company was not in existence, they both, appellants and respondents, thought that it was.[38]

A similar suggestion in the judgment of the majority was the subject of supportive comment by a judge of the Ontario Court of Appeal in a case discussed below.

That many early cases on pre-incorporation contract law seemed to emphasize formal distinctions has been the subject of much criticism.[39] In Canada, for example, this emphasis was the subject of a short, disparaging comment by the Lawrence committee in 1967:

Whether or not the contracting party has a remedy against the promoter (*to whom he may or may not have intended to look for liability*) depends, in the present state of the law, in large part upon caprice: the manner of execution of the particular contract.[40]

To similar effect were the observations of the Dickerson committee:

In practice, this means that a great deal may turn upon the form of a contract, and minor differences in wording may be decisive of the rights of the parties.[41]

---

36 See, e.g., ibid., at 749: "The distinction between a case where the execution of a document by a company is effected by the subscription of the company's name followed by the signature of a director or directors as such and the case where the document is executed by an agent on behalf of a company is well illustrated by ... *Richardson v. Landecker*. ... It is, in our view, clear from the written instrument that the respondents in this case did not enter into any contract."

37 Ibid., at 750.

38 Ibid., at 751.

39 Lord Denning recounts some of those criticisms in *Phonogram Ltd. v. Lane*, supra footnote 29, at 944.

40 *Interim Report of the Select Committee on Company Law*, at para. 1.5.5, p. 11 (emphasis added).

41 Robert W.V. Dickerson et al., *Proposals for a New Business Corporations Law for Canada*, vol. I, Commentary (Ottawa: Information Canada, 1971), at para. 69 (Dickerson committee).

Such rigid formalism is often found distasteful by many modern (or post-modern) lawyers, judges, and academic commentators. So, it is little wonder that in recent discussions of pre-incorporation contracts, the jurisprudence is more often explained in terms of the subjective intention of the contracting parties, for which formal features of the contract might well be one, among many, relevant considerations, but not necessarily the determinative factor.

Does this focus on intention represent the kind of jurisprudential revisionist history suggested by Gower?[42] Or does it, rather, as Oliver LJ in *Phonogram Ltd. v. Lane* suggests,[43] represent a more nuanced reading of the older authorities? It may at least be said that support for both positions may be found by selective reading of the same authorities. For example, although the form of the promoter's signature was of unquestionable significance in *Black v. Smallwood*,[44] one finds that a consideration of subjective contractual intention seems also significant in that case.

Borins JA alluded to this dual aspect of *Black v. Smallwood* in a recent Ontario Court of Appeal decision, *Sherwood Design Services Ltd. v. 872935 Ontario Ltd.*[45] There Borins JA reviewed the common law of pre-incorporation contracts, highlighting a portion of the majority judgment in *Black v. Smallwood*:

> The majority opinion of the High Court strongly suggests that it is not the form of the contract but the intention of the parties that is decisive. In the majority judgment ... the judgment of Fullager J in *Summergreene v. Parker* ... was quoted with approval. Fullager J said ... "the fundamental question in every case must be what the parties intended or must fairly be understood to have intended."
>
> Thus, in *Kelner v. Baxter* the parties intended, or were deemed to have intended, that the promoters would be personally liable. In *Newborne v. Sensolid* and *Black v. Smallwood* it was found to be the intention of the parties that the promoters would not be personally liable. The effect of these decisions was to challenge the long-held belief that *Kelner v. Baxter* laid down the categorical rule that a promoter is always personally liable on a pre-incorporation contract.[46]

In summary, the common law of pre-incorporation contracts appeared to run like this. In those cases where a promoter purported to contract as agent or trustee for a corporation to be formed, the promoter would be personally liable under the contract, because

---

42   See the text accompanying notes 30 and 31, supra.

43   *Phonogram*, supra footnote 29, at 945: "Speaking for myself, I am not convinced that the common law position ... depends upon the narrow distinction between a signature 'for and on behalf of' and a signature in the name of a company or an association. The question I think in each case is what is the real intent as revealed by the contract?"

44   Supra footnote 26.

45   *Sherwood Design Services Ltd. v. 872935 Ontario Ltd.* (1998), 39 OR (3d) 576 (CA). Application for leave to appeal to SCC discontinued, [1998] SCCA no. 318. Although Borins JA was writing in dissent, the majority took no issue with his summary of the common law of pre-incorporation contracts, and, indeed, this summary was specifically endorsed in a subsequent Court of Appeal decision, *Szecket v. Huang* (1998), 42 OR (3d) 400 (CA).

46   Ibid.

there was no basis on which the corporation, when formed, could validly adopt or ratify that contract (though it could, of course, by way of novation enter into a new contract on identical terms).[47] Perhaps the justification for imposing this liability was that it was consistent with the parties' intentions as conclusively evidenced by the form of signature used by the promoter (for example, promoter, "on behalf of" or "in trust for" a company to be incorporated). Perhaps, instead, liability flowed from the court's determination of the intention of the parties based on all surrounding circumstances. So, for example, where both parties knew no corporation yet existed, but clearly intended, as in *Kelner*, that the contract must be enforceable, the parties must be presumed to have intended the promoter to be personally liable, absent some other compelling evidence to the contrary. But, where the signatories appeared to intend that the non-existent corporation itself should be a party, one or both of them labouring under the mistaken impression that the corporation did exist, as in *Black v. Smallwood*, then the result was different. The parties in such a case could not be taken to have intended the promoter to be personally liable. The purported contract itself would be a nullity. In either event, the common law position was, at best, uncertain and, at worst, capricious.

Kelner v. Baxter Postscript

Before turning to consider the response of the legislators to this unsatisfactory state of affairs, it may be illuminating to mention one often-overlooked feature of the foundational

---

47   See, e.g., *Heinhuis v. Blacksheep Charters Ltd.* (1988), 19 BCLR (2d) 239 (CA), where McLachlin JA (as she then was), states, citing various authorities, "A pre-incorporation contract may be enforced where the company and the other party to the contract make a new contract after incorporation on the same terms as the pre-incorporation contract." The basis for the decision in *Heinhuis* was that the conduct of the corporation (and the third party) after incorporation was sufficient to establish a contract by conduct. In particular, the court focused on the fact that the corporation, having accepted the property that was the subject matter of the contract, must also be taken to have accepted the obligations that went with that. Alternatively (or perhaps additionally), the court suggested that the pre-incorporation contract could be characterized as a continuing offer to convey the property, which was subsequently accepted by the corporation. One troubling aspect of *Heinhuis*, in the context of the common law of pre-incorporation contracts, is that it appears to use the fact that acceptance of the property evidenced contractual intention that bound *the corporation*. But recall that in *Kelner v. Baxter* itself, the subject matter of the contract had also been accepted (and consumed) in the business of the new corporation. This fact was also seen as strong evidence of an intention to contract, but, in view of the fact that no contract with the corporation could have been validly made, this intention became the basis for imposing personal liability on the promoter. Of course, in *Heinhuis*, this "solution" would have been unsatisfactory, because the "promoter" was the plaintiff himself—who had conveyed the shares of the corporation in question to the individual defendants as part of the transaction in which the pre-incorporation contract arose. (Heinhuis, in other words, was in the unusual position of being both the promoter and the "third party" contractor on the facts of that case.) Prof. Ziegel et al. have generously suggested that the decision in *Heinhuis* "indicates a contemporary Canadian court's willingness to relax the strict common law requirements." See Ziegel et al., *supra* footnote 24, at 274. If, however, the conduct referred to in *Heinhuis* is sufficient to establish that a new contract between the corporation and the third party has been entered into, it is difficult to see on what basis in *Kelner v. Baxter* the individual defendants, and not the insolvent corporation, were held personally liable, other than, perhaps, the possibility that the wine in *Kelner v. Baxter* had been entirely consumed before the incorporation of the company had been completed, a fact that is difficult to determine with certainty from the reported decision.

pre-incorporation contract case, *Kelner v. Baxter*. The rationale conventionally thought to underlie *Kelner*, and the common law of pre-incorporation contracts more generally, is the need to ensure the protection of innocent third parties who might otherwise be prejudiced in their dealings with careless or unscrupulous corporate promoters. How, after all, could the wine seller in *Kelner v. Baxter* have protected himself from negligence or even chicanery on the part of the supposed promoters of the new hotel corporation? How could he know whether they had, or would, do everything in their power to bring about the incorporation of the company on behalf of which they claimed to be acting? Because he could not reasonably protect himself, it might be thought, the law must intervene to protect him.

There is, however, an intriguing feature of *Kelner v. Baxter* that is rarely highlighted in modern corporate law texts and casebooks. The plaintiff (Kelner) was not, in fact, merely a third party dealing at arm's length with the defendants while those defendants were in the process of forming a new corporation. Rather, the plaintiff was himself one of the promoters of the proposed corporation on whose behalf the defendants purported to contract. In fact, it appears that the plaintiff's role in the new hotel venture was far from peripheral; he was to be a director and the manager of the new corporation. It was the plaintiff (not the defendants) who had been operating the hotel business that was to be incorporated. What's more, it was the plaintiff whose letter had initially indicated that the sale was being made to the defendants on behalf of a proposed corporation. The defendants had merely, as Byles J indicated, "adopted" the words the plaintiff himself had used when they accepted his offer to sell wine. The plaintiff, in other words, was no stranger to the nascent corporation; he was—together with the defendants—one of its key promoters. It seems not an unreasonable inference from the background facts of the case that the only reason the defendants signed the contract at issue in *Kelner* was that the plaintiff, the seller, could hardly execute a sale agreement signing *both* as vendor and as purchaser.

When the proposed hotel corporation was duly formed (as it soon after was), it did dutifully purport to adopt the wine sale contract (and later still to "ratify" it); but when the new corporation failed shortly thereafter, it was unable to satisfy the payment obligations called for in the contract. Accordingly, the plaintiff's three hotel "partners" (that is, the defendants)—by denying any personal liability—were in effect attempting to impose on the plaintiff a disproportionate share of the financial burden arising from the collapse of their joint enterprise (namely, the full value of the wine he had supplied to the newly incorporated business).

This unique aspect of *Kelner v. Baxter* has for the most part been ignored in subsequent decisions and statutory reform initiatives. The pre-incorporation problem is typically conceived in terms of a third-party stranger contracting with a (perhaps shifty) promoter. Thus, a typical rationale suggested for imposing liability on promoters is that "[t]he promoter is almost always in the best position to determine if and when a corporation will come into existence."[48] It is intriguing to note that considerations of this sort were actually quite irrelevant to the outcome of the foundational common law case on the issue.

---

48   See Poonam Puri, "The Promise of Certainty in the Law of Pre-Incorporation Contracts" (2001), 80 *Canadian Bar Review* 1051, at 1061.

Whether the unusual facts in *Kelner v. Baxter* were more determinative to the outcome of the case than has been generally acknowledged must remain a matter of speculation. Admittedly, these facts were not recited in any of the judgments and so, in the purest common law tradition, cannot be taken to form part of the case's *ratio decidendi*. However, it is not unreasonable to suggest that it was the threatened inequity in the specific case posed by this unique set of facts that launched a legal problem that continues to defy the efforts of courts and, as will be seen in the next section, of legislators seeking to restore rationality and certainty to this area of the law.

Statutory Reform

The uncertainty of the common law relating to pre-incorporation contracts was recognized by statutory reformers, and has led to specific legislative changes in many Canadian jurisdictions. In Ontario, the Lawrence committee in 1967 proposed that Ontario's corporate legislation be amended to address the uncertainties of pre-incorporation contracts by expressly permitting a corporation, following its incorporation, to adopt or ratify a contract made on its behalf by a promoter. Failing such ratification or adoption, the promoter would remain liable. However, if the contract were ratified or adopted, the promoter would normally be relieved of personal liability.

The committee recognized that special circumstances may arise in which it might be appropriate for third parties to seek redress against the promoters even in cases where the corporation subsequently adopts the pre-incorporation contract. They therefore proposed a statutory provision to permit a third party to apply to the court for an order making the corporation and the promoter jointly and severally liable.[49] These recommendations were embodied in the new Ontario *Business Corporations Act* enacted in 1970,[50] and had a significant influence on the development of later federal proposals on the subject as well.

The Dickerson committee reached conclusions similar to those of the Lawrence committee, and proposed similar statutory language aimed at changing the common law rules in three specific ways.

First, all promoters would, *prima facie*, be subject to the burdens and entitled to the benefits of pre-incorporation contracts. The type 1/type 2 distinction suggested above—whether conclusively evidenced by formal differences in signatures or presumed differences in parties' subjective intentions—would be irrelevant. All pre-incorporation contracts would be treated in the same way.

Second, corporations would be entitled, within a reasonable time after incorporation, to effectively adopt pre-incorporation contracts. The theoretical bar to contractual ratification by a corporation that could not have executed the original contract would thus be swept away. Moreover, on adoption, the corporation, and the corporation alone, would become the contracting party. The promoter would be relieved of any exposure (and from entitlement to any benefits) under the contract.

---

49 Supra footnote 40, at para. 1.5.8, p. 12.

50 *Business Corporations Act* (Ont.), RSO 1970, c. 53, s. 20. Ontario subsequently adopted a pre-incorporation provision essentially based on the CBCA provision.

Third, it would be possible for the promoter and the third party to agree at the time the contract was made that the promoter would, under no circumstances, be liable under the contract. But an agreement to this effect would have to be specifically provided for. In the absence of any such agreement, the general rule of promoter liability would apply. In special cases, a court could apportion contractual liability between the promoter and the corporation appropriately.

The Dickerson committee's recommendations were embodied in s. 14 of the CBCA. The intent of s. 14 seemed clear. It was meant to spell an end to the uncertain and unsatisfactory common law pre-incorporation contract rules. The basic regime originally created by s. 14 (it has recently been amended, as discussed below) may be briefly summarized as follows:

- Subsection (1) provided that a promoter is personally liable for (and entitled to the benefits under) a pre-incorporation contract entered into on behalf of a corporation before it is incorporated, unless relieved of that liability pursuant to one of the other subsections of s. 14.
- Subsection (2) provided that a corporation, "within a reasonable time after it comes into existence," may adopt a written pre-incorporation contract. On adoption, the corporation becomes liable under the contract and entitled to its benefits, and the promoter is relieved of any such liability or entitlements, subject to subsection (3).
- Subsection (3) provided that a party to a pre-incorporation contract may apply to a court to apportion liabilities and obligations under the contract as between the promoter and the adopting corporation.
- Subsection (4) provided that "if expressly so provided in the written contract," a promoter who signs a contract on behalf of an as-yet-unformed corporation will not in any event be bound by the contract (that is, the promoter is relieved of liability, even if the contract is never subsequently adopted by a corporation as contemplated in subsection (2)).

Before considering how these new provisions fared in the courts, it is worth mentioning a sticky constitutional point identified by Professor Maloney.[51] Section 14 could surely be characterized as fundamentally a provision regulating contracts—a matter of property and civil rights and so within the legislative authority of the provinces and not the federal government. Nor would it appear to be saved—as other parts of the CBCA no doubt are—on the basis that this legislation is somehow vital to a corporation's existence,[52] because the provision is intended to apply even when no corporation is formed. Provincial pre-incorporation contract provisions, such as s. 21 of Ontario's *Business Corporations Act*, could perhaps effectively be amended so as to apply not only to corporations incorporated under the provincial statute itself, but to contracts purported to be made in the province on behalf of all bodies corporate wherever incorporated, or

---

51   M.A. Maloney, "Pre-incorporation Transactions: A Statutory Solution?" (1985), 10 *Canadian Business Law Journal* 409.

52   Dickerson committee, supra footnote 41, at para. 177.

intended to be incorporated.[53] But that is not currently the way in which the provincial pre-incorporation contract provisions are drafted. And, even if they were so amended, the problem of the non-incorporation would still persist.

Several Canadian jurisdictions—including Ontario—subsequently emulated the CBCA's approach to pre-incorporation contracts, sometimes with minor additions or modifications.[54] Ontario's new pre-incorporation contract regime, for example, applied to both oral and written contracts. The CBCA provision extended only to written contracts, a limitation that reflected a concern expressed by the Dickerson committee about the potential uncertainty surrounding the precise terms of an oral contract, which would make purported adoption or ratification of such a contract problematic and potentially unfair to the adopting corporation.[55] It scarcely deserves mention that this consideration is primarily important in those cases where the promoter was not the sole shareholder of the adopting corporation.[56]

A statutory provision dealing with pre-incorporation contracts was also introduced into the UK *Companies Act*, pursuant to an EC directive. The UK provision, now found in s. 36C of the *Companies Act, 1985*, is somewhat less detailed than the CBCA language. It reads as follows:

> (1) A contract which purports to be made by or on behalf of a company at a time when the company has not been formed has effect, subject to any agreement to the contrary, as one made with the person purporting to act for the company or as agent for it, and he is personally liable on the contract accordingly.

The new statutory provisions did not, however, immediately end the confusion in the courts on either side of the Atlantic. Many uncertainties still remained and became the

---

53 Extending the application of provincial corporate legislation to certain activities of bodies corporate from other jurisdictions would not be unprecedented. For example, see *Business Corporations Act* (Ont.), part VI.

54 See, e.g., *Business Corporations Act* (NB), s. 12; *The Business Corporations Act* (Sask.), s. 14; *Corporations Act* (NL), s. 26; *The Corporations Act* (Man.), s. 14; and *Business Corporations Act* (Ont.), s. 21. (The principal difference between Ontario's original pre-incorporation contract provision enacted in 1970 and s. 14 of the CBCA is that the original Ontario provision did not include a provision permitting the promoter to explicitly disclaim liability in the pre-incorporation contract.) Alberta's provision has been recently amended and is discussed in more detail below. (See also footnote 85, infra.)

55 Dickerson committee, supra footnote 41, at para. 71, p. 23. See, e.g., J.H. Gross, "Pre-incorporation Contracts" (1971), 87 *Law Quarterly Review* 367, at 368-69: "It is one thing to subject shareholders and creditors to the normal risks of the business, and quite another to increase these by saddling the corporation with burdens imposed upon it in advance by overly optimistic promoters. The management of the corporation elected by the shareholders should be free to decide for itself what obligations are to be assumed or incurred," cited with approval by Borins JA in *Sherwood Design Services Ltd.*, supra footnote 45. This is, of course, precisely the concern that underlies the promoters' cases.

56 However, it must be emphasized that, in all cases, the corporation itself must choose to adopt the contract. As Steele J noted in *Okinczyc v. Tessier* (1979), 8 RPR 249 (Ont. HC), at para. 17: "Even where a person is the sole owner of a company, for him to shift his personal liability to the company it must be shown that the company authorized such action. I realize that the company could only act by the force of its owner but it must so act. Otherwise the sole owner of a company could act in his own name and later elect to say whether or not he did it on behalf of the company. This would be totally unacceptable."

subject of debate and litigation. Among the more difficult questions raised by the statutory language were the following:

- Do the statutory pre-incorporation contract rules apply not only to pre-incorporation contracts (that is, contracts that are made shortly before a corporation is formed), but also to what might be called "non-incorporation contracts" (that is, cases where no corporation is subsequently formed by the promoter)?[57]
- If the statute does apply to "non-incorporation contracts," on what reasonable basis can it be argued that a contract ought to be governed by any particular jurisdiction's corporate law? For example, if no corporation is incorporated, is it reasonable to say that the CBCA's rules ought to apply? Does it make any sense, in other words, to contend that it was necessarily a CBCA corporation that was *not* incorporated?
- Because s. 14(1) of the CBCA (*as originally drafted*) referred to "contracts" entered into before a corporation comes into existence, should the provisions apply in cases where, applying common law rules, no "contract" is found to exist? (This ambiguity was eliminated under the CBCA in 2001 by adding to s. 14(1) language referring to cases where a promoter "purports to enter" into an agreement.)
- Section 14(2) of the CBCA operates to relieve a promoter of liability provided the corporation adopts the contract "within a reasonable period of time after it comes into existence." It does not, however, state that adoption must occur within a reasonable period of time after the contract is signed.
- Because the promoter's liability under a pre-incorporation contract ends if, but only if, the contract is subsequently adopted by the corporation, what precisely must a corporation do to indicate such "adoption"?
- Where the contract is not subsequently adopted by a corporation, the promoter may still be exempt from liability, so long as such exemption is "expressly so provided" in the pre-incorporation contract. What constitutes such an express exemption? Is it sufficient to infer from the parties' conduct that the promoter is never to be personally bound? Or is something more formal or more explicit required?

Each of these matters is discussed further below. However, quite apart from these specific technical concerns, there also appears to be an overriding fundamental (but generally ignored) problem inherent in the CBCA approach to pre-incorporation contracts. Canadian corporate law confers limited liability on a corporation's shareholders, but does not impose any minimum level of capitalization on corporations themselves. Therefore, it is not clear on what policy basis individual promoters ought to be held liable (absent fraud) to third parties when those third parties have willingly entered into pre-incorporation contracts with the promoter, knowing that the promoter purports to contract on behalf of a coming corporation. Such third parties necessarily anticipate that some not-yet-created corporation will, ultimately, be their counterparty. They have no reason to believe that the corporation will have substantial assets. Nothing in the CBCA or the common law (in the

---

57   This question was dealt with squarely in the United Kingdom in the first case interpreting s. 36C of the UK *Companies Act*. Solicitors for the defendant had argued that the EC Directive on which that section of the Act was based did not apply in cases where no company was in the process of being formed. Lord Denning expressly rejected this limitation. See *Phonogram Ltd. v. Lane*, supra footnote 29, at 943 (CA).

absence of fraud) prevents a promoter who has signed a pre-incorporation contract on behalf of a corporation to be incorporated from immediately establishing a shell corporation with no assets whatsoever, then causing that corporation to adopt the pre-incorporation contract. All of the statute's formal requirements would be satisfied, yet the third-party contractor would be left with no meaningful remedy in the event of breach by this new, judgment-proof corporation.

This possibility was not overlooked by the Dickerson committee. In fact, it is precisely the risk that a promoter might incorporate a worthless shell corporation to adopt a pre-incorporation contract that the committee identified as the principle mischief at which s. 14(3) was aimed:

[Section 14(3)] accordingly permits a third party to apply to court for an order that, in effect, renders the purported adoption either wholly or partially ineffectual, and authorizes the court to impose liability upon the promoter notwithstanding the adoption of the contract by the corporation.[58]

The policy underpinning this provision is, however, significantly undermined by the inclusion of s. 14(4). That subsection permits a promoter, in all events, to disclaim personal liability. This provision was justified, in the Dickerson committee's view, because, "an express written disclaimer should make the third party fully aware of the kind of arrangement he is getting himself into."[59] But, when a promoter signs a pre-incorporation contract, disclosing that he or she is acting on behalf of a corporate body that does not yet exist, is not the other party to that contract just as well aware of the "kind of arrangement he [or she] is getting ... into"? Why should such a third-party contractor ever expect to look to the assets of the promoter to satisfy any liabilities under such a contract? Individual officers and directors signing on behalf of corporations do not implicitly guarantee that the corporation on whose behalf they act has sufficient resources to honour any contract entered into by the corporation. Why should a party dealing with a promoter prior to incorporation be placed in any stronger position, simply because the promoter may have neglected to undertake the ritualistic step of incorporating a worthless shell company to adopt the contract?

In short, in those cases where it is the creditworthiness of the individual promoter that is considered essential to a third-party contractor, surely it is not unreasonable for the law to require that the third party take steps to explicitly contract with the individual in his or her personal capacity only. Imposing personal liability on a promoter of substantial means, in cases where that promoter has expressly indicated an intention *not* to contract in his personal capacity, appears to represent nothing less than a windfall for the third-party contractor. When the law imposes such liability, it, in effect, creates an unbargained-for personal guarantee.[60] What, then, is the policy basis on which a promoter (expressly contracting on behalf of a yet-to-be-formed corporation) ought ever to be held personally

58 Dickerson committee, supra footnote 41, at para. 72.

59 Ibid., at para. 73.

60 An analysis to this effect appears in *Bowstead on Agency*, and was specifically referenced by the Alberta Institute of Law Research and Reform in its proposals for a new Alberta business corporations statute. See infra footnote 90, at 40.

liable for anything more than nominal damages whether or not a corporation has subsequently adopted that contract?

Each of these matters is discussed in greater detail below.

Application to Non-incorporation Contracts

Canadian courts have implicitly interpreted s. 14 of the CBCA (and its provincial counterparts) to apply to pre-incorporation contracts whether or not the promoter subsequently takes steps to incorporate a corporation. Meaningful legislative reform of the common law demands such an interpretation. The drafters of the CBCA intended to introduce certainty into the law by making it clear that a promoter would be liable under a pre-incorporation contract under s. 14(1) unless a corporation adopted the contract pursuant to s. 14(2), or the parties to the contract expressly agreed under s. 14(4) that the promoter was not to be liable. It would be anomalous if a promoter could avoid personal liability, in the absence of a negotiated liability exemption pursuant to s. 14(4), merely by choosing never to incorporate a corporation.

If the statute did not apply to cases of "non-incorporation," there would be other curious problems, as well. Arguably, the statute might never operate to impose personal liability on promoters. To understand why, recall that s. 14(2) relieves the promoter from liability when a corporation subsequently adopts a pre-incorporation contract. Suppose that a promoter were to sign a pre-incorporation contract, then subsequently incorporate a corporation. Suppose further that the corporation chose not to adopt the pre-incorporation contract. Would it not be open to the promoter to argue that s. 14(1) nevertheless had no application? True, a corporation had been formed, and that corporation had not adopted the contract. But that corporation, the promoter might insist, was not, in fact, *the* particular corporation that had been anticipated by the pre-incorporation contract. The particular corporation anticipated by the contract had not, in fact, been formed after all. And so, if s. 14 did not apply to "non-incorporations," it could not be used against the promoter here. While one might well assume that courts would have little time for such metaphysical legerdemain, it must nevertheless be pointed out that it is hard to see a principled reason to reject this analysis if one accepts that s. 14 has no application to situations where a corporation is never formed.

So the provision, if it is to function at all, must surely apply to "non-incorporation" situations. The "non-incorporation" issue was raised in *Phonogram Ltd. v. Lane*,[61] the first UK case to consider s. 36C of the UK *Companies Act*. The English Court of Appeal explicitly rejected the notion that the statute was intended to apply only in those cases where a corporation was, indeed, subsequently formed. Significantly, the court reached this conclusion notwithstanding that there were strong suggestions, at least in the French-language version of the European directive upon which the English statutory provision was based, that the directive was indeed intended to govern only in those cases where companies were in the process of formation.

There is now little doubt that the Canadian provisions apply equally in the case of non-incorporation contracts, notwithstanding something of a false start on this issue intro-

---

61   Supra footnote 57.

duced by the Ontario Divisional Court in *Westcom Radio Group Ltd. v. MacIsaac et al.*,[62] in which the court commented:

> The learned trial judge questioned whether the OBCA had any application to the facts of this case because the purported company was never incorporated. The three Canadian cases noted above each involved a situation where the company was later incorporated. In *Phonogram*, the English Court of Appeal applied the relevant statute to circumstances in which there was no later incorporation.[63]

Doubt on the issue was laid to rest more recently when the Ontario Court of Appeal applied s. 21(1) of the Ontario *Business Corporations Act* (OBCA) in a case where the promoter failed to incorporate a company after the agreement in dispute was signed.[64] (Section 21(1) of the OBCA is substantially similar to the pre-2001 wording of s. 14(1) of the CBCA.)

Thus, coherent legislative policy and the most recent Canadian jurisprudence both support the notion that the "pre-incorporation contract" provisions of modern Canadian corporate statutes do apply to "non-incorporation" promoter's contracts. But, as sensible as that conclusion may be, it nevertheless does give rise to a kind of corporate law existential paradox. For, if no corporation is formed, how, exactly, may one contend that the corporation that was *not* formed was a CBCA corporation? Or an OBCA corporation? Or a Nova Scotia *Companies Act* corporation? Or, for that matter, a Delaware, New York, or Bermudian corporation?

The question is not a trivial one, because the pre-incorporation contract law rules differ from jurisdiction to jurisdiction. Even before the 2001 CBCA amendments, the CBCA and OBCA provisions have always differed in one critical respect—the OBCA rules apply to oral contracts, whereas the CBCA rules do not. Let us suppose that a promoter enters into an oral pre-incorporation contract with a third party in Ontario. The promoter takes no subsequent steps to form a corporation. The contract is not performed. Should the court apply the pre-incorporation provisions of the OBCA or the CBCA? Or, indeed, in appropriate cases, those of some other jurisdiction entirely?

Consider a somewhat more specific example. A promoter mistakenly believes that a corporation, "ABC Corp.," has already been formed. He had given clear instructions to his solicitors to incorporate ABC Corp. Alas, the incorporation was not completed. The unsuspecting promoter purports to enter into an oral contract with a third party. The promoter acts, not on his own personal behalf, but—as he wrongly supposes—as a duly appointed officer of ABC Corp.

The contract is not honoured and litigation begins. As the parties prepare for their courtroom battle they discover that ABC Corp. was never incorporated. Is the promoter liable? If the OBCA applies, the promoter will indeed be liable. If the CBCA applies, it appears that he will not be. The CBCA does not apply to oral contracts. The matter, therefore, would be decided in accordance with the common law. At common law, this

---

62   (1989), 70 OR (2d) 591 (Div. Ct.).

63   Ibid., at 597.

64   See *Szecket v. Huang*, supra footnote 45.

appears to be a *Black v. Smallwood* (type 2) case, in which the purported contract would be found to be a nullity.

On facts such as these, on what principled basis could a court sensibly declare that it was the CBCA, and not the OBCA, under which the corporation was *not* formed? No corporation, after all, was formed under either statute.[65] Should the plaintiff be entitled to choose the legislation most favourable to him or her? Or perhaps it is the promoter who should enjoy this privilege. No jurisdictional nexus test appears to solve the problem. The parties are no more closely connected to Ontario than to Canada.

This peculiar issue does not appear to have been definitively resolved in any of the decided "non-incorporation" cases. Perhaps counsel in these cases did not think to raise the issue; or perhaps the parties wisely decided to avoid this knotty issue by stipulating the applicable corporate law regime.

The paradox of the "non-incorporation's" true jurisdiction has not been overlooked by academic commentators, including, most recently, Professor Puri.[66] As she notes, however, although two possible solutions to this problem have been raised in earlier academic articles,[67] neither seems to deal with the problem sufficiently.[68]

The reason that the corporate jurisdiction problem is so difficult to solve in this context may stem from the fact that legislative attempts to regulate pre-incorporation

---

65   It may be thought that this conundrum could be addressed by avoiding the corporate law provisions altogether and seeking to impose liability on the promoter on the basis of breach of implied warranty of authority. Gower, in fact, raises this possibility. See Davies, supra footnote 30, at 141, note 66. However, this apparent solution does not seem to work either, because a claim for breach of warranty of authority entitles a plaintiff only to the remedy he or she would have had in the event that the agent did, indeed, have actual authority to bind the principal. But such a determination surely requires some assessment of the solvency of the principal, and in Canada, where corporations have no minimum capital requirements, the corporate principal could have well been a shell corporation with no assets at all.

66   Puri, supra footnote 48, at 1062-63.

67   Professor Maloney suggested that one ought to apply the law of the jurisdiction in which the promoter had intended to incorporate his or her corporation. See M.A. Maloney, supra footnote 51, at 433. Professor Ziegel favoured applying the law of the jurisdiction to which the transaction appeared to have the greatest nexus. See J.S. Ziegel, "Promoter's Liability and Preincorporation Contracts: *Westcom Group Ltd. v. MacIsaac*" (1990), 16 *Canadian Business Law Journal* 341, at 346-47. In a recent Ontario decision, the court appeared to accept the logic of an intentions test; however, the litigants were not disputing the application of Ontario law in any event, and although she specifically referred to the fact that the defendant had "intended to incorporate ... in Ontario," the judge in that case went on to state that it was this intention "and all other facts" that caused her "to conclude that Ontario is the governing law." See *1080409 Ontario Ltd. v. Hunter*, supra footnote 24, at para. 31.

68   Professor Puri argues that Maloney's approach is problematic because it requires the court to determine subjective intentions, a determination that "may be an inefficient use of judicial resources" (supra footnote 48, at 1063). Moreover, it will often be the case that the promoter had not actually directed his or her mind to the issue at the time of signing the contract in any event. (Ibid.) Anecdotally, this latter observation seems especially apt, because the choice of incorporating jurisdiction is rarely a decision that is made by business people except after obtaining the advice of legal counsel. Professor Ziegel's solution she finds problematic given the fact that it is common for corporations to be formed in jurisdictions that have no connection to proposed business transactions, and, indeed, in the United States, this fact has long been thought to underpin much of the "competitive federalism" found in the development of US state corporate statutes. (Ibid., at 1063 including note 62 and the authorities referred to therein.)

contracts are not properly characterized as corporate law at all. They are, instead, contract legislation, but contract legislation awkwardly grafted onto corporate statutes. And trying to address the problem of "non-incorporation" in corporate legislation is as unsatisfactory as trying to determine if one's microphone is working by asking everyone in the audience who *cannot* hear to raise his or her hand.

What Is a Pre-incorporation "Contract"?

Problems have occasionally arisen surrounding the murky legal status of a pre-incorporation contract as envisioned by CBCA s. 14 and similar provisions. The fundamental challenge of the courts is to try to place the system of statutorily mandated rights and obligations within the traditional rubric of contract law. It is an awkward fit. For example, as Professor Ziegel has pointed out, where a promoter effectively disclaims liability pursuant to CBCA s. 14(4) (or its provincial equivalents), what may be said to constitute the consideration that has been given for the third-party contractor's promise?[69] In such circumstances, the third party appears to have simply granted the promoter a fully transferable option.[70] But the promoter has paid nothing for this option. Worse still, as Professor Ziegel has pointed out, the situation is rather more onerous for the third party than would normally be the case where a traditional option had been granted because the third party may, in fact, have to perform some of its contractual obligations before the pre-incorporation contract "option" is exercised.[71]

Carthy JA, in *1394918 Ontario Limited v. 1310210 Ontario Inc.*,[72] recognized the potential inconsistency between traditional contract law principles and the obligations provided for under the OBCA's pre-incorporation contract rules. He asserted, however, that

> [t]he statutory scheme for pre-incorporation contracts throws off the confusion of the common law and shouldn't be thwarted to that end by concern, for instance, that a common law contract requires two parties with co-existent liabilities. If s. 21 calls for liability absent those features then those liabilities must flow and the "contract" referred to must be treated as a statutory creation.[73]

Elsewhere in his judgment, he used the term "nascent contract"[74] to describe the peculiar sort of agreement that is anticipated by the statute's pre-incorporation contract provisions that apply when the promoter has expressly disclaimed all liability.

It was the challenge of attempting to reconcile the sort of contract envisioned by s. 14 with traditional contract law principles that led to one of the most perplexing of all the

---

69   Jacob S. Ziegel, "Preincorporation Contracts: A Further Comment on *1394918 Ontario Ltd. v. 1310210 Ontario Inc.*" (2002), 37 *Canadian Business Law Journal* 445, at 448.

70   Indeed, in *1394918 Ontario Ltd. v. 1310210 Ontario Inc.* (2002), 57 OR (3d) 607 (CA), Carthy JA characterized a pre-incorporation contract under such circumstances as "effectively an option" (at para. 13).

71   Ziegel, supra footnote 69, at 448-49.

72   Supra footnote 70.

73   Ibid., at para. 5. Professor Ziegel found this characterization less than satisfactory.

74   Ibid., at para. 9. Again, Professor Ziegel took issue with this concept. Supra footnote 69, at 448.

cases decided under CBCA s. 14, *Westcom Radio Group Ltd. v. MacIsaac et al.*[75] *Westcom* involved a claim against an individual who had purported, in the name of a corporation, to sell radio advertising to the plaintiff. Unbeknownst to the plaintiff and defendant alike, the supposed corporation did not exist. The court could have reasonably concluded that the individual promoter ought to be found personally liable under the contract. Section 21(1) of the OBCA—like s. 14 of the CBCA—does provide for such personal liability when a contract has been signed on behalf of a corporation before it comes into existence unless (1) the contract has subsequently been ratified by the new corporation, or (2) the parties have expressly agreed to exempt the promoter from liability under s. 21(4). However, the court took quite a different tack.

Section 21(1), noted the court, refers to a "contract." And the word contract is a legal term of art. Where both parties to an agreement mistakenly believe—as they did in *Westcom*—that one of those parties is an incorporated entity, then the "purported 'contract'" is no contract at all. It is a "nullity." And without a contract, said the court, "there is nothing to which s. 21(1) of the OBCA can apply."

Thus, the individual promoter in *Westcom* was not found liable, despite s. 21 of the OBCA. The court held, instead, that the matter fell squarely within the common law principles established in *Newborne* and in *Black v. Smallwood*: the contract had been made between the third party and a non-existent entity and thus was a nullity. Although the legislative drafters may have thought they had ousted the common law in cases such as this, they were, in the Divisional Court's view, mistaken.

The judgment in *Westcom* attracted harsh criticism. Professor Ziegel suggested that the technical reading of "contract" on which the case turned was "misperceived for the plainest of reasons."[76] The word, Professor Ziegel argued, was surely used by the drafters in a colloquial, not a technical sense. Wilfred Estey was even less diplomatic in his critique of the case, condemning the court's approach to s. 21(1) as "a ludicrous conclusion."[77]

As ludicrous as it might have seemed to some, the *Westcom* decision was followed in a few subsequent decisions in Ontario. It appears, however, that, through a somewhat circuitous route, the Ontario Court of Appeal has, at last, laid to rest the uncertainties created by *Westcom*.

In 2002, the Court of Appeal considered the pre-incorporation contract provisions of the OBCA in *1394918 Ontario Ltd. v. 1310210 Ontario Inc.*[78] The case concerned an agreement for the purchase and sale of land. The agreement had been entered into on behalf of the defendant (vendor) and a promoter "in trust for a company to be incorporated and not in his personal capacity." The vendor allegedly repudiated the contract before the promoter had incorporated a corporation to function as the purchaser. Never-

---

75   Supra footnote 62.

76   Ziegel, supra footnote 67, at 345. Note that this issue was specifically addressed in the 2001 amendments to the CBCA that extended application of s. 14 to situations where a promoter "purports to enter" into an agreement.

77   Wilfred M. Estey, "Pre-incorporation Contracts: The Fog Is Finally Lifting" (2000), 33 *Canadian Business Law Journal* 3, at 15.

78   Supra footnote 70.

theless, the plaintiff, through his counsel, accepted the repudiation, and indicated that a claim for damages would be pursued.

Only then was the plaintiff (promoter's) company incorporated. Immediately on incorporation, the promoter purported to assign to the new corporation his rights under the repudiated contract. This new corporation then sued the vendor. The defendant argued that the plaintiff corporation had no capacity to commence an action for damages under the repudiated contract.

The court held, however, that the plaintiff corporation did indeed have status to bring the action, a decision that was significant for at least two reasons. First, it clarified that the rights of a promoter under a repudiated pre-incorporation contract could be validly assigned under s. 21(2) of the OBCA (the OBCA equivalent to CBCA s. 14(2)). Such rights, in other words, could be assigned to a corporation in the same manner, and with the same effect, as a pre-incorporation contract itself. This was a significant development. An earlier trial division decision in Saskatchewan had appeared to adopt the contrary position.[79]

More important, however, the decision also conclusively rejected the analytical approach that had been taken by the Divisional Court in *Westcom*, holding that

> *Szecket* ... established that common law contract principles should not be reintroduced into the analysis of s. 21 and rejected the two-stage approach in *Westcom* ... whereby the court first established that there was a valid contract at common law and only then applied the statutory rules.[80]

When one is pleased with the outcome of a judicial decision, it is tempting to overlook any inconvenient gaps in its reasoning; however, it is not perhaps entirely correct to assert, as the court in *1394918* did, that *Szecket v. Huang*[81] had "established" this salutary principle. Admittedly, one may find language in the *Szecket* judgment supportive of the conclusion reached by the Court of Appeal in *1394918*. Indeed, Wilfred M. Estey, commenting on this aspect of the case in 2000, cited the following passage from *Szecket* upon which he based his conclusion that "even though the court did not *expressly* overrule *Westcom*, it *effectively* did so":[82]

> We feel obliged to comment on the analysis undertaken by the trial judge in determining the appellant's liability. With respect, we question his reliance on the *Westcom* case, *supra*, which made his analysis of the evidence and s. 21(1) unnecessarily complex. We have not been asked to consider the correctness of the decision in *Westcom*, and, therefore, we decline to do so. ... As Borins JA concluded in his analysis of the law pertaining to pre-incorporation contracts in the *Sherwood* case, in a situation like this where the company is not incorporated and the contract is not performed, liability for breach of the

---

79   *Landmark Inns of Canada Ltd. v. Horeak*, [1982] 2 WWR 377 (Sask. QB). The case was referred to at the trial level, where the court expressed disagreement with it, but was able to distinguish it on the basis that in *Horeak* the issue related to the imposition of personal liability. *Horeak* was not referred to by the Appeal Court.

80   Supra footnote 70, at 612.

81   *Szecket v. Huang*, supra footnote 45.

82   Supra footnote 77, at 25.

pre-incorporation contract depends on the application of s. 21, which was enacted to replace the common law.

Accordingly, *Westcom* was of no assistance to the trial judge in resolving the issue of Mr. Huang's personal liability. There was no need for him to undertake the two-stage analysis suggested by *Westcom* and first determine whether it was the intention of the parties to the pre-incorporation contract that Mr. Huang incur personal liability before determining the ultimate issue of his liability through the application of s. 21(1). This represented one of the problems arising from the common law of pre-incorporation contracts, which the legislature intended to remedy by the enactment of s. 21.

This lengthy quotation has been reproduced just as it appears in Estey's article. No doubt the words in this passage do seem to constitute strong authority for the proposition for which he cites it.

But a few words that appeared in the judgment itself have been left out. (They are indicated by ellipsis ("…") in the passage quoted by Mr. Estey.) The omitted words show that the reference to *Westcom*, in a case such as *Szecket*, is essentially irrelevant. To use the terminology adopted earlier in this section, *Szecket* was a type 1 pre-incorporation contract case, similar to *Kelner v. Baxter*. *Westcom*, on the other hand, was a type 2 contract of the *Black v. Smallwood* variety. Nor was this sort of distinction lost on the *Szecket* court. Indeed, the words strategically omitted from the passage quoted by Mr. Estey were these:

In any event, [*Westcom*] is distinguishable on its facts from this appeal where there is no evidence that Mr. Huang believed he was contracting on behalf of an existing company that, in fact, did not exist, as was the case in *Westcom*. In this appeal, all the evidence pointed to only one conclusion—that the respondents and Mr. Huang knew, and, indeed, intended, that Mr. Huang, and his associates, were contracting on behalf of a company to be incorporated.[83]

Alas, then, *Szecket* "effectively" overruled *Westcom* only in those cases to which *Westcom* never would have applied in the first place.

Fortunately, however, the Court of Appeal in *1394918*, in what might be seen as something of a *felix culpa*, happily falls into the same error. By rather strategically "misreading" its own earlier decision, the court blissfully arrives at what is, regardless of the rocky path the court has taken to arrive there, surely the right destination: the problematic *Westcom* approach may safely be disregarded in the future (at least in Ontario). The statutory rules will apply in the case of all pre-incorporation contracts, whether of the type 1 (*Kelner*) or the type 2 (*Newborne*; *Black v. Smallwood*) variety.[84]

An Alternative Statutory Approach

The CBCA/OBCA approach to pre-incorporation contracts is undoubtedly the subject of most decided cases in this area. But an alternative statutory model has been developed in Canada, one that has attempted to address head on the perplexing problem of "non-incorporation."

---

83   Supra footnote 81, at 411.

84   Of course, this still leaves unresolved the jurisdictional question discussed earlier. See text accompanying footnotes 66 to 69, supra.

This alternative model is found in the Alberta *Business Corporations Act*.[85] (A similar approach was also adopted recently in the BC *Business Corporations Act*.) Subsections 15(1) and (2) of the Alberta Act read as follows:

(1) This section applies unless the person referred to in subsection (2) and all parties to the contract referred to in that subsection
(a) believe that the body corporate exists and is incorporated under, or
(b) intend that the body corporate is to be incorporated under
the laws of a jurisdiction other than Alberta.
(2) Except as provided in this section, if a person enters into a written contract in the name of or on behalf of a body corporate before it comes into existence,
(a) that person is deemed to warrant to the other party to the contract
(i) that the body corporate will come into existence within a reasonable time, and
(ii) that the contract will be adopted within a reasonable time after the body corporate comes into existence,
(b) that person is liable to the other party to the contract for damages for breach of that warranty, and
(c) the measure of damages for that breach of warranty shall be the same as if the body corporate existed when the contract was made, the person who made the contract on behalf of the body corporate had no authority to do so and the body corporate refused to ratify the contract.

One of the first points to note about this provision is that it refers to a "body corporate" rather than a "corporation." This is significant because the term "body corporate" is defined by the statute to mean an incorporated entity whether incorporated under the Alberta *Business Corporations Act* or otherwise.[86] In other words, subsections (1) and (2) are, strictly speaking, matters of contract law rather than merely provincial corporation law. The jurisdictional issue is thus dealt with using a subjective intention test such as had been suggested by Professor Maloney.[87]

The second distinguishing feature of the Alberta legislation is that the legal theory of promoter's liability differs somewhat from the theory underlying the CBCA. The Alberta statute does not provide—as does the CBCA and similar statutes—that the promoter is bound by the terms of an agreement purportedly made by or on behalf of the corporation. Rather, the promoter is to be liable on the basis of breach of warranty of authority.[88] What is not entirely clear, however, is how the provision dealing with the measure of

85   The new BC *Business Corporations Act*, supra footnote 2, adopts a pre-incorporation contract regime similar to Alberta's. (See s. 20 of the BC Act.)

86   *Business Corporations Act* (Alta.), s. 1(i), definition of "body corporate." It is interesting in this context to note that in the United Kingdom, the operation of the pre-incorporation contract provision in the *Companies Act* is made to apply to corporations incorporated outside the United Kingdom as well. See SI 1994/950.

87   Supra footnote 51.

88   That an action for breach of warranty of authority might be available in the case of a type 2 pre-incorporation contract case was specifically alluded to by Windeyer J in *Black v. Smallwood*, supra footnote 26, at 752.

damages, in paragraph 15(2)(c), would operate in such a case. In cases of breach of warranty of authority, where the principal has no means to satisfy a judgment, it has been held that the plaintiff can recover only nominal damages from the agent unless the agent is personally liable under the contract (and not liable merely for breach of warranty of authority).[89] The Alberta statute does not purport to extend personal liability to the promoter. It therefore seems possible that a promoter defendant might successfully be able to incorporate an empty shell corporation, then argue that nominal damages only were recoverable, despite the attempt in paragraph (c) to specify a measure of damages.

Although there do not appear to have been any relevant cases yet decided under the Alberta statute, it is evident that this aspect of the Alberta provision was carefully considered prior to enactment. In its 1980 *Proposals for a New Alberta Business Corporations Act*,[90] Alberta's Institute of Law Research and Reform (now the Alberta Law Reform Institute (ALRI)) considered the paradox of exposing individual promoters to liability within a regime in which shell corporations could be incorporated for the purpose of adopting previously signed pre-incorporation contracts. The report explicitly rejected the CBCA approach to the pre-incorporation contract problem. As the report points out, the central difficulty with the CBCA approach—in cases where there is no post-incorporation adoption—is that it deems a contract to exist between the promoter and the third-party contractor: a result that "will be contrary to the intention of both parties."[91] Thus, a different approach was taken in Alberta, one which is premised on a deemed warranty by the promoter that relates not only to the fact that the corporation will adopt the contract within a reasonable time after it comes into existence, but also to the fact that the corporation will, in fact, come into existence within a reasonable time. Recall that one important gap in the CBCA-style provisions is that they do not explicitly address cases in which a corporation is simply not formed for a considerable period of time after the pre-incorporation contract is signed.

Alberta's Institute of Law Research and Reform had recognized the challenge posed by the attempt to measure damages in such a case. It noted, for example, that in cases of non-incorporation, damages

> would usually be nominal if [the third party] did not stipulate that the corporation was to be incorporated with assets which would enable it to perform its obligations or to pay damages for failure to do so.[92]

---

89   See, e.g., Harvey McGregor, *McGregor on Damages*, 17th ed. (London: Sweet & Maxwell, 2003), at 1017-18. The rationale for this measure is explained by McGregor as reflecting a contract measure of damages, rather than a measure that would be applicable for the tort of deceit. In this regard, McGregor cites a passage from *Firbank's Executors v. Humphreys* in which Lord Esher explained that damages would be assessed, "under the general rule arrived at by considering the difference in the position he [the person acting in reliance on the warranty] would have been in had the representation been true and the position he is actually in in consequence of its being untrue." See McGregor, ibid., at 1018, citing *Firbank's Executors v. Humphreys* (1886), 18 QBD 54, at 60. (The parenthetical words are McGregor's.)

90   Alberta Institute of Law Research and Reform, Report no. 36, *Proposals for a New Alberta Business Corporations Act* (Edmonton: Alberta Institute of Law Research and Reform, 1980).

91   Ibid., at 41.

92   Ibid., at 42.

Surely any such representation would be peculiar—it would be equivalent to the promoter providing a personal guarantee. But, is it not precisely because promoters wish to *avoid* personal liability that pre-incorporation contracts are entered into on behalf of corporations to be incorporated in the first place? And can it not fairly be assumed that a third party has accepted the fact that the promoter is not to be personally liable when that third party, voluntarily dealing with a promoter, willingly agrees to enter into a contract that includes a specific statement that the contract is entered into, not simply on the promoter's personal behalf, but rather on behalf of a corporation to be incorporated? Are we to assume that the third-party contractor regards these qualifying words as meaningless?[93]

Furthermore, the ALRI report suggests that if a corporation with substantial assets is eventually incorporated, but fails to adopt the pre-incorporation contract, then the promoter ought to be liable for substantial damages. This conclusion is not illogical, but it is contestable.

Consider this simple example. A promoter (P) enters into a pre-incorporation contract "on behalf of a corporation to be formed." Later, P takes steps to incorporate a corporation, ABC Ltd. ABC Ltd. does not adopt the pre-incorporation contract. Since the contract was negotiated before ABC Ltd. had ever come into existence, how may it be said that the contract was entered into on behalf of that specific corporation, ABC Ltd.? All one knows is that ABC Corporation is a body corporate that has *not* adopted the contract. But surely ABC Ltd. is not the only corporate body in Canada that has *not* adopted the contract. The Royal Bank of Canada has *not* adopted it either. Nor has Nortel, General Motors, Corner Brook Bar and Grill Inc., nor any of the other hundreds of thousands of corporations currently in existence in Canada. On what basis, then, can ABC Ltd. be inextricably linked to a contract that it did *not* adopt?

The intuitive answer is obvious. ABC Ltd. is not just any corporation chosen at random. It is linked to the pre-incorporation contract negotiated by P, because, of course, P has incorporated ABC Ltd. But now suppose that, after signing the pre-incorporation contract, P actually incorporates not one, but two corporations—ABC Ltd. and XYZ Ltd. Suppose further that P capitalizes XYZ Ltd. with significant assets, but ABC Ltd. is left as an empty, valueless shell. Is ABC Ltd. still, clearly, *the* corporation that did *not* adopt the contract? Or is it XYZ? Or is it both? Or neither?

To push the example a little further, suppose that P is the sole shareholder of ABC Ltd. (the empty shell), but he is just one of two shareholders of XYZ Ltd. (the valuable corporation). Suppose P is one of three shareholders of XYZ Ltd. Suppose P is one of three thousand shareholders of XYZ Ltd. Can it be said that XYZ Ltd. in all or any of these cases is the corporation implicated by the section? Why? Why not?

It is easy to construct elusive examples of this kind because the pre-incorporation contract problem is grounded in a paradox. Courts (and legislatures, too) wish, on the one hand, to treat the corporation consistently as a distinct legal person, and not merely as an aggregate of shareholders. However, to solve the pre-incorporation contract puzzle, they

---

93   As Abella JA so aptly put it, "Individuals may negotiate an agreement in which one or the other, or both, do not wish to incur personal liability. Importantly, one side agrees to forgo security and deal with a shell company." See *Sherwood Designs v. 872935 Ontario Ltd.*, supra footnote 45, at 582.

must nevertheless link such a supposed distinct entity with the actions of a particular natural person. The result is an example of the logical fallacy of contradictory premises.[94]

In brief, it seems that the legislative measure *permitting* (though not requiring) a corporation to adopt pre-incorporation contracts is an eminently sensible one; but the case for imposing personal liability on a promoter in cases of non-adoption seems to melt away under close scrutiny.

Adoption of the Contract

Section 14(2) of the CBCA (and similar provisions in its provincial counterparts) provides that a corporation may effectively adopt a pre-incorporation contract "within a reasonable time after it [that is, the corporation] comes into existence, by any action or conduct signifying its intention to be bound thereby." Once so adopted, the corporation steps into the shoes of the promoter, and the promoter no longer has any rights or obligations under the contract.

The thorny question raised by s. 14(2) is what, precisely, constitutes "action or conduct signifying [the corporation's] intention to be bound"? It is customary for large corporate contracts to be authorized by way of a formal board of directors' resolution. Often a copy of the contract itself is attached as a schedule to this resolution and slipped into the corporate minute book to leave no doubt as to precisely what the board of directors authorized.

In the case of major corporate deals, the counterparty to such a contract will often demand to be given a "certified copy" of such an authorizing resolution.[95] And so a corporate officer—usually the corporate secretary—will duly sign a short certificate confirming the text of the directors' authorizing resolution. This certificate will then be delivered to the counterparty when the transaction contemplated by the contract closes.

This high level of formality and certainty is expected in major corporate transactions where both parties are represented by counsel; but there is no legal requirement that contract approval for purposes of s. 14(2) take the form of a specific, written directors' resolution. Indeed, the language of s. 14(2) clearly anticipates alternative—less formal—means of contract adoption.

Comparable wording in s. 21(2) of the Ontario *Business Corporations Act* was interpreted by the Ontario Court of Appeal in the remarkable case of *Sherwood Design Services Ltd. v. 872935 Ontario Ltd.*[96] The pre-incorporation contract in *Sherwood* was a purchase and sale agreement between the plaintiff (as vendor) and three promoters, "in trust for a corporation to be incorporated."

---

94   A well-known illustration of the informal logical fallacy of contradictory premises is to ask whether the following statement is true or false: "This statement is false." If the statement is false, then it is (paradoxically) true. But if the statement is true, then it must, alas, be false. There are many other commonly used examples. (For example, "if God can do anything, can he make a stone so heavy he cannot lift it?")

95   A certified copy of a resolution consists of a copy of the text of the resolution, along with a certificate—usually signed by the corporate secretary and affixed as a separate page to the document—certifying that the document is a copy of a resolution of the board of directors duly passed at a meeting held on the date specified, and still in force and in effect, unamended, as of the date of the certificate.

96   Supra footnote 45.

The promoters retained a law firm to set up a corporation to complete the transaction. The promoters' law firm, in common with many Canadian law firms, regularly incorporated generic "shelf companies" for use by their clients. A shelf company is a simple, numbered company (that is, a corporation incorporated under a designating number assigned by the government rather than a name)[97] that is incorporated by a law firm, and then placed on the "shelf" so that it may be turned over in future to a client who needs an incorporated entity on a timely basis.

The promoters' lawyer sent a letter to the plaintiff in which he advised that a particular numbered shelf company "has been assigned ... as the corporation that will complete the asset purchase." (As it happened, the shelf company had been incorporated *after* the date on which the contract had been entered into. This fortuitous fact made the pre-incorporation contract rules applicable.) The letter also included unsigned draft copies of a directors' resolution for the numbered company for the "review and consideration" of the plaintiff's lawyer. (The resolution, if passed by the directors of the numbered company, would approve the pre-incorporation contract that had previously been signed by the promoters and the plaintiff.)

The numbered company, in fact, was never assigned to the promoters—in other words, the promoters at no time became shareholders, officers, or directors of the numbered company. The purchase transaction fell through—that is, there was no closing—and therefore no apparent need for the promoters ever to assume control of the numbered company in order to complete the transaction. Accordingly, the numbered company was returned to the law firm's shelf company inventory to be available for some future client. Sure enough, one day another client of the firm needed such a corporation, so the law firm assigned the numbered company to this other client.

The plaintiffs eventually sued for breach of the purchase agreement. They named as a defendant the numbered company. But of course the numbered company was now being operated by the clients to which the law firm had later assigned it, and it possessed considerable assets. The current shareholders of the numbered company were complete strangers to the pre-incorporation contract upon which the plaintiff's legal action was based.

The Ontario Court of Appeal held, however, that the lawyer's letter to the plaintiffs had effectively constituted adoption of the purchase agreement by the numbered company. The practical result of this conclusion was, remarkably, that a company that was operated and had been capitalized by individuals who were complete strangers to the pre-incorporation contract was suddenly liable for breach of a pre-incorporation contract. Carthy JA, concurring in this result, acknowledged that the outcome meant "a windfall

---

97   The advantage of incorporating using a number rather than a name, as discussed in chapter 2, is that it saves the expense of obtaining a NUANS name search and also the sometimes lengthy process of identifying a name that is sufficiently distinct from those of other existing corporations that it can be "cleared." The authority to incorporate a numbered company under the CBCA is found in s. 11(2), which provides that "[i]f requested to do so by the incorporators of a corporation, the Director shall assign to the corporation as its name a designating number followed by the word 'Canada' and a word or expression, or the corresponding abbreviation, referred to in subsection 10(1)." The "name" of a company originally incorporated by number can (if the corporation wishes) later be changed when a permanent name is decided on.

recovery for the appellants,"[98] but, somewhat curiously, defended this decision on the basis that the statute's purpose was "related to business efficiency."[99]

Abella JA (as she then was), for the majority, emphasized in her reasons that nothing in the statute calls for any particular formal requirements to be observed before a pre-incorporation contract may be said to have been adopted. The lawyer's letter was enough.

Borins JA wrote a vigorous and well-reasoned dissent. He reasoned, correctly in my view, that the solicitor's letter simply did not constitute an act of the numbered corporation at all, and therefore could not signify adoption of the contract. In fact, although Borins JA did not make the point in quite this way, it appears that the judgment of the majority in *Sherwood* means that s. 14 has precisely the effect that the law of corporate promoters has always sought to avoid—namely, it enables an unauthorized individual to bind a corporation to a contract without the concurrence of the corporation itself.

If, for example, the solicitor in *Sherwood* had mistakenly named, say, General Motors or Microsoft as the corporation adopting the pre-incorporation contract (unbeknownst to anyone in authority at either of these large corporations), would the corporation so named in the letter really have become bound by the contract? Surely not. However, under the reasoning of the majority in *Sherwood* there would be no principled reason to avoid this outcome. After all, Abella JA said, "Parties should be able to take at face value letters such as the one sent—and received." Nor is it an answer to say that Microsoft or General Motors could not be bound because the lawyer in *Sherwood* had no authority to act for either of these two corporations. The lawyer had no authority to act for the numbered company either. The lawyer, it must be emphasized, was not an officer, director, or share-holder of the numbered company—*nor were any of the promoters who had signed the pre-incorporation contract*. Thus, no one with authority to bind the numbered corporation (as it happens, other individuals at the law firm) authorized the numbered company to adopt the pre-incorporation contract, or instructed the lawyer to send the letter in question.

Moreover, as Welling et al. have suggested,[100] it was entirely fortuitous that the numbered company in this case was incorporated after the contract was signed (thus bringing the pre-incorporation contract provisions into play). It would more commonly be the case that a law firm would transfer to a promoter client a shelf company that had previously been incorporated, and so was already in existence at the time the promoter entered into his or her contract with a third party. In every practical respect, from the perspective of the signatories to the contract, this minor difference would be irrelevant, and would go unnoticed. But, from a legal perspective, the difference is dramatic. The action of an individual purporting to act on behalf of a company in circumstances where he or she has no actual authority (such as the lawyer in *Sherwood*)—and has not been held out by the company itself as having ostensible authority—would not bind the company.

Perhaps the clearest indication that the reasoning of the majority in *Sherwood* is ill conceived is to consider how that reasoning could be used to utterly defeat the intention

---

98   *Sherwood Designs*, supra footnote 45, at 584.

99   Ibid.

100   Bruce L. Welling et al., *Canadian Corporate Law: Cases, Notes and Materials*, 2nd ed. (Markham, ON: Butterworths, 2001), at 236. In *Sherwood*, the agreement in question was signed on November 29, 1989. The corporation was incorporated on December 15, 1989.

of the legislation. Suppose, for example, an aggressive promoter enters into a pre-incorporation contract. He subsequently forms a corporation, of which he is just one of several shareholders. Unbeknownst to the other shareholders, the promoter then simply writes a letter to the other party to the pre-incorporation contract—in precisely the form of the letter in *Sherwood*. If such an unauthorized action truly is sufficient to bind the corporation (on the basis, as Abella JA suggested, that "parties should be able to take at face value letters such as the one sent—and received"), then over a century of law that has been developed to protect the integrity of the corporate form from exploitation by unauthorized promoters would have been wiped out by a three-page Ontario Court of Appeal judgment.

In sum, it appears that in *Sherwood*, as Wilfred Estey has (perhaps a touch harshly) put it, "Abella JA 'dropped the ball.'"[101] The dissent of Borins JA provides a much more careful analysis, and arrives at a more sensible and cogent conclusion.[102]

Disclaiming Promoter's Liability

Subsection 14(4) of the CBCA (and its provincial counterparts) permits a promoter to disclaim the personal liability to which he might otherwise be subject pursuant to s. 14(1). To be effective, such disclaimer of liability must be "expressly so provided" in the relevant contract.

At first, this simple provision might seem sensible enough. The "default rule" under s. 14(1) exposes the promoter to personal liability under a pre-incorporation contract. But surely this default rule, which is designed to protect the third-party contractor, may be modified with the agreement of the third-party contractor. That is surely a matter that the promoter and the third party may best decide on for themselves, and the law ought to respect that decision. This apparently straightforward and sensible proposition, however, actually introduces an element of incoherence to s. 14. Again, one emphasizes that this incoherence does not result from any failure on the part of the drafters to take sufficient care in the use of the statutory language. Rather, it arises from the contradictory premises that unavoidably thwart s. 14.

Before exploring the nature of this incoherence, one might first note that there is some uncertainty surrounding how precisely a promoter must disclaim liability to enjoy the protection of s. 14(4). In *Szecket v. Huang*,[103] the third-party contractor had, during pre-incorporation contract negotiations, specifically requested that the promoter provide a personal guarantee of the contractual obligations of the not-yet-formed corporation. The promoter refused. Provisions in an early draft of the agreement that called for such a personal guarantee were, accordingly, deleted from the version the parties ultimately signed.

---

101 Estey, supra footnote 77, at 21.

102 Perell has noted that a number of lower-court decisions in Ontario appear to have adopted more rigorous tests for contract adoption. See Paul M. Perell, "Pre-Incorporation Contracts and *1394918 Ontario Ltd. v. 1310210 Ontario Inc.*: Some Answers, Some Questions" (2002), 37 *Canadian Business Law Journal* 291, at 304, note 36. (The cases he cites in support of this proposition are: *Netmar Inc. v. Aquilina (c.o.b. as Smart Choice Furniture)*, [1999] OJ no. 790 (QL) (Gen. Div.); *Massey v. Smahel*, [1991] OJ no. 450 (QL) (Gen. Div.); *Canam Air Leakage Control Systems Corp. v. Tor-Can Conservation & Renovations Inc.*, [1989] OJ no. 1205 (QL) (Div. Ct.); and *Okinczyc v. Tessier*, supra footnote 56.)

103 *Szecket v. Huang*, supra footnote 45.

Despite this apparently clear evidence of the parties' intentions that the promoter not be personally liable, the Ontario Court of Appeal concluded that the promoter, who signed the agreement, "acting on behalf of a company to be formed," had not effectively disclaimed his liability under the OBCA equivalent of CBCA s. 14(4):

> To limit the liability of a person who enters into a pre-incorporation contract, an express provision to that effect must be contained in the pre-incorporation contract. The contract in this appeal did not contain such an express provision. Whatever may have been the result of the negotiations between the parties preceding the execution of the contract about the personal responsibility of Mr. Huang for the obligations of the company to be incorporated, the contract itself contained no express provision relieving Mr. Huang from personal liability under s. 21(1) if the company was not incorporated, or if it was incorporated, and failed to adopt the contract. Had he wished to avail himself of s. 21(4), Mr. Huang could have sought the consent of the respondents to include an appropriate provision in the agreement.[104]

Liability could not, in other words, be disclaimed merely by implication. To satisfy s. 14(4), the contract had to deal explicitly with the point.

The matter does not end there, however. In the subsequent case of *1394918 Ontario Ltd. v. 1310210 Ontario Inc.*,[105] the Court of Appeal held that the protection of subsection (4) applies to a promoter who had executed the pre-incorporation contract, "in trust for a company to be incorporated and not in his personal capacity." In other words, reciting this simple verbal formula was, apparently, enough to constitute an express agreement, within the meaning of subsection (4), such that the promoter was not to be held personally liable.

This conclusion, as Professor Ziegel has observed,[106] is somewhat curious. The mere statement by a promoter in a pre-incorporation contract that he is not acting in his personal capacity surely ought not to be sufficient to satisfy subsection (4). After all, s. 14 "does not require the promoter to contract in his personal capacity before holding him liable"[107] in the first place. Moreover, "the contract already states that the promoter is contracting on behalf of a future corporation."[108] Put another way, the only contracts that ever come to be scrutinized under the pre-incorporation provisions of the CBCA or OBCA are contracts *not* entered into in the promoter's personal capacity. How can reciting this fact, without more, invoke the protective language of subsection (4)?

Moreover, as Professor Ziegel once again has pointed out,[109] where a promoter has expressly disclaimed any liability under the pre-incorporation contract, the "contract" is a very peculiar beast indeed. The third-party contractor is, evidently, subject to obligations—to someone (or to something). But no one, evidently, has any reciprocal legal obligations to the contractor. If a third party who has entered into a pre-incorporation contract with a promoter seeks escape from a disclaimed contract before a corporation has

---

104 Ibid., at para. 31.

105 Supra footnote 70.

106 Ziegel, supra footnote 69.

107 Ibid., at 446.

108 Ibid., at 447.

109 Ibid.

adopted it, it cannot do so with impunity. It is somehow bound by the contract. However, it enjoys no corresponding legal rights to enforce the agreement against anyone else.

Now the reader might perhaps argue that this odd state of affairs—a contract enforceable only against one party, and unsupported by consideration—is a sensible solution to the pre-incorporation contract problem. The contractor can always avoid any unfairness that might arise from such a peculiar arrangement simply by refusing to contract with a promoter on this basis in the first place.

However, even if one is satisfied with such an analysis in the case of type 1 pre-incorporation contracts, matters break down rather badly when one recalls that s. 14 is also intended to apply to type 2 agreements. And it is here that the "incoherence" mentioned earlier becomes evident.

Recall that a type 2 agreement is the designation that has been used in this chapter to refer to agreements mistakenly made in the name of a non-existent corporation. Parties to such an agreement, of course, will never include an express disclaimer of the promoter's personal liability, because, simply put, neither party is actually aware that one of them *is* a promoter. In other words, there would be no reason for a party to disclaim personal liability where he or she had no reason to suspect that he or she has entered into the agreement in his personal capacity in the first place.

If the "logic" of subsection (4) is that it merely permits the express intention of the parties to govern, then in every type 2 case—where the parties' intentions unequivocally indicate that the promoter is not expected to be personally liable—the promoter surely ought never to be liable. That conclusion, however, is precisely the result one reaches by applying the discredited reasoning of *Westcom v. McIsaac*. And since the *Westcom v. McIsaac* analysis has been expressly rejected by the Court of Appeal, something quite astonishing has happened. The common law has, evidently, not simply been modified by s. 14—it has been quite literally reversed. For now, a promoter acting "on behalf of a corporation and not in his personal capacity" (that is, as in *Kelner*) will never be personally liable, thanks to the Court of Appeal's recent interpretation of subsection (4). Yet, at common law, such a promoter would always have been liable.

Meanwhile, a promoter who signs a contract purportedly as an officer of a non-existent corporation (and so, naturally, making no explicit attempt to disclaim personal liability) will *always* be personally liable. Yet, at common law, a person in this position (as in *Black v. Smallwood*) would never have been liable!

Did the legislature really intend not simply to clarify or refine the common law but rather to turn it completely on its head? To what do we owe this odd result? Have the courts simply laboured to divine the true intention of the parties to the pre-incorporation contract? Surely not. The intention of the parties in a type 2 case would never to be to impose personal liability on the "promoter." What explains the matter then?

The sad but surprising answer seems to be this: the personal liability issue now appears to turn to a significant extent on the mere form of words that appear in the signature block of the contract—the very capricious and uncertain thing that the statutory reform had been designed to cure in the first place. *Plus ça change, plus c'est la même chose.*

But could the legislation be re-drafted in some clever way to solve this problem?

Perhaps a pre-incorporation contract could be conceived either as nothing more or less than a fully assignable option, granted by the contractor to the promoter. For an option like that, the contractor should, quite reasonably, expect to be paid a premium. Or, again, we might perhaps conceive of these agreements as fully assignable contracts, on which the promoter will be liable unless and until they are assigned. This approach is functionally equivalent to the current statutory scheme provided for by section 14 of the CBCA. As for those cases, such as *Black v. Smallwood*, where the parties are simply mistaken about the existence of the corporation, perhaps traditional contract remedies or analysis will not do, and we should look to equitable principles, rather than legal principles. Or perhaps some other approach altogether might be taken, such as one of the suggestions put forward by Professor Ziegel.[110] Or perhaps we cannot effectively address the problem of pre-incorporation contracts at all as long as we insist on conceiving the problem in corporation rather than contractual terms.

CONCLUSION

Disputes involving opportunistic promoters and pre-incorporation contracts compel us to do some very hard thinking about the legal nature of a corporation. How seriously are we prepared to accept the traditional notion that a corporation is a separate legal entity if that doctrine leads to absurd, uncertain, and unfair results? Do these cases, in fact, prod us toward adopting an altogether more functional conception of the law governing corporations?

---

110 Ibid., at 450.

CHAPTER SIX

Contracting Authority, Corporate Seals, and Ultra Vires

INTRODUCTION

It is one of the most fundamental of corporate attributes, and traditionally one of its principal advantages: a corporation can enter into contracts in the corporate name. Historically, when contracts were in writing, the corporation's "signature" was represented by a seal. The seal was a raised impression that set out the corporation's name and perhaps the year in which it had been incorporated. It was pressed with a metal "seal maker" into a dab of sealing wax that had been strategically melted onto the document page at the appropriate spot. When a seal was affixed to a document in this way, it was clear that the corporation itself had become a party to the contract, not the individual corporate representative who had melted the wax and pressed the seal maker to the page.

The formal requirement that corporate documents be executed under corporate seal has now been dispensed with in most modern jurisdictions,[1] although most corporations today are still encouraged by their legal counsel to (and do in fact) adopt a form of corporate seal so that they may seal documents if they wish. This is not a major expense. For a cost of perhaps $60 or so, one can purchase a metal or plastic "seal-maker" from a legal stationer. (The use of sealing wax is no longer necessary or desirable.)

For most ordinary business contracts, the affixing of the corporate seal is of no legal significance whatsoever. It is sufficient for a corporation's duly authorized officers or agents simply to sign their names beneath the corporation's name in the contract signing block, conventionally noting beneath their signatures the offices or titles they hold in the corporation. Thus, when a corporation signs a document, a typical signature block might look like this:

ABC Corporation Limited

Per [or by]:   *I.M. Thepres*
          President

---

1   See, e.g., CBCA, s. 23. *Business Corporations Act* (Alta.), s. 25; *The Business Corporations Act* (Sask.), s. 23; *The Corporations Act* (Man.), s. 23; *Business Corporations Act* (Ont.), s. 13; *Business Corporations Act* (NB), s. 21; and *Business Corporations Act* (NL), s. 32.

Much of the law relating to contracts entered into by or on behalf of a corporation is not, strictly speaking, corporate law. It is contract law and is more properly dealt with in the context of the study of the law of contracts. Nevertheless, there are several particular topics in respect of which contract and corporate law principles have become inextricably linked. In chapter 5 we considered two of those topics—promoters' contracts and pre-incorporation contracts, which relate especially to events that occur before a corporation has even been created. In this chapter we explore three issues that concern the "post-incorporation" contracting activities of the corporation:

- the actual and ostensible authority of corporate signing officers;
- sealed documents and the corporate seal; and
- the historically significant, if increasingly unimportant, doctrine of *ultra vires*.

ACTUAL AND OSTENSIBLE AUTHORITY OF CORPORATE SIGNING OFFICERS

Framing the Issue

Corporations, as courts and textbook writers never tire of reminding us, are artificial legal persons that can act only through natural persons—that is, human beings. Accordingly, it is often a matter of considerable importance to determine whether the actions of an individual who purports to act on behalf of a corporation will, in fact, operate to bind the corporation. When, for example, a corporate officer negotiates with a third party for the provision of goods or services by that third party to the corporation, both the third-party contractor and the corporation itself will be understandably concerned to know whether or not the contract is enforceable as a matter of law against the corporation.

Where the corporate signing officer has been expressly authorized by the corporation to enter into the contract in the corporate name—for example, by way of an explicit authorizing directors' resolution—the matter is free from difficulty. The officer is said in such cases to enjoy "actual authority" to act for the corporation, and the corporation will be bound by the contract signed by the officer.

But where the officer purporting to act on behalf of the corporation had not, in fact, been expressly authorized to do so, the legal position of the parties becomes thornier. Should the corporation always be bound by any contract purportedly entered into on its behalf by one of its employees? Or should third-party contractors be obliged to verify that a corporate employee who claims to speak for the corporation does indeed have actual authority to conclude a contract on the corporation's behalf, and, if they fail to do so, accept the risk that they may not be able to enforce the contract against the corporation?

In the case of major transactions, it is standard practice for solicitors to require, at the closing of the transaction, that various documents be delivered confirming the actual authority of a corporation's signing officers. These documents might include: certified[2] copies of the corporation's so-called constating documents (namely, its articles of incor-

---

2   That is, certified by a corporate officer—usually the corporate secretary—as true copies of the originals, together with all amendments as of the date on which the certificate is signed.

poration or memorandum of association, and its bylaws or articles of association, and perhaps any unanimous shareholder agreement); certified copies of the text of a valid and subsisting directors' resolution specifically authorizing the signing officer to act, and, perhaps, approving the agreement itself; a "certificate of incumbency" in which the corporate secretary certifies the names of the corporation's officers, their corporate titles, and the forms of each of their signatures; and so on. This level of formality and documentation, however, makes commercial sense only where the financial stakes are relatively high. Furnishing such detailed paperwork for most smaller contracts would be impractical and prohibitively expensive.

Naturally, when a corporation honours the contractual obligations purportedly made on its behalf—as will undoubtedly be the usual case—no thought will ever be given as to whether, as a technical legal matter, the signing officer had sufficient authority to bind the corporation. But there will be those rare cases in which the corporation disavows the actions of its supposed agent. For those cases, there is need of a set of coherent legal principles pursuant to which disputes between third parties and the corporation can be resolved.

No third-party contractor would have any practical means of determining whether such an employee had been expressly authorized to enter into corporate contracts. Minutes of directors' meetings are, after all, neither publicly filed nor—unlike the minutes of shareholder meetings—otherwise available to an outside party (even to the corporation's own shareholders).[3] Accordingly, it might be tempting to conclude that the burden of any contract entered into by a corporate officer or employee ought fairly to be borne by the corporation. Is the corporation not in the best position to control the actions of its own employees? Surely, then, it would not be unreasonable, on this view, to hold the corporation responsible for the actions of those people it has chosen to employ.

Closer consideration of the matter, however, reveals that this simplistic analysis will not do. It is well understood that organizations—especially large organizations—employ vast numbers of workers at widely varying levels of seniority and responsibility. It would be absurd to suggest that every contract purportedly made by any employee should bind the corporation. No reasonable third-party contractor would expect such a result. No reasonable court would either.

Consider, for example, the giant American entertainment corporation, The Walt Disney Company. At the end of its 2002 financial year, The Walt Disney Company (and its consolidated subsidiaries) had assets totalling over US $50 billion, and some 112,000 employees.[4] Those 112,000 people include the company's most senior officer—the chief executive officer—as well as the men and women who delight children at Walt Disney theme parks by dressing up as Mickey Mouse, Donald Duck, and other "costumed characters."

Now, suppose, hypothetically, that a furniture maker were to enter into a contract with The Walt Disney Company to make a fine new desk to furnish the office of one of the firm's top executives. If that contract were signed on behalf of The Walt Disney Company by its chief executive officer, it would seem reasonable enough to expect that The Walt

---

3   See the discussion in chapter 4. As a result of recent amendments to the CBCA, there is one narrow, partial exception to the confidentiality of directors' minutes in the case of interested directors contracts. See CBCA, s. 120(6.1).

4   See letter to shareholders, *Disney Annual Report, 2002*.

Disney Company ought to be bound by such a contract. And it would strike most observers that the legal position ought to be no different even if one were to discover that, in fact, Walt Disney's board of directors—just hours before this contract was signed— had passed a resolution forbidding the chief executive officer from entering into any contracts relating to office furnishings. In such a case, although it appears that the CEO lacked *actual* authority to contract, it would be eminently reasonable for the furniture maker to assume that the CEO possessed the necessary contracting authority. Indeed it would have been all but impossible for anyone other than a member of the Disney board of directors to discover the true state of affairs.

But now consider a very different case. Suppose that an ambitious (though foolish) entrepreneur, is eager to entice The Walt Disney Company to acquire his innovative animation studio at a cost, he hopes, of some $5 billion. He begins negotiating the terms of such a sale with one of the energetic young "cast members" working at Disney World's Magic Kingdom—a costumed character proudly performing the role of cartoon icon, Mickey Mouse. Neither The Walt Disney Company (nor any other reasonable third-party observer) would ever imagine that such a significant agreement, signed by "Mickey Mouse" on behalf of his employer, would be legally effective. The fact that Mickey may be a genuine Disney employee is irrelevant. It is not reasonable to expect that an employee in such a junior position within the firm would have the authority to enter into a major agreement on behalf of his corporate employer.

These two hypothetical cases, though highly fanciful, do illustrate the key principle underlying this area of the law: where a corporate agent or employee lacks actual authority to conclude a contract on behalf of a corporation, he or she can, nevertheless, bind the corporation provided he or she has "apparent" or "ostensible" authority to do so. The corporate CEO in the above example would have ostensible authority to enter into a modest contract to purchase a desk; the costumed character, however, would clearly not have ostensible authority to enter into a multi-billion dollar acquisition contract. Not surprisingly, it is those circumstances where the position of the agent is not located at either of these two extreme ends of the ostensible authority spectrum that have been the subject of the litigated cases to which we now turn.

Constructive Notice and the Indoor Management Rule

The doctrine of "ostensible" or "apparent" authority is a feature of the law of agency, and the law of agency has been understood to be a critical element of the law of partnerships at least since the seminal case of *Cox v. Hickman*.[5] Agency is a characteristic of the partnership relationship now codified in provincial partnership statutes, which typically state that each partner is an agent of the partnership and of the other partners.[6] Within a partnership, any contract entered into by a partner in the course of the partnership business will normally bind the other partners, even if—as between the partners—it had been privately agreed that the particular partner purporting to make such a contract had no actual authority to do so.

---

5   (1860), 11 ER 431 (HL).

6   See, e.g., *Partnerships Act* (Ont.), RSO 1990, c. P.5, s. 6.

There are, however, two key exceptions to this partnership agency rule: a contract will not be binding on the other partners in those cases where (1) the other party to the contract (the "contractor") had actual knowledge that the partner with whom he or she was dealing lacked authority; or (2) the contractor did not know that the person with whom she or he was dealing was a partner.[7]

Following the enactment in England of the first general incorporation statutes—which provided for the incorporation of "joint stock companies"—these partnership agency principles were applied with some modifications to incorporated joint stock companies. One of the key modifications was the introduction of what has come to be known as the "constructive notice" rule.

The "constructive notice" rule was a legal development that recognized a fundamental difference between ordinary partnerships and incorporated joint stock companies: the constating documents of an incorporated joint stock company were a matter of public record (unlike partnership agreements, which were private contracts). The courts therefore reasoned that any third party dealing with a corporation ought to be expected to investigate these public records. If the public records revealed want of authority on the part of a person purporting to act on behalf of the company, the third party would be put on notice and so would not be able to enforce the contract against the company. More important, third parties would be *deemed* to be aware of any such lack of authority, even if they had not, in fact, taken the time to examine the corporation's public records.

There were limits, however, on the extent to which constructive notice would prevent third parties from enforcing contracts. The boundaries were defined in a key 19th century case, *The Royal British Bank v. Turquand*,[8] from which emerged an important qualification of the constructive notice doctrine now known as the "indoor management rule" or the "rule in *Turquand's* case." *Turquand's* case was decided in 1856, 12 years after the enactment of England's first general incorporation statute, the *Joint Stock Companies Act* of 1844, and virtually on the eve of the enactment of the first modern English companies statute.[9] By that time, it appears that the constructive notice doctrine had already become well established.

Turquand's case involved an action brought by a bank to enforce a bond that had been signed on behalf of the borrowing company by two of its directors. According to the borrowing company's constating document, directors were indeed permitted to borrow money by issuing bonds, but only when authorized to do so by a shareholders' resolution. The shareholders had, in fact, passed a resolution authorizing the directors, in general terms, to borrow money on behalf of the company, but the resolution did not authorize specific amounts to be borrowed. The failure to authorize a specific monetary amount was a defect that, in the view of the defendant company, meant that the action of its directors must be considered unauthorized.

It was arguable that the shareholders' general authorizing resolution was, without more, sufficient to confer actual signing authority on the company's directors. However,

---

7   Ibid.

8   (1856), 119 ER 886 (Ex. Ct.).

9   *The Joint Stock Companies Act, 1856*, 19 & 20 Vict., c. 47.

the court did not base its ruling exclusively on this broader interpretation of the corporate charter. Rather, the court endorsed, in general terms, the application of the constructive notice doctrine, but went on to hold that the doctrine could not apply to defeat the bank's claims in a case such as this, reasoning:

> We may now take for granted that the dealings with these companies [i.e., companies incorporated under the *Joint Stock Companies Act* of 1844] are not like dealings with other partnerships, and the parties dealing with them are bound to read the statute and the deed of settlement. But they are not bound to do more. And the party here, on reading the deed of settlement, would find, not a prohibition from borrowing, but a permission to do so on certain conditions. Finding that the authority might be made complete by a resolution, he would have a right to infer the fact of a resolution authorizing that which on the face of the document appeared to be legitimately done.[10]

This statement encapsulates what is known as the "indoor management rule": although a third party may be deemed to have constructive knowledge of the contents of a corporation's constating documents, he or she is nevertheless entitled to assume that all necessary internal corporate steps referred to in those documents have been properly complied with. Of course, if the third party has actual knowledge that the necessary authorizing steps were not undertaken, he or she can no longer rely on the protection of the indoor management rule.

Constructive notice was a common law doctrine. Lest there be any doubt about the matter, the doctrine of "constructive notice" in its strictest form has been abandoned under the CBCA, and many other provincial corporate statutes.[11] Section 17 of the CBCA, for example, reads:

> No person is affected by or is deemed to have notice or knowledge of the contents of a document concerning a corporation by reason only that the document has been filed by the Director or is available for inspection at an office of the corporation.

The fact that the constructive notice doctrine has been addressed this way by statute does not, however, mean that the indoor management problem has been eliminated. Section 17, after all, provides that no one is deemed to have knowledge of a corporation's publicly available documents "by reason *only*" that they have been filed. The Dickerson committee took the view that this language would not invariably oust the doctrine of constructive notice, but rather would, properly, "[leave] it open to the court, in an appropriate case, to apply the doctrine of constructive notice if there is a good reason for so doing."[12] Moreover, whether or not the actions of a corporate agent should bind the corporation may involve considerations that go well beyond anything that could be revealed by even the most careful reading of the corporation's publicly filed paperwork.

10   Supra footnote 8, at 888.

11   See, e.g., *Business Corporations Act* (Alta.), s. 18; *The Business Corporations Act* (Sask.), s. 17; *The Corporations Act* (Man.), s. 17; *Business Corporations Act* (Ont.), s. 18; *Business Corporations Act* (NB), s. 15; *Companies Act* (NS), s. 31; and *Corporations Act* (NL), s. 30.

12   Robert W.V. Dickerson et al., *Proposals for a New Business Corporations Law for Canada*, vol. I, Commentary (Ottawa: Information Canada, 1971), at para. 84 (Dickerson committee).

It will often be the case that some contracts executed by officers and directors on behalf of their corporation will have been properly authorized by the corporation, while others will not. Rules are needed to determine when third-party contractors dealing with unauthorized corporate agents will, or will not, be able to enforce contracts against the corporation. Thus, there is still scope for the "indoor management rule," a rule that has not only survived, but has been effectively codified in many modern Canadian corporate statutes, as discussed further below. The rule in *Turquand's* case, however, applies primarily in those cases where a corporate officer or director purporting to bind the corporation might have actual authority to contract, if, and only if, certain specified internal corporate authorizing procedures had been complied with. Application of the rule becomes necessary, of course, only in those cases where such internal authorizing procedures—unbeknownst to the third-party contractor—have not been satisfied. There is a broader question that is left unanswered by *Turquand's* case: under what additional circumstances will a corporate officer or director lacking actual authority be able to bind the corporation in contract? It is that question with which the next section deals.

Actual and Ostensible Authority of Corporate Agents

When will a corporate agent, lacking actual authority, be said, as a matter of law, to have apparent or "ostensible authority" to conclude a contract on behalf of the corporation with a third party? The law of the ostensible authority of corporate agents is based on agency law principles, of which the classic articulation may be found in the judgment of Diplock J in *Freeman & Lockyer v. Buckhurst Park Properties (Mangal) Ltd.*[13] At the heart of Diplock J's reasoning is the premise that, in order for a corporation to be bound by a contract entered into by a corporate agent (who lacks actual contracting authority), the corporation must, somehow, hold out or represent to the third-party contractor that the agent has the requisite authority. But because a corporation can act only through human beings, this holding out or representation must be done by some corporate agent who does, indeed, possess actual authority to make such a representation. The purported agent's own representation to a third party that he or she has authority to contract is simply not enough.[14]

The logic underpinning this conclusion is unassailable. Clearly, if a person who was a total stranger to the corporation audaciously claimed to have authority to enter into contracts on behalf of the corporation, we would hardly expect the corporation to be bound by any contract concluded by such a charlatan. The situation is not so very much different even if the charlatan happens, in fact, to be employed by the corporation in some junior capacity. (Like the costumed character in the hypothetical Walt Disney example.)

---

13   [1964] 2 WLR 618 (CA).

14   This statement must, however, be read carefully in the context of the discussion that follows. As Laskin CJC noted, infra footnote 16, at para. 22:

> I do not subscribe to the proposition, in so far as it purports to be a general statement of the law, that a representation by an agent himself as to the extent of his authority cannot amount to a holding out by the principal. It will depend on what it is an agent has been assigned to do by his principal, and an overreaching may very well inculpate the principal.

What then should the law require? What does a corporation need to do in order to enable a third-party contractor to argue successfully that an agent (who may, in fact, lack actual contracting authority) nevertheless has been held out or represented as having such authority, and so has been cloaked with *ostensible* authority? In the simplest case, a corporate officer—with actual authority to bind the corporation—might explicitly state to a third-party contractor that a particular corporate agent has power to contract. To return to our earlier example, suppose that the CEO of The Walt Disney Company were to tell a third party that the fellow wearing the Mickey Mouse costume has full authority, after all, to purchase paperclips on behalf of the corporation. This representation, as a matter of fact, might not be true. But it would not necessarily be unreasonable for a third-party paper-clip vendor to rely on this representation—made as it is by a corporate officer possessing actual authority—and so conclude a sale agreement with the costumed character. A court might well be disposed to find such an agreement binding on The Walt Disney Company.

But now let us suppose the facts are different. What if the representation or holding out is made in a somewhat more subtle or ambiguous way? For example, imagine that a corporation simply appoints a certain employee to the position of director of corporate purchasing, allowing her to represent herself with that fine-sounding title on her business cards, stationery, and so on. Of course, if she has actual authority to conclude purchasing contracts on behalf of the corporation, no interesting legal issues arise. There will be no doubt about the enforceability of contracts she negotiates on behalf of the corporation. However, if she does not have actual authority to conclude such contracts—despite what her corporate title might suggest to outsiders—will such contracts be binding on the corporation? No explicit representation of her authority has been made by a corporate officer with actual authority. Is the act of appointing her to a position with a particular sort of title enough to implicate the corporation, as it were? Perhaps. This example differs in one important way from the situation in which the purported agent himself simply (falsely) represents the extent of his contracting authority to a third party. The difference is this. When the corporation places an individual in a position of the sort that would normally give to the individual occupying it actual authority to enter into contracts of a particular kind, the law has recognized that third parties may be misled just as surely as if an express verbal "holding out" or representation had been made by a corporate official with actual authority to bind the corporation. As Diplock J explained in *Freeman & Lockyer*:

> The commonest form of representation by a principal creating an "apparent" authority of an agent is by conduct, viz., by permitting the agent to act in the management or conduct of the principal's business. Thus, if in the case of a company the board of directors who have "actual" authority under the memorandum and articles of association to manage the company's business permit the agent to act in the management or conduct of the company's business, they thereby represent to all persons dealing with such agent that he has authority to enter on behalf of the corporation into contracts of a kind which an agent authorised to do acts of the kind which he is in fact permitted to do normally enters into in the ordinary course of such business. The making of such a representation is itself an act of management of the company's business.[15]

---

15   Supra footnote 13, at 637-38.

Diplock J distilled the principles of ostensible (or apparent) authority into a fourfold proposition, consisting of these elements:

- representation;
- actual authority (of the representor);
- reliance by the third-party contractor; and
- the absence of any overriding incapacity (such as *ultra vires*) on the part of the corporation to undertake or perform the contract.

The fourth element is rarely relevant today because, for the reasons explained later in this chapter, concerns about the limitations of corporate capacity (*ultra vires*) have largely been eliminated in typical Canadian corporate statutes. At common law, then, a corporate agent lacking actual authority could still bind the corporation contractually if that agent had ostensible authority to do so; and an agent could be said to have ostensible authority if a representation of that authority, on which a third-party contractor were induced to rely, were made on behalf of the corporation by someone with actual authority. But that representation need not be an explicit verbal representation; it could include representation by conduct. The representation by the corporation of the agent's ostensible authority operates as an estoppel—that is, the corporation is estopped from denying the authority of the agent on which the third party has been induced to rely.

Not surprisingly, it is not always easy to determine whether there has been a "holding out" sufficient to cloak a corporate agent with ostensible authority to contract in the *Freeman & Lockyer* sense. Reasonable people, including reasonable Supreme Court justices, can disagree on whether such a holding out has or has not occurred. Consider, for example, the Supreme Court of Canada's decision in *Canadian Laboratory Supplies Limited v. Engelhard Industries of Canada Limited*.[16] There, the Supreme Court of Canada was asked to rule on whether purchase contracts entered into by a dishonest corporate employee—as part of an elaborate fraud scheme—would be binding on his corporate employer. Note that the employer was also a victim of the fraud.

Cook, the miscreant employee, was employed by Canadian Laboratories Ltd. ("Canlab") in its sales department. Cook concocted a scheme to deceive his employer by inventing a fictional customer—"Giles." Giles, he would claim, required sheets of platinum for some kind of (conveniently secret) scientific research. Canlab was to procure this platinum for Giles. Cook would thus negotiate the purchase of this platinum— ostensibly on behalf of Canlab—from Engelhard Industries. After one or two days, Giles (in reality, Cook) would resell the "used" platinum back as scrap to Engelhard. Engelhard would send a cheque for this used platinum directly to Giles, at an address supplied by Cook. These cheques, of course, were being delivered to Cook himself.

This deception continued undetected for almost seven years; when the fraud was finally uncovered, Canlab brought an action against Engelhard for conversion. (In other words, the platinum in question was found to belong to Canlab. The *purchase* transactions by Canlab had all been properly authorized; in every case, a purchase order was signed, not by Cook, but by a duly authorized employee of Canlab. The remaining question was whether the bogus sales by "Giles" of platinum that was owned by Canlab

---

16   [1979] 2 SCR 787.

constituted conversion. That Cook himself would have been liable there is no doubt; however, it may be assumed that Cook no longer had the financial means to make restitution to his employer.)

Engelhard's defence to this claim relied, in part, on an assertion that Cook had ostensible authority to enter into a deal with Engelhard on Canlab's behalf. Two matters were clear: one, a question of fact and the other, a question of law. First, Cook lacked actual authority from Canlab to enter into contracts of the kind in dispute (even if, it must be stressed, they had been genuine, good faith agreements). Second, in order to establish that Cook had ostensible authority to act for Canlab, some representation (or holding out) on the part of Canlab would have to be identified.

Writing for the majority, Estey J found the necessary holding out by Canlab in a series of communications between an Engelhard employee (McCullough) and a Canlab purchasing agent (Snook). To be sure, Snook had made no express verbal representation that Cook had authority to conclude the platinum purchase agreements on behalf of Canlab. However, in Estey J's view, the specific exchange he identified between Snook and McCullough was sufficient to clothe Cook with ostensible authority. This exchange had occurred in the context of a billing inquiry that had been made by Engelhard. (Canlab had been slow to pay Engelhard's invoices. Engelhard wanted them to settle up on a more timely basis.) Snook, a person with actual authority to authorize purchase transactions on behalf of Canlab, had referred McCullough's billing inquiry to Cook. By doing so, in Estey J's view, Snook cloaked Cook with ostensible authority from that point forward.

Chief Justice Laskin did not quite agree. On the applicable legal principles, he was completely in accord with the majority. But he had a different view on how those principles ought to be applied on these fact. Unlike Estey J, Laskin CJ did not accept that the conversation between Snook and McCullough constituted a holding out by Canlab (through Snook) of Cook's authority such that Cook's actions would thereafter bind Canlab. Laskin CJ did not accept that Snook had any "back-up" authority to make representations for Canlab. Snook, in other words, was not—in Chief Jusice Laskin's view—a person with actual authority either. It was only later, in Chief Justice Laskin's view, when the president of Engelhard called a more senior officer in Canlab's organization, that Canlab itself could be said to be implicated by Cook's scheme. Therefore, in his view, Canlab could not look to recover from Engelhard losses incurred from that moment forward.

Estey J was prepared to recognize that the requisite back-up authority could be provided by a rather lower-level employee. His reasoning for doing so reflects a policy of "devolution" that, in Estey J's view, is an essential part of commercial life, and so must be sanctioned by law:

> Persons, including corporate persons, dealing with a corporation must for practical reasons be able to deal in the ordinary course of trade with the personnel of that corporation secure in the knowledge that the law will match these practicalities with binding consequences. The law has long so provided. Both corporate sides to a contractual transaction must be able to make secure arrangements at the lowest level at which adequate business controls can operate. It is in the interest of both corporate and natural persons engaged in business that this be so.[17]

---

17   Ibid., at para. 51.

The *Canlab* decision did not involve a CBCA corporation. The incidents giving rise to the case all took place before the CBCA was enacted. However, although the corporate authority issue has been codified in the CBCA, the statutory tests involve the same sorts of qualitative judgments on which the *Canlab* decision turned.

One of the knottiest problems of all is the question when an agent without actual authority may be said to have been cloaked with ostensible authority—not by virtue of any express representation by the corporation—but rather in a more subtle way. Diplock J alluded to this subtler sort of representation when he referred to the corporation permitting "the agent to act in the management or conduct of the company's business" and so representing "to all persons dealing with such agent that he has authority to enter on behalf of the corporation into contracts of a kind *which an agent authorised to do acts of the kind which he is in fact permitted to do normally enters into in the ordinary course of such business.*"[18] The Supreme Court had occasion to consider this question of ostensible authority again in *Rockland Industries, Inc. v. Amerada Minerals Corporation of Canada Ltd.*[19]

Rockland involved a contract dispute between a vendor and a purchaser of a large quantity of sulphur. The vendor had failed to honour the contract, arguing that no valid agreement had ever been made because the employee who executed the contract on the vendor's behalf— that is, Kurtz—had no authority to do so. The court found as a fact that Kurtz did, in fact, originally have actual authority when negotiations first began with the purchaser. That authority was curtailed just two days before the contract in dispute was signed. The purchaser was not informed that Kurtz no longer had actual authority to bind his employer.

On these facts, the Supreme Court concluded that Kurtz—though lacking actual authority on the day the contract was made—nevertheless had ostensible authority. The contract was thus binding. The fact that Kurtz had previously had actual authority to contract was, for the court, the strongest possible indication that he had been represented by his employer as having continuing authority to act. In other words, once an agent is endowed with actual authority to conclude a contract, if that authority is later withdrawn, it is incumbent on the corporate employer to inform third parties with whom the agent has been dealing that the agent no longer possesses actual authority.

Statutory Codifications

The Dickerson committee recommended provisions that would, for the most part, codify the common law indoor management rule. The policy underlying the common law appears to reflect an attempt to determine which party—the corporation or the third-party contractor—is in the best position to protect itself from the actions of an employee who exceeds his authority. On that basis, decisions such as *Rockland* are surely sensible.

The relevant provisions of the CBCA are found in s. 18:

18(1) No corporation and no guarantor of an obligation of a corporation may assert against a person dealing with the corporation or against a person who acquired rights from the corporation that

---

18   Supra footnote 13 (emphasis added).

19   [1980] 2 SCR 2.

(a) the articles, by-laws and any unanimous shareholder agreement have not been complied with;

(b) the persons named in the most recent notice sent to the Director under section 106 or 113 are not the directors of the corporation;

(c) the place named in the most recent notice sent to the Director under section 19 is not the registered office of the corporation;

(d) a person held out by a corporation as a director, an officer or an agent of the corporation has not been duly appointed or has no authority to exercise the powers and perform the duties that are customary in the business of the corporation or usual for a director, officer or agent;

(e) a document issued by any director, officer or agent of a corporation with actual or usual authority to issue the document is not valid or not genuine; or

(f) a sale, lease or exchange of property referred to in subsection 189(3) was not authorized.

(2) Subsection (1) does not apply in respect of a person who has, or ought to have, knowledge of a situation described in that subsection by virtue of their relationship to the corporation.

With the exception of paragraph (1)(e), this provision primarily codifies the common law indoor management rule. The section does not, however, resolve a number of difficult factual issues. Paragraph (d), for example, states that a corporation may not deny the authority of a person "held out by a corporation." Accordingly, it will still be necessary to determine whether a representation or holding out that inculpates the corporation has or has not occurred. Moreover, later in that same paragraph, reference is made to the "duties that are customary in the business of the corporation or usual for a director, officer or agent." Once again, determining what is "customary" or "usual" in any given case will involve difficult judgments of fact.

However, it is perhaps paragraph (e) that is of the most interest. The Dickerson committee noted that common law authority existed for the proposition that the indoor management rule would not apply in cases of forgery.[20] "The justification for this view," they noted, "was that the outsider had better means of protecting himself against the loss."[21] They disagreed with this conclusion, and so the CBCA now adopts a different approach in cases of forgery by a corporate agent.

One such case involving the provision equivalent to CBCA s. 18(1)(e) found in the Ontario *Business Corporations Act* came before the Supreme Court of Canada in 1997.[22] The case involved a fraudulent debenture, issued in the name of a corporation (Artyork Limited) by B., one of the corporation's three officers and directors. The debenture purportedly secured a loan of $120,000 that had been made to Artyork Limited by the plaintiff. However, the $120,000 that the plaintiff had advanced had never reached the corporation. It had been appropriated by B. himself. At trial,[23] the court held that this

---

20   The case commonly cited as authority for this proposition is *Ruben v. Great Fingall Consolidated*, [1906] AC 439 (HL). See Dickerson et al., supra footnote 12, at para. 88.

21   Ibid., at para. 88.

22   *Martin v. Artyork Investments Ltd.*, [1997] 2 SCR 290.

23   *Martin v. Artyork Investments Ltd.*, [1991] OJ no. 1890 (QL) (Gen. Div.).

matter fell squarely within the words of ss. 19 (d) and (e) of the Ontario *Business Corporations Act* (provisions that are virtually identical to CBCA ss. 18(1)(d) and (e)). The trial court thus found in favour of the plaintiff, and so confirmed that the effect of s. 18(1)(e) was, as the Dickerson committee had intended, to overrule the forgery exception to the common law indoor management rule.

The Court of Appeal reversed the trial judge's decision.[24] For the Court of Appeal, the fact that the corporation had never actually received the funds in question was determinative of the matter. The debenture, on its face, only purported to secure amounts that had, in fact, been received by Artyork Limited. And Artyork Limited had never received any funds.

The problem with the Court of Appeal's reasoning is that it appears to render paragraph (e) largely ineffective. In any case where a corporate document is not "valid or genuine" that document will, by definition, misrepresent the true state of affairs. The Supreme Court of Canada reversed the Court of Appeal's decision[25] without providing much analysis. Indeed, the Supreme Court's judgment consisted of a single, curt paragraph, simply confirming that s. 19 applied to the issue, and restoring the judgment of the trial court.

SEALED DOCUMENTS AND
THE CORPORATE SEAL

At one level, a corporation's capacity to enter into contracts in the corporate name is one of the most straightforward aspects of corporate law. Yet the peculiar legal fiction that is the corporation also leads to some complications where practical expediency can result in logical paradoxes.

A corporation can act only through human agents, and so when a corporation enters into a contract it is the corporation's officers, directors, or other agents who must either put pen to paper, when the corporation enters into a written contract, or speak for the corporation, when it makes an oral agreement.

Historically, when a corporation entered into a written contract, the corporation's "signature" was the corporate seal, which would be duly affixed to the document by the officer or officers empowered by the corporation's bylaws to do so. The seal, as has often been observed, technically refers to the impression on paper made by the seal maker. In common parlance today, however, it is the seal maker that is often referred to as the corporate seal.

When the corporate seal was affixed to the document, the signing officers were typically attesting to the affixation. But it was the seal—and not the officers' signatures—that constituted the corporation's signature. A corporate seal was thus essential for every corporation.[26] A corporation could not enter into written contracts without one. One of the principal advantages of the seal, in the case of business corporations, was that

---

24 *Martin v. Artyork Investments Ltd.* (1995), 25 OR (3d) 705 (CA).

25 Supra footnote 22.

26 William Blackstone, *Commentaries on the Laws of England*, vol. 1 (published in a facsimile edition with an introduction by Stanley N. Katz) (Chicago: University of Chicago Press, 1979), at 475.

it was said to clearly delineate between actions taken on behalf of the corporation, and actions taken by the corporate officers or directors in their personal capacities.[27]

The necessity for the corporate seal, however, has in recent years been regarded as anachronistic.[28] Accordingly, many modern corporate statutes make adoption of a seal voluntary. The CBCA, for example, states:

> 23(1) A corporation may, but need not, adopt a corporate seal, and may change a corporate seal that is adopted.
>
> (2) A document executed on behalf of a corporation is not invalid merely because a corporate seal is not affixed to it.

However, although CBCA corporations are no longer required to adopt a corporate seal, it is probable that many, perhaps most, choose to do so for at least two reasons. First, for some time after the CBCA seal requirement was abolished, various commercial parties—including financial institutions—continued in accordance with longstanding practice to insist that corporations execute contracts under seal. Although with the passage of time the new rules have become more widely understood, given the modest cost associated with adopting a corporate seal (essentially, the cost of purchasing a seal maker from a legal stationer), many corporations may prefer to do so rather than incur the potential inconvenience of having to convince less-sophisticated or stubbornly conservative parties that such seals are no longer required.

More important, solicitors may counsel their corporate clients to adopt a seal so that they may, when required, effectively execute "specialties" or other instruments under seal. The use of a seal for this purpose raises special issues deserving of some brief explanation here.

Because the corporate seal traditionally constituted merely the corporation's signature, it seems reasonable enough to ask whether a corporate seal—without more—constitutes a seal for other purposes. Recall that, for historical reasons, Canadian contract law attaches especial significance to contracts made under seal. Such contracts need not be supported by consideration to be enforceable. Moreover, limitation periods for enforcement of "specialties" under seal may be longer in some jurisdictions.

The special status of sealed documents is thought to have been connected to the particular solemnity with which seals were originally affixed to documents—the delib-

---

27   See, e.g., William Robert Scott, *The Constitution and Finance of English, Scottish and Irish Joint-Stock Companies to 1720*, vol. 1 (Cambridge: Cambridge University Press, 1912), at 3.

28   The Dickerson committee, for example, referred to the corporate seal as "an anachronism carried over from a less literate age." See Dickerson et al., supra footnote 12, at para. 96. It is not entirely clear, however, that the use of corporate seals (as opposed to sealed documents executed by individuals) was in fact linked to the deficiencies of "a less literate age." Scott has suggested that the use of a common seal began at the time of the Anglo-Saxon or Anglo-Norman guilds, where it was used to give "visible expression ... to the corporate character [of guilds]," because "some method was required by which the act of the whole body could be identified." Scott, supra footnote 27, at 3. The Dickerson committee evidently considered recommending abolition of the corporate seal altogether, but ultimately determined that "[m]any people, bank managers in particular, are devoted to the seal and would be very upset if its use was prohibited," and so, after concluding that "[t]he law need not deprive people of such simple and harmless pleasures," ultimately resolved to recommend that corporate seals be permitted, though not made obligatory. Supra footnote 12, at para. 96.

erative process of melting sealing wax over parchment, then carefully pressing a signet into the still-warm mixture was presumed to focus the mind of the affixer.[29] Today, however, red wafer seals with self-adhesive backing may be easily unrolled from packets purchased cheaply from any stationery store. It seems unlikely that the act of affixing a seal like this involves any more considered thought than slapping a Post-it note onto a message board.

Although the supposed rationale for affording special status to sealed documents has long since been overtaken by time, the seal continues to have significance in Canadian contract law. The Supreme Court of Canada, for example, recently affirmed the so-called sealed contract rule—a principle evidently well known among many members of the practising real estate bar, but otherwise perhaps somewhat obscure. Simply put, the sealed contract rule operates as an exception to the ordinary rule of agency law under which a principal may both sue and be sued under a contract entered into on the principal's behalf by an agent acting within the scope of that agent's authority. Where the agent enters into a contract under seal, the principal can neither sue nor be sued under such a contract. In *Friedmann Equity Developments Inc. v. Final Note Ltd.*,[30] the Supreme Court of Canada not only affirmed the continuing validity of this old rule in general, but specifically affirmed its application to cases where the agent was a corporation.

The court was also called upon in *Friedmann* to consider the question whether, and under what circumstances, a contract to which a corporation had affixed its corporate seal can be considered, in the eyes of the law, a sealed document, noting that "[c]orporate seals have a different legal effect than the seal of an individual. The seal of a corporation, in many circumstances, is equivalent to the signature of a natural person … . Therefore, the affixing of a corporate seal may not in all cases be evidence of an intention to create a sealed instrument, within the meaning of the sealed contract rule."[31] One might note that, although this issue seems somewhat narrow when raised in the context of the sealed contract rule, it actually has a somewhat broader practical application. It is, for example, common for corporations to provide intercorporate guarantees in support of debt obligations incurred by affiliates. The consideration for the provision of such guarantees is often tenuous; and so lenders, and their counsel, might well insist that such guarantees be delivered under seal. Accordingly, determining what constitutes a sealed instrument when executed by a corporation can be critical.

The Supreme Court confirmed that a corporation is certainly

> capable of creating a sealed instrument and availing itself of the different legal consequences which flow from such an agreement. However, the attachment of its corporate seal, on its own, may not be sufficient to do so. Courts must examine the instrument itself and the circumstances surrounding its creation to determine whether the corporation intended to create a sealed instrument by affixing its corporate seal.[32]

---

29   This is the so-called cautionary effect. Some writers have, however, raised doubts about this explanation for the special status attached to sealed documents. See, e.g., G.H.L. Fridman, *The Law of Contract*, 4th ed. (Toronto: Carswell, 1999), at 128.

30   [2000] 1 SCR 842.

31   Ibid., at 867.

32   Ibid., at 868.

The court did not, however, note that the relevant incorporation legislation might also offer some guidance on the matter. For example, a now-repealed section of Ontario's *Business Corporations Act* specifically stated that a contract entered into by an individual that would require the individual's seal could validly be executed by a corporation under its corporate seal.[33] At least one general legal reference work has suggested (without citing any specific authorities) that this provision was "no more than declarative of the general law."[34]

The general law on this point is perhaps somewhat more ambiguous than this statement seems to suggest. The court in *Friedmann* noted that some statutes may render the intention of the corporation to create a sealed document irrelevant. Indeed, such a statute was said to be determinative in the *Friedmann* case.[35] Accordingly, although the court held that, at common law, the court's determination of the corporation's intention will govern, it was not necessary to formulate any bright-line test for determining whether a particular document executed by a corporation with its corporate seal was intended by the parties to be treated as a sealed document.

How might a corporation go about ensuring that its intention to execute a sealed document could not be mistaken? Would it be enough to recite the formalistic language "signed, sealed, and delivered"? Or is more required? Perhaps one might unambiguously signal an intention to execute a document under seal by affixing a "peel and stick" red wafer seal (such as those used by notaries) and then impressing the corporate seal on it. The corporate seal might even, for good measure, be impressed a second time elsewhere on the document as well, to suggest that one seal is intended to represent the corporation's "signature" while the other is meant to constitute the formal act of sealing. Doubtless, specific reference to the parties' express intention to create a sealed instrument— beyond the customary "signed, sealed, and delivered" language with which contracts are often concluded—would also be helpful.

Yet, such formalistic exercises seem almost to border on the superstitious. Perhaps what needs careful re-examination is the question whether any compelling reason remains for the law to attach any special significance to sealed documents, whether delivered by corporations or individuals.

---

33 RSO 1980, c. 54, s. 17(1) (since repealed).

34 6 *Canadian Encyclopedic Digest*, 3rd ed., title 36, s. 189.

35 The statutory provision in question was s. 13(1) of the *Land Registration Reform Act, 1984* (Ont.), SO 1984, c. 32 (now *Land Registration Reform Act*, RSO 1990, c. L.4). Section 13(1) essentially deems any land transfer document to have the same effect as a document under seal.

ULTRA VIRES

Introduction

The Supreme Court of Canada has described the concept of *ultra vires* as "a protection to no one and a trap for the unwary."[36] And, having so denounced the vile doctrine, the same court has been proud to pronounce it dead under the CBCA and most other Canadian corporate law statutes.[37] Indeed, many Canadian corporate lawyers would be pleased to dismiss *ultra vires* as an archaic and now wholly abandoned vestige of 19th century formalism. But, the doctrine continues to be relevant for certain "special act" or statutory corporations,[38] and even in the CBCA itself, some residual problems that have their roots in the traditional *ultra vires* concept remain.

Framing the Issue

Suppose that an imaginary entrepreneur, Harry Hops, has discovered a remarkable new recipe for brewing beer. He incorporates a corporation under the CBCA. The name of the corporation is "Nothing But Beer Brewing Inc."[39] The articles of the corporation include a restriction: "The business of the corporation is restricted to the brewing of beer." The corporation's slogan is: "We're the Beer Brewing Experts. That's all we do."

Harry is the sole director and sole officer of Nothing But Beer Brewing Inc. But there are a few other shareholders. Harry has managed, for example, to attract some beer brewing enthusiasts as investors.

Time passes and Harry decides that he would like to branch out. He thinks his corporation should begin manufacturing shoes. Nothing But Beer Brewing Inc. enters into a contract for the purchase of a large quantity of shoe leather. Harry is careful to emphasize to the vendor when signing the purchase contract that the leather must be suitable for making shoes because Nothing But Beer Brewing Inc. is buying the leather for that purpose.

The shoe market begins to go into freefall shortly after Harry signs this contract. He fears that he has made a terrible mistake. Even worse, his investors, who were only interested in investing in a beer brewing business, are shocked to discover that Harry is

---

36   *Communities Economic Development Fund v. Canadian Pickles Corp.*, [1991] 3 SCR 388, at 406. The doctrine has been denounced in similar terms by Gower and Davies: "a nuisance to the company and a trap for unwary third parties," Paul L. Davies, *Gower & Davies: Principles of Modern Company Law*, 7th ed. (London: Sweet & Maxwell, 2003), at 133; by the UK Cohen committee: "an illusory protection for the shareholders and yet may be a pitfall for third parties dealing with the company"; and by the Lawrence committee (citing Gower): "merely a trap for the unwary third party and a nuisance to the company itself," at para. 4.1.2.

37   *Continental Bank Leasing Corporation v. Her Majesty the Queen*, [1998] 2 SCR 298, at para. 57 and *Canadian Pickles*, supra footnote 36.

38   Indeed, note that the *Canadian Pickles* case itself involved such a statutory corporation and the Supreme Court did rule that this particular corporation had acted *ultra vires*. Supra footnote 36.

39   The specific choice of businesses in this example (beer brewing and shoe manufacturing) is borrowed from the Dickerson committee report, supra footnote 12, at para. 83.

using the corporation's funds to expand into shoe manufacturing. They remind Harry that the articles of the corporation specifically say that the corporation is not permitted to engage in any business other than beer brewing. Indeed, they insist, they placed great reliance on this constitutional restriction when they agreed to invest their money in the first place. The contract with the leather seller, they argue, was a contract that Nothing But Beer Brewing Inc. had no legal right to enter into. It was beyond the corporation's powers.

Should it be possible for Nothing But Beer Brewing Inc. to avoid its obligations under the shoe leather contract by claiming that such a contract was beyond the corporation's powers to enter into and must therefore be considered void? This is the issue raised by the corporate *ultra vires* doctrine.

Trap for the Unwary?

Students of Canadian constitutional law will be familiar with the Latin phrase *ultra* (beyond) *vires* (the powers). In the corporate law context, the term is used to refer to the principle that certain incorporated bodies have no power to perform actions (typically, involving entering into contracts with third parties) beyond those for which they were originally incorporated. Any attempt by such corporations to exceed their powers is a legal nullity.

Of course, the decision to engage in an *ultra vires* act would be a decision made for the corporation by the corporation's own officers or directors. However, the effect of the *ultra vires* rule was that an overreaching corporation could avoid what would otherwise be its contractual obligations. The obvious unfairness of this result was that innocent third parties contracting with the corporation would be forced to shoulder losses that had really arisen from the carelessness (or high handedness) of the corporation's own signing officers. It is for this reason that the Supreme Court of Canada—echoing the complaint of many academics and commentators—condemned the concept as a "trap for the unwary."

Protection to No One

The other half of the court's criticism—that the doctrine was a "protection to no one"—is also readily explained. Defenders of the *ultra vires* doctrine long insisted that allowing a company to exceed its stated objects would constitute a wrong to the shareholders (who might be presumed to have based their investment decision on the wording of the company's charter); to the company's creditors (whose assessment of the company's creditworthiness might, equally, have been based on a scrutiny of its charter); or to the public generally. It seems doubtful, however, that *ultra vires* really offers much (if any) protection to these constituents.

If the goal of *ultra vires* was to protect shareholders, for example, then one might have thought that shareholders—at least by unanimous consent—ought to be able to permit a corporation to deviate from its stated objects or ratify or adopt a contract that would otherwise be declared *ultra vires*. However, no such deviation, ratification, or adoption was permitted at common law.

The creditor-protection rationale does have a certain logic to it, but of a somewhat myopic sort. Creditors of a corporation, possessing fixed claims, do indeed have an interest in ensuring that the corporation does not materially alter its asset mix. A substantial change in a company's business could have the effect of increasing the volatility of the firm. Increased volatility (that is, increased riskiness) may well benefit the shareholders (who have the potential for unlimited gain, and limited liability to protect them from ruinous losses). However, an increase in the volatility of a corporation's assets is typically bad news for existing creditors, whose primary concern is their debtors' continued solvency, not its potential for earning spectacular future profits. Indeed, a standard feature of negotiated loan transactions and bond indentures is a provision prohibiting a borrowing company from substantially altering its asset mix without the lender's consent.

Although a rigid *ultra vires* rule might well protect a firm's *existing* creditors, if new obligations undertaken by a corporation could be voided by application of such a doctrine, then "new" creditors would actually be harmed. Perhaps such prospective creditors could protect themselves by carefully reviewing a corporation's charter before entering into contractual relations with it. However, it is the corporation itself that is in the best position to ensure that no offending transactions are undertaken. Accordingly, there seem to be few compelling reasons to, in effect, reward existing creditors for the improprieties of the corporation by prejudicing the interests of innocent "new" creditors.

As for the supposed "protection of the public" rationale, little needs to be said. If the corporation's own constituencies—its shareholders and its creditors in particular—cannot be seen clearly to benefit from the *ultra vires* doctrine, it is rather disingenuous to suggest that the principle is needed to protect the "public" at large. Surely third parties entering into contractual relations with corporations are the very members of the public with the most immediate interest in the conduct of a corporation's affairs; but it is their interests that are most likely to be harmed by rigid application of the *ultra vires* rule.

Despite the injustices to which *ultra vires* may lead, it is useful to recall just how central to corporate law this now largely ridiculed concept did once appear. In 1874, Seward Brice published a massive treatise on the doctrine of *ultra vires*, a treatise that had, by the time of the second edition in 1877, grown to over 900 pages.[40] In the preface to that second edition, Brice explains:

> Perhaps indeed the Law of Corporations may be considered for most practical purposes as in reality only the application and development of the Doctrine of Ultra Vires.[41]

Brice may perhaps be forgiven for an understandable desire to trumpet the importance of the subject in which he had obviously invested so much of his waking life. But if his remark is somewhat extravagant, it surely could not be dismissed, in 1877, as wholly ridiculous.

Moreover, *ultra vires* is appealing to the formalist. It is a very logical, internally consistent proposition: a legal person, whose existence is circumscribed by the legal documents that gave it life, cannot validly act in any manner not provided for in those documents. It is not, as early writers put it, a corporation at all for any purposes beyond those for which it was originally created.

---

40   Seward Brice, *A Treatise on the Doctrine of Ultra Vires*, 2nd ed. (London: Stevens & Haynes, 1877).

41   Ibid., at x.

However, with apologies to Emerson, "foolish consistency is the hobgoblin of the lawyer's mind." And, although the doctrine of *ultra vires* might seem quite consistent with the concept of an artificial legal person—even an indispensable part thereof—in fact, it appears that not all trading corporations were actually understood to have their operations delimited in this way.

Gower notes, for example, that before the year 1844, the doctrine of *ultra vires* had little practical application to commercial trading companies. This was so because, prior to 1844—the year the *Joint Stock Companies Act* was enacted—most companies were either created by royal charter (and thus were entities to which the limitations of *ultra vires* had never applied[42]) or were deed of settlement companies, which were not considered separate legal entities.[43] Companies could also, it is true, be created by special statute, but evidently the use of that device was very rare.

Companies created by royal charter—dubbed chartered companies or common law corporations—were not subject to any particular limits on their powers or capacity that would make application of the doctrine of *ultra vires* relevant, a fact mentioned by the Supreme Court of Canada in the brief survey of the history of *ultra vires* it offers in the *Canadian Pickles*[44] decision. If a common law corporation purported to exercise powers or pursue objects outside the scope of its charter, it could be sued for such wrongdoing; but the offending actions themselves were not rendered a nullity.

But should the same rule apply to corporations formed under the general incorporation statutes first promulgated in England in the mid-19th century? That was the question addressed by the House of Lords in the landmark case of *Ashbury Railway Carriage & Iron Co. v. Riche*.[45] The *Ashbury Railway* case involved a company incorporated under the *Companies Act, 1862*. The company's memorandum of association included an objects clause, as mandated by s. 8(3) of the 1862 Act. That clause itemized four types of businesses in which the company was permitted to engage: (1) making and selling railway equipment of various sorts; (2) carrying on business as mechanical engineers and general contractors; (3) trading in timber, coal, metals, and other materials; and (4) buying and selling materials on commission or as agents. The company sought to enter into a contract to build a railway line in Belgium. The company hired Riche to do construction work on this line. It was this construction contract that shareholders of the company argued was *ultra vires*.

The House of Lords found that the contract was, indeed, *ultra vires* the company. In so finding, the Law Lords drew a clear distinction between common law or chartered companies—which possessed "inherent common law rights"—and companies incorporated by memorandum of association, which had no such inherent rights. The latter sort of company was, accordingly, strictly confined to those objects set out in its memorandum.

What is sometimes overlooked or forgotten about the *Ashbury Railway* case is how closely focused the decision was on the specific wording of the corporate legislation

---

42   The traditional authority cited for this proposition is *Sutton's Hospital* (1612), 10 Co. Rep. 1a. Davies, supra footnote 36, at 130.

43   Davies, ibid., at 132.

44   Supra footnote 36.

45   (1875), 7 LRHL 653.

under which the company in question had been formed. In particular, the House of Lords drew particular attention to three sections of the 1862 Act that touched on the memorandum of association: s. 8 (which required every company to include an objects clause in its memorandum of association); s. 11 (which referred to the effect of the memorandum); and s. 12 (which permitted a company, following its incorporation, to amend some—but not all—of the provisions of its memorandum).

It is the effect, in particular, of s. 12 of the *Companies Act* that should not be overlooked. That section made it impossible for the shareholders of a company to effect any change to the objects of the corporation. Indeed, it does not seem unreasonable to suggest that the presence of this section was fundamental to the court's decision. Lord Cairns, for example, seems to ground his judgment on the wording of s. 12:

> [I]f there is a covenant that no change shall be made in the objects for which the company is established, I apprehend that that includes within it the engagement that no object shall be pursued by the company, or attempted to be attained by the company in practice, except an object which is mentioned in the memorandum of association.[46]

Indeed, Lord Cairns was careful to contrast the memorandum—of which the Act permitted few alterations—to the articles of association, the document regulating the internal governance of the corporation of which he declared the shareholders the "absolute masters."

The *Ashbury Railway* case is regularly cited as authority for the general proposition that the doctrine of *ultra vires* applies to (all) memorandum companies[47] and indeed such acts, according to commentators, would be void "even if ratified by all the members."[48] However, it appears that the existence of s. 12 of the 1862 Act—which is not a necessary feature of a statute providing for incorporation by memorandum—was pivotal to the House of Lords' reasoning.

Remarkably, the *Ashbury Railway* case is sometimes even cited as authority for the proposition that the objects of a corporation incorporated in a memorandum jurisdiction (such as the United Kingdom or Nova Scotia) cannot be varied, even with the unanimous consent of all the members. In other words, it is suggested that this restriction was somehow imposed by judicial fiat upon memorandum-style corporations. But of course no such general proposition arises from the decision. As indicated earlier, the conclusion that a company incorporated under the 1862 Act was prevented from changing its objects was no more than the court's paraphrasing of specific statutory language that governed the corporation involved in that case.

Many jurisdictions have subsequently promulgated memorandum-style incorporation statutes that do in fact permit the shareholders to amend the corporation's objects. The UK *Companies Act* now permits this. Thus, it is arguable that this particular aspect of *Ashbury Railway*—and possibly the case in its entirety—is now inapplicable to such statutes. But, the original case is so little read today in conjunction with the unique statute upon which it was based, that this critical limitation has been much unappreciated.

---

46   Ibid., at 670.

47   See, e.g., *Canadian Pickles*, supra footnote 36.

48   Davies, supra footnote 36, at 132.

In any event, the contractual underpinning of memorandum corporations was critical to the court's reasoning in *Ashbury Railway*—the *ultra vires* doctrine being said to
have no application to chartered companies. Recall from chapter 2, however, that there
are two other models of general incorporation statute in force in Canada today: letters
patent statutes (such as Prince Edward Island's *Companies Act*), and "New York-style"
registration statutes, such as the CBCA and the provincial statutes that followed it.
These historical distinctions become quite important to an understanding of the doctrine of *ultra vires*.

In *Bonanza Creek Gold Mining Co. v. R*,[49] the Privy Council held that the *ultra vires*
doctrine had no application to companies created by letters patent, except to the extent
that statutory restrictions (as opposed to restrictions in their constating documents) were
imposed on them. Such corporations would, in other words, have the powers of a natural
person unless those powers were circumscribed by statute.

The CBCA: The End of Ultra Vires?

What, then, of corporations incorporated under American-style statutes such as the
CBCA? How, if at all, does the doctrine of *ultra vires* apply to them? At first blush, the
answer seems straightforward. Recall that the Supreme Court of Canada has declared that
there is nothing left of *ultra vires* under the CBCA.[50] In the narrowest sense, the court's
pronouncement cannot be doubted. The Supreme Court itself acknowledged in *Canadian
Pickles* that the *ultra vires* doctrine could very well survive in the case of special act
corporations.[51] But entities created under the CBCA are not corporations of that kind. So,
ultra vires in its broadest sense is surely gone under the CBCA but, in some ways, its
legacy is not yet entirely forgotten.

The CBCA, and other modern Canadian corporate statutes, typically contain explicit
provisions denoting that the corporation has the powers of a natural person.[52] Those
provisions appear to be intended to codify the holding in *Bonanza Creek* and to provide
additional certainty to third parties dealing with corporations. But have they succeeded?
Has the CBCA, specifically, as the Dickerson committee evidently intended, and as the
Supreme Court has recently stated, abolished every vestige of the *ultra vires* doctrine?
The question proves less conclusive than one might expect.

To begin, the CBCA's declaration that a corporation is to have the capacity, rights,
powers, and privileges of a natural person is not absolute. The statement is qualified by
the phrase "subject to this Act."[53] And, although the old requirement that corporations
include specific corporate objects in their constating documents was abolished by the

---

49   [1916] 1 AC 566 (PC).

50   *Canadian Pickles*, supra footnote 36.

51   See also in this context, *Hazell v. Hammersmith and Fulham London Borough Council*, [1992] 2 AC 1
      (HL); and *Pacific National Investments Ltd. v. Victoria (City)*, [2000] 2 SCR 919.

52   See, e.g., s. 15(1) of the CBCA: "A corporation has the capacity and, subject to this Act, the rights,
      powers and privileges of a natural person."

53   Ibid.

CBCA, it is still possible for a CBCA corporation, if it so chooses, to specify in its articles of incorporation any restrictions to be place on the corporation's business.[54]

Anecdotal evidence suggests that it is highly unusual for corporations to elect to impose any such limiting restrictions on themselves. Nonetheless, what is the effect of such a restriction if incorporators do choose to include one?

Note that, unlike the statute under which the corporation in *Ashbury* had been created, the CBCA does not render a restriction in the articles immune from amendment by the shareholders. Furthermore, s. 16(2) of the CBCA provides that "[a] corporation shall not carry on any business or exercise any power that it is restricted by its articles from carrying on or exercising, nor shall the corporation exercise any of its powers in a manner contrary to its articles." However, this prohibition now seems to speak to matters of internal governance rather than to create a rule the breach of which is likely to affect third parties dealing with the corporation.

Certainly, the most odious effect of the *ultra vires* doctrine appears to have been removed, in the case of CBCA corporations, by s. 16(3). This section reads:

> No act of a corporation, including any transfer of property to or by a corporation is invalid by reason only that the act or transfer is contrary to its articles or this Act.

At first, this language seems to provide reassurance that *ultra vires* has been banned from the CBCA lexicon. But, the troublesome phrase "by reason *only*" hints that the matter may not yet be entirely free from doubt. More's the pity, because it appears that the general statutory features that were critical to the House of Lords' decision in *Ashbury* are noticeably absent from the CBCA. Thus, rather than abolishing *ultra vires* in toto—as the drafters of the CBCA claimed to have done—it appears that some vestige of the doctrine might inadvertently have been re-introduced through the inclusion of that short qualifying phrase in s. 16 as well as the further qualifying language in s. 18.

Paragraph 18(1)(a), for example, provides:

> 18(1) No corporation and no guarantor of an obligation of a corporation may assert against a person dealing with the corporation or against a person who acquired rights from the corporation that
>
> (a) the articles, by-laws and any unanimous shareholder agreement have not been complied with;

But, s. 18(2) provides an exception to s. 18(1) in cases that involve "a person who has, or ought to have, knowledge of a situation described in that subsection by virtue of their relationship to the corporation." Accordingly, where such a person acquires rights or property from a corporation in a transaction that is, for example, contrary to a restriction in that corporation's articles, would a subsequent transfer of those rights or property to a third person be voidable at the instance of the corporation or of a third party?

It may be useful to illustrate the potential uncertainty by introducing an (admittedly contrived) example. Assume that ABC Co. is a CBCA corporation. Its articles of incorporation provide that it is restricted from buying, *selling*, or holding real estate in the province of Ontario, and from borrowing money for any such purposes.

---

54   Ibid., s. 6(1)(f).

ABC Co., in flagrant breach of this restriction, borrows $1 million from a bank for the purpose of buying a property in Ontario. Shortly thereafter, sensing that the Ontario real estate market is overvalued, and wishing to maximize the value of the company, ABC Co. sells the property to one of its directors for $1.5 million. That director subsequently assigns his rights and obligations under the purchase contract to Assignee Ltd. Shortly before the deal is scheduled to close, the Ontario real estate market, in fact, experiences a rapid boom. The property is now worth over $3 million, and ABC Co., wishing to keep the property, refuses to complete the transaction with Assignee Ltd., arguing that the sale agreement was *ultra vires* ABC Co.'s corporate powers.

Now, if the *ultra vires* doctrine has truly been eliminated, ABC's argument will be to no avail; the contract is enforceable. However, under CBCA s. 18(2), ABC Co. can perhaps argue that the director to whom it sold knew, or ought to have known, that the sale was in breach of ABC Co.'s articles. Section 16(3) may not protect Assignee Ltd. in this case. ABC Co., after all, may argue that the transfer is not invalid *only* by virtue of its being *ultra vires*; it is, rather, invalid by virtue of its being an *ultra vires* transaction that, additionally, was initially settled with a corporate insider.

Section 15(1) may also not ensure that Assignee Ltd. is protected. This section is qualified by the language "subject to this Act," and s. 16(2) of the Act specifically says that a corporation may not carry on any business that it is restricted by its articles from carrying on. As a result, ABC Co. could, theoretically, be in the enviable position of being able to write free options for itself by engaging in such restricted transactions: if property values fall, it would choose to complete sales; if property values rise, it would claim that the transactions are *ultra vires* and promptly seek to avoid them.

Needless to say, if ABC Co. (or companies like it) were to attempt to engage in such devious activities, our courts could no doubt be relied on to thwart them, on a case-by-case basis. But this would involve litigation of the very sort that the drafters of the CBCA surely sought to eliminate. Thus, although the courts might well be trusted to sort such matters out, the point to be made here is only that the Act itself has not necessarily eliminated all uncertainty in the area.

CONCLUSION

A corporation can contract in its own name. The power to do so is, in no small measure, the very point of the corporation and lies at the heart of what Hansmann and Kraakman have identified as the "asset partitioning" function of the corporation.[55] Yet, although many modern Canadian corporate statutes declare a corporation to have the powers of a "natural person," a corporation is not, after all, able to contract in quite the same way as a human being. The signing mechanics that must be observed by a corporation are distinct. So they must be, since it is crucial to know when "the corporation" is truly acting. Indeed, all of the issues canvassed in this chapter remind us that it is important to establish when the corporation itself is acting. Even the troublesome doctrine of *ultra vires* is, at its core, a concept that relates to defining the true legal essence of a corporation that is purporting to enter into contractual relations.

---

55   Henry Hansmann and Reinier Kraakman, "The Essential Role of Organizational Law" (2000), 110 *Yale Law Journal* 387. See the discussion in chapter 1.

CHAPTER SEVEN

Piercing or Lifting the Corporate Veil

FRAMING THE ISSUE

The House of Lords' decision in *Salomon*[1] appeared to leave no doubt that the incorporated company was indeed—just as the English *Companies Act* had declared it to be[2]—a body corporate or corporation and, accordingly, a separate, distinct legal person. It is not inconceivable, perhaps, that later courts or legislators might have determined, in the interests of certainty or perhaps simply logical consistency, that no deviation from this principle ought ever to be permitted, no matter how harsh or unjust might be the result.

Suppose, for example, that a highly paid employee, as a condition of obtaining his well-remunerated position, were to agree to have special restrictions included in his employment contract. Specifically, in this contract, he expressly covenants never to compete with his employer. But this employee is cunning. Hoping to avoid the operation of this non-competition clause, he incorporates a business corporation—a corporation of which he is the sole shareholder, director, and officer. This new corporation, a separate legal entity after all, that has not signed any such inconvenient non-compete covenant, then enters into aggressive competition with the original employer.

We might perhaps imagine a world in which the courts felt obliged to apply the doctrine of *Salomon* inflexibly, and so hold that the disloyal but shrewd employee's covenant had not technically been breached. In such a world, the corporation—although under the complete control of the restricted employee—would be permitted to compete unabashedly with its sole shareholder's employer. This seems a rather hard result: a triumph of legal form over economic substance. But perhaps such strong medicine is just what business people need. Just as *Salomon's* case reminded creditors to be on their guard when dealing with corporate borrowers, so our (hypothetical) non-competition clause judgment could stand as a powerful warning to employers and solicitors. In future, they must take care to ensure that such covenants are drafted explicitly to catch corporate subterfuge of this sort.

---

1   [1897] AC 22 (HL). See the discussion of this case, and some of its implications, in chapter 3.

2   *The Companies Act, 1862,* 25 & 26 Vict., c. 89, s. 18.

Or, again, suppose that a holder of a certain unique piece of real estate, having entered into a binding agreement to sell the property to a buyer, experiences a sudden change of heart. He resolves to keep the property, and so dishonour the sale contract. He knows he will be found liable for breach of contract. He has steeled himself to the possibility that he will have to pay damages. But he wants to be sure that the property itself remains in his hands. To avoid any possible court order of specific enforcement of the contract, he quietly conveys the property to a corporation of which he is the sole shareholder, officer, and director. This conveyance is completed just days before the originally agreed sale transaction had been scheduled to close. If the corporation is to be treated as a truly separate legal person, a claim for specific performance of the original sale contract might appear—according to *Salomon*—to be quite impossible. The corporation itself—that is, the current owner of the disputed property—was never, after all, a party to the original sale contract sought to be enforced.

As the reader has no doubt suspected, the facts described in these examples are based (albeit rather loosely) on disputes that have come before the courts. However, in both of these cases, the real-world courts, in fact, were not prepared to let a rigid application of *Salomon* stand in the way of a just result. They chose, instead, to disregard or, at the least, to look behind the corporate form.

Nor are these isolated examples. Numerous courts have also been prepared to disregard the apparent rigidity of the separate legal entity doctrine, notwithstanding the fact that *Salomon's* case is said to continue to be good law and, indeed, is said to form the very cornerstone of Anglo-Canadian corporate law.

Thus, we see that although courts might have chosen, everywhere and always, to adhere to a strict formalistic interpretation of *Salomon* or, alternatively, might have chosen, more radically, to overrule *Salomon* altogether, they have, in practice, followed neither of these extreme paths. Instead, various judicial "exceptions" to the *Salomon* doctrine have been admitted. But the essential soundness of the doctrine itself has been consistently reaffirmed.

On those occasions (still rare) where courts have elected to relax the strictness of *Salomon*, they have come to refer to their decisions as instances in which they have decided to "pierce" or "lift" the veil of corporate personality. As Lord Denning put it in a famous (and oft critiqued) statement in *Littlewoods Mail Order Stores v. IRC*:[3]

> The doctrine laid down in *Salomon v. Salomon & Co.* ... has to be watched very carefully. It has often been supposed to cast a veil over the personality of a limited company through which the courts cannot see. But that is not true. The courts can and often do draw aside the veil. They can, and often do, pull off the mask. They look to see what really lies behind. The legislature has shown the way with group accounts[4] and the rest. And the courts should follow suit.

---

3   [1969] 1 WLR 1241, at 1254 (CA).

4   Lord Denning's reference is presumably to the use of consolidated financial statements. Accounting rules require a corporation that has subsidiaries to consolidate the financial results of these subsidiaries when preparing its financial statements. In other words, a parent company's balance sheet, for example, would include all of the assets and all of the liabilities (other than intercorporate liabilities) of its subsidiary companies. Thus, for accounting purposes, all of the separate companies in a corporate group are treated very much as though they are, collectively, a single corporation.

What, precisely, does it mean for a court to say that it has lifted or pierced the corporate veil? In certain cases, it means that courts have considered it appropriate to impose personal liability on a corporation's shareholders. In others, it means that courts have conferred on a corporation's shareholders some legal right or interest that—strictly speaking—belongs to the corporate entity itself. In still other instances, courts have decided to treat two or more otherwise separate (but somehow related) corporations just as though they were one aggregate or single enterprise.

Lord Denning's reference in *Littlewoods* to drawing aside the "corporate veil" (and variants of this expression such as "lifting" or "piercing" the corporate veil) had already become, many years before the *Littlewoods* case, conventional metaphors used by courts to describe decisions in which the separateness of the corporate entity was judicially disregarded. The now common phrase, "piercing the corporate veil," appears to be of American origin. Frederick Powell credited Professor Maurice Wormser with coining this metaphor.[5] The phrase, "Piercing the Veil of Corporate Entity" is, in fact, the title of an article by Professor Wormser that appeared in the *Columbia Law Review* in 1912,[6] an article in which the author also used the expression *"lift* the veil."[7]

But although Wormser may have introduced the phrase *"piercing* the veil" to the corporate legal lexicon, the veil metaphor itself appears to have pre-dated Wormser's paper by well over half a century. Wormser quotes an American judicial decision from 1839 in which the judge remarked that "courts have drawn aside the veil and looked at the character of the individual corporators."[8] The corporate veil metaphor may have gained currency in English jurisprudence following the publication of the first edition of Gower's influential text, *The Principles of Modern Company Law*,[9] although Gower noted in a footnote that "etymologically 'mask' might be [a better metaphor] since 'persona' is derived from the name for a mask worn by a player in the Greek theatre."[10]

There has been some esoteric debate about whether there is (or ought to be) a distinction drawn between use of the phrases "pierce the veil," on the one hand, and "lift the veil," on the other. Thus, for example, in *Atlas Maritime Co. SA v. Avalon Maritime Ltd. (No. 1)*,[11] Staughton LJ distinguishes between use of these two phrases. The phrase "piercing" the corporate veil, he "would reserve for treating the rights or liabilities or activities of a company as the rights or liabilities or activities of its shareholders."[12] As for the phrase, "lifting the corporate veil," that, in

---

5   Frederick J. Powell, *Parent and Subsidiary Corporations: Liability of a Parent Corporation for the Obligations of Its Subsidiary* (Chicago: Callaghan and Company, 1931), at 3, note 2.

6   (1912), 12 *Columbia Law Review* 496. The article was later reproduced as a chapter in Wormser's book, *Disregard of the Corporate Fiction and Allied Corporation Problems* (New York: Baker, Voorhis and Company, 1929), at 42.

7   Ibid., at 499 (emphasis added).

8   Ibid., at 498.

9   (London: Stevens & Sons Limited, 1954), at 197.

10   Ibid., at 197, note 2.

11   [1991] 4 All ER 769, at 779 (CA).

12   Ibid., at 779.

his view, "should mean to have regard to the shareholding in a company for some legal purpose."[13]

S. Ottonlenghi has attempted to craft an even more ambitious fourfold categorization, pursuant to which, depending on the facts, courts might be said to be "peeping behind," "penetrating," "extending," or "ignoring" the corporate veil.[14] One Canadian scholar has suggested that the veil metaphor may have sexist—even violent—overtones.[15]

Whatever its etymology, or indeed propriety, the corporate veil metaphor continues to be widely invoked by courts in Canada, the United States, and the United Kingdom in those cases contemplating judicial disregard of the separateness of the corporate entity. Still, the guiding principles underlying the cases in which courts have decided to "lift," "pierce," or "draw aside" the corporate veil remain elusive, as the following discussion illustrates.

JUDICIAL RELUCTANCE TO PIERCE THE CORPORATE VEIL

The most important preliminary point to be made about cases in which courts decide to "lift the corporate veil" is that they appear to be quite uncommon—at least in Canada and in the United Kingdom.[16] This is not surprising.

---

13   Ibid.

14   S. Ottonlenghi, "From Peeping Behind the Corporate Veil to Ignoring It Completely" (1990), 53 *Modern Law Review* 338.

15   See, e.g., Karen Busby, "The Maleness of Legal Language" (1989), 18 *Manitoba Law Journal* 191, at 204. The "veil," on this reading, is assumed to be a women's garment. However, the term "veil" also means curtain, and it appears that when Wormser originally coined the phrase, he had in mind the concept as it was used in the 1839 case he quoted in his article. That quotation—referring to the "drawing aside" of the veil—seems rather clearly to indicate a curtain, a use, it must be said, that is also more consistent with the earliest uses of phrases such as "behind" or "beyond" the veil. (See *Oxford English Dictionary*, s.v. "veil.") It is also intriguing to note that Nathaniel Hawthorne's haunting and widely read story, "The Minister's Black Veil," had been written in 1836. The story was included in the collection *Twice-Told Tales*, published in 1837. For a more recent reprint, see Nathaniel Hawthorne, "The Minister's Black Veil" in *Twice-Told Tales*, introduction by Roy Harvey Pearce (New York: Dutton, 1967), at 23. However, word use is malleable. Note, for example, a Canadian corporate law casebook in which the veil metaphor is expressly linked to a woman's garment: "Consider any one of a thousand women. Assume she is wearing a veil or a mask over her face. Rip it off. Whose face do you see?" Earl E. Palmer and Bruce L. Welling, *Canadian Company Law: Cases, Notes and Materials*, 3rd ed. (Toronto: Butterworths, 1986), at 3-26. One appreciates that speculating about a writer's intention is not fully responsive to Prof. Busby's point; but, such Derridian discussions of language and the law—although interesting and illuminating—are beyond the scope of this text.

16   It is occasionally suggested that American courts may be somewhat more willing to lift the corporate veil. The late L.C.B. Gower, a great English corporate law scholar, made such an assertion some years ago: "The case of *Salomon v. A. Salomon and Co.* ... laid down the corporate entity principle with such rigor that English judges have found much greater difficulty than their American colleagues in piercing the corporate veil when public policy so demands." L.C.B. Gower, "Some Contrasts Between British and American Corporate Law" (1956), 69 *Harvard Law Review* 1369, at 1379. This "observation" is perhaps based more on anecdotal than empirical evidence. In this regard, it is especially useful to note the empirical study of corporate veil piercing undertaken in the United States by Robert B. Thompson,

The foundational common law authority for the separate legal entity doctrine remains the House of Lords' decision in *Salomon*,[17] a case that has been described as "probably the most cited company law case in the jurisdictions of the Commonwealth."[18]

That case itself was decided upon facts that, at least in the view of some,[19] suggested a potentially egregious abuse by a shareholder of the corporate form to defeat the interests of his unsecured business creditors.[20] *Salomon*, in other words, was not a case in which principles of ordinary decency, natural justice, or common sense necessarily compelled the court to craft an otherwise legally tenuous solution in the interests of relieving the plight of an especially sympathetic litigant.[21] On the contrary, the House of Lords—or at any rate some members of the panel—appeared to conceive the matter as one in which the law respecting the separateness of the corporate entity must be applied rigidly, even, perhaps, if that rigid application might result in something of an *injustice* in the particular case.[22]

Thus, *Salomon* cannot be easily rationalized or read down as simply a hard case that made bad law in an effort to do justice in the particular circumstances.[23] And any residual doubts about the validity of the outcome of *Salomon's* case have surely been put to rest by the more than one hundred years of corporate law jurisprudence in which it has been regularly and repeatedly followed.

"Piercing the Corporate Veil: An Empirical Study" (1991), 76 *Cornell Law Review* 1036. Thompson discovered, among other things, that, perhaps surprisingly, "courts pierce less often in tort than in contract contexts, and a piercing decision is not less but more likely when the shareholder behind the veil is an individual rather than another corporation." Ibid., at 1038.

17 Supra footnote 1.

18 Charles E.F. Rickett and Ross B. Grantham, eds., *Corporate Personality in the 20th Century* (Oxford: Hart Publishing, 1998), at 1.

19 Including, as it will be recalled from chapter 3, judges in the English Court of Appeal ruling on the *Salomon* case itself.

20 Many of those supportive of the *Salomon* decision would, needless to say, take issue with this characterization of the facts in that case. One notes, for example, that Bonham and Soberman, in their synopsis of the facts indicate that the failure of Mr. Salomon's company was due to "a series of misfortunes not involving any misconduct on the part of Salomon," and that "[i]n fact Salomon pledged his debentures to raise further money in an effort to save the business." See David H. Bonham and Daniel A. Soberman, "The Nature of Corporate Personality," in J.S. Ziegel, ed., *Studies in Canadian Company Law* (Toronto: Butterworths, 1967), 1, at 14.

21 Of course, as discussed in chapter 3, Lord Macnaghten did clearly have sympathy for Aron Salomon, whom, he felt, had been "dealt with somewhat hardly." Supra footnote 1, at 47.

22 See, for example, the speech of Lord Herschell, supra footnote 1, at 47: "The issue of debentures to the vendor of a business as part of the price is certainly open to great abuse, and has often worked grave mischief. It may well be that some check should be placed upon the practice. ... But as the law at present stands, there is certainly nothing unlawful in the creation of such debentures." See also the speech of Lord Davey, ibid., at 54: "My Lords, it is possible, and (I think) probable, that the conclusion to which I feel constrained to come in this case may not have been contemplated by the Legislature, and may be due to some defect in the machinery of the Act."

23 As Seaton JA has aptly put it, "If it were possible to ignore the principles of corporate entity when a judge thought it unfair not to do so, *Salomon's* case would have afforded a good example for the application of that approach." *B.G. Preeco I (Pacific Coast) Ltd. v. Bon Street Holdings Ltd.* (1989), 60 DLR (4th) 30, at 37 (BCCA).

The robustness of the separate legal entity principle—already fully developed in the judgments rendered in *Salomon* itself—has become so firmly entrenched in Anglo-Canadian law and Anglo-Canadian commercial practice that it is only with the greatest reluctance that courts are prepared, on infrequent occasions, to depart from that principle by purporting to pierce the corporate veil. Moreover, as Professor Sealy has suggested,[24] whatever mild enthusiasm courts may have had to pierce the corporate veil in the not so distant past, that enthusiasm has abated considerably since the 1970s. Readers of corporate law reports are more likely today to encounter judicial explanations as to why courts ought to be generally unwilling to disregard the separateness of the corporate entity than they are to find actual examples of the corporate veil being successfully pierced. Indeed, even in cases where it certainly appears, for all practical purposes, that the courts have purposefully lifted the corporate veil, it is not unusual for the courts to deny that they have done any such thing.

Perhaps the best example of such judicial legerdemain may be found in the Supreme Court of Canada's decision in *Kosmopolous v. Constitution Insurance Co.*[25] To understand *Kosmopolous*, a little background is necessary. *Kosmopolous* involved the plight of a small, sole-shareholder business corporation, and the sole shareholder himself who became embroiled in a dispute with an insurance company.

(Parenthetically, note that challenges to the separate legal entity principle, especially in the case of the smallest private corporations, are not infrequently encountered in the insurance context.[26] Insurers, on occasion, have attempted to deny coverage under policies by arguing that a corporation and its individual controller (its "directing mind and will") are really one and the same person. Such was the basis for the dispute in *Lee v. Lee's Air Farming Ltd.*,[27] discussed in chapter 3. In that case, the insurer attempted to argue, unsuccessfully, that the deceased shareholder and the corporation that at once employed him and was controlled by him, ought to be treated as the same legal person. In other cases, however, insurers have attempted to deny coverage by arguing the contrary proposition. That is, they have sought to rely on the principle that a corporate business entity is a legal person separate and distinct from the human being who manages the business. They thus contend that only the corporation, not its shareholders, is entitled to obtain, and to receive benefits under, an insurance policy relating to the corporation's assets. *Kosmopolous* is an example of the latter sort of case.)

---

24   L.S. Sealy, *Cases and Materials in Company Law*, 7th ed. (London: Butterworths, 2001), at 58.

25   [1987] 1 SCR 2.

26   Although I refer here to traditional insurance products, recent media reports have indicated a related issue in the context of credit derivatives. A credit derivative is, in essence, a financial contract by which one party agrees to assume the risk of loan default on the part of a corporate borrower. Recent reports indicate that certain credit derivatives entered into by a major financial institution were, inadvertently, made in the name of the wrong corporate borrower. When the borrower defaulted, and the counterparty under the credit derivative sought payment from the financial institution, the institution balked on the basis that the wrong corporate entity was named in the instrument. (See "Credit Derivatives: What's in a Name?" *The Economist*, May 25, 2002, at 75.)

27   [1961] AC 12 (PC).

An important early example of a dispute of this type led to the House of Lords' 1925 judgment in *Macaura v. Northern Assurance Co. Ltd.*[28] This decision laid much of the legal groundwork on this matter and was for many years among the most significant authorities in the development of both Anglo-Canadian corporate and insurance law. In *Macaura*, fire had destroyed the assets of a corporation (a large quantity of timber). An individual who was the sole shareholder and principal creditor of the corporation was held to have no insurable interest in those corporate assets.

The *Macaura* decision was a fairly straightforward application of fundamental corporate law doctrine. Because no shareholder can be said to have a property interest in assets owned by a corporation, he or she ought likewise to have no insurable interest in those assets.[29] As Lord Wrenbury rather succinctly put it, "the corporator, even if he holds all the shares is not the corporation, and ... neither he nor any creditor of the company has any property legal or equitable in the assets of the corporation."[30]

It was precisely this issue that the Supreme Court of Canada was called upon in 1987 to revisit in *Kosmopolous*.[31] *Kosmopolous* involved an especially compelling set of facts. The plaintiff was the sole shareholder and sole director of a corporation that operated a leather goods store in Toronto, a business he had originally carried on (though only for a matter of months) as a sole proprietorship.

After forming a corporation to operate the business, the plaintiff, Mr. Kosmopolous, attempted to transfer the lease for the store premises to this new corporation. The lessor would not consent to such an assignment, so the plaintiff continued to hold the lease in his own name. The store had been operated for some five years on this basis when disaster struck. A fire in an adjacent building damaged the store and its merchandise.

The plaintiff's insurance policy, from the time the policy had first been obtained, had been held in the name of "Andreas Kosmopolous O/A [that is, operating as] Spring Leather Goods." But, in fact, at the time of the fire, the store was no longer being operated by the plaintiff in his personal capacity; it was being operated by the plaintiff's corporation, Kosmopolous Leather Goods Limited. The corporate name had never appeared on the insurance policy, despite the fact that "the insurance agency was well aware ... that the business was being carried on by an incorporated company."[32]

The insurers denied coverage. The damaged assets were owned by the corporation, they observed, and thus the individual named insured—according to the principles laid down so clearly in *Macaura*—had no insurable interest in them.

---

28   [1925] AC 619 (HL).

29   The traditional threefold rationale for requiring that a person purchasing insurance have an "insurable interest" was explained by Wilson J in *Kosmopolous*, supra footnote 25, at para. 31: "(1) the policy against wagering under the guise of insurance; (2) the policy favouring limitation of indemnity; and (3) the policy to prevent temptation to destroy the insured property."

30   Supra footnote 28, at 633.

31   *Macaura* had been referred to in at least two earlier Supreme Court of Canada cases, but in neither of those cases was the court required to confront squarely the insurable interest issue. See *Guarantee Co. of North America et al. v. Aqua-Land Exploration Ltd.*, [1966] SCR 133 and *Wandlyn Motels Ltd. v. Commerce General Ins. Co. et al.*, [1970] SCR 992.

32   Supra footnote 25, at 7.

When the matter came before the Supreme Court of Canada, counsel for Mr. Kosmopolous, the plaintiff, argued that the *Macaura* principle ought not to be applied. The court, he argued, should disregard the corporate entity entirely, "lift the corporate veil," and simply treat the corporation's business assets as though they belonged to the plaintiff in his individual capacity.

The court, however, was quite unwilling—so it said—to lift the corporate veil. But, Wilson J's consideration of this aspect of the plaintiff's arguments has often been recited and reproduced in later cases. In particular, much has been made of the following language that appears in her judgment:

> I have no doubt that theoretically the veil could be lifted in this case to do justice ... . But a number of factors lead me to think it would be unwise to do so.[33]

By refusing to lift the corporate veil, Wilson J expressly confirmed that the plaintiff, as sole shareholder of a corporate entity, "has neither a legal nor an equitable interest in the assets of the company."[34] Accordingly, if *Macaura* were the law in Ontario, the province in which the dispute arose, the plaintiff's claim would fail.

Wilson J went on, however, to reject the rigidity of the *Macaura* formulation.[35] She found (echoing language from the 1806 decision in *Lucena v. Craufurd et al.*)[36] that the individual plaintiff "had a moral certainty of advantage or benefit from those assets but for the fire. He had, therefore, an insurable interest in them."[37]

Thus, shareholder and corporation were distinct legal persons. Nevertheless, although the shareholder had no *ownership* interest in the corporation's assets, as a matter of insurance law, he could still be said to have an *insurable* interest in them. The corporate veil, in other words, was to be left quite unruffled, but Mr. Kosmopolous's claim would succeed all the same.

This rather dexterous bit of legal reasoning has led some to suggest that the *Kosmopolous* decision represents a triumph of form over substance, and may illustrate an abiding reluctance on the part of courts to admit that they are lifting the corporate veil,[38] a reluctance that bears witness to the near reverence with which *Salomon* continues to be regarded.

---

33   Ibid., at 11.

34   Ibid., at 13.

35   Wilson J expressly indicates that to the extent that the definition of insurable interest as adopted in *Kosmopolous* differs from that found in those earlier cases, "I respectfully suggest that [those earlier cases] should not be followed." Ibid., at 30. In so doing, it is interesting to note that she carefully scrutinizes the circumstances involved in the *Macaura* decision itself, a decision that she characterizes as "a rather odd case" (at 20). She notes, ibid., citing Robert Keeton, that the case began as an arbitration in which fraud had been alleged against the insured, and so raises the possibility that, although the fraud allegation could not be entirely made out, the court may have had some reason to find against the plaintiff and was so motivated to interpret the law of insurable interest narrowly.

36   (1806), 127 ER 630, at 643 (HL).

37   Supra footnote 25, at 30.

38   Harry Glasbeek, Comments on "The Limits of Limited Liability," in *The Future of Corporation Law: Issues and Perspectives*, Papers Presented at the Queen's Annual Business Law Symposium 1997 (Toronto: Carswell, 1999), 30, at 31, note 4.

A more recent example of similar judicial inclination (or disinclination) may be found in the Ontario Court of Appeal's 1999 decision in *Tony and Jim's Holdings Ltd. v. Silva*.[39] The nominal plaintiff[40] leased premises to a corporation of which the defendant, Silva, was evidently the "president and directing mind" although he was not, in fact, a shareholder. Fire broke out in the leased premises, allegedly the result of Silva's negligence.

Owing to an implied covenant on the part of the landlord to insure the leased property, the landlord was barred from pursuing an action against the corporate tenant for damage to the leased premises caused by this fire. However, the plaintiff reasoned that nothing stood in the way of pursuing a claim against the individual defendant personally. That is precisely what the plaintiff did.

The defendant countered by arguing that the corporate veil ought to be lifted. He and the corporate tenant of which he was the "directing mind" should, he said, be treated as one and the same person for purposes of the leasing agreement. If he and the corporation were treated as one person, then he (the individual) would benefit from the same immunity from the landlord's claim that the corporation enjoyed.

The Court of Appeal said that there was no "valid juristic reason"[41] to lift the corporate veil, and thus refused to do so. But that was not the end of the story. The court went on to uphold the trial judge's decision to dismiss the plaintiff's claim after all. The court reasoned that there was "such an identity of interest between Silva and the tenant [that is, the corporation] with respect to the landlord's implied covenant to insure as to justify extending the benefit to both."[42] In other words, just as in *Kosmopolous*, the court declined to characterize its decision as an exercise in corporate veil lifting, preferring, in this case, to base its conclusion on contractual interpretation.

Explicit "veil piercing" by the courts, then, is rare. Even when courts appear, in fact, to be lifting the corporate veil, they often prefer to insist that they have come to their decision on some other basis that fully respects the integrity of the corporation as a separate legal entity. However, as the discussion below indicates, there are also some cases—including very recent Canadian cases—in which the courts have been prepared to expressly disregard the separateness of the corporate personality. These cases are deserving of careful study because they raise and perhaps answer critical questions about the legal nature of the corporation. There have also been a number of recent reiterations of the wariness with which courts approach requests by litigants to lift the corporate veil, and a small sample of those cases also punctuates the following discussion.

---

39   (1999), 43 OR (3d) 633 (CA).

40   The claim was, in fact, being pursued by the plaintiff corporation's insurance company, which had previously paid a claim to the plaintiff, and thereupon exercised a right of subrogation so as to seek recovery against the defendant.

41   Supra footnote 39, at para. 14.

42   Ibid.

CLASSIFYING THE "VEIL" CASES

As Wilson J's reasoning in *Kosmopolous* illustrates, the prospect of lifting the corporate veil poses a particular jurisprudential challenge. For some, the importance of the separate legal entity principle is so fundamental that any departure from it is flatly unacceptable,[43] and generally unnecessary.[44] To others, it seems sensible that the courts should exercise a fairly flexible power to lift the corporate veil, "especially," as Professor Sealy puts it, "when it enables the court to counter fraud, oppression or sharp practice or to condone informality in the affairs of small companies."[45]

Commentators and judges have searched diligently (but largely in vain) to find some clear and abiding principle that reconciles those cases in which the courts have lifted the corporate veil, not only with other such decisions rendered in the past, but also with the more general principles underlying the separate legal entity doctrine from which they necessarily depart. The utility of this exercise, it must fairly be said, has been doubted by some.[46]

Nevertheless, law and economics scholars, for example, have contended that the secret to the veil-piercing cases is to be found in the court's implicit promotion of economic efficiency: the veil will be pierced, on this view, in those very instances where the economic justification for limited liability is least compelling. Thus, Easterbrook and Fischel suggest that veil-piercing decisions, in the United States at any rate,

> may be understood, at least roughly, as attempts to balance the benefits of limited liability against its costs. Courts are more likely to allow creditors to reach the assets of shareholders where limited liability provides minimal gains from improved liquidity and diversification, while creating a high probability that a firm will engage in a socially excessive level of risk taking.[47]

---

43   See, e.g., Bruce L. Welling, *Corporate Law in Canada: The Governing Principles*, 2nd ed. (Toronto: Butterworths, 1991), at 122: "[Twentieth century judges] have claimed authority to ignore [corporate personality] on numerous occasions. I can't see where they get such power; I deny that they have it. Their talk about 'the corporate veil' is pure mystification and leads the analysis astray."

44   It has been suggested that in many of the cases in which the courts have based their conclusions on a decision to pierce the corporate veil the same outcome could have been achieved using other traditional doctrinal tools. See, e.g., Welling, ibid., at 135; and Jason W. Neyers, "Canadian Corporate Law: Veil-Piercing and the Private Law Model" (2000), 50 *University of Toronto Law Journal* 173, at 217ff. See also, in this regard, *B.G. Preeco I (Pacific Coast) Ltd. v. Bon Street Holdings Ltd.*, supra footnote 23, at 37: "A number of [veil lifting] cases ... turn on particular legislation and do not assist this argument. Some of the cases referred to by counsel used corporate veil language but in truth seem to have been based on holding out, estoppel or agency."

45   Sealy, supra footnote 24, at 58.

46   See, e.g., Brian Cheffins, *Company Law: Theory, Structure and Operation* (Oxford: Clarendon Press, 1997), at 333-34:

> Commentators have for many years struggled to reconcile the English cases dealing with [lifting the veil]. Perhaps because of this, judges have been criticized for using vague standards ... rather than identifying precisely the factors which will cause a court to disregard corporate personality. It may be, however, that such pleas are futile. The factual variations which can arise in lifting the veil cases are substantial. Correspondingly, it is questionable whether the judiciary will ever be able to formulate detailed guidelines which account for all relevant considerations. [Footnotes omitted.]

47   Frank Easterbrook and Daniel Fischel, *Economic Structure of Corporate Law* (Cambridge, MA: Harvard University Press, 1991), at 55. See also Richard A. Posner, *Economic Analysis of Law*, 6th ed. (New York: Aspen Publishers, 2003), at 423ff.

Less ambitious attempts to rationalize the veil-piercing cases range from short pro-nouncements to detailed taxonomies. An example of the former may be found in an early edition of Gower's *Principles of Modern Company Law*. The author there suggested that the veil might be lifted where strict adherence to the *Salomon* principle would lead to a result "too flagrantly opposed to justice, convenience or the interests of the Revenue."[48] As for more ambitious taxonomies, some of these are mentioned below.

It might be useful to begin the classification exercise with this general observation. There are—at the broadest level—two different classes of cases in which courts declare that they are being invited or urged to "lift the corporate veil":

- First, there are those in which a corporation's shareholders, either directly or indi-rectly (that is, through their interests in related corporations), seek some benefit or right that would be denied them if the corporate entity were respected. I will call these sorts of cases "shareholder or enterprise benefit" cases.
- Second, there are those in which some third party seeks to compel the corporation's shareholders, either directly or indirectly (that is, through their interests in related corpora-tions), to satisfy some debt or other obligation that, strictly speaking, is an obligation only of the corporation. These are often called "shareholder or enterprise liability" cases.

The policy considerations engaged by these two, distinct types of "veil-piercing" cases differ. It appears that it is only in cases of the second sort (that is, the shareholder or enterprise liability cases) that veil piercing threatens the fundamental "asset partitioning"[49] function performed by the corporation. In cases of the first type, where the consequence of piercing the veil is to confer some shareholder or enterprise benefit, the usefulness of the corporation as an economic institution is not compromised. At most, judgments that ignore the corporate form when doing so benefits the corporation or its controllers might offend some concept of legal symmetry. Such judgments might thereby run afoul of broad notions of fairness too, for, as Professor Sealy has said, "Those who adopt the corporate form should surely be expected to take the rough with the smooth."[50]

It might also appear, as some have argued, that in a number of those cases that are cited as examples of veil piercing—both of the benefit[51] and liability[52] variety—the

---

48 L.C.B. Gower, *Gower's Principles of Modern Company Law*, 4th ed. (London: Stevens, 1979), at 112. Note that this passage does not appear in the current (7th) edition of this work. Indeed, the current edition disclaims such a proposition. See the discussion accompanying footnote 72, *infra*.

49 Henry Hansmann and Reinier Kraakman, "The Essential Role of Organizational Law" (2000), 110 *Yale Law Journal* 387.

50 Sealy, *supra* footnote 24, at 58.

51 It has been argued, however, that even in these cases, the courts could achieve the results they wished without in any way infringing on the integrity of the separate legal entity principle, by resort, for example, to principles of agency or partnership law or, perhaps, to the kind of very technical reasoning employed by Wilson J in *Kosmopolous*. See, for example, Welling, *supra* footnote 43, at 135.

52 For example, as Jason Neyers has noted, it is peculiar that "agency" is ever seen as an example of veil piercing. "Although agency, as currently applied, has the same effect as veil-piercing ... it is arguably not a real violation of the separate legal entity principle. Rather, it is a reaffirmation of that principle because it allows that one legal person, a corporation, may be the agent of another legal person, just as a natural person might." Neyers, *supra* footnote 44, at 181.

courts have (or could have, with no significant stretch of imagination or established legal doctrine) treated the corporations involved as distinct legal persons in every way, but nevertheless determined that, for appropriate juridical reasons, shareholders ought to be granted some particular right or be made subject to some particular liability. No "veil of corporate entity" would necessarily have to be "lifted" to arrive at the appropriate conclusion in such cases, any more than it is necessary, for example, to "lift the veil" of human personal identity in those cases where individual human principals are found liable for the deeds or misdeeds of their agents.

It is important to stress, however, that while the courts *might* have chosen to draw careful distinctions between true "veil-lifting" cases, on the one hand, and "good juridical reasons" cases, on the other, that is not, in fact, the way in which courts have typically characterized their decisions.

Another point bears mentioning. Historically, the term "lifting the veil" referred to those situations where the courts would look behind the corporation to its *shareholders*. Courts today, however, frequently use the phrase in other sorts of cases too. For example, courts frequently speak of corporate veil piercing in those cases in which liability has been imposed not on a corporation's shareholders, but on a corporation's officers, directors, or employees. However, as Professor Sealy has pointed out, cases of this latter sort almost invariably do not involve any disregard of the corporate entity at all; liability is imposed on the relevant individuals *as well as* (not instead of) on the corporation.[53] Further, these directors' and officers' liability cases pose very distinct and difficult legal and policy questions of their own,[54] questions that typically transcend corporate law as such,[55] and are perhaps best understood within a more general discussion of directors' and officers' responsibilities rather than within the more limited analytical parameters appropriate to the study of the more traditional "veil-piercing" decisions. The directors' and officers' liability cases are, accordingly, dealt with elsewhere in this book.

Finally, it is often suggested that veil piercing occurs almost exclusively in the context of small, privately held corporations, where the line between shareholder and corporation can be the most murky.[56] This observation is surely accurate, provided that one recalls, as discussed in chapter 4, that not all private corporations are the vehicles of small business. In fact, a good number of private corporations are actually subsidiaries or affiliates of very large public corporations. Nevertheless, it is the private corporation—in particular the single-shareholder corporation—in which the artificiality of the corporate entity doctrine is seen in its sharpest relief.

---

53   Sealy, supra footnote 24, at 57.

54   See Christopher C. Nicholls, "Liability of Corporate Officers and Directors to Third Parties" (2001), 35 *Canadian Business Law Journal* 1.

55   See, e.g., Neil Campbell and John Armour, "Demystifying the Civil Liability of Corporate Agents" (2003), 62 *Cambridge Law Journal* 290, at 291: "The problem seems to us to be that courts and commentators have treated questions of corporate agents' liability as turning on some special principle of *company law*, and consequently have paid insufficient attention to the cause of action pleaded against the agent. In our view company law has nothing useful to say in this area."

56   So, for example, Robert Thompson, in his empirical analysis of US veil-piercing cases, concluded that in the "entire data set" that he examined, "piercing did not occur in a publicly held corporation." Rather, he concluded, "piercing of the corporate veil is limited to close corporations and corporate groups (parent/ subsidiary or sibling corporations)." See Thompson, supra footnote 16, at 1047.

With these observations and caveats in mind, it is now time to consider the numerous attempts that have been made to classify or categorize the veil-piercing cases.[57] Some of the more frequently encountered categories of these cases include:

- when equity or the *interests of justice* are served by disregarding the corporate entity;
- where the corporation in question is a *sham* or a mere *facade* concealing the true facts, or is merely the *alias* or *alter ego* of a shareholder or, perhaps, of some other individual;
- where the corporation has been formed in order to engage in *fraud* or to carry out some other *improper purpose*;
- where the corporation in question is merely the *agent* of its shareholders or of some other related corporation;
- where the corporation is *thinly or inadequately capitalized* in view of the type of business in which it is engaged;
- where the corporation is one of a group of related corporations that are viewed, collectively, as a *group enterprise* or *single economic unit*;
- in the case of certain *tort* claims; and
- in the interpretation of *taxation* (and perhaps other) *statutes*. (It should be noted that there are a number of specific Canadian tax cases that often feature prominently in discussions of corporate veil piercing.[58] These cases were decided, however, before a series of important recent Supreme Court of Canada tax judgments,[59] and equally important amendments to the *Income Tax Act*. Accordingly, it would seem to be imprudent to discuss these older cases, except in the context of a careful analysis of these more recent developments, and such a comprehensive analysis is beyond the scope of this chapter.)

Categorizations like these have formed the bases for empirical examinations of veil-piercing cases in the United States[60] and the United Kingdom;[61] although, to my knowledge, no similar empirical study has yet been carried out in Canada. It is important to

---

57   See, e.g., Paul L. Davies, *Gower & Davies: Principles of Modern Company Law*, 7th ed. (London: Sweet & Maxwell, 2003), at 184-89; Sealy, supra footnote 24, at 58-75; Jacob S. Ziegel et al., *Cases and Materials on Partnerships and Canadian Business Corporations*, 3rd ed., vol. 1 (Toronto: Carswell, 1994), at 166-67; Welling, supra footnote 43, at 124-27; Harry Sutherland et al., *Fraser & Stewart: Company Law of Canada*, 6th ed. (Toronto: Carswell, 1993), at 21-30; William P. Friedman, "The Limits of Limited Liability," in *The Future of Corporation Law: Issues and Perspectives*, Papers Presented at the Queen's Annual Business Law Symposium 1997 (Toronto: Carswell, 1999), 1; and Neyers, supra footnote 44, at 216-37.

58   For example, *Covert v. Minister of Finance (NS)* (sub nom. *Jodrey Estate v. Nova Scotia (Minister of Finance)*), [1980] 2 SCR 774; *De Salaberry Realties Ltd. v. MNR* (1974), 46 DLR (3d) 100 (FCTD), aff'd. (1976), 70 DLR (3d) 706 (FCA).

59   *Neuman v. Canada*, [1998] 1 SCR 770; *Duha Printers (Western) Ltd. v. Canada*, [1998] 1 SCR 795; and *Shell Canada Ltd. v. Canada*, [1999] 3 SCR 622.

60   See Thompson, supra footnote 16.

61   See Charles Mitchell, "Lifting the Corporate Veil in the English Courts: An Empirical Study" (1999), 3 *Company, Financial and Insolvency Law Review* 15.

emphasize, though, that this list is presented here purely as an attempt to describe previous attempts made by others at detailed categorization. Whether such efforts are meaningful, valuable, or even coherent is another question.

Commentators, and indeed courts, have frequently been critical of the overly liberal invocation of supposed exceptions to the separate entity principle, and have even suggested that veil-piercing cases that courts themselves have described as falling within one of the above-mentioned categories could, in fact, have been satisfactorily resolved without purporting to disregard the corporate entity at all.

Moreover, these categories are far from watertight compartments. A judge may well recite a string of veil-piercing epithets within a single case. A court might, for example, characterize one corporation as a mere puppet of another, proclaim the first corporation a sham, condemn them both for their attempt to deceive or defraud, and then end by declaring the second corporation to be an agent of the first. Consider, for example, the judgment in one of the "classic" English veil-piercing cases, *Gilford Motor Co. Ltd. v. Horne*.[62] Horne signed an agreement with his employer promising not to solicit his employer's customers after his employment terminated. When his employment ended, Horne began running a competing business through a corporation in which he ostensibly had no legal interest. (Horne's wife and another employee were the shareholders and directors of the new corporation.) Lord Hanworth condemned this competing company, calling it "a device, a stratagem … a cloak or sham." He then went on to enforce the non-solicitation covenant against the company on the basis that it was Horne's "agent."

Moreover, the most recent Canadian veil-piercing cases defy any sort of ready categorization. They appear to reflect a more holistic approach to the question. Accordingly, the following section, while discussing a number of cases in each of these putative categories, will make no attempt to neatly pigeonhole all of them. Rather, it will sketch out in slightly broader terms how the courts have grappled with the veil-piercing issue. This discussion will resist the twin temptations of overstating the significance of organizing categories, on the one hand, and of wrongly suggesting, on the other hand, that courts simply apply some ill-defined, intuitive notion of individual fairness.

Equity or the Interests of Justice

It is necessary to raise and, one hopes, dispose of this category first. It is no doubt true that a case-by-case study of examples in which the courts have pierced the corporate veil would reveal situations where only an unyielding formalist imbued with both a knowledge of, and perhaps reverence for, *Salomon's* case would rigorously object to the ultimate outcomes. The common sense and fairness of the *results* reached in veil-piercing cases is, in other words, usually quite evident. Little wonder that some observers have been tempted to conclude that the courts simply choose to pierce the corporate veil whenever justice demands it. If this explanation were both accurate and complete, no more systematic analysis of these cases would be either possible or desirable.

Such a broad "fair and equitable" test, however, is plainly unsatisfactory and has generally been rejected as a meaningful rationale for the veil-piercing cases by the

---

62   [1933] Ch. 935 (CA).

courts[63] as well as by careful commentators in England[64] and Canada.[65] Recall that the dispute in *Salomon's* case itself, as members of the English Court of Appeal had apparently been convinced,[66] could easily be characterized as a situation where the interests of justice ought not to be thwarted by the technical protections afforded to a shareholder by incorporation. Yet *Salomon* continues to be invoked today as foundational authority for the proposition that the law must respect the sanctity of corporate "personhood."

It is trite, of course, to observe that in every case in which judges choose to lift the corporate veil, they must surely have considered it just to do so; but one must attempt to define with as much clarity and precision as possible which perceived "injustices" have been sufficient to prompt courts to conclude that they ought to depart from the *Salomon* principle. As Paul Davies has rather nicely put it:

> Although the interests of justice may provide the policy impetus for creating exceptions to the doctrines of separate legal personality and limited liability, as an exception in itself it suffers from the defect of being inherently vague and providing to neither courts nor those engaged in business any clear guidance as to when the normal company law rules should be displaced. Consequently, it is difficult to find cases in which "the interests of justice" have represented more than simply a way of referring to [other specifically enumerated grounds] in which the veil of incorporation has been pierced.[67]

In Canada, the suggestion that there might be a loose "just and equitable" test for piercing the corporate veil is sometimes linked to the short passage from Wilson J's judgment in *Kosmopolous*, cited earlier. But it should not be forgotten that Wilson J's obiter statement occurred in the context of a case in which the court, in fact, expressly refused to pierce the corporate veil, notwithstanding obviously compelling circumstances. The court was still able to achieve a just result, but preferred to grant the appropriate relief on a basis that did explicitly involve lifting the corporate veil.

The suggestion that a vague "just and equitable" test is an appropriate basis for disregarding the corporate entity was expressly rejected in *Transamerica Life Insurance Company of Canada v. Canada Life Assurance Company et al.*[68] The plaintiff, Transamerica Life Insurance Company of Canada, had made a number of mortgage loans to borrowers who ultimately defaulted on those loans. The defendant, Canada Life Mortgage Services Ltd., had acted as the broker with respect to those loans. The plaintiff contended that the defendant was in breach of its obligation to the plaintiff to properly investigate the creditworthiness of the borrowers.

---

63   See, e.g., *B.G. Preeco I (Pacific Coast) Ltd.*, supra footnote 23, at 37: "I do not subscribe to the 'Deep Rock Doctrine' that permits the corporate veil to be lifted whenever to do otherwise is not fair."

64   Davies, supra footnote 57, at 187.

65   See, e.g., Welling, supra footnote 43, at 124: "Little need be said about this rationale, other than it simply will not do. There are, so far as I know, no broadly enforceable standards of 'fair play and good conscience,' at least in Canadian corporate law."

66   A Court of Appeal, as Professor Sealy has noted, where "the judges concerned were outstanding company lawyers of considerable experience." Sealy, supra footnote 24, at 56. Indeed, the Court of Appeal bench included Lord Lindley.

67   Davies, supra footnote 57, at 187.

68   (1996), 28 OR (3d) 423 (Gen. Div.), aff'd. [1997] OJ no. 3754 (QL) (CA).

Canada Life Mortgage Services Ltd. was a wholly owned subsidiary of Canada Life Assurance Company. The plaintiff also sought to hold the parent company liable for the wrongs of its subsidiary. The plaintiff's counsel argued that the corporate veil could be pierced when it is "just and equitable to do so,"[69] citing for this proposition the oft-quoted words of Wilson J in *Kosmopolous*.[70]

Sharpe J categorically rejected the suggestion that the corporate entity may be disregarded so readily, saying,

> [i]n my view, the argument advanced by Transamerica reads far too much into a dictum plainly not intended to constitute an in-depth analysis of an important area of the law or to reverse a legal principle which, for almost 100 years, has served as a cornerstone of corporate law.[71]

Sharpe J scrutinized the relevant language from Wilson J's judgment and made some important observations. He noted that Wilson J, in support of her comments, had cited a passage from an early edition of L.C.B. Gower's influential company law text, which, in a subsequent edition, no longer suggested that the corporate veil might be pierced merely on "just and equitable" grounds.[72] Sharpe J concluded that although "[t]here are undoubtedly situations where justice requires that the corporate veil be lifted,"[73] it would not be proper for a court "to act as it pleases on some loosely defined 'just and equitable' standard."[74]

Sharpe J suggested that liability of a corporate parent may, in certain cases, be based on the application of agency principles, or in cases where it is necessary to give effect to statutes, especially tax statutes.[75] Since neither of these two "exceptions" were relevant in *Transamerica*, Sharpe J also discussed in more general terms the basis on which a parent company might be held liable for the actions of its subsidiaries. His comments make it clear that the circumstances under which such recovery will be permitted will be comparably rare, and will require evidence of nefarious conduct:

---

69   Ibid., at 431.

70   Supra footnote 25. The passage cited appears at 10-11.

71   Supra footnote 68, at 431.

72   Indeed, by the sixth edition of Gower's text (published subsequent to the court's decision in *Transamerica*), the author explicitly rejected such a proposition: "The court cannot lift the veil merely because it considers that justice so requires." See Paul L. Davies, *Gower's Principles of Modern Company Law*, 6th ed. (London: Sweet & Maxwell, 1997), at 173-74. Still later, in the 7th edition of the work released in 2003, the author argues that an "interests of justice" exception to limited liability "suffers from the defect of being inherently vague and providing to neither courts nor those engaged in business any clear guidance as to when the normal company law rules should be displaced," concluding that even in those cases where "the interests of justice" have been referred to as justification for lifting the corporate veil, this formulation was nothing more than "simply a way of referring to the [more specific] grounds identified above." Davies, supra footnote 57, at 187.

73   Supra note 68, at 433.

74   Ibid.

75   For this latter proposition, he cites the case of *Jodrey's Estate v. Nova Scotia*, supra footnote 58. However, in light of three more recent Supreme Court of Canada decisions—*Neuman*, *Duha*, and *Shell Canada*, supra footnote 59—one wonders whether this "exception" (if it ever really existed) may still be regarded as robust.

[T]he courts will disregard the separate legal personality of a corporate entity where it is completely dominated and controlled and being used as a shield for fraudulent or improper conduct. The first element, "complete control," requires more than ownership. It must be shown that there is complete domination and that the subsidiary company does not, in fact, function independently ... . The second element relates to the nature of the conduct: is there "conduct akin to fraud that would otherwise unjustly deprive claimants of their rights"?[76]

Finding neither of these elements satisfied in the case at hand, Sharpe J granted the motion for summary judgment in Canada Life's favour, a decision upheld by the Court of Appeal.[77]

Facade or Sham; Fraud or Improper Purpose

Cases traditionally included as examples of several of the supposed veil-piercing "categories" have in common some element of sharp practice or outright deceit. Courts may, in some of these cases, but not all, make specific findings of "fraud" or "improper purpose." They may prefer instead to use such words as "facade," "cloak," "mask," or "sham." But some element of deliberate wrongdoing seems to be a commonly recurring feature.

Some English decisions have given prominence to the finding of a "facade." In the House of Lords decision *Woolfson v. Strathclyde Regional Council*,[78] for example, Lord Keith declared that

it is appropriate to pierce the corporate veil only where special circumstances exist indicating that it is a mere façade concealing the true facts.[79]

Such a statement might suggest that the finding of "facade" is, at least, a necessary condition if not a sufficient condition for piercing the corporate veil; however, note two preliminary points.

First, the reference to the corporation as a facade is often a conclusion posing as a premise. That is, it is apparent that courts in certain cases—especially those involving sharp practice of some sort—have first determined the appropriate legal outcome. Working backward from this desired outcome, they have then defined the supposed "true facts" that they then triumphantly declare have been "concealed" by the corporate facade.

Second, to speak of the "true facts" or the "reality" of a corporate structure is inevitably a somewhat disingenuous exercise. The concept of a corporation—as a wholly distinct legal person—is entirely an artificial construct in the first place.[80] Every corporation

---

76   Supra footnote 68, at 433-34.

77   [1997] OJ no. 3754 (QL) (CA).

78   [1979] 38 P & CR 521 (HL).

79   Ibid., at 526.

80   This statement should, of course, be readily endorsed by proponents of the "fiction" theory. However, even from the realist perspective, although the corporation's personality cannot necessarily be identified with any particular human being, it is understood as being somehow inextricably linked to the human beings whose collective will has given it whatever existence it may be said to have. Accordingly, to say that the corporate form "conceals" in any meaningful way the existence of those who comprise the corporation is surely to suggest an artificiality of corporate existence, which the realists would also readily acknowledge.

"conceals" the human beings behind it. Accordingly, in the shareholder or enterprise *liability* cases, it is not really meaningful to complain merely that the corporation "conceals" something; there must typically be some indication of deliberate deception as well that goes beyond the simple decision to use the corporate form as a liability shield, the very purpose, after all, for which it is intended.[81]

Certainly, in the shareholder or enterprise liability context, it does indeed seem that some wilful attempt to obfuscate or deceive is frequently a feature of those cases in which the veil is lifted. Consider, for example, the frequently cited English case of *Jones v. Lipman*.[82] An owner of real estate, who had entered into an agreement to sell the real estate to the plaintiffs, transferred the property to a corporation that he controlled prior to the date on which the sale to the plaintiff was to be completed. That the seller was in breach of the original sale contract there was no doubt; indeed, the seller had offered to pay the plaintiff damages. The issue, however, was whether the purchaser could obtain an order for specific performance of the contract, or whether such a remedy was simply out of reach given that the property was in the hands of a corporation that had never been a party to the original contract.

The court concluded that it could, and indeed it did, make an order for specific performance of the contract against the corporation, notwithstanding, as Welling has pointed out, that it appears that the same conclusion might have been reached simply by ordering that the individual defendant cause the corporation, that he clearly controlled, to convey the subject property.[83]

Surely, however, it was not merely because the corporation was a facade that the court was prepared to lift the veil. How, after all, would one characterize the "true facts" that such a facade attempted to conceal? Would one argue that the corporation was, in truth, the individual defendant, because it was under the individual defendant's control? If so, how could one reasonably distinguish *Jones v. Lipman* from *Salomon's* case itself?[84] How, indeed, could the separate personality of any sole-shareholder corporation ever be respected?

---

81   This assessment seems to accord with Jennifer Payne's analysis of the so-called fraud exception to the *Salomon* principle, in which she argues that in order for the veil to be lifted, there must be a finding that a corporation was used with an intent to deceive (and, she goes on to argue, more particularly a deception aimed at avoiding a pre-existing legal obligation). See Jennifer Payne, "Lifting the Corporate Veil: A Reassessment of the Fraud Exception" (1997), 56 *Cambridge Law Journal* 284.

82   [1962] 1 WLR 832 (Ch. D).

83   Welling, supra footnote 43, at 148. Russell J clearly recognized that there was authority for making such an order against an individual who controlled a corporation holding an asset under dispute (supra footnote 82, at 835), yet nonetheless thought it appropriate to make an order of specific performance not only against the individual defendant, but also against the corporation itself.

84   A recent Canadian case raising issues somewhat similar to those in *Jones v. Lipman* was *369413 Alberta Limited v. Pocklington* (2000), 194 DLR (4th) 109 (Alta. CA). Pocklington controlled a corporation (Gainers) which owned, in turn, the shares of a numbered company ("350 Ltd."). 350 Ltd. had acquired certain valuable property (the Carma Lands). Gainers granted a security interest in all of its property to 369413 Alberta Limited (369413) to secure a loan made by 369413. Just one day before 369413 served notice of its intention to realize on its security (and seize, among other things, the share of 350 Ltd.

In some "veil-piercing" cases, the *de facto* controller of the corporation—perhaps having received the advice of legal counsel—has attempted to distance himself or herself from the corporation altogether. The *Gilford Motor Co.* case discussed earlier offers one well-known example: the employee who was subject to the non-competition covenant at issue in that case held no shares at all in the corporation through which, the court found, he was effectively flaunting that covenant. For a more recent Canadian decision raising similar issues, consider *Rogers Cantel Inc. v. Elbanna Sales Inc.*[85]

In *Elbanna*, Rogers Cantel had entered into a sales agency agreement with a corporation (Elbanna) controlled by a Mr. Annable. Under the terms of this agreement, neither Elbanna nor any of its affiliates was permitted to enter into an agreement with a competitor of Rogers Cantel. Breach of this provision would entitle Rogers Cantel to terminate the sales agency agreement.

Annable subsequently became, as the Court of Appeal put it, "deeply involved" in a second, numbered company that entered into an agreement with Rogers Cantel's principal competitor, Bell Mobility. As in *Gilford*, Annable was evidently not a shareholder of this numbered company; his mother and two friends were the shareholders. Accordingly, the agreement made by this second company with a Cantel competitor did not, technically, violate the non-compete clause in the Elbanna/Rogers Cantel contract.

Nonetheless, the Court of Appeal determined that Annable "in this case was indistinguishable from Elbanna insofar as the performance of the [Rogers Cantel sales agency] contract was concerned."[86] Thus, Rogers Cantel was justified in considering Annable's actions as a breach of the non-competition clause that would justify terminating the agreement. One final intriguing note about *Elbanna* merits a brief mention. This case arose in Quebec, and the court, in reaching this conclusion, drew support from the references to use of corporate entities contained in article 317 of the Quebec *Civil Code* as well as to the principles contained in article 318.

Certainly, then, as the Alberta Court of Appeal has recently put it, "[t]he exposure of dishonest, deceitful and corrupt conduct, is, in our view, a compelling reason to disregard the corporate veil."[87] But how critical is such a finding to a decision to ignore the corporate personality? The Ontario courts have frequently reiterated the need for a finding of fraudulent or wrongful conduct as a prerequisite to a decision to disregard the corporate entity. Sharpe J, for example, in *Transamerica*,[88] spoke of the need to identify "conduct akin to fraud," and explained:

---

owned by Gainers), Pocklington—as sole director of Gainers—passed a resolution transferring the share in 350 Ltd. to another company controlled by him ("Holdings"). Holdings had not granted a security interest to 369413. Therefore, 369413 could not seize the share of 350 Ltd. that it had always expected to stand as security for its loan. However, in this case, 369413 sued Pocklington for the tort of inducing breach of contract, and the court's analysis was focused on that tort, rather than on the sort of veil-piercing analysis found in *Jones v. Lipman*.

85   [2003] RJQ 745 (CA). Leave to appeal to Supreme Court of Canada dismissed April 14, 2003.

86   Ibid.

87   *Colborne Capital Corporation v. 542775 Alberta Ltd.*, [1999] 8 WWR 222 (Alta. CA).

88   Supra footnote 68.

Typically, the corporate veil is pierced when the company is incorporated for an illegal, fraudulent or improper purpose. But it can also be pierced if when incorporated "those in control expressly direct a wrongful thing to be done."[89]

A more recent example of the court's unwillingness to allow the corporate form to be used to improperly evade obligations is *642947 Ontario Ltd. v. Fleischer*.[90] *Fleischer* arose from an aborted property sale. The plaintiffs had entered into an agreement to purchase land from the defendants. The land was under lease to a third-party corporation, Sweet Dreams Delights Inc. ("Sweet Dreams"). The lease contained a right of first refusal that entitled Sweet Dreams, if it wished, to match any offer to purchase the land received by the defendants.

Sweet Dreams, at first, did purport to match the offer made by the plaintiffs. But when Sweet Dreams failed to proceed with the purchase, the plaintiffs made a second (identical) purchase offer. The defendants chose to accept this second offer. Sweet Dreams was not given the opportunity to match the second offer because the defendants had decided that Sweet Dreams's right of first refusal had been "spent" following its failure to complete the purchase the first time around.

Sweet Dreams then sought an interlocutory injunction to prevent the plaintiff from purchasing the land, pending a hearing on the status of its right of first refusal. It is customary for an applicant who is seeking such an interlocutory injunction to provide an undertaking to pay any amount that might become necessary to compensate the responding party for damages suffered by that responding party as a result of the granting of the injunction. Note that this undertaking as to damages is not made directly to the responding party. It is, in fact, an undertaking made by the applicant to the court itself, to "abide by any Order concerning damages that the Court may make."[91]

Sweet Dreams gave such an undertaking. However, at the time of giving the undertaking, Sweet Dreams had no assets, or at least had insufficient assets to honour such an undertaking. Accordingly, the undertaking was worthless.

As a factual matter, the Court of Appeal ultimately found that damages suffered by the plaintiff did not arise from the granting of the injunction. In other words, the undertaking as to damages did not have to be called on. Nevertheless, the court went on to state that, if these damages *had* in fact resulted from the injunction, the shareholders of Sweet Dreams would have been personally liable to pay them—that is, the shareholders would not have been permitted to shield themselves behind a worthless corporate shell; the court would be prepared to look behind that shell.

The fact that the obligation in question arose from an undertaking made to the court, and not merely from a contractual obligation, influenced the court's decision. Such an undertaking is very different from a commercial contract. In the case of an ordinary commercial contract, if a contracting party is not satisfied with the creditworthiness of a corporate counterparty, it is free to insist on receiving personal guarantees from that corporation's shareholders. Such a contractor can simply refuse to enter into a contract

---

89   Ibid., at 438. The quoted language is from *Clarkson v. Zhelka*, [1967] 2 OR 565, at 578 (HCJ).

90   (2001), 56 OR (3d) 417 (CA).

91   *Rules of Civil Procedure*, RRO 1990, reg. 194, rule 40.03.

with the corporation if such guarantees are not provided. (Bank lenders, for example, routinely demand such guarantees as a pre-condition to extending credit to small corporations.) Thus, in the commercial context, if a contracting party chooses not to seek such a guarantee, there is usually no compelling reason for a court to, in effect, create such an unbargained-for guarantee in favour of the contractor.

Piercing the corporate veil has the same economic effect as creating such a guarantee. In both cases, shareholders are exposed to personal liability with respect to a contract entered into by their corporation. Courts should, indeed, be reluctant to disregard the corporate form in the ordinary commercial context. After all, the comfort of receiving a personal guarantee from a corporation's shareholders has value. If a contracting party wishes to obtain such a valuable concession, surely he or she ought to be expected to pay something for it, either by way of an express guarantee fee or by making some sort of contractual concession. Where no such guarantee has been sought or obtained, a judicial decision to pierce the corporate veil bestows a windfall on the contracting party.

However, matters are quite different in the case of an undertaking provided to the court itself. A court is not engaged in a commercial negotiation with an injunction applicant. It is not seeking to "price" the undertaking so provided; nor would it be in any position to attempt to do so. Representations made to a court do not arise from a market transaction. The court has the right to expect candour from litigating parties and, as the Court of Appeal puts it,

> [b]y undertaking to "abide by any Order concerning damages that the Court may make," Sweet Dreams implicitly represented that it had sufficient assets to honour that undertaking.[92]

The court affirmed the general proposition that "the separate legal personality of the corporation cannot be lightly set aside,"[93] and asserted that "[o]nly exceptional cases—cases where applying the *Salomon* principle would be 'flagrantly' unjust—warrant going behind the company and imposing personal liability."[94] Again the court emphasized that the veil ought not usually to be pierced in the absence of some finding of wrongdoing.[95]

Accordingly, the court found that, had Sweet Dreams been liable under the undertaking, the shareholders of Sweet Dreams would have been personally liable as well.

A recent Ontario Court of Appeal decision again underscores the importance of a finding of wrongdoing as a prerequisite to lifting the corporate veil. In *Haskett v. Equifax Canada Inc.*,[96] the plaintiff sued two credit reporting agencies, alleging that they had improperly included information in the plaintiff's credit report that had, in turn, resulted in damage to the plaintiff. The plaintiff brought the action not only against the Canadian

---

92 Supra footnote 90, at 438.

93 Ibid., at 440.

94 Ibid., at 439.

95 In support of its statement that the corporate veil should be pierced only in cases where the corporation is being used for a wrongful purpose, the court cited *Transamerica*, supra footnote 68 and *Clarkson*, supra footnote 89.

96 (2003), 63 OR (3d) 577 (CA). Application for leave to appeal to SCC dismissed, [2003] SCCA no. 208 (QL).

credit reporting agencies alleged to have included the incorrect information, but also against the US parent corporations of these agencies. The defendants sought to have the plaintiff's statement of claim struck on the basis that it did not disclose a reasonable cause of action. With respect to the claim against the parent companies only, the Court of Appeal held that the pleadings should indeed be struck out. The court stated:

> In order to found liability by a parent corporation for the actions of a subsidiary, there typically must be both complete control so that the subsidiary does not function independently and the subsidiary must have been incorporated for a fraudulent or improper purpose or be used by the parent as a shield for improper activity.[97]

However, it must be emphasized that taking full advantage of the benefits of organizing one's affairs through separate corporate entities does not constitute the sort of wrongdoing that will prompt a court to find that a corporation is a mere facade. In *Adams v. Cape Industries PLC*,[98] for example, the English Court of Appeal,[99] offered an extended discussion of "facade" as an exception—indeed, as it was there suggested the "one well-recognised exception"[100]—to the normal rule that a corporation must be treated as a distinct legal entity. The court, however, expressly disavowed any attempt to provide "a comprehensive definition"[101] of the applicable principles.

The *Adams* case concerned a claim for damages arising from losses allegedly suffered by a number of people from exposure to asbestos fibres emitted from a plant in the United States.

Cape Industries PLC ("Cape"), an English company, held shares in two subsidiary companies that had mined and marketed asbestos in the United States. One of these subsidiaries had been incorporated in England, the second, in the United States. The plaintiffs sought damages against Cape essentially for selling asbestos without giving adequate warnings about its dangers.

The plaintiffs had obtained default judgment against the English companies in an earlier US proceeding. The English companies contested the jurisdiction of the US court over them, and so argued in the English court that this judgment was not enforceable against them. Accordingly, the court was called upon to consider, among other things, whether the English companies had been present in the United States, such that the US court would have jurisdiction over them.

The corporate structure put in place by the defendants was very complicated. Essentially, the aspects of that structure relevant to the court's analysis of the corporate veil were these. The English parent company, Cape, had caused two corporations to be incorporated. The first, A.M.C., was a Liechtenstein corporation the shares of which were held by a Liechtenstein lawyer, in trust for a wholly owned subsidiary of Cape. The second, C.P.C., was an Illinois corporation, the shares of which were held by Morgan, who had formerly been the president of a Cape subsidiary in the United States.

---

97   Ibid., at 598.

98   [1990] 2 WLR 657 (CA).

99   Leave to appeal to the House of Lords was dismissed.

100   Supra footnote 98, at 755.

101   Ibid., at 759.

C.P.C. had entered into an agency agreement with A.M.C. Under the agreement, C.P.C. was appointed an agent for A.M.C. for purposes of making asbestos sales in the United States. The corporate veil issue before the court came down to this. Could the operations of C.P.C. and A.M.C. in the United States be construed as operations of Cape itself, such that Cape could be said to have been present in the United States (and, therefore, subject to the jurisdiction of the US court in which the plaintiffs had obtained their prior judgment)? Put another way, was it appropriate to "pierce the corporate veil" and so treat C.P.C. not as an independent corporate entity, but merely as a conduit for Cape that should simply be looked through?

The Court of Appeal declined to lift the corporate veil. It recognized that this complex structure had been put in place quite deliberately with a view of shielding Cape from liability emanating from the United States. The court endorsed the finding of the judge at first instance that Cape had purposefully structured its corporate affairs so that it might continue to reap the benefits of selling asbestos in the United States, while "reducing the appearance of any involvement therein of Cape or its subsidiaries," and further inferred that Cape had also hoped to reduce "by any lawful means available to it the risk of any subsidiary or of Cape as parent company being held liable for United States taxation or subject to the jurisdiction of the United States courts … and the risk of any default judgment by such a court being held to be enforceable in this country."[102]

Moreover, the court did find that A.M.C. was a mere facade—a corporation with no real existence of its own. (As the trial judge had put it, "A.M.C. was no more than a corporate name,"[103] and a "creature of Cape."[104]) But this finding availed the plaintiff little, because A.M.C. was not found to be carrying on business in the United States. C.P.C., on the other hand, clearly was carrying on business in the United States. If it, like A.M.C., was a mere facade, then Cape would indeed be subject to the jurisdiction of the US courts.

The Court of Appeal declined, however, to find that C.P.C. was a facade in this sense. This conclusion was significantly influenced by the fact that the shares of C.P.C. were held, not by Cape, but by Morgan. (Morgan's ownership of the shares both as a legal and equitable matter was not impugned.) Though Cape had clearly structured its affairs expressly for the purpose of insulating itself from liability for its US sales, this did not compromise the legal status of C.P.C. As the Court of Appeal noted,

> we do not accept as a matter of law that the court is entitled to lift the corporate veil as against a defendant company which is the member of a corporate group merely because the corporate structure has been used so as to ensure that the legal liability (if any) in respect of particular future activities of the group (and correspondingly the risk of enforcement of that liability) will fall on another member of the group rather than the defendant company. Whether or not this is desirable, the right to use a corporate structure in this manner is inherent in our corporate law … . [I]n our judgment, Cape was in law entitled to organise the group's affairs in that manner and (save in the case of A.M.C. to which special considerations

---

102 Ibid., at 757.

103 Ibid., at 699.

104 Ibid., at 702. Both of these comments were endorsed by the Court of Appeal, ibid., at 759.

apply) to expect that the court would apply the principle of *Salomon v. A. Salomon & Co. Ltd.* ... in the ordinary way.[105]

Thus, taking full advantage of the liability shield offered by the corporate form does not, without more, constitute a corporation a facade or sham for purposes of disregarding the corporate form. When the corporate veil has been pierced on the basis that a corporation was a facade or sham, there is almost invariably the presence of some additional evidence of wrongdoing or deception. However, deception is not apparently a sufficient condition for piercing of the corporate veil. This proposition may be illustrated by the rather remarkable facts of *B.G. Preeco I (Pacific Coast) Ltd. v. Bon Street Holdings Ltd.*[106]

The plaintiff in *Bon Street Holdings* wished to sell a certain property, and so had entered into sale negotiations with principals of a corporation called Bon Street Developments Ltd., a substantial corporation. A deal was reached, and a written agreement prepared for signature.

However, unbeknownst to the plaintiff, the corporation with which the plaintiff *presumed* it was dealing had quietly changed its name (twice in fact), and was now actually named Bon Street *Holdings* Ltd. ("Holdings"). The shareholders of Holdings—that is, the human beings with whom the plaintiff had been dealing—had then incorporated a new shell company with no substantial assets. To this new shell company they had given the name Bon Street Developments Ltd. In other words, the new shell company, which had no significant assets, was given a name identical to the original name of the substantial corporation with which the plaintiff had assumed it had been dealing all along.

The effect of these contrivances was this. When the sale agreement for the property was signed, the *name* of the purchaser that appeared on the contract was the very name the vendor (plaintiff) had always expected to see there—namely, Bon Street Developments Ltd. The name was the same; however, sadly for the vendor, the corporation that was now using this name was a very different entity from the one with which the vendor had assumed it was dealing. This new Bon Street Developments Ltd.—the only entity the vendor would have a contractual right to sue—had no assets. Therefore, if the purchaser were to fail to perform its contractual obligations, it would not be able to satisfy any judgment the plaintiff might ultimately win against it for breach of contract.

And indeed, the purchaser did default. It repudiated the sale contract. The plaintiff (vendor) sued and won. Judgment was entered against Bon Street Developments Ltd. But alas, *this* Bon Street Developments Ltd. had no assets. The judgment was worthless to the plaintiff. The plaintiff therefore sought to hold the original Bon Street Developments Ltd. (the company that had since been renamed, Bon Street Holdings Ltd.) liable. The plaintiff sought remedies against individual officers and directors of that company as well.

The plaintiff succeeded in an action based on fraud. However, damages in a fraud action are calculated differently from damages in an action for breach of contract. Contract damages would be higher. So the plaintiff sought, more specifically, to have the corporate veil lifted in order that it could obtain (higher) breach of contract damages from Bon Street Holdings Ltd. and its shareholders.

105 Ibid., at 760.

106 Supra footnote 23.

The BC Court of Appeal, despite the finding of fraud, did not consider this an appropriate case to lift the corporate veil. The court acknowledged that fraud or improper conduct had been recognized as a basis on which the corporate veil could be lifted, but determined that the corporate veil would be lifted only "where a corporation is used to effect a purpose or commit an act which the shareholder could not effect or commit."[107] That was not, in the court's view, what had happened in this case.[108]

As well, it is apparent that the Court of Appeal interpreted the phrase "lifting the veil" to mean looking behind a corporation to its shareholders, commenting at one point that "[l]ifting the veil is no help—when it is lifted the old company is not to be seen. Neither company had shares in the other."[109]

Is the key to the outcome in *B.G. Preeco* (and cases like it) that the corporation's obligation to the plaintiff was, to use Payne's form of analysis, not a pre-existing legal right?[110] That is, the corporation was not formed *after* the legal obligation of the defendant had been incurred, and so with a view to avoiding that obligation. At least one passage from the *B.G. Preeco* trial judge's decision, quoted by the Court of Appeal, would support such an explanation.[111] Or is it, rather, a case in which it could not necessarily be said that the use by the defendants of the shell corporation had made it impossible for the plaintiff to take the steps necessary to protect itself through normal contract terms?[112] Or, is it simply that *B.G. Preeco* is an anomalous case?

Single Economic Entity and Other Veil-Piercing Considerations

Emphasis on the element of corporate wrongdoing found in many veil-piercing cases should not obscure the fact that the corporate veil is not always pierced for the purpose of imposing liability on a corporation's shareholders or controllers. The veil is also lifted in some cases at the request of the corporation itself. And the presence of deliberate deception can hardly account for the outcome of these shareholder or enterprise *benefit* cases.

---

107 Ibid., at 38.

108 Note that although it might, perhaps, have been possible to find Bon Street Holdings Ltd. liable on the contract on the basis that it had held itself out to the plaintiff as the contracting party, it had been found as a fact at trial that the plaintiff had not, in fact, been misled as to the *identity* of the contracting party, but rather only as to the *assets* owned by the contracting party, and the plaintiffs did not seek to appeal this finding. See ibid., at 40 and 41.

109 Ibid., at 40. On this basis, presumably neither *Gilford*, supra footnote 62, nor *Rogers Cantel*, supra footnote 85, could be regarded as veil-piercing cases either. This is curious in view of the fact that Seaton JA cited *Gilford*, evidently in support of the statement accompanying footnote 107, supra.

110 Payne, supra footnote 81, at 287.

111 "[T]he [new] company was a properly incorporated legal entity whose principals intended to operate through it for specific purposes which I have described. It had no significant assets—it was a 'shell' company—but of course that, *per se*, does not mean it did not have the power to contract to purchase real estate. ... Furthermore, the fact that the principals of the company may have intended even at the time of undertaking the obligation on behalf of the company to take advantage of the limited liability of the company if it suited their purposes does not *per se* make the company a sham, i.e., does not expose its principals to liability for the company's obligations." Extract from the trial decision, quoted by the Court of Appeal, supra footnote 23, at 37.

112 See Friedman, supra footnote 57, at 16.

There are a number of circumstances in which corporate groups have sought to have the "separateness" of the corporate form disregarded—when it is to their advantage to do so—by arguing that various affiliated corporations ought to be treated, for some legal purposes, as though they constituted a single economic entity. Perhaps the most well-known English example of such a case is *DHN Food Distributors v. Tower Hamlets*.[113] Very briefly put, this case concerned a proposed expropriation of business premises by a local government authority. Under the terms of the relevant statute, when land was expropriated, the owner of that land was entitled to compensation. Compensation was available not only for the loss of the land itself, but also for disturbance to any business run on that land. The problem was that the DHN group's corporate structure was such that one company in the group owned the land, and a second company ran the business on the land. But, no compensation was payable under the statute for disturbance of a business unless the operator of the business also had an interest in the land.

The Court of Appeal held that the group of companies could, in effect, be treated as a single entity, and therefore be entitled to compensation. Two subsequent English cases are said to have cast doubt on the broadness of the single economic unit principle apparently articulated in *DHN*, if not on the correctness of the decision itself.[114]

One of those cases, the *Adams v. Cape* decision, referred to above, includes a discussion of the single economic unit argument. The Court of Appeal is wary of the proposition, noting:

> There is no general principle that all companies in a group of companies are to be regarded as one. On the contrary, the fundamental principle is that "each company in a group of companies (a relatively modern concept) is a separate legal entity possessed of separate legal rights and liabilities."[115]

In the second of these cases, *Woolfson v. Strathclyde Regional Council*,[116] the court declined to find that the corporations constituted a single economic entity on the particular facts before it, but without providing significant illumination as to when such an argument might otherwise be successfully advanced.

In Canada, the Supreme Court of Canada did affirm in its 1944 decision in *Aluminum Company of Canada Limited v. City of Toronto (Alcan)*[117] that

> the business of one company can embrace the apparent or nominal business of another company where the conditions are such that it can be said that the second company is in fact the puppet of the first. ... In such a case it is not accurate to describe the business as being

---

113   [1976] 3 All ER 462 (CA).

114   See *Woolfson v. Strathclyde*, supra footnote 78 and *Adams v. Cape PLC*, supra footnote 98.

115   *Adams*, ibid., at 749. The passage quoted by the court is taken from the judgment of Roskill LJ in *The Albazero*, [1977] AC 774, at 807.

116   Supra footnote 78.

117   [1944] SCR 267. The court cited as authority for this proposition the Supreme Court's earlier decision in *City of Toronto v. Famous Players' Canadian Corporation Ltd.*, [1936] SCR 141. The Supreme Court's judgment in *Famous Players'* did not include any analysis of this point, as it rather summarily dismissed an appeal from the Ontario Court of Appeal.

carried on by the puppet for the benefit of the dominant company. The business is in fact that of the latter.[118]

However, in the *Alcan* case itself, the court was not in fact prepared to treat the business carried on by a corporation's subsidiary as though it were business carried on by the parent corporation itself.

Moreover, the BC Court of Appeal, in an expropriation case with some similarities to *DHN*, expressly rejected the broad "group enterprise theory" articulated by Lord Denning in *DHN*, commenting that this approach "has not been endorsed by this Court."[119]

The Federal Court did invoke a group enterprise analysis for taxation purposes in *De Salaberry Realties Ltd. v. MNR*[120]—not to benefit the corporate group, but rather for the purpose of increasing its tax liabilities. That case, though, as suggested earlier, is best analyzed within the context of a more extended discussion of Canadian tax law than is possible here.

The "single enterprise" cases are perhaps *sui generis* in the sense that the corporate veil is lifted for rather limited purposes frequently to accord a benefit to the corporate group as a whole, rather than to impose a liability; although, to be sure, the group enterprise analysis has frequently been commingled with arguments of "sham," "cloak," and "puppet" in cases involving attempts to impose liabilities as well. Yet, it is noteworthy that even in those cases, the liabilities are imposed on other corporations, and not on individuals who, ultimately, lie at the top of the corporate shareholding pyramid.

Gale CJO in *Canada Life Assurance Co. v. Canadian Imperial Bank of Commerce*[121] suggested various factors that would lead a court to treat two (or more) corporations as a single entity:

> I do not suggest that the foregoing represent all of the cases relating to whether, in particular circumstances, the corporate form and independence are to be respected. They do, however, provide sufficient basis on which to tentatively catalogue factors relevant to this determination. By way of a tentative catalogue, I offer the following as relevant criteria:
>
> (1) the capitalization of the subsidiary;
> (2) the degree of observance of corporate formalities;
> (3) the extent of the relationship between the business of parent and subsidiary;
> (4) the nature and extent of the business dealings between parent and subsidiary;
> (5) the corporate histories of both parent and subsidiary;
> (6) the relationship between the boards of directors and upper management personnel of parent and subsidiary; and
> (7) the extent of the ownership interest of the parent in the subsidiary; it appears from Scrutton LJ's judgment in *Com'rs of Inland Revenue v. Sansom*, ... that, despite the

---

118 Ibid., at 271.

119 *Actton Petroleum Sales Ltd. v. B.C. (Minister of Transportation and Highways)* (1998), 161 DLR (4th) 481 (BCCA).

120 Supra footnote 58.

121 (1974), 3 OR (2d) 70 (CA).

comments of the Court in the *Gramophone* case, ... the presence of an independent
minority interest may still be of some relevance.

Of overriding importance, considering that what one seeks to determine is whether the
subsidiary is, as Rand J put it, a "puppet," will be the respect accorded the legal independence of the subsidiary by its parent; that is, whether on a full view of the facts the subsidiary
looks as though it has its own business, rather than being completely subservient to and
dependent upon its parent. Also important will be the purpose for which it is sought to
impugn the subsidiary's integrity, and the position of the applicant.[122]

This sort of reasoning was invoked by the Ontario Court of Appeal in *Gregorio v.
Intrans-Corp. et al.*,[123] but in a rather peculiar context. The plaintiff had purchased a
defective truck from a dealer, Intrans Corp. The dealer had, in turn, acquired the truck
through Paccar Canada Ltd., the Canadian subsidiary of the American corporation that
had manufactured the truck. That parent company was not a defendant in the action.

Both the dealer, Intrans, and the manufacturer's Canadian subsidiary, Paccar Canada
Ltd., were found liable at trial. It was the liability of the manufacturer's subsidiary that
raised the "veil-piercing" issue. The trial judge had based his judgment on a finding that
Paccar Canada Ltd. was the mere alter ego of its parent company (the American manufacturer) and therefore ought to be liable for its parent company's negligence. The
Ontario Court of Appeal disagreed. Paccar Canada Ltd., the court held, could not be
regarded in law as the alter ego of its parent company:

> Generally, a subsidiary, even a wholly owned subsidiary, will not be found to be the alter
> ego of its parent unless the subsidiary is under the complete control of the parent and is
> nothing more than a conduit used by the parent to avoid liability. The alter ego principle is
> applied to prevent conduct akin to fraud that would otherwise unjustly deprive claimants of
> their rights.[124]

The court cited one American[125] and two Canadian cases[126] as authority for this
proposition. What is sometimes overlooked about *Gregorio* is that it did not involve an
attempt to undermine the principle of limited liability at all. That is, it was not a case in
which an attempt was made to hold a shareholder liable for the negligence of a corporation. Rather, it was a case in which an attempt was made to hold the corporation liable for
the failings of its shareholder. Note that the court refers in the passage quoted above to
situations where the subsidiary has been "used by the parent to avoid liability." But in
Gregorio, the parent's liability was never in issue—the parent had not been sued. Indeed
Gregorio is a contemporary example not of the importance of limited liability, but rather
of Hansmann and Kraakman's concept of "asset partitioning" or "entity shielding."[127]

---

122 Ibid., at 84-85.

123 (1994), 18 OR (3d) 527 (CA).

124 Ibid., at 536.

125 *Pauley Petroleum Inc. v. Continental Oil Co.*, 239 A 2d 629 (Del. SC 1968).

126 *Canada Life Assurance Co.*, supra footnote 121 and *Aluminum Co. of Canada*, supra footnote 117.

127 Hansmann and Kraakman, supra footnote 49.

In any event, although the courts have, on occasion, been willing to allow corporations to avoid what would otherwise appear to be the legal consequences of their own choice of corporate structure,[128] judges have warned that

> [t]he "group enterprise" concept must obviously be carefully limited so that companies who seek the advantages of separate corporate personality must generally accept the corresponding burdens and limitations.[129]

A recent Ontario Court of Appeal decision indicates the considerable judicial wariness of too readily ignoring the separateness of corporate holding companies and their subsidiaries.

In *Meditrust Healthcare Inc. v. Shoppers Drug Mart*,[130] the court would not allow a parent company to invoke the notion that it and its subsidiaries together constituted a single economic entity that would enable the parent company to bring an action for wrongs committed against its subsidiaries. The court noted what it described as "the difference between economic reality and legal reality":

> A parent company that owns all the shares of its subsidiaries may exercise complete and constant control over them. That control, however, does not clothe the parent with the right to sue for the subsidiaries.[131]

The court suggested that separate corporate entities could normally be ignored only for "the benefit of innocent third parties"[132] or "where the corporate structure has been used by the corporation's principals as a sham or to perpetrate a fraud."[133] In this case, however, the parent company

> must be held to the corporate structure that it created. It created a structure in which it operated the business through subsidiaries. It must take not only the benefits of that structure, but also the burdens.[134]

CONCLUSION

The categorization of veil-piercing cases, though conventional, is, in the end, a somewhat dissatisfying exercise. Certainly, if the formalistic concept of the corporation as a separate legal entity is to be preserved, departures from that principle must be minimized and rationalized. But perhaps in place of dogged adherence to the notion that a corporation must normally be respected as a separate legal person because *Salomon* says so, what is

---

128 In addition to the *DHN* case, supra footnote 113, see also *Manley Inc. v. Fallis* (1977), 2 BLR 277 (Ont. CA).

129 *Manley*, ibid.

130 (2002), 61 OR (3d) 786 (CA).

131 Ibid., at 794.

132 Ibid.

133 Ibid.

134 Ibid.

needed is a more refined concept of why the law ought to respect that proposition. And, from that more refined concept, a more coherent theory could likewise be developed to explain judicial departures from this norm. This exercise requires more than simply identifying, as some law and economics scholars have done, those instances where the arguments favouring limited liability are most compelling. A comprehensive solution to the puzzle of when a corporation is, and when it is not, always to be regarded as a thing apart from its controllers requires a fully specified theory of the organizational form itself.

CHAPTER EIGHT

Criminal and Tortious Liability of Corporations

INTRODUCTION

A woman is badly burned when she is splashed by scalding hot coffee served at a well-known fast-food restaurant. She successfully sues the company for damages.

A certain brand of automobile is found to roll over rather too easily under certain driving conditions. Injured drivers and passengers launch lawsuits against the manufacturer.

A famous national retailer falsely advertises sale prices for some of its merchandise. The company is charged with an offence, tried, and sentenced to pay a large fine.

We have become well accustomed to reading or hearing media stories about legal actions such as these in which large, often well-known corporations are found liable for committing torts or crimes. So commonplace have such stories become, that it is difficult to imagine that there might have been a time when the law struggled with the question of whether it would ever be possible for an artificial legal person such as a corporation to be said to have committed a tort or a crime.

But in fact, the law did sometimes struggle with these issues. The central problem confronted by early jurists was one of trying to apply rules designed to punish and correct human behaviour to the actions of the distinctly non-human corporation. The challenge is nicely articulated in a quotation usually attributed to Baron Thurlow, which tends to appear with great regularity in commentaries on the subject of corporate criminal responsibility. A corporation, he is supposed to have observed, can have no conscience because "it has no soul to be damned, and no body to be kicked."[1]

---

1 The provenance of this well-worn statement is a little shadowy. Many of the modern authors who have repeated the quotation either do so without citing any authority, or cite as their source another modern, secondary source. (See, e.g., Joseph Groia and Kellie Seaman, "Enron, Fear and Loathing on Bay Street," in Anita Anand and William Flanagan, eds., *The Corporation in the 21st Century: Papers Presented at the 9th Queen's Annual Business Law Symposium 2002* (Kingston, ON: Queen's University, 2003) 241, at 257, citing as their source for the Thurlow quotation J.C. Coffee Jr., "No Soul To Damn, No Body To Kick: An Unscandalized Inquiry into the Problem of Corporate Punishment" (1981), 79 *Michigan Law Review* 386, at 386. But Coffee himself had cited as his source for this quotation, a 1977 publication, *Public Policy and the Corporation* by M. King. The quotation does indeed appear on page 1 of King's book, but the author offers no source for the quotation (London: Chapman and Hall, 1977), at 1.) Lord Denning invoked a version of the maxim in *British Steel Corp. v. Granada Television,* [1981] 1 All ER 417, at 439 (CA), with no mention of Baron Thurlow. Sedgwick J of the Ontario Superior Court

Issues of corporate liability and corporate punishment continue to pose practical problems. Even if one can articulate a coherent and meaningful basis on which to impose liability on an abstract entity such as a corporation, an even greater challenge comes at the stage of assessing penalties or damages.

Consider the likely effects of corporate criminal sanctions, for example. Although individual corporate officers can, of course, be fined or imprisoned for their role in corporate crimes,[2] sentencing the corporation itself is rather trickier. A corporation cannot be hanged, electrocuted, given a lethal injection, or even imprisoned for its crimes, so there appear to be only two forms of punishment available: (1) fines and (2) dissolution. Whenever punishment of either sort is imposed on a corporation, the human beings who will likely suffer most are those who were unlikely to have had any role to play in the criminal wrongdoing.

After all, if a corporation were to be dissolved as a result of its crimes, its employees would be thrown out of work. The most highly skilled among them may well be able to find jobs elsewhere. But the most vulnerable members of a large corporation's workforce—its most junior, unskilled workers—may find it very difficult to find alternative employment. And yet, these are precisely the people who are *least likely* to be among those who have taken the critical decisions that exposed the corporation to criminal prosecution in the first place.

Commentators such as Harry Glasbeek remind us that it is not unknown for criminal punishment of individuals to adversely affect innocent people: when a father is sentenced to jail, for example, his innocent children are bound to suffer.[3] However, there is surely a critical difference here that Professor Glasbeek too quickly glosses over. When a corporation is penalized, it is not simply that innocent people may *also* suffer; on the contrary, it is most likely that *only* innocent people will suffer. The "corporation" itself can no more suffer the burden of penalties than can a stone, or, for that matter, a clever thought, or a well-phrased metaphor—because a "corporation" is an equally abstract concept.

Attempts to articulate the goals and efficacy of corporate criminal liability and punishment have prompted theoretical discussions at a far more nuanced and sophisticated level than this rather simplistic example. The aim of this chapter, however, is not to undertake a synthesis of this vast academic literature, but to offer a brief sketch of the doctrinal developments to which much of this literature responds and reacts.

---

of Justice gives J. Poynder, *Literary Extracts*, vol. 1 (1844), 268 as the source of the quotation. See *Kennedy v. Canada Customs and Revenue Agency*, [2000] 4 CTC 186, at 190-91 (Ont. SCJ). Yet another 19th century source suggests somewhat different wording: "You remember Thurlow's answer to some one complaining of the injustice of a corporation. 'Why, you never expected justice from a company, did you? they [*sic*] have neither a soul to lose, nor a body to kick.'" See Lady Holland, *A Memoir of the Reverend Sydney Smith*, vol. 1 (New York: Harper & Brothers, 1855), at 33.

2   See, e.g., *R v. Bata Industries Ltd.* (1992), 9 OR (3d) 330 (Prov. Div.).

3   See, e.g., Henry J. Glasbeek, "Why Corporate Deviance Is Not Treated as a Crime: The Need To Make 'Profits' a Dirty Word" (1984), 22 *Osgoode Hall Law Journal* 343.

CORPORATE LIABILITY FOR TORTS

Framing the Issue

Imagine that a hypothetical Canadian corporation, ABC Corp., owns and operates an (equally hypothetical) chain of pizza restaurants. The pizza delivery business is competitive. Some time ago, to try to attract more customers, ABC Corp. decided to offer the most aggressive pizza delivery guarantee in the business: every customer who orders an ABC Corp. pizza is guaranteed that the pizza will be delivered within 15 minutes, or the customer will receive double his or her money back.

One foggy evening, ABC Corp.'s top pizza delivery driver, Merrill, rushes to make a delivery, determined to meet the company's 15-minute deadline. Perhaps being on time has become a matter of personal pride for Merrill, or perhaps ABC Corp. has threatened to fire him if he should ever arrive late and trigger the customer's double-your-money-back guarantee. Whatever the reason, speeding through town on his way to make a delivery, Merrill fails to stop at a red light, collides with a pedestrian, and seriously injures her. Merrill has certainly been negligent. But Merrill is uninsured and does not have sufficient personal assets to compensate the victim. Can the injured pedestrian successfully sue ABC Corp.? Will the law hold ABC Corp. liable for the negligence of one of its employees?

Readers familiar with general principles of tort law will know the answer. Of course ABC Corp. may be held responsible for Merrill's negligence. The governing legal principle here is the doctrine of vicarious liability—that is, an employer (or other principal) can be held vicariously liable for torts committed by an employee (or other agent) acting within the scope of his or her assigned duties.

The classic statement of the law on this point, as applied to corporate employers or principals, is Lord Lindley's comment in *Citizens' Life Assurance Company, Ltd. v. Brown*:[4]

> If it is once granted that corporations are for civil purposes to be regarded as persons, i.e., as principals acting by agents and servants, it is difficult to see why the ordinary doctrines of agency and of master and servant are not to be applied to corporations as well as to ordinary individuals.[5]

So a corporate employer (or corporate principal) may be found vicariously liable for the negligent acts of its agents or employees just as a human employer or principal may be. But for some torts, the law has not been prepared to impose vicarious liability, whether on human beings or on other non-human legal persons. And certainly, in the criminal law sphere, our courts have been extremely reluctant to punish one person for the criminal wrongs of another. Thus it can often be important to determine whether a corporation may be said to be *personally*, and not merely vicariously, liable for committing some wrong. Put another way, in the case of certain torts and in the case of criminal offences generally, the law requires that we determine whether the corporation *itself* committed the wrongful act; the plaintiffs (or the prosecutors, as the case may be) will

---

4   [1904] AC 423 (PC).

5   Ibid., at 426.

not prevail if they are able to establish nothing beyond the fact that some other person (such as an agent or employee of the corporation) has committed the tort or crime in question.

Atiyah has suggested that in the early 19th century the courts were not really troubled by this distinction between holding corporations vicariously liable or personally liable.[6] That is, in some torts cases where, today, no determination of corporate liability would be tenable in the absence of an express finding of the corporation's actual or *personal* liability, courts of a bygone area seemed not to regard themselves as subject to any such technical constraints. They were quite prepared to find corporations liable without agonizing over a personal/vicarious liability distinction, and indeed without apparently seeing any need to try to articulate a theory of how, technically speaking, a finding of personal liability against a corporation would ever be possible.

By the 20th century the courts had both articulated the need for a coherent legal theory that would support finding a corporation personally liable for certain torts (and indeed crimes) and had proceeded to develop such a theory—the identification theory—basing it on the concept of the corporation's "directing mind and will."

Organic or Personal Liability of Corporations and the "Directing Mind and Will"

The proposition at which English and Canadian courts eventually arrived may be summarized simply. A corporation may be found *personally* (not merely vicariously) liable for a tort (or, as discussed later, a crime) if (among other things) the human being who took the actions on which the tort claim (or criminal prosecution) was based may fairly be described as a "directing mind and will" of the corporation. There is rather more to the matter than just this and, as discussed below, the analysis in the Canadian criminal law context has recently been changed by statute. But, for the moment, it is useful to focus on the threshold question of precisely what is meant by the common law concept of "directing mind and will."

The idea, as many courts have explained, is that within every corporation there are some human actors or decision makers who are "not merely [servants] or [agents] for whom the company is liable upon the footing *respondeat superior*, but ... for whom the company is liable because [their actions are] the very action of the company itself."[7]

Who are these people? Certainly it cannot be the case that every corporate employee— no matter how junior—can be said to be a "directing mind and will" of the corporation. Such a conclusion would make any distinction between vicarious and personal liability of corporations meaningless. So, how low down the proverbial corporate ladder may one go in one's search for a human being whose actions may be said to constitute the actions of the corporation itself? Lord Denning famously tried to express the distinction between

---

6   P.S. Atiyah, *Vicarious Liability in the Law of Torts* (London: Butterworths, 1967), at 381-82: "Throughout the nineteenth century little attempt was made to analyze the nature of the liability thus imposed on corporations or to decide whether it was vicarious liability or personal liability."

7   *Lennard's Carrying Co., Ltd. v. Asiatic Petroleum Co., Ltd.*, [1915] AC 705 (HL).

those corporate actors who could fairly be identified as the corporation's "directing mind and will" and those who could not by analogizing the corporate body to a human body:

> A company may in many ways be likened to a human body. It has a brain and nerve centre which controls what it does. It also has hands which hold the tools and act in accordance with directions from the centre. Some of the people in the company are mere servants and agents who are nothing more than hands to do the work and cannot be said to represent the mind or will. Others are directors and managers who represent the directing mind and will of the company, and control what it does. The state of mind of these managers is the state of mind of the company and is treated by the law as such.[8]

Metaphors like this are a useful beginning for legal analysis, but they go only so far. Subsequent courts have continued to grapple with this issue, the resolution of which has proved to be of particular significance in the context of corporate criminal liability, which is discussed later in this chapter.

A BRIEF DIGRESSION: PERSONAL LIABILITY OF CORPORATE OFFICERS AND DIRECTORS TO THIRD PARTIES

Before turning to the issue of corporate criminal liability, however, one other issue should perhaps be mentioned. As we have seen, corporations may be found liable for torts on the basis of actions committed by certain of their directors, officers, employees, or agents. In some cases, the corporation's liability is vicarious: the human actor has committed the "wrong," but the law holds that the corporation is liable to the injured party *in addition to* (not instead of) the human tortfeasor. But, when the liability of the corporation is based on the identification theory—that is, when the human corporate actor is said to be the corporation itself for purposes of imposing liability—will that human actor (the directing mind and will) also be held personally liable? Or, is his or her identification with the corporation complete, such that the corporation, and only the corporation, may be found liable?

The question of the personal liability of a corporate agent, acting within the scope of his or her duties, is an intriguing issue that has been the subject in the United Kingdom of recent House of Lords decisions,[9] and an enlightening research paper prepared for the UK Department of Trade and Industry as part of its recent company law reform initiative.[10] The issue has also been the source of a plethora of recent Canadian cases.[11] This issue is dealt with in chapter 11, within the context of director and officer liability more

---

8   *H.L. Bolton (Engineering) Co. v. T.J. Graham & Sons Ltd.*, [1957] 1 QB 159, at 172.

9   See *Williams v. Natural Life Health Foods*, [1998] 1 WLR 830 (HL); *Standard Chartered Bank v. Pakistan National Shipping Corpn. (Nos. 2 and 4)*, [2003] 1 AC 959 (HL).

10   Ian Glick QC, Advice, "Company Law Review Attribution of Liability." Available online at http://www.dti.gov.uk/cld/other_information.htm.

11   See, e.g., *Blacklaws v. Morrow* (2000), 84 ALR (3d) 220 (CA); *Lana International Ltd. v. Menasco Aerospace Ltd.* (2000), 50 OR (3d) 97 (CA); *Immocreek Corp. v. Pretiosa Enterprises Ltd.* (2000), 186 DLR (4th) 36 (Ont. CA); *ADGA Systems International Ltd. v. Valcom Ltd.* (1999), 43 OR (3d) 101 (CA); *Montreal Trust Co. of Canada v. ScotiaMcLeod Inc.* (1995), 26 OR (3d) 481 (CA); *Normart Management*

generally, and little more will be said about it here. The subject is one of considerable interest to this author,[12] but the issues involved are not, first and foremost, corporate law issues at all. Or, as Neil Campbell and John Armour have curtly put it:

> Company law has nothing useful to say in this area: the liability questions should be resolved simply by applying the established rules relating to the particular head of liability, with due regard paid to the defendant's capacity as an agent.[13]

CORPORATE CRIMINAL LIABILITY

Introduction

In the early morning hours of a spring day in 1987, a 23-year-old man climbed into his car and drove about 23 kilometres from Pickering, Ontario to the residence of his mother-in-law and father-in-law in Scarborough. When he arrived, he parked his car and entered his in-laws' home. He paused in the kitchen to pick up a knife before proceeding to the bedroom where his mother-in-law and father-in-law were fast asleep. Then the horror began. He strangled his father-in-law until his defenceless victim lost consciousness. He next stabbed and beat his mother-in-law to death.

The young man was charged with the murder of his mother-in-law, and the attempted murder of his father-in-law. He was eventually acquitted of both offences. Why? The court was satisfied that these attacks had been committed while the accused was sleepwalking. (An appeal of this acquittal was dismissed by the Ontario Court of Appeal and a further appeal to the Supreme Court of Canada was also dismissed.)[14]

It may seem odd to begin a discussion of corporate criminal liability with a summary of the facts of this rather extraordinary homicide trial. However, this unusual example does illustrate a fundamental proposition of Canadian criminal law: to be convicted of a criminal offence, an accused must have had the requisite intent to commit that offence, and where that mental element is lacking—as it was in the case of this sleepwalking (indeed sleep-driving) killer—there can be no conviction.

Now, if it is possible for a court to acquit a human being because the requisite mental element of the crime cannot be established, consider how much more challenging is the prospect of convicting a corporation of a criminal offence. Simply put, how can one prove *mens rea* (guilty mind) in the absence of any *mens*? Historically, it was generally thought that corporations could not be convicted of criminal offences, a principle grandly expressed in the ponderous Latin maxim "*societas delinquere non potest*." Vicarious

---

Ltd. v. West Hill Redevelopment Co. (1998), 37 OR (3d) 97 (CA); *NBD Bank, Canada v. Dofasco Inc.* (1999), 46 OR (3d) 514 (CA); *London Drugs Ltd. v. Kuehne & Nagel International Ltd.*, [1992] 3 SCR 299; and *Berger v. Willowdale A.M.C.* (1983), 41 OR (2d) 89 (CA).

12 See Christopher C. Nicholls, "Liability of Corporate Officers and Directors to Third Parties" (2001), 35 *Canadian Business Law Journal* 1.

13 Neil Campbell and John Armour, "Demystifying the Civil Liability of Corporate Agents" (2003), 62 *Cambridge Law Journal* 290, at 291.

14 *R v. Parks* (1992), 95 DLR (4th) 27 (SCC).

liability, which made the analysis of most corporate tort liabilities fairly straightforward, did not apply to criminal offences.

The world has moved on. Corporations can be, and frequently are, convicted of criminal offences. Nor has this development always required the courts to grapple with the issue of corporate *mens rea*, because certain offences—especially of the regulatory variety—require no proof of such a mental element, regardless of whether the accused is a natural or an artificial person.

Indeed, the Supreme Court of Canada in two leading cases from 1978 and 1985 noted[15] that criminal (and quasi-criminal) offences can generally be divided into the following three categories:

- *Absolute liability offences*: offences for which the commission of the guilty "act" constitutes the entire offence. No mental element need be shown in order to secure a conviction. Minor parking offences offer simple examples of such offences. One is liable to pay a fine for overstaying one's welcome at a parking meter regardless of whether one did or did not have any intention to commit the offence.
- *Strict liability offences*: offences for which, to obtain a conviction, the prosecution need prove only that the accused committed the culpable act (or *actus reus*). The accused may still avoid conviction for such offences if he or she is able to success-fully establish a due diligence defence. A number of regulatory offences fall into this category, including certain offences under environmental protection legislation.
- *Full* mens rea *offences*: traditional serious criminal offences in respect of which, to obtain a conviction, the prosecution must not only establish that the accused com-mitted the culpable act, but must also demonstrate the requisite mental element or *mens rea*.

No novel legal theory is needed to find a corporation guilty of offences in either of the first two categories, because those offences do not require the prosecution to prove that the accused—human or corporate—acted with intent; proof that the accused committed the prohibited act warrants a conviction, subject, in the case of strict liability offences, to the possibility that the accused might successfully raise a due diligence defence.

Still, for offences in the third category, the most serious offences, for which conviction requires proof of intent (or *mens rea*), determining the purpose and means of prosecuting corporations has fuelled considerable debate.

Important amendments to the *Criminal Code* concerning corporate criminal liability were recently proclaimed into force.[16] Some of the implications of this new legislation are discussed later in this chapter. It is, however, important to understand the context in which this legislation emerged; and that, in turn, requires an examination of the judicially created doctrine "identification theory."

---

15   See, e.g., *Canadian Dredge & Dock Company v. R*, [1985] 1 SCR 662 and *R v. Sault St. Marie*, [1978] 2 SCR 1299.

16   SC 2003, c. 21. (Proclaimed into force March 31, 2004.)

Identification Theory

The principle underlying identification theory is easily explained: some corporate actors are more than mere employees or agents of the corporation; for all practical purposes, they *are* the corporation, or at least, they represent the corporation's directing mind. Thus, their actions are the corporation's actions and their intentions may be considered the corporation's intentions.

The identification theory, once so central to corporate criminal liability, appears to have its origin in a civil case: *Lennard's Carrying Co. Ltd. v. Asiatic Petroleum Co. Ltd.*[17] This case arose out of a shipping accident. A ship, carrying a cargo of benzene, caught fire. The court determined that the cause of the fire was the unseaworthiness of the ship. The cargo was lost, and the owners of the cargo sued the owner of the ship, a corporation, for damages. Under the *Merchant Shipping Act*, an owner of a ship was not liable for any loss or damage that happened "without his actual fault or privity." In other words, proving that someone—even an employee of the owner corporation—had been negligent would *not* be enough to implicate the corporation itself. To succeed, the plaintiff somehow had to establish that the owner corporation itself was "personally" at fault.

As it happened, the ship was managed by a second corporation. A Mr. Lennard was described as "the active director"[18] and the "active spirit"[19] of the managing corporation. He was also a director of the corporation that owned the ship (a corporation that includes "Lennard" in its corporate name). Mr. Lennard's was the name that appeared in the ship's register.[20] Could the fault of Mr. Lennard be attributed to the corporation itself?

In considering whether the damage in this case had resulted from the corporate owner's actual fault or privity, Viscount Haldane made the following now famous remarks:

> My Lords, a corporation is an abstraction. It has no mind of its own any more than it has a body of its own; its active and directing will must consequently be sought in the person of somebody who for some purposes may be called an agent, but who is really the directing mind and will of the corporation, the very ego and centre of the personality of the corporation.[21]

Of Mr. Lennard, Viscount Haldane concluded,

> [I]f Mr. Lennard was the directing mind of the company, then his action must, unless a corporation is not to be liable at all, have been an action which was the action of the company itself within the meaning of [the statute] ... . It must be ... in such a case as the present one that the fault or privity is the fault or privity of somebody who is not merely a servant or agent for whom the company is liable upon the footing respondeat superior, but somebody for whom the company is liable because his action is the very action of the company itself.[22]

---

17   [1915] AC 705 (HL).

18   Ibid., at 712.

19   Ibid.

20   Ibid.

21   Ibid., at 713.

22   Ibid., at 713-14.

Mr. Lennard was, in the court's view, such a directing mind. Thus, his misfeasance constituted the "actual fault" of the corporation itself. The House of Lords thus upheld the Appeal Court's judgment in favour of the plaintiffs. (Not surprisingly, the English law on this point has evolved since *Lennard's Carrying Co. Ltd.* was decided.[23])

The same reasoning has been used to attribute the criminal intent of individuals who may be said to be a corporation's "directing mind and will" to the corporation itself for the purpose of imposing criminal liability on the corporation.

However, it was not enough merely to identify an employee of the corporation as the guilty actor. Imposing liability on corporations for the criminal acts of any employee, no matter how junior, would be tantamount to imposing criminal liability on the corporation vicariously. No human employer would be held vicariously liable for the (full *mens rea*) crimes committed by his or her employees. It has thus been argued that there is, similarly, no compelling reason for the law to make corporate employers vicariously liable for all of their employees' crimes either.

Identification theory, and the resulting proposition that a corporation may be convicted of full *mens rea* offences, thus represented a kind of compromise between two extremes: complete immunity for corporations from criminal prosecution, on the one hand, and criminal liability for all criminal acts committed by corporate agents or employees, no matter how junior, on the other. Estey J expressly acknowledged the intermediate nature of the identification theory in *Canadian Dredge & Dock Company v. R*,[24] dubbing identification theory a "median rule" that "is but a legal fiction invented for pragmatic reasons."[25]

Who Is a Corporation's Directing Mind and Will?

Once it had been determined that a corporation may be held "personally" (or perhaps corporately) liable for the criminal actions of some, but not all, of its human "agents," it next became critical for the law to develop some criteria upon which to determine the category in which any particular corporate employee or agent will fall.

The Supreme Court of Canada attempted to articulate some general principles on this subject in two important cases: *Canadian Dredge & Dock Company v. R*[26] and, more recently, *The "Rhone" v. The "Peter A.B. Widener."*[27] One may abstract several important concepts concerning the application of the identification doctrine from these cases:

- *"Governing executive authority"*: "The individual who is identified as the corporation's directing mind and will must have been delegated the 'governing executive authority' of the company within the scope of his or her authority."[28] As Iacobucci J

---

23   See, in particular, *Meridian Global Funds Management Asia Ltd. v. Securities Commission*, [1995] 2 AC 500 (PC).

24   *Canadian Dredge & Dock*, supra footnote 15.

25   Ibid., at para. 14.

26   Ibid.

27   [1993] 1 SCR 497.

28   Ibid., at para. 32.

put it: "The key factor which distinguishes directing minds from normal employees is the capacity to exercise decision-making authority on matters of corporate policy, rather than merely to give effect to such policy on an operational basis."[29]

• *Acting within the scope of authority*: Before the criminal actions of a "directing mind" may be attributed to a corporation, the directing mind must be acting "within the scope of his authority." But this does not mean that he or she was operating "within the scope of his or her employment." Rather, the question is whether the directing mind or will was acting "within the field [or sector] of operations delegated to the operating mind. ... The sector may be functional, or geographic, or may embrace the entire undertaking of the corporation."[30] "Acts of the *ego* of a corporation taken within the assigned managerial area may give rise to corporate criminal responsibility, whether or not there be formal delegation; whether or not there be awareness of the activity in the board of directors or the officers of the company; and ... whether or not there be express prohibition."

• *Defence where a criminal act of the directing mind is in fraud of the corporation*: One difficulty frequently encountered in cases of alleged criminal liability is that the corporation itself may be among the victims of the wrongful actions of the "directing mind." Clearly, where the corporation is the *only* victim (as, for example, in the case of embezzlement by a senior officer), there is no issue of the corporation's criminal liability. But occasionally, the directing mind may be engaged in acts that are partly designed to benefit the corporation, and partly for the directing mind's own benefit. In those cases, the inquiry becomes especially complex. The Supreme Court has suggested:

> Where the criminal act is totally in fraud of the corporate employer and where the act is intended to and does result in benefit exclusively to the employee–manager, the employee–directing mind, from the outset of the design and execution of the criminal plan, ceases to be a directing mind of the corporation and consequently his acts could not be attributed to the corporation under the identification doctrine. ... [T]he identification doctrine only operates where the Crown demonstrates that the action taken by the directing mind (a) was within the field of operation assigned to him; (b) was not totally in fraud of the corporation; and (c) was by design or result partly for the benefit of the company.[31]

The *Rhone* was decided in 1993, prior to the important decision of the Privy Council in *Meridian Global Funds Management Asia Ltd. v. Securities Commission*.[32] However, there is little need to speculate on how Canadian identification theory might thereafter have evolved had the matter been left entirely to the courts. In 2004, a new *Criminal Code* provision dealing with this subject came into force. Armed with this brief summary

---

29   Ibid., at para. 42.

30   Ibid., at para. 22. This concept is said by the court to echo the concept of acting "within the scope of delegation" as that phrase is used by Lord Reid in *Tesco Supermarkets Ltd. v. Nattrass*, [1972] AC 153 (HL).

31   *Canadian Dredge & Dock*, supra footnote 15, at para. 68.

32   Supra footnote 23.

of identification theory, we now turn to consider the recent amendments to Canada's *Criminal Code* aimed at addressing perceived shortcomings in the common law.

Bill C-45

In 2003, Parliament introduced a series of important changes to the *Criminal Code* in Bill C-45. These amendments were prompted in no small part by reactions to the 1992 Westray mine disaster in Plymouth, Nova Scotia, when 26 miners were killed in a coal mine explosion. Bill C-45 received Royal Assent in November 2003, and was proclaimed into force on March 31, 2004.

The Department of Justice summarized the principle features of Bill C-45 as follows:

- The criminal liability of corporations and other organizations will no longer depend on a senior member of the organization with policy-making authority (i.e., a "directing mind" of the organization) having committed the offence.
- The physical and mental elements of criminal offences attributable to corporations and other organizations will no longer need to be derived from the same individual.
- The class of personnel whose acts or omissions can supply the physical element of a crime (*actus reus*) attributable to a corporation or other organization will be expanded to include all employees, agents and contractors.
- For negligence-based crimes, the mental element of the offence (*mens rea*) will be attributable to corporations and other organizations through the aggregate fault of the organization's "senior officers" (which will include those members of management with operational, as well as policy-making, authority).
- For crimes of intent or recklessness, criminal intent will be attributable to a corporation or other organization where a senior officer is a party to the offence, or where a senior officer has knowledge of the commission of the offence by other members of the organization and fails to take all reasonable steps to prevent or stop the commission of the offence.
- Sentencing principles specifically designed for corporate/organizational offenders will be adopted.
- Special rules of criminal liability for corporate executives will be rejected.
- An explicit legal duty will be established on the part of those with responsibility for directing the work of others, requiring such individuals to take reasonable steps to prevent bodily harm arising from such work.[33]

Because the purpose of this book is to introduce the principles of corporate law, not criminal law, little more will be said about Bill C-45 here. Note, however, that the common law concept of the directing mind has been broadened by the bill in at least two respects. First, in the case of offences that require proof of negligence, the legislation introduces the concept of aggregation. That is, it is not necessary to find a single "directing mind" upon whose conduct corporate liability will turn. Rather, a corporation

---

33   Quoted in the legislative summary of Bill C-45 prepared on behalf of the Parliamentary Research Bureau. See David Goetz, *Legislative Summary, Bill C-45: An Act to Amend the Criminal Code* (July 3, 2003). Available online at http://www.parl.gc.ca/.

(or other organization) may be party to an offence (assuming the responsible senior officer or officers have departed from the appropriate standard of care that "could reasonably be expected to prevent a representative ... from being a party to the offence"[34]) if

> two or more of its representatives engage in conduct, whether by act or omission, such that, if it had been the conduct of only one representative, that representative would have been a party to the offence.[35]

The use of the word "representative" in this context is especially significant since this term includes directors, partners, employees, members, agents, and even contractors of an organization.[36]

Second, for offences that require the proof of fault other than negligence, the common law concept of directing mind has been replaced with a statutorily defined term, "senior officer." A senior officer is defined as

> a representative who plays an important role in the establishment of an organization's policies or is responsible for managing an important aspect of the organization's activities and, in the case of a body corporate, includes a director, its chief executive officer and its chief financial officer.[37]

Whether this definition of senior officer will prove, in practice, to extend to a wider or indeed narrower range of individuals than the common law concept of a corporation's "directing mind" remains to be seen. Criminal liability will be attributed to a corporation for crimes of this sort if one of its senior officers "with the intent at least in part to benefit the organization"[38] is either himself or herself a party to the offence (acting within the scope of his or her authority), has the requisite mental state, directs the work of other representatives such that they commit acts or make omissions relating to the offence, or fails to "take all reasonable measures"[39] to stop a representative from being party to the offence in cases where the senior officer knows that representative "is or is about to be a party to the offence."[40]

Implications of Corporate Criminal Liability

Although corporate liability for crimes is based essentially on an analogy to individual human liability, it would be unwise to deny the essential difference between the two.[41] But, when once it is established that a corporation may be charged with a criminal

---

34   Supra footnote 16, s. 2. The quoted language is from the *Criminal Code* (as amended), s. 22.1(b).

35   Ibid., s. 22.1(a).

36   Ibid., *Criminal Code* (as amended), s. 2, definition of "representative."

37   Ibid. The language quoted is from the new *Criminal Code*, s. 2 definition of "senior officer."

38   Ibid., s. 22.2.

39   Ibid., s. 22.2(c).

40   Ibid.

41   See, e.g., Victor V. Ramraj, "Disentangling Corporate Criminal Liability and Individual Rights" (2001), 45 *Criminal Law Quarterly* 29, arguing that this important distinction could justify "a separate corporate criminal code, governing corporate criminal liability and reflecting its distinct character" (at 52).

offence, a host of related legal questions follow along swiftly including issues such as the compellability of witnesses,[42] and, of course, the application of the *Canadian Charter of Rights and Freedoms*.[43] These issues, though undeniably important, are fundamentally matters of constitutional law and the law of evidence, and are most appropriately dealt with in those contexts (and by experts in those respective fields) rather than within the necessarily narrower perspective of the law of business corporations.

The Animating Logic of Corporate Criminal Liability and Punishment

The foregoing discussion may well give the inaccurate impression that identification doctrine is highly formalistic: determine if the guilty party satisfies some judicially approved list of "directing mind" attributes, and the crime is automatically attributed to the corporation. But attributing criminal liability to a corporation in any particular case is far from such a formalistic exercise, as the Privy Council's judgment in *Meridian Global Funds Management Asia Ltd.*[44] and the recent legislative initiatives embodied in Bill C-45 illustrate. Judicial and legislative approaches to corporate criminal liability inevitably involve implicit policy decisions about how the goals of criminal law are properly achieved by prosecuting non-human entities.

The process of determining whether a particular corporate actor is, as a matter of law, a "directing mind" (or, in some cases under Bill C-45, a "senior officer") for purposes of imposing criminal liability on a corporation in any specific case must be informed by the broader question of whether prosecution of the corporation in that case will likely achieve appropriate criminal law objectives.[45]

Is corporate crime fundamentally different from human crime? Chief Justice Lamer (as he then was) suggested in *R v. Wholesale Travel Group*[46] that "when the criminal law is applied to a corporation, it loses much of its 'criminal' nature and becomes, in essence, a 'vigorous' form of administrative law. With the possibility of imprisonment removed, and the stigma which attaches to conviction effectively reduced to a loss of *money*, the corporation is in a completely different situation than is an individual."[47]

Even before the 2004 legislation, it had been suggested that considerations of Canadian public policy objectives argued for a wider scope for corporate criminal liability than had

---

42   See, e.g., *R v. N.M. Paterson and Sons Ltd.*, [1980] 2 SCR 679; *R v. Amway Corp.*, [1989] 1 SCR 21.

43   See, e.g., *R v. Big M Drug Mart Ltd.*, [1985] 1 SCR 295; *Irwin Toy Ltd. v. Quebec (Attorney General)*, [1989] 1 SCR 927; *R v. CIP Inc.*, [1992] 1 SCR 843.

44   Supra footnote 23.

45   Thus, as Glanville Williams observed (in a passage quoted by Iacobucci J in *The Rhone*, supra footnote 27), exonerating corporations from criminal liability on the basis that the wrongdoer could not reasonably be considered a "directing mind" was probably of little consequence, because, as he put it, "[i]n crimes requiring *mens rea* it does not greatly matter if the range of persons inculpating the company is restricted, since the purposes of deterrence are generally best served by prosecuting those who are responsible" (that is, the individual human being himself or herself). See Glanville Williams, *Textbook of Criminal Law*, 2nd ed. (London: Stevens & Sons, 1983), at 973, quoted in *The Rhone*, supra footnote 27, at para. 30.

46   [1991] 3 SCR 154.

47   Ibid., at 182. (Emphasis in original.)

traditionally been recognized in England and, accordingly, for a broadening of the range of corporate actors who might properly be found to constitute a corporation's "directing mind."[48]

Of course, assessing the efficacy of applying the criminal law to corporations involves not only pondering theories of liability, but also considering questions of sentencing. For a recent extended discussion by a Canadian court of the goals and principles of sentencing corporations, see *R v. General Scrap Iron and Metals Ltd.*[49] Bill C-45 also includes a list of specific factors to be considered by a court when sentencing an organization. These factors clearly attempt to deal both with social cost–benefit analysis and the unintended effects of corporate sentencing of innocent corporate actors. Some factors to be considered by courts include, for example: "any advantage realized by the organization as a result of the offence"; "the impact that the sentence would have on the economic viability of the organization and the continued employment of its employees"; "the cost to public authorities of the investigation and prosecution of the offence"; and "any measures that the organization has taken to reduce the likelihood of it committing a subsequent offence."[50]

The issue of corporate crime and punishment has not, however, been of interest only to the courts. It is well beyond the scope of this introductory book to fairly canvass the extensive academic debate over the goals and efficacy of imposing criminal liability on corporations.[51] Suffice it to say that the literature on this subject is immense. In recent years, law and economics scholars in particular have taken a considerable interest in this subject.[52] Not surprisingly, the concern raised in the law and economics literature relates to the potential inefficiencies resulting from corporate criminal liability, and the corresponding question of how and when criminal sanctions ought to be imposed in the corporate sphere so that they do at least as much good as harm.

A competing literature examines the issue from a rather different perspective. Some scholars have challenged many of the premises underlying traditional analysis of corporate criminal liability. Some commentators, for example, roundly denounced the identification doctrine as a basis for corporate criminal liability in the first place, arguing that its focus on individuals within the corporation might usefully give way to a truly "corporate" notion of criminal liability.[53]

---

48   See, e.g., *Canadian Dredge & Dock*, supra footnote 15, at 693 and *The Rhone*, supra footnote 27, at para. 31. See Kent Roach, *Criminal Law*, 3rd ed. (Toronto: Irwin, 2004), at 201. The English position to which the Supreme Court referred was the position articulated in *Tesco Supermarkets Ltd. v. Nattrass*, supra footnote 30. More recently, however, the matter has been revisited by the Privy Council in *Meridian Global Funds Management Asia Ltd.*, supra footnote 23. For a discussion of this case, see Paul L. Davies, *Gower & Davies' Principles of Modern Company Law*, 7th ed. (London: Sweet & Maxwell, 2003), at 172ff.

49   2003 ABQB 22.

50   Supra footnote 16, s. 14. This section adds section 718.21 to the *Criminal Code*.

51   See, e.g., V.S. Khanna, "Corporate Criminal Liability: What Purpose Does It Serve?" (1996), 109 *Harvard Law Review* 1477.

52   See, e.g., D. Fischel and A. Sykes, "Corporate Crime" (1996), 25 *Journal of Legal Studies* 328; and Jennifer Arlen, "The Potentially Perverse Effects of Corporate Criminal Liability" (1994), 23 *Journal of Legal Studies* 833.

53   See, e.g., Jennifer A. Quaid, "The Assessment of Corporate Criminal Liability on the Basis of Corporate Identity: An Analysis" (1998), 43 *McGill Law Journal* 67. See also text accompanying footnote 54, infra.

As the earlier discussion indicates, the "problem" of corporate criminal responsibility emerges because the framework of our criminal law assumes that crimes are committed by human beings. As Celia Wells has suggested, however,

> [o]nly if autonomy and rationality ... were both necessary and sufficient for criminal responsibility would corporations have to be excluded *ex necessitate*. There may be good reasons why corporate liability should neither flow from nor depend on the same arguments as those which serve for individuals.[54]

Essentially, Wells cautions that it is misguided to mistake for a principle of corporate law the usual justification for requiring proof of intent to commit a criminal offence— namely, to avoid convicting someone who ought not to be convicted. The critical issue, in her view, is: whom do we want to be able to convict? We should not, she points out, substitute for that critical inquiry the formalistic question, "can we find a mind to which to attach *mens rea*?" Wells, in other words, suggests that it might be possible to devise a uniquely corporate theory of criminal responsibility that goes beyond finding the corporation's intent within the mind of an individual guilty actor. Drawing on the work of other authors, she suggests that "corporations exhibit their own special kind of intentionality, namely corporate policy."[55]

Evidently, Australian federal criminal law has adopted tests for corporate *mens rea* that take into account a facilitative corporate culture.[56] As we have seen, the most recent Canadian *Criminal Code* amendments do not go this far, still focusing, in large measure, on the role played by "senior officers."

CONCLUSION

Corporate liability for tort and crime challenge our conceptions of "fault" and responsibility. But perhaps, more fundamentally, a careful consideration of these issues ought to lead us to reconsider and redefine the precise social benefit of tort and criminal law and, of course, of the modern business corporation as well.

---

54   Celia Wells, *Corporations and Criminal Responsibility*, 2nd ed. (Oxford: Oxford University Press, 2001).

55   Ibid., at 71.

56   See Goetz, supra footnote 33. Goetz notes, however, that in Australia, criminal law is still primarily a matter of state, rather than federal, authority and this modification has not been adopted at the state level.

CHAPTER NINE

The Basic Structure of the Modern Business Corporation

INTRODUCTION

If the importance of a subject can be judged by the number of government and industry reports it has generated, then corporate governance is on its way to becoming the single, most important topic in all of corporate law. An unprecedented rise in the market price of publicly traded shares reached its apex in the first quarter of 2000. This equity price boom was followed by a general slide in the market, a slide that was exacerbated by the turmoil caused by the stunning terrorist attacks of September 11, 2001. Soon thereafter came a series of high-profile US corporate scandals and failures in 2001 and 2002, and these were popularly blamed for further depressing prices and stalling the market's recovery.[1]

Angry investors and the politicians who court their votes soon catapulted the issue of how business corporations govern themselves to the top of the political agenda. What was once a question of limited popular interest, suddenly became a matter of apparent urgency. Indeed, the public observed an especially poignant sign of the profile this issue had acquired in the summer of 2002, when the president of the United States addressed a national audience standing in front of a banner trumpeting the phrase "corporate responsibility." A subject once considered the exclusive preserve of corporate lawyers, regulators, and business executives had managed to gain pride of place on the public agenda.

This chapter, and the two chapters following it, will outline many of the issues that are conventionally discussed under the "corporate governance" rubric, and will briefly discuss a number of the specific legal, regulatory, and industry measures introduced to address these issues.

Corporate governance is often bifurcated into two essential considerations: "shareholder voice"[2] (the principal topic of chapter 10) and "director (and officer) obligations"

---

1   Some (including the present author) have questioned whether the link between these scandals and low stock prices is really the simple "cause and effect" relationship that has been favoured by the press and some legislators. That argument is, however, well beyond the scope of this book.

2   The term "voice" in the organizational context is usually attributed to Albert O. Hirschman's book, *Exit, Voice, and Loyalty* (Cambridge, MA: Harvard University Press, 1970), in which he examined responses to organizational failure as taking one of two forms: exit or voice. Hirschman did not confine the use of exit and voice options to organization members (such as shareholders); he noted that these two options were also broadly available to the consumers of an organization's products or services.

(the principal topic of chapter 11). More fundamentally, at the heart of all corporate governance concerns lies the so-called agency issue, as discussed in chapter 1. Recall in this context that "agency" is an economic term—it is quite distinct from the legal definition of agency. Agency concerns, as an economic matter, arise when assets are owned by one person (the economic "principal"), but are under the control of another (the economic "agent"). This separation of ownership and control imposes costs—agency costs—that do not exist when ownership and control rest in the same hands.[3] In the corporate context, agency costs include monitoring costs incurred by shareholders, bonding costs incurred by corporate officers and directors, and the remaining residual losses that cannot be eliminated.[4] As one considers the array of corporate governance mechanisms that exist in Canada and elsewhere, it is useful to consider to what extent they represent monitoring or bonding mechanisms.

The following sections consider each of the basic building blocks in the corporate governance structure. The canvass of these basic structural features is then followed by a discussion of a number of more specific parts of the governance equation. Chapter 10 will focus in particular on "shareholder voice," and will provide an outline of some of the principal methods by which that voice may be heard—whether as a whisper or a shout—using the *Canada Business Corporations Act* (CBCA) provisions as a convenient example. Discussion of corporate governance will then continue in chapter 11, where the emphasis will be on the duties, responsibilities, and potential liabilities of the corporation's directors and officers.

THE BUILDING BLOCKS OF CORPORATE GOVERNANCE

The basic structure of the modern business corporation in Canada, the United States, and the United Kingdom is well established. Shareholders elect the corporation's directors. The directors then appoint the corporation's officers, and the officers hire employees and run the business. This pattern is conventional, though it is not invariably mandated by statute. As Gower and Davies point out, referring to the English *Companies Act*,

> contrary to popular belief, the Act requires neither that directors be elected by the shareholders in general meeting nor that they submit themselves periodically to re-election by the shareholders.[5]

Though true of the UK *Companies Act*, this statement is no longer an accurate description of the law in many Canadian jurisdictions. The CBCA and many other Canadian corporate statutes now do expressly provide that the shareholders must vote to elect directors, and that this vote is to occur at the annual meeting of shareholders.[6] (The

---

3   Michael Jensen and William Meckling, "Theory of the Firm: Managerial Behavior, Agency Costs and Ownership Structure" (1976), 3 *Journal of Financial Economics* 305.

4   Ibid.

5   Paul L. Davies, *Gower & Davies: Principles of Modern Company Law*, 7th ed. (London: Sweet & Maxwell, 2003), at 307.

6   See, e.g., *The Business Corporations Act* (Sask.), s. 101(3); CBCA, s. 106(3); *Business Corporations Act* (Alta.), s. 106(3) (but for an important exception, see text accompanying footnote 7, infra); *The*

Alberta *Business Corporations Act*, however, does state that, if the articles or a unanimous shareholder agreement so provide, directors may be elected "by creditors or employees of the corporation or by a class or classes of those creditors or employees,"[7] a provision that is reflected in the Alberta statute's articulation of directors' fiduciary duties as mentioned in chapter 10.) Even where a statute does not explicitly require it, however, convention and the financial markets demand that the holders of at least one class of shares enjoy the right to elect the corporation's directors.

Although the formal roles played by shareholders (as shareholders), directors (as directors), and officers (as officers) are distinct, there is no requirement—legal or otherwise—that different human beings occupy these various positions. It is quite possible, and indeed not at all uncommon, for an individual to be a shareholder, a director, and an officer of the same corporation. In small, private corporations, it is, in fact, very much the norm for each of the major participants to function simultaneously in all of these roles.

The situation is different in large, public corporations. Most shareholders of public companies have neither the time, the talent, nor the inclination to become directors or officers of the corporation. Most shareholders of public corporations thus take no part whatsoever in the management of those corporations, preferring instead to remain passive investors. And, although it is no longer typically a legal requirement that directors or senior officers hold shares in their corporations, as a matter of business practice, officers and directors of public corporations are usually expected to hold shares. In fact, it is not uncommon for some portion of their remuneration to come to them in the form of share interests of one sort or another.

Shareholders Elect the Board of Directors

Shareholders, in return for their investment of capital—that is, the money they have paid to the corporation to purchase their shares[8]—acquire a bundle of rights. Those rights may

---

Corporations Act (Man.), s. 101(2); *Business Corporations Act* (Ont.), s. 119(4); *Corporations Act* (NL), s. 175(3); and *Companies Act* (PEI), s. 24. It should be noted that, although annual meetings are mandated, directors may be elected for terms longer than one year, but not typically longer than three years.

7   *Business Corporations Act* (Alta.), s. 109(b).

8   Of course, when a person purchases shares in the secondary market (such as through the facilities of a stock exchange), the money he or she pays does not go to the corporation that has issued those shares; it goes to the person from whom those shares have been purchased. Nevertheless, the purchaser has become an investor in the corporation because he or she has, in effect, stepped into the shoes of the former shareholder, and has paid a price for this privilege. Although corporations receive no new money when their shares change hands in secondary markets, corporations are far from indifferent about the operation of those secondary securities markets. The stock markets support the "primary markets"—that is, the market for new shares first issued by a corporation—in essential ways: the price a purchaser of new shares will be willing to pay will be strongly affected by the purchaser's expectation that he or she will be able to resell the share at a time of his or her choosing in the secondary market. Furthermore, the price at which a public corporation's shares are traded in the capital markets provides important signals to the corporation, and reflects, among other things, the market's view of the success or failure of the corporation's managers.

include (at least in the case of common or ordinary shares)[9] the right to elect the directors of the corporation. That election normally occurs at the company's annual meeting.

The directors of the corporation manage, or supervise the management of, the corporation's business.[10] In the case of large, public corporations, *supervision* of management is the only function that the board can realistically perform.[11] The actual operational management of such corporations is left to the corporation's full-time officers.

In small, private corporations, the election of directors is not necessarily such a formal matter. The principals of the company (that is, the people who established the corporation, typically own most or all of the shares, and actively run the business) agree in advance to take all necessary steps to ensure that they are all elected as directors,[12] and are appointed to specified corporate offices.[13] The corporate governance issues encountered within small, private corporations are very different from those of large, public corporations. Within private corporations, governance issues often relate to intershareholder disputes rather than, as in the case of public corporations, to conflicts between shareholders and managers that arise from the separation of ownership and control in those large corporations.

The election of directors of a large, public corporation is very different from the election of people to political office, at least as those political elections occur in democratic countries. To begin with, the shareholders are not usually asked to choose between

---

9   As discussed in chapter 12, the terms "common" shares and "ordinary" shares are not used in the CBCA. However, as a matter of convention, these terms are used when referring to equity shares conferring on the holders, among other things, the right to vote for the election of the corporation's directors. This brief statement, however, skirts over a very significant policy debate concerning the meaning of "common" or "ordinary" or "equity" shares, and whether a corporation should be permitted to issue shares so designated that carry no voting rights. This matter was the subject of some discussion in the 1962 *Report of the Company Law Committee* (the Jenkins committee), at paras. 123-136, and that discussion, in turn, prompted the Lawrence committee, in 1967, to consider the matter as well. (See *1967 Interim Report of the Select Committee on Company Law*, at 30-33.)

10   See, e.g., CBCA, s. 102; *Business Corporations Act* (Ont.), s. 115. *The Corporations Act* (Man.) and the *Corporations Act* (NL) have slightly different wordings. They provide that the directors are to "exercise the powers of the corporation directly or indirectly" and "direct the management of the business and affairs of the corporation." See *The Corporations Act* (Man.), s. 97(1) and *Corporations Act* (NL), s. 167.

11   The Dey report, in fact, had recommended that the language of Canadian corporate statutes expressly acknowledge that directors of public corporations need only supervise the management of corporations. *Where Were the Directors? Guidelines for Improved Corporate Governance* (Toronto: Toronto Stock Exchange, 1994). Language to this effect was added to s. 102 of the CBCA in 2001. The comparable provision in the Ontario *Business Corporations Act* already provided that directors must either manage or supervise the management of the corporation. The New Brunswick *Business Corporations Act* and the Alberta *Business Corporations Act* still have the older form of language, indicating that the directors are to manage "the business and affairs of the corporation." See *Business Corporations Act* (NB), s. 60(1) and *Business Corporations Act* (Alta.), s. 101(1).

12   In fact, there may be few formalities associated with this "vote." The parties may simply draft a simple written resolution, to be included in the company's minute book, stating that the shareholders have elected certain directors to hold office until the next annual meeting or until their successors are elected or appointed.

13   The mechanics of shareholder agreements, including unanimous shareholder agreements, are canvassed in chapter 4.

competing candidates. Instead, a slate of directors, endorsed by the corporation's management, is typically put forward. At most, then, the shareholders are asked to endorse the choice of these directors, or to withhold their endorsement. However, for reasons discussed later, it has been very difficult for shareholders—on their own—to nominate rival candidates of their own choosing. Recently, there have been a number of proposals and initiatives aimed at enhancing the role of shareholders in the choice of directors, and some of these measures are discussed below.

Removal of Directors

Shareholders not only elect directors, they may also remove them. At common law, shareholders did not enjoy the right to remove a director before that director's term had expired. If, for example, a director was elected to a three-year term, then, at least in the absence of fraud, that director—like a member of Parliament—would be entitled to stay in office until the expiration of that term, unless power to remove directors was conferred by statute or by the corporation's bylaws.[14]

The Dickerson committee thought that this limit on the power of shareholders was inappropriate. They considered the right of shareholders to remove directors before their term had expired to be "elementary and necessary, and that it should not depend on fortuitous provision for removal in the corporate constitution."[15] Accordingly, the CBCA gives shareholders the right to remove directors at any time by ordinary resolution (that is, by a simple majority vote).[16] There are two exceptions to this rule. First, when the corporation's articles provide for cumulative voting rights, special rules apply. These rules are needed to ensure that the protection that cumulative voting rights is intended to give to minority shareholders in the first place is not completely undone by director removal rules. Put simply, there would be little point in ensuring that minority shareholders could elect directors to the board if the majority shareholders could immediately thereafter remove any such directors from office.[17] Similarly, where the corporation has issued a class (or series) of shares that gives holders the right to elect a director to the board, that director may only be removed by a vote of the holders of that same class (or series) of shares.[18]

Statutory Requirements Concerning Directors

Number of Directors

A CBCA corporation must have at least one director.[19] This is the usual minimum requirement in provincial corporation statutes as well. Public corporations, or "distributing

---

14 See, e.g., *Imperial Hydropathic Hotel Co. v. Hampson* (1882), 23 Ch. D 1.

15 Robert W.V. Dickerson et al., *Proposals for a New Business Corporations Law for Canada*, vol. I, Commentary (Ottawa: Information Canada, 1971), at para. 209 (Dickerson committee).

16 CBCA, s. 109.

17 Ibid., and s. 107(g).

18 CBCA, s. 109(2).

19 CBCA, s. 102(2).

corporations" as they are called in the CBCA, must have at least three directors.[20] At least two directors of a distributing corporation must be neither officers nor employees of the corporation or its affiliates.[21]

Subject to these fairly minimal restrictions, the CBCA, and other Canadian provincial corporate statues, permit corporations to decide for themselves how large or how small they prefer their board of directors to be. The CBCA requires the size of the corporation's board to be set out in its articles but, as discussed in chapter 2, this does not necessarily mean that the articles must state a fixed number of directors. Instead, the Act permits the articles to state, if so desired, merely a "minimum and a maximum number of directors"—a choice often referred to by practitioners as a "flexible board." A flexible board is not permitted, however, if the articles provide for "cumulative voting," a concept that is discussed in the next section of this chapter.

It is common for incorporators to choose such a flexible board. The articles of many CBCA corporations, therefore, provide for a minimum of one director, and a maximum of some larger number of directors. How the actual size of the board, at any time, is to be determined varies slightly among Canadian corporate jurisdictions. For example, under the Ontario *Business Corporations Act*, when the articles provide for a flexible board, the actual number of directors to be elected at any time must be set by way of a special resolution of the shareholders, or, if the power to set the number has been delegated to the board by special resolution, by the board itself.[22] The CBCA contains no such explicit rules on how the size of the board, within the minimum and maximum number set out in the articles, is to be fixed. It is the usual practice, however, to include in the articles of incorporation a provision permitting the actual number to be fixed from time to time by directors' resolution.[23]

---

20   Ibid.

21   Ibid. Note that the CBCA requires only that a corporation has at least two directors who are neither officers or employees, regardless of how large the board is. Thus, whether a public corporation has a board of three or of thirty, it is still not required as a matter of corporate law to have more than two such non-employee, non-officer directors. However, as discussed below, a public corporation may be subject to pressures other than those contained in its governing statute that may lead it to ensure that its board includes a greater number of independent directors. An interesting issue that may arise, however, is precisely what should be done in cases where a public corporation does not have the requisite number of independent directors. Clearly, such a corporation would be in violation of the CBCA, but it may well be the case that a corporation is simply unable to find suitable independent candidates to sit on the board, owing, perhaps, to liability or reputational concerns. It is difficult to see how, as a practical matter, a corporation can be "forced" to find independent directors that simply may not be available. For a recent example of the quandary facing a public corporation when a series of board resignations leaves it without the requisite number of independent directors, see Paul Waldie, Richard Blackwell, and Sinclair Stewart, "Investor Opposes Black Sitting on CanWest Board," *Globe and Mail*, January 15, 2004, B1.

22   This mechanic is set out explicitly in the *Business Corporations Act* (Ont.), s. 125(3). The CBCA has no comparable explicit provisions.

23   There are other variations. *The Corporations Act* (Man.), for example, provides that the number of directors may be varied by special resolution (s. 107).

Flexible Boards and Cumulative Voting

Flexible boards are not permitted where a corporation's articles provide for cumulative voting.[24] To fully understand this exception, one needs to understand how cumulative voting works. Unfortunately, cumulative voting is difficult to explain other than by way of a numerical example.[25] Rather than setting out such an example, here is a general explanation. Cumulative voting is a technique by which a corporation may give minority shareholders more voting power to elect directors than the ordinary "one share–one vote" rule permits. Without the cumulative voting option, when a shareholders' meeting is held to elect directors, each shareholder is typically entitled to cast one vote with respect to each share that he or she holds;[26] a shareholder (or a group of shareholders voting together) holding a bare minority of the corporation's voting shares (that is, 50 percent of the total plus 1 share) can thus elect every one of the directors they choose. In other words, holding 51 percent of a corporation's voting shares will not simply entitle the holder to elect 51 percent of the directors; it will normally enable the shareholder to elect 100 percent of the directors.

With cumulative voting, however, a kind of "proportional representation" becomes possible. The number of votes to which each shareholder is entitled under cumulative voting depends on the total number of directors to be elected at the meeting. Specifically, each share will carry the same number of votes as the number of directorships to be filled. If three directors are to be elected, each share carries three votes. If 10 directors are to be elected, each share carries 10 votes, and so on. "Candidates" are then voted for individually, not as a slate.[27] What this means is that, the greater the number of directors to be elected at a meeting, the greater the influence of the minority shareholders. (For proof of this statement, the reader is, once again, referred to the Dickerson committee's detailed numerical example.[28])

Where a corporation has adopted cumulative voting, the CBCA imposes special rules designed to make it difficult for the majority shareholders to reduce the size of the board, because if the size of the board is decreased, the benefit of cumulative voting to the minority shareholders is diluted. Normally, where a corporation has a flexible board, the directors themselves can change the number of directors at any time; no amendment to the articles is necessary and no shareholder approval is required. If it were possible to vary the number of directors this easily in the case of a corporation that had adopted cumulative voting, then any protection of cumulative voting would be lost.

---

24 See, e.g., CBCA, s. 107(a).

25 The Dickerson committee provides such an example, supra footnote 15, at para. 216.

26 It is possible, of course, for special classes of shares to be issued that carry greater voting rights per share. This simple example, however, assumes that a corporation has only one class of voting shares outstanding and that all of these shares, therefore, are equal in all respects and entitle each holder to one vote.

27 CBCA, s. 107(c). The requirement to vote on candidates individually can be varied, but only if *all* shareholders (including, obviously, every minority shareholder) agree.

28 Dickerson committee, supra footnote 15, at para. 216.

No more will be said about cumulative voting here. The decision to provide cumulative voting provisions in a corporation's articles in the first place is entirely optional, at least under most Canadian corporate statutes.[29] Because such a decision does not favour majority shareholders, it is unclear why such provisions would ever be adopted voluntarily. It is theoretically possible that the existence of cumulative voting rights might become critical to the marketing of new shares to prospective purchasers. However, there is no evidence that cumulative voting shares are the norm in the Canadian capital markets, nor does there seem to be evidence that investors are willing to pay a premium significant enough to entice corporations widely to adopt cumulative voting.

Can a Corporation Have No Directors?

At one time, based on what seemed, at least, to this author and many other lawyers, to be a strained and disingenuous reading of the Ontario *Business Corporations Act*, some creative Ontario lawyers were prepared to argue that a private Ontario corporation was not actually required to have any directors at all. This interpretation was, evidently, welcome news to some entrepreneurs. Because the names of directors must be disclosed in public filings, and because corporate directors may be exposed to personal liability in some circumstances, the possibility of running a corporation with no directors seemed quite advantageous.

Not all members of the bar agreed that this approach was necessarily permissible or even desirable.[30] Little more needs to be said about the point here, however, because the Ontario *Business Corporations Act* was ultimately amended to leave no doubt that the appointment of at least one director is mandatory,[31] and indeed—to eliminate any residual uncertainty—to deem anyone functioning as a director (whether officially appointed to the position or not) to *be* a director for purposes of the Act.[32]

There is one context, however, in which the requirement that a corporation must have at least one director is of dubious use. As discussed in chapter 4, it is possible for the shareholders of a CBCA corporation to enter into a unanimous shareholder agreement, which restricts the directors' powers to manage the corporation in whole or in part.[33] In those instances in which the shareholders of a CBCA corporation—or of a corporation with similar unanimous shareholder agreement rules—have chosen to restrict the powers

---

29   One notable exception is New Brunswick. The New Brunswick *Business Corporations Act*, s. 65, makes cumulative voting mandatory for corporations incorporated under it.

30   Among other things, many of the personal liabilities to which "directors" were exposed, attached to anyone who was acting as a director in fact, regardless of whether he or she had ever been formally given such a title.

31   *Business Corporations Act* (Ont.), s. 115(2). To similar effect, see CBCA, s. 102(2); *The Corporations Act* (Man.), s. 97(2); *Corporations Act* (NL), s. 168; *Companies Act* (NS), s. 93; and *Business Corporations Act* (Alta.), s. 101(2).

32   *Business Corporations Act* (Ont.), s. 115(4).

33   Many other provincial statutes also allow for the restriction of directors' powers by unanimous shareholders agreements or, perhaps, by including such a restriction in the articles themselves. See, e.g., *Corporations Act* (NL), s. 169.

of the directors in their entirety, it is not at all clear what purpose is served by requiring such a corporation to elect a (powerless) director nonetheless.[34]

As mentioned in chapter 4, the Dickerson committee had evidently been prepared to recommend that a corporation in such circumstances not be required to have a board of directors, but such an approach was regarded as an unacceptable undermining of the rule that all CBCA corporations were to have a majority of resident Canadians on their board of directors. It must be said that it has long been well known to Canadian corporate law practitioners that it is rather easy for Canadian subsidiaries of foreign corporations to circumvent the Canadian-majority director requirement for all practical purposes. The foreign parent simply needs to execute a unanimous shareholder agreement taking all powers away from the board of the Canadian corporation. Then, although a resident Canadian (such as the corporation's lawyer) would still technically be appointed to the board, that person would simply be a "cipher" or placeholder with no duties or responsibilities.

The efficacy of the CBCA's director residency requirement in the case of such corporations where the directors' powers have been effectively eliminated by a comprehensive unanimous shareholder agreement was always doubtful. Following the 2001 amendments to the CBCA that softened the director residency rules,[35] the argument for relaxing the requirement to have even one director where the board's powers have been completely stripped away is even more compelling.

In fact, insisting on the election of directors in circumstances where, as a matter of law, they would be forbidden[36] from exercising any directorial duties, also raises the spectre of potentially unavoidable liabilities. For example, suppose that the shareholders of a corporation have entered into a unanimous shareholder agreement by which they have restricted the directors' powers in their entirety. It is the shareholders' intention to run the business themselves, a possibility that the CBCA clearly anticipates. However, the shareholders elect a director nonetheless, so that they may be sure that the corporation is in full compliance with the CBCA provisions. The director is, perhaps, the lawyer who originally incorporated the company. Now, suppose that circumstances unfold that trigger the operation of some statutory provision that imposes personal liability on a corporation's directors. Perhaps, for example, the corporation has failed to withhold and remit source deductions from its employees' wages, thus exposing the corporation's directors to personal liability for the amounts that ought to have been withheld pursuant to s. 227.1 of the *Income Tax Act*. Directors are normally entitled to a "due diligence" defence under s. 227.1. But would a director with no authority to manage the corporation's business be able to demonstrate that he or she had taken any steps to make out such

---

34   For discussion of this point, including the comments of Robert Dickerson to the effect that his committee would have preferred to relax the requirement to appoint directors in such a case, see chapter 4.

35   These rules are discussed further below. See the text accompanying footnotes 46 to 48, infra.

36   The directors' power to manage or supervise the management of the corporation is expressly made subject to "any unanimous shareholder agreement." (CBCA, s. 102(1).) Moreover, CBCA s. 122(2) provides that "[e]very director and officer of a corporation shall comply with ... any unanimous shareholder agreement." Failure to abide by this provision would constitute an offence under the CBCA, punishable on summary conviction. (See CBCA, s. 251.)

a defence? Happily, in this particular context there appears to be some authority for the proposition that, where a director is powerless to act, he or she has satisfied the due diligence defence because he or she has done what any reasonable person in the circumstances would have done (as it happens, nothing).[37] And, of course, one assumes that the Canada Revenue Agency would never be so unreasonable as to attempt to recover unremitted source deductions from a director under such circumstances in any event. However, there are many other examples of statutes purporting to impose personal liability on directors, and though one certainly hopes that the prospect of personal liability for powerless directors under such statutes is equally remote, nonetheless, there seems to be little reason for the CBCA to retain the needless requirement for a corporation to elect a director who is unable to discharge any directorial duties.

Qualifications of Directors

BASIC QUALIFICATIONS

The statutory qualifications that must be satisfied by directors are not onerous. Under the CBCA, to be eligible to serve as a director, an individual must be at least 18 years of age, of sound mind, and not bankrupt.[38] There are similar requirements in some,[39] but not all, other Canadian corporate statutes.[40]

One particularly intriguing question is whether one corporation can serve as the director of another corporation and, if so, what the practical import of that would be. Of course, under the CBCA, only an individual (that is, a human being) may act as a director. In fact, the Dickerson committee expressly addressed this issue, and recommended this requirement so as to ensure that no practice of appointing corporations as directors would ever develop.[41] But no such express provision appears, for example, in the Nova Scotia *Companies Act*. In the United Kingdom, there is no prohibition against corporations acting as directors of other corporations, and according to Gower and Davies, parent corporations are, indeed, sometimes appointed as directors of their subsidiaries.[42] In

---

37   See, e.g., *Chempeval v. MNR*, [1990] 1 CTC 2385 (TCC). To similar effect, see also *Canada v. McKinnon*, [2001] 2 FC 203 (FCA) in which it is clear that the liability of directors under s. 227.1 of the *Income Tax Act* is predicated on their ability to freely choose a course of action—a freedom that the director of a corporation whose powers have been removed by a unanimous shareholder agreement would not enjoy.

38   CBCA, s. 105(1).

39   See, e.g., *Business Corporations Act* (Ont.), s. 118(1) and *Corporations Act* (NL), s. 119 (note that under the Newfoundland and Labrador statute, a director must be at least 19 years old).

40   The Nova Scotia *Companies Act*, for example, like the UK *Companies Act*, does not even specify a minimum age for directors.

41   Dickerson committee, supra footnote 15, at para. 199.

42   See Davies, supra footnote 5, at 308. The authors note, however, that this practice has likely waned since the passage of ss. 213 and 214 of the UK *Insolvency Act*, 1986. The brief explanation for this is that these sections create an offence of "wrongful trading" and s. 214 in particular imposes liability on a "shadow director," one in accordance with whom the corporation is accustomed to act. See ibid., at 194-200. Thus, the less autonomy a subsidiary corporation enjoys, the more likely it is that the parent corporation will be considered a "shadow director" and thus exposed to the very liability that it presumably sought to avoid by incorporating a separate limited liability subsidiary in the first place.

fact, a recent government report in the United Kingdom indicated that about 2 percent of the directors of UK companies are corporations.[43]

QUALIFYING SHARES

At one time, it was customary for corporations to require that every director hold at least one share. Indeed, many corporate statutes—including the Canadian federal statute that preceded the CBCA—made it mandatory for each director to hold at least one share. Many directors held no more than the single share they were obliged to own, and such a share was typically known as a "qualifying share."

The Dickerson committee noted that the share-holding requirement, unless it involved a significant number of shares, was "meaningless," and recommended that such a requirement was best left to the discretion of the incorporators.[44] Accordingly, the CBCA no longer requires that directors hold any shares in their corporations, but the Act does permit any corporation that wishes to include such a requirement in its articles to do so.[45]

RESIDENCY REQUIREMENTS

Some Canadian corporate law statutes require some proportion of the corporation's directors to be Canadian residents or, in the case of one provincial statute, to be residents of the province of incorporation. The value of a residency requirement is dubious, and there is little evidence that those provinces that do not impose such a requirement are somehow the worse for it. In fact, foreign corporations establishing subsidiaries in Canada have been known to choose to incorporate those subsidiaries in Canadian jurisdictions with no director residency requirements,[46] making the efficacy of insisting on such requirements in the remaining jurisdictions questionable indeed. The Dickerson committee cast considerable doubt on the value of imposing onerous director residency requirements on every corporation,[47] noting that if there are special concerns in particularly sensitive industries or sectors, those can be dealt with in more specific legislation.[48]

Nevertheless, the CBCA, prior to recent amendments in 2001, did require that every CBCA corporation have a majority of resident Canadian directors. Although the 2001

---

43 Secretary of State for Trade and Industry, *Modernising Company Law*, Command Paper CM 5553 (July 2002), at 3:32. Available online at http://www.dti.gov.uk/companiesbill/whitepaper.htm.

44 Dickerson committee, supra footnote 15, at para. 200.

45 CBCA, s. 105(2). There are similar provisions in other Canadian statutes. See, e.g., *Business Corporations Act* (Ont.), s. 118(2).

46 Wayne Gray has suggested that the "leading" choices for a foreign corporation in such circumstances are the corporate statutes of New Brunswick, and the three territories because these jurisdictions combine an otherwise "CBCA-style" statute with the freedom to have no resident Canadian directors. Three other Canadian jurisdictions also allow corporations the freedom to choose directors regardless of their residency, but none of these three—Nova Scotia, Prince Edward Island, and Quebec—has a statute based on the CBCA model. See Wayne D. Gray, "Corporations as Winners Under CBCA Reform" (2003), 39 *Canadian Business Law Journal* 4, at 25.

47 See Dickerson committee, supra footnote 15, at para. 201: "Canadian industry being what it is, it seems a futile gesture to impose a general requirement that directors of federally incorporated corporations should be citizens or residents of Canada."

48 Ibid.

amendments have softened the residency requirement, they did not totally eliminate it. According to the briefing book on the 2001 amendments prepared by Industry Canada, the rationale underlying the resident Canadian director requirement was "to specifically promote a Canadian viewpoint at meetings of directors of corporations controlled by non-resident Canadians."[49] However, that same source went on to explain that "this requirement is now posing a constraint on Canadian corporations which are growing to global size and expanding their investments. More and more, corporations require a board that reflects the international character of their business."[50] Thus, the board residency requirement was reduced so that boards of CBCA corporations must now include at least 25 percent resident Canadians,[51] and the requirement that committees of the board include resident Canadians was eliminated completely.

Some, but not all, other Canadian statutes also include some residency requirements. The Ontario statute,[52] for example, still requires not only that a majority of the board as a whole be resident Canadians, but also that a majority of the members of any board committee also be resident Canadians,[53] a requirement also found in Alberta,[54] Manitoba,[55] Newfoundland and Labrador,[56] and Saskatchewan.[57]

To complicate matters further, the definition of "resident Canadian" is not the same in every statute. The Ontario Act, for example, defines "resident Canadian" as

(a) a Canadian citizen ordinarily resident in Canada,

(b) a Canadian citizen not ordinarily resident in Canada who is a member of a prescribed class of persons, or

(c) a permanent resident within the meaning of the *Immigration Act* (Canada) and ordinarily resident in Canada.[58]

---

49   See Clause-by-Clause Briefing Book: Bill S-11, part 10, available online at http://strategis.ic.gc.ca/epic/internet/incilp-pdci.nsf/en/cl00284e.html.

50   Ibid.

51   CBCA, s. 105(3). Where a corporation has three or fewer directors, at least one of those directors must be a resident Canadian. Ibid. There are special rules in place for corporations engaged in certain businesses in which ownership restrictions are in place or in the following nationally sensitive business sectors, as prescribed in s. 16 of the *Canada Business Corporations Act Regulations, 2001*:

(a) uranium mining;

(b) book publishing or distribution; and

(c) book sales, where the sale of books is the primary part of the corporation's business; and

(d) film or video distribution

Those special rules will not be dealt with further here. See CBCA, ss. 105(3.1) and (4).

52   *Business Corporations Act* (Ont.), s. 118(3).

53   Ibid., s. 127(2).

54   *Business Corporations Act* (Alta.), s. 105(3) (board) and s. 115(2) (committees).

55   *The Corporations Act* (Man.), s. 100(3) (board) and s. 110(2) (committees).

56   *Corporations Act* (NL), s. 174(1) (board) and s. 189(2) (committees).

57   *The Business Corporations Act* (Sask.), s. 100(3) (board) and s. 110(2) (committees).

58   *Business Corporations Act* (Ont.), s. 1(1), definition of "resident Canadian."

The CBCA definition, however, is distinctly different in at least one important respect. Unlike the Ontario definition, which includes all permanent residents who are ordinarily resident in Canada, the CBCA definition states that a permanent resident *ceases* to qualify as a resident Canadian one year after he or she becomes eligible to apply for Canadian citizenship.[59] The somewhat odd effect of this definition is that a permanent resident of Canada might be appointed to the board of a CBCA corporation, fully complying with the resident Canadian definition, then, after some years have passed, that same person—although he or she has lived continuously in Canada—would suddenly cease to be a resident Canadian for CBCA purposes. At that moment, the corporation could potentially find itself running afoul of the CBCA requirement that at least 25 percent of the board members be resident Canadians.

The rationale for this particular requirement is somewhat baffling. As Iacobucci et al. noted in 1977,

> The [CBCA] thus continues to create a disability which seems designed to pressure landed immigrants into becoming citizens rather than to ensure that corporate decision-makers are cognizant of Canadian interests and needs.[60]

DEFECT IN DIRECTOR'S APPOINTMENT

Where there is some defect in a director's appointment, the Act makes it clear that the corporation ought not to be able to take advantage of that defect to defeat the interests of third parties dealing with the corporation through that putative director. Thus, s. 116 of the CBCA provides that, "an act of a director or officer is valid notwithstanding an irregularity in their election or appointment or a defect in their qualification." This provision is in addition to s. 18(1)(d), which was discussed in chapter 6.

Directors Manage or Supervise the Management of the Corporation

Directors' Authority To Manage

Perhaps one of the most important features of the modern Canadian corporation is the extent to which the directors—and not the shareholders—generally enjoy residual managerial authority. The directors, to be sure, are permitted to delegate many of their management functions. But the shareholders—notwithstanding that they are sometimes characterized as the "owners" of the corporation—typically have no right to participate in the management of the corporation. (There are exceptions to this statement, particularly in the case of private corporations in which the shareholders have entered into a unanimous shareholder agreement. This type of arrangement was discussed in chapter 4.)

---

59 CBCA, s. 2(1), definition of "resident Canadian." It goes without saying that if such a person does obtain Canadian citizenship he or she would continue to be a resident Canadian by virtue of the earlier part of the definition that includes all Canadian citizens ordinarily resident in Canada.

60 Frank Iacobucci, Marilyn Pilkington, and J. Robert S. Prichard, *Canadian Business Corporations: An Analysis of Recent Legislative Developments* (Toronto: Canada Law Book, 1977), at 248.

The dominant role played by directors (and by senior officers) seems an almost inevitable result of the increasing size and complexity of corporations, with the attendant need for specialized, professional managers. It makes no more sense to attempt to run a major corporation by shareholder plebiscite than to try to run a major nation-state in that way.

With respect to the allocation of shareholder and director authority, however, there is an important theoretical distinction that must be drawn among the governance structures of corporations incorporated under each of the three distinct types of Canadian incorporation jurisdictions: (1) memorandum and articles of association (such as those of the Nova Scotia and British Columbia corporate statutes); (2) letters patent (such as that of the PEI corporate statute); and (3) articles of incorporation—or "New York Style" (such as that of the CBCA and most other Canadian jurisdictions).

Theoretically, the directors of companies that have been formed in memorandum jurisdictions exercise only those powers that have been delegated to them by the shareholders. In contrast, in letters patent jurisdictions, the charter of the corporation has, as a technical matter, been granted to the incorporators by the Crown. The corporate constitution is not simply a matter of private agreement among the shareholders. In articles of incorporation jurisdictions (such as the CBCA), the directors' powers to manage are conferred on them by the incorporating statute itself. They are not simply delegated to them by the shareholders. However, there is considerable flexibility under the CBCA not only for the directors to delegate their managerial authority to others, but also for the shareholders to assume some or all of the directors' powers themselves by choosing to enter into a unanimous shareholder agreement, as discussed in chapter 4. A unanimous shareholder agreement is a practical possibility only in the case of private corporations, of course, and has no part to play in the governance of large, public corporations in which the issues relating to the separation of ownership and control are typically encountered.

It is useful to be aware of the theoretical differences in governance structures that reflect underlying differences in Canadian corporate statutes because in marginal cases it can often be helpful to return to first principles in the analysis of legal rules. At the same time, it would be misleading to suggest that these theoretical distinctions result in major differences in the way in which most Canadian corporations are actually managed today. In other words, Canadian corporations—whether incorporated under the CBCA, the Nova Scotia *Companies Act*, the PEI *Companies Act*, or otherwise—are very likely to be characterized by centralized managerial authority vested in a board of directors, with no significant role for shareholders to play in ongoing management.

One of the clearest articulations of the significance of the shareholders' delegation of managerial powers to the directors of a "memorandum"-style corporation (of which Nova Scotia and British Columbia are the two remaining Canadian examples) occurred in the early 20th century English decision *Automatic Self-Cleansing Filter Syndicate Co. v. Cuninghame*.[61] The *Cuninghame* case involved a dispute between the majority share-

---

61 [1906] 2 Ch. 34, at 34-37 and 41-45 (CA). The Supreme Court of Canada recently cited *Cuninghame* in support of the proposition that the "clear demarcation between the respective roles of shareholders and directors long predates the 1975 enactment of the CBCA." *Peoples Department Stores v. Wise*, 2004 SCC 68, at para. 31. What the court did not make clear is that the demarcation of power in that case arose from the terms of the corporation's articles, and not from the governing corporate statute itself.

holders of a company and its board of directors. The majority shareholders (and, in particular, the largest single shareholder, McDiarmid) wanted the company to sell all of its assets. A buyer had been found. It is possible that this buyer was a corporation incorporated by McDiarmid, although this is not expressly stated in the law report. In any event, McDiarmid, together with other shareholders who supported him, requisitioned the directors to call a shareholders' meeting to consider the proposed sale. At that meeting, a resolution was passed by simple majority vote authorizing the sale, and directing the directors of the company to take the steps necessary to complete it.

The directors refused to follow the shareholders' resolution. They evidently believed that the proposed sale was not in the best interests of the company. The shareholders initiated a legal action against the directors. In this action, the shareholders sought to force the directors to comply with the resolution that had been passed at the shareholders' meeting. The directors, however, prevailed, both at first instance and in the Court of Appeal.

The judgment of the Court of Appeal relied mainly on a specific provision in the company's articles of association, a provision similar to one still found today in the Table A articles contained in the First Schedule of the Nova Scotia *Companies Act*.[62] The court found, in effect, that the directors' authority to manage the corporation, as specified by the articles of association, could not be usurped on an *ad hoc* basis by the shareholders. If the shareholders wished to alter the power of the directors, they could certainly do so.

---

62   *Companies Act* (NS), First Schedule of Table A, reg. 147, reads as follows:

> The management of the business of the Company shall be vested in the Directors, who, in addition to the powers and authorities by these Articles or otherwise expressly conferred upon them, may exercise all such powers and do all such acts and things as may be exercised or done by the Company and are not hereby or by statute expressly directed or required to be exercised or done by the Company in general meeting, but subject nevertheless to the provisions of the applicable statutes, and of these Articles and to any Articles from time to time made by the Company in general meeting; provided that no Article so made shall invalidate any prior act of the Directors, which would have been valid if such Article had not been made.

Three points should be noted about this provision. First, the Nova Scotia provision differs from the provision considered by the court in *Cuninghame* in that, in place of the references to "Articles" in the Nova Scotia provision, the provision in *Cuninghame* used the word "regulations," a term, as Professor Sealy has noted, the meaning of which "in this context was never settled." L.S. Sealy, *Cases and Materials in Company Law*, 7th ed. (London: Butterworths, 2001), at 205. Second, note that the Table A regulations are not mandatory provisions; they *may* be adopted by corporations if they wish to do so, and, in the case of Nova Scotia companies, they are the "default rules" that will apply to a corporation limited by shares if it does not elect to adopt its own tailor-made articles of association (see *Companies Act* (NS), s. 21). Finally, the Nova Scotia provision was based on an older version of the UK *Companies Act*. This provision has subsequently been amended in the British Act, essentially to reflect the cases interpreting the older version. Thus, the current version of this provision in the UK *Companies Act, 1985*, table A, art. 70, reads as follows:

> Subject to the provisions of the Act, the memorandum and the articles and to any directions given by special resolution, the business of the company shall be managed by the directors who may exercise all the powers of the company. No alteration of the memorandum or articles and no such direction shall invalidate any prior act of the directors which would have been valid if that alteration had not been made or that direction had not been given. The powers given by this regulation shall not be limited by any special power given to the directors by the articles and a meeting of directors at which a quorum is present may exercise all powers exercisable by the directors.

They would, however, need to take those steps called for in the articles; and for this purpose, the articles required an extraordinary resolution (that is, a resolution passed by three-quarters of the shareholders). It was simply not enough for the shareholders to attempt to curtail a particular exercise of the directors' powers by a mere majority shareholder vote.

Alternatively, the court noted, if the shareholders had lost confidence in their directors, they were certainly entitled under the articles to remove them. But once again, the articles specified the method by which directors could be removed, and such removal required a special resolution (that is, as the term was defined in the English *Companies Act*, a resolution first passed by three-quarters of the shareholders, then, at a subsequent meeting, ratified by at least a simple majority).[63]

Because the underlying theory of a memorandum statute, such as the one involved in *Cuninghame*, is that the corporation's constitution is a contract between all the members (that is, the shareholders), the directors enjoy only those powers that have been delegated to them by the shareholders. So, even though the directors in *Cuninghame* were, theoretically, mere delegates, a majority of the shareholders were not entitled to step in and pre-empt their managerial decisions. The shareholders could remove the directors (as long as they did so in accordance with the constitution); the shareholders could amend the articles by which the directors exercised their powers (again, as long as they did so in accordance with the constitution); but a mere majority vote of shareholders taken at the general meeting did not give the shareholders the power to overrule decisions made by the directors exercising the management authority previously delegated to them. This was so, even though such a vote in many other circumstances might be said to constitute the will of the company.

This proposition, and its implications for the shareholder/director relationship under English company law, was reinforced by later courts. For example, as Buckley LJ put it in *Gramophone & Typewriter, Ltd. v. Stanley*:[64]

> [E]ven a resolution of a numerical majority at a general meeting of the company cannot impose its will upon the directors when the articles have confided to them the control of the company's affairs. The directors are not servants to obey directions given by the shareholders as individuals; they are not agents appointed by and bound to serve the shareholders as their principals. They are persons who may by the regulations be entrusted with the control of the business, and if so entrusted they can be dispossessed from that control only by the statutory majority which can alter the articles. Directors are not, I think, bound to comply with the directions even of all the corporators acting as individuals.[65]

---

63   Section 87 of the Nova Scotia *Companies Act* maintains this definition of "special resolution," though the number of matters that now require approval by such a "special resolution"—as opposed to the affirmative vote of two-thirds of the shareholders, with no subsequent ratifying vote—is now fairly limited. The phrase "special resolution" is also used in the CBCA; but there it simply refers to the affirmative vote of two-thirds of the shareholders (or a unanimous signed resolution). See CBCA, s. 2(1), definition of "special resolution."

64   [1908] 2 KB 89.

65   Ibid., at 105-6.

It soon became clear that the directors' authority was not only complete with respect to the matters specifically delegated to them, but, in fact, that it was they, and not the shareholders in general meeting, in whom resided residual managerial authority.

In *Scott v. Scott*,[66] for example, the shareholders of a corporation had passed a resolution directing cash distributions to be made to the shareholders. The power to declare dividends had been expressly delegated to the directors by the company's articles; so if these payments were properly characterized as dividends, the shareholders would have had no authority to pass such a resolution. However, the payments might, alternatively, have been properly characterized as loans from the company to the shareholders. Unlike the power to declare dividends, the power to make loans had not been expressly delegated to the directors.

Nevertheless, Clauson LJ held that, because the general power to manage the business of the company *had* been given to the directors, such a power must necessarily include the authority to manage its finances. Thus, even if these proposed payments were loans, it was not within the shareholders' power to interfere with the directors' managerial authority by attempting to compel the corporation to make such payments.

Gower and Davies have noted a curious feature of cases such as *Scott v. Scott*. They actually seem to be quite inconsistent with the provision in Table A on which they purport to rely.[67] Moreover, they note, the fact that shareholders lack the authority to give operative instructions or directions to the board of directors by passing shareholders' resolutions seems, today, difficult to reconcile with the fact that the shareholders can readily remove directors altogether by ordinary resolution—that is, by a simple majority vote[68]—a power that shareholders of corporations under consideration in these early cases did not have.

For our purposes, however, the central point is this. Beginning in the early part of the 20th century, the courts clearly recognized that residual managerial authority in the corporation properly resided in the board of directors, not in the shareholders, at least when the articles had delegated managerial authority to the directors in the first place. Professor Sealy argues that the new relationship between directors and shareholders heralded by *Cuninghame* and confirmed by the cases that followed it, did not result from a change in the law, but rather, from a judicial recognition of a change in business practice.[69]

Of course, under the CBCA, and statutes like it, the directors of a corporation are not simply delegates; their managerial authority is conferred on them by the statute itself.[70]

---

66 [1943] 1 All ER 582 (Ch. D).

67 See Davies, supra footnote 5, at 302.

68 Ibid., at 304: "[I]t seems strange that members in general meeting can dismiss the board by an ordinary resolution but cannot take a less extreme step except by a special resolution."

69 L.S. Sealy, supra footnote 62, at 204.

70 See, e.g., CBCA, s. 102. Although the shareholders do not delegate authority to directors in a CBCA-style jurisdiction, they may, of course, take such authority by entering into a unanimous shareholder agreement. It might also be mentioned that the *Companies Act* of Prince Edward Island, a letters patent statute, also expressly confers managerial power on the directors. Section 28 of that statute states: "The directors of the company have full power in all things to administer the affairs of the company, and may make or cause to be made for the company any description of contract which the company may by law enter into."

As Madam Justice Fraser of the Alberta Court of Appeal remarked in *Canadian Jorex Ltd. v. 477749 Alberta Ltd.*:[71]

> Under the corporate model adopted by the CBCA, the residual power to manage the corporation's affairs rests with the directors. This power is given by statute and is not derived from the delegation of powers by the shareholders. This must be contrasted with the British model of corporate law under which the directors enjoy only those powers delegated to them by the shareholders.[72]

Indeed, in large, public corporations, the role of shareholders is especially limited.

Directors' Meetings/Directors' Resolutions

Recall that directors are not full-time employees of the corporation (although, as noted above, some members of the board may very well hold, in addition to their positions on the board, other full-time corporate offices). Accordingly, the directors do not—and are not expected to—for example, report to the company for work each day, or even each week. Their supervisory role is largely performed in two ways: (1) at formal meetings of the board of directors held, in the case of large, public corporations, perhaps once every month or quarter (that is, every three months), or more often if required; and (2) as members of committees of the board of directors charged with specific responsibilities. For example, the boards of large, public corporations will have a number of important committees, including, for example, an audit committee, a compensation committee, and a nominating and corporate governance committee.

At a directors' meeting, the chairperson of the corporation typically presides as chair. In respect of each item of business that requires a formal decision by the directors, a resolution is placed before the meeting. So, for example, if the board decides to appoint a new corporate treasurer, the directors formally pass a resolution that might state,

> RESOLVED that Jane Doe is hereby appointed Treasurer of the Corporation.

---

71   (1991), 85 Alta. LR (2d) 313 (CA). There have, however, been some legislative aberrations. For example, an earlier version of Ontario's *Business Corporations Act* contained a provision (s. 101) that authorized holders of at least 10 percent of the corporation's voting shares to requisition the directors to convene a board meeting "for the purpose of passing any by-law or resolution that may properly be passed at a meeting of the directors duly called, constituted and held for that purpose." In the event that the directors failed to hold such a meeting, or failed to pass the bylaw or resolution at the meeting within 21 days, any of the original requisitionists were then empowered to call a general meeting of the shareholders at which they could pass the requested bylaw or resolution themselves, and that bylaw or resolution would be "as valid and effective as if it had been passed at a meeting of directors duly called, constituted and held for that purpose and confirmed at a meeting of the shareholders." This approach attracted some academic support. Professor Ziegel likened it to a parliamentary private member's bill (Jacob S. Ziegel, "New Look in Canadian Corporation Laws," in Jacob S. Ziegel, ed., *2 Studies in Canadian Company Law* (Toronto: Butterworths, 1973), 1, at 60). Iacobucci et al. noted that "[t]he difficulties of obtaining majority support for a resolution initiated by a minority group mean that even if this procedure is available, it will rarely be used successfully," and so concluded that "[t]he procedure's primary value may be largely symbolic, a reminder to management of its accountability and to all shareholders of their participatory status," and so supported it (Iacobucci et al., *Canadian Business Corporations* (Toronto: Canada Law Book, 1977), at 161).

72   *Canadian Jorex Ltd.*, supra footnote 71, at 316.

At the conclusion of the meeting, the person who acted as secretary of the meeting (typically the person holding the office of corporate secretary) prepares a document recording the outcome of the meeting. The form of this document (the "minutes" of the meeting) is not prescribed by the CBCA, but the minutes generally recite the date, time, and place of the meeting; the names of those present at the meeting; and include a copy of the notice of the meeting, perhaps with proof of timely delivery of notice (to indicate that the meeting was properly called). Most important, the minutes record the text of the resolution that was passed, prefaced by some language such as "on motion duly made and seconded," and perhaps including the names of the individual directors who made and seconded the motion.

If there are no other items of business to deal with at the meeting, this fact is indicated, followed by a statement that the meeting is now adjourned. Once prepared, this document, by convention, is then dated and signed by the person who chaired the meeting and by the secretary of the meeting. The signed minutes are then placed in the corporation's minute book to serve as a permanent record of the business transacted at the meeting.

It perhaps goes without saying that the level of formality observed at directors' meetings varies widely from board to board, although a review of meeting minutes tends to give the impression that board meetings are invariably conducted in a rigidly formal manner, with due regard to all of the niceties of *Robert's Rules of Order*.[73] In fact, meetings, especially of small, private companies, may be conducted quite informally.

Place and Notice of Directors' Meetings

Meetings of its board of directors are typically called by one or more of the corporation's officers (as specified in the corporate bylaws) or directors. When a meeting is called, a notice of the meeting is sent to each director setting out the time and the place of the meeting. The place of the meeting is generally the office of the corporation, or perhaps the office of the corporation's solicitors. However, meetings of a CBCA corporation may in fact be held anywhere unless there is some restriction in the corporation's articles or bylaws. Some provincial statutes impose general constraints on the place of directors' meetings. For example, the Ontario *Business Corporations Act* requires that a majority of a resident corporation's directors meetings each year must be held in Canada.[74]

The amount of notice required for a directors' meeting is not regulated by the CBCA, except in the case of the very first directors' organizational meeting, which is held just after a corporation is first incorporated.[75] Typically, the amount of notice required for a directors' meeting will be specified in the corporation's bylaws and is likely to be considerably shorter than the notice period required for shareholders' meetings.[76]

---

73   Henry M. Robert, *Robert's Rules of Order*, revised by Darwin Patnode (New York: Berkley Publishing Group, 1993).

74   *Business Corporations Act* (Ont.), s. 126(2).

75   CBCA, s. 104(3) requires that at least five days' notice be given for such a meeting. In fact, it is usually the case that the organizational matters to be dealt with at such a meeting are, instead, consented to by written resolution as discussed below.

76   For example, a typical minimum notice period for the calling of a directors' meeting of a CBCA corporation is 48 hours.

The CBCA does not require that any particular disclosure document be sent to the directors in advance of a directors' meeting, although if any of the non-delegable matters (discussed under the heading "Directors Appoint the Corporation's Officers" below) are to be dealt with, notice of the meeting must specify this.[77] In fact, though, it is common practice for managers of public corporations, at any rate, to prepare for each of the directors a "board book." The board book will include information on the matters to be discussed at the meeting including, in the case of a meeting called to consider a business transaction, copies of drafts of the operative documents or appropriately detailed summaries. A board book might be sent to each of the directors at the same time as the notice of meeting or, where the notice is given well in advance of the meeting, closer in time to the meeting date.

Sometimes, urgent matters may arise. It will simply not be possible to provide the amount of advance notice of a directors' meeting required by the corporation's bylaws. This does not usually pose any practical problem, provided there is no dissent within the board. Directors may simply waive notice of a directors' meeting, and the broad wording of the CBCA seems to permit such a waiver to be delivered at any time—even conceivably *after* the meeting has taken place. Moreover, attendance at the meeting in and of itself constitutes waiver of notice, except where a director has attended the meeting expressly for the purpose of objecting to any business being transacted on the basis that the meeting has been unlawfully convened.[78]

Unfortunately, board meetings are not always harmonious. Occasionally, dissension may develop within a board. Some directors may begin to openly oppose other directors. When this happens, it might be very tempting for the majority members of the board to agree among themselves to call a meeting on very short (or on no) notice, in an attempt to meet without the presence of the dissenting minority. However, all directors have a right to attend and be heard at every directors' meeting. If the majority directors were to succumb to the temptation to exclude the minority by not giving proper notice of a meeting, the dissenters would predictably withhold their waiver of notice. Thus, the meeting held in their absence would not be lawfully constituted, and any business transacted at it would be invalid.[79]

Telephone and Electronic Meetings

Directors' meetings need not necessarily be of the traditional, in-person, face-to-face variety. It is often possible for directors to "attend" meetings by conference telephone call or videoconference facilities. Subsection 114(9) of the CBCA deals expressly with this possibility. That subsection permits directors, subject to the corporation's bylaws, to consent to participate in meetings by "means of a telephonic, electronic or other communication facility that permits all participants to communicate adequately with each other

---

77   CBCA, s. 114(5).

78   CBCA, s. 114(6).

79   But, this is not altogether the end of the story because if the corporation were to act on a resolution taken at such an unlawfully constituted meeting and enter into a contract with a bona fide third party, unaware of the internal dispute, the indoor management rules would need to be considered.

during the meeting." That same subsection also contemplates that regulations may be promulgated affecting such meetings, but no such regulations have yet been issued.

Quorum

The concept of a quorum required for a valid meeting is not unique to corporate law. It is a concept encountered whenever groups of people are required or are entitled to hold formal meetings to make decisions. The word quorum has an interesting etymology. According to the *Oxford English Dictionary*, it comes from the Latin word meaning "of whom"—a word that evidently appeared in "commissions in which certain persons were specially designated as members of a body." The word has thus come to mean those people whose presence is essential.

In the context of meetings (whether of directors, of shareholders, or of anyone else), quorum usually refers not to any specific people, but rather to some previously agreed (or mandated) minimum *number* of people. It would, of course, be possible for organizations to demand that every voting member must be present at a meeting before any decisions can be taken. But such a demanding rule would be impractical. One person, for example, might be ill on the day fixed for the meeting, another might be off on holiday, and so on. Worse still, such a rule could also subject the meeting to a sort of "tyranny by truancy" if manipulative members were to absent themselves strategically, so as to hold up the conduct of business. Put simply, any single member could bring the organization's business to a standstill merely by refusing ever to attend a meeting.

Accordingly, it has long been recognized that it is quite fair and proper that a meeting be empowered to make binding decisions even if fewer than all the voting members are in attendance.[80] At common law, a quorum was typically a majority of those people eligible to attend the meeting. So, for example, if a board consisted of a total of seven directors, a quorum—at common law—would be four directors. As long as at least four directors were present at a meeting for which proper notice had been given, that meeting would be properly constituted and any business transacted at the meeting would be valid.

The CBCA now allows even greater flexibility. A corporation can specify whatever quorum it chooses for directors' meetings in its articles or bylaws. If no such quorum is specified, the CBCA states that a quorum consists of a majority of the directors or minimum number of directors required by the articles.[81]

Written Resolution in Lieu of Meetings

In a world of telephones and videoconferencing facilities, it is easy for people to virtually "meet" at the same time. It is, nevertheless, sometimes more convenient to dispense with a meeting altogether in favour of simply consenting to proposed directors' resolutions in writing. There are many instances where conducting business by signed written resolutions will be more convenient than organizing a formal meeting of directors: where the

---

80   Provided, of course, that proper notice of the meeting has been given so that those eligible to attend can decide whether they wish to be present.

81   CBCA, s. 114(2).

business to be completed is of a routine nature on which no useful discussion is apt to take place; or, perhaps, where the board's formal approval is needed to finalize a business transaction and the matter is one on which all directors are already fully briefed and have had multiple meetings; and, of course, in the case of small, private corporations, it may be far more efficient and convenient for directors to sign written resolutions than to pull themselves away from their operational duties for an in-person meeting.

Whatever the reason, provided that *all* the directors sign, a written resolution signed by the directors of a CBCA corporation would be as valid as if it had passed at a meeting.[82] What must be stressed, however, is that such written resolutions must be unanimous. Even though a mere majority of directors could pass an identical resolution at a directors' meeting, the CBCA does not authorize a majority of directors to consent to a written resolution. The reason for requiring unanimity is presumably to recognize each director's right to be heard at a meeting; a dissenting director, if able to present his or her opposing views to his or her fellow directors, might conceivably be able to sway some of them to change their votes. At the very least, the opportunity for full discussion helps ensure that whatever decision is taken is based on a full understanding of pitfalls and possible adverse consequences. If a mere majority of directors could transact business by signed resolution, they could cease having potentially unpleasant meetings with dissenting directors altogether, thus rendering meaningless such protections as the meeting notice requirements.

Dissenting Directors

At a meeting of the board of directors, the decision of the majority normally governs. However, some decisions taken by the board could in fact expose the directors to personal liability.[83] Clearly, it would be unjust if a director who opposed such an action, but was outvoted, was nevertheless subject to the same liability as those directors who supported the impugned action. Conversely, if a director is absent from a meeting at which an action is taken, mere absence alone should not shield that director from any liability that might arise out of decisions taken at the meeting. Otherwise, there would obviously be an undesirable incentive for directors to avoid attending meetings where controversial matters are to be debated.[84]

---

82   CBCA, s. 117(1).

83   For example, purchasing, redeeming, or acquiring shares in contravention of s. 34, 35, or 36; payment of a commission contrary to s. 41; payment of a dividend contrary to s. 42; payment of an indemnity in contravention of s. 124; payment to a shareholder in contravention of s. 190 or 241; and issuing a share for non-cash consideration equal to less than the value of the share contrary to s. 25. See CBCA, ss. 118(1) and (2).

84   Indeed, absenting oneself from a meeting was hardly discouraged at common law. See, e.g., *Re Denham & Co.* (1883), 25 Ch. D 752, where a director who had not attended a board meeting in some four years, and had never looked at the corporation's books, was, nevertheless, not held liable for breach of his duty of care when it was eventually discovered that the corporation's financial records were fraudulent and that dividends had been improperly paid. (Note in passing, however, that there are two rarely mentioned features of this frequently cited case that indicate that the court was by no means wholly indifferent to the director's somewhat cavalier attitude. First, the court does in fact state that the director "has been

Accordingly, those provisions of the CBCA that expose directors to the risk of personal liability in respect of certain actions impose such personal liability only on those directors who *consented* to the relevant action.[85] The CBCA also provides that any director who is present at a meeting is deemed to have consented to any resolution passed at that meeting, unless he notes his dissent in one of the ways specified in s. 123(1).

Moreover, a director who is absent from a meeting is also deemed to have consented to any resolution passed at the meeting unless, within seven days of becoming aware of the resolution, the director takes steps to note his dissent in accordance with s. 123(3).[86]

Directors Appoint the Corporation's Officers

Officers are a corporation's senior administrative officials. The corporation's officers are appointed by the board of directors,[87] and directors are expressly permitted by the CBCA to delegate many (but not all) of their functions to officers.[88] As the Dickerson committee explained it, "certain aspects of management ... are sufficiently important to warrant the attention of all directors."[89] Many of the matters on the CBCA's "non-delegable list"

---

guilty of considerable negligence in the discharge of the duties of his office" (at 766), albeit not enough to constitute the sort of "gross and willful negligence" that would be sufficient to find him liable. Second, the fact that the director, Mr. Crook, had been absent from so many board meetings and was so inattentive to his duties were both factors cited by Chitty J as he denied Mr. Crook any award for costs (at 768).) As Gower put it (in a passage from the third edition of *Modern Company Law* quoted by the Dickerson committee, supra footnote 15, at para. 224): "Though it is said that (directors) ought to attend these meetings (of the board) whenever they can, the cases suggest that this is little more than a pious hope. As in other walks of life, if anything is going wrong there are great advantages in not being there." An even more remarkable example of directorial non-attendance is found in the case of *Re Cardiff Savings Bank*, [1892] 2 Ch. 100. There the Marquis of Bute evidently became president of the Cardiff Savings Bank at the age of six months (following the death of his father, the bank's founder). He attended only one board meeting of the company in his life (a few months after turning 21).

85 See CBCA, ss. 118(1) and (2).

86 The method for registering dissents varies from jurisdiction to jurisdiction. For example, in Prince Edward Island, when a dividend is declared contrary to s. 65 of the *Companies Act*, to escape personal liability, a dissenting director present at the meeting must register his or her protest "forthwith," and an absent director must do so within 24 hours and within ten days thereafter publish such protest in a newspaper. See *Companies Act* (PEI), s. 66.

87 See, e.g., CBCA, s. 121.

88 CBCA, ss. 115(3) and 121(a).

89 Dickerson committee, supra footnote 15, at para. 220. The matters that are not delegable are listed in CBCA, s. 115(3). That subsection provides that no one but the directors shall have authority to

　　(a) submit to the shareholders any question or matter requiring the approval of the shareholders;

　　(b) fill a vacancy among the directors or in the office of auditor, or appoint additional directors;

　　(c) issue securities except as authorized by the directors;

　　(c.1) issue shares of a series under section 27 except as authorized by the directors;

　　(d) declare dividends;

　　(e) purchase, redeem or otherwise acquire shares issued by the corporation;

　　(f) pay a commission referred to in section 41 except as authorized by the directors;

relate, in any event, to issues in respect of which the directors are potentially exposed to personal liability; so, it is very much in the directors' own interests that the directors alone are authorized to deal with them. At one time, it was not unusual for Canadian corporate statutes to specifically require that all corporations appoint at least two officers to be designated, respectively, as the corporation's president and secretary.[90] There is no longer such a requirement in the CBCA. In fact, the CBCA is extremely flexible on the question of a corporation's officers, leaving it to each corporation to craft the management structure best suited to it. Thus, the board of directors is free to designate whatever offices it wishes, and to determine the functions to be performed by the office holders.[91] By convention, however, corporations typically still choose to appoint a president and secretary (as well as other corporate officers). One person is, however, permitted to occupy more than one corporate office,[92] and in small, private corporations it is common for one person to hold multiple offices.

In the case of public corporations, the most senior officer is typically known as the chief executive officer, a title that may or may not be combined with the office of president and sometimes with that of chairman (or chairperson) of the board. Other offices typically found in public companies include chief financial officer, vice-president, secretary, and treasurer. Another key corporate office is that of chairman (or chairperson) of the board of directors. The role of this person, unlike some of the other officers named above, does not typically involve any active participation in the corporation's business, as such, but rather involves setting the agenda for, and chairing, meetings of the board of directors. The CBCA and the Ontario Act both include a definition of "officer," which refers to a number of these conventional office designations,[93] as well as to individuals performing the sorts of functions normally performed by someone occupying these traditional corporate offices.[94]

(g) approve a management proxy circular referred to in Part XIII;

(h) approve a take-over bid circular or directors' circular referred to in Part XVII;

(i) approve any financial statements referred to in section 155; or

(j) adopt, amend or repeal by-laws.

90 The *Companies Act* of Prince Edward Island still includes a requirement for the board of directors to appoint, from among themselves, a president; but this requirement may be varied in the letters patent or bylaws of the company. (*Companies Act* (PEI), s. 25(f).) The Nova Scotia *Companies Act* has numerous references to the role of such officers as the president and the secretary, in the First Schedule, Table A regulations, and indeed reg. 125(1) of the First Schedule, Table A states that the directors are to elect a president. However, remember that the Table A regulations are in some respects more akin, in a memorandum jurisdiction such as Nova Scotia, to the bylaws in articles of incorporation statutes such as the CBCA and the Ontario *Business Corporation's Act*. Moreover, although the Table A regulations are default rules, which function as a corporation's articles of association in the absence of any alternative articles filed by the corporation, it is always possible for a corporation to vary the rules in Table A in whole or in part. See *Companies Act* (NS), s. 21.

91 CBCA, s. 121(a).

92 See, e.g., CBCA, s. 121.

93 The two lists are not identical. The CBCA provision includes several additional officers.

94 CBCA, s. 2(1), definition of "officer."

Corporate officers are, in one respect, employees of the corporation. For example, with the likely exception of the chairperson, each officer is likely to be on the company payroll.[95] If he or she is also the president or chief executive officer, the chairperson will be on the payroll as well. In the case of large, public companies, these officers are often generously compensated. Like the corporation's more junior employees, officers are expected to devote their full time and attention to the affairs of the company. However, as "top management" they differ rather significantly from regular employees in other ways. They do not work under the same kind of active supervision that has traditionally defined the employment relationship. To use the archaic legal language of a bygone era, the most senior corporate officers, especially the chief executive officer, function rather more like "masters" and rather less like "servants."

In a typical Canadian or American public corporation, the most senior officers, although appointed by the board, will also be members of the board. This, too, is expressly permitted by the CBCA.[96] The chief executive officer of a large public corporation, for example, is invariably a member of the board of directors of her or his company. This does not mean, however, that the senior officers are simply hiring themselves, or one other. In addition to these inside or management directors, the boards of publicly traded corporations will also include a number of "outside," "unrelated," or "independent" directors who are not company insiders.[97] These outside or independent directors are not full-time employees of the company. In fact, they are not employees of the company at all. They are not expected to devote their full time and attention to the business of the company. In the case of large, public companies, these directors typically hold full-time senior positions at other large companies.

In large corporations, it is not only the directors whose role it is to supervise management. The most senior officers, especially the chief executive officer, also typically perform primarily a supervisory role. The senior officers—in particular the chief executive officer—report to the board of directors. But, the relationship between senior managers and the board of directors is actually a very complex one. It has frequently been suggested by governance critics that it is the chief executive officer that actually controls the board of directors, rather than the reverse, except at rare times of public governance crises.

It is to the senior officers that other, lower-level managers report. And these managers in turn are responsible for hiring the employees needed to carry out the corporation's business operations effectively.

---

95 In some cases, the chairperson will be an outside or independent director. He or she will certainly receive a fee in respect of his or her services (just as all directors of public corporations do) and may even receive additional remuneration for acting as chair of the board, but will not be engaged in full-time employment with the corporation. The corporate secretary is also, typically, employed by a public corporation in some other capacity, not infrequently as the corporation's general counsel.

96 CBCA, s. 121(b).

97 The governing corporate statute or stock exchange rules will affect the minimum number of outside directors on the corporation's board of directors.

CONCLUSION

The basic corporate management structure—shareholders electing directors, who, in turn, appoint officers, who are actively engaged in running the business—apparently has its genesis in the so-called deed of settlement companies.[98]

From this basic structure the two central components of corporate governance emerge: shareholders' "voice," and directors' (and officers') obligations. An important adjunct to both of these components is the concept of external monitoring. These two components will be discussed, in turn, in the next two chapters. But an important preliminary word of warning is necessary. As we saw in chapter 1, one of the recurring issues in corporate law is the question of whether the corporation ought to be governed solely in the interests of its shareholders or whether, instead, corporate managers should have due regard as well for other important "stakeholders" or "corporate constituents." This question has aroused considerable public interest, as political and legal questions of "corporate social responsibility" have assumed prominence in both scholarly writing and the popular media. Advocates on either side of this "shareholder primacy" debate often find it genuinely difficult to understand how anyone can seriously champion the other's position. The result is a curious combination of disinterested scholarship, polemic, and dogma.

Indeed, the question of the proper goal of the business corporation has spawned such an immense body of literature that it would be impossible to do the matter justice even in a book considerably more ambitious than the present work. Chapters 10 and 11 will, therefore, offer a modest introduction to this topic, and invite the reader with an interest in this timely intellectual, political, and legal controversy to consult the articles on the subject that are noted briefly there.

---

98   Deed of settlement companies were an early form of trust-based business organization that pre-dated the first 19th century general incorporation statutes. Gower indicates that in these early non-incorporated companies the members' joint stock was held in trust and placed, by contract, under the management of directors, some of whom, but by no means all of whom, might also have been trustees. L.C.B. Gower, *Gower's Principles of Modern Company Law*, 5th ed. (London: Sweet & Maxwell, 1992), at 30.

CHAPTER TEN

"Best Interests of the Corporation": Shareholder Voice and Directors' Duties

INTRODUCTION

Shareholders are often described, at least colloquially, as the "owners" of business corporations. That description, as discussed in chapter 1, is not accurate as a matter of law, and is rejected as fundamentally flawed by law and economics scholars. But, although it may not, strictly speaking, be correct to characterize shareholders as "owners" of the corporation, it cannot be denied that shareholders have important financial interests in the corporations in which they hold shares. They occupy a unique position in the corporate governance structure. Shareholders have the power to elect and to remove the corporation's directors, and they hold the residual economic interest in the corporation, a "claim" to whatever value might remain in the corporation after the corporation's fixed claimants have been paid.

This power to elect and remove directors, coupled with the general legal attributes of share ownership prescribed by corporate statutes and developed at common law, provides shareholders with an incentive to monitor the performance of a corporation's managers, and tools with which to try to discipline those managers. But, a number of practical constraints frequently make it difficult for shareholders to perform an effective monitoring or disciplinary role.

The corporation's directors and officers, in turn, are subject to a specific set of obligations intended to ensure that they remain accountable for their actions. Shareholders are the direct beneficiaries of corporate managerial prowess and of the corporation's financial success. Well-run, successful corporations also create employment opportunities; purchase goods and services from other businesses—incorporated and unincorporated, large and small; pay taxes; and contribute to universities, hospitals, and other philanthropic causes. And, in a broader sense, it is hoped that by generating wealth to meet people's material needs, the operation of corporations will contribute to the betterment of society generally. The recent series of corporate scandals in the United States and elsewhere has provided a sobering reminder, however, that individual officers and directors may have significant incentives to mislead investors and to divert corporate value to themselves.

Although this chapter focuses on the role of shareholders and the basic duties of directors and corporate managers, it is important to remember from the outset that scholars have identified a host of factors that might operate to constrain managers from the temptation to shirk their duties or, worse, to divert corporate assets into their own hands. These factors include:

- *The capital markets*:[1] Corporations that are poorly managed, it is argued, will have difficulty finding financing in the capital markets. The cost of capital for such corporations will increase, making it difficult for them to remain competitive and so, ultimately, placing their future in jeopardy.
- *Product and labour markets*:[2] If a corporation is not competitive because of the inefficiency or dishonesty of its managers, the cost of its products will increase, its sales and so its revenues will decrease, and it may eventually be driven out of business. Similarly, if poor profitability constrains the corporation's ability to offer its employees competitive wages and benefits, it will not be able to attract and retain competent employees.
- *The market for corporate managers*:[3] If a company underperforms or fails, this failure will adversely affect the reputation of the corporation's managers, and, accordingly, adversely affect their ability to secure other positions except, perhaps, at a significantly lower income level.
- *The market for corporate control*:[4] If a corporation is poorly managed, the market price of its shares will fall. Such a fall in price may then entice a bidder to seek to acquire the corporation's outstanding shares and replace its underperforming managers.

What is important to remember about these factors is that one may presume that managers are well aware of them and, thus, it has been argued, managers have significant incentives to perform their duties wisely and well, notwithstanding the well-known obstacles that stand in the way of effective monitoring by shareholders. However, as Easterbrook and Fischel note, "[t]hese mechanisms reduce but do not eliminate the divergence of interests."[5] Nevertheless, these market and external constraints operate within the context of the traditional shareholder/director relationship, and so we now turn to consider some of the well-known general characteristics of "shareholder voice" and directors' and officers' duties.

---

1   See, e.g., Frank H. Easterbrook and Daniel R. Fischel, *The Economic Structure of Corporate Law* (Cambridge, MA: Harvard University Press, 1991), 95.

2   See, e.g., Eugene F. Fama, "Agency Problems and Theory of the Firm" (1980), 88 *Journal of Political Economy* 288.

3   See, e.g., Eugene F. Fama and Michael C. Jensen, "Separation of Ownership and Control" (1983), 26 *Journal of Law and Economics* 301, at 315.

4   The seminal academic paper on this topic is Henry Manne, infra footnote 9.

5   Supra footnote 1, at 91.

SHAREHOLDER VOICE

Introduction

The modern corporation—in particular the modern public corporation—is one in which the directors (and, through them, the managers more generally) are clearly in control. This consolidation of control in the hands of corporate managers has been praised by many as a key virtue of the modern corporation because it allows for the development of specialized professional managers and greater operating efficiency. However, in the view of some shareholder activists, the increasing power and lack of effective accountability of corporate directors is woefully anti-democratic.

Of course, shareholders do have the power to vote their shares,[6] and may use this voting power to elect and to remove corporate directors. In large, public corporations, however, this theoretical power is subject to important practical restrictions. If a corporation's shares are widely held, most shareholders will be total strangers to one another, separated by large geographical distances. Coordinated action would be difficult enough under such circumstances, and the likelihood of shareholders taking prompt collective action to discipline underperforming managers is further reduced if each shareholder holds only a small number of a corporation's shares. There is little incentive for any small shareholder to expend time and energy (and possibly money) in an attempt to communicate with other shareholders with a view to crafting a strategic voting plan. The problem is a classic example of "rational apathy," and it makes effective collective action by shareholders of widely held corporations problematic.

There are additional hurdles standing in the way of effective shareholder discipline of managers of widely held corporations. The corporation's managers, as it has often been noted, control the proxy process.[7] This means that the corporation's existing managers decide when and where to hold shareholders' meetings. It is the managers who prepare the information package (the information circular) and forms of proxy that are sent to shareholders in connection with these meetings. And it is, effectively, the managers and the existing directors who propose the names of the directors who are to be elected at the meeting. It is the managers, too, that effectively set the agenda of the meeting itself.

---

6   The concept of "one share, one vote" to which we are accustomed today was not always the norm. At one time, evidently, it seems that "one share*holder*, one vote" was the preferred method of conduct. Indeed, an English statute was passed in 1767 explicitly to prevent

> the most unfair and mischievous Practice … of splitting large Quantities of Stock, and making separate and temporary Conveyances of the Parts thereof, for the Purpose of multiplying or making occasional Votes immediately before the time of declaring a Dividend, or chusing [*sic*] Directors, or of deciding any other important Question.

Such a practice was derided by the statute as "subversive of every Principle upon which the Establishment of such General Courts is founded." (See *An Act for regulating the Proceedings of certain Public Companies and Corporations carrying on Trade or Dealings with Joint Stocks, in respect to the Declaring of Dividends; and for further regulating the Qualification of Members for voting in their respective General Courts*, 1767, 7 Geo. III, c. 48.)

7   For a detailed description of the proxy solicitation process, see Jeffrey G. MacIntosh and Christopher C. Nicholls, *Securities Law* (Toronto: Irwin, 2002), at 262ff.

(Recently, in the United States, the Securities and Exchange Commission launched a controversial proposal to allow shareholders direct proxy access to nominate corporate directors.[8])

In addition to all of this, the managers are able to use the company's own resources to call and convene shareholders' meetings. With some limited exceptions, if the shareholders themselves wish to convene a meeting that is not sanctioned by the managers, the shareholders must personally bear the costs.

Because of these practical impediments to participatory shareholder democracy, it was long thought that when shareholders were disappointed with a corporation's perform-ance, they had only one practical recourse: they would simply have to sell their underperforming shares, rather than try to replace underperforming managers. This better-to-sell-than-fight attitude is often referred to as the "Wall Street rule."

The Wall Street rule is not necessarily a mere counsel of despair. If the "market for corporate control"[9] functions efficiently, the market price of the shares of poorly man-aged corporations should fall as disaffected shareholders sell their interests. If the price sinks low enough, a hostile bidder might well be tempted to step in and attempt to acquire all the outstanding shares, with a view to replacing the managers and using the corporation's assets to better advantage. Because managers are aware of this possibility, they ought to have considerable incentive to work honestly and diligently to ensure that disgruntled shareholders do not drive down the price of the corporation's shares by selling their interests.

The supposed disciplining effect exerted by the market for corporate control cannot, however, be expected to prevent all managerial shirking problems. First, many large, public corporations in Canada have controlling shareholders. If the underperforming managers are favoured by those controlling shareholders, the possibility that they will be cowed by the prospect of a hostile takeover bid is seriously constrained. Second, in order to succeed, the price offered for shares by a hostile bidder must represent a significant premium over the recent trading price for those shares. The requisite premium is gener-ally thought to be high enough to leave considerable room for directors to engage in a significant amount of value-destroying, self-serving behaviour before share values erode sufficiently to make the company an attractive takeover target.[10] Third, for many large institutional shareholders (such as pension funds), the decision to sell shares in a poorly managed corporation is not a simple one. Where such a shareholder holds a sufficiently large block of shares, any sale of those shares will have market repercussions. Put more simply, the very fact that holders of large blocks of shares wish to sell will tend to drive

---

8   See Securities and Exchange Commission, *Proposed Rule: Security Holder Director Nomination*, release
     nos. 34-48626 and IC 26206. Available online at http://www.sec.gov/rules/proposed/34-48626.htm.

9   Henry Manne, "Mergers and the Market for Corporate Control" (1965), 3 *Journal of Political Economy*
     110.

10   As Richard Posner has put it, "tender offers [i.e., formal takeover bids] are made at very high premiums
     over the current market price of the target firm's stock—thirty percent being a generally accepted
     average figure. This suggests a large margin within which managers can divert wealth from the share-
     holders to themselves without worrying about inviting a takeover that may cost them their jobs." See
     Richard Posner, "Law and the Theory of Finance: Some Intersections" (1986), 54 *The George Washing-
     ton Law Review* 160, at 167 (footnotes omitted).

down the price of the very shares they are selling. There are various sophisticated techniques used by institutions, and sometimes facilitated by stock exchanges, that may make it possible to unwind a large position gradually in order to avoid some of this market impact; but this is nonetheless an important friction that cannot simply be ignored.

Furthermore, some institutional shareholders have no real choice but to retain the shares of certain companies, regardless of sub-par share performance. For example, if a shareholder is "indexing"—that is, holding shares in corporations so as to mirror the performance of a particular stock index (such as the S&P 500, the Dow Jones Industrial Average, or the S&P/TSX MidCap Index)—then that shareholder must continue to hold the appropriate number of shares of every corporation that is included within that index.

The practical constraints under which increasingly large institutional shareholders must operate go some way to explaining the increased levels of shareholder activism that have been observed in recent years. Institutional shareholders have come to recognize the need, at least in some circumstances, to take active steps to encourage better corporate governance practices in the corporations in which they have taken positions, and to put pressure on poorly performing officers and directors of those corporations. There is help available, too. Service providers, such as Institutional Shareholder Services, provide assistance in such matters as analyzing the voluminous and detailed proxy materials produced by public corporations and making specific shareholder voting recommendations.[11]

The increasing activism of institutional shareholders has not been entirely without controversy. Many corporate managers argue that there is a fine line between responsible shareholder monitoring and undue (and value-destroying) interference. The proper location and breadth of such a line, needless to say, lies very much in the eye of the beholder (and perhaps the beholden).

Shareholders—whether individuals or institutions—that wish to use their voting power to take a more active role in holding a corporation's management to account generally have the following corporate law tools[12] available to them:

- access to certain corporate records;
- shareholder meeting requisition procedures;
- right of discussion at shareholder meetings;
- shareholder proposal rules; and
- shareholder power to make bylaws or amend articles.

Access to Certain Corporate Records

Corporate statutes allow shareholders to have access to some (but by no means all) corporate records. For example, under the CBCA, shareholders are permitted to examine the following corporate records:

---

11   See, e.g., the Institutional Shareholder Services Web site, online at http://www.issproxy.com/.

12   Needless to say, there are a host of other strategies that shareholders can and do employ. For example, some shareholders may put pressure on management through the media, or by lobbying regulators and legislators.

- the articles, the bylaws, and any unanimous shareholder agreement;[13]
- minutes of shareholders' meetings and any shareholders' resolutions;[14]
- copies of notices of the corporation's directors, and notices of change of directors, filed with the CBCA Director;[15]
- the corporation's securities register (with information concerning the names and addresses of holders of the corporation's securities, the number of securities held, and transfer details);[16] and
- portions of any minutes of directors' or committee meetings, or other documents in which disclosures by directors or officers have been made of their interest in material contracts with the corporation.[17] (Note that this is a limited exception to the general rule that shareholders are *not* permitted to see minutes of directors' meetings. The law concerning interested directors' contracts is dealt with further in chapter 11.)

What should not be overlooked, however, is that shareholders' access to corporate information is confined to a limited number of specific corporate records. Shareholders—no matter how loudly they may assert that they are the corporation's "owners"—are not entitled to have access to most parts of the minutes of directors' meetings or to any of the corporation's sensitive commercial information. The reason that shareholders are prevented from seeing most corporate information is understandable. Disclosure of information to shareholders of publicly traded corporations is tantamount to disclosure to the public generally. There would be nothing, for example, to prevent a publicly traded corporation's chief competitor from purchasing a single share in the corporation. If a corporation's shareholders were generally entitled to review commercially sensitive information, a competitor could thus gain access to such information.

Shareholders' Meetings: Requisitions and Proxies

One of the most visible ways in which shareholders may voice their concerns about the management of the corporation is by attending, speaking, and voting at shareholders' meetings. However, although shareholders' meetings are the most symbolic (some would say ritualistic) form of shareholder activism, it is the rare shareholders' meeting that has a significant effect on the running of a major, public corporation.[18] It is for that reason that

---

13 CBCA, s. 21(1); s. 20(1)(a). Creditors are also permitted access to these records.

14 CBCA, s. 21(1); s. 20(1)(b). Creditors are also permitted access to these records.

15 CBCA, s. 21(1); s. 20(1)(c); s. 106; s. 113. Creditors are also permitted access to these records.

16 CBCA, s. 21(1); s. 20(1)(d); s. 50. Creditors are also permitted access to these records.

17 CBCA, s. 120(6.1).

18 There are, of course, notable exceptions. For example, at the March 2004 shareholders' meeting of The Walt Disney Company, 43 percent of the shareholders withheld their votes for the re-election to the board of Disney CEO Michael Eisner. (See "Death by Proxy? Vote on Eisner Causes a Stir," *Wall Street Journal*, March 4, 2004.) Although Eisner still won enough votes to retain his board seat, this remarkable show of shareholder opposition prompted Eisner, who had previously held the positions of CEO and chairman of the board, to resign as board chairman. He did, however, continue as CEO. See Press Release, "Statement for the Board of Directors of the Walt Disney Company," March 3, 2004. Available online at http://psc.disney.go.com/corporate/communications/releases/pdfs/StatementBoard.pdf.

annual shareholders' meetings in particular are often regarded by corporate CEOs as largely a rather expensive waste of time.

To understand this dichotomy between the shareholder democratic ideal and the usual mundane reality, it is important to consider some of the legal mechanics and practicalities of convening a shareholders' meeting in Canada.

First, it is normally the directors who call shareholders' meetings, not the shareholders themselves.[19] There are some constraints placed on directorial control of meetings. For example, annual meetings of shareholders must be held regularly (although, as a technical matter, each "annual" meeting could, under typical Canadian corporate statutes, follow the previous meeting by more than a year).[20]

Corporate statutes also prescribe minimum and maximum periods of advance notice of an upcoming shareholders' meeting. The CBCA and its related regulations, for example, specify that directors must provide notice of a shareholders' meeting at least 21 days, but not more than 60 days, before the date of the meeting.[21] For public corporations, the logistics involved in sending a notice to shareholders along with proxy materials is subject to additional securities law requirements intended to protect the interests of shareholders whose shares are registered, not in their own names, but in the names of their brokers or a securities depository, such as the Canadian Depository for Securities.[22]

Under certain circumstances, however, shareholders have the right to require that a shareholders' meeting be convened. So, for example, if shareholders wish to attempt to replace a corporation's directors, they need not rely on those same directors to call the necessary meeting. The right of shareholders to initiate a shareholders' meeting is therefore an important safeguard of corporate democracy.

But shareholders' meetings are expensive. They involve the significant out-of-pocket costs of printing and mailing notices and information circulars, renting an appropriate meeting space (a hotel or convention centre meeting room), and paying any necessary fees, for example, to proxy solicitation firms or outside scrutineers to ensure the integrity of any balloting at the meeting. They also create costs indirectly by diverting the time and attention of directors and managers in preparing for and attending such meetings. In short, in the hands of irresponsible corporate shareholders, an unconstrained power to call shareholder meetings could prove a wasteful nuisance.

Accordingly, modern corporate statutes attempt to balance the legitimate interests of responsible shareholders to ensure that they may, in exceptional circumstances, convene a meeting against the potential for abuse. The CBCA, for example, provides that shareholders

19   See, e.g., CBCA, s. 133.

20   See, e.g., CBCA, s. 133(1)(b), which provides that each annual meeting must be held "not later than fifteen months after holding the last preceding annual meeting but no later than six months after the end of the corporation's preceding financial year."

21   CBCA, s. 135(1); *Canada Business Corporations Regulations, 2001*, s. 44.

22   Canadian Securities Administrators, the umbrella organization of all of Canada's provincial and territorial securities regulators, has dealt with these matters in two national regulatory instruments: National Instrument 54-101 (2002), 25 OSCB 3361 and National Instrument 54-102 (2002), 25 OSCB 3402. For a discussion of these instruments and their operation, see MacIntosh and Nicholls, supra footnote 7, at 372-76.

may requisition a shareholders' meeting only if certain specific criteria are satisfied.[23] As a threshold requirement, the request must be made by holders of at least 5 percent of the corporation's issued shares. A 5 percent share interest—particularly in the case of a large, widely held corporation—represents a significant equity investment. (At one time, the federal corporate statute required that requisitioners hold at least 10 percent of a corporation's outstanding shares.) It is unlikely that so large an interest would be in the hands of a shareholder who merely seeks to call a meeting for its nuisance value, or who is holding what are sometimes called "action shares"—that is, shares purchased in a corporation by opponents of the corporation's business or policies solely for the purpose of enabling the holder to attend (and perhaps disrupt) shareholders' meetings to publicize such opposition.

However, even where holders of at least 5 percent of the corporation's shares request the directors to call a meeting, the CBCA provides that this request may be denied in any one of three circumstances. The first exception is understandable enough: a meeting need not be called when the purpose for which the shareholders have requisitioned the meeting is inappropriate.[24]

The other two exceptions also appear, on their face, to be uncontentious: directors are not required to call a shareholders' meeting at the request of shareholders if a record date for a shareholders' meeting has already been fixed and notice of that record date has been provided, or if, in fact, the directors have already given notice of a shareholders' meeting themselves.[25] Clearly, if directors (who, after all, have primary responsibility for calling shareholders' meetings) are already in the process of calling a meeting, shareholders should not be able to hijack the process by requisitioning a meeting of their own.

However, what is perhaps implicit, but not made explicit, in this statutory language are two rather important assumptions that:

- nothing critical turns on any difference in timing between the shareholders' meeting called by the directors and the meeting proposed by the shareholder requisitioners; and
- the business in respect of which the shareholders wish to convene a meeting can also be fully and fairly dealt with at the meeting called by the directors.

The first of these assumptions was flatly rejected in *RioCan Real Estate v. Realfund*.[26] The second was challenged in *Airline Industry Revitalization Co. v. Air Canada*.[27]

The *Air Canada* case arose from the 1999 attempted takeover of Air Canada and Canadian Airlines by Onex Corporation. Although Air Canada was a CBCA corporation, it was subject to a special federal statute that prohibited any single shareholder from acquiring more than 10 percent of shares that may be voted to elect directors.[28] That

23   CBCA, s. 143(1).

24   CBCA, s. 143(3). Specifically, a meeting need not be called if the proposed business for the meeting includes any of the matters in respect of which a shareholder proposal may be rejected by directors pursuant to ss. 137(5)(b)-(e).

25   Ibid., ss. 143(3)(a) and (b).

26   [1999] OJ no. 1349 (QL) (Gen. Div.).

27   (1999), 45 OR (3d) 370 (SCJ).

28   *Air Canada Public Participation Act*, RSC 1985, c. 35 (4th Supp.).

prohibition made it impossible for Onex Corporation simply to launch a takeover bid for all the shares of Air Canada. Given the fragile state of Canada's airline industry at the time, the federal government had indicated that it might be willing to remove this restriction to accommodate a transaction that would prevent Canadian Airlines from failing. Accordingly, Onex formulated a strategy that would allow it to move its proposed transaction forward, while awaiting removal of the statutory ownership restrictions.

That plan involved, among other things, a somewhat complicated restructuring of Air Canada's shares. This restructuring required shareholder approval. It was critical, in Onex's view, that the meeting to seek such approval be held before November 10, 1999, the date on which a special federal cabinet order exempting merger discussions between Canadian Airlines and Air Canada from the *Competition Act* was set to expire.

But there was a snag—the directors of Air Canada opposed the Onex bid. On August 30, the Air Canada board adopted a special takeover defence often referred to as a "poison pill plan,"[29] the effect of which was to render impossible any transaction by which Onex might obtain control. The Air Canada directors then set and gave notice of a record date for a shareholders' meeting to be held on January 7, 2000, well after the date on which the November 10 Cabinet order was expected to expire. To be clear, the Air Canada directors had called this meeting immediately before—not after—the shareholders' requisition was made. Thus, the directors argued, they were under no obligation to call the meeting sought by the shareholders, relying on the explicit wording of s. 143(3)(a) of the CBCA.

The court held that the directors of Air Canada were obliged to call a meeting in accordance with the requisition, and the "record date" exception did not apply to exempt them from such an obligation. Blair J reasoned that

> a "record date" as contemplated in s. 143(3)(a) must be a "record date" for a meeting at which there is some reasonable chance that the business stated in the requisition will be considered.[30]

---

29 For a discussion of the nature of "poison pills" as a takeover defence, and the legal issues such defences raise, see Christopher C. Nicholls, *Corporate Finance and Canadian Law* (Toronto: Carswell, 2000), at 351ff.

30 Supra footnote 27, at 380. Under Delaware law, there is an alternative method of obtaining majority shareholder approval without convening a shareholders meeting. That method is the consent solicitation. Under s. 228 of Delaware's *General Corporation Law*, a corporation may undertake any action that would otherwise need to be taken at an annual or special meeting to be approved by written consent signed by shareholders with at least the same number of votes that would have been required had such a meeting been held. Although the consent solicitation process is available for the approval of any *action* that could be taken at an annual or special meeting, Delaware courts originally held that the consent solicitation procedure could be used to circumvent the requirement in s. 211(b) of the statute for an annual meeting to be held. (See, e.g., *Hoschett v. Int'l Software Ltd.*, 683 A 2d 43 (Del. Ch. 1996).) However, s. 211(b) was recently amended to add the qualifying phrase, "unless directors are elected by written consent in lieu of annual meeting as permitted by this subsection" and specific language permitting directors to be elected by written consent in lieu of an annual meeting, subject to certain qualification in cases where such consents constitute less than unanimous votes. It might also be noted that, in the United Kingdom, it has been held that the informal unanimous consent of a corporation's shareholders—even in the absence of any meeting or written consent—may be effective, and that this common law concept has survived the recent introduction of a statutory provision allowing for unanimous

Blair J also commented on CBCA s. 143(4). That subsection states that, if the directors do not call a meeting within 21 days of receiving a shareholder requisition, any shareholder who signed the requisition may call the meeting. Blair J interpreted this language to mean that even if the directors of the corporation were not obliged to call a shareholders' meeting pursuant to a requisition because of the availability of one of the exceptions in s. 143(3), the shareholders could, nevertheless, still call the meeting themselves pursuant to s. 143(4) within 21 days.[31] In other words, the shareholders' right to call a meeting on their own, in his view, did not depend on the directors' *wrongful* refusal to call a meeting. It was triggered by *any* directors' refusal, even if that refusal was perfectly justified. This is a somewhat curious outcome, because it suggests, among other things, that shareholders may properly call a shareholders' meeting even if the primary purpose of that meeting is to conduct business that is inappropriate for a shareholders' meeting. For example, if shareholders requisitioned a meeting primarily for the purpose of redressing a personal grievance against one of the corporation's directors,[32] the directors could quite rightly refuse to call such a meeting, but, on Blair J's reasoning, the shareholders themselves could then proceed to hold such an improper meeting. It seems unlikely that the CBCA drafters intended such a result. Certainly, the Dickerson committee had designed their shareholder requisition rules to facilitate meetings "for legitimate corporate purposes"[33] and, in crafting the prohibited grounds for shareholder proposals (which are also the grounds for refusing a shareholders' meeting requisition), "to make it clear that the machinery of [the shareholder proposal section] cannot be used to authorize the taking of decisions by the general meeting which the shareholders are not otherwise competent to make."[34]

Right of Discussion at Shareholders' Meetings

The CBCA provides that registered or beneficial owners of voting shares are entitled to discuss any matter at a shareholders' meeting in respect of which a shareholder proposal

---

written resolutions. See Paul L. Davies, *Gower & Davies: Principles of Modern Company Law*, 7th ed. (London: Sweet & Maxwell, 2003), at 334. The possibility of informal unanimous shareholders' consent appears to have been recognized at one time in Canada as well. (See, e.g., *Eisenberg v. Bank of Nova Scotia*, [1965] SCR 681.) However, it is not entirely clear whether such consent would continue to be recognized where the corporate statute itself provides for unanimous, written shareholder resolutions. The BC *Business Corporations Act* also allows for written consent resolutions passed by the majority of shareholders (s. 180).

31   Blair J noted that the comparable provision of the Ontario *Business Corporations Act* on this point is slightly different. It states that the shareholders' right to call a meeting themselves is "subject to subsection (3)." (See *Business Corporations Act* (Ont.), s. 105(4).) Blair J commented that "this difference in wording suggests that under the OBCA regime, a requisitioned meeting which the directors are properly exempted from calling may not be called by the requisitioning shareholder, whereas under the CBCA regime the opposite is the case." Ibid., at 386.

32   See CBCA, s. 137(5)(b).

33   Robert W.V. Dickerson et al., *Proposals for a New Business Corporations Law for Canada*, vol. I, Commentary (Ottawa: Information Canada, 1971), at para. 289 (Dickerson committee).

34   Ibid., at para. 277.

may be submitted.[35] (The shareholder proposal rules are discussed in the next section.) The right of discussion has important symbolic value, although at meetings of many publicly traded companies, it is not unusual for proxies to have been deposited in advance of the meeting that make the outcome of most votes to be taken at the meeting a foregone conclusion.

Shareholder Proposal Rules

The shareholder proposal rules provide a means by which shareholders can seek to have a matter voted on at the shareholders' meeting without having to incur the expense of preparing and mailing an information circular of their own to their fellow shareholders. Where a shareholder proposal satisfies the requirements of the statute, it must be included by the corporation's managers in the management information circular. Thus, the shareholders who have crafted the proposal are not subject to any printing or mailing costs.

The key features of the CBCA shareholder proposal rules[36] are:

- *Minimum shareholding requirement*: To be eligible to submit a proposal, a person must be the registered holder or beneficial owner, or have the support of others who are registered holders or beneficial owners, of voting shares representing either 1 percent of the total number of outstanding shares or with a fair market value of at least $2,000.[37] In addition, the shareholders must have held their shares for at least six months before the date on which the proposal is submitted.[38] (These requirements are intended to limit access to the shareholder proposal device to those shareholders who have made some meaningful, economic investment in the corporation, and have not, for example, simply purchased a single share (sometimes, as discussed above, called an "action share") solely for the purpose of attacking the corporation or its managers.)
- *Proposal and supporting statement included in management information circular*: Subject to certain exemptions discussed below, a corporation that solicits proxies must include the proposal in the management proxy circular, or attach the proposal to the circular, together with a written statement by the shareholder in support of the proposal that, together with the proposal itself, does not exceed 500 words.[39]
- *Higher shareholding threshold required for director nominations*: If the proposal includes nominations for the election of directors, the proposal must be signed by shareholders holding in the aggregate at least 5 percent of the shares of a class of voting shares.

---

35   CBCA, s. 137(1)(b).

36   There are similar, though not necessarily identical, rules in many provincial corporate statutes as well. See, e.g., *Business Corporations Act* (Alta.), s. 136; *The Business Corporations Act* (Sask.), s. 131; *The Corporations Act* (Man.), s. 131; *Business Corporations Act* (Ont.), s. 99; *Business Corporations Act* (NB), s. 89; *Companies Act* (NS), Third Schedule, s. 9; *Corporations Act* (NL), s. 224; and *Business Corporations Act* (BC), s. 188.

37   CBCA, s. 137(1.1); *Canada Business Corporations Regulations, 2001*, s. 46(a).

38   CBCA, s. 137(1.1); *Canada Business Corporations Regulations, 2001*, s. 46(b).

39   CBCA, ss. 137(2) and (3); *Canada Business Corporations Regulations, 2001*, s. 48.

- *Prohibited grounds*: The corporation is not required to include certain proposals in the management proxy circular. Specifically, a proposal need not be included if:

  – the proposal is not submitted in a timely fashion (at least 90 days before the anniversary date of the previous year's notice of the annual meeting of share-holders);[40]
  – the primary purpose of the proposal is to enforce a personal claim or grievance against the corporation, its officers, directors, or securityholders;[41]
  – the proposal "does not relate in a significant way to the business or affairs of the corporation";[42] (This "prohibited grounds" exception was added to the CBCA in 2001. It replaced broader language that allowed proposals to be excluded where they clearly appeared to have been submitted "primarily for the purpose of promoting general economic, political, racial, religious, social or similar causes." The older language reflected the Dickerson committee's concern that "the share-holders' meeting is not an appropriate forum for discussing personal grievances or life in general."[43] Indeed, that older language was successfully relied on by a corporation to block a proposal condemning apartheid in South Africa and a corporation's business interests in South Africa in *Varity Corp. v. Jesuit Fathers of Upper Canada*.[44])
  – the proposal has been submitted by someone who had submitted another pro-posal within the previous two years, but subsequently failed to appear and present that earlier proposal at the relevant shareholders' meeting;[45]
  – the proposal is substantially the same as a proposal submitted to shareholders in a management proxy circular or dissident's proxy circular relating to a share-holders' meeting held within the previous five years, if that earlier proposal did not receive certain minimum amounts of shareholder support at that meeting, as specified in the *Canada Business Corporations Regulations, 2001*;[46]
  – the proposal rules "are being abused to secure publicity";[47] or
  – the proposal is submitted by a person who had previously submitted a proposal in connection with a meeting held within two years prior to the scheduled meeting date, if that person failed to hold the requisite minimum number of shares needed to be eligible to submit a proposal continuously from the date of submitting that previous proposal until the day of that previous meeting.[48]

---

40   CBCA, s. 137(5)(a); *Canada Business Corporations Regulations, 2001*, s. 49.

41   CBCA, s. 137(5)(b).

42   CBCA, s. 137(5)(b.1).

43   Dickerson committee, supra footnote 33, at para. 278.

44   (1987), 59 OR (2d) 459 (HC), aff'd. (1987), 60 OR (2d) 640 (CA). Note, however, that Tarnopolsky JA dissented in the Court of Appeal.

45   CBCA, s. 137(5)(c); *Canada Business Corporation Regulations, 2001*, s. 50.

46   CBCA, s. 137(5)(d); *Canada Business Corporation Regulations, 2001*, s. 51.

47   CBCA, s. 137(5)(e).

48   CBCA, s. 137(5.1); *Canada Business Corporations Regulations, 2001*, s. 52.

The Dickerson committee made it clear that it was not the intention of the proposal rules to "authorize the taking of decisions by the general meeting which the shareholders are not otherwise competent to make."[49] To the extent that a proposal touches on a matter within the authority of the corporation's directors (such as, for example, determining the remuneration of officers), even if the proposal were to be "passed" by a majority of the corporation's shareholders, presumably it could constitute no more than advice to the board of directors. Any matter attracting majority shareholder support, however, could not, as a practical matter, be simply ignored by a corporation's board of directors.

In the United States, there is an active shareholder proposal "culture." Proxy circulars for large, US corporations often contain many shareholder proposals, covering a wide range of subjects. Some of these proposals are sensible enough. But many are ill advised, and whether the marginal gains for shareholder democracy justify the resources that must be expended in responding to uninformed shareholder proposals seems very much an open question.

Brian Cheffins, commenting in 1998 on a then high-profile shareholder proposal decision, *Michaud v. Banque Nationale du Canada*,[50] suggested that the shareholder proposal regime might not prove to be as widely used a tool in Canada as in the United States, and he further suggested that this should not necessarily "be a cause for substantial regret."[51] More recently, Janis Sarra has noted that the shareholder proposal mechanism has rarely been used in Canada, but she suggests that the 2001 amendments to the CBCA shareholder proposal rules might lead to greater use of the mechanism to try to effect improvements in corporate governance.[52] Perhaps. In any event, institutional investors have other avenues of discussion and persuasion available to them that seem to offer more practical and more efficient means of addressing corporate governance concerns. While it is politically expedient to applaud the activism of small, retail investors, it does not seem unreasonable to ask whether the benefits of such shareholder participation outweigh the costs of wasted resources expended in dealing with misinformed-shareholder proposals. Additional empirical research is needed, however, to attempt to quantify the cost to corporations of responding to shareholder proposals—wise or foolish. It may well be that the cost is manageable, and, accordingly, justifiable in the interests of facilitating shareholder democracy.

Shareholder proposal rules in most Canadian provincial corporate statutes are similar to the CBCA provisions.[53] However, some minor variations can be found, particularly in the British Columbia *Business Corporations Act*. Under the BC statute, a proposal must be made by a "qualified shareholder,"[54] a term that refers to a shareholder who, among

---

49   Dickerson committee, supra footnote 33, at para. 277.

50   [1997] RJQ 547 (SC).

51   Brian R. Cheffins, "Michaud v. National Bank of Canada and Canadian Corporate Governance: A 'Victory' for Shareholder Rights?" (1998), 30 *Canadian Business Law Journal* 20, at 72.

52   See Janis Sarra, "Shareholders as Winners and Losers Under the Amended Canada Business Corporations Act" (2003), 39 *Canadian Business Law Journal* 52, at 75.

53   See supra footnote 36.

54   *Business Corporations Act* (BC), s. 187(1).

other things, has owned shares for at least two full years before the date on which the proposal is signed. The other basic threshold requirements are almost identical—that is, a valid proposal must be submitted by qualified shareholders holding at least 1 percent of the corporation's voting shares,[55] or a fair market value in excess of $2,000[56] (the CBCA requires a market value of "at least" $2,000). However, the supporting statement for a BC proposal may be longer: 1,000[57] words rather than the CBCA's 500. The BC Act also makes explicit what is surely implicit in the case of CBCA proposals—namely, that a proposal is improper in cases where it deals with matters beyond the company's powers[58] or, if implemented, it would cause the company to commit an offence.[59]

Shareholders' Power To Make Bylaws or Amend Articles

A CBCA corporation's bylaws are normally made, in the first instance, by directors' resolution.[60] Bylaws made by the directors in this way must then be submitted to the shareholders at the next shareholders' meeting, and the shareholders may confirm, amend, or reject the bylaws.[61] However, the CBCA also preserves the right of shareholders to make bylaws of their own initiative, theoretically even against the will of the directors.[62] To be sure, a proposal to make a bylaw must satisfy the same requirements as other shareholder proposals.[63] Nevertheless, this power represents, at least in theory, a significant challenge to the notion that managerial authority rests exclusively with the board of directors.

Many practical hurdles would stand in the way of any dissident shareholders who sought to propose a bylaw that did not enjoy management's support. Among the most significant is the formidable challenge of waging a successful proxy contest, as discussed in the next section. Accordingly, it is unclear how often this power has been exercised (indeed, if ever) in the case of large, Canadian, public corporations.

Shareholders of CBCA corporations also have the power, in theory, to propose amendments to the articles of the corporation[64] in accordance with the s. 137 shareholder proposal rules. However, because certain amendments to the articles would trigger dissent and appraisal rights,[65] it is not entirely clear how, as a practical matter, amendments of this sort could be successfully advanced against the wishes of the corporation's directors.[66]

---

55   Ibid., s. 188(1)(b)(i).

56   Ibid., s. 188(1)(b)(ii); *Business Corporations Regulation*, BC Reg. 65/2004, s. 17.

57   Ibid., s. 188(3).

58   Ibid., s. 189(5)(h).

59   Ibid., s. 189(5)(g).

60   See, e.g., CBCA, s. 103(1).

61   See CBCA, s. 103(2).

62   See CBCA, s. 103(5).

63   These requirements are set out in CBCA, s. 137.

64   CBCA, s. 175(1).

65   See CBCA, s. 175(2); s. 190(1); s. 173; s. 174; and s. 176.

66   Attempts by shareholders to call meetings for the purpose of amending the articles are not, however, unheard of. Recall that the meeting requisition in the *Air Canada* case, supra footnote 27, included such a proposal.

NON-SHAREHOLDER CONSTITUENTS AND THE "BEST INTERESTS OF THE CORPORATION"

Shareholders have always been concerned with the corporation's financial performance. Since they hold the residual economic interest in the corporation, there are good reasons to provide shareholders with the tools they need to hold management to account, and to prevent managerial shirking or opportunism. The prospect of institutional shareholders, such as pension funds, exercising an effective monitoring role has seemed to offer particular promise.[67]

It has also been suggested, however, that many shareholders, when making their investment decisions, are motivated by non-financial concerns as well.[68] To the extent that shareholders seek to influence the corporation's actions in areas that are not necessarily related to improving the corporation's financial performance, it might be said that shareholders are, in effect, acting as advocates on behalf of broader societal interests.

Not all corporations have such noble-minded shareholders, however. Many shareholders are motivated more by the quick buck than by the quixotic. Should this be of any concern to the law of the business corporation? Should corporations be legally obliged to take into account such broader interests, even if their shareholders have no desire to press for such benevolent corporate behaviour? The question of precisely what interests the business corporation ought to serve has generated considerable debate throughout this century. Canadian directors and officers are, after all, typically charged with the duty to act in the "best interests of the corporation,"[69] not (expressly) "in the best interests of the shareholders."

Family law practitioners are familiar with the general principle that decisions affecting children must always be made with a view to the best interests of the child. Reasonable people can, and often do, disagree about how, in any particular case, these "best interests" are to be fairly determined. But they are never in any doubt about the identity of the person (the child) whose interests they seek to protect.

In the case of a business corporation, matters are less clear. How can an artificial legal concept such as a corporation be truly said to have "interests"? A corporation is not a

---

67   See, e.g., Roberta Romano, "Less Is More: Making Institutional Investor Activism a Valuable Mechanism of Corporate Governance" (2001), 18 *Yale Journal of Regulation* 174. For a Canadian perspective on this subject, see Jeffrey G. MacIntosh, "Institutional Shareholders and Corporate Governance in Canada" (1996), 26 *Canadian Business Law Journal* 145. It is interesting to note that institutional shareholder activism has not always been encouraged by the courts. Consider, for example, the following comments from the English Court of Appeal in *Prudential Assurance Co. v. Newman Industries Ltd. (No. 2)*, [1981] Ch. 257 (CA):

> We were invited to give judicial approval to the public spirit of the plaintiffs who, it was said, are pioneering a method of controlling companies in the public interest without involving regulation by a statutory body. In our view the voluntary regulation of companies is a matter for the City. The compulsory regulation of companies is a matter for Parliament. We decline to draw general conclusions from the exceptional circumstances of the present case. But the results of the present action give food for thought.

68   For a discussion of shareholders' non-financial interests, and the relevance of corporations' public disclosure obligations in that context, see Cynthia A. Williams, "The Securities and Exchange Commission and Corporate Social Transparency" (1999), 112 *Harvard Law Review* 1197.

69   See, e.g., CBCA, s. 122(1)(a).

sentient being with feelings, desires, or aspirations. How, then, does one translate vague language such as "best interests of the corporation" into something operational? As Gower and Davies put it, "In effect, the core duty of directors ... which is a duty to exercise their powers in the interests of the company, becomes of little value because of its imprecision, except perhaps as a tool of ideological discussion."[70]

The attempt to define in a practical way what it means for directors and officers to serve the "best interests of the corporation" has generated a body of literature so vast and so varied that it will be impossible to do it justice. All that will be attempted here is to introduce one or two of the more intriguing themes raised by the competing arguments.

Earlier this century one of the most famous examples of the shareholder/stakeholder debate was played out in the pages of the *Harvard Law Review*, in a short series of articles by Adolf Berle (advocating the view that directors ought to serve the shareholders alone)[71] and E. Merrick Dodd (who argued in favour of recognizing that corporations have broader social service goals beyond maximizing profits for their shareholders).[72]

Although Berle and Dodd are no longer with us, their debate has been taken up by successive generations of scholars, business leaders, legal practitioners, and, as it will be seen, courts. At its broadest, the dispute turns on differing notions of accountability and the proper role of the corporation in modern society. For some commentators, the economic power of the modern corporation (specifically, the modern public corporation) ought to carry with it a corresponding obligation to serve broader social interests; this is especially so, some maintain, given the way in which resources are mobilized within the corporate form.

For others, corporations are seen as critical components in the production of wealth through which prosperity is attained and the material needs of society are met; any dilution of the corporation's primary function—to generate wealth for its shareholders— will not only lessen prosperity, but will also insulate corporate managers from accountability. It would always be possible, for example, for corporate managers to explain their inability to produce strong financial results by asserting that they were, instead, serving some non-shareholder interest. And mixing the wealth-creation and wealth-distribution functions in this way may reduce society's collective power to perform either function well. In other words, the best way for business corporations to benefit society as a whole is to perform the specific function for which they are best suited—increasing the wealth of their shareholders. As Milton Friedman famously put it, "The Social Responsibility of Business Is To Increase Its Profits."[73] Within these very broad parameters, however, highly detailed and sophisticated arguments have been formulated and refined.

First, it seems fair to suggest that when the phrase "best interests of the company" was originally used, the "company" was understood to mean the company of shareholders in general meeting. In other words, the shareholders—as a collective—*were* the company.

---

70   Davies, supra footnote 30, at 371.

71   Adolf A. Berle, "Corporate Powers in Trust" (1931), 44 *Harvard Law Review* 1049 and "For Whom Corporate Managers Are Trustees: A Note" (1932), 45 *Harvard Law Review* 1365.

72   E. Merrick Dodd, "For Whom Are Corporate Managers Trustees?" (1932), 45 *Harvard Law Review* 1145.

73   Milton Friedman, "The Social Responsibility of Business Is To Increase Its Profits," *New York Times Magazine*, September 13, 1970, 32.

They could decide, as a body, what they considered to be in the company's (that is, their own) best interests. The identification of "the best interests of the company" with the "best interests of the shareholders" is still found today in the judgments of many courts[74] and the works of many commentators;[75] but even the proponents of this view recognize that this principle needs to be qualified (or at least refined) in some respects.

For example, the law cannot sanction a regime where shareholders, by majority vote, are permitted to trample the interests of the minority shareholders. Accordingly, even if the "best interests of the corporation" is understood to mean "the best interests of the share-holders," it is clear that this principle must take account of the interests of *all* the shareholders, and not simply the interests of the current majority or controlling shareholders.

The implications of the concept must also be evaluated in the context of the evolution of the practical operation and legal understanding of business corporations. The notion that the shareholders, collectively, are the company (or the corporation) itself, is an idea that originated before the theory of the corporation as a distinct legal person had fully crystallized, and, perhaps more importantly, before business practice and eventually statutory law (at least in some jurisdictions) unequivocally devolved residual managerial powers on the board of directors rather than on the shareholders. Shareholders of a modern, Canadian, publicly traded corporation are, therefore, not in the same position as members of a 19th century joint stock company. Shareholders of publicly held corporations today are not equipped, legally or practically, to discern, let alone conclusively define, the corporation's interests. Rather, it is the directors and officers who speak for modern corporations (at least modern, public corporations). The foundations on which the concept of the "best interests of the company" was originally formulated, then, has changed.

---

74   The classic American case perhaps most often cited for this proposition is *Dodge v. Ford Motor Co.*, 170 NW 668 (1919). It is interesting to note that *Dodge* was referred to by E. Merrick Dodd, who in fact argued that "[n]either the language of the opinion nor the relief granted necessarily involves an unqualified acceptance of the maximum-profit-for stockholders formula." See Dodd, supra footnote 72, at 1158n. One of the most well-known English authorities on this point is *Parke v. Daily News (No. 2)*, [1962] 3 WLR 566 (Ch. D), in which the court disallowed an attempt by a corporation to use proceeds of the sale of its assets to compensate employees who lost their jobs when the corporation ceased its business operations. As Gower and Davies point out, in the United Kingdom, the legislature responded to this case by enacting legislation to provide additional protection to employees. See Davies, supra footnote 30, at 133. For a recent Canadian example, see the judgment of the Alberta Court of Appeal in *Colborne Capital Corp. v. 542775 Alberta Ltd.* (1999), 69 ALR (3d) 265, at 315:

> Only the board acting collectively can decide what is in the best interests of the corporation. The best interests of a corporation include the interests of the shareholders collectively. Where there is but one shareholder, the best interests of the corporation will accord with the best interests of that shareholder: *Gainers Inc. v. Pocklington Holdings Inc.* ... . A director's duty to preserve the value of the corporation does not permit the director to ignore the collective interests of its shareholders. Nor do we agree that *Teck* stands for the proposition that directors will never owe a fiduciary duty to the shareholders. Where the relationship between the shareholder and director is unique a director may owe a direct fiduciary duty to the shareholders: *Tongue v. Vencap Equities Alberta Ltd.*

However, note the recent observations of the Supreme Court of Canada in *Peoples Department Stores Inc. v. Wise*, infra footnote 94.

75   For a canvass of the literature on this subject, see, e.g., D. Gordon Smith, "The Shareholder Primacy Norm" (1998), 23(2) *Journal of Corporation Law* 277.

But has the nature of the duty itself changed? When the Dickerson committee recommended including express statutory language in the CBCA obliging directors to act "in the best interests of the corporation," they recognized the malleability of the phrase they were proposing. They declined to offer any guidance as to how the words ought to be interpreted, suggesting that it was best to leave it to the courts to develop the appropriate principles.[76] The drafters of the report, however, did express the hope that their broad formulation would allow the courts to "escape from the constraints of what has somewhat charitably been described as the 'anachronistic' view that has developed in the English courts."[77] The Dickerson committee did not explain what they meant by the "anachronistic" view, but their meaning becomes clear when one consults the source they cited for this characterization: an early edition of Gower's English company law text. The "anachronistic" view of which Gower complained was the view that the best interests of the company meant nothing more than the best interests of the company's shareholders.[78]

A full explication of the goal or purpose of the corporation involves consideration of theories of the corporation more generally. In chapter 1, several of these theories were discussed. This chapter, at the risk of oversimplification, notes only that the debate over the proper goal of the corporation (and, by extension, the proper goal of a corporation's directors and officers) may be said to have been linked to at least three competing theories of the corporation (with many variations of opinion within each):

- the corporation as entity;
- the stakeholder constituency model; and
- the shareholder primacy view.

Corporation as Entity

As noted above, some commentators place great emphasis on the (uncontentious) fact that Canadian corporate statutes typically require directors and officers to act in the best interests of the corporate entity itself. This duty, they contend, though perhaps ambiguous, has the advantage of flexibility. Though such a duty may be difficult to define with precision, they nevertheless suggest that, at the very least, it contemplates a reasonable balancing of the interests of a corporation's various constituents with a view to preserving the long-term viability and profitability of the corporation as an entity. However, the greatest strength of this position, its flexibility, is also surely its greatest weakness. For as Adolf Berle noted over 70 years ago,

> you cannot abandon emphasis on "the view that business corporations exist for the sole purpose of making profits for their stockholders" until such time as you are prepared to offer a clear and reasonably enforceable scheme of responsibilities to someone else.[79]

---

76   Dickerson committee, supra footnote 33, at para. 241.

77   Ibid.

78   L.C.B. Gower, *The Principles of Modern Company Law*, 3rd ed. (London: Stevens, 1969), at 522.

79   Berle, "For Whom Corporate Managers Are Trustees: A Note," supra footnote 71, at 1367.

Stakeholder Constituency

We have become well accustomed to pleas for enhanced "corporate social responsibility." The idea is not a new one. In 1931, Merrick Dodd extolled the virtues of viewing "the business corporation as an economic institution which has a social service as well as a profit-making function,"[80] and in 1959, Edward S. Mason outlined the notions of corporate social responsibility in *The Corporation in Modern Society*.[81] Quite recently, editorial writers, academics, and—cynics might say—not a few self-serving corporate governance "consultants" have trumpeted the virtues of corporate social responsibility and the supposed antidote that such an enlightened philosophy offers to the greed and plunder revealed by the recent series of major corporate scandals. Though the meaning of the term "corporate social responsibility" is infinitely pliable, most versions involve a recognition that corporations ought to be regarded as more than unidimensional vehicles for maximizing shareholder value.

It is important, first of all, to distinguish the stakeholder constituency view from that of mere "enlightened shareholder interest." Needless to say, every business needs to be concerned about nurturing its relationships with employees, customers, suppliers, and the community, because it is in the long-term interests of the corporation—and therefore in the long-term interests of the shareholders—to do so. If the stakeholder constituency view involved nothing more than wise concern for this "long-term shareholder interest," then it would not be at all inconsistent with the shareholder primacy paradigm; considering non-shareholder interests would simply represent an important means by which shareholder value was ultimately enhanced. The stakeholder constituency view is only important and interesting, however, to the extent that it goes further, and implies that a corporation is entitled, if not obliged, to take non-shareholder views into account even where doing so does not necessarily advance short- or even long-term shareholder interests.[82]

It is easy to understand the appeal of the stakeholder constituency view. Many commentators are uncomfortable about the unconstrained operation of a shareholder primacy rule. A corporation is more than just its shareholders, they insist. They reject as unrealistic

---

80 Dodd, supra footnote 72, at 1148.

81 Edward S. Mason, *The Corporation in Modern Society* (Cambridge, MA: Harvard University Press, 1959).

82 Merrick Dodd had been careful to distinguish between the rather uninteresting notion of enlightened shareholder interest and the more challenging concept of genuine stakeholder constituency:

> No doubt it is to a large extent true that an attempt by business managers to take into consideration the welfare of employees and consumers ... will in the long run increase the profits of stockholders. ... If the social responsibility of business means merely a more enlightened view as to the ultimate advantage of the stockholder-owners, then obviously corporate managers may accept such social responsibility without any departure from the traditional view that their function is to seek to obtain the maximum amount of profits for their stockholders.
>
> *And yet one need not be unduly credulous to feel that there is more to this talk of social responsibility on the part of corporate managers than merely a more intelligent appreciation of what tends to the ultimate benefit of their stockholders.*

Dodd, supra footnote 72, at 1156-57 (emphasis added).

the argument that other corporate "stakeholders" (such as creditors, employees, suppliers, and customers) can invariably protect themselves by contract. Many people, including employees, who deal with a corporation are not in a position to bargain effectively, or fairly, to ensure that their interests are fairly protected. Some important stakeholder interests cannot bargain at all. Local communities and the natural environment, for example, may both be affected significantly by corporate activity; however, their interests cannot typically be protected by consensual agreements with the corporation.

Corporations, say proponents of the stakeholder view, are entities that we, as a society, only suffer to exist because of a presumption that they promote social welfare. How, then, can we allow corporations to ultimately destroy social welfare in the pursuit of private profit?

A partial answer is that many of the "harms" that such commentators fear are—rightly and more effectively—prevented not by imposing incoherent and potentially conflicting fiduciary duties on corporate directors, but rather through appropriate regulation—worker safety regulation, environmental protection laws, and so on.

Over time, the stakeholder constituency philosophy has given rise to theories far more sophisticated than the saccharine, bumper-sticker slogans of the "doing good by doing well" variety. One especially intriguing argument in favour of defining the duty of directors as extending to constituents other than the corporation's shareholders is the "team production" model.[83] The team production model is premised on the notion that corporations must induce non-diversifiable, firm-specific investment from various constituents. Attracting this kind of investment is possible only if a mechanism exists to distribute corporate wealth that is credible and that is not dominated by those whose judgment is clouded by self-interest. Although complex contracts could, theoretically, provide the necessary distribution formula, contracts must necessarily be incomplete— that is, it is simply not possible in real life to write contracts that will provide for every possible state of the world and, indeed, it is not possible even to draft contracts that anticipate a significant enough number of possible states of the world except by incurring prohibitive transaction costs. Accordingly, because contracting cannot solve the problem, some other mechanism is needed. That mechanism is what Blair and Stout have described as a "mediating hierarchy"[84]—a structure in which the corporation's various constituents (or "team members") assign control rights to the corporation's board of directors—a board that, on this matter, is not (and should not be) directly controlled by the shareholders or any other specific constituency.

The team production model is, to date in Canada, chiefly of academic rather than of doctrinal interest. Not all the academic assessments of this model have been positive.[85] However, one non-shareholder constituency that has attracted the attention of courts and commentators is the corporation's creditors. A series of cases from the United King-

---

83   See Margaret M. Blair and Lynn A. Stout, "A Team Production Theory of Corporate Law" (1999), 85 *Virginia Law Review* 247.

84   Ibid., at 276.

85   See, e.g., Jeffrey G. MacIntosh, "The End of Corporate Existence: Should Boards Act as Mediating Hierarchs? A Comment on Yalden" in Anita Anand and William F. Flanagan, eds., *The Corporation in the 21st Century: Papers Presented at the 9th Queen's Annual Business Law Symposium 2002*, 37.

dom,[86] the United States,[87] Australia,[88] and New Zealand[89] suggest that, in those jurisdictions, directors of a corporation might well owe duties to a corporation's creditors either directly or, more probably, as a corollary to their duties to act in the best interests of the corporation, at least in cases where the corporation is in "the vicinity of insolvency." The rationale for such a putative duty, simply put, is that when a corporation nears insolvency, shareholders—as residual claimants—no longer have any meaningful economic interest in the corporation. Accordingly, the basis on which directors' duties to shareholders is grounded falls away when the corporation nears insolvency. At that point, it is the corporation's creditors, not its shareholders, that retain an economic interest in the corporation.

In Canada in recent years, there were some suggestions of a growing willingness by some courts to consider the possibility that directors must, indeed, take account of creditors' interests when an insolvency approaches.[90] Then, in 1998, the Quebec Superior Court, in *People's Department Stores Inc. (Trustee of) v. Wise*,[91] held that breach of such a duty could expose directors to personal liability. That decision, however, was reversed by the Quebec Court of Appeal.[92] The Court of Appeal's judgment generated significant interest among members of the practising bar and corporate law scholars,[93] and was, in

---

86   See, e.g., *Lonrho Ltd. v. Shell Petroleum Co.*, [1980] 1 WLR 627 (HL); *Re Horsley & Weight*, [1982] Ch. 442 (CA); *Winkworth v. Edward Baron Development Co.*, [1987] 1 All ER 114 (HL); and *West Mercia Safetywear (Liquidator of) v. Dodd*, [1988] BCLC 250 (CA). Note that Professor Sealy has dismissed the comments of Lord Templeman in *Winkworth* relating to directors' duties to creditors as "little more than so much hot air." See L.S. Sealy, "Personal Liability of Directors and Officers for Debts of Insolvent Corporations: A Jurisdictional Perspective (England)" in Jacob S. Ziegel, ed., *Current Developments in International and Comparative Corporate Insolvency Law* (Oxford: Clarendon Press, 1994), 485, at 487. Also note that the UK *Companies Act* includes an express fraudulent trading provision, making it an offence for the business of a company to be "carried on with intent to defraud creditors of the company or creditors of any other person." See UK *Companies Act, 1985*, at s. 458.

87   See e.g., *Credit Lyonnais Bank v. Pathe Communications*, Del. Ch. LEXIS 215 (1991); *Miramar Resources, Inc. v. Schultz*, 208 BR 723 (Bankr. MD Fla. 1997); and *Weaver v. Kellogg*, 216 BR 563 (SD Texas 1997). For a discussion of this issue in the US context, see Royce de Barondes, "Fiduciary Duties of Officers and Directors of Distressed Corporations" (1998), 7 *George Mason Law Review* 45.

88   See, e.g., *Walker v. Wimbourne* (1976), 137 CLR 1 (HC) and *Kinsela v. Russell Kinsela Pty. Ltd. (In Liq.)* (1986), 4 NSWLR 722 (SC).

89   *Nicholson v. Permakraft (New Zealand) Ltd.*, [1985] 1 NZLR 242 (CA).

90   See, e.g., *Canbook Distribution Corp. v. Borins* (1999), 45 OR (3d) 565 (SCJ); *Downtown Eatery (1993) Ltd. v. Ontario* (2001), 54 OR (3d) 161 (CA), leave to appeal to Supreme Court of Canada dismissed [2001] SCCA no. 392 (QL); and *Dylex Ltd. (Trustee of) v. Anderson* (2003), 63 OR (3d) 659 (SCJ); Jacob S. Ziegel, "Creditors as Corporate Stakeholders: The Quiet Revolution—An Anglo-Canadian Perspective" (1993), 43 *University of Toronto Law Journal* 511; James C. Baillie, "In Support of Striking a Balance Between Unlimited Flexibility and Rigid Statutory Prescriptions," in *Corporate Restructurings and Insolvencies: Issues and Perspectives*, Papers Presented at the Queen's Annual Business Law Symposium 1995 (Toronto: Carswell, 1996).

91   (1998), 23 CBR (4th) 200 (Que. SC).

92   (2003), 224 DLR (4th) 509 (Que. CA).

93   See, e.g., Brian Morgan and Harry Underwood, "Directors' Liability to Creditors on a Corporation's Insolvency in Light of the *Dylex* and *Peoples Department Stores* Litigation" (2004), 39 *Canadian*

turn, appealed to the Supreme Court of Canada. In the fall of 2004, the Supreme Court
released its long-awaited judgment in that case,[94] upholding the judgment of the Court of
Appeal and rejecting the notion that directors owe a fiduciary duty to the corporation's
creditors when the corporation is in the vicinity of insolvency. The decision also touched
on a number of other matters relating to corporate stakeholders' interests more generally,
and the directors' duties toward creditors specifically. Some of the implications of the
Peoples Department Stores case are discussed later in this chapter and in a number of
sections elsewhere in this book.

On the legislative side, many US states enacted so-called constituency legislation in
response to an increasing wave of hostile takeover bids in the 1980s. Those statutes
expressly permit directors of a company that is the target of a hostile takeover bid to
consider the intererests of non-shareholder constituents when deciding whether, and how,
to defend against such a bid. However, it remains an open question as to whether this
legislation was genuinely passed with a view to protecting vulnerable non-shareholder
interests, or, rather, whether these statutes were implemented at the behest of corporate
managers who sought to insulate themselves from the market for corporate control.[95]
Although proposals have occasionally been put forward urging similar changes in Canada,
thus far similar constituency legislation has not yet been enacted in Canada.

In the Canadian courts, prior to the Supreme Court's recent judgment in *Peoples
Department Stores*, there was little judicial endorsement of the stakeholder constituency
notion. One notable exception may be found in certain language of Berger J in the 1973
case of *Teck Corporation Limited v. Millar*,[96] language that the Supreme Court expressly
endorsed in *Peoples Department Stores*.

Before setting out this important language, however, it may be useful to consider the
context from which it emerged. *Teck* involved a junior mining company, Afton Mines
Ltd. Afton owned an interest in a valuable copper deposit, and was seeking a senior
mining company to assist it in developing this property. There were two rival suitors:
Teck Corporation and Placer Developments Ltd. The managers of Afton favoured a deal
with Placer. However, there was a snag. Teck Corporation had begun purchasing shares
of Afton Mines Ltd. Indeed, Teck acquired over 50 percent of the voting shares of
Afton—enough to replace Afton's board of directors with its own nominees, and thus be
assured of securing a contract with Afton to develop the copper property.

However, before Teck had time to convene a shareholders' meeting to replace the
Afton board, the directors of Afton made plans of their own. They negotiated and signed
a contract with a subsidiary of Placer, and granted an option to that subsidiary permitting
it to purchase a 30 percent share interest in Afton. In other words, by exercising its share

Business Law Journal 336; Stephane Rousseau, "The Duties of Directors of Financially Distressed Corporations: A Quebec Perspective on the *Peoples* Case" (2004), 39 *Canadian Business Law Journal* 368; Christopher C. Nicholls, "Liability of Corporate Officers and Directors to Third Parties" (2001), 35 *Canadian Business Law Journal* 1, at 30ff.

94   *Peoples Department Stores Inc. v. Wise*, 2004 SCC 68.

95   See, e.g., Roberta Romano, "The Political Economy of Takeover Statutes" (1987), 73 *Virginia Law Review* 111; *The Genius of American Corporate Law* (Washington: AEI Press, 1993), at 58-59.

96   [1973] 2 WWR 385 (BCSC).

purchase option, Placer would be able to acquire enough shares to end Teck's voting control over Afton.

Teck objected to the actions of Afton's directors. It brought an action against these directors, among others, alleging that they had breached their fiduciary duties. The action was dismissed. In the course of his written reasons, Berger J made the following statement, which has come to be heralded by many as an endorsement of the stakeholder constituency view:

> The classical theory is that the directors' duty is to the company. The company's shareholders are the company (Boyd C in *Martin v. Gibson* (1907), 15 OLR 623) and therefore no interests outside those of the shareholders can legitimately be considered by the directors. ... In defining the fiduciary duties of directors, the law ought to take into account the fact that the corporation provides the legal framework for the development of resources and the generation of wealth in the private sector of the Canadian economy. ... A classical theory that once was unchallengeable must yield to the facts of modern life. In fact, of course, it has. If today the directors of a company were to consider the interests of its employees no one would argue that in doing so they were not acting bona fide in the interests of the company itself. Similarly, if the directors were to consider the consequences to the community of any policy that the company intended to pursue, and were deflected in their commitment to that policy as a result, it could not be said that they had not considered bona fide the interests of the shareholders.[97]

The Supreme Court of Canada quoted the latter part of this language from *Teck*, accepting "as an accurate statement of law that in determining whether they are acting with a view to the best interests of the corporation, it may be legitimate, given all the circumstances of a given case, for the board of directors to consider, *inter alia,* the interests of shareholders, employees, suppliers, creditors, consumers, governments and the environment."[98] What the Supreme Court has so recently blessed, no lower court may now lightly ignore. But it is, at the very least, curious to note that Berger J's original pronouncement appears to have had little to do with the facts at issue in *Teck*. *Teck* involved a dispute between two competing joint venture partners. There was no apparent issue of employee or any other non-shareholder interests for the managers to consider. What is more, earlier in the judgment, Berger J summarized the position of Teck's counsel as follows:

> [Teck's counsel] says the defendant directors believed that Teck would use its dominant position to compel Afton to give Teck the ultimate deal. They believed that under Teck's management the property would not be developed as profitably as it would under Placer's management. They also believed that the value of Afton's shares, including their own, would decline, under Teck's management. Therefore, the argument goes, the defendant directors entered into the contract with Canex so that shares would be allotted under the contract to defeat Teck's majority.[99]

---

97 Ibid., at 412-13.

98 Supra footnote 94, at para. 42.

99 Supra footnote 96, at 409.

The plaintiff had thus conceded that the defendant directors had been pursuing the goal of maximizing the value of Afton's shares. Such a goal, of course, is consistent with the shareholder primacy norm. In other words, the decision reached by the court in *Teck* did not require the court to balance the directors' concern for non-shareholder interests against their concern for maximizing shareholder wealth. The actions of Afton's directors to which the plaintiff objected were, by the plaintiff's own admission, aimed at increasing the value of Afton's shares. And it was those entirely pro-shareholder actions that the court in *Teck* upheld.

Shareholder Primacy

We have already alluded generally to the shareholder primacy view above. A few additional observations and considerations will be offered in this section. The shareholder primacy[100] norm refers to the idea that it is the shareholders, and only the shareholders, whose interests the directors and officers of a corporation should seek to serve. Advocates of this view note, first, that the shareholders hold the residual economic interest in the corporation. Put simply, the shareholders' financial claims rank last. They are entitled only to whatever value happens to remain in the corporation after all other claimants— the creditors—have been paid in full. If the corporation is thus managed with a view to maximizing the value of the interests held by those who, as it were, stand at the end of the queue, then the interests of all other prior-ranking stakeholders must necessarily be maximized as well.

Before the principle of shareholder primacy may be fairly critiqued, it is important to define as a practical matter what it means to say that directors ought to act in the interests of the shareholders. At one time, it was suggested that this duty to shareholders could be translated into a duty to maximize the corporation's profits.[101] But, the dominant view today is that maximizing shareholder welfare does not simply mean maximizing profits—at least if "profits" means short-term accounting earnings. The duty is not, in other words, "to make a quick buck for shareholders."[102] Rather, the modern conception of the shareholder primacy norm is usually understood today in terms of efforts aimed at increasing the market price of the corporation's shares (which inevitably means, among other things, sustaining the corporation's productive capacity).[103] Such a view obviates

---

100 In 2001, Henry Hansmann and Reinier Kraakman boldly proclaimed that the ideological battle was over, and that the shareholder primacy view now prevailed. As they put it, "[t]here is no longer any serious competitor to the view that corporate law should principally strive to increase long-term shareholder value." And, elsewhere in that same paper, that "as a consequence of both logic and experience, there is convergence on a consensus that the best means to [the] end (that is, the pursuit of aggregate social welfare) is to make corporate managers strongly accountable to shareholder interests and, at least in direct terms, only to those interests." See Henry Hansmann and Reinier Kraakman, "The End of History for Corporate Law" (2001), 89 *Georgetown Law Journal* 439, at 441.

101 See Friedman, supra footnote 73.

102 Steven M.H. Wallman, "Understanding the Purpose of a Corporation: An Introduction" (1999), 24 *Journal of Corporation Law* 807, at 818.

103 See, e.g., Zvi Bodie and Robert C. Merton, *Corporate Finance* (Upper Saddle River, NJ: Prentice Hall, 2000), at 10ff.

the need to consider whether a corporation's shareholders are long-term investors or short-term speculators. Because share prices ought to represent the market's view of the future earnings of the corporation, all shareholders—whether long-term investors or short-term speculators—will be equally well served by a policy aimed at maximizing the corporation's current share price. Needless to say, this reliance on the share price implicitly assumes the efficiency of the securities markets in which those shares trade.[104] Not surprisingly, that assumption—essential to the efficient capital markets hypothesis—has been rather hotly debated,[105] and some commentators have suggested alternative methods of framing the duty of directors to maximize shareholder wealth.[106]

In addition to arguments raised by those who view the efficient capital markets hypothesis with skepticism, there are at least two other well-known objections to the shareholder primacy model of corporate law. The first turns chiefly on a matter of semantics. Some commentators note that it is clear, as a matter of law, that directors do not owe a fiduciary duty to shareholders at all; they owe a fiduciary duty to the corporation itself, a proposition in support of which numerous legislative and judicial authorities may be cited.

This rejoinder is entirely correct, but, in this context, unhelpful. It cannot be disputed that, as a matter of Canadian law, directors do not owe a fiduciary duty to shareholders personally.[107] It is precisely for this reason that shareholders must typically pursue their claims against wayward directors by way of derivative action, as discussed in chapter 13. However, what is at issue is how corporate directors are properly to interpret and so fulfill an ambiguous duty. Those who support the shareholder primacy norm thus argue that to make practical sense of the proposition that directors are under a duty to act in the best interests of the corporation, that duty must be understood to be synonymous with a duty to act in the best interests of the shareholders as a whole whose interests, as a matter of history and logic, define the corporation's interests.

---

104 The seminal paper on the impact of efficient market theory on corporate law is Ronald J. Gilson and Reinier H. Kraakman, "The Mechanisms of Market Efficiency" (1984), 70 *Virginia Law Review* 549. In 2003, the *Journal of Corporation Law* published a "Symposium" issue dedicated to Gilson and Kraakman's article. See (2003), 28 *Journal of Corporation Law*.

105 See, e.g., the papers published in the *Journal of Corporation Law*, ibid., especially Lynn A. Stout, "The Mechanisms of Market Inefficiency" (2003), 28 *Journal of Corporation Law* 635.

106 For example, Henry Hu has advocated what he calls "blissful shareholder wealth maximization," a term that he derives from the notion that corporation managers should "blissfully ignore" the occasional irrationality that distorts the trading price of their corporation's shares, and attempt, instead, to maximize the "blissful price" at which the shares *would* trade if the markets were perfectly efficient. See Henry Hu, "New Financial Products, the Modern Process of Financial Innovation, and the Puzzle of Shareholder Welfare" (1991), 69 *Texas Law Review* 1273, at 1285-86.

107 The classic Anglo-Canadian authority for this proposition is said to be *Percival v. Wright*, [1902] 2 Ch. 421, where the directors of a corporation purchased shares from their shareholders without disclosing that a sale of the company's undertaking—which would have resulted in a greater gain for the shareholders—was pending. Note that the actions of the directors in *Percival v. Wright* would, if attempted by directors of a CBCA corporation today, be prohibited by various statutory provisions, such as CBCA s. 131 or, in the case of publicly traded corporations, by the insider-trading provisions of provincial securities statutes.

There is a second well-known, if somewhat technical, objection to the supposed efficacy of the shareholder primacy position. This objection is often illustrated through the use of stylized numerical examples. The examples are intended to prove that, at least for certain corporate investment decisions, the interests of a corporation's shareholders and the interests of its fixed claimants (that is, its employees, creditors, and so on) actually diverge. On this view, a legal rule that obligates directors to act only in the interests of shareholders could, in some cases, erode the value of the corporation as a whole (the enterprise value), not increase it. In addition to this general admonition, however, some commentators have observed that merely demonstrating that pursuit of shareholder wealth might not *always* maximize firm wealth is not an effective rebuttal of the shareholder primacy norm if it cannot, further, be demonstrated that some alternative corporate goal results in firm wealth maximization more consistently than the shareholder primacy model.[108] These sorts of examples also typically suffer from a fundamental flaw. To illustrate this flaw, it is necessary to reproduce one such typical example in some detail (see table below). The figures used in this example are taken from a 1999 paper by Steven M.H. Wallman.[109]

Wallman's illustration works in this way. The reader is asked to assume that a certain hypothetical corporation has before it two alternative (but mutually exclusive) investment options: option A and option B. The table shows the expected return and probabilities of returns for each of these options. One is invited to make two further assumptions: (1) that the shareholders of this hypothetical corporation have, collectively, invested a total of $100,000 in the corporation; and (2) that the cost to the corporation of pursuing either of these two possible investment projects is $2.1 million. (That is, the cost to the corporation of investing in either option A or option B is exactly $2.1 million. That cost might include an expenditure of cash—which the corporation would have to borrow from a lender—or other cost elements such as labour, etc.)

Based on these assumptions, which of the two investment options is truly in the best interests of the corporation? If the only goal of the corporation is to maximize the value of the shareholders' interests, says Wallman, the answer appears to be A. However, this outcome is perverse. The pursuit of option A, he observes, will actually result in a fall in the value of the corporation as a whole, because the expected return of option A is lower than the expected return of option B:

Project	Optimistic scenario (50% probability)	Pessimistic scenario (50% probability)	Expected return
A	$2.5 million return	$1.5 million return	$2 million (i.e., $0.5 \times \$2.5$ million + $0.5 \times \$1.5$ million)
B	$2.2 million	$2.2 million	$2.2 million

---

108   See MacIntosh, supra footnote 85, at 68.

109   Wallman, supra footnote 102, at 811.

Why would the shareholders prefer the corporation to pursue the option with a lower expected return? The answer, on Wallman's analysis, is that even though option A's expected return is lower than option B's *from the corporation's perspective*, it is actually higher than option B's *from the shareholders' perspective*.

How can this be? Remember that the cost to the corporation of pursuing either option is $2.1 million. That cost must be paid before the corporation receives any return. That means that $2.1 million must, from the shareholders' perspective, be subtracted from the total expected return of each project. In other words, under Wallman's analysis, the expected return of option A, from the shareholders' perspective, is not $2 million after all. Rather, it is only $150,000, calculated as follows:

$$[0.5 \times (\$2.5 \text{ million} - \$2.1 \text{ million})] + (0.5 \times -\$100,000) = \$150,000.$$

The second term in this equation perhaps requires a brief explanation. This term indicates that if option A is pursued, there is a 50 percent chance that the shareholders will lose the entire amount of their share investment ($100,000). The potential loss *to the corporation* would be much higher. There is a 50 percent chance that the corporation will lose $600,000 (that is, $1.5 million minus the $2.1 million project cost). But the shareholders can never lose more than the amount of their initial $100,000 investment, no matter how much the corporation itself stands to lose. That, of course, is the significance of the fact that the shareholders enjoy limited liability.

Now consider the expected return of pursuing option B from the perspective of the shareholders, rather than from the perspective of the corporation itself. Using this same analysis, the expected return to the shareholders if the corporation pursues option B would be:

$$[0.5 \times (\$2.2 \text{ million} - \$2.1 \text{ million})] + (0.5 \times (\$2.2 \text{ million} - \$2.1 \text{ million}) = \$100,000.$$

According to Wallman, the upshot of this analysis is that we must assume that the shareholders would elect to pursue option A, because pursuing that option has a higher expected return from their perspective. But, pursuing option A would, at the time the corporation makes its investment decision, actually decrease the value of the corporation. Thus, he argues, an uncompromising rule that a corporation ought to maximize *shareholder* value could actually destroy *firm* value.

Wallman, however, overlooks one rather important factor. Pursuing the "wrong" investment option will surely have an adverse effect on the market price of the corporation's shares. This is a critical omission, because the value that shareholders attach to their shares is dependent on the shares' market price, not the amount they happened to pay originally for the shares. In this example, then, the $100,000 price paid by the shareholders when they initially acquired their shares is a red herring. The market does not care what a shareholder has originally paid for his or her shares. The market price is determined by an assessment of the corporation's current value.

To illustrate the effect of this critical oversight in Wallman's argument, re-examine his example, this time from the perspective of a hypothetical purchaser of the corporation's shares. We will need to add one further simplifying assumption to take account of the fact that the payoffs from investment projects in the real world are rarely (indeed never) instantaneous. So, suppose that the return on either of the two available investment options will be realized by the corporation in precisely one year's time. Also assume that, whichever investment option is chosen, the returns from that project will represent the firm's entire undertaking for that year.

Now, any prospective purchaser of the corporation's outstanding shares would calculate the price he or she would be willing to pay for the shares on the basis of the expected return on this proposed investment. Let us suppose that prospective purchasers of this corporation's shares require a 20 percent annual return on equity investments of this kind. We know, from the calculation above, that the shareholders' overall expected return if the corporation pursues option B will be $100,000. Therefore, if the corporation decides to pursue option B, our hypothetical purchaser would be prepared to pay $500,000 to acquire all of the corporation's outstanding shares, because an expected return of $100,000 would represent a 20 percent return on an investment of $500,000. (Obviously, the $100,000 represents just a single year's return. We might assume, for the sake of simplicity, that the firm is to be wound up at the end of the year, or perhaps that prospective purchasers forecast that the corporation's managers will make similar investment decisions on behalf of the corporation in future years as well.)

Would this prospective purchaser be prepared to pay as much for the corporation's shares if option A were pursued instead? No. If a shareholder were to pay $500,000 to acquire shares in the corporation, the expected return on that shareholder's investment, if option A is pursued, would be:

$$(0.5 \times \$400,000) + (0.5 \times -\$500,000) = -\$50,000.$$

The expected return is a negative number because it is possible (though not certain) that the new shareholder will lose his or her entire investment. (If the new shareholder were certain to lose the entire $500,000 he or she had paid for the shares, the expected return would be equal to -$500,000.)

Clearly, then, no purchaser who requires a 20 percent expected annual return on its investments would pay $500,000 for these shares. In fact, in order for the shares of a corporation that pursues option A to offer the required 20 percent expected return, the shares cannot be sold for more than $285,714.30.

Put simply, if the corporation pursues option B, its outstanding shares will be worth $500,000. If it pursues option A, its outstanding shares will be worth considerably less (only $285,714.30). Because it is the price at which shares can be sold in the market that matters to a corporation's existing shareholders (and *not* the price at which they originally purchased their shares), existing shareholders of this corporation will—contrary to Wallman's prediction—*always* prefer that the corporation pursue option B. That is the investment option that will maximize the value of their share price, and so increase their current wealth.

Therefore, a rule that requires directors to work to maximize the corporation's share price will, in fact, be consistent with maximizing firm value as a whole. To be clear, this argument should not be taken to suggest that the interests of creditors and shareholders will never diverge. Of course they will. Creditors will typically prefer the corporation to pursue lower risk strategies than the shareholders. The problem, however, is that creditors may be expected to favour such lower risk strategies even where higher risk investments offer the firm superior risk-adjusted returns. Indulging the creditors' understandable conservatism, therefore, would reduce the firm's value.

Three caveats should be mentioned here. First, if a corporation is a small, private corporation, the shares of which cannot be easily bought and sold, then the market price of the shares cannot be expected to act as a reasonable discipline on managerial behaviour. However, in fact, in small, private corporations—where the shareholders and the managers are typically the same people—the corporation will predictably be run in the interests of the shareholders in any event (subject to possible disputes between majority and minority shareholders). Second, this example assumes that the market can accurately assess information about the corporation and instantaneously reflect that information in the share price. But, even if the market does not function with perfect efficiency, there is still no reason to suppose that share prices are more likely to rise if the corporation pursues a value-destroying investment option, or are more likely to fall if it does not. Finally, the analysis of the economic interests of a corporation's shareholders becomes murkier when a corporation begins to approach insolvency. In such circumstances, the corporation's shares may be, for all practical purposes, worthless regardless of which investment option the corporation chooses. That particular case is considered further below.

The interests of shareholders and the duties of directors are, thus, carefully interwoven. And so we now move on from a consideration of shareholder interests to consider directors' and officers' duties.

DIRECTORS' AND OFFICERS' DUTIES

Introduction

Corporate law imposes two (or, on some reckonings, three[110]) sorts of duties on corporate directors and corporate officers: (1) a duty of care, diligence and skill and (2) a duty of loyalty and good faith. These duties are occasionally spoken of collectively as directors' and officers' "fiduciary duties";[111] but, more conventional usage (recently endorsed by the Supreme Court of Canada)[112] is to reserve the phrase "fiduciary duty" as a label to be applied only to the duty (or duties) of good faith and loyalty.

Most reported cases in which directors are alleged to have breached their duties have involved breaches (or alleged breaches) of the duty of loyalty and good faith. Courts,

---

110 There has been some technical discussion in recent US cases as to whether the duty of good faith is separate from, or simply forms part of, the duty of loyalty. See, e.g., *In re The Walt Disney Company Derivative Litigation* (Del. Ch. May 28, 2003); *Emerald Partners v. Berlin* (Del. Ch. April 28, 2003).

111 The Delaware Supreme Court, for example, has spoken of "the board of directors' triad of fiduciary duties, loyalty, good faith or due care." See *Emerald Partners v. Berlin*, 726 A 2d 1215 (Del. SC 1999).

112 *Peoples Department Stores*, supra footnote 94, at para. 3: "In our view, it has not been established that the directors of Peoples violated either the fiduciary duty or the duty of care imposed by s. 122(1) of the CBCA." And later, at para. 32: "Subsection 122(1) of the CBCA establishes two distinct duties to be discharged by directors and officers in managing, or supervising the management of, the corporation ... . The first duty has been referred to in this case as the 'fiduciary duty.' It is better described as the 'duty of loyalty.' We will use the expression 'statutory fiduciary duty' for purposes of clarity when referring to the duty under the CBCA."

shareholders, and the public generally seem more concerned about punishing dishonesty than mere incompetence. Could this apparent tolerance for directorial inattentiveness be changing? The cluster of US corporate scandals that began with the 2001 restatement by Enron Corp. of its third-quarter financial results has renewed public interest in shoring up directors' duty of care obligations. There have been signs, and not always welcome signs, that some shareholders have become rather eager to punish directors and managers not only when they have been guilty of fraud and overreaching, but also when they have been inactive, inattentive, or obsequious individuals on whose watch financial scandals have occurred. One reading of history suggests that this keen interest in directors' duty of care may melt away if the stock markets stage a strong and sustained rally, but time alone will tell.

The Duty of Care, Diligence, and Skill

Introduction

At common law, the standard of competence demanded of corporate directors was not onerous. Courts recognized that corporate directors are not members of an accredited profession for which special qualifications or credentials are required, and were quite forgiving of the honest director, however inept. Several lines of judicial reasoning tended to make successful claims against honest yet incompetent directors as rare as sunshine during a Reykjavik winter.

First, courts emphasized that the shareholders' choice of directors was a private matter. Because the shareholders themselves chose their directors, why, then, should those same shareholders be entitled to compensation for the consequences of their own poor choice (unless, of course, the director had engaged in dishonest behaviour)?[113]

Second, in assessing the standard of care that directors might be expected to meet, it was thought inappropriate to apply the kind of objective yardstick against which the actions of accredited professionals (like physicians, lawyers, or engineers) must be measured. Rather, the actions of each director were to be judged against the standard of what might be expected of someone of that particular director's ability and experience.

The concept of the "business judgment rule," discussed below, has also presented a barrier to those seeking to sue (honest) directors for (mere) breaches of their duty of care, although the Canadian version of the "business judgment rule," as it has evolved and is evolving, does not appear to offer much comfort to directors who have failed to implement appropriate systems and follow proper procedures.

Finally, corporate directors have, as a general rule, been permitted to rely on the representations of managers, in the absence of any reasonable grounds for suspicion, and may, in certain cases, also have specific statutory due diligence and reliance defences

---

113 As Gower and Davies correctly note, whatever validity this view may have (or have had) in the context of small, private corporations, it is wholly unrealistic in the context of large, public corporations where shareholders are, at best, given the opportunity to ratify management's choice of directors, rather than any effective opportunity of electing directors of their own choosing. See Davies, supra footnote 30, at 433.

available to them. That said, recent cases in Delaware[114] and elsewhere[115] have signalled the importance of directors taking proactive steps to prevent corporate wrongdoing by ensuring that adequate and effective systems have been put in place. The most recent pronouncement of the Supreme Court of Canada on this subject has also signalled the importance to directors and officers of ensuring that sound governance standards and systems have been established.[116]

To these liability considerations, one might perhaps add a further practical problem facing plaintiffs seeking to sue directors for breach of their duty of care: the challenge of proving damages. Even if a plaintiff can successfully establish that a director has breached his or her duty of care, it may be inordinately difficult to show that such a breach actually caused any damages suffered by the plaintiff.[117]

Finally, much of whatever sting might have remained in the law has been considerably softened by corporate indemnification provisions and the availability of directors' and officers' insurance. Still, neither indemnification nor insurance can completely eliminate the risk of personal liability, and neither can address the risk of reputational harm that might still act to deter potential public company directors from accepting board seats.

The Subjective Standard at Common Law

A relatively low standard of directorial care was articulated in a series of English cases of which *Re Denham & Co.*,[118] *Re Cardiff Savings Bank*,[119] *Dovey v. Corey*,[120] and *In re Brazilian Rubber Plantations and Estates, Ltd.*[121] are some of the most well known. The classic common law statement of the corporate director's duty of care, though, is found in *Re City Equitable Fire Insurance Company Limited*.[122] That case involved a company that had been the victim of fraud on the part of one of its directors. The issue before the court was whether the remaining directors (and indeed the corporation's auditors) ought to be held personally liable for negligence. That is, although they had not participated in

---

114 See *In re Caremark Inc. Derivative Litigation*, 698 A 2d 959 (Del. Ch. 1996). For a discussion of *Caremark* and its significance, see H. Lowell Brown, "The Corporate Director's Compliance Oversight Responsibility in the Post *Caremark* Era" (2001), 26 *Delaware Journal of Corporate Law* 1.

115 See Nicholls, infra footnote 154, at 343.

116 *Peoples Department Stores*, supra footnote 94, at para. 64: "The establishment of good corporate governance rules should be a shield that protects directors from allegations that they have breached their duty of care."

117 The classic American authority on this point is *Barnes v. Andrews*, 298 F. 614, at 616 (1924): "The plaintiff must, however, go further than to show that [the defendant director] should have been more active in his duties. … The plaintiff must accept the burden of showing that the performance of the defendant's duties would have avoided loss, and what loss it would have avoided."

118 (1883), 25 Ch. D 752.

119 [1892] 2 Ch. 100.

120 [1901] AC 477 (HL).

121 [1925] 1 Ch. 407 (CA).

122 [1925] 1 Ch. 407.

the fraudulent conduct themselves, were they, nevertheless, negligent in having failed to detect the fraud of others?

There had been some older authorities, adverted to by Romer J, to the effect that a director (otherwise honest and loyal) would not be held liable unless guilty of "gross negligence."[123] Romer J was wary of attempting to assign any precise meaning to the term:

> But if it be said that of two men one is only liable to a third person for gross negligence, and the other is liable for mere negligence, this, I think, means no more than that the duties of the two men are different. The one owes a duty to take a greater degree of care than does the other.[124]

The issue, then, for Romer J was to determine what degree of care a corporate director was expected to exercise. In considering this question, he articulated three key propositions:

(1) A director need not exhibit in the performance of his duties a greater degree of skill than may reasonably be expected from a person of his knowledge and experience.[125]
(2) A director is not bound to give continuous attention to the affairs of his company. His duties are of an intermittent nature to be performed at periodical board meetings, and at meetings of any committee of the board upon which he happens to be placed.[126]
(3) In respect of all duties that, having regard to the exigencies of business, and the articles of association, may properly be left to some other official, a director is, in the absence of grounds for suspicion, justified in trusting that official to perform such duties honestly.[127]

This early English common law view has been characterized by one leading English commentator as having "framed the directors' duties of skill and care with non-executive [that is, an outside, independent director who is not an employee of the company] rather than executive directors in mind and, moreover, on the basis of a view that the non-executive director had no serious role to play within the company but was simply a piece of window-dressing aimed at promoting the company's image."[128]

A more demanding standard for directors' duties of care was eventually developed by the English courts. However, as Gower and Davies suggest, that new approach did not begin to emerge until the late 1970s.[129] By that time, in Canada, a statutory standard had

---

123 Parenthetically, the term "gross negligence"—although today found in American judicial decisions—has a somewhat doubtful meaning in Canada. The term has been considered by Canadian courts in some contexts (often involving statutory standards).

124 Supra footnote 122, at 428.

125 Ibid.

126 Ibid.

127 Ibid. Recall here, however, that the CBCA makes it unlawful for the directors to delegate certain of their powers. (CBCA s. 115(3).) Thus, as the Dickerson committee noted, it is not possible for directors of a CBCA corporation to avoid liability simply by claiming that any of these matters had been delegated. See Dickerson committee, supra footnote 33, at para. 221.

128 Davies, supra footnote 30, at 433.

129 Ibid., at 434, referring, in particular, to *Dorchester Finance Co. v. Stebbing*, [1989] BCLC 498. (As the authors point out, although reported in 1989, the case was actually decided more than a decade earlier.)

been introduced in the Ontario *Business Corporations Act* and, soon thereafter, in the CBCA and other provincial statutes as well.

Statutory Duty of Care Standard

In 1967, the Lawrence committee, in its review of Ontario corporate law, considered that the common law standard as articulated in *Re City Equitable* was no longer appropriate. The committee recommended that the standard be upgraded and, specifically, that it be replaced with a statutory requirement that directors exhibit the degree of care, diligence, and skill of a "reasonably prudent director in comparable circumstances."[130] The language actually adopted in the 1970 Ontario *Business Corporations Act*, however, differed from the language proposed by the Lawrence committee in two respects. First, it applied not only to directors, but also to officers. Second, the standard against which each director's and officer's actions were to be measured was that of a "reasonably prudent *person*" rather than of a "reasonably prudent *director*" in comparable circumstances.

The significance of the substitution of the word "person" for the word "director" may not be immediately apparent. In fact, one might think that this change was no more than a routine conforming amendment that had become necessary because of the inclusion, earlier in the section, of the reference to officers. In other words, it would make no sense to say that each officer was required to exhibit the skill of a reasonably prudent *director*. But much greater significance came to be attached to the modified wording.

The Lawrence committee's proposed reference to "director" was thought by many to set an unduly high standard—a standard akin to that of a credentialed professional, such as a physician or lawyer. Many directors, it was feared—including, in particular, many entrepreneurs who originally launched business enterprises—might not realistically be able to meet such a heightened standard. Changing the standard to that of a reasonably prudent *person* was, accordingly, regarded as something of a victory for corporate directors. Indeed, the Federal Court of Appeal in *Soper v. Canada*, discussed below, explicitly endorsed the notion that the statutory reference to the standard of a "reasonably prudent person," rather than the "reasonably prudent director," "was not intended to seriously alter the common law."[131]

When the Dickerson committee later made its proposals for a new CBCA, its views on the standard of care to be required of directors echoed those of the Lawrence committee.

---

130 *Interim Report of the Select Committee on Company Law*, Allan F. Lawrence, chair (1967), at 56, para. 7.2.4.

131 *Soper v. Canada*, [1998] 1 FC 124 (CA), at para. 38. Oddly, however, the court went on to conclude that "[s]ince the language of the *Canada Business Corporations Act* mirrors that of the OBCA, it seems logical to infer that the federal Parliament intended to send out the very same message to existing and potential directors" (that is, the message that the common law standard has not been upgraded). The court did not take note of (or perhaps was not directed to) the clear statement of the Dickerson committee to the contrary. See Dickerson committee, supra footnote 33, at para. 242: "The principal change here is that whereas at present the law seems to be that a director is only required to demonstrate the degree of care, skill and diligence that could reasonably be expected from him, having regard to his knowledge and experience ... under [the new language] he is required to conform to the standard of a reasonably prudent man."

The Dickerson committee, like the Lawrence committee before it, argued that its proposed statutory codification would upgrade the common law standard of care.[132] The Dickerson committee was dismissive of the argument that moving away from the common law's subjective standard would impose such an onerous burden on corporate directors that competent candidates would be frightened away from agreeing to serve on corporate boards. As the Dickerson report wryly put it, "It is ... cold comfort to a shareholder to know that there is a steady supply of marginally competent people available under present law to manage his investment."[133]

However, the "upgrading" statutory language recommended by the Dickerson committee differed from the Lawrence committee's language in one significant way. The Dickerson committee's proposed language did not include the final phrase, "in comparable circumstances."[134]

When the CBCA was enacted, however, the drafters chose to include the phrase "in comparable circumstances" after all. That language is now found in s. 122(1)(b) of the CBCA. It is identical to the language found in the Ontario statute (and indeed mirrors similar provisions in many other provincial corporate statutes).[135] The section, in its current form, reads as follows:

> 122.(1) Every director and officer of a corporation in exercising their powers and discharging their duties shall ...
>
> (b) exercise the care, diligence and skill that a reasonably prudent person would exercise in comparable circumstances.

How significant is the inclusion of the qualifying phrase, "in comparable circumstances"? That language for a time was thought by some to preserve a subjective element to the duty of care standard.[136]

Prior to the Supreme Court's 2004 ruling in *Peoples Department Stores*, certain Canadian courts—interpreting virtually identical due diligence language in s. 227.1(3) of

---

132   Dickerson committee, ibid., at para. 242.

133   Ibid.

134   Ibid., vol. II, at 74, para. 9.19:

> (1) Every director and officer of a corporation in exercising his powers and discharging his duties shall
>
> (a) act honestly and in good faith with a view to the best interests of the corporation, and
>
> (b) exercise the care, diligence and skill of a reasonably prudent person.

135   See, e.g., *Business Corporations Act* (Alta.), s. 122(1)(b); *The Business Corporations Act* (Sask.), s. 117(1)(b); *The Corporations Act* (Man.), s. 117(1)(b); *Business Corporations Act* (NB), s. 79(1)(b); *Corporations Act* (NL), s. 203(1)(b); and *Business Corporations Act* (BC), s. 142(1)(b). Neither the Prince Edward Island *Companies Act* nor the Nova Scotia *Companies Act* includes comparable provisions.

136   The BC *Business Corporations Act* provides that the statutory standard of care "is in addition to, and not in derogation of" any other rule of law or equity (s. 142(2)). Its predecessor, the BC *Company Act*, contained similar language. The Federal Court of Appeal, in *Soper*, supra footnote 131, attached significance to this provision as well and—perhaps more importantly—to the fact that no similar provision appeared in the federal legislation, suggesting that the federal legislation was more of a codification, rather than an expansion, of the common law.

the *Income Tax Act*—held that this wording contemplated a mixed objective and subjective standard of care.[137] For example, the Federal Court of Appeal in *Soper v. Canada*[138] explicitly considered whether the s. 227.1(3) language, which the court noted was "virtually identical"[139] to the CBCA language in s. 122, upgraded the common law director's standard of care. The court considered, in particular, whether the subjective element of the common law standard had been eliminated by the statutory prescription.[140] Referring to interpretations of s. 122 of the CBCA, the court concluded that whatever "upgrading" may have occurred had been modest, and that the statutory test had "retained much of [the] original subjective character" of the common law test.[141]

The basis for the court's conclusion on this point was twofold. First, the phrase "in comparable circumstances," in the court's view, was suggestive of a subjective test. Second, the statutory language referred to a "reasonably *prudent* person" not to a "reasonably *skilled* person."[142] This choice of words, again, was thought to imply that the drafters were not attempting to prescribe an objective standard of competence as opposed, perhaps, to an objective standard of care.

To end, the Federal Court of Appeal concluded that the s. 227.1(3) language created a standard that was neither purely objective nor purely subjective:

> It is not enough for a director to say he or she did his or her best, for that is an invocation of the purely subjective standard. Equally clear is that honesty is not enough. However, the standard is not a professional one. Nor is it the negligence law standard that governs these cases. Rather, the Act contains both objective elements, embodied in the reasonable person language, and subjective elements, inherent in individual considerations like "skill" and the idea of "comparable circumstances." Accordingly, the standard can be properly described as "objective subjective."[143]

This phrase—"objective subjective"—was especially revealing. It was the very phrase that had been used in the same decision when the court described the old common law standard of care.[144]

The "objective subjective" standard was applied in subsequent cases considering s. 227.1(3) of the *Income Tax Act*. In one such recent case, for example, the Federal Court of Appeal succinctly stated that, "[g]enerally, a person who is experienced in business

---

137 See, e.g., *Corsano v. Canada* (1999), 172 DLR (4th) 708 (FCA) and *Soper*, supra footnote 131. In fact, Robertson JA, in *Soper*, described the common law test as articulated in *Re City Equitable* as "a hybrid 'objective subjective standard.'" (Ibid., at para. 25.) But by "objective" he meant only that, at common law, the actions of each director were judged against those of a *reasonable* person of that director's knowledge and experience. Thus the "objective" component of this standard at common law was, as described earlier, very modest indeed.

138 Supra footnote 131.

139 Ibid., at para. 29.

140 Ibid.

141 Ibid., at para. 31.

142 Ibid., at para. 33.

143 Ibid., at para. 41.

144 Ibid., at para. 25.

and financial matters is likely to be held to a higher standard than a person with no business acumen or experience whose presence on the board of directors reflects nothing more, for example, than a family connection."[145]

Until the Supreme Court recently clarified this issue, a curious situation obtained. Although the intention of the Lawrence committee and the Dickerson committee had been to upgrade the standard of care from the very low common law threshold, it was not at all clear that they had succeeded. Each director's own personal level of skill appeared to constitute, as it were, a "ceiling": the law seemed to demand no level of skill higher than that already possessed by each individual director. The Supreme Court has now, however, laid to rest the suggestion that inclusion of the phrase "in comparable circumstances" somehow undercuts the original intention of the CBCA and Ontario *Business Corporations Act* drafters to upgrade the standard of care. The phrase, according to the Supreme Court, "is not the introduction of a subjective element relating to the competence of the director, but rather the introduction of a contextual element into the statutory duty of care."[146] The court even had some gentle criticism for Robertson JA, who had delivered the Federal Court of Appeal's judgment in *Soper,* suggesting that his reference in that judgment to an "objective subjective" standard "could lead to confusion. We prefer to describe it as an objective standard."[147]

In the meantime, and in the absence of any comparable British attempt to statutorily upgrade the director's standard of care, the English courts appear to have gone some way to enhance the common law standard of care. It has been suggested that, in England, each director's personal level of skill functions not simply as a "ceiling" for the standard of care required of that director but, instead, operates more as a "floor." That is, if the director's personal abilities are higher than the base standard to be expected of the reasonable director, he or she will be subject to his or her own higher personal standard. Conversely, if the director's personal level of skill is lower than the base standard of the reasonable director, he or she should, presumably, either immediately take steps aimed at self-improvement, or decline directorial service because his or her performance will be measured against the higher (objective) standard.[148]

Differing Standards of Duty of Care?

Profit and Non-profit/Large and Small Corporations

It had often been assumed (or at least hoped) by legal practitioners that a lower standard of care ought to apply to voluntary directors of non-profit corporations than to directors of business corporations. This assumption was seriously undermined by the Federal Court of Appeal's decision in *Corsano v. Canada,*[149] at least in the context of the

---

145 *Smith v. Canada*, 2001 FCA 84, at para. 10.

146 *Peoples Department Stores Inc.*, supra footnote 94, at para. 62.

147 Ibid., at para. 63.

148 See Davies, supra footnote 30, at 434-35.

149 *Corsano*, supra footnote 137.

personal liability of directors under s. 227.1 of the *Income Tax Act* when a corporation has failed to withhold and remit employee income tax source deductions.

Similarly, in a recent decision by the Ontario Securities Commission, the commissioners noted that directors of smaller companies were not to be less attentive to their responsibilities than the directors of larger enterprises:

> Whether the issues facing a board involve a TSE 300 company, a smaller public company or an unlisted company, a director's attention to his or her obligations is still the essence of diligence.[150]

In short, the subjective element of the statutory duty of "care, diligence, and skill" seems to be especially relevant to the director's level of *skill*, rather than to the director's required level of *care and diligence*.

"Inside" and "Outside" Directors and Members of Board Committees

The boards of every public corporation, and even some private corporations, include two different types of directors:

- inside (or executive) directors—that is, directors who are also managers of the corporation; and
- outside (or non-executive) directors—that is, directors who are not managers of, or otherwise employed by, the corporation.

The CBCA specifically requires that every CBCA corporation that is a "distributing corporation"[151] and that has shares outstanding in the hands of at least two people, must have at least two directors who are not officers or employees of the corporation or its affiliates.[152] Outside directors of public corporations may be subject to further rules and classifications if, for example, the corporation's shares are listed on a securities exchange such as the Toronto Stock Exchange or the New York Stock Exchange. Outside directors might, for example, be further classified as "independent" or "unrelated" directors.[153] These more specific categories could take into account such considerations as whether a particular director is related to any of the corporation's senior managers, to a major

---

150 *Re YBM Magnex* (2003), 26 OSCB 5285 (Ont. Sec. Comm.), at 5327.

151 A distributing corporation is one that has issued its securities to the public, as opposed to a private, closely held corporation. For a more precise definition of the term "distributing corporation," see *Canada Business Corporations Regulations, 2001*, s. 2. See also the discussion of public and private corporations in chapter 4.

152 CBCA, s. 102(2).

153 See, e.g., TSX *Company Manual*, at ss. 472 to 475. In October 2004, the Canadian Securities Administrators published for comment Proposed National Instrument 58-101 and Proposed National Policy 58-201. When this instrument and policy become effective, the TSX will revoke its own corporate governance guidelines. See (2004), 27 OSCB 8825. If approved, it is anticipated that the proposed National Instrument and proposed policy would apply to companies' Annual Information Forms or information circulars filed after financial year-ends falling on or after June 30, 2005. See CSA *Staff Notice* 58-302 (2005), 28 OSCB 835.

shareholder of the corporation, or to a firm that is a major supplier or customer of the corporation, and so on.[154]

In addition, the boards of public corporations typically appoint special subcommittees of directors to exercise specific functions. In some cases, boards are required by law or stock exchange listing requirements to create certain special committees. In other cases, such committees are created as a sensible way for the board members to manage their diverse responsibilities. Among the most important public corporation board committees[155] are:

- the audit committee (the principal point of contact between the corporation's auditors and the board of directors);
- the compensation committee (the committee that reviews and makes recommendations to the board regarding compensation arrangements for the corporation's senior executives); and
- the nominating/corporate governance committee (the committee that, among other things, seeks to identify suitable candidates for board positions).

It is especially important for these committees to be able to function without undue influence or interference from the corporation's managers. Thus, in the case of public corporations, legal or stock exchange requirements typically mandate that a majority of the members of each of these committees must be outside directors and, in some cases, that the entire committee be composed of outside directors.

Outside (Non-executive) Directors

Small, private corporations rarely include outsiders on their boards, although large, private corporations do, from time to time, choose to invite independent outsiders. There are several reasons that a large, private corporation might choose to do this. First, as a private business grows very large, the scale and complexity of the corporation becomes similar to that of a public corporation. The entrepreneurs who have founded these businesses may thus find that they need the ongoing counsel of experienced, independent professional business managers. Second, if a private corporation has obtained financing from a venture capital or similar firm, that firm will typically require board representation as a condition to providing financing. Third, if a large, private corporation anticipates offering its securities to the public in the foreseeable future ("going public" as such an exercise is commonly described), it can be useful to have put into place in advance the sorts of formal board structures that will become mandatory once it becomes a public corporation.

Nevertheless, although some private corporations may choose to include non-executive directors on their boards, issues relating to representation on the board by outside as opposed to inside directors are primarily of concern to publicly traded corporations. The

---

154 For a more detailed discussion of these sorts of classifications, see Christopher C. Nicholls, "The Outside Director: Policeman or Policebo" (2003), 38 *Canadian Business Law Journal* 323.

155 This is a generic, hypothetical list of public corporation committees. Although the boards of public corporations form committees generally carrying out the functions of the committees described in this list, needless to say, there is some variation in the names they adopt for certain of these committees and in the combination of functions they perform.

role, effectiveness, and even the putative value of outside directors on the boards of public corporations have been the subject of considerable scholarly and industry debate.[156] But, in the absence of other tangible, workable means of counterbalancing the power of corporate managers, corporate governance proposals continue to champion the role of the outside corporate director.[157]

What role is the outside director expected to play? It has long been argued that outside directors are essential to protecting the interests of public corporations' shareholders, especially its non-controlling or minority shareholders. Because the board of directors is required to supervise the management of the corporation, if all board members were also executives of the corporation, directors would, in effect, be placed in the untenable role of supervising themselves. The supervision problem is especially acute when the chief executive officer of a corporation—typically the corporation's most senior executive—is also a member of the board of directors (as he or she inevitably is). The other management directors then find themselves in an especially unenviable position. As directors, it is their responsibility, in theory, to monitor and supervise the performance of the chief executive officer; however, in their capacity as full-time officers of the company, they are, in fact, the chief executive officer's subordinates.

In light of such obvious conflicts, one might well ask why inside directors are permitted to sit on corporate boards at all. Newcomers to corporate governance practices might be even more surprised to learn that the chief executive officer, particularly in the case of many US corporations, is not only typically a member of the board, but often serves as the board's chair. The conflicts inherent in such board structures are obvious. However, a board composed entirely of outside directors—with no detailed understanding of the corporation's business and limited time to devote to the corporation's affairs—could not be expected to perform a meaningful strategic or supervisory role. Worse still, the relationship between the corporation's senior executives and a board composed entirely of outsiders could easily become confrontational, leading to potentially distracting and unproductive squabbles.

There must, then, be some optimal mix of executive (inside) and non-executive (outside) directors on the board of a distributing corporation. But finding that optimal mix is no simple task. Moreover, once it is conceded that a board ought to include both inside and outside directors, a perplexing legal issue must be confronted. Should "inside" directors be subject to a higher duty of care, diligence, and skill than "outside" directors? Is the fact that one is an inside or an outside director a relevant consideration for a court when assessing the appropriate "comparable circumstances" within which to judge a defendant director's actions (or inaction)? The court in *Soper* alluded to this issue. There

---

156 See Nicholls, supra footnote 154.

157 Various corporate governance studies have emphasized the importance of outside or non-executive directors, including: the Cadbury Committee Report (UK); the Hampel Committee Report and the Combined Code (UK); the Higgs Report (UK); the American Law Institute's *Principles of Corporate Governance* (US); the Organisation for Economic Co-operation and Development's *Principles of Corporate Governance*; the Toronto Stock Exchange Committee on Corporate Governance in Canada, "Where Were the Directors? Guidelines for Improved Corporate Governance in Canada" (the "Dey report"); and the Joint Committee on Corporate Governance, Final Report, *Beyond Compliance: Building a Corporate Governance Culture* (the "Saucier report"). See Nicholls, ibid., at 331.

it was suggested that inside directors would find it especially difficult to satisfy the due diligence defence in s. 227.1(3) of the *Income Tax Act*.[158] Inside directors, in other words, would be held to a higher standard than their outside director colleagues at least in the source deduction withholding context. Language to similar effect may also be found in the Federal Court of Appeal's recent decision in *Smith v. Canada*.[159]

Tax cases such as *Soper* and *Smith* are illuminating and useful. However, they are focused only on the specific sorts of steps a director is or is not expected to take to ensure that source deductions are duly remitted to the Canadian tax authorities. They do not purport to speak to more general aspects of a director's duty of care. Nevertheless, it may fairly be said that the judgments in *Soper* and *Smith* are supportive of the idea that outside directors may have greater scope than their inside director colleagues to rely on the competence and integrity of the corporation's managers, in the absence of any grounds for suspicion. The Supreme Court's recent comments on the duty of care in *Peoples Department Stores*[160] do not appear to shed much additional light on this issue. There were, in that case, no outside directors on the board in question.

A recent decision of the Ontario Securities Commission (OSC) in *YBM Magnex*[161] alludes to differing standards of care for outside and inside directors. The OSC is, of course, an administrative tribunal, not a court. Moreover, the particular issue before the panel—whether or not to make an order under s. 127 of the Ontario *Securities Act*[162]— did not involve the application of any statutorily mandated standard of director's care. However, the decision is still noteworthy because the standard of care that the OSC regarded as appropriate in the circumstances was identical to the CBCA standard.

The OSC panel's discussion of directors' duties echoed the language of the Federal Court of Appeal in *Soper*. The panel's comments on differing standards of care are illuminating, and so are reproduced at some length as follows:

> The standard of care for directors and officers is not a professional standard nor is it the negligence standard; *Soper* at para. 41. Each director and officer owes a duty to take reasonable care in the performance of the office and in some circumstances that duty will require a director or officer to take action. That action may in some circumstances even call for a resignation.
>
> Directors are not obliged to give continuous attention to the company's affairs. ... However, their duties are awakened when information and events that require further investigation become known to them. The standard of care encourages responsibility not passivity, ...

---

158 Supra footnote 131, at para. 44.

159 Supra footnote 145, at para. 12: "[I]t may be appropriate to impose a higher standard on an 'inside director' (for example, a director with a practice of hands-on management) than an 'outside director' (such as a director who has only superficial knowledge of and involvement in the affairs of the corporation)."

160 Supra footnote 94.

161 Supra footnote 150.

162 For a discussion of the significance of a s. 127 order, see MacIntosh and Nicholls, supra footnote 7, at 350ff.

Directors act collectively as a board in the supervision of a company. Directors, however, are not a homogenous group. Their conduct is not to be governed by a single objective standard but rather one that embraces elements of personal knowledge and background, as well as board processes. More may be expected of persons with superior qualifications, such as experienced businesspersons. As such, not all directors stand in the same position. ...

In addition, more may be expected of inside directors than outside directors; ... . Similarly, a CFO who is on the board may be held to a higher standard than one who is not, particularly if he or she is involved in the public offering.

When dealing with legal matters, more may be expected of a director who is a lawyer. A lawyer-director may be in a better position to assess the materiality of certain facts. Due to improved access to information, more may sometimes be expected of directors depending on the function they are performing, for example those who sit on board committees, such as a special committee or audit committee. An outside director who takes on committee duties may be treated like an inside director with respect to matters that are covered by the committee's work; ... .

Directors may rely on the members of a special committee if the committee is comprised of disinterested directors in a position to base their decisions on the merits of the issue free of extraneous considerations and influences so that the committee's integrity and processes are beyond challenge; ... . In the absence of grounds for suspicion, it is not improper for a director to rely on management to honestly perform their duties; *Re Standard Trustco Ltd.* (1992), 15 OSCB 4322 at 4364-4365 (*Standard Trustco*). Directors are entitled to rely on professional outside advisers, including legal counsel and underwriters; *Standard Trustco* at 4364-4365. Reliance would be unreasonable if the director was aware of facts or circumstances of such character that a prudent person would not rely on the professional advice.[163]

Common sense and common experience argue for differing standards of care. But the law on this issue, like so many others, is clearly in a fluid state. The expectations placed on all directors appear to be rising and, accordingly, whatever reasonable gap may exist between the standards of care against which directors of different sorts are to be evaluated, that gap is surely narrowing.

Relative Infrequency of "Duty of Care" Cases

Cases in which honest, disinterested directors have been found liable for a breach of their duty of care are rare. That is true not only in Canada, but in the United States as well. Klein and Coffee have even suggested, in the US context, that "the reality of the duty [of care] may be that courts will in fact impose liability only when they sense that the officer or director had a hidden conflict of interest that explains his or her behaviour or was otherwise knowingly inattentive."[164] They do also note, though, that the courts may be more willing to find a breach of the duty of care when the remedy sought is not damages from the director, but rather an injunction to restrain some pending corporate action.[165]

---

163 Supra footnote 150, at paras. 181-186.

164 William A. Klein and John C. Coffee Jr., *Business Organization and Finance*, 7th ed. (New York: Foundation Press, 2000), at 149.

165 Ibid., at 151.

Part of the explanation for the paucity of cases in which directors have been exposed to personal liability for breach of their duty of care is that, in order to determine that disinterested directors have erred, courts would necessarily need to assess the substance of the board's business decisions. Courts have historically been reluctant to second-guess the substance of good faith business decisions. The basis for this judicial reluctance has been expressed in a number of different ways. In American jurisprudence, judicial deference to board decision making has long been articulated in the form of the "business judgment rule." In Canada, courts have historically expressed similar wariness about interfering with directors' good faith decisions, but only comparatively recently have they begun to refer to the relevant legal principles using the phrase "business judgment rule." The Canadian "business judgment rule" is discussed later in this chapter.

In a recent decision of the Delaware Chancery Court,[166] it was suggested that, in unusual circumstances, a director's breach of his or her duty of care can be so egregious that it raises the possibility that the director has, in fact, breached his or her duty of loyalty. The significance of this in the context of Delaware corporations is that the Delaware *General Corporation Law* permits corporations to include in their certificate of incorporation a provision eliminating a director's personal liability "for breach of fiduciary duty as a director"[167] other than breaches relating to breach of loyalty and conflicts of interest. Essentially, then, such a provision in a corporation's articles relieves a director of personal liability for duty of care breaches. But if an act of omission or lack of diligence is characterized by the court as a breach that rises to a breach of the duty of loyalty, this exemption provision would be of no protection to the director. Moreover, such a breach would also not be subject to the protection of the business judgment rule because that rule, once again, is not intended to shield directors who have breached their duty of loyalty.

Duty of Care: Owed to Whom?

One of the most provocative aspects of the Supreme Court of Canada's recent decision in *Peoples Department Stores* was the court's comment on the potential "beneficiaries" of corporate directors' duty of care. The court made the curious observation that

> unlike the statement of the fiduciary duty in s. 122(1)(a) of the CBCA, which specifies that directors and officers must act with a view to the best interests of the corporation, the statement of the duty of care in s. 122(1)(b) of the CBCA does not specifically refer to an identifiable party as the beneficiary of the duty. ... Thus, the identity of the beneficiary of the duty of care is much more open-ended, and it appears obvious that it must include creditors.[168]

One wonders if two somewhat different concepts have been conflated here—namely, the tort concept of "duty of care," which clearly anticipates many potential "beneficiaries,"

---

166 *In re The Walt Disney Company Derivative Litig.*, CA no. 15452 (Del. Ch. Ct. May 28, 2003).

167 Delaware *General Corporation Law*, s. 102(b)(7). For a longer extract from this provision, see infra footnote 172.

168 *Peoples Department Stores*, supra footnote 94, at para. 57.

and the duty to perform one's work duties attentively, skillfully, and diligently (that is, with care), a concept that surely implies an obligation to the corporation itself. Directors and officers, after all, would already be subject to the normal duties of care—to which we are all subject and at all times—to avoid taking actions that could reasonably be foreseen to cause others harm. How, then, and more to the point why, should a corporate statute impose on the directors an additional layer of personal duties intended to protect parties other than the corporation itself? Although the Supreme Court at two points in its judgment affirmed that the CBCA "does not provide a direct remedy for creditors against directors for breach of their duties,"[169] the *Peoples Department Stores* case arose in Quebec, so what the CBCA was unable to provide in terms of direct recourse to the directors, in the court's view, art. 1457 of the Quebec Civil Code could certainly supply.[170] Although, in the end, the court did not find the directors in *Peoples Department Stores* liable, the judgment has raised some rather unsettling questions that will almost surely spawn future litigation.

Directors' Indemnification and Insurance

Although directors' duty of care cases have, to date, been infrequent, they have not been non-existent. Moreover, even a single decided case can have a significant effect on the market for corporate directors if the amounts involved are large enough and the profile of the corporation high enough. The 1985 Delaware Supreme Court's judgment in *Smith v. Van Gorkom*,[171] for example, remains almost two decades after it was rendered, a poignant reminder that a prestigious directorship is not a sinecure. But the benefits of board membership are not so great that material risks of liability can be ignored. If directors are to be enticed into serving on corporate boards, they must have some assurance that that service will not expose them to disproportionate risk of personal liability. Since the Delaware Supreme Court rendered its judgment in *Smith v. Van Gorkom*, the Delaware legislature has amended the state's corporate statute to permit corporations to include a provision in the corporate charter effectively relieving directors of any liability for breach of their duty of care.[172] This provision is in addition to statutory provisions permitting indemnification and insurance.

---

169 Ibid., at para. 54. See also ibid., at para. 29.

170 Ibid., at para. 54 et seq.

171 488 A 2d 858 (Del SC 1985).

172 Delaware *General Corporation Law*, s. 102(b)(7) permits a corporation to include in its certificate of incorporation:

> (7) A provision eliminating or limiting the personal liability of a director to the corporation or its stockholders for monetary damages for breach of fiduciary duty as a director, provided that such provision shall not eliminate or limit the liability of a director: (i) For any breach of the director's duty of loyalty to the corporation or its stockholders; (ii) for acts or omissions not in good faith or which involve intentional misconduct or a knowing violation of law; (iii) under §174 of this title; or (iv) for any transaction from which the director derived an improper personal benefit. No such provision shall eliminate or limit the liability of a director for any act or omission occurring prior to the date when such provision becomes effective. All references in this paragraph to a director shall also be deemed to refer (x) to a member of the governing body of a

Although the CBCA does not provide for such express relief of a director's duty of care, it does, nevertheless, permit corporations to indemnify directors and officers and to obtain directors' and officers' liability insurance. The Dickerson committee described the indemnification of corporate officers and directors as "one of the most complex and most controversial problems of contemporary corporation law."[173] The indemnity provisions are typically subject to some important limitations. Section 124 of the CBCA,[174] for example, permits the corporation to indemnify officers or directors (or former officers or directors) only in cases where they have acted honestly and in good faith with a view to the best interests of the corporation, and in the case of criminal or administrative penalties, only where they had reasonable grounds to believe their conduct was lawful, and on completion of a court approval process that enables interested persons to intervene.[175] Where the director or officer is being sued by the corporation itself, indemnity is permitted only with the approval of the court, and extends only to the director's or officer's costs, not—as in the case of actions brought against the officer or director by third parties—to amounts paid to satisfy a judgment or settle a claim.[176]

However, directors and officers are entitled to a right of indemnity for their costs and expenses incurred in defending a claim where they have, in effect, been exonerated by a court in respect of that claim.[177] (This indemnity extends only to costs and not to payments to satisfy a judgment or settle a claim for the obvious reason that the right of indemnity is predicated on the director or officer having successfully defended an action, and thus having no need to settle or satisfy a judgment.)

In *Consolidated Enfield v. Blair*,[178] the president of a public corporation, when chairing a shareholder meeting, ruled that certain proxy votes cast at the meeting in respect of the election of directors were invalid. The effect of the chairman's ruling was that he, the chairman himself, was re-elected as a director of the corporation. Had the proxy votes in question been valid, the chairman would have lost his seat on the board. Following a court challenge, it was determined that the chairman's ruling had been wrong in law, and that he had been in breach of his fiduciary duties. When the corporation, in a subsequent proceeding, sought to recover its costs against the chairman, the chairman argued that he was entitled to be indemnified for those costs by the corporation.

---

corporation which is not authorized to issue capital stock, and (y) to such other person or persons, if any, who, pursuant to a provision of the certificate of incorporation in accordance with §141(a) of this title, exercise or perform any of the powers or duties otherwise conferred or imposed upon the board of directors by this title.

173 Dickerson committee, supra footnote 33, at para. 243.

174 For similar provisions in provincial corporate statutes, see *Business Corporations Act* (Alta.), s. 124; *The Business Corporations Act* (Sask.), s. 119; *The Corporations Act* (Man.), s. 119; *Business Corporations Act* (Ont.), s. 136; *Business Corporations Act* (NB), s. 81; *Corporations Act* (NL), ss. 205-209; and *Business Corporations Act* (BC), s. 163(1). The *Companies Act* (PEI) also includes a somewhat less detailed provision dealing with indemnification of directors (at s. 64).

175 CBCA, ss. 124(7)-(9).

176 CBCA, s. 124(4).

177 CBCA, s. 124(5).

178 Infra footnote 193.

The Supreme Court of Canada held that the chairman was, indeed, entitled to indemnification because his ruling had been made "with the bona fide intent that the corporation should have a lawfully elected Board of Directors."[179] The court held that to deny him indemnification would require a finding of "actual mala fides ... such that the director did not act with a view to the best interests of the corporation."[180]

Now, as a practical matter, an indemnity can never be worth more than the party that has granted it. And directors will typically be at greatest risk of personal liability when the corporation itself has become insolvent and thus judgment-proof. Therefore, although indemnification is important, it does not provide complete protection. Many corporations have been known to establish trust funds in favour of their directors and officers to provide protection for unindemnified or uninsurable liabilities, including the risk of being personally liable for unpaid employee wages.[181] And, of course, corporations also obtain insurance for their directors, as specifically contemplated by corporate statutes,[182] and without which few (if any) credible directors would be prepared to serve on the boards of large, public corporations. The wording of the CBCA provision dealing with directors' insurance is exceedingly broad and, at first glance, appears to permit a corporation to insure a director against any claim whatsoever. However, as the Dickerson committee noted, in responding to critics of such broad provisions,

> [t]hese criticisms have validity if no account is taken of the insurance policies that are available. But they largely beg the question by assuming that insurers are in business only to shield directors and officers from liability for their own misconduct.[183]

That said, many provincial corporate statutes prefer to take no chances. They include provisions specifying that insurance may not be obtained to cover losses arising from a director's breach of his or her duty of loyalty and good faith.[184] While directors' and officers' insurance is crucial to attracting qualified directors, concerns have frequently been raised about gaps both in availability and in coverage offered by conventional insurance policies that may leave directors exposed to risks that may greatly exceed the personal benefits they derive from serving on a public corporation board.[185] This problem may have been significantly more acute some years ago than it is today, but it remains a subject of concern.

---

179   Ibid., at para. 76.

180   Ibid.

181   See, e.g., *Re Westar Mining Ltd.* (1996), 136 DLR (4th) 564 (BCCA).

182   The CBCA expressly permits a corporation to obtain such insurance. See CBCA, s. 124(6).

183   Dickerson committee, supra footnote 33, at para. 250.

184   See, e.g., *Business Corporations Act* (Alta.), s. 124(4); *The Business Corporations Act* (Sask.), s. 119(4); *The Corporations Act* (Man.), s. 119(4); *Corporations Act* (NL), s. 208; *Business Corporations Act* (Ont.), s. 136(4); and *Business Corporations Act* (NB), s. 81(4).

185   For a discussion of this topic and related issues of directors risks and board service, see Ronald J. Daniels and Susan M. Hutton, "The Capricious Cushion: The Implication of the Directors' and Officers' Insurance Liability Crisis on Canadian Corporate Governance" (1993), 22 *Canadian Business Law Journal* 18; Warren Grover, "The Canadian Outside Director: Great Expectations" (2003), 38 *Canadian Business Law Journal* 349; and Ronald J. Daniels, "Must Boards Go Overboard? An Economic Analysis of the Effects of Burgeoning Statutory Liability on the Role of Directors in Corporate Governance" (1994), 24 *Canadian Business Law Journal* 229.

Due Diligence and Good Faith Reliance Defences

For many years, the CBCA offered directors a specific defence to claims brought against them under certain provisions of the Act (including under s. 122, the section that prescribes the directors' general duties). This defence was available where the director had relied in good faith on financial statements, an auditor's report, or a report of some credible professional, such as a lawyer, accountant, engineer, or appraiser. The existence of this defence was, needless to say, regularly brought to the attention of corporate directors by their legal counsel, and was a source of no small comfort to lawyer and client alike.

The good faith reliance defence, however, came to be regarded by some as too narrow. The provision was amended in 2001. Now, instead of a single good faith reliance defence, the Act provides two separate directors' defences: a due diligence defence (of which good faith reliance may be a part), and a straightforward good faith reliance defence.

The new due diligence defence is found in s. 123(4). It provides that directors will not be liable under s. 118 (which provides for personal liability when directors agree to issue shares at an undervalue or vote for or consent to resolutions under a number of other provisions of the Act), s. 119 (which provides for personal liability to employees for debts not exceeding six months' wages), or s. 122(2) (which provides that directors must comply with the CBCA, the regulations, the articles, the bylaws, and any unanimous shareholder agreement) provided that the director has "exercised the care, diligence and skill that a reasonably prudent person would have exercised in comparable circumstances." This due diligence defence may specifically include reliance in good faith on financial statements and experts' reports of the same sort that are referred to in the new "good faith reliance" section, discussed below. In a briefing book produced by Industry Canada in connection with the 2001 amendments, this change was explained as follows:

> The due diligence defence provides more fairness to directors than does the good faith reliance defence. The due diligence defence recognizes that the nature and extent of the expected precaution will vary under each circumstance. These precautions can include such things as relying on financial statements presented to directors by an officer, putting in place appropriate controls and systems to monitor and ensure that policies are being implemented, requiring a proper review or periodic reports, and taking appropriate action when a problem is brought to the directors' attention.[186]

By making good faith reliance simply one means of satisfying the due diligence defence, the drafters were evidently persuaded by the words of the 1994 Dey committee and the 1995 Industry Canada discussion paper on directors' liability, both of which suggested that the availability of a general due diligence defence would encourage boards to put in place appropriate controls and systems that could significantly lessen the risk that losses would occur.[187]

---

186   Available online at http://strategis.ic.gc.ca/epic/internet/incilp-pdci.nsf/en/cl00284e.html.

187   Toronto Stock Exchange, Committee on Corporate Governance in Canada, *Where Were the Directors? Guidelines for Improved Corporate Governance* (Toronto: Toronto Stock Exchange, 1994), at para. 5.62; Industry Canada, *Canada Business Corporations Act*, Discussion Paper, *Directors' Liability* (hereinafter

The 2001 amendments to the CBCA also maintained, in slightly different form, a good faith reliance defence. This defence is now found in s. 123(5). This provision states that a director has complied with his or her duties under s. 122(1) (that is, with the duties of care, good faith, and loyalty) if he or she has relied in good faith on financial statements represented to the director by an officer or in a written auditor's report as fairly reflecting the corporation's financial condition, or on the report of a person "whose profession lends credibility to a statement made by the professional person." The Supreme Court of Canada has recently emphasized that the statute refers to reports by a member of a "profession," a term suggestive of someone "subject to the regulatory overview of [a] professional organization and … [carrying] independent insurance coverage."[188] Thus, a senior employee of an organization, regardless of his or her experience, would not constitute such a professional for purposes of the statute. This provision does not, however, mean that a director is exonerated whenever an acceptable legal or other opinion is obtained. Obviously, the expert providing the opinion must have been fully apprised of all relevant information.[189] One might also suggest that good faith reliance assumes that the expert's report was not prepared with undue haste.[190] In addition, good faith reliance, it has been suggested, also requires the director to exercise his or her judgment after receiving the expert's advice.[191] Where the director himself or herself has special expertise, the extent to which it is reasonable for him or her to rely on an expert report will be affected.[192]

The Business Judgment Rule

There are many good reasons for judges not to interfere with the decisions taken by corporate managers. There is, first, the question of institutional competence. Judges are not appointed to the bench on the basis of their business experience or managerial acumen. This is not to say that judges necessarily lack these qualities; it is only to say that such qualities are not regarded as essential for those holding judicial office. Business executives are not expected to be able to write legal judgments; judges are not expected to be able to run businesses.

Furthermore, if courts were given free rein to examine the decisions of business people, there would be a very real danger of hindsight bias. Business decisions must be

---

"Discussion Paper"), November 1995, at 24-25. This material is summarized in a research paper prepared by the Parliamentary Research Branch. See Margaret Smith, "Directors' Liability," Parliamentary Research Branch, Law and Government Division, February 29, 2000. See also the Industry Canada briefing book, which was prepared in connection with the 2001 CBCA amendments, supra footnote 186.

188 *Peoples Department Stores*, supra footnote 94, at para. 78.

189 See *Westfair Foods Ltd. v. Watt* (1990), 73 ALR (2d) 326, at 349-50 (QB).

190 See, for example, the comments of Iacobucci J in *Blair*, infra footnote 193, at para. 61.

191 *Northern Central Gas Corp. v. Hillcrest Collieries Ltd.* (1975), 59 DLR (3d) 533, at 597-98 (Alta. SCTD).

192 See *In re Emerging Communications Inc. Shareholders Litigation*, CA no. 16415 (Del. Ch. Ct. June 4, 2004), at 107ff.

made on the basis of incomplete information. Urgent decisions, in particular, must necessarily be taken before all possible information has time to be gathered. If a decision, honestly made, turns out to have disappointing or even disastrous consequences, it may be tempting, but unfair, to conclude that the decision makers were incompetent. If managers expected their good faith decisions to be mercilessly dissected by the courts, the cost to business efficiency and to the economy generally could be horrendous. Managers might become overly risk averse. Decision making could be unnecessarily delayed. Excessive corporate resources might be expended on justificatory documentation, expensive expert opinions, or fruitless, even symbolic "research." Finally, but just as significant, is the critical question of the proper limits of the court's jurisdiction. Business enterprises are essentially a matter of private ordering.[193] In the absence of unlawful behaviour, courts generally have no more jurisdiction to second guess the decisions of a corporate director than they have the power, say, to decree that a family change the design of the wallpaper in their living room.

Courts are aware of these considerations and of their own institutional limitations. Historically, they have shown great deference to the honest decisions of directors and managers, even where those decisions, in hindsight, appear to have been mistaken. As one court has aptly put it,

> [t]here is no appeal on merits from management decisions to courts of law: nor will courts of law assume to act as a kind of supervisory board over decisions within the powers of management honestly arrived at.[194]

In the United States, the deference of courts to managerial decision making has been formalized in the "business judgment rule." The American business judgment rule is a concept of considerable complexity. The Delaware Supreme Court, for example, has said of the business judgment rule that it operates "as both a procedural guide for litigants and a substantive rule of law."[195] Melvin Eisenberg has contrasted the business judgment rule to the standard of care. The former he characterizes as a "standard of review"; the latter, he sees as a "standard of conduct."[196] Law and economics scholar Stephen Bainbridge has noted that the courts have, indeed, at times seen the business judgment rule as prescribing a "standard of review," but at other times have regarded it merely as "doctrine of abstention."[197]

---

193 As Iacobucci J said, for a unanimous Supreme Court of Canada in *Blair v. Consolidated Enfield Corp.*, [1995] 4 SCR 5, at para 50: "The detailed organization of a corporation is essentially a private contractual matter."

194 *Howard Smith Ltd. v. Ampol Petroleum Ltd.*, [1974] 2 WLR 689 (PC) (per Lord Wilberforce).

195 *McMullin v. Beran*, 765 A 2d 910 (Del. SC 2000).

196 Melvin A. Eisenberg, "Whether the Business-Judgment Rule Should Be Codified," Background Study Prepared for the California Law Revision Commission, May 1995, in "Business Judgment Rule" (1998), 28 *California Law Revision Commission Reports* 1, at 33. Available online at http://www.clrc.ca.gov/pub/BKST/BKST-EisenbergBJR.pdf.

197 Stephen M. Bainbridge, "The Business Judgment Rule as Abstention Doctrine," UCLA School of Law, Law and Economics Research Paper No. 03-18. Available online at http://ssrn.com/.

A review of the complexities of the Delaware business judgment rule is well beyond the scope of this text.[198] In any event, although the phrase "business judgment rule" has been borrowed by Canadian lawyers and judges from the American jurisprudence—even the Supreme Court of Canada has referred to it[199]—not all the nuances of that phrase have necessarily been imported across the border.

The Supreme Court of Canada has recently described the Canadian business judgment rule in this way:

> Many decisions made in the course of business, although ultimately unsuccessful, are reasonable and defensible at the time they are made. Business decisions must sometimes be made, with high stakes and under considerable time pressure, in circumstances in which detailed information is not available. It might be tempting for some to see unsuccessful business decisions as unreasonable or imprudent in light of information that becomes available *ex post facto*. Because of this risk of hindsight bias, Canadian courts have developed a rule of deference to business decisions called the "business judgment rule," adopting the American name for the rule.[200]

The Supreme Court quoted from an earlier Ontario Court of Appeal decision, in which the Court of Appeal had summarized the effect of the business judgment rule in this way:

> The court looks to see that the directors made a reasonable decision not a perfect decision. Provided the decision taken is within a range of reasonableness, the court ought not to substitute its opinion for that of the board even though subsequent events may have cast doubt on the board's determination. As long as the directors have selected one of several reasonable alternatives, deference is accorded to the board's decision. ... This formulation of deference to the decision of the Board is known as the "business judgment rule." The fact that alternative transactions were rejected by the directors is irrelevant unless it can be shown that a particular alternative was definitely available and clearly more beneficial to the company than the chosen transaction.[201]

Generally speaking, it appears that the term "business judgment rule" has been used by Canadian courts in two senses:

- To refer generally (and perhaps somewhat vaguely) to a traditional principle of Anglo-Canadian law that courts ought not to second-guess the substance of decisions taken by corporate directors and officers. This is, to be sure, the same principle that underlies the American business judgment rule as well. However, the Delaware business judgment rule operates more formally as a rebuttable presumption that directors' decisions have been made honestly and in good faith by a disinterested board of directors exercising due care. Unless a plaintiff can rebut this presumption

---

198 Much has been written about the Delaware business judgment rule, including at least one recent book-length treatment of the issue. See Dennis J. Block et al., *The Business Judgment Rule: Fiduciary Duties of Corporate Directors* (New York: Aspen Law & Business, 1998).

199 *Peoples Department Stores*, supra footnote 94.

200 Ibid., at para. 64.

201 *Maple Leaf Foods Inc. v. Schneider Corp.* (1998), 42 OR (3d) 177 (CA).

by "providing evidence that directors, in reaching their challenged decision, breached any one of the triad of their fiduciary duties—good faith, loyalty, or due care"[202]—the business decision will not be challenged as long as it can be rationally connected to some business purpose. That same sort of presumption does not appear to form part of the Canadian business judgment rule.

• More specifically, to refer to a principle of judicial deference to the substance of directors' decisions that is *pre-conditioned* on the establishment of certain conditions—namely, that the decision was made "honestly, prudently, in good faith, and on reasonable grounds" by disinterested directors, on an informed basis. Directors' decisions, then, are not (as in the case of the Delaware rule) presumed to have been made in good faith on an informed basis by independent directors. Rather, it seems that *if* a business decision has been made honestly, with due care, and on an informed basis, then the substance of that decision will not be challenged. Thus, as was recently stated in an Ontario decision:

> It is, in my view, clear from this decision and similar decisions applying the business judgment rule that it is a *precondition* to the application of the rule that the court must determine that the directors have acted honestly, prudently, in good faith and on a reasonable belief that the transaction is in the best interest of the company.[203]

In that same case, however, the judge referred to the business judgment rule as "in addition, ... a presumption only which can be rebutted by evidence which may cast doubt as to the honesty, prudence and good faith of the directors in approving or entering into the challenged transaction." The use of the word "presumption" in this context does raise some question as to who carries the burden in a business judgment case. Clearly, if it is the plaintiff who must "rebut," then the Canadian business judgment rule appears to be very similar to the Delaware version. However, although the law on this point continues to evolve, it appears that, at present, directors who wish to rely on the business judgment rule in Canada will need to ensure that the pre-conditions have been established.[204] It is equally clear, however, that the directors will need to demonstrate only that the process they followed was appropriate; they are not required to justify the substance of their business decisions.

To determine whether the pre-conditions have been satisfied, Canadian courts have been led to consider the processes adopted and followed by corporate boards. Where the directors' decision-making process is flawed in some fundamental way, the board's decision may be impugned. So, for example, it has been said that "[t]he business judgment rule cannot apply where the Board of Directors acts on the advice of a director's committee that makes an uninformed recommendation."[205] At the same time, no process

---

202 *Cede & Co. v. Technicolor, Inc.*, 634 A 2d 345, at 361 (Del. SC 1993).

203 *Corporacion Americana de Equipamientos Urbanos S.L. v. Olifas Marketing Group Inc., et al.* (2003), 66 OR (3d) 352 (SCJ) (emphasis added).

204 For a further discussion of some of these issues, see Lorie Waisberg and Robert Vaux, "Board Governance: The Importance of Process," in *The Future of Corporation Law Issues and Perspectives*, Papers Presented at the Queen's Annual Business Law Symposium 1997 (Toronto: Carswell, 1999), at 97.

205 *UPM-Kymmene Corp. v. UPM-Kymmene Miramichi Inc.*, [2002] OJ no. 2412, at para. 155 (QL) (SCJ), aff'd. (2004), 42 BLR (3d) 34 (Ont. CA).

designed and implemented by human beings will ever be flawless. The standard against which boards are measured is not one of perfection.

Missteps in a board's process will not, therefore, necessarily prove fatal. In *CW Shareholdings*,[206] for example, a supposedly independent special committee struck by the board to consider a takeover offer improperly included the corporation's chief executive officer as a member. Although the court acknowledged that the CEO's conflict of interest made his position on the special committee inappropriate, this procedural gaffe was not fatal to the committee's, and ultimately the board's, decision.

Duty of Loyalty and Good Faith

Directors and officers also have fiduciary obligations to act honestly and in good faith with a view to the best interests of the corporations on whose boards they sit. Directors were subject to such a duty at common law, but this obligation has now also been explicitly written into a number of Canadian corporate statutes.[207] So, for example, s. 122(1)(a) of the CBCA provides that

> (1) Every director and officer of a corporation in exercising their powers and discharging their duties shall
>   (a) act honestly and in good faith with a view to the best interests of the corporation; ... .

At its core, this statutory duty speaks to the obligation of corporate officers and directors to put the interests of the corporation they serve ahead of their own. Our law gives them the benefit of the doubt in most cases, because, as a general proposition, people are assumed to act in good faith, unless it is proved otherwise.[208]

In many instances, this general duty is translated into an obligation upon directors and officers to avoid situations where their duty to their corporations does (or might) conflict with their personal interests. Conflicts between corporate duty and personal interest are especially common in the following four particular contexts:

- interested director (or officer) contracts (that is, contracts entered into between the corporation and one of its directors or officers, or between the corporation and another business organization in which one of the corporation's directors or officers has a material interest);
- directors' and officers' remuneration;
- corporate opportunities (that is, cases in which a director or officer personally pursues a business opportunity that, in some sense, properly "belonged" to the corporation instead); and

---

206 (1998), 39 OR (3d) 755 (Gen. Div.).

207 See, e.g., *Business Corporations Act* (BC), s. 142(1)(a) (see also supra footnote 136); *Business Corporations Act* (Alta.), s. 122(1)(a); *The Business Corporations Act* (Sask.), s. 117(1)(a); *The Corporations Act* (Man.), s. 117(1)(a); *Business Corporations Act* (Ont.), s. 134(1)(a); *Business Corporations Act* (NB), s. 79(1)(a); and *Corporations Act* (NL), s. 203(1)(a).

208 *General Motors of Canada Ltd. v. Brunet*, [1977] 2 SCR 537, at 548 and *Blair v. Consolidated Enfield*, supra footnote 193, at para. 35.

- hostile takeover bids (that is, where a bidder (usually a corporation) attempts to gain control of a second corporation (the "target") against the wishes of the directors and officers of the target. A conflict of duty and interest arises for directors of the target, because it is presumed that once control of the target changes hands, the target's directors and most senior officers are almost certain to be replaced. Aware of the potential effect of a takeover on their own career aspirations, there is a concern that directors and officers may have an incentive to prevent takeover bids that would, in fact, be of real benefit to the target corporation and to its shareholders).

Interested directors' contracts, corporate opportunities, and directors' and officers' remuneration are discussed in further detail in chapter 11. With respect to the role and duties of the directors of a corporation subject to a hostile takeover bid, many of the Canadian cases on this subject come before the courts as oppression applications, a subject dealt with in chapter 13. It is also important to understand how the securities law rules surrounding takeover bids intersect with the law of directors' fiduciary obligations. A detailed discussion of this topic is beyond the scope of this text.[209]

The long-standing debate over the precise meaning of "best interests of the corporation" was discussed earlier in this chapter. The Supreme Court of Canada, it will be recalled, has now declared that—whatever this nebulous phrase might mean—it may not simply be read to mean "best interests of the shareholders."[210] The corporation's interests, the court says, "are not to be confused with the interests of the creditors or those of any other stakeholders."[211] Although the interests of a corporation's various stakeholders may generally align when a corporation is healthy and viable, conflicts become manifest when a corporation begins to struggle financially. It is then that the directors must take special care, in the court's words, "to attempt to act in [the corporation's] best interests by creating a 'better' corporation, and not to favour the interests of any one group of stakeholders."[212] The court sheds little light, however, on the concept of what makes for a "better corporation" under these circumstances. Nor do they make clear whose judgment of "better" is to govern. Is this an assessment best left to the business decision makers? Does the duty of loyalty, in other words, merge with the duty of care on this point, and so enjoy the protection of the business judgment rule? Or would that take matters too far? Perhaps a "better corporation" is a phenomenon readily identified by any intelligent observer and so the courts should be ready and willing to correct wayward directors who are making matters "worse" for some (although, one assumes not for all) of the corporation's many stakeholders.

If the beneficiaries of the directors' fiduciary duties do not shift when the corporation nears insolvency, is there any other major event that might occasion any such shift? Students of Delaware corporate law are very familiar with the so-called *Revlon* duty—a duty said to be imposed on corporate directors when sale of the corporation is imminent

---

209   See Christopher C. Nicholls, *Corporate Finance and Canadian Law* (Toronto: Carswell, 2000), at 341-67.

210   *Peoples Department Stores*, supra footnote 94, at para. 42.

211   Ibid., at para. 43.

212   Ibid., at para. 47.

(and in other comparable situations).[213] When the corporation enters this mysterious Revlon zone, the duty of the directors, it is said, is to act so as to maximize the (short-term) value of the corporation for the benefit of its (current) shareholders. The status of the Revlon duty in Canada is rather unclear. As I have noted elsewhere,[214] in 1998 the Ontario Court of Appeal declared that *"Revlon* is not the law in Ontario"[215] before proceeding to undertake an analysis that seemed very consistent with the *Revlon* duty as it has evolved in the Delaware jurisprudence. More recently, that same court, without mentioning the troublesome *Revlon* case itself, stated, as an apparently non-contentious fact, that once a company "was 'in play,' its legal obligation was to try to maximize value for shareholders ... ."[216] It must be cautioned that this case was decided a number of months before the Supreme Court rendered its judgment in *Peoples Department Stores*, discussed earlier. On the other hand, perhaps it might be argued that maximizing share-holder value is the only way to make a "better corporation" under such circumstances.

Nominee Directors

Frequently, directors of corporations are elected by a particular subset of the corporation's shareholders: perhaps a class of shares carries with it the right to elect a member to the board; perhaps dividends have been in arrears for some time with respect to a class of (usually) non-voting preference shares, and so the holders have become entitled, under the share conditions, to elect one or more directors; or perhaps a major investor requires the right to have his or her "nominee" on the board. Whatever the reason, it will frequently be the case that a board member has not been elected by the shareholders as a whole, but by some specific subgroup of shareholders. In such a case, should (or may) the director pay greater attention to the interests of those who elected him or her than to the corporation as a whole? Although common sense (and common experience) suggest that such special allegiance is all but unavoidable, the legal answer—at least under the CBCA—is clear: each and every director owes a duty to act in the best interests of the corporation and may not favour any particular group of shareholders, regardless of whether or not the director owes his or her place on the board to them. As Farley J has rightly noted,

> [i]t may well be that the corporate life of a nominee director who votes against the interest of his "appointing" shareholder will be neither happy nor long. However, the role that any director must play (whether or not a nominee director) is that he must act in the best interests of the corporation. If the interests of the corporation (and indirectly the interests of

---

213 The term *"Revlon* duty" comes from the first case in which it was applied, *Revlon Inc. v. MacAndrews & Forbes Holdings*, 506 A 2d 173 (Del. SC 1986). For a discussion of the circumstances under which directors are said to be subject to *Revlon* duties, see Ronald J. Gilson and Reinier Kraakman, "What Triggers *Revlon*?" (1990), 25 *Wake Forest Law Review* 37.

214 Nicholls, supra footnote 209, at 351.

215 *Maple Leaf Foods Inc. v. Schneider Corp.*, supra footnote 201, at 199.

216 *Casurina Limited Partnership v. Rio Algom Limited* (2004), Ontario Court of Appeal Docket C38844, at para. 27.

the shareholders as a whole) require that the director vote in a certain way, it must be the way that he conscientiously believes after a reasonable review is the best for the corporation. The nominee director's obligation to his "appointing" shareholder would seem to me to include the duty to tell the appointer that his requested course of action is wrong if the director in fact feels this way. Such advice, although likely initially unwelcome, may well be valuable to the appointer in the long run. The nominee director cannot be a "Yes man"; he must be an analytical person who can say "Yes" or "No" as the occasion requires (or to put it another way, as the corporation requires).[217]

Note that the situation may be viewed differently under the Alberta *Business Corporations Act*. Section 122(4) of the Alberta statute provides:

> In determining whether a particular transaction or course of action is in the best interests of the corporation, a director, if the director is elected or appointed by the holders of a class or series of shares or by employees or creditors or a class of employees or creditors, may give special, but not exclusive, consideration to the interests of those who elected or appointed the director.

Proper Purpose/Collateral Purpose Doctrine

One particularly puzzling line of fiduciary duty cases deserves at least a brief mention. This line of cases concerns the "proper purpose" or "collateral purpose" doctrine. The proper purpose doctrine may be understood as a rule, or principle, to the effect that when directors of a corporation exercise a power that has been granted to them, they are entitled to exercise that power only for its proper purpose—that is, the purpose for which that power was intended in the first place.[218]

Most of the cases in this area involve the exercise by the directors of their power to issue shares in the corporation. Clearly, the directors have the power to issue shares; the question that these cases discuss is whether a share issuance can be set aside where the directors have exercised this power for some improper purpose—for example, to dilute a particular shareholder's existing majority ownership interest.

Canadian courts appear to have diverged from UK courts on the application of the proper purpose doctrine. In *Teck v. Millar*,[219] for example, a case decided shortly after the Dickerson committee released its report (though not in the context of a CBCA corporation), the court appeared simply to equate the proper purpose doctrine with the duty of the directors to act in the best interests of the corporation. That is, as long as the directors are acting in what they honestly believe to be the corporation's best interests, provided they

---

217 *820099 Ontario Inc. v. Harold E. Ballard Ltd.* (1991), 3 BLR (2d) 113, at 172 (Ont. Ct. Gen. Div.).

218 See, e.g., *Hogg v. Cramphorn Ltd.*, [1967] Ch. 254 (Ch. D); *Howard Smith Ltd.*, supra footnote 194; *Exco Corporation v. Nova Scotia Savings & Loan Company* (1987), 35 BLR 149 (NSSCTD); and *347883 Alberta Ltd. v. Producers Pipelines* (1991), 80 DLR (4th) 359 (Sask. CA). The issue is also discussed in *Teck v. Millar*, supra footnote 96. See also Davies, supra footnote 30.

219 Supra footnote 96.

have reasonable grounds for that belief,[220] they are acting for a proper purpose. That, indeed, is precisely how *Teck* has been interpreted by one leading English authority.[221]

The principle authority relied on by the court in *Teck* in reaching that conclusion was *Re Smith and Fawcett Ltd.*[222] However, it is not clear that *Re Smith and Fawcett* really stands for such a broad proposition.[223] In any event, it seems clear that, in the United Kingdom, there is a clear distinction between the proper purpose doctrine and the general duty of directors to act in the best interests of the company.[224] Moreover, other Canadian authorities[225] suggest that there are still some important questions surrounding the proper purpose rule that must await a more extended explication than can be offered here.

RECENT CORPORATE GOVERNANCE DEVELOPMENTS

Beginning in late 2001, a series of corporate governance scandals rocked the US capital markets. The companies most prominently associated with these scandals included Enron, WorldCom, Tyco, and Adelphia. These scandals prompted a series of legislative and regulatory reforms in both the United States and Canada. At the centre of these regulatory initiatives was the US *Sarbanes-Oxley Act of 2002*[226] (SOX). The specific governance changes introduced by SOX, as well as by the series of rules promulgated by the US Securities and Exchange Commission to implement those initiatives, are too voluminous to itemize in an introductory text on Canadian corporate law. In Canada, the Canadian response to SOX has thus far primarily been from securities regulators.[227] Among the most significant of the Canadian initiatives adopted in response to SOX are:

- A requirement that the chief executive officer and chief financial officer of reporting issuers personally certify the accuracy of the corporation's annual and interim

---

220 See also, *Maple Leaf*, supra footnote 201: "If there are no reasonable grounds to support an assertion by the directors that they have acted in the best interests of the company, a court will be justified in finding that the directors acted for an improper purpose."

221 See Davies, supra footnote 30, at 385, note 75: "The 'improper purpose' test, as a requirement distinct from subjective good faith, has been rejected ... in British Columbia."

222 [1942] Ch. 304 (CA).

223 See, e.g., Davies, supra footnote 30, at 386-87.

224 See, e.g., R.C. Nolan, "The Proper Purpose Doctrine and Company Directors," in B.A.K. Rider, ed., *The Realm of Company Law* (London: Kluwer, 1998), 1, at 3: "[T]he proper purpose doctrine is not simply an alternative description of a duty to act *bona fide* in the interests of the company." Nolan does acknowledge that this proposition "has been doubted," but contends that such doubts have been expressed "with less conviction as time progresses." Ibid.

225 See, especially, *Exco*, supra footnote 218 and *Producers Pipelines*, supra footnote 218.

226 United States, Pub. L. no. 107-204 (2002).

227 For a discussion of the interplay between certain of the US initiatives and the Canadian regulatory response, see, Christopher C. Nicholls, "The Canadian Response to Sarbanes-Oxley," Capital Markets Institute Policy Comment (January 14, 2003); Philip Anisman, "Regulation of Lawyers by Securities Commissions: Sarbanes-Oxley in Canada," Capital Markets Institute Policy Comment (March 13, 2003), both available online at http://www.rotman.utoronto.ca/cmi/news/index.htm. Since the foregoing was written, the Canadian Securities Administrators have also issued for comment proposed Multilateral

publicly filed documents (that is, the corporation's annual information form, financial statements, MD&A, etc.).[228]
- A requirement that, subject to certain exemptions, audit committees of reporting
  issuers, other than reporting issuers whose shares trade only on the TSX Venture
  Exchange, have at least three directors, all of whom must be independent and
  financially literate.[229]

Not all of these reforms have been adopted in every Canadian province, and more
reform proposals are pending. What is clear, however, is that the US statutory reforms,
and the impact of the scandals that prompted them, will in the coming months and
perhaps years have a significant effect on the corporate governance initiatives of legislators and regulators and the governance practices of Canadian public corporations.

Instrument 52-111, dealing with the sensitive issue of internal corporate controls, an issue that Ontario
Securities Commission Chair David Brown has described as, "the most difficult issue I've seen in my
time as Chair." See David Brown, "The State of Corporate Governance in Canada," online at http://
www.osc.gov.on.ca/About/Speeches/sp_20050310_db-corp-gov-in-cdn.pdf.

228 See Multilateral Instrument 52-109, "Certification of Disclosure in Issuers' Annual and Interim Filings"
     (2004), 27 OSCB 3230.

229 See Multilateral Instrument 52-110, "Audit Committees" (2004), 27 OSCB 3252. "Independence" for
     this purpose is defined in s. 1.4 of the instrument.

CHAPTER ELEVEN

Interested Directors' Contracts, Corporate Opportunities, and Directors' and Officers' Personal Liability

INTRODUCTION

Chapter 10 introduced the general principles that underlie the legal duties of a corporation's directors and officers. This chapter will look at the role of directors and officers from a different perspective, focusing on three areas of potential liability for directors and officers:

- interested directors' and officers' contracts (that is, contracts between the corporation and one of its own directors or officers);
- corporate opportunities (that is, cases in which a corporate director or senior officer seizes for his or her own benefit a profitable business opportunity in which the corporation itself may be said to have had the prior right or interest); and
- personal liability of directors and officers to third parties.

INTERESTED DIRECTORS' CONTRACTS

Framing the Issue

Corporate directors may, from time to time, have goods or services that they wish to sell to the corporation on whose board they sit. Alternatively, the corporation may have assets or services that it wishes to sell, and that one of its directors is willing and able to buy. Transactions like these inevitably place the directors involved in a position where their personal interests may conflict with their duty to the corporation. If a director is selling an asset to the corporation, for example, the director's duty to the corporation requires him or her to try to negotiate the *lowest* possible purchase price. But, the director's personal interest, as seller, is to try to obtain the *highest* possible sale price.

The law has always taken a dim view of such conflicts of interest. Honourable directors, it was long thought, ought never to permit their duty to come into conflict with their personal interest. As will be seen below, historically, the law would often treat such

313

transactions between a corporation and any of its directors as voidable at the instance of the corporation.

This harsh common law rule is understandable in the case of a corporation that has multiple shareholders but only one director. That director might well be tempted to use her position to enrich herself personally by committing the corporation to one-sided contracts in her own favour. But suppose a corporation has not one director, but many. If those directors, acting in the best interests of the corporation, collectively decide that the corporation ought to enter into some contract or other transaction with one member of the board, is it clear that the law should always forbid such matters? Why should the corporation not be permitted to decide for itself (through its impartial directors) whether it wishes to deal with an "interested director"? After all, the non-interested directors would surely be no less aware of their fellow directors' conflicts than are judges or legislators. If the non-interested directors, acting in good faith, are satisfied that a contract with one of their own is, all things considered, to the benefit of the corporation, why should courts or statutes interfere with that business judgment?

Two answers to this question are sometimes suggested. First, it has been argued that a corporation has a right to expect the full attention and decision-making skills of *all* of its directors.[1] In other words, if a corporation has, for example, a board of five directors, it is not right for one of them—the interested director—to remove himself or herself from the business decision-making dynamic by proposing to deal with the corporation. There is also a second consideration. Many doubt whether it is ever really possible for directors of a corporation to deal objectively and independently with one of their colleagues. These doubts are especially poignant when the interested director is also a senior manager of the corporation. The interested director may exercise a degree of undue influence on the remaining board members—sometimes subtle, even unconscious, and sometimes, sadly, not subtle at all.

If the influence, or pressure, exerted by one director over his or her fellows were always overt or heavy handed, then perhaps the legality of such contracts could be dealt with on a case-by-case basis. But, more often than not, directors approving a contract between the corporation and a member of the board may be subject to influence that is quite incapable of proof after the fact. Better, then, to equip non-interested directors with a ready answer to the aggressive "interested" director by imposing an unforgiving rule of contract voidability.

It seems, however, both impractical and unnecessary to forbid all contracts between corporations and directors. And such a total ban also does seem to be an excessive intrusion into private business relationships. Accordingly, the law of interested directors' contracts attempts to balance and resolve these tensions. Judges and legislators do not wish to interfere unduly with what are, after all, private organizations that must normally be permitted to make (and live with) their decisions. However, at the same time, this laissez-faire ideal must be balanced against an awareness that we do not live in a utopian world of philanthropy and altruism, and that things are not always what they seem. A board's decision to permit a corporation to enter into a contract with one of its own

---

1   As Lord Radcliffe put it in *Gray v. Augarita Porcupine Mines Ltd.*, [1952] 3 DLR 1 (PC), "The company, it has been said, has a right to the services of its directors as an entire Board."

directors can be made to appear honest, well-informed, and undertaken with the utmost good faith. But, the reality may be very different. A contract between a corporation and an interested director could well lead to unfair prejudice to the interests of the corporation and an unfair enrichment of the interested director.

Interested Directors' Contracts at Common Law

At common law, directors were not permitted to enter into contracts with the corporations they served. Any contract purported to be made in violation of this prohibition was voidable at the instance of the company,[2] and, as it has been observed, "so strictly [was] this principle adhered to that no question [was] allowed to be raised as to the fairness or unfairness of a contract so entered into."[3]

In some cases, however, a contract like this could not be avoided because events had occurred that made rescission of the contract impossible. In these cases, the interested director was said to remain accountable for any profits he or she made under the contract.[4] As well, the principle of accountability appeared to apply not only to situations where the director was entering into a contract with the corporation in his personal capacity, but also to instances where the corporation was contracting with another incorporated entity in which the director had some proprietary interest.[5]

This harsh, apparently inflexible common law rule was subject to a rather important qualification. The members (that is, the shareholders) of a corporation could, if they wished, adopt or ratify any such contract. To be effective, this adoption had to have been obtained by proper means; but, perhaps surprisingly, it was quite proper for an interested director who also held shares to vote as a shareholder on such a ratification.[6]

There are conflicting authorities on what, precisely, was the effect of ratification on the director's obligation to account for his or her profits under the contract. Some cases, it is true, indicate that full disclosure to shareholders, followed by ratification by the shareholders, would relieve interested directors from the otherwise harsh operation of the common law restrictions.[7] However, one notes that the Privy Council in *Gray v. New*

---

2   See L.S. Sealy, *Cases and Materials in Company Law*, 7th ed. (London: Butterworths, 2001), at 270. The Dickerson committee indicated that such a contract was void. Robert W.V. Dickerson et al., *Proposals for a New Business Corporations Law for Canada*, vol. I, Commentary (Ottawa: Information Canada, 1971), at para. 226 (Dickerson committee).

3   See *Aberdeen Railway v. Blaikie* (1854), 1 Macq. 461, at 471 (HL).

4   *Gray*, supra footnote 1.

5   See, e.g., *Transvaal Lands Company v. New Belgium (Transvaal) Land & Development Co.*, [1914] 2 Ch. 488 (CA).

6   *North-West Transportation Co. Ltd. v. Beatty* (1887), 12 App. Cas. 589 (PC). Len Sealy, however, has noted that, in fact, the *North-West Transportation* case did not actually involve a ratification of a contract. Rather, the "ratification" in that case was the ratification of a bylaw approving the purchase of the ship that was the transaction in question. (See Sealy, supra footnote 2, at 273-74. However, it may at least be said that *North-West Transportation* is consistent with the proposition that shareholders in a general meeting may ratify a contract entered into between the company and an interested director.)

7   See, e.g., Paul L. Davies, *Gower & Davies: Principles of Modern Company Law*, 7th ed. (London: Sweet & Maxwell, 2003), at 395.

Augarita Porcupine Mines Ltd.[8] gave as a specific example of a circumstance in which an interested director would be obliged to account for profits, the case of a contract that the corporation had elected to affirm.

In any event, a company's articles could exempt interested directors from any duty to account for profits arising from such contracts. They could even relieve directors of any obligation to disclose their interest in such a contract to the corporation. Evidently, including such exemption provisions in company articles started to become a common practice in the United Kingdom.[9] In time, the use of these charter provisions to render interested directors wholly unaccountable came to be viewed as too lax by the legislators.

UK Statutory Reform

The UK Parliament responded to this proliferation of permissive company charter provisions by amending the UK *Companies Act* to deal explicitly with the subject of interested directors' contracts.[10] The new legislative provision required that directors disclose their interest in such contracts to the board.[11] Failure to do so could render the offending director liable to pay a fine of up to £100.[12]

So non-disclosing directors were to be subject to what would presumably have been, at the time, a significant fine. But the statute said nothing about what effect, if any, a failure to comply with the Act would have on the validity or invalidity of the contract itself. This rather important detail was evidently left for the courts to sort out. The legislation said only that "nothing in this section shall be taken to prejudice the operation of any rule of law restricting directors of a company from having any interest in contracts with the company."[13]

This effect of the original UK provision was considered in the well-known case of *Hely-Hutchinson v. Brayhead Ltd.*[14] The plaintiff, Hely-Hutchinson (styled Lord Suirdale) had been involved with an electronics company known as Perdio. An investment banking firm had loaned money to Perdio, and Lord Suirdale had provided a personal guarantee of this loan in favour of the investment bank.

A second company, Brayhead Ltd., became interested in Perdio. Brayhead purchased a large number of Perdio's shares. Lord Suirdale joined Brayhead's board of directors. Brayhead, as a substantial shareholder of Perdio, now had a direct interest in the fortunes of Perdio. Perdio was struggling financially. Lord Suirdale, while a director of Brayhead, agreed to help Perdio by making a personal loan to the company. He was willing to make this loan, however, only if Brayhead would (1) indemnify him against losses he might suffer under the guarantee he had previously provided to the investment bank, and (2) guarantee the repayment of his new loan to Perdio as well.

---

8   Supra footnote 1.

9   See Dickerson committee, supra footnote 2, at para. 226 and Davies, supra footnote 7, at 395-96.

10   Dickerson committee, supra footnote 2, at para. 226.

11   This provision was originally found in s. 149 of the UK *Companies Act*, 1929.

12   Ibid., s. 149(4).

13   Ibid., s. 149(5).

14   [1968] QB 549 (CA).

Naturally, Brayhead was eager to see its investment in Perdio saved. The chairman of Brayhead, therefore, agreed to both of Lord Suirdale's conditions. However, the negotiation of these terms—between Lord Suirdale and the chairman—occurred *after* a Brayhead directors' meeting, in an office without, apparently, other Brayhead directors present.

Perdio ultimately collapsed. Lord Suirdale thus called on Brayhead to honour the guarantee and the indemnity that he had negotiated with Brayhead's chairman. Brayhead refused to honour these commitments. Among other things,[15] Brayhead argued that the contracts that Lord Suirdale sought to enforce were contracts that had been entered into when he, Lord Suirdale, was a director of Brayhead. As a director, entering into such interested contracts, Lord Suirdale was obliged by the terms of Brayhead's articles to expressly disclose his interest at a directors' meeting, and he had failed to do so.

On this factual point, there was no dispute. Lord Suirdale had not disclosed his interest at a directors' meeting. (The arrangements with Brayhead's chairman had all been made *after* the directors' meeting.) The critical legal issue was what the consequence of such a failure to disclose ought to be. The Court of Appeal determined that the effect of this failure to disclose was that the contract was voidable at the option of the company. However, as in the case of any voidable contract, if the company wished to exercise its right to avoid it, appropriate steps needed to be taken; it would need to be possible to put the parties back into their original position, and there must be no prejudice to the rights of third parties.[16]

Brayhead could not satisfy these requirements. Thus, the court concluded that the contracts—that is, the guarantee and the indemnity—although voidable by Brayhead, had not, in fact, been avoided in time. Accordingly, they were enforceable by Lord Suirdale, notwithstanding his failure to comply with the applicable disclosure obligations.

Canadian Statutory Reform
Overview

It was against this legal backdrop that the Dickerson committee put forward its proposals for what is now s. 120 of the CBCA.[17] The goal of s. 120 was to improve on the earlier UK legislative approach, still with a view to balancing the rights of the corporation, as a private enterprise, to make its own business decisions, against the need to protect the interests of shareholders who cannot easily monitor boardroom behaviour.

The view taken by the Dickerson committee was that it would be a mistake to adopt an overly rigid rule that would inevitably render all interested directors' contracts void *ab initio*, or even voidable at the option of the corporation. Evidently, the committee recognized that not every corporate contract entered into with an interested director necessarily harms the corporation. The corporation ought generally to be able to decide for itself if it wishes to accept such contracts—provided that some formal rules are in place to ensure that the corporation's acceptance is based on complete information.

---

15   Brayhead also argued that the chairman had neither actual nor ostensible authority to bind Brayhead. The Court of Appeal rejected Brayhead's argument on this point.

16   Davies suggests that it may even be "doubted how strong a bar *restitutio in integrum* really is, given the wide powers the court has to order financial adjustments when directing rescission." See Davies, supra footnote 7, at 427.

17   Section 120 was materially amended in 2001, as discussed further below.

Those formal rules proposed by the Dickerson committee, like those of the original UK legislation, emphasized the importance of disclosure of the director's interest. But they did not rely on disclosure alone. They also included a requirement of substantive fairness. The disclosure regime proposed by the Dickerson committee was not, of course, the final word on this subject in Canada. Provincial corporate statutes introduced important variations, and s. 120 itself was amended as part of the 2001 CBCA reforms. Although the following discussion will focus first on CBCA s. 120, some of the innovations introduced in other Canadian statutes will also be briefly canvassed.

CBCA Section 120

Section 120 of the CBCA is thus premised on the notion that, if a corporation accepts a contract with an interested director (or indeed an interested officer), the contract will not necessarily be voidable by the corporation provided that

- the interested director or officer has fully disclosed his or her interest in that contract; and
- the contract is reasonable and fair to the corporation.

The section is not, however, intended to operate as a "safe harbour." In other words, mere formal compliance with the procedures in s. 120 does not relieve directors of their overriding obligation to act in the best interests of the corporation.[18] A more detailed consideration of s. 120 follows.

Applies to Officers and Directors

Section 120 applies not only to contracts entered into between a corporation and one of its directors, but also to contracts between a corporation and any of its officers.[19] Both directors and officers are subject to fiduciary duties under s. 122, and so it is sensible and consistent to extend the conflict of interest provisions to officers.

Applies to "Material Contracts" or "Material Transactions" with the Corporation

Section 120 does not apply to all contracts or transactions, but only to those contracts or transactions that are "material."[20] The test of materiality is obviously to be judged from

---

18 Specifically, the Dickerson committee noted that, although s. 120 states that a contract must be "reasonable and fair" to the corporation to come within the ambit of s. 120, this was language intended "only to underline the director's specific duties in the circumstances." (Dickerson committee, supra footnote 2, at para. 228.) In other words, any directors who permitted a corporation to enter into a contract that was *not* reasonable and fair to the corporation would be in breach of their fiduciary duties, whether or not s. 120 had included this language.

19 The term "officer" is defined in s. 2(1) of the CBCA.

20 Reference to "material" contracts or transactions is also found in sections comparable to s. 120 in many provincial corporate statutes. See, e.g., *Business Corporations Act* (Alta.), s. 120; *The Business Corporations Act* (Sask.), s. 115; *The Corporations Act* (Man.), s. 115; *Business Corporations Act* (Ont.), s. 132; *Business Corporations Act* (NB), s. 77; and *Corporations Act* (NL), s. 198.

the perspective of the corporation, and only a pedant would be bothered by the fact that the statutory language does not expressly state this. Of rather more significance, however, is that the CBCA makes no attempt to define the word "material" for this purpose, and there has been little judicial insight into the meaning of this term, at least in the context of disclosure of interested directors' contracts. Certainly, questions of "materiality" confront accountants and lawyers every day, especially in the context of financial statement and securities law disclosure requirements.[21] However, it is unlikely that the test for determining whether a fact or a change is "material" for securities law purposes is the appropriate test to apply in determining whether or not a contract or transaction with an interested director or officer is material for purposes of s. 120. Any contract or transaction that is not trivial or insignificant ought to be subject to the rules of s. 120, even if entering into such a contract or transaction would not otherwise trigger a public disclosure requirement.

Applies to Contracts with Officers and Directors and with Other "Entities" in Which the Officers or Directors Have an Interest

Section 120 applies not only when a director or officer is a party in his or her personal capacity to a contract or transaction with the corporation, but also where he or she

- is a director or officer of, or acts in a similar capacity with, a party to the contract or transaction (that party could, of course, be another corporation, but it could also be an unincorporated entity such as a partnership, limited partnership, limited liability partnership (LLP), an American-style limited liability company (LLC), a trust, etc.[22]); or
- has a "material interest" in a party to such a contract or transaction.

Again, the Act does not define precisely what "material interest" means for the purpose of this second category of contracts or transactions. Professor Welling has suggested that

---

21   For a discussion of the obligation to disclose "material facts" or "material changes," see Jeffrey G. MacIntosh and Christopher C. Nicholls, *Securities Law* (Toronto: Irwin, 2002), at 270ff.

22   Section 120, as it was worded prior to the 2001 amendments, applied to situations where non-corporate entities were parties, but the current language provides additional clarity. Prior to 2001, the CBCA referred to situations where a director or officer of a corporation was "a director or an officer of or [had] a material interest in any person who is a party to a material contract or proposed material contract with the corporation." The word "person" was broadly defined under s. 2 of the pre-2001 CBCA, and included not only individuals and incorporated entities but also a "partnership, association, body corporate, trustee, executor, administrator or legal representative." Moreover, even this definition did not purport to be exhaustive—that is, person was defined to "include" these terms, rather than to "mean" these terms. Thus, where a non-corporate party was involved, the courts needed to determine if the director or officer in question had a "material interest" in such a person; but this did not appear to be an overly troublesome restriction. (See, e.g., *McAteer v. Devoncroft Developments* (2001), 24 BLR (3d) 1 (Alta. QB) where the comparable section of the Alberta *Business Corporations Act* was held to include a trust in which the director in question had no beneficial interest, but of which the director was a trustee.) Amendments in 2001 considerably narrowed the definition of "person" in s. 2. However, the language in s. 120 was broadened to make clear that a director or officer would be in a position of conflict if he or she was "a director or an officer, *or an individual acting in a similar capacity, of a party* [i.e., not necessarily a "person" as defined in the CBCA] to the contract or transaction."

this wording could extend even to "interests" in natural persons. That is, in his view, the provision would apply to contracts entered into, for example, with a close relative of a director or officer.[23] Indeed, one court has recently cited Professor Welling's views on this topic with apparent agreement.[24]

With respect, however, this conclusion is problematic. While it may well be *good policy* to extend the application of s. 120 to contracts or transactions between corporations and those with whom their directors and officers have personal relationships, it is surely straining the statutory language to argue that the relationship between two human beings could be described in terms of one having "a material interest in" another. Had the drafters intended the provision to extend to contracts entered into with relatives or friends of a director, surely they would have used more conventional language indicating human, rather than commercial, relationships. Remember, too, that the failure to include contracts with directors' friends or relatives within the section does not mean that the legislature has blessed or even permitted such contracts. It means only that the specific provisions of s. 120 will not be applicable to them. It should go without saying that the failure on the part of a director to disclose the existence of such a personal relationship may well mean, in appropriate circumstances, that such a director is himself or herself in breach of his or her general fiduciary duties—fiduciary duties, as the Dickerson committee emphasized, that are not overridden or pre-empted in any way by the provisions of s. 120.[25]

Obligation To Disclose

A director must disclose any interest that he or she may have in a material contract or material transaction either to the board of directors or to a committee[26] of the board. That disclosure must include not only the fact of the director's interest, but also the nature and the extent of that interest.[27] As Lord Radcliffe stated in *Gray v. New Augarita Porcupine Mines Ltd.*:[28]

> It can rarely be enough for a director to say, "I must remind you that I am interested" and to leave it at that. ... His declaration must make his colleagues "fully informed of the real state of things." ... If it is material to their judgment that they should know not merely that he has an interest, but what it is and how far it goes, then he must see to it that they are informed.[29]

23   See Bruce Welling, *Corporate Law in Canada: The Governing Principles*, 2nd ed. (Toronto: Butterworths, 1991), at 452.

24   See *Zysko v. Thorarinson*, [2003] AJ no. 1375 (QL) (Alta. QB). This judgment is somewhat unclear, however, because it appears to conflate the terms "material contract" and "material interest" in some sections.

25   Dickerson committee, supra footnote 2, at para. 228.

26   CBCA, s. 120(1).

27   This provision reverses the effect of cases such as *Guinness PLC v. Ward* (1990), 108 NR 44 (HL), in which the court regarded as ineffective disclosure made by the interested director to a subcommittee of the board, but not to the board as a whole.

28   Supra footnote 1.

29   Ibid., at 14. This passage was cited with approval by Lax J of the Ontario Superior Court of Justice in *UPM-Kymmene Corp. v. UPM-Kymmene Miramichi Inc.*, [2002] OJ 2412, at para. 115 (QL) (SCJ), aff'd. (2004), 42 BLR (3d) 34 (Ont. CA).

In the recent highly publicized Ontario case, *UPM-Kymmene v. UPM-Kymmene Miramichi Inc.*,[30] the court found that a director had fallen short of the disclosure standard mandated by CBCA s. 120 in connection with two contracts—an executive employment agreement and a stock option grant agreement—entered into between the corporation and the director. The board in that case was obviously aware of the fact that the director had an interest in these contracts. However, several important facts had not been disclosed to the board at the meeting at which these contracts were approved.

Among the matters not disclosed were the following facts:

- at an earlier board meeting—when the board had been differently constituted— strong opposition had been expressed over the substance of these proposed agreements;
- the corporation's managers had raised concerns about the agreements with former members of the board;
- a compensation consultant who had been engaged to provide expert advice concerning these agreements had, in fact, been unable to perform any due diligence on which to provide an authoritative opinion and, thus, although an opinion was indeed before the board, it was not one on which the board could (if properly informed) have placed much weight; and
- the agreements that the board was asked to approve actually differed in material ways from drafts that had previously been provided for review.

Some of these matters—in particular the differences between the final and draft versions of the agreements—were undoubtedly things that the directors could have discovered on their own. However, in Lax J's view, "It is no answer to the duty to disclose to say the directors could have discovered this for themselves. The duty to disclose is an absolute one, because, without full disclosure, any investigation into whether the beneficiary would have acted in the same manner is impossible."[31]

METHOD OF DISCLOSURE

Section 120 provides a fairly detailed disclosure protocol. Without attempting to parse through these rules rigorously, it is sufficient here to suggest that the two fundamental principles underlying these detailed rules appear to be that

- disclosure must be made by the interested officer or director at the earliest opportunity after the potential conflict has been identified; and
- a once-for-all-time general disclosure to the board may be made of the fact that a director or officer is interested in an entity with which the corporation might enter into contracts or transactions. So, for example, a director of one public corporation (ABC Ltd.) might also be a significant shareholder of another corporation (XYZ Ltd.) that is a major supplier or major customer of ABC Ltd. The director may thus declare once to the board of ABC Ltd. that he or she is to be regarded as interested in any contract or transaction entered into between ABC Ltd. and XYZ Ltd. Thereafter, it

---

30   Ibid.

31   Ibid., at para. 116.

is not necessary for that director to remember to ensure that the nature of his or her interest is repeated each and every time a contract or transaction with XYZ Ltd. comes before the ABC Ltd. board. Needless to say, there would be no harm in reminding the board of this interest each time a contract or transaction is entered into; but requiring such redundant disclosure would be at best fruitless. At worst, requiring such ritualistic disclosure could tempt some corporations to act opportunistically. For example, if an interested director inadvertently neglected to formally disclose his or her interest in one particular contract or transaction (though every member of the board was, in fact, well aware of that interest because of dozens of identical prior disclosures) an opportunistic corporation might attempt to seize on that oversight to avoid a contract that, with the benefit of hindsight, had proven to be unprofitable.

It has sometimes been suggested that disclosure by one director to his or her board colleagues is not, without more, sufficient protection from the potential abuses that s. 120 aimed to prevent. The Alberta Institute of Law Research and Reform (as it was then called) recognized this problem in its 1980 report, *Proposals for a New Alberta Business Corporations Act.*[32] They noted, in particular, a unique feature of the Ghana Code (which had been drafted by the eminent English corporate law scholar L.C.B. Gower). The Ghana Code, as they explained, "requires more detailed disclosure to be put in a special book which is then made available for inspection by the shareholders."[33] They recommended that a similar approach be adopted in Alberta. When the CBCA was amended in 2001, express provision was made for access by shareholders of disclosures made by directors or officers under s. 120.[34]

Abstention from Voting

An interested director is not permitted to vote on a contract or transaction in which he or she has an interest unless the contract or transaction:

(a) relates primarily to his or her remuneration as a director, officer, employee or agent of the corporation or an affiliate;

(b) is for indemnity or insurance under section 124; or

(c) is with an affiliate.[35]

---

32   Institute of Law Research and Reform, *Proposals for a New Alberta Business Corporations Act*, report no. 36, vol. 1 (Edmonton: Institute of Law Research and Reform, 1980), at 64.

33   Ibid., at 64.

34   CBCA, s. 120(6.1).

35   CBCA, s. 120(5). Note that this section on "Abstention from Voting" was written in March 2004. Many months later, following my appointment in the summer of 2004 as associate editor of the *Canadian Business Law Journal*, I received for edit the manuscript of an excellent forthcoming article by an experienced practitioner, Paul Wickens, in which he independently reached some very similar conclusions concerning the rationale for the s. 120 treatment of remuneration contracts or transactions. See Paul D. Wickens, "Policing Director and Officer Conflicts" (forthcoming), *Canadian Business Law Journal*.

(This restriction does not apply to interested officers for the simple reason that officers who are not also directors do not attend and vote at directors' meetings in any event.) It may at first seem curious that a director is permitted to vote in connection with the two matters in which his or her financial interest is the greatest of all: remuneration and indemnity. However, remember that it is the responsibility of the board to determine both of these matters and, in the case of directors' remuneration and indemnity and insurance, all members of the board would be subject to virtually identical treatment.[36] Thus, a provision that precluded directors from voting in these cases would lead to the artificial and rather absurd result that each director would be obliged to abstain, in turn, as the board approved his or her remuneration and his or her right to receive indemnity.

Nevertheless, when a board is voting with respect to the remuneration of a senior officer who is also a member of the board, it is surely best practice for the affected director to abstain from voting, notwithstanding that the specific provisions of s. 120 would not be engaged by such a vote.

Contract or Transaction Must Be "Reasonable and Fair to the Corporation"

At common law, it will be recalled, the fairness or reasonableness of a contract with an interested director was an irrelevant consideration. Under s. 120, however, the matter of fairness and reasonableness is of critical importance. A contract or transaction between a corporation and an interested director or officer will be voidable, even if the disclosure/ vote abstention requirements of s. 120 are met, unless the contract or transaction "was reasonable and fair to the corporation at the time it was approved."[37]

The Dickerson committee maintained that this substantive fairness requirement was needed to prevent what they called the risk of "mutual 'back-scratching' by directors who might otherwise tacitly agree to approve one another's contracts with the corporation."[38] Directors' general fiduciary duties would, in any event, oblige them to take steps to ensure that the corporation did not enter into improvident contracts. The Dickerson committee acknowledged this fact, suggesting that the only real purpose of this additional "reasonable and fair standard" was to "underline the director's specific duties in the circumstances."[39]

This "reasonable and fair" requirement, or equivalent language in provincial corporate statutes, has been the subject of a few judicial interpretations. It has been noted that such a test must not be limited merely to an examination of the words of the agreement being assessed, but must also take account of the surrounding facts and circumstances under which it was entered,[40] or, as it has sometimes been said, the "factual matrix."[41]

---

36 It is true that the fees paid to the chair and to chairs of individual board committees may be higher than fees paid to ordinary members of the board. These fees would typically be based on the office held, rather than the office holder.

37 CBCA, s. 120(7)(c).

38 Dickerson committee, supra footnote 2, at para. 228.

39 Ibid.

40 *Cannaday v. Sun Peaks Resort Corp.* (1998), 44 BCLR (3d) 195 (CA).

41 *UPM-Kymmene Corp. v. UPM-Kymmene Miramichi Inc.*, supra footnote 29, at para. 190.

324 Chapter 11 Directors' Contracts, Corporate Opportunities, Personal Liability

In *Rooney v. Cree Lake Resources Corp.*,[42] Dilks J indicated that, in determining whether a contract was reasonable and fair to a corporation, courts must apply a facts and circumstances test.[43] Dilks J further noted that a paucity of Canadian cases on the meaning of "reasonable and fair" had led commentators to consider US jurisprudence. The effect of the American decisions was briefly summarized in *Rooney* in this way:

> ... whether or not in all the circumstances the transaction carries the earmarks of an arm's length bargain. See *Pepper v. Litton* 308 US 295, or whether, in other words, the transaction would have recommended itself to an independent board of directors that was acting in good faith and had the best interests of the corporation in mind. See *Summa Corp. v. Trans World Airlines, Inc.* at 540 A. (2d) 218.[44]

In addition to the US authorities mentioned in *Rooney*, it is also useful to consider the approach of the Delaware Supreme Court in *Weinberger v. UOP, Inc.*[45] in determining whether a contract with an interested director or officer is reasonable and fair. In particular, attention must be paid to the process used in formulating and entering into the agreement ("fair dealing") as well as the substantive fairness of the contract ("fair price").[46]

Contract Not Invalid; Director Under No Duty To Account

Unlike older legislative measures concerning interested directors' contracts, s. 120 deals explicitly with the effect of compliance on the enforceability of the interested contract. If the disclosure, abstention from voting, and substantive fairness rules reviewed above have been dutifully followed, the contract or transaction will not be invalid.[47] Moreover, the interested director or officer in such a case is under no obligation to account to the corporation for any profit he or she may have earned.

Even if disclosure to the board has not been made properly, the contract or transaction will not necessarily be void. It might still be saved, provided that three conditions are satisfied:

- the contract or transaction is reasonable and fair to the corporation;
- full disclosure has been made to the corporation's shareholders; and
- with the benefit of that full disclosure, the shareholders have approved or confirmed the contract or transaction by special resolution (that is, by the affirmative vote of at least two-thirds of the shareholders voting on the matter at a meeting, or by unanimous written resolution).

The statutory language dealing with the effect of compliance with these shareholder disclosure/approval procedures on the validity of an interested director's or officer's

---

42 [1998] 40 CCEL 96 (Ont. Ct. Gen. Div.).

43 Ibid., at para. 52: "one must examine all the surrounding circumstances including the purpose of the agreement and its possible ramifications for the corporation."

44 Ibid., at para. 46.

45 457 A 2d 701 (Del. SC 1983).

46 Supra footnote 29, at para. 195.

47 CBCA, s. 120(7).

contract must be read carefully, however. It differs in a subtle, but rather important, respect from the language that is used to describe the effect of compliance with the more conventional *directors'* disclosure procedures. As discussed above, when proper disclosure is made *to the directors*, the contract is reasonable and fair, and the interested director refrains from voting, then the contract will be valid (unless, of course, there is some other defect—unrelated to the directors' interest—that might render it void). The statute is more equivocal, however, in dealing with those cases in which shareholder disclosure and approval, rather than director disclosure and approval, are relied on.

Subsection 120(7.1) states that, where the shareholder disclosure/approval/reasonable and fair requirements have been met, the contract is not invalid and the director is not required to account *by reason only* of the director's interest. In other words, the contract might still be invalidated under certain circumstances. Prior to 2001, this same language (and thus this same ambiguity) applied to interested directors' or officers' contracts that had been properly disclosed to the board as well, and indeed many provincial corporate statutes are still subject to this limitation.[48]

The statutory language is puzzling. What remaining reason might there be for holding such a contract invalid, especially when one recalls that the contract or transaction must, by the terms of the section, be reasonable and fair to the corporation?

The intended scope of this language is not entirely clear. Perhaps the drafters considered it prudent to leave open the possibility that a contract or transaction that had not been properly disclosed to the board might be held invalid, even if it were ultimately approved by the shareholders, so that interested directors and officers would have appropriate incentives to disclose their interests to the board in the first place. The risk of nondisclosure might be especially great in cases where the interested director also controls a significant number of shares, so that he or she could be reasonably assured that at a shareholders' meeting—as opposed to a directors' meeting—approval of the contract or transaction would be forthcoming. Under most Canadian corporate statutes, an interested director who is also a shareholder would, after all, be permitted to vote as a shareholder to approve such a contract. Under New Brunswick's *Business Corporations Act*, however, approval of the contract by the disinterested shareholders is necessary in such cases to relieve the director from his or her duty to account.[49]

Other Canadian Jurisdictions

The corporate statutes in most of the common law provinces have provisions that are comparable to s. 120 of the CBCA, at least in its pre-2001 form. There are, however, some interesting variations, in addition to those noted earlier. For example, the BC *Business Corporations Act* deals explicitly with certain issues that are left unstated or ambiguous under the CBCA, and also refines the circumstances under which the disclosure obligations will apply. The BC provisions, first, make clear that the contracts that are

48   See, e.g., *Business Corporations Act* (Alta.), s. 120(8); *The Business Corporations Act* (Sask.), s. 115(7); *The Corporations Act* (Man.), s. 115(7); *Business Corporations Act* (Ont.), s. 132(7); and *Corporations Act* (NL), s. 200.

49   *Business Corporations Act* (NB), s. 77(9).

relevant are those that are material *to the company*.[50] Moreover, the obligation to disclose falls upon all directors, but only upon *senior* officers, a term defined in s. 1(1) of the BC statute. The Act also makes explicit that a director or senior officer who is the sole shareholder of the company or any corporation of which the company is a wholly owned subsidiary does not hold a disclosable interest.[51] Further, the BC Act provides that contracts that relate to security granted by the company in respect of director or officer loans, indemnity, director/officer remuneration, loans to the company that a director or officer has guaranteed, and certain affiliate transactions, do not necessarily constitute matters in respect of which a director or senior officer will be said to have a "disclosable interest" in any event.[52] Recall that under the CBCA, a director or officer's interest in contracts of this sort (although the list is not identical) must be disclosed, although the relevant director is not precluded from voting on a resolution to approve them.

The BC provisions also make explicit that a director or senior officer is not liable to account, and is entitled to retain the profit from any contract or transaction in which he or she had a disclosable interest, provided certain requirements are met. Those requirements include providing proper disclosure of the matter to the directors, and receiving their approval[53] or disclosing the matter to the shareholders, and receiving the shareholders' approval by special resolution.[54] Alternatively, in cases where the contract or transaction was entered into before the interested person became a director or senior officer, the requirements will be satisfied if disclosure has been made to the directors or the shareholders, and the senior officer or director in question has not voted or otherwise taken part in any decision or resolution relating to the contract or transaction.[55] Normally, a director with a disclosable interest is not permitted to vote in respect of such a matter;[56] however, this requirement is, not surprisingly, not applicable where all directors have a disclosable interest in the same contract or transaction.[57] Finally, the question of whether such a contract or transaction was "fair and reasonable" to the company is only relevant in the context of certain applications made to the court, including in the case of such a contract or transaction that was not properly disclosed and approved in accordance with s. 148(2).[58]

There are other noteworthy provincial variations, too. The Alberta *Business Corporations Act* provides that the interested director's contract regime is made subject to any

---

50   *Business Corporations Act* (BC), s. 147(1)(a).

51   Ibid., s. 147(2)(e).

52   Ibid., s. 147(4).

53   Ibid., s. 148(2)(b). Note that this provision does not apply to contracts or transactions approved by the directors in those cases where every director has a disclosable interest and where the Act, accordingly, must permit all of them to vote in respect of the matter because there would otherwise be no way for the board to consider such matters at all. (See ibid., s. 149(3).)

54   Ibid., s. 148(2)(c).

55   Ibid., s. 148(2)(d).

56   Ibid., s. 149(2).

57   Ibid., s. 149(3).

58   Ibid., s. 150.

unanimous shareholder agreement.[59] In Saskatchewan, *The Business Corporations Act* also makes the interested director provisions subject to the provisions of any unanimous shareholder agreement. But the Saskatchewan legislation goes further still by making explicit that, where the statutory disclosure and approval rules are excluded by the terms of such an agreement, the rules of common law and equity are not to apply to the interested contracts or proposed contracts either.[60] Moreover, the Saskatchewan Act provides that the shareholders may by *unanimous* resolution *at a meeting* approve a contract that the directors of the corporation would be unable to approve by reason of the interest of some or all of them in the matter. Presumably, this provision is included to deal with situations where the number of interested directors is such that there are insufficient non-interested directors to constitute a quorum.

Under the Manitoba *Corporations Act*, if a director votes in respect of any contract in which he or she has an interest, other than in respect of the usual exempted contracts (that is, those relating to remuneration, indemnity, and so on), the resolution to approve that contract is not effective unless approved by a vote of at least two-thirds of the shareholders to whom appropriate disclosure has been made.[61]

The Ontario *Business Corporations Act*, like the pre-2001 CBCA, says only that, if the disclosure and approval regime is properly adhered to, and the contract or transaction is reasonable and fair, that contract or transaction is not voidable, and the interested director or officer is not required to account, *by reason only* of the director's or officer's interest.[62] The Ontario *Business Corporations Act* also includes in the list of contracts on which interested directors are permitted to vote, "an arrangement by way of security for money lent or obligations undertaken by the director for the benefit of the corporation or an affiliate." [63] Similar language appeared in the CBCA prior to the 2001 amendments. An Industry Canada briefing book on the 2001 amendments explained that this provision was deleted essentially because any such transaction that was *not* for the benefit of the corporation would presumably be improper in any event.[64] At the very least, trying to determine whether such a contract or transaction was for the benefit of the corporation (as opposed to the interested director) seemed to the drafters to create unnecessary uncertainty; and forbidding interested directors from voting in cases of such a potential conflict appeared to be a superior approach.[65]

One of the more significant variations is found in the New Brunswick *Business Corporations Act*. That legislation provides that a director or officer is not accountable

59 *Business Corporations Act* (Alta.), s. 120(10). (The Alberta statute applies to contracts or proposed contracts, not to transactions.)

60 *The Business Corporations Act* (Sask.), s. 115(10). Note that the Saskatchewan Act refers only to contracts or proposed contracts, not to transactions.

61 *The Corporations Act* (Man.), s. 115(5).

62 *Business Corporations Act* (Ont.), s. 132.

63 *Business Corporations Act* (Ont.), s. 132(5)(a).

64 Industry Canada, *Clause-by-Clause Briefing Book: Bill S-11*, Part 10: Directors and Officers (clauses 35-51). Available online at http://strategis.ic.gc.ca/epic/internet/incilp-pdci.nsf/en/h_cl00269e.html.

65 Ibid.

for profits made under a contract, even where the normal disclosure and approval process is *not* followed, provided that the contract is approved by the majority of votes cast by *disinterested shareholders*.[66] The New Brunswick Act also exempts sole shareholder corporations from the provisions of the interested director sections.[67] It is not entirely clear why, as a practical matter, such an exemption was considered necessary; although, as discussed above, the BC Act also provides a special exception for directors and senior officers who are sole shareholders.

The provisions in the Nova Scotia *Companies Act* are very different from those in the CBCA-style statutes. The Nova Scotia provisions are based on an older UK model.[68] They require directors directly or indirectly interested in contracts or proposed contracts with the corporation to disclose the nature of that interest at a directors' meeting, and they provide for a penalty of up to $100 for failure to do so.[69] But the Nova Scotia provision does not explicitly apply to corporate officers, nor does it deal with the effect of compliance (or non-compliance) on the validity of the contract itself. Indeed, s. 99(5) of the Nova Scotia legislation expressly states that

> [n]othing in this Section shall be taken to prejudice the operation of any rule of law restricting directors of a company from having any interest in contracts with the company.

The Table A regulations set out in the First Schedule to the Act contain very liberal rules permitting directors to enter into contracts with the corporation.[70] Recall that the Table A regulations function as the regulations of any Nova Scotia company (limited by shares) that has not adopted articles of association that exclude or modify the Table A provisions.[71]

CORPORATE OPPORTUNITIES

Framing the Issue

Business executives are rarely chosen for their posts because of their monastic commitment to a life of self-denial. So when these men and women show up for work each day, we should not be surprised to learn that they do not necessarily check their self-interest at the door. The very ambition and business savvy that make such people an asset to their employer can also, if unchecked, make them a liability.

Consider this simple example. Suppose that XYZ Corp. is a corporation engaged in the widget consulting business. XYZ Corp.'s chief executive officer, Mia, is not only a senior administrator, but is also a highly skilled consultant in her own right. Mia is approached by a potential client. The client is about to undertake a sizable and lucrative project, one for which the client will require the attention and expertise of a single widget

---

66   *Business Corporations Act* (NB), s. 77(9).

67   Ibid., s. 77(10).

68   See supra footnote 11.

69   *Companies Act* (NS), s. 99(4).

70   Ibid., First Schedule, Table A, reg. 115.

71   Ibid., s. 21.

consultant. The project could, of course, be undertaken by XYZ Corp., and the day-to-day work simply assigned to one of XYZ's many staff consultants. But Mia reckons that she personally could perform the consulting work, and knows that she would be paid handsomely for it. Should Mia be permitted to take this contract for herself? Or, if she does so, will she be required to account to XYZ Corp. as the contract ought, in some sense, to have come to XYZ Corp. in the first place?

Instances in which directors and, in some cases, top managers of corporations have appropriated business or investment opportunities that might have gone to the corporations they serve have come to be known as "corporate opportunity" cases. The law, not surprisingly, has taken a fairly harsh line with directors and officers who have wrongfully seized corporate opportunities, but has not always developed precise guidelines with respect to cases lying within the greyer areas.

One of the most famous of the corporate opportunities cases is *Regal (Hastings) Ltd. v. Gulliver*.[72] *Regal* involved a corporation that owned and operated a movie theatre. The corporation wished to acquire a long-term lease on two additional theatres. To that end, it incorporated a new corporation—Amalgamated—to acquire these leases. Regal, the parent company, invested £2,000 in shares of Amalgamated, but was not able to put more money than that into the new company.

The landlord of the two theatres was understandably nervous about dealing with such a thinly capitalized company as Amalgamated, and sought comfort that Amalgamated would be able to make its regular lease payments. To this end, the landlord demanded that the directors of Regal personally guarantee the lease payments, until such time as Amalgamated had paid-up capital of at least £5,000. One of the Regal directors refused to provide a personal guarantee. So, to satisfy the landlord's requirements, each of the five Regal directors subscribed for £500 of Amalgamated shares.[73] Regal's solicitor agreed to subscribe for an additional £500 of shares, bringing Amalgamated's paid-up capital (including Regal's own original £2,000 investment) up to the required minimum of £5,000, thus obviating the need for the directors to provide personal guarantees.

The shares of Regal and of Amalgamated were subsequently sold to the same purchaser. The Amalgamated shareholders each earned a considerable profit on the sale of £2 16s. 1d. per share (roughly £2.81 using post-1971 decimal notation).[74] The new owners of the corporation then caused the company to launch a lawsuit against its former directors (and their solicitor). The suit was brought to recover the profit these individuals had made on their sale of the Amalgamated shares.

The essence of the claim was this. The directors had taken for themselves an investment or an asset that properly belonged to the very corporation (Regal) that they were supposed to serve. The assets in question were, of course, the 3,000 shares in Amalgamated

---

72   [1942] 1 All ER 378 (HL).

73   In fact, one of the directors, instead of subscribing personally, was able to place the shares with three third parties—a friend of his, and two private corporations in which he held some shares, but not, evidently, a controlling interest.

74   Prior to the decimalization of the English money system in 1971, there were 20 shillings in a pound, and 12 pence in a shilling. So, expressed in decimal form, the sum received for the shares would have represented a profit of just under £2.81 per share.

that the directors had bought and then sold at a profit. The plaintiff complained that Regal itself should have owned all of these shares, and that these directors should not be entitled to profit from such a seizure of a corporate opportunity.

The House of Lords agreed with the plaintiff, and granted judgment against four of the five directors. They were ordered to pay an amount equal to the entire profit they had received on their sale of the Amalgamated shares. The fifth director was not held liable because, although he had arranged for shares to be purchased by a friend and companies in which he had some interest, he had not, himself, profited from the sale. The solicitor who had purchased shares, similarly, escaped personal liability. He was found to have acted solely at the behest of his client.

It is important to recognize that the House of Lords concluded that the directors must repay the amount of the profits they had earned on the sale of the shares, despite an express finding that the directors had acted honestly and in good faith throughout. The directors' liability, in other words, was in no way intended to punish morally wrongful conduct; rather, it was the result of a rather strict principle drawn by analogy to the law governing trustees, and in particular the rule articulated in the old trust case, *Keech v. Sandford*.[75] Lord Russell put the matter this way:

> I am of opinion that the directors standing in a fiduciary relationship to Regal in regard to the exercise of their powers as directors, and having obtained these shares by reason and only by reason of the fact that they were directors of Regal and in the course of the execution of that office, are accountable for the profits which they have made out of them.[76]

There are a number of curious and apparent injustices that arise from the specific facts of *Regal*.[77] But the general principle that appears from the case is rigid and uncompromising. When directors pursue a business opportunity that has come to them in their capacity as directors, their personal interests and their directorial duties are in potential conflict. They are bound to restore to the company any profits they have realized from pursuing this opportunity.

The measure of recovery is based on the amount of profits the directors have realized. That is, it is not necessary for the corporation to prove the amount of any "loss" it may

---

75   (1726), Scl. Cas. Ch. 61.

76   *Regal (Hastings) Ltd. v. Gulliver*, supra footnote 72, at 389.

77   Davies notes three particular practical problems with this outcome: (1) The effect of the judgment is an unbargained for reduction in the purchase price for the Regal/Amalgamated shares. If anyone had suffered a loss as a result of the Regal directors' actions, it was surely the *former* shareholders of Regal (Hastings) Ltd., not the new shareholders; however, it was the new shareholders who would benefit from the order that the directors pay moneys to Regal (Hastings) Ltd. (2) The only reason the directors had invested in the Amalgamated shares in the first place was that one director—Gulliver—had refused to provide the personal guarantee of the lease that the other directors had, apparently, been prepared to offer as a condition for obtaining the two valuable theatre leases. But that same director, Gulliver, was the only one of the five directors who was not required to repay amounts to the corporation (because the court had accepted his evidence that the purchasers he had procured for the shares were not merely his nominees but were genuine third parties). (3) The solicitor, Garton, was not required to disgorge the profits he had made, though he had, evidently, advised (one might say ill-advised) the other directors on the legalities of these transactions. See Davies, supra footnote 7, at 417-18.

have suffered. Indeed, for all practical purposes, the corporation may have suffered no loss at all. In fact, even if the corporation itself may not have been able to secure that profit for itself, this still is no answer to the claim, just as it was no answer to the claim made against the trustee in *Keech v. Sandford*.

Much more could be said about *Regal*. Indeed, much more has been said. But for the purposes of this chapter, what is of most interest is the question of just how broad this corporate opportunity principle actually is. Certainly, it cannot be the case that from the moment a person becomes a director or top manager of a corporation, any business or investment opportunity that comes his or her way—no matter how unrelated to the corporation—must either be passed along to the corporation or ignored altogether. There must, in other words, be some basis on which a particular opportunity may be meaning-fully said to have been a *corporate* opportunity. That aspect of the doctrine was further explored and tested in two Supreme Court of Canada cases discussed below.

Another intriguing aspect of the *Regal* decision was the suggestion of how the direc-tors might have protected themselves from legal attack. It is Lord Russell who makes this somewhat surprising comment:

> They could, had they wished, have protected themselves by a resolution (either antecedent or subsequent) of the Regal shareholders in general meeting. In default of such approval, the liability to account must remain.[78]

This statement is curious because it implies that directors (who may also be shareholders) could effectively approve—as shareholders—of their own directorial wrongdoing. In fact, on the particular facts of *Regal*, the directors did, indeed, also have voting control over the corporation at the time of the impugned transaction. This was a fact, as Professor Sealy notes, that was stated in the lower courts' judgments, and would therefore have been known to Lord Russell.[79] Should such wildly different legal consequences ensue simply because the directors failed to undertake the ritual of voting, as shareholders, to approve their purchase (as directors) of the Amalgamated shares?

On this point, commentators often contrast *Regal* with the earlier case of *Cook v. Deeks*.[80] There, the impugned directors did use their controlling votes as shareholders to ratify the actions they had taken, as directors, to seize a corporate opportunity. The court rejected the efficacy of this approval, however, saying, in effect, that directors cannot make gifts of the company's property to themselves. Davies, noting the discrepancy between *Regal* and *Cook* on this issue of shareholder approval, concedes that it is difficult to reconcile these cases.[81] He nevertheless attempts an explanation that seeks to distinguish between misappropriation of property (as in *Cook*), and merely making an incidental profit (as in *Regal*). The problem with this distinction, however, is that it appears to beg the question: why were the shares of Amalgamated that were acquired by the directors in *Regal* any less the property of the corporation than the contract pursued by the directors in *Cook*?

---

78   *Regal*, supra footnote 72.

79   Sealy, supra footnote 2, at 286.

80   [1916] 1 AC 554 (PC).

81   Davies, supra footnote 7, at 439.

The Supreme Court of Canada has dealt with the corporate opportunity issue in four cases: *Midcon Oil & Gas Ltd. v. New British Dominion Oil Co. Ltd. et al.*,[82] *Zwicker v. Stanbury*,[83] *Peso Silver Mines Ltd. v. Cropper*,[84] and *Canadian Aero Services Ltd. v. O'Malley*,[85] and has commented on the animating principle underlying these cases most recently in a fifth case, *Peoples Department Stores Inc. v. Wise*.[86]

Of these, *Peso Silver Mines* might be regarded as a case that defines the outermost boundary of permissible behaviour in the corporate opportunities context.[87] It has never seriously been contended that a director of a corporation is totally forbidden from pursuing any business opportunities in his personal capacity that might come his way while he continues to hold a seat on a corporate board. Only those opportunities that may be said to rightly belong to the corporation are so restricted. But at what point does a corporate opportunity cease to belong to the corporation and so become "fair game" for the individual directors?

In *Peso*, a corporation ("Peso") in the business of promoting mining ventures had rejected an offer to purchase certain mining claims. One of the Peso directors then formed a new company and, through this new company, purchased the claims the Peso board had previously rejected.

Peso underwent a change of control. The new owners sued the director. The Supreme Court found that the defendant director was not liable. How did this case differ from *Regal*, a decision that had previously been followed by the Supreme Court? Among other things, significance was attached to the fact that mining claims were regularly offered to the board of Peso—three to four a week, in fact. It was also found, and evidently considered important, that, at the time the claims in dispute were offered to Peso, Peso was labouring under financial strain. In other words, it may not have had the financial means with which to pursue the opportunity in any event. Furthermore, it was empha-sized that the mining properties in question were of a highly speculative nature. The speculative nature of the opportunity seems an especially important consideration when linked to the company's precarious financial position because it suggests that the com-pany may have been unlikely to raise the funds necessary to acquire the disputed claims. Obtaining additional financing to purchase a speculative mining claim is, after all, a rather different proposition from seeking financing to pursue, say, a lease of cinemas. While it is certainly possible that cinema operations may not perform as well as expected, it is rather less likely that they will prove in the end to be worth nothing at all. The same cannot be said about speculative mining claims. Another possible consideration, although not one mentioned by the court, is that the riskiness of the asset might have made it quite

---

82   [1958] SCR 314.

83   [1953] 2 SCR 438.

84   [1966] SCR 673.

85   [1974] SCR 592.

86   2004 SCC 68.

87   There are many, in fact, who go further and suggest that *Peso Silver Mines* may not have been rightly decided at all; but when the Supreme Court of Canada had the opportunity to consider the issue again in *Canaero* it cast no doubt on the propriety of the principle articulated in *Peso Silver Mines*.

an unsuitable investment for one investor (the corporation) even though an attractive investment for another (the director).

The Supreme Court also noted that the suggestion to start another company to pursue the claim was made by the defendant director only after "the matter had passed out of [his] mind."[88] While it is, of course, easy enough to second-guess this finding of fact, it is crucial to recognize that the legal principles articulated in the case were, nevertheless, based on that factual finding.

The court, in other words, concluded that, by the time the director took up the business opportunity for himself, whatever interest in it that the corporation might previously have possessed had been extinguished. Accordingly, Cartwright J, for a unanimous court concluded:

> On the facts of the case at bar I find it impossible to say that the respondent obtained the interests he holds in Cross Bow and Mayo by reason of the fact that he was a director of the appellant and in the course of the execution of that office.[89]

The Supreme Court did not quarrel with the House of Lords' decision in *Regal*. In fact, they purported to find some support for their judgment in *Regal*. In the *Regal* case, Lord Russell had referred to a *reductio ad absurdum* argument that had been raised by Lord Greene in the Court of Appeal:

> One final observation I desire to make. In his judgment Lord Greene MR, stated that a decision adverse to the directors in the present case involved the proposition that, if directors *bona fide* decide not to invest their company's funds in some proposed investment, a director who thereafter embarks his own money therein is accountable for any profits which he may derive therefrom. As to this, I can only say that to my mind the facts of this hypothetical case bear but little resemblance to the story with which we have had to deal.[90]

Cartwright J, alluding to Lord Greene's comments, remarked in *Peso*:

> The facts of the case at bar appear to me in all material respects identical with those in the hypothetical case stated by Lord Greene and I share the view which he expressed that in such circumstances the director is under no liability.[91]

The Supreme Court's most recent specific consideration of the issue of corporate opportunities is found in the case of *Canadian Aero Services Ltd. v. O'Malley* ("*Canaero*"). In *Canaero*, two senior officers of the plaintiff corporation (Canaero) had been involved in attempting to secure for the corporation a contract to map Guyana. They subsequently resigned from Canaero, and incorporated a new company of their own ("Terra"). Terra then submitted its own proposal to survey Guyana, and it was this proposal (not Canaero's) that was accepted.

---

88   *Peso Silver Mines Ltd. v. Cropper*, supra footnote 84, at 677.

89   Ibid., at. 682.

90   *Regal*, supra footnote 72, at 391.

91   *Peso*, supra footnote 84, at 683.

The *Canaero* case provides useful analysis on and insight into a number of issues, including:

- the fiduciary duties of a corporation's senior officers, as well as its directors;
- the effect of resignation on a corporate officer's fiduciary duties;
- the considerations relevant to assessing when a contract or transaction pursued by a corporation's directors or officers may be properly considered an opportunity in which the corporation has a prior and continuing interest;
- the relevance in the corporate opportunities context of the fact that the corporation may not, in fact, have been able to avail itself of the opportunity seized by its officers or directors; and
- the general importance of fiduciary duties in the corporate governance equation.

There was a factual dispute over whether the defendants had ever actually been appointed as directors of Canaero. But Laskin J (as he then was)[92] took the view that whether or not they were directors was irrelevant. They were certainly "top management" as opposed to mere employees of the corporation and thus subject to fiduciary duties comparable to those of corporate directors. Those duties, he argued, meant, at the very least, that

> a director or a senior officer like O'Malley or Zarzycki is precluded from obtaining for himself, either secretly or without the approval of the company (which would have to be properly manifested upon full disclosure of the facts), any property or business advantage either belonging to the company or for which it has been negotiating; and especially is this so where the director or officer is a participant in the negotiations on behalf of the company.
>
> An examination of the case law in this Court and in the Courts of other like jurisdictions on the fiduciary duties of directors and senior officers shows the pervasiveness of a strict ethic in this area of the law. In my opinion, this ethic disqualifies a director or senior officer from usurping for himself or diverting to another person or company with whom or with which he is associated a maturing business opportunity which his company is actively pursuing; he is also precluded from so acting even after his resignation where the resignation may fairly be said to have been prompted or influenced by a wish to acquire for himself the opportunity sought by the company, or where it was his position with the company rather than a fresh initiative that led him to the opportunity which he later acquired.[93]

Of course, when once it is determined that senior officers, as well as directors, may be sued for seizing a corporate opportunity, it becomes important to establish precisely which senior officers are subject to such liability. Although Laskin J characterized the two defendants in *Canaero* as "top management," a rather different picture emerges from the Court of Appeal's judgment. There it was noted that decision making for the Canadian corporation in question had, essentially, been taken over by its ultimate American parent,

---

92   Though *Canaero* was reported in 1974, the decision was rendered by the Supreme Court of Canada in June 1973. Bora Laskin was appointed Chief Justice in December of that year. See the Supreme Court of Canada Web site, "Judges of the Court—Current and Former Chief Justices," online at http://www.scc-csc.gc.ca/AboutCourt/judges/curformchief/index_e.asp.

93   *Canaero*, supra footnote 85, at 606-7.

Lytton Industries, Inc., leaving the two defendants with little authority typical of the offices they ostensibly held—offices, in fact, to which they had not been formally appointed by either the directors or the shareholders. Indeed, the Court of Appeal boldly concluded:

> In these circumstances, in so far as the plaintiff company is concerned I am of the opinion that it is not open to it to say that either of these defendants were in fact either directors or president and vice-president, respectively, of the company.[94]

The *Canaero* court was also obliged to deal with the *Peso* precedent, which seemed to signal a more relaxed judicial attitude toward the pursuit by directors of business opportunities that had once been within the ambit of the corporation. Laskin J suggested, however, at least two distinctions that separated the *Canaero* facts from the situation in *Peso*. First, in *Peso*, whatever equitable interest the corporation might have had in the mining interest under dispute had ceased when the board of directors rejected the opportunity. The Peso board, after all, as the court had expressly found, had been acting in good faith when it made this decision.

Second, *Peso* involved a corporation that regularly considered many opportunities of the sort in question. Furthermore, the particular mining claim at issue in *Peso* "could not be said to be essential to the success of the company."[95]

Canaero offers a useful delineation of some of the key factors to be considered in determining whether directors or officers ought to be found liable for seizing a corporate opportunity, although Laskin J did go to some pains to emphasize how fact specific such cases as these were, and how wrong it would be to interpret the Supreme Court's decision as a kind of code or statute regulating the matter. Nevertheless, it is inevitable that when the Supreme Court has spoken on an issue, lawyers and commentators are keen to attempt to formalize the result and so the non-exhaustive list of considerations referred to by Laskin J are often recited as though they were meant to comprise a liability checklist. Laskin J's remarks on these considerations were prefaced with the important qualification that

> [t]he general standards of loyalty, good faith and avoidance of a conflict of duty and self-interest to which the conduct of a director or senior officer must conform, must be tested in each case by many factors which it would be reckless to attempt to enumerate exhaustively.[96]

It was in this context, then, that Laskin J spoke of some relevant considerations:

> Among them are the factor of position or office held, the nature of the corporate opportunity, its ripeness, its specificness and the director's or managerial officer's relation to it, the amount of knowledge possessed, the circumstances in which it was obtained and whether it was special or, indeed, even private, the factor of time in the continuation of fiduciary duty where the alleged breach occurs after termination of the relationship with the company, and the circumstances under which the relationship was terminated, that is whether by retirement or resignation or discharge.[97]

---

94   *Canadian Aero Services Ltd. v. O'Malley*, [1972] 1 OR 592 (CA).

95   *Canaero*, supra footnote 85, at 618.

96   Ibid., at 620.

97   Ibid.

Canaero also raises an issue as to the legal relevance of the corporation's own ability or likelihood to obtain the improperly seized opportunity. What is not immediately apparent from the Supreme Court's judgment, but is discussed in some detail in the lower court's judgment, is that Canaero was a subsidiary of Aero Service Corporation, an American company that, since 1961, was itself a subsidiary of Lytton Industries, Inc. The significance of this is that the mapping contract under dispute was to be financed by the Canadian government, pursuant to a program, to which the Court of Appeal referred, by which such contracts would be awarded only to Canadian-owned firms unless foreign-owned firms were better qualified. Although this fact is not dealt with in any detailed way by the Supreme Court of Canada, is it alluded to in at least two places in Laskin J's judgment. These passages cast doubt, as a factual matter, on the conclusion that Canaero would never have been able to obtain the contract for itself.[98] What is perhaps more telling, though, is an earlier statement to the effect that the former director's and officer's duties would not necessarily be different even if their former employer had been unable to avail itself of the contract in question:

> [T]here may be situations where a profit must be disgorged, although not gained at the expense of the company, on the ground that a director must not be allowed to use his position as such to make a profit even if it was not open to the company, as for example, by reason of legal disability, to participate in the transaction.[99]

Canaero thus teaches that a corporation's senior officers (and not merely its directors) are constrained from seizing corporate opportunities; that these restrictions may apply even to opportunities that are realized after an officer or director has resigned his or her position, at least "where the resignation may fairly be said to be prompted or influenced by a wish to acquire for himself the opportunity sought by the company, or where it was his position with the company rather than a fresh initiative which led him to the opportunity which he later acquired;"[100] that the contract actually obtained by the former officer or director need not be precisely identical to the contract that had originally been pursued by the corporation; and that the basis for the director's or officer's liability is to be the gain he or she has reaped from the seized opportunity, not any proven loss suffered by the corporation.

Finally, in addition to the specific discussion of factors relevant to corporate opportunity cases, Laskin J's judgment in *Canaero* also articulates a more general proposition concerning the importance of fiduciary duties in the corporate governance equation. This statement seems especially poignant in the current post-*Enron* environment:

---

98   Ibid. Laskin J states at 617: "There was, however, no certain knowledge at the time O'Malley and Zarzycki resigned that the Guyana project was beyond Canaero's grasp. Canaero had not abandoned its hope of capturing it, even if Wells was of opinion, expressed during his luncheon with O'Malley and Zarzycki on August 6, 1966, that it would not get a foreign aid contract from the Canadian Government." Then again, at 619, His Lordship notes: "Since Canaero had been invited to make a proposal on the Guyana project, there is no basis for contending that it could not, in any event, have obtained the contract or that there was any unwillingness to deal with it."

99   Ibid., at 609.

100 Ibid., at 607.

Strict application against directors and senior management officials is simply recognition of the degree of control which their positions give them in corporate operations, a control which rises above day to day accountability to owning shareholders and which comes under some scrutiny only at annual general or at special meetings. It is a necessary supplement, in the public interest, of statutory regulation and accountability which themselves are, at one and the same time, an acknowledgment of the importance of the corporation in the life of the community and of the need to compel obedience by it and by its promoters, directors and managers to norms of exemplary behaviour.[101]

Ultimately, of course, the law of "corporate opportunities" is simply a well-recognized example of the strictness with which the courts treat the fiduciary obligations imposed on corporate directors, a fact recently reiterated by the Supreme Court of Canada in *Peoples Department Stores Inc. v. Wise*.[102] In that same case, however, the Supreme Court also pointed out that "it is not required that directors in all cases avoid personal gain as a direct or indirect result of their honest and good faith supervision or management of the corporation. In many cases the interests of directors and officers will innocently and genuinely coincide with those of the corporation."[103] The key to determining when directors and officers will or will not be liable, therefore, lies, as discussed in chapter 10, in a careful scrutiny of their actions, "to determine whether [they] have acted honestly and in good faith with a view to the best interests of the corporation."[104]

PERSONAL LIABILITY OF DIRECTORS AND OFFICERS TO THIRD PARTIES

Statutory Liabilities

Corporate directors are subject to personal liability under a number of statutory provisions. Some of those provisions are found within corporate legislation itself. For example, directors of a CBCA corporation may be personally liable to corporate employees for debts equal to up to six months' wages.[105] They may also be personally liable if they vote for or consent to authorize various payments such as dividends or share repurchases in contravention of the statutory rules respecting such payments.[106]

But directors are also subject to potential personal liability under many other statutes as well. Directors' liability under s. 227.1 of the *Income Tax Act* for failure to withhold and remit employee source deductions probably accounts for the largest number of decided cases in this area. But as Ron Daniels noted some years ago, citing a practitioner's memorandum, "in Ontario alone more than 100 different federal and provincial

---

101 Ibid., at 610.

102 Supra footnote 86, at para 38.

103 Ibid., at para. 39.

104 Ibid., at para. 39.

105 CBCA, s. 119.

106 CBCA, s. 118(2).

statutes prescribe some type of directors' liability."[107] Indeed, legislators seem quite prepared to seek to regulate corporate conduct through the threat of personal sanctions against corporate directors, a legislative proclivity that is not likely to abate in the aftermath of the scandals at Enron, WorldCom, etc.

Many commentators have argued that whenever statutes impose personal liability on directors, they should provide directors with a due diligence defence.[108] It was considerations of this sort that led to the 2001 amendments of the directors' defences under the CBCA that were discussed in chapter 10.

Tort Liability

When a corporate officer or director, acting within the scope of his or her corporate duties, commits a tort—a tort for which the corporation itself might be found liable[109]— is that officer or director also personally liable? There have been a series of rather interesting cases on this topic in Canada[110] and in the United Kingdom.[111] But, as Campbell and Armour have noted, "company law has nothing useful to say in this area."[112] They are surely correct. The imposition of liability, whether for the commission of crimes or the commission of torts, must be based on an assessment of the appropriate goals of criminal and tort law, respectively, rather than on an assessment of corporate law. Thus, only the very briefest of comments will be offered here.

First, it may be useful to recall the basis on which corporations themselves are liable in tort. As discussed in chapter 8, corporations may be liable vicariously for the torts of their agents or employees, and they may be liable directly (or "personally") for torts committed by certain corporate actors who may be regarded as the "directing mind and will" of the corporation, on the basis of identification theory.

---

107 Ronald J. Daniels, "Must Boards Go Overboard? An Economic Analysis of the Effects of Burgeoning Statutory Liability on the Role of Directors in Corporate Governance," in J.S. Ziegel, ed., *Current Developments in International and Comparative Insolvency Law* (Oxford: Clarendon Press, 1994), at 548.

108 See, e.g., The Toronto Stock Exchange, Committee on Corporate Governance in Canada, *Where Were the Directors?* December 1994, at 36, para. 5.62; Industry Canada, *Canada Business Corporations Act*, Discussion Paper, *Directors' Liability* (November 1995), at 24-25; and Margaret Smith, *Directors Liability*, Parliament Research Branch Paper PRB 99-44E (February 29, 2000).

109 The basis on which corporations themselves may be found liable in tort is discussed in chapter 8.

110 See., e.g., *ADGA Systems International Ltd. v. Valcom Ltd.* (1999), 43 OR (3d) 101 (CA), leave to appeal to SCC refused (2000), 51 OR (3d) xvii; *NBD Bank, Canada v. Dofasco Inc.* (1999), 46 OR (3d) 514 (CA), leave to appeal to SCC refused [2000] 1 SCR x; *Meditrust Healthcare Inc. v. Shoppers Drug Mart*, [1999] OJ no. 3243 (QL) (CA); *Immocreek Corp. v. Pretiosa Enterprises Ltd.* (2000), 186 DLR (4th) 36 (Ont. CA); *Lana International Ltd. v. Menasco Aerospace Ltd.* (2000), 185 DLR (4th) 255 (Ont. CA); *Blacklaws v. Morrow* (2000), 84 Alta. LR (3d) 270 (CA); *Kapuscinski v. Aristos Capital Corp.*, [2000] OJ no. 3493 (QL) (CA); *Anger v. Berkshire Investment Group Inc.*, [2001] OJ no. 379 (QL) (CA); *Unisys Canada Inc. v. York Three Associates Inc.* (2001), 44 RPR (3d) 138 (Ont. CA); and *Glenayre Manufacturing Ltd. v. Pilot Pacific Properties Inc.*, 2003 BCSC 303.

111 See, especially, *Williams v. Natural Life Health Foods Ltd.*, [1998] 1 WLR 830 (HL); and *Standard Chartered Bank v. Pakistan National Shipping Corp. (Nos. 2 and 4)*, [2003] 1 AC 959 (HL).

112 Neil Campbell and John Armour, "Demystifying the Civil Liability of Corporate Agents" (2003), 62 *Cambridge Law Journal* 290, at 291.

Now, the essence of vicarious liability is that the employer (or principal) is responsible for the wrong committed by the employee (or agent). Thus, *ex hypothesi*, the employee or agent has committed an actionable wrong himself or herself. The employer in such a case is merely an additional defendant, as it were, not a substitute defendant.

But is the situation different when the corporation is said to have primary or personal liability? In such a case, the corporate actor's actions are said to be the actions of the corporation itself. This theory of liability, therefore, does not necessarily require that the actor in his or her individual capacity has committed a wrong (for which the corporation must also answer). Rather, it is the corporation itself that has committed the wrong. Note, however, that although the courts have certainly expanded the range of corporate employees who might be considered a corporate "directing mind and will," the concept has not been expanded so far as to make it irrelevant. In other words, only the actions of relatively senior employees will expose the corporation to such "personal" (rather than merely vicarious) liability. Thus, simplistic sequential reasoning might lead us to the uncomfortable conclusion that the most junior employees of a corporation can be personally liable for actions they take in the course of carrying out their duties as employees, but the most senior officers and directors of the corporation may not be.[113]

This logic has not been uniformly followed by the courts, however. Identification theory perhaps had its roots in civil cases, but it is fair to say that it came into full bloom in the criminal sphere; and, as a criminal law doctrine, it is clear that identification theory by no means implied that the individual "directing mind and will" was somehow exonerated from personal accountability merely because, through his or her actions, the corporation for which he or she was working could also be found guilty of an offence.[114]

So the question remains, if "identification doctrine"—as a basis for certain tortious liability—was based on the concept that had developed under criminal law, and if the criminal law doctrine had *not* implied that the individual actor was somehow freed from liability if he or she was acting as a directing mind or will, how then did the notion arise that the individual directing mind and will might *not* be liable for a tort in instances where he or she was acting within the scope of his or her corporate duties and, indeed, pursuing the interests of the corporation itself?

Could it be that the prospect of potential liability of corporate directors, particularly in the case of small, private corporations (and most especially sole-shareholder corporations), was regarded as such a threat to the usefulness of the corporate form for such smaller ventures that commentators eagerly strained early authorities to find support for

---

113 This paradox has not gone unnoticed by commentators. See, e.g., Colin Feasby, "Corporate Agents' Liability in Tort: A Comment on *ADGA Systems International Ltd. v. Valcom Ltd.*" (1999), 32 *Canadian Business Law Journal* 291, at 291.

114 Note, for example, the following comments of Estey J from *Canadian Dredge & Dock Company v. R*, [1985] 1 SCR 662, at para. 21:

> In order to trigger its operation and through it corporate criminal liability for the actions of the employee (*who must generally be liable himself*), the actor-employee who physically committed the offence must be the "*ego*," the "centre" of the corporate personality, the "vital organ" of the body corporate, the "*alter ego*" of the employer corporation or its "directing mind." [Emphasis in parenthetical phrase added.]

And again at 685, "Generally the directing mind is also guilty of the criminal offence in question."

the proposition that, where the liability of a corporation is personal and not vicarious, the individual "directing mind and will" is not himself or herself personally liable?[115]

It is interesting to observe that Wegenast was of the view, writing in 1931, that there was an important difference between Quebec law and the law of the common law provinces on this issue. He wrote:

> Where a company, through its directors, commits a fraud or other wrong upon a third party, the directors as well as the company, are liable to the third party. This is on the general principle that in cases of tort if the principal is liable the agent is liable also. And, in particular, "all persons concerned in the commission of a fraud are to be treated as principals."
>
> In Quebec the rule is different, and it has been laid down that the directors of a company are not, as a general rule, responsible for its torts; and that to render them so there must have been some individual fault on their part personal to themselves; and that in the absence of such gross fault or fraud there is no *lien de droit* between the directors and non-shareholders; and that the directors occupy merely the position of agents of a disclosed principal, *viz.* the company.[116]

It is unfortunate that Wegenast specifically included in his language reference to the tort of fraud, because it is not clear that Canadian common law courts have been prepared to relieve directors or officers of personal liability when their actions are fraudulent. But in the case of other corporate torts, it appears that the Canadian common law position, in Ontario at any rate, has moved rather closer to what Wegenast described as the law of Quebec at the time that he wrote.

The story of the imposition of personal liability in some way begins with a case that created an express *exception* to such liability. From the 1920 English case of *Said v. Butt*[117] emerged the proposition that, where a corporation was liable for breach of contract, the corporate director that caused the corporation to dishonour the contract in question could not be held personally liable for the tort of inducing breach of contract, provided that he or she was acting in the best interests of the company. Professor Welling has noted, rightly enough, that the famous principle today associated with *Said v. Butt* is based on language in the case that was undoubtedly *obiter dicta*.[118] But the sense of the principle has been so frequently endorsed and reaffirmed by Canadian courts, that a wholesale reversal of the so-called *Said v. Butt* exception seems quite out of the question. And while this principle might, perhaps, have been expanded to insulate directors and officers more generally from personal liability, it appears that, in Ontario at any rate, the *Said v. Butt* exception was fairly narrowly confined to the tort of inducing breach of contract.

In a series of Ontario cases in the late 1990s,[119] the Ontario Court of Appeal indicated that the directing minds of a corporation could *not* be held liable for the actions of the

---

115   Feasby, supra footnote 113, at 306-7, for example, argues that an unconstrained principle of personal liability would undermine the purposes of incorporation in the case of sole-shareholder companies.

116   F.W. Wegenast, *The Law of Canadian Companies* (Toronto: Carswell, 1979), at 393.

117   [1920] 3 KB 497.

118   Bruce Welling, "Individual Liability for Corporate Acts: The Defence of Hobson's Choice" (2000), 12 *Supreme Court Law Review* 55, at 59.

119   See especially, *Normart Management Ltd. v. West Hill Redevelopment Co.* (1998), 37 OR (3d) 97 (CA) and *ScotiaMcLeod Inc. v. Peoples Jewellers Ltd.* (1995), 26 OR (3d) 481 (CA).

corporation unless their actions were "themselves tortious or exhibit a separate identity or interest from that of the company."[120] That proposition, in the view of many, implied that a directing mind and will was generally not exposed to personal liability while acting within the scope of his or her responsibilities and in the best interests of the corporation.

However, in the 1999 decision of *ADGA Systems International Ltd. v. Valcom Ltd.*,[121] the Court of Appeal dismissed such suggestions. Carthy JA there noted that a corporate officer or director might indeed be found personally liable for tortious conduct,

> even though that conduct was directed in a *bona fide* manner to the best interests of the company, always subject to the *Said v. Butt* exception.[122]

More recently, Finlayson JA has attempted to articulate the current position of the law in Ontario on this point in this way:

> It is well established that the directing minds of a corporation cannot be held civilly liable for the actions of the corporations they control and direct, unless it can be shown that their actions are themselves tortious or exhibit a separate identity or interest from that of the corporation so as to make the acts or conduct complained of those of the directing minds: see *Normart Management Ltd. v. West Hill Redevelopment Co.* ... ; *ScotiaMcLeod Inc. v. Peoples Jewellers Ltd.* ... Therefore, a claim in tort may proceed against the directing minds of corporations for acts performed in the course of their duties. This court has recently confirmed that in all events, directors, officers and employees of corporations are responsible for their tortious conduct, even though that conduct was directed in a bona fide manner to the best interests of the company, provided that the evidence justifies an allegation of a personal tort: see *ADGA Systems International Ltd. v. Valcom Ltd.*[123]

Directors and officers can, therefore, be held liable in tort to third parties, even in cases where they have acted bona fide in the best interests of the corporation. But such liability, not surprisingly, will flow only from their own tortious conduct and not, for example, merely from the fact that they occupied their corporate offices at the time a tort was committed. Needless to say, a statement such as this does not go very far in defining in any practical way the ambit of personal liability of directors and officers to third parties. In addition to the formalistic considerations of the corporation as a "separate legal entity" and the supposed implications of this doctrine in the context of identification theory, as discussed above, some combination of the following principles and practical considerations appear to have influenced judicial considerations of the directors' and officers' liability question. First, directors and officers should not be held vicariously liable for the corporation's torts. Second, plaintiffs may well, for tactical reasons, name directors personally as defendants, even in circumstances when the directors so named had no part to play whatsoever in the commission of the tort; courts wish to discourage such tactics.

At one time it was thought that "the rule from the law of agency that an agent is personally liable for his own tortious acts, even if the company is also vicariously liable,

---

120 *ScotiaMcLeod*, ibid., at 491.

121 Supra footnote 110.

122 Ibid., at 107.

123 *Unisys Canada Inc. v. York Three Associates Inc.*, supra footnote 110.

cannot be simply applied to the case of the director."[124] That statement—quoted with approval by an Ontario court—was taken from the 25th edition of Palmer's *Company Law.*[125] But the current version of that same eminent authority reads rather differently with respect to this point.[126] And little wonder. Two recent House of Lords decisions rendered since the publication of Palmer's 25th edition have offered further judicial insights. In particular, they have sought to address the role of assumption of personal responsibility in the context of imposition of directors' and officers' personal liability in certain circumstances. But it now appears clear that the scope of this analysis is narrow and, critically, properly to be understood within the ambit of tort principles, not corporate law principles. As Lord Hoffman put it in the second of those two cases, *Standard Chartered Bank,*[127] referring to the earlier House of Lords decision in *Williams,*[128] that case "had nothing to do with company law. It was an application of the law of principal and agent to the requirement of assumption of responsibility under the *Hedley Byrne* principle."[129]

Much more could be, and has been, written about this topic. And, for more considered analysis and discussion, the reader is invited to consult more specialized sources.[130]

---

124 From *Palmer's Company Law*, 25th ed. (London: Sweet and Maxwell, 1992), at 8153. Quoted by Farley J in *Montreal Trust Co. v. ScotiaMcLeod Inc.* (1994), 15 BLR (2d) 160, at 190 (Ont. Ct. Gen. Div.).

125 Ibid.

126 The current version (looseleaf) suggests that there are now "two competing approaches to the issue of personal liability" of which one (the agency approach rejected in the earlier version of the text) is the "simplest" and, indeed, is "the approach now approved by the House of Lords."

127 Supra footnote 111.

128 Supra footnote 111.

129 Supra footnote 111, at 969.

130 For a discussion of the apparent progression of the Ontario case law, see Christopher C. Nicholls, "Liability of Corporate Officers and Directors to Third Parties" (2001), 35 *Canadian Business Law Journal* 1. For an excellent analysis of these issues, see Robert Flannigan, "The Personal Tort Liability of Directors" (2002), 81 *Canadian Bar Review* 247. See also Campbell and Armour, supra footnote 112; Ian Glick and Orlando Gledhill, "Company Law Review: Attribution of Liability," advice to the Company Law Review, October 2000 (available online at http://www.dti.gov.uk/cld/glick.pdf); and Ross Grantham and Charles Rickett, "Directors' Tortious Liability: Contract, Tort, or Company Law?" (1999), 62 *Modern Law Review* 133. See also La Forest's lengthy dissenting opinion in *London Drugs Ltd. v. Kuehne & Nagel International Ltd.*, [1992] 3 SCR 299.

CHAPTER TWELVE

Financing the Corporation

INTRODUCTION[1]

The business corporation is, perhaps above all, a means of pooling capital from many investors to carry on productive business. Financial pooling lies at the heart of the corporate form, although the law has been willing to permit the "separate entity" metaphor to be carried to its logical conclusion in the case of sole-shareholder companies.[2]

Legal rules concerning a corporation's finances are related to the law that governs the protection of those who buy and sell corporate financial instruments, such as shares, debentures, and other securities. Investor protection, since the early 20th century, has become the subject of a separate branch of law: securities regulation.[3] The boundaries of corporate law and securities regulation are often rather hazy.[4] This chapter, however, will endeavour to focus on the corporate law rules surrounding corporate finance, leaving the reader to seek an introduction to Canadian securities regulation from other sources.[5]

---

1   The subject of corporate finance can be, and indeed has been, the subject of book-length studies, including one by the present author. See, e.g., Christopher C. Nicholls, *Corporate Finance and Canadian Law* (Toronto: Carswell, 2000). The discussion in this chapter offers only a very brief summary of some of the broad principles affecting the financing of the corporation.

2   But see Hansmann and Kraakman's discussion of asset partitioning as a rationale for sole-shareholder business corporations. Henry Hansmann and Reinier Kraakman, "The Essential Role of Organizational Law" (2000), 110 *Yale Law Journal* 387, at 404-10. The authors of this paper refer to a sole-shareholder business corporation as a "corporation sole." This use of the phrase "corporation sole" is unconventional. Traditionally, a corporation sole was said to be "always the holder of a public office" such as the English monarchy. (John Burke, *Jowitt's Dictionary of English Law*, 2nd ed. (London: Sweet & Maxwell, 1977.) Thus, as Professor Sealy has said, "[t]he newly-sanctioned single-member company seems to be an anomalous institution which does not fit the criteria for either of these traditional classifications" (that is, the corporation aggregate or the corporation sole). L.S. Sealy, *Cases and Materials in Company Law*, 7th ed. (London: Butterworths, 2001), at 77.

3   The phrase "securities regulation" was coined by the late Professor Louis Loss. See Louis Loss, *Anecdotes of a Securities Lawyer* (Boston: Little, Brown and Company, 1995), at 51.

4   For an excellent examination of the close relationship between corporate law and securities regulation, see Philip Anisman, "Regulation of Public Corporations: The Boundaries of Corporate and Securities Law," in *The Future of Corporation Law: Issues and Perspectives*, Papers Presented at the Queen's Annual Business Law Symposium 1997 (Toronto: Carswell, 1999), 63.

5   The author will, one hopes, be forgiven for suggesting one book in particular for this edifying purpose: Jeffrey G. MacIntosh and Christopher C. Nicholls, *Securities Law* (Toronto: Irwin, 2002).

Corporations invariably need money to carry on their business operations. Of course, as they sell their goods or are paid for their services, cash will flow into the business. But, often, corporations will need more money than they generate in the ordinary course of their business operations. The need for additional cash does not arise simply because corporations wish to "live beyond their means." More often, this need relates to a timing mismatch: the corporation may have bills that it must pay today, even though payment from its own customers or clients is still some days or weeks away. Or, again, the need for more money may have nothing at all to do with paying ordinary expenses. The corporation may have identified an excellent investment opportunity—a project or perhaps even another whole business that will cost it a great deal of money to acquire, but that will, over time, enable it to save or earn even more money.

Just as many Canadian families need financial help when they buy a home, so when business corporations decide to make major investments, they too may need to raise additional cash. In the broadest sense, corporations that need to raise money over and above amounts generated from their operations have three choices: they may sell or lease some of their corporate assets; they may borrow cash from a bank or other lender; or they may issue shares or some other type of corporate securities.[6]

We will not say much here about the first option, selling corporate assets. Selling assets does not raise many uniquely *corporate* law issues, unless, perhaps, the sale involves the sale of "all or substantially all" of the corporation's property, as discussed further in chapter 14. It is true that asset sales are actually an important aspect of a very sophisticated form of financing—securitization. But, again, the many interesting and challenging legal issues that securitizations raise do not relate primarily to corporate law.[7] The focus here will be instead on corporate borrowing and, more particularly, on some of the corporate law issues surrounding the issue of corporate securities, especially corporate shares.

In an economic sense, deciding how a corporation is to be financed Klein has described as an exercise in negotiating the terms of one or more implicit or explicit contracts with a view to determining how to allocate *risk*, how to allocate *returns* from the business, determining where *control* of the business will lie, and specifying the *duration* of each participant's investment.[8] It is useful to keep this helpful fourfold paradigm in mind when reviewing the various methods by which corporations may finance their businesses.

---

6   There are other methods of financing available to corporations as well, such as factoring and asset securitization. But even these techniques involve some combination of asset sale or lease, borrowing, and sale of securities.

7   For a brief introduction to securitization, see Nicholls, supra footnote 1, at 60ff.

8   See William A. Klein, "The Modern Business Organization: Bargaining Under Constraints" (1982), 91 *Yale Law Journal* 1521.

DEBT AND EQUITY

When a corporation borrows money, the obligation to repay the money is a debt. Raising money by borrowing is referred to as debt financing. When a corporation raises money by offering new shares to purchasers, the shareholders' interest in the corporation is referred to as equity. Raising money in this way is referred to as equity financing.

It is often helpful to introduce the concepts of debt and equity by comparing the differences between them from the perspective of the corporation as well as from the perspective of investors. Some of the major differences are discussed below.

Debt Ranks Ahead of Equity

Perhaps the most fundamental difference between debt and equity is this: when a corporation that has borrowed money is wound up or liquidated, the assets of the corporation are sold. The proceeds of sale go first to satisfy the claims of outstanding creditors. Until all the creditors of the corporation have been repaid every penny they are owed, the corporation's shareholders receive nothing at all. This is true even if the shareholders hold so-called preferred shares, as discussed later in the chapter.

Debt Must Be Repaid

When a corporation borrows money, it is under a legal obligation to repay it. However, when a corporation raises money by selling equity—at least in its humblest form, common or ordinary shares—the money received from investors never needs to be repaid. It becomes part of the corporation's permanent capital.[9]

Interest Payment Deductibility

When a corporation makes interest payments on any money it has borrowed, the amount of those payments may be deducted from the corporation's income calculated for tax purposes. As a result, the corporation will pay less income tax. That means that, for a taxpaying corporation, every dollar distributed to a lender in interest actually costs the corporation something less than a dollar after taxes. By contrast, when a corporation makes a distribution to its shareholders, that distribution—a dividend—is not deductible by the corporation in calculating its income for tax purposes.

Taxation of Interest Payments and Dividend Payments

Interest payments received by debtholders are taxed as ordinary income. Dividend payments, on the other hand, benefit from the *Income Tax Act*'s "dividend tax credit." The

---

9   This statement is subject to two qualifications. Shares can be created with "redemption" or "retraction" features that anticipate that the corporation may, at some future date, return the shareholders' capital and cancel the shares. Common or ordinary shares would not typically have such features, however. Furthermore, as discussed in chapter 14, in certain circumstances, shareholders may be entitled to dissent from certain corporate decisions and seek an appraisal remedy. When a shareholder is entitled to an appraisal remedy, the corporation will be required to purchase his or her shares for fair value.

dividend tax credit attempts to integrate Canadian corporate income tax and Canadian personal income tax by taking account of the fact that, when a shareholder receives a dividend payment, that payment has come from income on which the corporation has already been required to pay tax. Because of the dividend tax credit, $1 received by a taxpayer in the form of a dividend is normally worth more, after tax, than $1 received by the same taxpayer in the form of interest.

"Dilution" of Ownership

Equity in its simplest form (common or ordinary shares) typically entitles the shareholder to voting rights—in particular, the right to vote at annual meetings to elect directors of the corporation. Thus, when a corporation raises money by issuing more shares, it is also issuing more votes. The effect of increasing the number of voting shares may be to undermine the existing shareholders' control over the corporation. There are many ways, however, in which a corporation may raise equity capital without diluting the ownership or control of its existing shareholders. For example, shares may be issued that carry no voting rights except in exceptional circumstances. Or, the controlling shareholders may issue to themselves a separate class of shares that have enhanced voting rights so that they can maintain voting control even though they may not hold an overall majority of the corporation's shares. The only point to remember here is that when a corporation has decided to raise equity, it must consider not only the financial implications of that decision, but also the potential impact that issuing new equity may have on control of the corporation. Concern about dilution of ownership or control is not typically an issue when a corporation is issuing debt—that is, borrowing money. It is rare for debt instruments, such as bonds or debentures, to carry rights to elect the corporation's directors. Indeed, as discussed in chapter 9, in many Canadian jurisdictions, the governing statute requires that only shareholders can elect directors. (There are exceptions to this proposition, however, as discussed in chapter 9.)

"Dilution" of Earnings

When a corporation issues the simplest form of equity (common or ordinary shares) those shares are typically said to represent a residual economic interest in the corporation. Put more simply, whatever earnings a corporation has left after it has provided for the payment of all of its fixed claimants (its creditors, employees, and so on) *notionally* accrues to the shareholders. This does not mean that the corporation is under any obligation to distribute this money to the shareholders. However, as the earnings of a company increase, this increase should be reflected in the value of the company's shares.

Corporations—particularly public corporations—typically calculate and include in their financial statements the amount of their "earnings per share." Thus, a corporation that has earnings of $1 million and has 100,000 common shares outstanding, would report earnings of $10 per share. Obviously, if the earnings of a corporation remain the same, while the number of shares the corporation has issued increases, then "earnings per share" will fall. The corporation's earnings may thus be said to have been "diluted" by the issue of more shares.

The arithmetic that leads to this conclusion is unassailable. The conclusion that issuing more shares will, therefore, dilute earnings in any meaningful way is, however, a bit more suspect. It is only meaningful to say that corporate earnings have been "diluted" if one assumes that the corporation's future earnings would have been precisely the same regardless of whether or not the corporation had chosen to issue more equity. But, if the corporation's future earnings really will remain unchanged, whether additional shares are or are not issued, then one might reasonably ask whatever possessed the corporation to issue more shares in the first place? Put another way, why would a corporation incur the time and considerable expense of selling more of its shares if the use to which the corporation intends to put the additional funds is not expected to have any impact on the corporation's earnings? Of course, it is true that, immediately after issuing new equity, any calculation of earnings per share based on *past* profits will, by definition, be affected. And it is also true that corporations can sometimes be pressured by their lenders into issuing more equity, as a condition for the extension of loan facilities. However, if lender pressure is the corporation's motivation for issuing equity, then balancing the relative advantages and disadvantages of debt and equity would be irrelevant to the financing decision in such a case, because it is equity that the corporation must issue in any event.

Financial Statement Implications

Corporations regularly prepare financial statements that are in standardized form and that are subject to standardized accounting conventions. Typically, directors of a corporation must ensure that financial statements are placed before the shareholders at every annual meeting.[10] The basic financial statements that must typically be prepared by corporations are:

- a balance sheet,
- a statement of retained earnings,
- an income statement, and
- a statement of changes in financial position (that is, a cash flow statement).[11]

In the case of corporations with publicly traded shares, Canadian securities laws impose additional financial reporting requirements, including public reporting requirements.[12] Financial statements are intended to present the corporation's financial position and its income in a form that makes it possible for readers of those statements (shareholders, prospective investors, creditors, banks, and so on) to assess the financial health of the corporation. Standardized financial statements also make it easier to compare the financial results of one corporation with those of others.

The differing ways in which debt and equity must be accounted for on a corporation's financial statements, and the implications of these differences, flow from the legal distinctions between debt and equity canvassed above.

---

10   See, e.g., CBCA, s. 155.

11   See, e.g., *Canada Business Corporations Regulations, 2001*, s. 72(1).

12   See, e.g., National Instrument 51-102, part 4, (2004), 27 OSCB 3439.

One of the ways in which financial analysts and lenders extract meaning from financial statements is through "ratio analysis"—that is, they compare various specific numbers on a corporation's financial statements that are thought to be indicative of a corporation's solvency or profitability. For example, one commonly used financial indicator is a corporation's "debt-to-equity" ratio. To calculate this ratio, an analyst will simply compare the total dollar amount of debt as it appears on a corporation's balance sheet, to the total dollar amount of that corporation's equity. From a lender's perspective, the lower the debt-to-equity ratio, the better, because the less total debt a corporation owes, the less likely it is that the corporation will default on any of its debt payments.

When corporations borrow money, the loan agreements they are required to sign will often contain specific covenants by which the corporation promises to maintain certain financial statement ratios. For example, a corporate borrower might promise not to allow its debt-to-equity ratio to rise to more than some amount specified in the loan agreement. If the borrower fails to comply with such a covenant, an event of default may be triggered. The lender may then be entitled to call for the immediate repayment of the entire amount owing under its loan, and the defaulting corporation could well be forced into insolvency.

In the case of large, public corporations that issue debt instruments or preferred shares to the public, credit rating agencies will use financial statements as an important part of their assessment of the corporation's ability to service its debt.

The use (and indeed misuse) of financial statements is a topic that has recently received significant attention owing to a number of high-profile corporate scandals in which the integrity of the financial statements of a number of public corporations—such as Enron, WorldCom, and, more recently, Parmalat—has been impugned.

Effects of "Leverage"

The concept of leverage is a little difficult to explain, but it is quite important to understand. When corporations issue debt, they are said to be able to "lever" their equity. That is, by using debt (what might be thought of as "other people's money"), a corporation can greatly increase the percentage return on their shareholders' equity. Consider this simplified example. Imagine two "identical twin" corporations: Unleveraged Ltd. and Leveraged Inc. Assume that each corporation needs exactly $1,000 to operate its business, and that each corporation will earn exactly $100 per year from its business. (To simplify the example, ignore any tax implications.)

Now, suppose that Unleveraged Ltd. decides to raise the $1,000 it needs by selling shares. Shareholders invest a total of $1,000. At the end of the year, Unleveraged Ltd. has earned $100; so the return on its shareholders' equity is $100/$1,000 = 10 percent.

Unlike Unleveraged Ltd., Leveraged Inc. decides to finance its business using debt. Leveraged Inc. borrows $990 from a bank at an annual interest rate of 5 percent. Leveraged Inc. issues just a single share to its incorporator for $10. At the end of the year, Leveraged Inc. has also earned $100. But, unlike Unleveraged Ltd., Leveraged Inc. must use some of those "gross" earnings to pay interest on the money it has borrowed.

Leveraged Inc.'s interest expense will be $990 × 0.05 = $49.50.

This leaves Leveraged Inc. with earnings, after paying its interest expenses of $51.50. The return on Leveraged Inc.'s shareholders' equity is therefore $51.50/$10 = 515 percent. Leveraged Inc.'s shareholder invested only $10, yet has notionally earned, through the corporation, over $50.

Remember that Unleveraged Ltd. and Leveraged Inc. are identical in every way *except* for their capital structure. But the shareholders of Unleveraged Ltd. saw a return on their equity of just 10 percent, while Leveraged Inc.'s shareholders saw an astronomical return on equity of over 500 percent. This enhanced return is what is meant by leverage—in effect, the result of putting the lender's money to work for the shareholders.

It is critical to remember, however, that leverage can work in both directions. In other words, leverage, as we have seen, can greatly increase rates of return on equity when things go well; but leverage can also magnify rates of loss when things go sour. To understand why, let us modify our example slightly.

Let us now suppose that the fates have conspired against Unleveraged Ltd. and Leveraged Inc. Instead of earning $100 this year, as they had hoped, each company earned just $49.50. This will mean that the return on Unleveraged Ltd.'s shareholders' equity will be $49.50/$1,000 = 4.95 percent. Disappointing, certainly. But not disastrous.

But what about Leveraged Inc.? Remember that Leveraged Inc. is obliged to repay its lender $49.50 in interest at the end of the year. But under this new scenario, Leveraged Inc. has only earned $49.50 in total. Every penny will have to be paid over to the lenders. Leveraged Inc.'s pre-interest earnings have only fallen by just over 50 percent, but it's return on equity has been completely wiped out.

The lesson is a simple one: Leverage benefits shareholders only so long as leveraged corporations can generate returns in excess of their required interest payments.

DEBT FINANCING

Basic Elements of Debt

Like any borrower—business or individual—a corporation will be concerned about the fundamental terms of the loans it negotiates: the interest rate; the timing of required payments (whether these are interest payments or repayments of the principal amount borrowed); any covenants or restrictions the loan agreement may impose on the corporation, especially because the violation of these provisions might constitute an event of default, which could entitle the lender to demand immediate repayment of the entire loan; and so on.

A corporation's decision to borrow money, rather than to issue shares, is a complex one. Much has been written about it by legal and finance academics as well as by legal and finance practitioners.[13] Here, however, the principal focus is not on the business considerations but on the corporate law implications of the financing decision.

Corporation's Power To Borrow

The CBCA and those Canadian corporate statutes similar to it provide, as a default rule, that the directors of the corporation have the authority to borrow money on the credit of the

---

13   For a discussion of the considerations surrounding the choice of whether to finance by way of debt or
     equity, see Nicholls, supra footnote 1, at 5ff.

corporation, to issue debt securities, and to grant a security interest in the corporation's property to secure any corporate obligation.[14] This default position can, however, be varied by the articles, the bylaws, or the provisions of a unanimous shareholder agreement.

Negotiated Loan or Debt Security

When a corporation borrows money, it may either enter into a negotiated loan agreement with a bank or other lender, or it may sell corporate securities (such as bonds or debentures). From a corporate law perspective, there is no distinction between these two forms of debt, unless, in the case of debt securities, they are issued pursuant to a trust indenture, as discussed below. There are, however, important differences from a securities law perspective, because the sale of debt securities is subject to provincial securities laws, while borrowing money by way of a negotiated loan agreement is not. The securities law implications will not be dealt with here.

The word "security" has a broad and somewhat complicated definition for the purposes of provincial securities regulation,[15] but a fairly simple definition for corporate law purposes. So, for example, under the CBCA, "security" means:

> a share of any class or series of shares or a debt obligation of a corporation and includes a certificate evidencing such a share or debt obligation.[16]

Debt securities include bonds, debentures, and notes. The significance of issuing debt securities, rather than entering into a negotiated loan agreement with a financial institution or other lender, is discussed in the next section.

Debt Securities and Trust Indentures

A corporation may prefer to raise debt capital in the capital markets rather than borrow money from a lender. In other words, a corporation may issue and sell debt securities to the public, just as it might choose to issue and sell equity securities (shares) to the public. There are several conventional names for corporate debt securities, including bonds,

---

14   See, e.g., CBCA, s. 189(1); *Business Corporations Act* (Alta.), s. 103(1); *The Business Corporations Act* (Sask.) (articles are deemed to include such a provision); *The Corporations Act* (Man.), s. 183(1) (stating that the articles are deemed to include a provision so empowering the directors); *Business Corporations Act* (Ont.), s. 184(1) (deeming articles to include such a provision); *Business Corporations Act* (NB), s. 61(6) (deeming articles to include such a provision); and *Corporations Act* (NL), s. 302(1) (articles "presumed" to include such a provision). Under the Nova Scotia *Companies Act*, there is no statutory default rule; however, s. 106(1) of that Act empowers the company to borrow, and companies would normally bestow such powers on their directors pursuant to the articles of association. Indeed, art. 71 of the Table A regulations in the First Schedule contains such a provision. A similar provision is found in art. 6.1 of the Table 1 articles, prescribed by the British Columbia *Business Corporations Regulations*, BC Reg. 65/2004, s. 42. As in Nova Scotia, the Table 1 articles apply in default of any other articles adopted by a corporation. See *Business Corporations Act* (BC), ss. 12(4), 16(b), and 261.

15   See, e.g., the definition of "security" in the Ontario *Securities Act*, RSO 1990, c. S.5, s. 1(1). See also the discussion of the jurisprudence surrounding this term in MacIntosh and Nicholls, supra footnote 5, at 23 ff.

16   CBCA, s. 2(1), definition of "security."

debentures, and notes. Although it is sometimes claimed by people in the financial industry that each of these words has a well-understood meaning, as a matter of law there is no clearly settled legal distinction between these terms.[17] However, for our purposes, all that matters is that, whatever name is used, a debt security represents a right to receive periodic payments of interest and a return of principal on specified dates and in accordance with the other terms of their issue.

The main advantage to a corporation in issuing debt securities, rather than negotiating a loan, is that very large amounts of money may be borrowed through the issue of securities without the need to identify a single lender (or a relatively small lending syndicate) that is prepared to advance the entire amount. There may be other advantages, too. By issuing an instrument in the capital markets, rather than negotiating with a financial institution, the borrowing corporation is, in effect, getting direct access to savers, rather than going through a financial intermediary such as a bank. The borrowing corporation may therefore be able to obtain funds at more attractive rates.[18]

When a large loan is carved up into smaller pieces by the issue of debt securities, it is more difficult for the "lenders" (that is the holders of the debt securities) to act in concert to try to monitor or discipline the corporate borrower. Individual holders of debt securities—each holding a relatively modest amount of the corporation's debt and perhaps living very far apart from other debtholders—may have insufficient incentive, insufficient information, or insufficient resources to act effectively to prevent or respond to defaults by the corporate borrower. This collective-action problem does not hurt only the debtholders. It can also hurt the borrowing corporations when they are trying to attract people to purchase debt securities from them in the first place. Thus, a device has been developed to try to address the collective-action problems facing corporate debt securityholders. That device involves the use of a "trust indenture" or "trust deed."

A trust indenture is an agreement entered into between a corporation that is issuing debt securities (such as debentures) and a trustee, normally a regulated trust company.

---

17   For a discussion of the vagueness of the term "debenture," see *Levy v. Abercorris Slate and Slab Company* (1887), 37 Ch. D 260, at 263-64:

> Now what is a "debenture"? I am unable to add anything to what I have already stated on this point in *Edmonds v. Blaina Finances Company*. My attention has been called to extracts from *Skeat's Etymological Dictionary* and *Blount's Law Dictionary* as to the derivation of the word "debenture," from which it appears that the term is a very old one and is derived from the Latin "*debentur*," because it is said "these receipts began with the words '*debentur mihi*.'" ... In my opinion a debenture means a document which either creates a debt or acknowledges it, and any document which fulfils either of these conditions is a "debenture." I cannot find any precise legal definition of the term, it is not either in law or commerce a strictly technical term, or what is called a term of art.

In a recent case, Cronk JA of the Ontario Court of Appeal noted that "[d]ebentures, by definition, either create or acknowledge a debt. They are often, but not invariably, coupled with a charge or security interest against the debtor's property." *Canadian Broadcasting Corp. Pension Plan v. BF Realty Holdings Ltd.* (2002), 214 DLR (4th) 121, at para. 109 (Ont. CA).

18   The supposed advantages of such direct access to investors should not, however, be exaggerated. In a public debt offering, an issuing corporation typically retains the services of an investment banking firm (or firms) to place the debt securities. That firm (or those firms) will generally assume an active role in structuring and, indeed, negotiating the terms of the debt as well as the language of the trust indenture.

The trust indenture sets out the financial terms of the debt securities. Those terms will include the interest rate, the repayment terms, and financial covenants (promises) similar to those that might be found in a loan agreement. The indenture trustee's role is to protect the interests of the securityholders. In theory, then, the individual securityholders are no longer left to fend for themselves in the event of a default by the issuer. The indenture trustee can coordinate enforcement or take other actions.

There is, however, a practical problem with this structure. The indenture trustee must be selected before any securities have been issued, because the securities cannot be created until the trust indenture, which contains the terms of the debt, has been finalized. Therefore, the securityholders cannot select the indenture trustee for themselves. It is the corporation issuing the securities that selects the indenture trustee.

The fact that the issuing corporation engages the trustee inevitably leads to the possibility of a conflict of interest. There is more. The indenture trustee has little monetary incentive to diligently enforce the trust indenture and, in fact, cannot reasonably be expected to expend its own resources to enforce the securityholders' rights. Concerns such as these led legislators and regulators to propose specific rules governing trust indentures. Many Canadian corporate statutes—including the CBCA—include provisions governing the use of trust indentures.

The CBCA's trust indenture provisions are found in part VIII of the Act.[19] Trust indenture provisions were introduced into the federal statute following a recommendation of the Dickerson committee.[20] The committee was influenced in framing their recommendation by the earlier report of the Lawrence committee in Ontario. The Lawrence committee, in turn, had been inspired by the US federal *Trust Indenture Act of 1939*.

Briefly summarized, the CBCA's provisions, which apply only when debt securities are part of a distribution to the public,[21] deal with the following matters:

- *Trustee conflict*: A trustee is not to be appointed, or continue to act, if it has a material conflict of interest.[22]
- *Regulated trust company*: An indenture trustee must be a regulated trust company (or, if there is more than one trustee, at least one of the trustees must be a trust company).[23]
- *Trustee's fiduciary duties*: An indenture trustee is subject to the duties of care and good faith,[24] and the trustee may not contract out of these duties.[25]

---

19 There are similar provisions in part V of the *Business Corporations Act* (Ont.); part VII of the *Corporations Act* (NL); part VII of *The Corporations Act* (Man.); part 7 of the *Business Corporations Act* (Alta.); and division VII of *The Business Corporations Act* (Sask.).

20 Robert W.V. Dickerson et al., *Proposals for a New Business Corporations Law for Canada*, vol. I, Commentary (Ottawa: Information Canada, 1971), at para. 178 (Dickerson committee).

21 CBCA, s. 82(3).

22 CBCA, s. 83.

23 CBCA, s. 84.

24 CBCA, s. 91.

25 CBCA, s. 93.

- *Evidence by issuer of compliance*: The issuer must provide the trustee with evidence that the issuer has complied with all the conditions in the trust indenture before: (1) issuing any debt securities under the trust indenture, (2) releasing or substituting any security interest in property under the trust indenture, or (3) discharging the trust indenture.[26] As well, the issuer must provide the trustee each year with a certificate indicating that the issuer is in compliance with all provisions of the trust indenture, the breach of which would trigger an event of default. As well, the issuer must provide the trustee with evidence of compliance at any other time that the trustee demands.[27]
- *Trustee to notify holders of events of default*: An indenture trustee must notify the holders of debt securities within 30 days of learning of any events of default committed by the issuer, unless it is considered to be not in the best interests of the debtholders to do so.[28]
- *List of debtholders*: A holder of debt may obtain from the trustee a list of all outstanding debtholders. This information may be used, among other things, to enable one debt holder to contact others in an effort to influence their voting at a meeting of debtholders.[29] (Debtholders' meetings, unlike shareholders' meetings, are convened and conducted in accordance with the terms of the trust indenture itself, and not the corporate statute. Moreover, the issues considered at debtholders' meetings relate entirely to the terms of their debt instrument—for example, whether to amend the trust indenture, whether to waive a default or enforce their debt obligations, etc.)

Voting by Debtholders

When common or ordinary shareholders of a corporation exercise their votes at a meeting of shareholders, they are normally permitted to vote in accordance with their own self-interest.[30] There is a suggestion in some older case law, however, that holders of debt

---

26   CBCA, ss. 86-88.

27   CBCA, s. 89.

28   CBCA, s. 90.

29   CBCA, s. 85.

30   The classic statement of this principle comes from *Pender v. Lushington* (1877), LR 6 Ch. D 70. Janet Dine has noted that the passage in *Pender v. Lushington* on which this proposition rests, is expressed to have been supported by *Menier v. Hooper's Telegraph Works* (1874), LR 9 Ch. 250. But, Professor Dine suggests that in fact that earlier case appeared to "set limitations on the selfish exercise of rights." Janet Dine, *The Governance of Corporate Groups* (Cambridge: Cambridge University Press, 2000), at 31, note 158. There have occasionally been suggestions that majority shareholders might have some constraints on their actions. In *Allen v. Gold Reefs, Ltd.*, [1900] 1 Ch. 656, at 671 (CA), the court, referring to the broad power conferred by s. 50 of the *Companies Act, 1862* for shareholders of a corporation, by special resolution, to amend the company's regulations, noted, "Wide, however, as the language of s. 50 is, the power conferred by it must, like all other powers, be exercised subject to those general principles of law and equity which are applicable to all powers conferred on majorities and enabling them to bind minorities. It must be exercised, not only in the manner required by law, but also bona fide for the benefit of the company as a whole." This precept was adopted by several other English courts, notably in *Greenhalgh v. Arderne Cinemas, Ltd.*, [1945] 2 All ER 719. Professor Welling has rejected the idea that

securities might not enjoy such an unrestrained voting privilege when they vote on matters relating to the terms of their debt. In *British American Nickel Corp. v. O'Brien*,[31] the Privy Council held that when a majority of bondholders vote on a matter that will bind all bondholders (majority and minority alike) pursuant to the powers granted under a trust indenture, "the power given must be exercised for the purpose of benefiting the class as a whole, and not merely individual members only."[32] The reasoning in the decision is subtle, and its nuances cannot be explored in detail here. Among other things, issues remain as to the applicability of this principle to votes of special classes of *shares*, as well as debt instruments. The only point here is that one must be mindful of the possibility that voting rights may, in certain circumstances, be subject to some constraint of this nature.

EQUITY FINANCING

Introduction

A corporate "share" is a unique type of corporate investment, and a complex form of personal property. It is widely known even by those otherwise unfamiliar with corporate law or the investment industry, that corporate shares are usually represented by ornate certificates, printed on crisp bank-note-type paper, bearing fancy engraved borders and

---

any such constraints are (or should be) imposed on shareholders of Canadian corporations, maintaining that a share vote "can be cast on any whim that the shareholder fancies, subject only to specific limitations imposed by either the corporate constitution or by previous commitments the shareholder has imposed upon himself." Bruce Welling, *Corporate Law in Canada: The Governing Principles*, 2nd ed. (Toronto: Butterworths, 1991), at 640. In particular he notes, rightly in my view, that any judicially imposed constraint on the free exercise of majority shareholders' voting power would undermine the careful legislative compromise represented by such minority shareholder protections as the appraisal remedy, discussed further in chapter 14. Ibid., at 638. Nevertheless, at least one recent Ontario case has suggested, albeit in obiter, that "if one ... gets into a situation where one is voting in a corporate situation and the vote [a]ffects the class within which one is voting, then Viscount Haldane in *British America Corporation v. M.J. O'Brien Ltd.* ... would appear to place a restriction on a shareholder's discretion to act in his own interests." See *Pente Investment Management Ltd. v. Schneider Corp.* (1998), 40 BLR (2d) 244 (Ont. Ct. Gen. Div.), at 255-56. At one time, there was considerable debate in Canada surrounding the general issue of whether majority shareholders of a corporation might owe fiduciary duties to minority shareholders. One Ontario case, in particular, seemed to point very much toward the existence of such a duty: *Goldex Mines Ltd. v. Revill* (1974), 7 OR (2d) 216 (CA). However, later courts have suggested that the broad Canadian corporate oppression remedy, discussed in chapter 13, has obviated the need for the law to recognize a fiduciary duty owing to minority shareholders by majority shareholders. See, e.g., *Brant Investments Ltd. v. KeepRite Inc.* (1991), 3 OR (3d) 289, at 302 (CA). See also J.G. MacIntosh, J. Holmes, and S. Thompson, "The Puzzle of Shareholder Fiduciary Duties" (1991), 19 *Canadian Business Law Journal* 86.

31   [1927] 1 DLR 1121 (PC).

32   Ibid., at 1123. In that case, the affirmative vote of a bondholder was obtained by a promise that he would receive a large number of common shares in the issuer corporation. It was clear that, but for this promise (which was made only to this particular bondholder and not to any other member of the class), he would have opposed the bond amendments being proposed. The Privy Council thus affirmed the judgments of the lower courts to the effect that the resolutions passed by the bondholders were not binding on the minority.

curious illustrations of men or women surrounded by various symbols of industrial progress—wheels, turbines, automobiles, and so on.[33]

Some traditional attributes of share ownership are also popularly understood. For example, it is well known that corporate shareholders may from time to time receive cash distributions (known as dividends) from the corporation, and that they are occasionally invited to attend shareholders' meetings at which they are given an opportunity to vote on certain matters affecting the corporation.

But the precise legal nature of a corporate share and the rights to which its owner is entitled are actually more difficult to describe or define than is the distinctive appearance of a typical paper share certificate.

The concept of a corporate share (and indeed the word "share" itself) connotes a common, divided, participation interest in the corporation's business—an interest ultimately connected in some way to an investment of money that has been made in the corporation. That investment may have been made by the current shareholder herself. But it need not have been. The current shareholder may have acquired her shares not from the issuing corporation itself, but from another shareholder. The money paid to acquire a transferred share would not have gone to the corporation. It would have gone to the former shareholder who sold the share. At some point in the past, however, when that share was first issued by the corporation to its original holder, that original holder would have paid the corporation the share price.

One often hears the "capital" of a corporation described as being "divided into shares." And it has been authoritatively declared that "[a] share is, therefore, a fractional part of the capital."[34] However, this description is of little explanatory value because the word "capital" is also a word with a somewhat elusive meaning. It is without doubt that share ownership does *not* represent a proportionate share in the assets owned by the corporation; the corporation, and only the corporation, owns those assets. Even when a corporation is dissolved, and its assets liquidated, shareholders do not have any right to receive a distribution of those specific assets. They are entitled only to receive a proportionate distribution of the *value* of those assets—and then, only such value as remains after all of the corporation's debts and other liabilities have been satisfied.

So, for example, in *United Fuel Investments Ltd. v. Union Gas Company of Canada Ltd.*,[35] United Fuel Investments Ltd. ("United Fuel") was being wound up. United Fuel was a holding company—that is, a corporation that does not carry on active business operations itself, but is created for the purpose of holding shares in other companies. United Fuel's principal asset consisted of shares in its wholly owned subsidiary, United Gas. As part of the winding up, these shares in United Gas were to be sold. The proceeds of the sale were to be used first to satisfy any outstanding obligations of United Fuel. The balance remaining would then be distributed to United Fuel's shareholders.

The holders of a small number of United Fuel's shares were not interested in receiving cash from United Fuel. They wanted, instead, to receive shares of United Gas. They

---

33   These pictures are known as "vignettes." Increasingly, the use of paper share certificates has become less common in Canada as more efficient book-based systems take the place of paper-based systems.

34   *Bradbury v. English Sewing Cotton Co.*, [1923] AC 744, at 767 (HL), per Lord Wrenbury.

35   [1966] 1 OR 165 (CA).

therefore argued against the liquidation (that is, the sale) of the whole block of United Gas shares owned by United Fuel. They asked that only a small portion of the shares be sold—a portion just large enough to raise the cash needed to pay all of the outstanding debts of United Fuel. The remaining shares, they said, should then be distributed to the United Fuel shareholders.[36]

The Ontario Court of Appeal held that the minority shareholders had no right to call for the property of the corporation in which they held shares to be distributed directly to them. As Schroeder JA put it:

> The contention that the appellants are entitled to a distribution of the shares of United Gas *in specie* is based upon a complete misconception of the rights of corporate shareholders. They have no title to the assets of the company, but in common with all shareholders they are entitled on dissolution of the company to receive a *pro rata* share of the proceeds remaining in the hands of the liquidator after payment of debts, the costs of winding-up and the liquidator's remuneration.[37]

The minority shareholders were mistaken to think that they had any proprietary interest in the assets held by the corporation.

What, then, is the legal nature of the property interest represented by a corporate share? A corporate share has been described as a "bundle of rights," and a "chose in action."[38] When once it is accepted, however, that a share is a type of personal property,[39] the conclusion that it is a chose in action seems to follow necessarily. The nature of the interest of a corporate shareholder, after all, seems not to fit at all easily within the alternative characterization of personal property—namely, that of a chose in possession.

In memoranda and articles of association jurisdictions, such as Great Britain and Nova Scotia, the contractual nature of the shareholders' relationship with each other and the company appears to have special significance in defining the nature of the corporate share.[40] However, because the theory underlying the CBCA and most other Canadian provincial corporate statutes today is no longer this kind of contractarian model, the

---

36   Evidently, these shareholders wanted to continue to participate as investors in the United Gas business and, according to the Court of Appeal, felt that they were, in effect, being squeezed out by the majority shareholder. The majority shareholder was itself a large company. It was apparent that, if the shares of United Gas were put up for auction as proposed, the majority shareholder of United Fuel would likely obtain all of the outstanding United Gas shares.

37   Supra footnote 35, at 169-70.

38   See, e.g., F.W. Wegenast, *The Law of Canadian Companies*, reprinted with an introduction by Margaret P. Hyndman (Toronto: Carswell Company Limited, 1979), at 445 and Paul Davies, *Gower & Davies: Principles of Modern Company Law*, 7th ed. (London: Sweet & Maxwell, 2004), at 615.

39   See, e.g. *Business Corporations Act* (Ont.), s. 41. It is intriguing to note that, at one point in the past, there was "considerable doubt as to whether shares in certain sorts of companies were realty or personalty." See Ronald Ralph Formoy, *The Historical Foundations of Modern Company Law* (London: Sweet & Maxwell, 1923), at 7.

40   See the statement of Farwell J in *Borland's Trustee v. Steel Brothers & Co. Limited*, [1901] 1 Ch. 279, at 288 (Ch. D):

> A share is the interest of a shareholder in the company measured by a sum of money, for the purpose of liability in the first place, and of interest in the second, but also consisting of a series

rights and obligations of the shareholder of these CBCA-type corporations is best understood in property law, not contract law, terms. Still, it would be misleading to underestimate the extent to which the contractual origins of the corporation have profoundly influenced Canadian corporate law.[41]

The Dickerson committee described a share as "simply a proportionate interest in the net worth of a business."[42] That definition is accurate enough, at least in the case of a corporation that has chosen to issue only one class of shares. But, even in this simplest of cases, the Dickerson committee's description is somewhat imprecise.

One way to develop an intuitive understanding of the concept of a corporate "share" is to consider the shareholder's position in functional terms, and in particular to contrast the position of the corporate shareholder with that of a sole proprietor of an unincorporated business or of a partner in a partnership.

Suppose someone (call her "Owner") wishes to open up a new restaurant. Owner launches her new restaurant business as a sole proprietorship—that is, she does not intend to incorporate the business, and she does not intend to run her business in partnership with anyone else.

Whenever there are any decisions to be made about the restaurant, Owner makes them on her own. She reports to no one. She is accountable to no one. At the end of the year, if the restaurant has made a profit, all of that profit belongs to Owner. If Owner decides one day that she would like to leave the restaurant business, she can decide for herself to sell the restaurant, and when the sale is completed, the sale proceeds are hers and hers alone.

Of course, if she has borrowed money at some point to finance her business and has granted to her lenders a mortgage in her restaurant building or some other security interest in the property she uses in her business, all of these debts will need to be satisfied out of the proceeds of the sale. Indeed, the secured lenders might even have a right, given to them under the security agreements Owner has made with them, to be consulted about a proposed sale of Owner's business. But these matters all arise from the loan contract. Any such rights enjoyed by the lenders are rights that Owner herself has granted to those lenders in return for their agreement to lend Owner money to operate her business.

Now suppose that Owner has decided that, instead of running her restaurant as a sole proprietorship, she would prefer to incorporate her new business. Owner will be the "incorporator" and will fill out the necessary incorporation documents discussed in chapter 2 (that is, in the case of a CBCA corporation, the articles of incorporation and the notices that must be filed along with the articles).

---

of mutual covenants entered into by all the shareholders *inter se* in accordance with s. 16 of the *Companies Act*, 1862. The contract contained in the articles of association is one of the original incidents of the share.

However, to be sure, it should be noted that in both of Canada's two remaining memorandum-style jurisdictions (British Columbia and Nova Scotia), there are express statutory provisions declaring corporate shares to be personal property. See *Companies Act* (NS), s. 32 and *Business Corporations Act* (BC), s. 56.

41 Consider, for example, the statement of Iacobucci J in *Blair v. Consolidated Enfield*, [1995] 4 SCR 5, at para. 50: "The detailed organization of a corporation is essentially a private contractual matter." The corporation that was the subject of this case had been incorporated under the Ontario *Business Corporations Act*, a "CBCA-style" statute.

42 Dickerson committee, supra footnote 20, at para. 98.

Once she has filed the necessary forms and paid the appropriate fee, Owner will receive from the appropriate government official a certificate of incorporation, indicating that her corporation now exists. Suppose the name of this new corporation is Ownerco Limited. Thus, Ownerco Limited, and not Owner herself, will become the owner of the restaurant business.

If Owner had started running the business as a sole proprietorship, Ownerco Limited would purchase the restaurant from Owner herself. But how will Ownerco Limited acquire the funds it needs to purchase the restaurant? There are several possibilities. If Ownerco Limited is purchasing the restaurant from Owner herself, there is one simple and very common way for the corporation to "pay." Ownerco Limited will issue Owner new shares in Ownerco Limited, and the value of those shares will be equal to the value of the assets being acquired.[43] The decision to issue these shares will be made by the board of directors of Ownerco Limited. Of course, if Ownerco Limited is a single shareholder company, it will almost certainly have only one director, and that director will be Owner herself. In other words, Owner, *in her capacity as director of Ownerco Limited*, will resolve to issue new shares of Ownerco Limited to herself, but to herself in her personal capacity.

But suppose that Owner had not purchased the restaurant assets in advance. Suppose, instead, that Ownerco Limited is being established for the purpose of owning the restaurant business from the very beginning. In this case, Ownerco Limited can raise the funds it needs either by borrowing the money from a bank or other lender,[44] or by selling shares in itself (presumably, to Owner) for cash. The corporation might find it difficult to persuade a lender to provide a loan sufficient to pay the entire purchase price. But even if such a loan can be arranged, Owner will still need to take up at the very least a single share in the new corporation. In order to function, every business corporation must have at least one shareholder. Also, as will be seen, it is through share ownership that Owner will benefit from any business success enjoyed by the new restaurant owned by Ownerco Limited.[45] Regardless of how Ownerco Limited comes to own the restaurant business, Owner can, if she wishes, always be the one and only shareholder of Ownerco Limited.

43   If Owner were to be the first (and initially only) shareholder of this new corporation, then any number of shares issued in "payment" would, necessarily, be equal in value to the assets being acquired. After all, whatever number of shares are issued to Owner—whether a single share, 1,000 shares, or a million shares—those shares will reflect the net value of the underlying assets owned by the corporation that issued them. In this example, the only assets of the new corporation will be the restaurant business that the corporation is acquiring from Owner. Assuming that the new corporation has no liabilities, the shares issued to Owner must, by definition, have the same value as the assets Owner has transferred to the corporation.

44   As a practical matter, when a sole-shareholder corporation borrows money from a bank or other financial institution, the lender almost invariably requires the sole shareholder to provide a personal guarantee of the loan. Thus, although incorporation theoretically shields the shareholder from the business's liabilities, as a practical matter, that protection proves quite illusory in the case of the business's bank loan. This is especially significant when one considers that, for small private corporations, typically the corporation's largest single liability will be such a bank loan.

45   An important qualification is needed here. It is not unusual, in small, closely held corporations, for the effective "controllers" of that corporation to extract benefits in forms that do not necessarily flow from their ownership of shares. For example, the corporation might choose to pay such individuals high salaries, provide them with perquisites such as "company" automobiles, personal computers, and mobile

Once Ownerco Limited is up and running, it will need a board of directors to satisfy corporate statutory requirements. For example, if Ownerco Limited is a CBCA corporation, s. 102(2) of the CBCA requires it to have at least one director. As mentioned earlier, Owner, as the sole shareholder, will undoubtedly elect herself to be Ownerco Limited's sole director. There is no legal impediment to the sole shareholder of a corporation also serving as that corporation's sole director. Therefore, even though the restaurant business is now securely in the hands of the new corporation, as a practical matter, Owner will still be the human being making all the decisions concerning the restaurant business, just as she would have done if she had continued to run the business as a sole proprietorship. What's more, as a practical matter, she will be able to receive the profits earned by the business, too, although the legal characterization of payments of money made to her by the corporation is a little more complicated.

Though, as a practical matter, Owner's position as a sole shareholder does not appear very different from her position as a sole proprietor, as a legal matter, there has been a very important change. There is now a new legal person—the corporation, Ownerco Limited—that stands between Owner and the business itself. If the restaurant earns a profit, that profit belongs to Ownerco Limited. Ownerco Limited, as a separate legal person, is also a separate tax-paying entity, and will have to pay its own taxes on that profit. Once those corporate taxes are paid, if Owner wishes to have the after-tax profits available for her own personal use (just as she would have when the restaurant was operated as a sole proprietorship), she will have to comply with one or two technical legal requirements. First, Ownerco Limited must decide to pay money over to her. This "decision" is going to seem a little artificial. After all, Owner is the sole director and sole shareholder of the corporation. In other words, she is going to be authorizing the corporation to distribute money to herself. Nevertheless, artificial or not, certain formalities must be complied with. Although there is only one human being involved (Owner), as a matter of law, there are two distinct legal persons interacting—Owner and Ownerco Limited.

When a corporation makes a payment from its earnings[46] to its shareholders, that payment is referred to as a "dividend." Dividend payments are discussed in some detail later in this chapter.

In order to pay a dividend, the directors of the corporation must first "declare" a dividend to be payable. This the directors do by way of directors' resolution.[47] Important legal consequences turn on the making of such a declaration, and these are discussed

---

telephones, or fund frequent travel to attractive destinations—ostensibly for business purposes. Needless to say, the provision of some of these benefits—in particular the use of automobiles, telecommunications services, and business travel with a significant personal component—may raise serious income tax issues, which are beyond the scope of this book. The only point to be noted here is that share ownership is not the only means by which value may be abstracted from a corporation.

46 The significance of making a payment or distribution from earnings is discussed below. In fact, dividends may often be paid even in years where a corporation has no earnings; again, this is discussed below.

47 A directors' resolution is a formal statement of a decision taken by the directors of a corporation. The resolution can take the form of a written resolution, signed by all of the directors. Alternatively, if there is more than one director, the directors can pass the resolution at a directors' meeting, and the resolution is then recorded in the minutes of the meeting. Indeed, the CBCA even makes it possible for one director to "constitute a meeting." CBCA, s. 114(8).

later. For the moment, however, it is sufficient to note that Owner, in her capacity as sole director of the corporation, will be able to declare a dividend to be paid to Ownerco Limited's sole shareholder (that is, to Owner herself, in her capacity as sole shareholder). That dividend will be paid on the date specified in the director's resolution. Now, because Owner is the sole shareholder of the corporation, the entire amount of the dividend declared will be paid to her and her alone. If, however, Ownerco Limited had issued additional shares at some point to other people, each shareholder, holding the same class of shares as Owner, would be entitled to share in the dividend too. In fact, the amount of any dividend paid on each share of the same class would have to be identical.

Finally, the day may come when Owner decides to sell the restaurant and retire. But, because the restaurant is owned, not by Owner in her personal capacity, but by Ownerco Limited, it is Ownerco Limited that will need to sell the restaurant. Of course, because Owner is the sole director of the corporation, it is she who will, as a practical matter, make all of Ownerco Limited's business decisions. And, if the restaurant property is sold, it will be she who will eventually sign the sale agreement. However, she will not be signing that agreement in her own individual capacity, or, for that matter, in her capacity as a shareholder of the corporation. Rather, she will sign as the authorized signatory of the corporation, and that will be clearly indicated by the way in which the signature section of the document is structured.[48] Canadian corporate statutes typically provide that when a sale of this sort is proposed—that is, a sale of all the corporation's assets—the shareholders are entitled to vote on whether it ought to proceed.[49] Again, in our Ownerco Limited example, the requirement to obtain shareholder approval would be artificial and formalistic. Owner herself—the only shareholder—was the very person who decided (in her capacity as sole director) to sell the assets of Ownerco Limited to begin with. Nevertheless, as a technical matter, Owner will need to give her approval to this sale transaction in her capacity as shareholder as well.

Once the sale is completed, and the proceeds are safely in hand (that is, in the corporation's "hands"), Owner will perhaps decide to wind up her corporation. After all, it has served its purpose. It no longer has any operating assets; it no longer has a business to run; it simply has some cash in the bank (namely, the proceeds received from the sale of the restaurant business). Accordingly, if she wishes to wind up and dissolve Ownerco Limited, and pay out all of the proceeds to herself, she may do so. Of course, before the proceeds may be distributed to Owner, all of the corporation's debts and other obligations must first be paid in full.

From this Owner/Ownerco Limited example, one observes the following aspects of share ownership. First, the economic interests of a shareholder of a business corporation are in some ways similar, but by no means identical, to the interests of an owner (or owners) of an unincorporated business. It is the shareholders that are entitled to decide *who* will be given authority to make decisions on behalf of the corporation. But the shareholders do not make those business decisions themselves directly, unless they are also directors or officers. Even then, their decision-making authority derives from their

---

48   To be more precise, it is the corporation itself that would execute the document. Owner would simply sign as a corporate officer, as discussed in chapter 6.

49   See, e.g., CBCA, s. 189(3). This requirement is discussed in more detail in chapter 14.

position as officers or directors, not from their position as shareholders. (Of course, as discussed in chapter 4, it is possible for shareholders of private corporations to take management authority away from the directors in whole or in part by executing a unanimous shareholder agreement.)

When the corporation makes a profit, it is the shareholders to whom that profit may be paid out in the form of dividends. It is, however, critical to understand that dividends will be paid to shareholders only if the corporation chooses to pay them. Shareholders are not *entitled* to receive a distribution of the corporation's profits by way of dividends. The corporation, for example, might choose to retain its profits in the business, and there is usually nothing shareholders can do about that.[50]

Finally, when the business is to be sold, the shareholders must give their approval to such a sale transaction. However, this right of approval should not be confused with the right to *propose* or *initiate* such a transaction: proposing such transactions is usually within the domain of the directors, not the shareholders. This issue was canvassed in *Automatic Self-Cleansing Filter Syndicate Co. v. Cuninghame*,[51] a case discussed further in chapter 9.

The shareholder of a corporation, in other words, has a significant economic interest in the corporation—both while it is a going concern, and when it comes time to be wound up. The value of a corporation's shares is clearly dependent on the value of the business owned by the corporation. This unique combination of rights and the link they create between the value of a shareholder's shares and the value of the underlying business itself lie at the heart of the Dickerson committee's description of a share as a "proportionate share in the net worth of a business."

Vocal shareholders of large, publicly traded corporations, of the sort whose shares are traded on the Toronto Stock Exchange or the New York Stock Exchange, sometimes refer to themselves as the corporation's "owners." The owner metaphor is indeed widely encountered and enjoys a distinguished history. A judge of the Ontario Court of Appeal has recently acknowledged that shareholders "in popular terminology are considered to be the owners of the corporation."[52]

But, as Margaret Blair has observed, the corporate shareholder's position is not, in any meaningful sense, accurately described as ownership of the corporation itself.[53] The ownership characterization is sometimes a useful analogy, but can often be seriously misleading. As we have seen, the shareholder's rights of control over the corporation and the corporation's assets are largely circumscribed by the law, except in the limited case of a private corporation in which a comprehensive unanimous shareholder agreement has been put in place, stripping directors of all of their managerial authority.

Shareholders are not, then, the "owners" of the corporation. Rather, they are the owners of a special kind of personal property—shares—which represent a bundle of

---

50   There is a very famous American case, *Dodge v. Ford*, 170 NW 668 (1919), in which minority shareholders were in fact successful in compelling a corporation to make a very large dividend payment to them. The facts in this case were, needless to say, unique.

51   [1906] 2 Ch. 34 (CA).

52   *Re Central Capital Corporation* (1996), 27 OR (3d) 494 (CA), per Finlayson JA (dissenting).

53   Margaret M. Blair, "A Contractarian Defense of Corporate Philanthropy" (1998), 28 *Stetson Law Review* 27, at 31.

rights the value of which is directly related to the value of the corporation's underlying assets and business. Those rights entitle the owner:

- to a proportionate (but qualified) ownership interest in:
  - the earnings stream of that corporation while the corporation is a going concern, and
  - the residual value of the corporation's assets in the event of a winding up or liquidation of the corporation after the corporation's creditors have been paid in full;
- to participate in the election of the directors of the corporation (whose job it is to manage or supervise the management of the corporation); and
- to vote on certain fundamental corporate transactions, such as a sale of all or substantially all of the corporation's assets.

One might also say, along with R.M. Bryden,[54] that there is a fourth right of ownership: the right to transfer one's shares, and thereby realize their value.

Share Capital

Minimum Capital Requirements

Some jurisdictions impose minimum capital requirements on business corporations. That is, a corporation may not be incorporated unless shareholders are prepared to invest at least some specified minimum amount of money in the corporation. For example, in the United Kingdom, public corporations (though not private corporations) are required to satisfy a minimum capital requirement of £50,000.[55]

No Canadian jurisdiction currently imposes minimum capital requirements on ordinary business corporations—public or private. Minimum capital requirements are, however, imposed on certain special types of corporations such as banks, insurance companies, and trust companies.

Theoretically, the purpose of a minimum capital requirement is to offer some protection to creditors of the corporation and to other claimants such as victims of corporate torts. In other words, a minimum capital requirement is, in some ways, thought to be a partial "antidote" to limited liability. Because Canadian business corporations can be established without satisfying a minimum capital requirement, it is possible to establish thinly capitalized corporations or shell corporations in which the shareholders have invested no more than some nominal amount such as $1. Such corporations may carry on business and incur liabilities that they have no reasonable means to satisfy. The shareholders of those corporations may rest secure in the knowledge that the protection of limited liability will *normally* make it impossible for unsatisfied creditors or tort claimants to look beyond the empty corporate shell for a remedy.[56]

---

54   R.M. Bryden, "The Law of Dividends," in J.S. Ziegel, ed., *Studies in Canadian Company Law* (Toronto: Butterworths, 1967), at 270.

55   Davies, supra footnote 38, at 229.

56   For the limited exceptions to the protections of limited liability, see the discussion of "lifting the corporate veil" in chapter 7.

In the view of some commentators, to prevent the potential abuse of the privilege of limited liability, corporations ought only to be permitted to be formed if incorporators are prepared to invest a meaningful, minimum amount of capital.

While superficially attractive, the argument in favour of imposing minimum capital requirements is, on closer examination, profoundly flawed. First, a minimum capital requirement would be of real protection to creditors and others only if the law required corporations to *maintain* minimum capital levels. That is, simply requiring corporations to meet minimum capital requirements on the day of incorporation would be of little use. As the corporation carried on business, it would expend resources. If the business was not profitable, its resources would be depleted and unavailable to satisfy subsequent judgments regardless of whatever nominal value appeared on its financial statements as "stated capital."

Second, requiring all businesses to satisfy minimum capital requirements would arguably discriminate against small entrepreneurs of lesser means.

Third, it is unclear how one could justify the imposition of minimum capital requirements for *incorporated* businesses when we do not, for example, forbid sole proprietors or partners from carrying on business when their personal assets are less than some specified minimum amount.

Accordingly, although the debate surrounding minimum capital requirements will no doubt continue, it is not entirely clear that imposing such requirements would be of net benefit to society.

Authorized Capital

How does a corporation go about creating shares in itself? Typically, a corporation creates shares (before they are ever issued or owned by anyone) by including a description of the attributes of the shares in its constating documents. Consider, for example, a CBCA corporation. A CBCA corporation is created by filing articles of incorporation in the form fixed by the Director appointed under the Act.[57] That form (Form 1) includes, among other things, a space in which the incorporators are required to fill in two pieces of information: the name of any shares (for example, "common," "preferred," "Class A," etc.) and any maximum number of such shares that the corporation is authorized to issue.

In the case of the restaurant corporation referred to in the earlier example, Owner might have filled in this box with a phrase such as, "The corporation is authorized to issue an unlimited number of common shares." This simple sentence would now define the new corporation's "authorized share capital" because it specifies the maximum number of shares that the corporation is entitled (that is, authorized) to issue.

Note that, under the CBCA, a corporation is permitted to specify that its authorized capital consists of an unlimited number of shares.[58] This is a significant innovation. Only comparatively recently have Canadian corporations been permitted to define their authorized share capital without reference to some fixed dollar amount. It was required under older corporate statutes—and is still the practice today in some jurisdictions—that a corporation specify an actual dollar/number amount of shares as its authorized capital.

---

57   CBCA, s. 6(1).

58   CBCA, s. 6(1)(c).

So, for example, the authorized capital clause in the articles of a corporation in such a jurisdiction might read:

The corporation is authorized to issue 1,000,000 shares, having a par value of $1.00 each; or

The corporation's authorized capital consists of $1,000,000, consisting of (or divided into) 1,000,000 shares with par value of $1.00 each.

Note that the "authorized share capital" refers only to the maximum number of shares that a corporation *may* issue. It has nothing to do with the number of shares that a corporation actually *has* issued. Thus, for example, the articles of many small, private CBCA corporations include a provision with wording similar to the hypothetical language suggested above authorizing the corporation to issue an unlimited number of shares. However, such corporations are often formed as sole-shareholder corporations, and only ever issue a single share to a single shareholder.

In fact, one might well wonder what possible purpose is served by requiring a CBCA corporation to specify authorized capital in its articles of incorporation. Would it not be simpler for the statute to provide that every CBCA corporation is authorized to issue an unlimited number of shares of any class? There are several answers to this question. First, a modern CBCA corporation needs an authorized capital clause in its articles not primarily for the purpose of defining the total *number* or *amount* of shares that the corporation is permitted to issue, but rather to delineate specific, distinct *classes* of shares. We assumed in our previous example that Owner had decided that her corporation would have only one class of authorized shares—common shares. But many corporations find it desirable to authorize the creation of several different classes of shares. The authorized capital clause in the articles of such a corporation might provide, for example, that the corporation is authorized to issue an unlimited number of common shares, an unlimited number of Class A preferred shares, and an unlimited number of Class B preferred shares.[59]

Moreover, private corporations may wish to provide for limitations on the corporation's authorized capital as a means of ensuring, for example, that relative voting powers remain unchanged or perhaps for estate planning, tax, or even legal considerations relevant to foreign jurisdictions in which the corporation intends to carry on its business.

Share Conditions

A glance at the CBCA articles of incorporation form, Form 1, suggests that incorporators are required only to set out "the classes and any maximum number of shares that the corporation is authorized to issue." In fact, much more is required than simply a statement of the name of the share classes and the number of authorized shares.

As the Act[60] and Form 1's instructions indicate, the incorporators must also include the conditions attaching to each class of share that the corporation is authorized to issue, at least if the corporation is to be authorized to issue more than one class of

---

59   The elusive meaning of "preferred" or "preference" shares is discussed later in this chapter.

60   CBCA, s. 6(1)(c).

shares.[61] As a practical matter, the space provided on Form 1 to recite these share conditions is quite small; so it is usual for incorporators (or, more typically, their lawyers) to attach additional pages in which the detailed share conditions are described. Where this technique is used, a short sentence will be included in the small space on the face of Form 1 itself, directing the reader of the form to those attached pages. Such a sentence might read, for example, "The rights, privileges, restrictions, and conditions attached to the [Class A] shares are set out in the annexed Schedule 1."

If a CBCA corporation is authorized to issue only one class of shares, the statute itself requires that those shares have three fundamental attributes: the right to vote for the election of directors, the right to receive dividends if and when they are declared, and the right to receive the remaining property of the corporation when it is wound up after the payment of the corporation's debts.[62] Moreover, where the corporation has more than one class of shares, all of these share attributes must either be possessed by one class of shares, or distributed among two or more classes. In other words, it is not necessary that every corporation have one single class of shares that enjoys all three of these rights. Each of the three rights may be enjoyed by the holders of a different class of shares. (The meaning and implications of different share classes are dealt with later in this chapter.) The point here is that a corporation cannot, for example, have no voting shares whatsoever.

Issuance of Shares

The issuance of shares by a corporation to a new shareholder consists, in law, of three distinct steps: subscription, allotment, and issuance.

Subscription

The subscription is the offer to purchase some number of shares—when issued—at the price per share specified in the share subscription document. In the case of the subscription of shares in a small, closely held corporation, the share subscription will be a very simple document, often consisting of a single sentence in which the subscriber indicates his or her willingness to subscribe for a certain number of shares. In the case of private placements of shares by public companies, however, the share subscription document can be very long and sophisticated.[63]

---

61 If there is only one class of shares, it is not necessary to include a description of the share conditions because, in the absence of any such description, the share conditions for a single class of share are provided by the statute. See CBCA, s. 24(3). Although, as a technical matter, the CBCA does not require a corporation with only one class of shares to include share conditions in its articles, it is surely the case that if a corporation wishes to have a single class of shares with rights in addition to those specified in s. 24(3) (such as, for example, cumulative voting rights (s. 107), or pre-emptive rights (s. 28(1)), these would need to be set out in the articles.

62 CBCA, s. 24(3).

63 Part of the reason for this complexity is the need for the issuing corporation to satisfy itself that the subscriber satisfies certain requirements under provincial securities laws so that the issue of shares may be lawfully made to him or her without the requirement that the issuer produce, file, and deliver a prospectus under applicable securities legislation. For a detailed discussion of these requirements, and the rules applying to such "exempt distributions," see MacIntosh and Nicholls, supra footnote 5, at 175ff.

Allotment and Issuance

When the corporation accepts the offer to purchase represented by the subscription agreement, and has received the share price from the subscriber, it will allot and then issue shares to the subscriber.

It has been held that "what is termed 'allotment' is generally neither more nor less than the acceptance by the company of the offer to take shares."[64] One modern Canadian secondary source has suggested that "[i]n modern corporate practice shares are no longer allotted but rather the subscription or application for shares is accepted and the shares are issued."[65] To some extent, however, this is a rather semantic distinction without a difference; and one notes that the same source in which this statement appears goes on to refer to allotment of shares by issuing corporations.

DIRECTORS' AUTHORITY

The CBCA states that, subject to the articles, bylaws, and any unanimous shareholder agreement, it is the directors who have the authority to decide to whom to issue the corporation's shares, and on what financial terms.[66] Of course, the exercise of the directors' power to issue such shares is subject, as are all of the directors' powers, to the overriding obligation to act honestly, in good faith, and with a view to the best interests of the corporation.

PARTLY PAID AND FULLY PAID SHARES

At one time, it was common practice to issue shares on an unpaid or partly paid basis. In other words, the directors of the corporation would determine the price at which shares were to be issued, but subscribers would not be required to pay that price in full. Instead, they would pay some smaller amount at the time of issue; then, at some future date when the corporation required additional funds, calls would be made requiring payment from shareholders with amounts left unpaid on their shares.

The CBCA no longer permits corporations to issue shares on an unpaid or partly paid basis—before a corporation is permitted to issue shares, consideration for those shares must have been received in full.[67] At the time of the Dickerson committee's report, the

---

64   See *In re Florence Land and Public Works Company (Nicol's Case)* (1885), 29 Ch. D 421, at 426 (CA), per Chitty J.

65   Harry Sutherland et al., *Fraser & Stewart Company Law of Canada*, 6th ed. (Toronto: Carswell, 1993), at 176.

66   CBCA, s. 25(1).

67   CBCA, s. 25(3). There is some debate surrounding the question of what ought to be the effect on the validity of the share itself if it is issued for less than full consideration, in contravention of this provision—particularly in cases where full consideration is received by the corporation at a later date. Some argued that a share issued for less than full consideration was a nullity and that no subsequent payment could rehabilitate the initial defective issuance. Others maintained that such a hard and fast rule was overly harsh, and was not necessary to fulfill the purposes of the statute. Professor Welling was in the former camp. He has written that "[d]irectors cannot issue shares where the statutory requirement has not been fulfilled and any attempt to issue shares before full consideration has been paid will fail." Bruce Welling, supra footnote 30, at 607. He recognizes that s. 118(1) of the Act appears, at first, to contradict this hypothesis because it makes a director who has consented to the issuance of shares in exchange for

use of partly paid shares had already been effectively eliminated for public corporations by securities commissions rules. As the drafters of the report thus concluded, "We can see no point in retaining in the law complications created by commercial practices which are no longer followed and which are widely prohibited already by other legislation."[68]

Since that time, another financing technique—namely, installment receipts—has been developed that is, at least from the subscriber's perspective, economically similar to the partly paid share. Installment receipt transactions have been considered useful by corporations in a number of circumstances. However, corporations using installment receipt transactions must put structures in place to ensure that the law prohibiting the issuance of shares on a partly paid basis is not offended.

To ensure that the rules against issuing shares on a partly paid basis are not readily avoided, the CBCA provides that a promissory note or a promise to pay from the person to whom shares are being issued does not constitute "property" for the purpose of determining whether a corporation has received payment for the issue of shares.[69]

PAR VALUE

Under some Canadian corporate statutes, it is possible to issue "par value" shares.[70] Under others, including the CBCA, the concept of par value shares has now been abolished.

Par value means nominal or face value. So, for example, in a jurisdiction that allows par value shares to be created, a corporation might create a class of shares having a par value of $10 each. When these shares are first sold to investors, the corporation might very well issue them at par—that is, at a price equal to their nominal or face value.

---

property of inadequate value liable to the corporation for the difference. If such shares were never, in fact, issued, why would a director ever need to make up such a shortfall? On this point, Welling argues that if a share *certificate* has been issued, the holder of the certificate (though not, in fact, a shareholder until full consideration has been paid) nevertheless has a legal right to compel the corporation to issue a share to him, and the director, he says, in that case will be liable to pay whatever amount necessary to enable the corporation to validly issue the share on a fully paid basis. Ibid., at 711-12. The automatic nullity hypothesis, however, seems unduly flexible; and the suggestion that wholly different consequences obtain depending on whether or not a paper share certificate is or is not delivered to a supposed purchaser seems regrettably formalistic. Although some courts have adopted Professor Welling's view, the better view of the law appears to be that expressed recently by the Alberta Court of Appeal in *Pearson Finance Group Ltd. v. Takla Star Resources Ltd.* (2002), 22 BLR (3d) 174. As the court points out, it would, among other things, be possible to violate the provision requiring full payment "in trivial ways." The example the court gives is one familiar to all corporate lawyers—the initial subscription for one share by the incorporator at a price of $1. Is this nominal $1 always and everywhere duly delivered to "the corporation" on or prior to the moment of share issuance? If the restriction against issuing shares that are not fully paid was as rigid as some have suggested, the legitimacy of the organizational steps of many (or most) shelf companies might well be subject to challenge. The court also notes that, if the rule is an inflexible one, "shares properly subscribed for at a price of $47,513.27 might be a nullity because the cheque to pay for them missed the 27 cents." Accordingly, the more sensible view appears to be that the legal effect of failure to pay full consideration must depend on the circumstances under which the failure occurred.

68   Dickerson committee, supra footnote 20, at para. 104.

69   CBCA, s. 25(5). This subsection was amended in 2001 to make it abundantly clear that only promissory notes or promises to pay from the shareholder himself or herself do not constitute property.

70   The corporate statutes of New Brunswick, Nova Scotia, and British Columbia permit the issuance of par value shares.

However, there is a problem with par value shares: a share's par value is generally of little interest to an investor. What matters is the share's market value—the amount at which the share can be sold. And the market value of a share will depend on the underlying value of the corporation's business. The par value of the share is totally irrelevant.

To understand why, consider this example. Imagine a company, XYZ Ltd., that wishes to raise $1,000 to launch a business. XYZ Ltd. decides to issue 100 shares, each with a par value of $10. Those shares are issued at par—that is, at a price of $10 each. Each share represents a 1 percent proportional interest in the value of XYZ Ltd. As long as XYZ Ltd. is worth $1,000 in total, each share will be worth $10. But, as XYZ Ltd. carries on its operations, it is very unlikely that it will continue to be worth exactly $1,000. Perhaps its business will be a runaway success, and its value will skyrocket. If XYZ Ltd. becomes worth, say $100,000, each of its 100 shares will be worth $1,000, not $10. The "par value" stated on the share certificate would grossly *understate* the share's actual value. Conversely, if XYZ Ltd. falls on hard times and the total value of the company plummets to, say, $100, then each of its 100 shares will be worth only $1, not $10. Now the "par value" stated on each share certificate would grossly *overstate* the share's actual value.

Moreover, if XYZ Ltd. wants to issue more shares of the same class in the future, it will have a problem. Will it be able to issue $10 par value shares for less than $10? If the value of the business has fallen, no one will be willing to pay $10 for each XYZ Ltd. share. But how can $10 shares be issued for less than $10? Is it proper, in other words, to issue such shares at an apparent "discount"?

Conversely, if the business has gone well, XYZ Ltd. will certainly not be prepared to issue new shares (which are worth perhaps $1,000 each) for a mere $10 each, just because $10 is the "par value" of these shares. But, if XYZ Ltd. issues the shares for more than their par value, how should it account for this "premium" or "surplus" in its financial statements?

Considerations of this sort prompted the Dickerson committee to denounce the concept of par value as "utterly useless"[71] and to conclude that "par values are arbitrary and misleading."[72] It recommended that the CBCA forbid the issuance of par value shares, and this recommendation was accepted.[73] Many other Canadian jurisdictions followed suit.[74] However, it has been suggested that, for a narrow range of transactions, there may indeed be some use for par value shares and, accordingly, the Canadian jurisdictions that still permit the use of such shares have been known to flag this fact as a potential advantage to incorporators.

STATED CAPITAL ACCOUNT

When shares are issued, a CBCA corporation is required (subject to some limited exceptions)[75] to add the consideration that is received for those shares to a "stated capital

71   Dickerson committee, supra footnote 20, para. 24.

72   Ibid., at para. 98.

73   See CBCA, s. 24(1).

74   See, e.g., *Business Corporations Act* (Alta.), s. 26(1); *The Business Corporations Act* (Sask.), s. 24(1); *The Corporations Act* (Man.), s. 24(1); *Business Corporations Act* (Ont.), s. 22(1); and *Corporations Act* (NL), s. 46(1).

75   CBCA, s. 26(3).

account."[76] The stated capital account maintained by a corporation in respect of each class of its issued shares plays an important role, among other things, in certain solvency tests that the corporation is required to meet before it may lawfully pay dividends,[77] or redeem or repurchase outstanding shares.[78]

Class Rights

Thus far, the discussion in this chapter has focused on share rights and conditions in general terms, without considering the complications that arise when a corporation has decided to create and issue shares of more than one class.

When a corporation has only one outstanding class of shares, those shares, as a matter of business convention rather than legal requirement, are typically referred to as common or perhaps—especially in the United Kingdom—ordinary shares. But most Canadian corporate statutes include no definition of either term and, indeed, typically make no mention of "common" or "ordinary" shares.

When a corporation chooses to issue more than one class of shares, a number of technical legal issues come into play. For one thing, it becomes necessary to define what precisely is meant by a "class" of shares. Furthermore, because corporations and their legal and financial advisers have become increasingly sophisticated, share conditions have become more complex. The distinction between certain types of "shares" and other forms of corporate securities (such as traditional debt securities) has become blurred.

What Is a "Class" of Shares?

As a general matter, all shares are presumed to be equal.[79] That presumption may be rebutted if the share conditions provide otherwise, but it is permissible to vary rights and privileges only between differing classes of shares. Shares of the same class must all be treated alike, at least as regards class as oppposed to "series" rights, as discussed in the next section. What, then, is a class of shares?

In *Sovereign Life Assurance Co. v. Dodd*,[80] Bowen LJ suggested that the term "class"

must be confined to those persons whose rights are not so dissimilar as to make it impossible for them to consult together with a view to their common interest.[81]

Of course, when a corporation creates shares (by including a description of them in its articles), the shares will be designated in a way that indicates that they are shares of a distinct class. For example, a certain corporation's articles might indicate that the corporation is authorized to issue common shares, with certain attributes; preferred shares,

---

76   CBCA, s. 26(2).

77   CBCA, s. 42.

78   CBCA, ss. 34-38.

79   *Birch v. Cropper* (1889), 14 App. Cas. 525 (HL).

80   [1892] 2 QB 573 (CA).

81   Ibid.

with certain (different) attributes; Class "A" shares, with yet further attributes; and so on. Obviously, the drafters of this corporation's articles intend that each of these designated categories of shares constitutes a separate class.

The Supreme Court of Canada has described a class of shares in this way:

> The concept of share "classes" is not technical in nature, but rather is simply the accepted means by which differential treatment of shares is recognized in the Articles of Incorporation of a company. As Professor Welling ... succinctly explains, at p. 583, "a class is simply a sub-group of shares with rights and conditions in common which distinguish them from other shares."[82]

In other words, shares of the same class must be treated equally. Therefore, the purpose of creating more than one class of shares is to enable the corporation to assign different rights and privileges to different classes of shares. It is critical to understand that share rights attach to the shares themselves, and not to the individual holders of those shares. Two well-known Canadian cases help to illustrate this foundational principle.

In *Muljo v. Sunwest Projects Ltd.*,[83] two shareholders each held 200 common shares in a corporation. However, they had purchased these shares at different times and the underlying value of the corporation had changed significantly in the intervening time period. Thus, the first shareholder paid a total of $200 for his 200 shares, while the second shareholder paid $375,000 for his 200 shares. Relations between the shareholders soured and the second shareholder sought to have the corporation wound up. However, he did not simply want the residual value of the corporation divided evenly between himself and the first shareholder. Instead, he asked the court to order that the corporation first repay to each shareholder the amount that he had paid for his common shares, and that only after that payment should the remaining assets of the corporation be divided equally between the shareholders.

The court rejected this request and ordered instead that the property of the corporation be distributed equally to the two common shareholders, regardless of the amount of capital paid on any particular share or class of shares. In other words, the rights attached to each share were to be identical. There was no need to look behind the share itself to ask, for example, whether the holder of one block of shares had paid more than the holder of another block of shares of the same class.

To similar effect is *Bowater Canadian Ltd. v. R.L. Crain Inc.*[84] *Bowater* concerned the legality of so-called step-down shares. These were shares that, according to the share conditions, entitled the original holder to 10 votes per share. If the shares were transferred to anyone else, however, the transferee was entitled to only 1 vote per share. The court held that the step-down provision was invalid because it violated a fundamental corporate law principle. Shares of the same class are equal in all respects, and rights attach to the shares themselves, not to the individual holders of those shares.

The court in *Bowater* believed it was appropriate to sever the offending provision of the share conditions. The effect of this severance was that each share was entitled to 10

---

82   *McClurg v. Canada*, [1990] 3 SCR 1020, at para. 25.

83   (1991), 60 BCLR (2d) 343, at 346-49 (CA).

84   (1987), 62 OR (2d) 752 (CA).

votes, even in the hands of a transferee. The court felt compelled to make this finding even though the purchaser of the shares had acquired them with full knowledge of the step-down provision in the share conditions. Among other things, the court expressed concern that "if there was not equality rights within a class of shareholders, there would be great opportunity of fraud."[85]

What is curious is that the *Bowater* court made no mention of the House of Lords' 1970 decision in *Bushell v. Faith*.[86] *Bushell v. Faith* is by no means an obscure English case, although it is usually considered in the context of shareholders' authority to remove directors rather than in the context of the rights of holders of shares of the same class.

In *Bushell*, the articles of a corporation provided that, in the case of any resolution proposed to remove a director from office, the shares held by that director would carry the right to three votes per share. Normally, each share of the corporation entitled the holder to only one vote per share. The corporation in question was a small, family-owned corporation with three directors and three shareholders, each holding an equal number of shares. Accordingly, the practical effect of this special voting provision, if valid, was that no director could be removed against his or her will. This consequence was significant because the UK *Companies Act* expressly stated that a director could always be removed by ordinary resolution, notwithstanding any provision in its articles. This special voting provision was, thus, a transparent attempt to do indirectly what could not be done directly. The House of Lords held that the special voting provision was valid.

Many of the speeches delivered in that case are strongly supportive of the notion that differential voting rights, even among shares of the same class, are perfectly acceptable. Lord Upjohn, for example, referred to a provision in the company's articles "which gives to the company a completely unfettered right to attach to any share or class of shares special voting rights upon a poll or to restrict those rights as the company may think fit."[87] He also noted that "Parliament has never sought to fetter the right of the company to issue a share with such rights or restrictions as it may think fit. There is no fetter which compels the company to make the voting rights or restrictions of general application and it seems to me clear that such rights or restrictions can be attached to special circumstances and to particular types of resolution."[88]

Similarly, Lord Donovan noted that it was only the unique conflict between this special voting provision and an explicit statutory rule on directors' removal that even made the matter contestable: "A provision for such 'weighting' of votes which applies generally, that is as part of the normal pattern of voting, is accepted by the appellant as unobjectionable."[89]

It may be thought that the distinction between *Bushell v. Faith* and *Bowater* might be explained on the basis of some specific statutory difference between the UK *Companies Act* and the CBCA. Certainly, the court in *Bowater* purports to rely to some extent on s. 24(4) of the CBCA. But that provision states only that if the articles provide for more

---

85   Ibid., at 755.

86   [1970] AC 1099 (HL).

87   Ibid., at 1109.

88   Ibid.

89   Ibid., at 1110.

than one class of shares, the rights attached to each class must be set out in the articles and must ensure that the three fundamental share rights referred to in s. 24(3) are attached to at least one class of shares. There is nothing, in other words, specifically requiring that voting rights cannot be specially weighted.

In the case of private corporations, different classes of shares have been used, among other reasons, to facilitate a corporation's cash flows to the shareholders in a tax-efficient way. For example, in *McClurg v. Canada*,[90] Revenue Canada (the predecessor to the Canada Revenue Agency) challenged the way in which a private corporation used a "discretionary dividend" clause in its articles' share conditions to split the income from the corporation's business between the corporation's two shareholders, a husband and wife. The amount of dividends paid in any year was evidently based on the respective tax positions of the shareholders as individuals. Revenue Canada argued that such a clause, which purported to permit the directors of the corporation to pay dividends to the holder of one class of the corporation's shares to the exclusion of another class, violated the corporate law rule that all shares of a class must be treated equally. The Supreme Court of Canada, by a narrow 4–3 majority, held that the discretionary dividend clause was sufficient to rebut what would otherwise be the corporate law presumption of equality between the classes of shares.[91]

Series of Shares

Closely related to the concept of "classes" of shares is the concept of share series. Section 27 of the CBCA provides as follows:

(1) The articles may authorize, subject to any limitations set out in them, the issue of any class of shares in one or more series and may do either or both of the following:

(a) fix the number of shares in, and determine the designation, rights, privileges, restrictions and conditions attaching to the shares of, each series; or

(b) authorize the directors to fix the number of shares in, and determine the designation, rights, privileges, restrictions and conditions attaching to the shares of, each series.

A series of shares, then, is a "subclass" of shares. That is, one class of shares may be subdivided into several different share series. These shares will have some common class rights, but will also have distinct series rights attached to them. The series rights might relate, for example, to such things as dividend rates or other market features. The purpose of providing for the issue of shares in series is to enable the directors of a corporation to respond quickly to financial market conditions. Without the flexibility offered by share series, directors who want to issue a class of shares with a dividend rate tied to current market conditions would be required to propose an amendment to the corporation's

---

90   [1990] 3 SCR 1020.

91   A similar income-splitting scheme was upheld more recently by the Supreme Court in *Neuman v. MNR*, [1998] 1 SCR 770. However, the court was careful to warn in that decision that changes in the *Income Tax Act* enacted subsequent to the events under dispute in *Neuman* might well change the outcome from a tax perspective. Accordingly, these cases are mentioned here solely from a corporate law, not a tax law, perspective.

articles. Such an amendment would require shareholder approval. By the time this approval is obtained, market conditions may well change, and financing opportunities may be lost.

Payment of Dividends

Meaning of "Dividend"

A dividend originally appeared to be a division of a corporation's profits distributed to shareholders. In *Re Carson*,[92] Wells J, of the Ontario High Court, made the following observations about the meaning of a dividend:

> The word "dividend" is not a word of art or one which under prior decisions of the Courts has any precise, definite or rigid meaning. As it has been said, it is a broad generic term and must be construed in its normal and ordinary meaning as one of the words of the English language. Primarily, the word "dividend" means that which is to be divided. In Murray's Oxford Dictionary it is described as a number or quantity which is to be divided by another and in addition as a sum of money which is to be divided among a number of persons especially the total sum payable as interest on a loan, or the profit of a joint-stock company divided periodically among the holders (usually reckoned at a certain rate per cent); also the sum divided among the creditors of an insolvent estate. It is also described as a portion or share of anything divided especially the share of anything divided among a number of persons that falls to each to receive or pay and is also described as the portion of interest on a loan or the profit from a joint-stock company received by an individual holder as his share. The word apparently includes the action of dividing among a number of persons, distribution of profits or assets. In the third edition of the Shorter Oxford Dictionary the definition which appears to be most prominent is that of describing a dividend as a sum of money to be divided among a number of persons especially the total sum payable as interest on a loan or as the profit of a joint-stock company. This edition of the dictionary has been corrected up to the year 1955 and it also describes a dividend as a portion or share of anything divided.[93]

The Mechanics of Declaring a Dividend

We often talk about corporations declaring dividends without explaining, as a practical matter, how exactly this takes place. At one time, deciding on the declaration of dividends was actually within the control of the shareholders. But as the corporation evolved and management became centralized in the board of directors, the declaration of dividends became recognized as a matter of internal management that is within the discretion of the directors, unless the corporation's articles declared otherwise.[94] Today, under the CBCA, and those statutes like it, it is the directors who decide whether or not to declare a dividend.[95]

---

92   [1963] 1 OR 373 (HC).

93   Ibid., at 379.

94   See *McClurg*, supra footnote 82, at para. 21, citing *Burland v. Earle*, [1902] AC 83 (PC).

95   Ibid., at para. 22.

Once the directors decide whether or not to declare a dividend, that decision will be evidenced—like all board decisions—by a formal resolution. If the decision is reached at a meeting of the board, the resolution will be voted on and then written up in the "minutes" prepared to record the business of the meeting. Alternatively, the directors might act by way of a unanimous written resolution, in which case all of the directors will sign their name to a piece of paper on which the resolution is written, and that piece of paper will then be placed in the corporation's minute book.

The resolution declaring a dividend will specify three things:

- the amount of the dividend to be paid on each share,
- the date on which the dividend is to be paid, and
- the record date (that is, the date on which the names of the shareholders entitled to receive the dividend will be determined).

The first two items are straightforward, but it may be useful to say something about the "record date." The setting of a record date is normally of little consequence in the case of a small private corporation, the shares of which trade infrequently, if at all. However, the matter is quite important in the case of corporations with publicly traded shares. The shares of a large, public corporation change hands daily—even hourly—as traders buy and sell them on securities exchanges (such as the Toronto Stock Exchange). If the directors simply declared a dividend on day one to be paid to all the people who were shareholders on the very day of the declaration, by the time the dividend cheque had been prepared, issued, and mailed, many of those lucky dividend recipients would no longer be shareholders at all. Imagine how a purchaser of those shares would feel. Not only would he or she not receive any cash dividend payment, but, worse still, he or she would have purchased shares in a company that now has less cash than it did on the day of the purchase.

Of course, dividend recipients who have sold their shares after the date of declaration but before the dividend cheque was actually mailed out to them would be delighted. They would receive a surprising windfall. If dividends were routinely paid in this way, the securities markets would be adversely affected. Share buyers would, in effect, have to discount the price they would be willing to pay to allow for the possibility that a dividend might be paid to the former shareholder. Needless to say, buyers and sellers could agree, as part of the contract for sale of the shares, that the seller would turn over any dividends received after the date of sale to the new owner. But when shares are traded on a stock exchange, the process is anonymous; there is no face-to-face negotiation. Moreover, even if private negotiation of every such share sale were always possible, this would be less than an ideal solution, because the buyers might still have problems enforcing the dividend-allocation contract. In addition, creditors of an insolvent seller might seize the dividend proceeds before they could be turned over to the new owner, leading to further disputes.

These problems are resolved when a corporation announces *in advance* the record date that will be used for the purpose of determining which shareholders will be entitled to receive a dividend. A person who sells his or her share before that record date (or, more precisely, whose share sale settles before that date) will not receive the dividend; similarly, a person whose share purchase settles after the record date will not be entitled to receive the dividend.

Restrictions on the Payment of Dividends

When a corporation distributes money to its shareholders, that distribution (assuming it *is* a distribution, and not a loan) must take one of two forms: (1) a return of the capital originally invested in the corporation by the shareholder, or (2) a dividend.

In either case, the holders of a corporation's fixed claims (that is, the corporation's creditors) will have reason to be concerned. It is a fundamental principle of corporate finance that debt ranks ahead of equity. If a corporation were free to return money to its equityholders at any time, that principle would be totally undermined, and if the priority of debt claims were not respected, the debt markets themselves would presumably collapse. Who, after all, would be prepared to accept the limited upside offered by a debt instrument without the offsetting advantage of additional security that comes from the knowledge that the corporation's funds are to be used first to satisfy the claims of its debtholders?

At the same time, it would be equally destructive if the law were to forbid a corporation from making any cash distributions to shareholders at any time that the corporation had debt outstanding. Equity investors, reasonably, seek returns on their capital. In certain cases, those returns will properly come to them in the form of dividends. Provided that a corporation's debt obligations are being serviced regularly and the corporation has financial resources sufficient to render the prospect of insolvency unlikely, no sensible public policy goal is served by forbidding the corporation from making any distributions whatsoever to its shareholders.

As is so often the case in law, however, it is easy enough to articulate sensible general principles. It is much more difficult to reduce those general principles to a reasonably certain legal rule. When should a corporation be free to pay dividends to its shareholders or to return a portion of their invested capital to them?

These issues are now dealt with specifically by the CBCA and other CBCA-style statutes. However, at common law, the rules were rather opaque. The Dickerson committee, writing in 1971, declared the law of dividends to have been "in a confused mess for years."[96] The "mess" to which they were specifically referring actually arose from earlier statutory provisions rather than from common law rules, but the common law was hardly more tidy.

The general principle was that payments of dividends were not to impair a corporation's capital.[97] The problem with that formulation, though, was that it was not at all clear what a corporation's capital was meant to include or exclude.[98] Dividends were properly paid, it was said, if they were paid out of a corporation's "profits." But what profits? If, for example, a corporation had suffered steady losses for nine years followed by a one-off profit in year 10, would it be permitted to pay a dividend in year 10 out of the "profits" earned that year? An early case, cited by the Dickerson committee, seemed to say that this might well be acceptable.[99]

---

96   Dickerson committee, supra footnote 20, at para. 140.

97   This test still applies to corporations incorporated under the PEI *Companies Act*. See *Companies Act* (PEI), s. 62.

98   As Davies observes, "'capital' as an item in the company's accounts exists only as a notional liability and nothing can be paid out of a liability—actual or notional." Davies, supra footnote 38, at 275.

99   *Ammonia Soda Co. v. Chamberlain*, [1918] 1 Ch. 266, cited in Dickerson committee, supra footnote 20, at para. 140.

It is still the case that common law rules on dividends apply in those jurisdictions (notably Nova Scotia) that have not adopted CBCA-style dividend provisions.[100] However, most Canadian statutes now include specific statutory rules on the matter, and those statutory rules wholly replace the old common law rules.[101]

CBCA Section 42

For CBCA corporations, the question of when dividends may lawfully be declared and paid is addressed by s. 42, which reads as follows:

> A corporation shall not declare or pay a dividend if there are reasonable grounds for believing that
>
>   (a) the corporation is, or would after the payment be, unable to pay its liabilities as they become due; or
>
>   (b) the realizable value of the corporation's assets would thereby be less than the aggregate of its liabilities and stated capital of all classes.

If a dividend is paid in contravention of s. 42, the directors of the corporation may be held personally liable.[102] A director found liable on this basis may, however, apply to a court for an order that shareholders who received such dividends be obliged to return the amounts received to the director.[103]

At the most general level, paragraph (a) provides a *liquidity test* (that is, will payment of the dividend leave the corporation short of cash in the short term so that it cannot meet its obligations as they come due), while paragraph (b) provides a *solvency/impairment of capital test* (that is, will the payment of the dividend result in reducing the corporation's assets below the amount it would need to have in a liquidation to repay all of its outstanding debts, and return to shareholders their capital).

These two tests are meant to be straightforward, but they do raise several points of interpretation. For example, note that it appears the tests must be satisfied *twice*—both at the time when the dividend is first declared and again at the moment at which the dividend is actually paid.[104]

This two-stage test is significant because, as a general proposition, once a dividend has been declared, it becomes a debt of the corporation.[105] But, if the statutory tests could

---

100 Although the Nova Scotia *Companies Act* itself does not specifically deal with the subject, reg. 159 of First Schedule, Table A, provides that dividends are only to be paid out of profits. Needless to say, no corporation is required to adopt Table A as its articles of association (essentially, equivalent to bylaws in a CBCA-style jurisdiction), but it is deemed to have adopted them unless it specifically varies them. *Companies Act* (NS), s. 21.

101 See *McClurg*, supra footnote 82, at para. 22; *Re Central Capital*, supra footnote 52, at 530 (per Weiler JA).

102 CBCA, s. 118(2)(c).

103 CBCA, ss. 118(4) and (5).

104 This interpretation is based on the phrase "shall not declare or pay." See also Nicholls, supra footnote 1, at 23-25.

105 See, e.g., *The Custodian v. Blucher*, [1927] SCR 420, at 425, citing *Severn & Wye & Severn Bridge Railway Co.*, [1896] 1 Ch. 559 (Ch. D).

not be satisfied at the time set for payment, the corporation would appear to be in a curious position: obliged to make the payment (which became a debt when it was declared), yet forbidden from making the payment because of s. 42. The only sensible course for directors to take under such circumstances would be to delay paying the dividend until the solvency tests are met; any other decision could expose them to personal liability[106] and would seem contrary to the policy underlying the statute and the judicial interpretations of the provision.[107]

The reference to "realizable value" in s. 42(b) raises some issues because it suggests that the value to be taken into account is not simply the value of assets as they appear on the corporation's financial statements. (It is customary to refer to asset values as they appear on a corporation's balance sheet as "book values." Book values are recorded in accordance with accounting rules that are not intended to represent the values at which the assets could actually be sold at any time. The term "realizable value" seems to represent something different from book value.) It was evidently the intent of the Dickerson committee to base the solvency tests on a consideration of asset values beyond their historical cost,[108] which was traditionally the basis on which asset book values were reported.

A more interesting question is whether the two tests in s. 42 need to be satisfied if the corporation is issuing a stock dividend rather than a dividend in money or property.[109] The reason for this distinction may seem obvious to some, but a brief explanation is offered here for the benefit of readers who are less familiar with the concept of a stock dividend.

When a corporation declares and pays a dividend to its shareholders in cash (or in assets having a value equal to the amount the corporation would have paid in cash), the corporation's assets are reduced. To put the matter in its starkest terms, if the corporation were to be liquidated the day after such a dividend was paid, there would be fewer assets available to satisfy the corporation's creditors than there would have been had the dividend not been

---

106 Ibid.

107 See, e.g., *Re Central Capital*, supra footnote 52, at 530 (per Weiler JA). However, it could, nevertheless, be relevant in some circumstances to determine whether a dividend that has been properly declared under s. 42 but that, by the time scheduled for payment, cannot properly be paid is rightly characterized as a "debt" of the corporation. The issue does not appear to have been definitively resolved by the courts. It is regularly reiterated that a dividend becomes a debt once declared, but little attention is paid to the fact that a CBCA corporation must satisfy the s. 42 solvency tests a second time immediately before paying the dividend. While the matter is not free from doubt, it seems probable that a declared dividend would be properly characterized as "debt" even if the corporation, between the date of declaration and date of payment, were no longer able to satisfy the s. 42 tests. The basis for this conclusion is twofold. First, as a general proposition, it has never been doubted that a dividend becomes a debt once properly declared. Second, the Supreme Court of Canada's decision in *The Custodian v. Blucher*, supra footnote 105, seems consistent with this conclusion. In *Blucher*, a dividend had been declared before the commencement of World War I, but not paid because of the intervening war. The Supreme Court held (at 425) that "[t]he right of recovery was in suspense during the War, but the debt nevertheless existed." See also the recent decision of the Ontario Court of Appeal in *Shahinian v. Precinda*, [2004] OJ no. 476 (QL) (CA) in which the court, in discussing conflicting interpretations of language in a shareholders' agreement concerning "default in payment of dividends," commented that "[o]ne is not ordinarily described as being in default for failing to do something prohibited by legislation." Ibid., at para. 26.

108 Dickerson committee, supra footnote 20, at para. 128.

109 CBCA, s. 43.

paid.[110] In other words, a dividend paid in cash or in property is precisely the sort of dividend that could jeopardize the position of fixed claimants and so must be controlled.

A stock dividend is quite different. The payment of a stock dividend has no effect on the assets of a corporation. Creditors and fixed claimants are quite indifferent to the payment of stock dividends. Consider this simple example. Suppose a corporation, ABC Limited, owns property worth precisely $1,000—$300 in cash and $700 in other assets. ABC Limited has exactly 1,000 common shares issued and outstanding, and also has outstanding debt obligations totalling $800. Now, if ABC Limited were to declare and pay a cash dividend of 30 cents per share (or $300 in total), the holders of ABC Limited's debt obligations would be very worried. ABC Limited's property would now be worth only $700. If the company were to be wound up and liquidated, there would not be enough money to pay all of ABC's debts in full.

But suppose that ABC, instead of paying a cash dividend, issued a stock dividend: every ABC Limited shareholder, for example, was issued a second ABC Limited share. After paying the dividend, ABC Limited would have 2,000 shares outstanding instead of 1,000; but the value of ABC Limited's assets would be unchanged. And from the perspective of ABC Limited's shareholders, although they would have a greater *number* of shares, the total value of this larger number of shares would be exactly the same as the total value of the smaller number of shares. A shareholder who owned, for example, 10 shares, would now own 20. But these 20 shares, in total, would not be worth any more than the holder's 10 shares had been worth in total before the stock dividend.

A stock dividend like this would have the same effect as a stock split—it would be an economic non-event. It would be as if a child at a birthday party with a piece of cake on her plate were to have that piece split in two, and then was told that she now had two pieces instead of one. The total amount of cake, of course, would not have changed.

That is not to say that a stock dividend never raises issues *between* shareholders. For example, if a corporation with two different classes of outstanding shares (Class A and Class B), were to make a stock dividend to all of the Class A shareholders, but not to the Class B shareholders, or were to pay a dividend of Class B shares to holders of the Class A shares, there could be a significant effect on the relative rights and interests of the shareholders of these two classes. The only point is that, from the perspective of creditors and other fixed claim holders, the payment of a stock dividend does not deplete the corporation's assets.

Accordingly, there do not seem to be compelling policy reasons to apply the s. 42 tests to the payment of a stock dividend. But does the CBCA require that they be applied

---

110 In the absence of information asymmetries (that is, if shareholders of corporations always had as much information about those corporations as the directors and officers), the payment of a dividend in cash or property should also reduce the total market value of the corporation's outstanding shares by an amount equal to the total amount of the dividend. In the case of large, public corporations, the payment of dividends may not necessarily have this effect. There is a rather sophisticated body of financial economic literature on the topic of dividends, why corporations declare them, and the economic effect of so doing. For example, one possibility is that the very fact that the corporation has declared a dividend might be interpreted as a positive signal that will in fact lead to an *increase* in the market price for the corporation's shares, notwithstanding the decrease in its assets. See, e.g., William W. Bratton, *Corporate Finance*, 5th ed. (New York: Foundation Press, 2003), at 553ff.

nonetheless? Sutherland et al. take the view that s. 43(1) does, indeed, require that the tests must be satisfied before a stock dividend may be paid, although they concede that that requirement "is not entirely certain."[111]

Repurchase or Redemption of Shares and Reduction of Capital

It has traditionally been thought that a corporation's share capital stands as a kind of notional "fund" for the protection of a corporation's creditors. As Sir George Jessel explained in *Flitcroft's* case,[112] the creditor of a corporation

> gives credit to the company on the faith of the representation that the capital shall be applied only for the purposes of the business, and he has therefore a right to say that the corporation shall keep its capital and not return it to the shareholders.[113]

Thus, corporations were not traditionally permitted to return shareholders' capital to them. Indeed, corporations were not even permitted to purchase their own outstanding shares in market transactions. Corporations were forbidden from "trafficking in their own shares"[114] in this way, because it was feared that if corporations were permitted to buy their own shares in the markets, they would be able to manipulate their trading price.

The CBCA now permits corporations to repurchase or redeem their outstanding shares, subject to specifically prescribed rules. These rules are intended to ensure that a share repurchase or redemption does not render the corporation insolvent. The rules differ slightly depending on whether shares are being redeemed in accordance with redemption features specified in the share conditions,[115] repurchased for certain specified purposes (such as to settle a debt, eliminate fractional shares, or to fulfill the terms of an agreement under which the corporation has an option or an obligation to purchase shares from its directors, officers, or employees),[116] or otherwise purchased for cancellation.[117] In every case, the Act forbids a corporation from repurchasing or redeeming its shares if there are reasonable grounds for believing that, after doing so, the corporation would be unable to pay its liabilities as they become due. Where the three tests differ, however, is with respect to the extent to which the corporation's assets must exceed the sum of its liabilities and stated capital. For share repurchases that are made neither in accordance with pre-existing redemption rights nor for any of the particular purposes specified in s. 35(1), the realizable value of the assets must not be less than the sum of the corporation's liabilities and the stated capital of all classes.[118] Where a

---

111 Sutherland, supra footnote 65, at 223.

112 (1882), 21 Ch. D 519.

113 Ibid., at 533-34.

114 The classic statement of this principle is found in *Trevor v. Whitworth* (1887), 12 App. Cas. 409 (HL). See also the discussion of the Dickerson committee, supra footnote 20, at para. 121ff.

115 CBCA, s. 36.

116 CBCA, s. 35(1).

117 CBCA, s. 34.

118 CBCA, s. 34.

share is repurchased or redeemed pursuant to previously granted redemption rights (and at a price not greater than the agreed redemption price), the test is somewhat easier for the corporation to satisfy—namely, the realizable value of the assets need only be at least equal to the sum of the liabilities and "the amount that would be required to pay ... on a redemption or liquidation" to holders of shares that rank prior to, or rateably with, the shares being redeemed.[119] Where the shares are being repurchased to compromise a debt, eliminate fractional shares, or fulfill an option or other agreement with a director, officer or employee, the test is more lenient still: realizable assets need only equal at least the sum of liabilities and the amount required to pay on a redemption or liquidation to holders of prior ranking shares.[120] Where a repurchase of shares is made in accordance with an appraisal or oppression remedy, the test is the easiest of all. Realizable assets need only, following the purchase, be equal at least to the corporation's liabilities.[121]

Unlike in the United States, where corporations often retain repurchased shares as "treasury shares,"[122] typically, Canadian corporate statutes require a corporation that repurchases its shares to cancel them, unless the corporation's articles impose a limit on the number of the corporation's authorized shares, in which case the shares may be "restored to the status of authorized but unissued shares of the class."[123] When the term "treasury shares" is used in Canada, it typically refers to previously unissued shares, rather than previously issued shares that have been repurchased or redeemed by the issuing corporation.[124]

Note, too, that when a public corporation offers to purchase its own shares, such an offer constitutes an "issuer bid" for securities law purposes, and so may be subject to a series of special rules intended to ensure that shareholders are not unfairly dealt with.[125]

---

119   CBCA, s. 36(2)(b). The subsection includes additional language, qualifying the reference to amounts required to be paid to holders of other shares, "to the extent that the amount has not been included in [the corporation's] liabilities." This language was added to the CBCA in 2001 to deal with a technical concern that arises under Canadian accounting rules. Canadian generally accepted accounting principles require that certain hybrid shares issued by a corporation may be required to be reported, in whole or in part, as debt on the corporation's financial statements. Accordingly, an amount in respect of such shares would already be included as liabilities on the corporation's balance sheet, and so need not (and should not) be counted a second time—as equity—when performing the solvency test for purposes of s. 36(2). See Wayne D. Gray and Casey W. Halladay, *Guide to CBCA Reform: Analysis and Precedents* (Toronto: Carswell, 2002), 19.

120   CBCA, s. 35(3). This subsection also contains language to prevent double-counting as explained in footnote 119, supra.

121   CBCA, ss. 35(2), 190(26), and 241(6).

122   See, e.g., Bratton, supra footnote 110, at 588: "Once repurchased, shares may be placed in the corporation's 'treasury,' an accounting zone where they are authorized and issued but no longer outstanding. Treasury shares may be reissued."

123   CBCA, s. 39(6).

124   See, e.g., George R.D. Goulet, *Public Share Offerings and Stock Exchange Listings in Canada* (Toronto: CCH Canadian Limited, 1994), 8, at note 2.

125   For further discussion of the securities law implications of issuer bids, see MacIntosh and Nicholls, supra footnote 5, at 330ff.

Financial Assistance

Until relatively recently, most Canadian corporate statutes contained a provision declaring it unlawful for a corporation to provide financial assistance in connection with a purchase made by any person of any shares of the company. This provision came into Canadian law directly (and almost verbatim) from the UK *Companies Act*, but the origin of the provision in the UK Act was soon forgotten. The provision was assumed by many practitioners to have been intended to apply primarily or even exclusively in the case of purchases of new shares from treasury—that is, by subscription. However, there is evidence that these restrictions were actually originally introduced to curb an early form of "leveraged buyout" transaction. Lord Greene, in *In re V.G.M. Holdings*,[126] offered the following explanation for the provision:

> Those whose memories enable them to recall what had been happening after the last war for several years will remember that a very common form of transaction in connection with companies was one by which persons—call them financiers, speculators, or what you will—finding a company with a substantial cash balance or easily realizable assets such as a war loan, bought up the whole or the greater part of the shares of the company for cash and so arranged matters that the purchase money which they then became bound to provide was advanced to them by the company whose shares they were acquiring, either out of its cash balance or by realization of its liquid investments. That type of transaction was a common one, and it gave rise to great dissatisfaction and, in some cases, great scandals.[127]

The *V.G.M. Holdings* case was controversial. It was criticized by commentators who regarded the financial assistance rules as part of a broader scheme of ensuring that the corporation's capital would stand as a kind of unimpaired "guarantee" or "fund" for creditors. Thus, Kahn-Freund argued that the case had revealed a "gap in the law."[128] Similarly, Eilis Ferran cited the case to illustrate the point that "loopholes emerged in the drafting"[129] of the early statutory prohibitions on financial assistance.

Statutory Approaches to Financial Assistance

Although most Canadian corporate statutes have liberalized their approach to financial assistance, they have not approached the matter in a uniform way. The Ontario *Business Corporations Act*, the Alberta *Business Corporations Act*, the British Columbia *Business Corporations Act*, and the Saskatchewan *Business Corporations Act*, for example, explicitly permit corporations to give financial assistance,[130] but require disclosure to be made to the shareholders of any material financial assistance (subject

---

126 [1942] 1 Ch. 235.

127 Ibid., at 239.

128 O. Kahn-Freund, "Some Reflections on Company Law Reform" (1944), 7 *Modern Law Review* 54, at 60, note 29.

129 Eilis Ferran, *Company Law and Corporate Finance* (Oxford: Oxford University Press, 1999), at 374.

130 *Business Corporations Act* (Ont.), s. 20(1); *Business Corporations Act* (Alta.), s. 45(1); *Business Corporations Act* (BC), s. 195; and *The Business Corporations Act* (Sask.), s. 42(1).

to some exceptions)[131] given to a shareholder, director, officer, or employee, or given to anyone in connection with the purchase of shares, or securities convertible into shares, issued by the corporation or an affiliate.[132] The Supreme Court of Canada has recently confirmed that even where a corporate statute expressly permits financial assistance to be given in certain circumstances, "it is incumbent upon directors and officers to exercise their powers in conformity with the duties" of care and loyalty otherwise imposed on them.[133] In the *Peoples Department Stores* case, the Supreme Court was considering the effect of the financial assistance provisions as they existed in the CBCA prior to the 2001 amendments. Those provisions included a statement to the effect that a corporation could give financial assistance "to a holding body corporate if the corporation is a wholly-owned subsidiary of the holding body corporate." The Supreme Court held that this exception could not serve as "a blanket legitimization of financial assistance given by wholly-owned subsidiaries to parent corporations."[134]

The CBCA adopted a different approach. In 2001, references to financial assistance were simply repealed altogether. It was clearly the intention of this repeal to remove any restrictions on financial assistance, subject, as always, to the constraints placed on directors by their fiduciary duties. Some questions have been raised as to whether the repeal of provisions that did not codify the common law might have the unintended consequence of reviving the common law dealing with financial assistance (whatever that might have been). However, it seems doubtful that a court would adopt such an approach and unclear, in any event, what precisely would be the result even if the prior law were said to have been revived.

Preference Shares

The term "preference shares" is not defined in the CBCA or any other Canadian corporate statute. Indeed, the term is not even mentioned in the CBCA, although it does appear in some provincial statutes.[135] The term "preference shares" (or "preferred shares") is used very loosely to refer to a class of shares that entitles its holder to *some* rights in preference to the rights of more junior classes of shares, such as common or ordinary shares. This rather unhelpful description, in fact, is made explicit in the New Brunswick *Business Corporations Act*.[136]

In the case of public corporations, provincial securities laws are also relevant. Ontario Securities Commission rule 56-501, for example, states that reporting issuers (that is, public corporations) must not use the term "preference shares" or "preferred shares" to

---

131 *Business Corporations Act* (Ont.), s. 20(3) and *Business Corporations Act* (Alta.), s. 45(4). The exceptions essentially mirror the situations in which financial assistance was permitted under prior legislation. The Saskatchewan provision is structured somewhat differently.

132 *Business Corporations Act* (Ont.), s. 20(2) and *Business Corporations Act* (Alta.), s. 45(3).

133 *Peoples Department Stores Inc. v. Wise*, 2004 SCC 68, at para. 74.

134 Ibid.

135 See, e.g., *Companies Act* (PEI), s. 87; *Companies Act* (NS), s. 50; and *Business Corporations Act* (NB), s. 22(4).

136 *Business Corporations Act* (NB), s. 22(4).

refer to shares in various documents, unless the shares they describe (1) are non-equity shares (that is, shares that have no residual right to participate in the earnings of the issuer and in its assets on its winding up) and (2) carry some preference or right over a class of the corporation's equity shares.[137]

The statutory and regulatory framework surrounding preference shares is very thin. But as a matter of business convention, preference shares are generally thought to have the following characteristics:

- At the most general level, they are thought to have much in common with "fixed-income" securities (that is, debt instruments, such as bonds and debentures). Indeed, as Laskin JA put it in *Re Central Capital Corporation*,[138] "[p]referred shares have been called 'compromise securities' ... the conditions attaching to preferred shares contain attributes of equity and, at least in an economic sense, attributes of debt."[139] The reason that they are often compared to fixed income securities is that they conventionally (though not invariably) have three features that are typical of debt:
  - *Regular, fixed payments*: Generally, preferred shares entitle their holders to a regular, fixed dividend payment; that regular payment is similar to the regular payment of interest that a bondholder or debentureholder would receive. (Although, it must be emphasized, payments of dividends on preferred shares are not, as a matter of law, treated in the same way as payments of interest. A dividend payment is not deductible by the paying corporation in calculating its taxable income. An interest payment is deductible. If a corporation determines that it cannot (or will not) declare and pay a dividend, a preferred shareholder cannot sue to force payment. A debtholder can sue whenever an issuer misses a scheduled interest payment. As explained above, a dividend is taxed differently in the hands of the recipient than a payment of interest.)
  - *Non-voting*: Commonly, preferred shares, like bonds or debentures, do not entitle the holders to vote at annual meetings of the corporation, although in the cases of certain proposed fundamental corporate changes, corporate legislation may bestow voting privileges on shares that are normally non-voting. As well, it is common for non-voting, preferred shares to be given limited voting rights in the event that the corporation has failed to pay dividends for some specified period of time.
  - *Fixed amount payable on redemption or winding up*: Preferred shares, like debt, typically entitle their holders to only a fixed return of capital in the event that the corporation is wound up, rather than the sort of "unlimited potential upside" right to participate in a distribution of the corporation's property after its debts have been paid that is a defining characteristic of equity shares (such as those shares typically called common or ordinary shares). If preferred shares are "redeemable," the corporation may redeem them (that is, repurchase the shares and cancel them) at a price specified in the share conditions. This sort of redemption right at a fixed price is economically similar to a right to prepay a loan or debt

137 OSC rule 56-501, s. 2.1(1)(b).

138 Supra footnote 52.

139 Ibid., at 536.

instrument. It is a right that a corporation may wish to exercise if market interest rates (and dividend rates) fall, thus making an outstanding class of preference shares with an above-market stated dividend rate an expensive form of financing. Because a corporation would be tempted to redeem such shares at the very time when redemption would be most inconvenient for investors (namely, when market interest rates are low), redeemable preferred shares typically include features to protect or compensate holders in some way.

- Preference shares typically confer on their holders a preference as to payment of dividends. In other words, the share conditions will typically provide that holders of the shares are entitled to receive regular dividends in an amount equal to some specified percentage of a fixed dollar amount. That fixed dollar amount (which might be referred to as the "redemption price") will typically be linked to the price at which the preferred shares were originally issued. The payment of this dividend is said to be "preferred" in the sense that it ranks in priority to the dividend rights of more junior shares. Put more simply, the corporation must satisfy its obligation to pay dividends on its preference shares before it is permitted to pay any dividends on its ordinary equity shares, such as its common shares.
- Preference shares typically confer on their holders a preference as to return of capital on a winding up of the corporation. In other words, when a corporation with outstanding preference shares is dissolved or wound up, its assets sold, and its creditors paid, it is the preference shareholders who then stand at the head of line, entitled to receive a return of their invested capital. This amount they receive only after all the corporation's creditors have been paid in full, but before any distribution is made from the corporation's assets to the holders of equity shares, such as common or ordinary shares.

These preference share conditions are typical, but by no means invariable. The only limits placed on the flexibility of preference share attributes are those of the human imagination and the desires of share investors who, after all, must ultimately be persuaded to purchase the shares created by a corporation. Nor should this short list mislead anyone into thinking that one should expect that any share called a preference share will necessarily have all or any of these conventional features. It is impossible to know (and foolish to speculate on or assume) the characteristics of *any* corporate security without specifically examining the document by which they have been created. In the case of preference shares (or any other equity security), the rights, privileges, and conditions attaching to those shares are contained in the share conditions. Those share conditions are found, in the case of a CBCA corporation, in the articles of the corporation.

There is a well-known series of English and Canadian cases that deal with the residual rights of preference shareholders to participate with the common shareholders in receiving dividends and in a distribution of the corporation's assets when the corporation is wound up. Those cases are relevant only when the preference share conditions are silent on certain matters, or ambiguous on others. It would be very rare today to find share conditions suffering from the deficiencies to which the courts in those cases were compelled to respond. Accordingly, it seems to be an imprudent use of space and time to say much about these old cases here. I provide only the briefest of summaries, and invite interested readers to pursue the original judgments themselves. In summary then, *if, and only if the share conditions do not specify otherwise*:

- Preference shares that entitle the holder to a fixed preferential dividend do *not* entitle the holder, after having received this dividend, to participate rateably with the holders of the common or ordinary equity shares in any further dividend.[140]
- Where preference shares entitle the holder to a fixed return of capital on a winding up, there is English authority providing that such shares do *not* entitle the holder, after having received this fixed return of capital, to further participate rateably with the holders of the common or ordinary equity shares in the distribution of any remaining property of the corporation.[141] A Supreme Court of Canada case decided to the contrary,[142] but that case was decided in 1946, at a time when decisions of the Supreme Court of Canada could still be appealed to the Judicial Committee of the Privy Council. This technical observation may be significant, because the contrary position was subsequently articulated by the House of Lords in 1949 and the matter has not come before the Supreme Court since then. Thus, the Canadian position is not necessarily free from doubt.
- Where preference shares entitle their holders to receive cumulative dividends, and those dividends are in arrears at the time that a corporation is wound up, the shareholders are *not*, in theory, entitled to receive the unpaid arrears of dividends; however, the English courts have been prepared to interpret share conditions very liberally in order to "find" an express share condition that would entitle shareholders to receive such cumulated and unpaid dividends.[143]

CONCLUSION

This whirlwind tour of corporate finance has been aimed only at providing a broad general background rather than a careful analysis of the many technical legal issues that surround the financing of a corporation. Although this review is necessarily brief and incomplete, it is hoped that it will provide some context within which to understand, among other things, the dynamic underlying modern corporate governance debates discussed in earlier chapters, and the mechanisms of corporate statutory remedies introduced in chapters 13 and 14.

---

140 *Will v. United Lankat Plantations Co. Ltd.*, [1914] AC 11 (HL).

141 *Scottish Insurance Corporation v. Wilsons & Clyde Coal Co. Ltd.*, [1949] AC 462 (HL).

142 *International Power Co. v. McMaster University*, [1946] SCR 178.

143 As Davies put it, "this presumption [that is, that the shareholders are not entitled to the cumulated dividends] may be rebutted by the slightest indication to the contrary." See Davies, supra footnote 38, at 623. This proposition was evidently adopted by the Ontario High Court (a predecessor of the Superior Court of Justice) in *Re Canada Tea Co.* (1959), 21 DLR (2d) 90 (Ont. HC), albeit the court there did not find in the articles before it, to use Davies's phrase, even "the slightest indication to the contrary."

CHAPTER THIRTEEN

Corporate Statutory Remedies: Derivative Actions and Oppression Remedies

INTRODUCTION

As we have seen in earlier chapters, when a corporation interacts with third parties—entering into contractual relations, engaging in tortious conduct, and even, on occasion, committing crimes—it is subject to traditional legal remedies and is entitled to many traditional legal protections. These remedies and protections, must, of course, be tweaked from time to time to ensure that they will apply appropriately to an artificial person rather than to the sort of natural (that is, human) person for which they were originally developed.

But disputes often arise within the proverbial walls of the corporation itself: disputes, not just between the corporation and arm's-length third parties, but also, for example, between the corporation and those who manage its business and affairs. Disputes may even involve one or more of the corporation's principal constituents. When conflicts of this sort arise, a special set of rules and remedies is sometimes called for.

Intracorporate disputes between the corporation and its investors are especially frequent. The term "investor" is sometimes used as a synonym for shareholder, but as we saw in chapter 12, corporate investors may, broadly speaking, be divided into two categories: creditors and shareholders.

Creditors of a corporation enjoy contractual rights. If their corporate debtors fail to make a payment of interest or principal on time, or otherwise commit some act of default, creditors may sue to enforce the terms of their loan agreement, debt security or instrument, or trust indenture (subject to restrictions imposed by the indenture), as the case may be.

However, the relationship between shareholders and the corporation in which they hold shares is not contractual in the conventional sense.[1] As discussed in chapter 10, corporate statutes accord shareholders various rights to exercise their "voice" in the

---

1   This statement is subject to two qualifications. First, provincial corporate statutes in British Columbia and Nova Scotia still adhere to the English memorandum/articles of association model of incorporation, pursuant to which the memorandum and articles of association are, as a technical matter, said to constitute a contract between the members. (See *Companies Act* (NS), s. 24 and *Business Corporations Act* (BC), s. 19(3).) Second, as discussed at some length in chapter 4, many Canadian corporate statutes now provide for creation, and recognition, of a unanimous shareholder agreement. (See, e.g., CBCA, s. 146.)

governance of the corporation on a regular (if not an ongoing) basis. These statutory measures include voting, proxy, and shareholder proposal rules. Shareholders also have the same rights as any other person dealing with a corporation to pursue personal actions against the corporation when some wrong has been done to them personally.

But when shareholders have been subject to unfair actions taken by the corporation, its directors, or its officers, they cannot turn to the enforcement of contractual covenants for protection. When shareholders' economic interests are placed in jeopardy by the very managers they entrusted to safeguard them, they suddenly find themselves barred by the gates of the fortress of separate legal entity that had originally been constructed for their own protection.

In cases such as these, the corporate structure creates obstacles to justice. Accordingly, a number of special avenues of redress have been developed and are, in Canada, typically included within the corporate legislation. These protections are often referred to, collectively, as "shareholder remedies." However, this term has become a misnomer because, although shareholders are still the primary beneficiaries of these measures, in many cases aggrieved parties other than shareholders are also permitted to make use of them.

To be clear, the corporate remedies with which this chapter is concerned are civil remedies. There are, of course, also a host of penalty provisions in Canadian corporate statutes intended to ensure that corporate managers and others comply with the applicable law.[2] But the philosophy underlying most modern corporate law statutes is that they ought to be, so far as possible, "self-enforcing"—relying mainly on the initiative of those who are aggrieved to ensure that appropriate legal proceedings are undertaken, rather than depending on a detailed regime of harsh penalty provisions. The Dickerson committee, for example, explicitly advocated such an approach in its report that led to the enactment of the CBCA.[3]

AN OVERVIEW OF KEY CORPORATE CIVIL REMEDIES

Among the most important of the special corporate civil remedies found in the CBCA and most other Canadian corporate statutes, are the following:

- *Derivative actions*: Derivative actions are initiated by a *complainant*,[4] as defined by statute, when a wrong has allegedly been done *to* a corporation. At common law,

---

2   See, e.g., CBCA, s. 251 (a general provision making it an offence to contravene the CBCA or the regulations). In addition to this general provision, there are a host of more specific penalty provisions including s. 20(6), s. 21(10), s. 22(3), s. 32(4), s. 85(6), s. 130(4), s. 149(3), s. 149(4), s. 150(3), s. 150(4), s. 152(4), s. 153(8), s. 159(2), s. 160(3), s. 168(4), s. 171(9), s. 225(2), and s. 235(4).

3   See Robert W.V. Dickerson et al., *Proposals for a New Business Corporations Law for Canada*, vol. I, Commentary (Ottawa: Information Canada, 1971), at para. 476 (Dickerson committee): "we think that the best means of enforcing a corporation law is to confer reasonable power upon the allegedly aggrieved party to initiate legal action to resolve his problem, making the Draft Act largely self-enforcing, obviating the need for sweeping administrative discretion and harsh penal sanctions, and, at the same time, forcing resolution of the issues before the courts, which have the procedures, the machinery and the experience that enable them better than any other institution to deal with such problems."

4   The term "complainant" is used in most Canadian corporate statutes. It might be noted that under s. 232 of the *Business Corporations Act* (BC), a derivative action may be initiated by a "complainant," a term

such actions were circumscribed by the rule in *Foss v. Harbottle*.[5] Canadian corporate statutes today now specifically prescribe the procedures and conditions to be followed when commencing derivative actions.

- *Oppression remedy*: Oppression applications may be initiated by a *complainant*,[6] as defined by statute, in cases where, among other things, acts or omissions of a corporation, or its affiliates, or the exercise of directors' powers effect a result that is "oppressive or unfairly prejudicial or that unfairly disregards the interests of any securityholder, creditor, director, or officer."

- *Dissent and appraisal rights*: Dissent and appraisal rights are available to dissenting *shareholders* when certain *specified* fundamental changes have been undertaken by the corporation; the appraisal remedy refers to a requirement that the corporation purchase the dissenting shareholders' shares for *fair value*.

- *Compliance orders*: Compliance orders are available to a *complainant*, as defined by statute, or to a *creditor*, when certain fundamental corporate documents (for example, articles, bylaws, or unanimous shareholder agreements) or the provisions of the corporate statute itself are not being complied with by the corporation. The remedy sought is an order to comply with the document or provision in question.

- *Liquidation or dissolution (winding-up orders)*: Action can be taken by a *shareholder* seeking dissolution of the corporation in cases where an "oppression" remedy would be available, where a unanimous shareholder agreement permits the shareholders to demand dissolution, or where it is otherwise "just and equitable" to do so.

This chapter will discuss the first two of these remedies, the derivative action and the oppression remedy. Chapter 14 will canvass the other statutory remedies. The availability in certain circumstances of an investigation order will also be touched on briefly in chapter 14. An investigation order is not, strictly speaking, a remedy, but it is another statutorily prescribed arrow in the quiver of aggrieved corporate investors.

DERIVATIVE ACTIONS

Framing the Issue

From time to time the directors or officers of a corporation will be tempted to act in selfish disregard of the corporate interests they were elected or appointed to protect. They might, for example, wrongly seize for themselves a business or investment opportunity that properly belongs to the corporation. "Corporate opportunity" cases of this sort were

---

defined to mean "a shareholder or director of the company." However, the term "shareholder" is given an extended definition for this purpose and includes not only a beneficial owner of the company's shares, but also any other "appropriate person" as determined by the court in its discretion (s. 232(1)).

5   *Foss v. Harbottle* (1843), 2 Hare 461.

6   Again, as in the case of the derivative action, the BC *Business Corporations Act* differs from most other Canadian corporate statutes that provide an oppression remedy. Such an action can be initiated only by a "shareholder"; but the term "shareholder" includes both a beneficial owner of shares and any other "appropriate person" as determined by the court (*Business Corporations Act* (BC), s. 227(1)).

discussed in chapter 11. They might opportunistically cause the corporation to purchase property from them at a large overvalue (or, alternatively, to sell valuable corporate property to them at a gross undervalue). Chapter 11 included a discussion of such "interested directors' and officers' contracts" as well. Many more examples could be offered. The opportunities for raiding the corporate till, literally or figuratively, are all too plentiful for faithless fiduciaries.

The fiduciary duties of officers and directors are owed to the corporation, not to its shareholders, or to any other corporate stakeholder, for that matter. As discussed in chapter 10, it has been an enduring challenge in corporate law to define—for practical purposes—what it means to owe duties to a legal abstraction. However, it is clear enough that when directors or officers act in breach of their duties, it is the corporation, as a matter of law, that has been wronged.[7]

But who speaks for the corporation in such cases? Who will ensure that the corporation takes the steps necessary to seek damages from the wrongdoer? Usually when a corporation is the victim of an actionable wrong, it falls to the managers—that is, the officers and directors—to initiate the appropriate legal action. Shareholders typically have no say in such matters. But when the corporation has suffered harm at the hands of the directors or senior officers themselves, enforcement of the corporation's rights is problematic. Wayward managers, who have already shown no compunction in violating their fiduciary duties, are unlikely to repent at once and, in a fit of self-sacrificing propriety, promptly authorize the corporation to launch a legal action to which they, the managers themselves, will be the defendants. It is for situations such as these that the derivative action was principally designed.

A derivative action is a lawsuit initiated by a shareholder (or other eligible "complainant," as defined by statute) effectively on behalf of the corporation, in cases where a wrong has been done *to* the corporation, but where, for some reason, the usual corporate decision makers have declined to initiate proceedings on the corporation's behalf.

This type of legal action is described as "derivative" because the complainant derives his or her right to bring the action from the corporation itself. The corporation, in other words, is really the proper plaintiff—it is the corporation that has been directly harmed, not the complainant. The complainant, to be sure, has almost surely been harmed indirectly in some way. For example, when a corporation suffers a loss, the value of its shares will tumble, reflecting the corporation's misfortunes. That is precisely why complainants, especially shareholders, have an incentive to put things right.

Today in Canada, the rules governing derivative actions are typically prescribed by corporate statute. But, to understand the rationale underlying specific aspects of the typical Canadian statutory derivative action provisions, it is helpful to look back briefly to the older common law concerning derivative actions. This glimpse into the past brings us rather hastily to the notorious rule in *Foss v. Harbottle*.

---

7   Note, however, with respect to the duty of care, the recent observation by the Supreme Court of Canada in *Peoples Department Stores Inc. v. Wise*, 2004 SCC 68 that "the statement of the duty of care in s. 122(1)(b) of the CBCA does not specifically refer to an identifiable party as the beneficiary of the duty." Ibid., at para. 57. Some of the implications of this decision are explored in chapter 10.

The Common Law Derivative Action and the Rule in Foss v. Harbottle

"Any event, once it has occurred," said scenic designer Lee Simonson, "can be made to appear inevitable by a competent historian." This might be said of any legal development as well. The common law of derivative actions is often said to have arisen inevitably from the doctrine of separate corporate personality, but surely the law might just as easily have developed along very different lines. For example, when the value of a corporation's shares falls, as a result of some wrong committed against that corporation, some pragmatic judge might well have chosen to characterize the shareholders' resulting financial loss as personal in nature, and thus actionable at the instance of each and every affected shareholder. No special "derivative action" rules, in this alternative legal universe, would ever have been required, although there might well have been a need for special procedural safeguards to deal with joinder of claims and other matters.

The law went in a different direction, though. Specifically, at common law, it became almost impossible for shareholders to pursue a claim when a wrong had been done to the corporation in which they held shares, notwithstanding that they might well have suffered significant financial loss (in the form of a collapse in the value of those shares). The formidable barriers placed in their way by the courts were embodied in the so-called rule in *Foss v. Harbottle*,[8] named for the 19th century case in which it was originally articulated.

Foss v. Harbottle involved an enterprise called the Victoria Park Company. This business had begun its "life" as an unincorporated joint stock company (that is, as discussed in chapter 1, a kind of partnership).[9] Later, according to the case reporter,

> in order to avoid the responsibilities of an ordinary partnership, the Defendants Harbottle and others suggested to the subscribers the propriety of applying for an Act of Incorporation, which was accordingly done.[10]

So the company came to be incorporated under a special act of Parliament[11] for the purposes of "laying out and maintaining an ornamental park" in Lancaster. The plaintiffs were shareholders of this company. The basis for their claim, simply put, was that the defendants—including a number of directors of the corporation—had conceived and engineered a fraudulent scheme: they had caused this new company, so the plaintiffs alleged, to purchase land from them (that is, from the defendants themselves) at inflated prices, and to finance this purchase by mortgaging the very lands purchased. (This mortgage transaction was, in and of itself, alleged to be improper.)

The court concluded that, even if the company itself had a right to sue the directors in respect of these transactions, the plaintiffs (as shareholders) were not entitled in their

---

8   Supra footnote 5.

9   There were important distinctions between joint stock companies and ordinary general partnerships, as canvassed briefly in chapter 1. Those distinctions, however, are not germane to a discussion of *Foss v. Harbottle*.

10   Supra footnote 5, at 463.

11   Special act companies are discussed in chapter 1. *Foss v. Harbottle* was decided before the enactment of the first general incorporation statute in England—the *Joint Stock Companies Act* of 1844.

individual capacities to bring this action. The action was intended to right a wrong allegedly suffered, not by the plaintiff shareholders in their individual capacities, but rather by the corporation of which they (and a number of others who were not plaintiffs) were merely members. The court was careful to allow that there might be cases in which individual shareholders could sue in similar circumstances.[12] However, two factors in particular seemed to persuade the court that *Foss v. Harbottle* was not such a case. First, the specific wording of the Victoria Park Company's incorporating statute, among other things, conferred power on the shareholders *in general meeting* to commence legal proceedings.[13] Furthermore, it was still possible that the sale contract entered into between the director defendants and the corporation could, at some future time, be adopted (or confirmed) by the shareholders at a general meeting. Because no attempt had been made to place the matter before any such meeting, it was improper, in the court's view, to permit individual shareholders to sue to have it set aside.

The rule in *Foss v. Harbottle*, as it has since come to be known, thus has two distinct prongs. First, it is said to stand for the proposition that, where a corporation has been wronged, the corporation alone may sue in respect of that wrong. Individual shareholders, in particular, normally lack standing to bring a lawsuit against those who have allegedly injured the corporation, notwithstanding that the effect of the actions complained of may well include a diminution in the value of the corporation's shares. Second, where a wrong is done to a corporation, that wrong may be cleansed if it is, in effect, "waived" (or perhaps confirmed) by the shareholders in general meeting.

The first prong of the "rule" might seem at first to constitute a rather straightforward application of what today is often called the *Salomon* principle: if a corporation is truly a distinct legal person, then naturally a court should not permit some different person to sue for damages when the corporation has been injured. Indeed, when the Supreme Court of Canada recently adverted to the *Foss v. Harbottle* rule, it was this narrow aspect of the first prong, and this aspect alone, that they appeared to have in mind:

> The rule in *Foss v. Harbottle* provides that individual shareholders have no cause of action in law for any wrongs done to the corporation and that if an action is to be brought in respect of such losses, it must be brought either by the corporation itself (through management) or by way of a derivative action.[14]

In that same decision, the Supreme Court cited with approval a passage from the English Court of Appeal's judgment in *Prudential Assurance Co. v. Newman Industries Ltd. (No. 2)*,[15] in which the court declared the *Foss v. Harbottle* rule to be "the consequence of the fact that a corporation is a separate legal entity."[16]

More recently still, the Ontario Court of Appeal expressly linked the logic underlying the rule in *Foss v. Harbottle* with that of the celebrated *Salomon* principle:

---

12   Supra footnote 5, at 491-92.

13   Ibid., at 492-93.

14   See *Hercules Management Ltd. v. Ernst & Young*, [1997] 2 SCR 165, at 211-12.

15   [1982] 1 All ER 354, at 367.

16   Ibid.

The rule in *Foss v. Harbottle* provides simply that a shareholder of a corporation—even a controlling shareholder or the sole shareholder—does not have a personal cause of action for a wrong done to the corporation. The rule respects a basic principle of corporate law: a corporation has a legal existence separate from that of its shareholders. See *Salomon v. Salomon & Co.*[17]

In both of these recent Canadian cases, the courts invoked *Foss v. Harbottle* to explain why, as a legal matter, shareholders, whose shares have lost value as a result of a wrong done to a corporation, are nevertheless not permitted in their personal capacity to bring an action against the alleged wrongdoer. This aspect of the rule in *Foss v. Harbottle*, and the hurdles it creates in the case of wrongs committed by a corporation's directors and officers, is by no means trivial. Nevertheless, two points deserve mention. First, it is not entirely correct to say, as the Ontario Court of Appeal suggests, that this first prong of *Foss v. Harbottle* is all that the rule "simply" "provides." The rule's second prong is surely just as important and, indeed, has historically garnered even more attention (and criticism) from courts, commentators, and legislators. Second, the articulation of the rule—merely as a special case of the *Salomon* separate entity doctrine—is somewhat incomplete because it does not reflect the extent to which it was the principle of majority shareholder rule (and not merely the separate legal entity concept) that informed the reasoning of the court in *Foss v. Harbottle*.

In fact, the apparent simplicity and inflexibility of the first prong of the rule appear to have been much doubted in the *Foss* case itself. On this matter the vice-chancellor had this to say:

> The first objection taken in the argument for the Defendants was that the individual members of the corporation cannot in any case sue in the form in which this bill is framed. During the argument I intimated an opinion to which, upon further consideration, I fully adhere, *that the rule was much too broadly stated on the part of the Defendants. I think there are cases in which a suit might properly be so framed.* Corporations like this, of a private nature, are in truth little more than private partnerships; and in cases which may easily be suggested it would be too much to hold that a society of private persons associated together in undertakings which, though certainly beneficial to the public, are nevertheless matters of private property, are to be deprived of their civil rights, *inter se*, because, in order to make their common objects more attainable, the Crown or the Legislature may have conferred upon them the benefit of a corporate character. *If a case should arise of injury to a corporation by some of its members, for which no adequate remedy remained, except that of a suit by individual corporators in their private characters, and asking in such character the protection of those rights to which in their corporate character they were entitled, I cannot but think that the principle so forcibly laid down by Lord Cottenham in Wallworth v. Holt ... and other cases would apply, and the claims of justice would be found superior to any difficulties arising out of technical rules respecting the mode in which corporations are required to sue.*[18]

---

17   *Meditrust Healthcare Inc. v. Shoppers Drug Mart* (2002), 61 OR (3d) 786, at 790 (CA).

18   Supra footnote 5, at 491-92 (emphasis added).

To be sure, the court went on to make it clear that such long-standing principles ought only to be departed from if there are "reasons of a very urgent character."[19] However, in the analysis that follows thereafter, it becomes increasingly clear that the court's decision in *Foss* did not turn simply on a dogged adherence to the notion that the corporation—as a legal entity, distinct from its shareholders—was therefore the only entity that could sue for alleged wrongs. Instead, it rested more specifically on the fact that by the terms of incorporation of *this particular corporation*, the shareholders in general meeting retained the right to adopt or confirm the impugned contracts (and retained the right to commence legal proceedings too, for that matter).

Thus, *Foss v. Harbottle*, a case that was decided more than half a century before *Salomon*, was far from a mere dogmatic application of the doctrine of separate corporate personality. The court in *Foss* instead made generous use of the concept of the business corporation as a company or collective of its members—likening it, and other such private corporations, to "in truth little more than private partnerships,"[20] associations in which the will of the majority ought properly to bind the minority.

Indeed, one may venture even a little further. The court in *Foss v. Harbottle* seems actually to have preferred this "majority rule" rationale over the more technical assertion that the corporation, as a distinct legal entity, was the only party to which the corporation's directors owed their duties. Consider, for example, the following passage from the judgment:

> Now, who are the *cestui que trusts* in this case? The corporation, in a sense, is undoubtedly the *cestui que trust*; but the majority of the proprietors at a special general meeting assembled, independently of any general rules of law upon the subject, by the very terms of the incorporation in the present case, has the power to bind the whole body, and every individual corporator must be taken to have come into the corporation upon the terms of being liable to be so bound.[21]

The shareholders in general meeting (not, as in the modern corporation, the board of directors) had the authority to commence litigation on behalf of the corporation, but had not yet been given the opportunity to consider the matter. They had said neither "yea" nor "nay" to the question of whether litigation ought to be commenced in the corporation's name, or, for that matter, to the issue of whether, in their judgment, the transactions complained of had, in fact, caused injury to the corporation justifying any such action.

Careful commentators have provided useful insights into the teaching of *Foss v. Harbottle*. A two-part article on the "rule" by K.W. Wedderburn published in the *Cambridge Law Review* in the 1950s was once said by Gower to constitute the "classic analysis of the rule."[22] The Wedderburn article nicely articulates how one part of the rule derives from traditional corporate law, and the other from the law of partnership.

---

19   Ibid., at 492.

20   Ibid., at 491.

21   Ibid., at 494.

22   Paul L. Davies, *Gower's Principles of Modern Company Law*, 6th ed. (London: Sweet & Maxwell, 1997), at 659, note 10.

The notion that the corporation is the proper plaintiff in any action commenced to address a wrong done to the corporation is the part of the rule solidly grounded in corporate law principles, under Wedderburn's analysis. But a judicial reluctance to interfere in a company's internal management—a reluctance that owes much to partnership law principles—underpins the second part of the rule. What Wedderburn notes, however, is that these two separate sources really merge in what may be said to be a complete and precise restatement of the rule in *Foss v. Harbottle*—namely, that "an internal 'irregularity' can be expressed in terms of a 'wrong against the corporation' alone, *because* [that is to say, *only* because] the majority might [subsequently] regularise it by adoption."[23]

Furthermore, it appears that application of the rule in *Foss v. Harbottle* has not been limited to incorporated bodies. Note that *Edwards v. Halliwell*,[24] a case that is routinely referred to in discussions of *Foss v. Harbottle*, actually concerned a trade union, not a business corporation, and, in that case, Jenkins LJ, of the English Court of Appeal, articulated the first prong of the rule of *Foss v. Harbottle* in this way:

> [T]he proper plaintiff in an action in respect of a wrong alleged to be done to a company *or association of persons* is prima facie the company *or the association of persons* itself.[25]

We thus mistake and misinterpret the rule in *Foss v. Harbottle* if we say that it speaks only to the fact that a shareholder has no cause of action for wrongs done to a corporation because a corporation is a distinct legal entity. Gower's articulation[26] of the rule appears rather better and certainly more consistent with the reasoning found in that famous case itself, rather than in other secondary source summaries of it:

> Driven by fears that such a rule [that is, an alternative to the rule in *Foss v. Harbottle*, that would allow suit by individual shareholders in cases where directors have control over the general meeting] would generate a multiplicity of suits and encourage wasted litigation, [English law] has developed a much more elaborate and restrictive set of criteria for determining when an individual shareholder may sue to enforce the company's rights against the wrongdoing directors. Those criteria are referred to compendiously as the "rule in *Foss v. Harbottle*," after the case in which the principle was first clearly articulated that the decision on suit ought normally be taken by the majority of the shareholders in general meeting.[27]

The corporate constitution (that is, the special act of Parliament) under which the corporation in *Foss v. Harbottle* was created, vested the power to commence legal

---

23   K.W. Wedderburn, "Shareholders' Rights and the Rule in *Foss v. Harbottle*," [1957] *Cambridge Law Journal* 194, at 198.

24   [1950] 2 All ER 1064 (CA).

25   Ibid., at 1066 (emphasis added).

26   The Dickerson committee, highlighting the interpretive problems raised by *Foss v. Harbottle*, cited a comment made by Professor Gower in the preface to the second edition of his text: "[A]n attempt has been made to elucidate the mysteries of the rule in *Foss v. Harbottle*; I believe that I now understand this rule, but have little confidence that readers will share this belief." L.C.B. Gower, *Principles of Modern Company Law*, 2nd ed., "Preface," at v, cited in Dickerson committee, supra footnote 3, at para. 482.

27   Davies, supra footnote 22, at 659 (footnotes omitted).

proceedings in the shareholders in general meeting. And it was this residual power of the shareholders to commence proceedings in the corporate name that was critical to the reasoning and the result in *Foss v. Harbottle*. As the Lawrence committee observed, that fact is "absolutely essential to an understanding of the Rule and the difficulties which surround it."[28] But typically, in modern Canadian corporations, the shareholders would never have such powers; it would be the responsibility of the directors to make the final determination as to whether a corporation should pursue legal action. Thus, unlike the situation that obtained at the time of *Foss v. Harbottle*, "there is no means whereby a majority of the shareholders in a [modern Canadian] company can authorize an action in the corporate name on behalf of the company against the wishes of the board of directors."[29]

The importance of this observation is simply this. The key premise underlying the holding in *Foss v. Harbottle* has no application to most Canadian corporations. This is not to suggest, of course, that there are not very good reasons for Canadian courts to prevent shareholders in the normal course from bringing actions based on the alleged diminution in value of their shares. There clearly are. Such a prohibition might well avoid multiplicity of suits,[30] for example, or inconsistent verdicts, or an unfair transfer of corporate assets (namely, the proceeds of the value of litigation) to some shareholders (the plaintiffs) to the prejudice of the remaining shareholders,[31] or a host of other administrative or substantive problems. But, perhaps it is these policy considerations that ought to be expressly invoked by courts today as they attempt to frame a useful and economically sensible approach to standing, rather than the now somewhat dubious authority of the supposed "rule" in *Foss v. Harbottle*.

Exceptions to the Rule in Foss v. Harbottle

No discussion of *Foss v. Harbottle* would be complete without reference to the famous exceptions to the rule that developed at common law. And so, despite the diminished significance of the rule under modern Canadian statutory derivative action regimes, a brief discussion of these oft-repeated four "exceptions" is offered here. The most fre-

---

28   *Interim Report of the Select Committee on Company Law*, Allan F. Lawrence Chair (1967), at 56, para. 7.3.4 (hereinafter "Lawrence committee report").

29   Lawrence committee report, ibid., at 57, para. 7.3.5. Note that Stanley M. Beck had prepared a research paper for the Lawrence committee analyzing the rule in *Foss v. Harbottle*. See Stanley M. Beck, "An Analysis of *Foss v. Harbottle*," in Jacob S. Ziegel, ed., *Studies in Canadian Company Law* (Toronto: Butterworths, 1967), at 545. Echoes of that paper are obvious within the final report itself. Beck noted that "exclusive director control of corporate litigation raises a situation not contemplated at the time *Foss v. Harbottle* was decided." At the time Beck wrote, however, Ontario law did not permit (as English law did) the removal of corporate directors by ordinary resolution, a power that, in Beck's view, would return to shareholders power of a kind comparable to that enjoyed by the corporation at the centre of the *Foss v. Harbottle* dispute. (Ibid., at 554.) Of course, Canadian corporate statutes now typically provide that directors may be removed by ordinary resolution. See, e.g., CBCA, s. 109(1).

30   See *Meditrust*, supra footnote 17, at para. 13: "The rule in *Foss v. Harbottle* also avoids multiple lawsuits. Indeed, without the rule, a shareholder would always be able to sue for harm to the corporation because any harm to the corporation indirectly harms the shareholders."

31   This point is made by Paul L. Davies, *Gower & Davies: Principles of Modern Company Law*, 7th ed. (London: Sweet & Maxwell, 2003), at 456.

quently cited articulation of those exceptions is taken from the judgment of Jenkins LJ in *Edwards v. Halliwell*:[32]

- where the impugned action involved an illegal act, or an act *ultra vires* the corporation;
- where the impugned act was not one that could be sanctioned by a simple majority of the company's members, but required, instead, the approval of some special majority vote;
- where the impugned act gave rise to a personal right of action on the part of the individual plaintiff; and
- where the impugned act constituted a fraud on the minority.

Where any of these "exceptions" applied, the law recognized the shareholder's personal right to commence a legal action, and that action would not be hindered by application of the *Foss v. Harbottle* rule. As Wedderburn and others[33] have observed, however, at least three of these "exceptions" are not true exceptions at all. They are really examples of situations where the rule would never have had any application in the first place. For example, at the core of the rule is the principle that no individual shareholder can sue over a transaction that the shareholders in general meeting might ultimately choose to ratify or confirm; so clearly the rule could never apply to instances involving illegal or *ultra vires* acts. Shareholders would never have the authority to authorize *ultra vires* or illegal actions, a fact specifically adverted to in the *Foss v. Harbottle* decision itself.[34]

Similarly, the rule cannot apply where a corporate action requires approval by some kind of super-majority vote (for example, by the affirmative vote of at least two-thirds of the corporation's shareholders, rather than by simple majority vote (50 percent of the voting shares plus 1)). After all, it would be absurd for a court to hold that failure to obtain shareholder approval by the specified super-majority could later be waived by a simple majority vote. So, once again, the "rule" could never be engaged in a case like that because it would never have been possible for the shareholders in general meeting (by simple majority) to ratify the disputed transaction.[35]

Finally, in those cases where an individual shareholder is pursuing a *personal* action, *ex hypothesi*, the *Foss v. Harbottle* rule would not apply. The alleged wrong would have been committed against the individual plaintiff personally. It would not be the corporation that had suffered injury in the first place. Indeed, Jenkins LJ, in *Edwards v. Halliwell*, noted that such a case was

---

32 Supra footnote 24, at 1067.

33 See, e.g., M.A. Maloney, "Whither the Statutory Derivative Action?" (1986), 64 *Canadian Bar Review* 309, at 311.

34 Supra footnote 5, at 493: "The second ground of complaint may stand in a different position; I allude to the mortgaging in a manner not authorized by the powers of the Act. This, being beyond the powers of the corporation, may admit of no confirmation whilst any one dissenting voice is raised against it." Again, of course, if the rule is articulated in this way, then it would not, without more, stand in the way of the sort of actions that had been launched in *Meditrust*, supra footnote 17 or *Hercules*, supra footnote 14, either. In both of these cases, the shareholders had no power either to commence legal proceedings or to waive the wrongs allegedly done to the respective corporations.

35 See Wedderburn, supra footnote 23, at 207.

of a kind which is not even within the general ambit of the rule. It is not a case where what is complained of is a wrong done to the union, a matter in respect of which the cause of action would primarily and properly belong to the union. It is a case in which certain members of a trade union complain that the union ... has invaded the individual rights of the complainant members.[36]

The only real exceptions to the rule in *Foss v. Harbottle*, then, as has often been observed, are cases falling within the fourth category—that is, cases involving a fraud on the minority.

The Rule in Foss v. Harbottle: Gone but Not Forgotten?

Were it not for occasional references to *Foss v. Harbottle* by Canadian judges—such as the two recent examples mentioned earlier (neither of which actually concerned derivative actions)—good reasons would exist for concluding that the rule had become a historical relic. Canadian corporate law statutes now typically include specific derivative action provisions. It is thus corporate legislation, and not the antique common law rule in *Foss v. Harbottle*, that should determine when an action can, or cannot, be brought in the corporate name. Certainly, the Dickerson committee appeared to be of the view that the new CBCA had

[r]elegated the rule [in *Foss v. Harbottle*] to legal limbo without compunction, convinced that the alternative system recommended is preferable to the uncertainties—and obvious injustice—engendered by that infamous doctrine.[37]

The "obvious injustice" refers to problems arising from adherence to the second prong of the rule. Taken to its logical extreme, that aspect of the rule would countenance a situation in which the shareholders, by majority vote, might ratify the misfeasance of a corporate director, even though that very director (if he were also a major shareholder) may have participated in the vote at the ratifying shareholders' meeting, and so ensured an outcome favourable to his or her own interests.

The CBCA drafters intended their statutorily prescribed derivative action to constitute a complete code, one that would entirely replace the pre-existing common law derivative action rules. There appears to be ample subsequent judicial authority to support the view that the framers accomplished their objective.[38]

Accordingly, although *Foss v. Harbottle* and the famous four "exceptions" occupy an important place in Canadian corporate law history, for practical purposes it is to the

---

36   Supra footnote 24, at 1067.

37   Dickerson committee, supra footnote 3, at para. 482.

38   See, e.g., *Farnham v. Fingold et al.* (1973), 33 DLR (3d) 156 (Ont. CA), in which the Ontario Court of Appeal rejected the argument that a derivative action of the type "exemplified by *Foss v. Harbottle*" could be maintained in Ontario, despite the existence of a statutory derivative action (with specific procedural requirements) in the governing corporate legislation. Jessup CA held, referring to the derivative action provision in the Ontario legislation at that time, that this provision "embraces all causes of action under any statute or in law or in equity, that a shareholder may sue for on behalf of a corporation. All forms of derivative actions purporting to be brought on behalf of and for the benefit of the corporation come within it." (Ibid., at 159.)

statutory derivative action that we must typically look in Canadian jurisdictions today. The CBCA's derivative action provisions offer a convenient and representative example. They will be the focus of discussion in the next section. Similar provisions may be found in most provincial corporate statutes as well.

Statutory Derivative Action

Introduction

The corporation at the centre of the dispute in *Foss v. Harbottle* had been incorporated by special act of Parliament, before the existence of a general English incorporation statute.[39] Today, the CBCA and similar provincial general corporate statutes set out a specific statutory regime for the bringing of derivative actions. Section 239 of the CBCA, for example, provides that

> (1) Subject to subsection (2), a complainant may apply to a court for leave to bring an action in the name and on behalf of a corporation or any of its subsidiaries, or intervene in an action to which any such body corporate is a party, for the purpose of prosecuting, defending or discontinuing the action on behalf of the body corporate.
>
> (2) No action may be brought and no intervention in an action may be made under subsection (1) unless the court is satisfied that
>
> (a) the complainant has given notice to the directors of the corporation or its subsidiary of the complainant's intention to apply to the court under subsection (1) not less than fourteen days before bringing the application, or as otherwise ordered by the court, if the directors of the corporation or its subsidiary do not bring, diligently prosecute or defend or discontinue the action;
>
> (b) the complainant is acting in good faith; and
>
> (c) it appears to be in the interests of the corporation or its subsidiary that the action be brought, prosecuted, defended or discontinued.

Three other sections of the statute also bear importantly on the CBCA's derivative action regime: s. 238, in which the critical term "complainant" is defined, as discussed below; s. 240, which sets out the remedies that may be ordered by a court in connection with a derivative action; and s. 242, which refers to a number of procedural matters.

Key Legal Issues in Connection with a Statutory Derivative Action

Introduction

The most important legal issues that arise in the context of statutory derivative actions are probably these:

- Who may commence such an action? (Who is a "complainant"?)

---

39 Parliament had passed what is sometimes called the *Trading Companies Act* of 1834 (4 & 5 Wm. IV, c. 94) and the *Chartered Companies Act* of 1837 (1 Vict., c. 73). These short, barebones statutes, however, did little more than empower the Crown to issue charters and were in no sense general incorporation statutes.

- What procedural steps must be satisfied by a complainant seeking to bring a derivative action?
- Who pays the costs of such an action?
- What is the scope of the orders that may be made?
- What is the relationship between the derivative action and the oppression remedy?

Who May Commence a Derivative Action?

"COMPLAINANT"

Under the CBCA, only a "complainant," as defined, may commence a derivative action. The term "complainant" is also found in most, but not all, of the provincial corporate statutes.[40] The word "complainant" is defined in the CBCA as follows:

"complainant" means

(a) a registered holder or beneficial owner, and a former registered holder or beneficial owner, of a security of a corporation or any of its affiliates,

(b) a director or an officer or a former director or officer of a corporation or any of its affiliates,

(c) the Director, or

(d) any other person who, in the discretion of a court, is a proper person to make an application under this Part.[41]

REGISTERED HOLDER OR BENEFICIAL OWNER OF SECURITIES

A shareholder—either as a registered or beneficial owner of a "security"—would at first appear always to satisfy the complainant's definitional requirements. Two important points merit attention here. The first concerns the phrase "beneficial owner." Shareholders of Canadian public corporations rarely hold their shares in registered form. Instead, their ownership interest is recorded on the books of their securities broker. Their broker's interest, in turn, is recorded on the books of a securities depository company (the Canadian Depository for Securities Limited). In Canada, the depository is frequently the registered shareholder of most of a public corporation's shares. A search of the share register of such a corporation would show the name of that depository or its nominee—not the names of the individual shareholders or even of their brokers—as the registered holder of those shares.

Specific reference to "beneficial owners" in the definition of complainant ensures, among other things, that the typical (unregistered) shareholder of a Canadian public corporation is not deprived of the same right to initiate a derivative action enjoyed by registered shareholders.

It no doubt seems eminently fair to ensure that a beneficial owner of shares enjoys the same rights to commence a derivative action as a registered holder. However, the

---

40   See, e.g., *Business Corporations Act* (Alta.), s. 239; *The Corporations Act* (Man.), s. 231; *Business Corporations Act* (NB), s. 163; *Corporations Act* (NL), s. 368; *Companies Act* (NS), s. 7; *Business Corporations Act* (Ont.), s. 245; and *The Business Corporations Act* (Sask.), s. 231.

41   CBCA, s. 238, definition of "complainant."

legislative decision to permit this is by no means an obvious one. Canadian corporate law has, historically, emphasized the virtual sanctity of the share register, from the corporation's perspective. It was long considered reasonable, efficient, and consistent with the goals of a system of registered share ownership that the corporation ought to be able to rely entirely on the names of its shareholders as they appeared in the share register. The corporation was not required to look behind the names on the register to determine whether there were any holders of beneficial interests in the corporation's shares.[42]

Prior to legislative amendments in 2001, the courts had generally supported the view that, whenever the CBCA used the word "shareholder," it referred only to registered shareholders, unless the statutory provision in question made specific reference to holders of beneficial interests in shares. Beneficial owners of shares were accordingly denied certain statutory shareholder rights, including, for example, the right to put forward a proposal at a shareholders' meeting.[43]

From the point of view of the corporation, this emphasis on registered ownership may not seem unreasonable. After all, share owners have a choice. They may always, if they wish, take steps to ensure that their names are entered on the corporation's share register.[44] Corporations, however, often have no way to determine who the beneficial owners of their outstanding shares might be.[45] To require corporations to second guess the integrity of their own share registers whenever they are required to give notice to their shareholders would be inefficient, expensive, and in many cases simply absurd.

However, there are competing concerns. It is very much in the interests of the Canadian capital markets that the settlement of share trades of public companies be fast and efficient. In other words, when shares of public companies are bought and sold, it is important that buyers receive their purchased shares promptly, and sellers receive their sale proceeds equally promptly. It would be very unwise if corporate statutes were to contain provisions that, inadvertently, created incentives for shareholders to insist that their shares be registered in their own names, rather than be held in "book form" through their brokers. The depository system described earlier facilitates faster, more efficient clearance and settlement of share trades. In the case of launching a derivative action, the balance is weighted on the side of expressly extending rights to beneficial shareholders. As the initiator of the action, the onus will presumably fall on the

---

42 CBCA, s. 51(1).

43 See *Verdun v. Toronto-Dominion Bank*, [1996] 3 SCR 550. Although this case was decided under the federal *Bank Act*, rather than under a general business corporation statute, the statutory provision in question was identical to the CBCA provisions, as the Supreme Court explicitly noted. The shareholder proposal provisions were subsequently amended in 2001 to reverse the effect of *Verdun* and to permit beneficial owners of shares to make shareholder proposals. See now CBCA, s. 137(1).

44 A shareholder can, for example, request that his or her broker register shares in the shareholder's name. Note, however, that choosing to hold shares in one's own name almost invariably involves additional fees.

45 For a further discussion of this issue, including the initiatives of Canadian securities regulators to ensure that beneficial owners of shares are not disenfranchised, see Jeffrey G. MacIntosh and Christopher C. Nicholls, *Securities Law* (Toronto: Irwin, 2002), at 267ff.

shareholder—not on the corporation—to confirm his or her status. And of course, although the foregoing discussion has focused on public companies, the reference, in paragraph (a) of the definition of "complainant," to "beneficial owners" extends to all those who hold a beneficial interest in shares—whether the issuing corporation is public or private. It is not limited to those whose shares of public corporations are held through a depository.[46]

The second aspect of paragraph (a) of the complainant definition that deserves closer scrutiny is the purpose and scope of the reference to "former" securityholders. The very sort of wrongful act that would justify launching a derivative action might well occur, for example, in the course of a transaction in which many of the corporation's shares also change hands. Consider, for example, the dispute that arose in *Regal (Hastings) Ltd. v. Gulliver*,[47] as discussed in chapter 11. The directors in that case were said to have seized for themselves a valuable investment opportunity that properly belonged to the corporation. The directors' profit from this investment was realized only when the corporation's shares were sold. At the time of this sale, the value of the corporation—and, therefore, the price paid by the new owners to acquire the corporation's shares—did not reflect the value of this lost investment. In other words, if anyone could be said to have suffered a loss as a result of the directors' actions, it was surely the "old" shareholders of the corporation—those who had sold their shares too cheaply. No real loss had been sustained by the corporation's new shareholders, who had, in fact, evidently acquired their shares at a bargain price.

Because of the inclusion of "former" securityholders within the definition of "complainant," had this case arisen under the CBCA, those former shareholders would have had status to bring a derivative action. As discussed later in this chapter, they would have had an oppression remedy available to them as well.

However, it has been held that not *every* former securityholder (or indeed former director) will necessarily enjoy complainant status. For example, in *Jacobs Farms Ltd. v. Jacobs*,[48] Blair J held that "it could not have been the intention of the Legislature ... to clothe every former shareholder and every former director with the status of complainant for purposes of bringing a derivative action."[49] Blair J suggested that there would need to be some connection between the "timing" of the complained of events, and the applicant's status as a director or shareholder.

In many circumstanes, former securityholders may be permitted to initiate a derivative action provided they had an interest in the corporation at the time it allegedly suffered injury. Should similar reasoning be used to *prevent current* shareholders of the corporation from launching a derivative action if they did not in fact acquire their shares until after the occurrence of a transaction alleged to have injured the corporation? In other words, to be a "complainant," should a securityholder be required to show that he or she had an interest in the corporation at the time of the act complained of?

---

46   See the definition of "beneficial ownership," CBCA, s. 1(1).

47   [1942] 1 All ER 378 (HL).

48   [1992] OJ no. 813 (QL) (Gen. Div.).

49   Ibid.

Certainly, in some foreign jurisdictions, notably Delaware, a shareholder cannot initiate a derivative action in such circumstances.[50] And there had been some suggestions in earlier Canadian cases, too, that to be a complainant, one must have had an interest at the time of the act complained of.[51] However, more recently, this fact was held not to be a per se bar to bringing a derivative action. In *Richardson Greenshields of Canada Ltd. v. Kalmacoff*,[52] for example, the Ontario Court of Appeal held:

> The Act does not impose a condition of ownership contemporaneous with the acts complained of and, in any event, it may be noted that the breaches complained of are of an ongoing nature. It is sufficient that Richardson Greenshields is "a registered holder ... of a security of [the] company" at the time it brings the application.[53]

Reasonable people might well differ on the wisdom of allowing securityholders who acquired their shares after the transaction complained of to initiate derivative actions. But it is clear, as the Court of Appeal rightly noted, that the CBCA contains no words of limitation comparable to those that appear, for example, in the Delaware corporate statute.

SECURITYHOLDERS OTHER THAN SHAREHOLDERS

A "complainant" need not be a shareholder. Paragraph (a) of the complainant definition refers to holders of any "security." All shares are securities, of course, but not all securities are shares. The term "security" is defined for purposes of the CBCA in s. 1(1) of the Act. This definition is shorter and far less comprehensive than the definitions of that same word found in Canada's provincial securities statutes.[54] The CBCA definition reads as follows:

> "security" means a share of any class or series of shares or a debt obligation of a corporation and includes a certificate evidencing such share or debt obligation.

The reference to a "debt obligation" might, at first glance, suggest that any creditor of the corporation is per se eligible to pursue a derivative action; however, this conclusion is clearly incorrect. The term "debt obligation" is itself defined in s. 1(1) of the CBCA to mean "a bond, debenture, note or other evidence of indebtedness or guarantee of a corporation, whether secured or unsecured." One notes that this definition does not

---

50   Section 327 of the Delaware *General Corporation Law* provides as follows:

> In any derivative suit instituted by a stockholder of a corporation, it shall be averred in the complaint that the plaintiff was a stockholder of the corporation at the time of the transaction of which such stockholder complains or that such stockholder's stock thereafter devolved upon such stockholder by operation of law.

51   *Royal Trust Corp. of Canada v. Hordo* (1993), 10 BLR (2d) 86 (Ont. Ct. Gen. Div.).

52   (1995), 22 OR (3d) 577 (CA).

53   Ibid., at 583-84. See also *A.E. Realisations (1985) Ltd. v. Time Air Inc.*, [1995] 3 WWR 527 (Sask. QB), aff'd. (1995), 131 Sask. R 249 (CA).

54   See, e.g., *Securities Act*, RSO 1990, c. S.5, s. 1(1). For a discussion of the concept of "security" for purposes of Canadian securities laws, see MacIntosh and Nicholls, supra footnote 45, at 23ff.

sweep in all debts owed by the corporation; it is, instead, limited to those corporate debts evidenced by specific types of debt instruments (bonds, debentures, and notes) and other *evidences* of indebtedness. Many creditors, of course, such as trade creditors, suppliers, or employees whose wages have not been paid, would not typically be the holders of such corporate securities.

The Alberta Court of Queen's Bench considered similar language in the derivative action provision of Alberta's *Business Corporations Act* (as it was then worded)[55] in *First Edmonton Place Ltd. v. 315888 Alberta Ltd.*[56] The conclusion the court drew was that "a creditor can be a 'complainant' under [paragraph (a) of the definition] only if it holds or is the beneficial owner of a security of the corporation, and if the security is of a type *which is capable of being registered.*"[57]

This restrictive interpretation of the word "security" does not mean that a creditor will never be permitted to commence a derivative action under the CBCA (or indeed under the Alberta statute, especially as currently drafted). Quite the contrary. It will always be possible for a creditor of a CBCA corporation to seek to satisfy the court that he or she is a "proper person" to commence such an action within the meaning of paragraph (d) of the "complainant" definition. Creditors have frequently been successful in making such arguments. The only point is that, unlike a shareholder (or, indeed, a holder of a debt security such as a bond or debenture), an ordinary creditor of a CBCA corporation does not enjoy per se "complainant" status.

There seems to be little or no compelling reason that holders of debt securities ought always to qualify as "complainants," while other creditors may qualify as complainants only if they are able to satisfy a court that they are "proper persons" within the meaning of paragraph (d) of the "complainant" definition. (The "proper person" test is discussed later in this chapter.) Indeed, two Canadian provincial corporate statutes—the New Brunswick *Business Corporations Act*[58] and the Alberta *Business Corporations Act*[59]— now explicitly include all creditors (not simply those who hold debt securities) within the definition of "complainant" for purposes of commencing a derivative action. The Dickerson committee's only explanation for the wording they had proposed for the CBCA's complainant definition was that it was "broadened to encompass the persons who clearly might be interested"[60] in the corporation's affairs. Surely, however, a creditor whose debt does not happen to be represented by a debt security is no less interested in the affairs of his corporate debtor than a creditor whose debt happens to take the form of such a debt security.

---

55   This provision was subsequently amended. See infra footnote 59.

56   (1989), 40 BLR 28 (Alta. QB), rev'd. on other grounds (1989), 45 BLR 110 (Alta. CA).

57   Ibid., at 61.

58   Section 163(c), definition of "complainant."

59   Section 239(iii), definition of "complainant." The Alberta statute is unique in that it includes creditors in this way *only* for the purposes of the derivative action. For purposes of commencing an oppression remedy, a creditor will qualify as a "complainant" only if it is found by the court to be a "proper person" to bring such an action.

60   Dickerson committee, supra footnote 3, at para. 480.

Although a creditor's interest in a corporation is a fixed claim, rather than a residual interest such as that of a traditional equityholder,[61] a creditor may frequently have very legitimate reasons for wishing to ensure that the corporation diligently pursues legal action against third parties who may have wronged it. In extreme cases, the corporation's ultimate ability to honour its debt obligations may depend on whether it is able to obtain compensation from third parties. In such a case, the interests of the corporation's creditors in seeing the corporation seek redress and those of the corporation itself will clearly align.

Fortunately, construing the definition of "security" narrowly may not have significant practical consequences. As discussed below, all derivative actions require leave of the court in any event. If a creditor—whether or not the holder of a debt security—is able to satisfy a court in the course of such a leave application that he or she is a proper person to commence a derivative action, he or she may be accorded complainant status.

"OF A CORPORATION OR ANY OF ITS AFFILIATES"

Note that a complainant includes not only a shareholder of the corporation that is itself the subject of the dispute, but also a shareholder of any of the corporation's affiliates. The term "affiliate" is defined in s. 2 of the CBCA:

(2) For the purposes of this Act,

(a) one body corporate is affiliated with another body corporate if one of them is the *subsidiary* of the other or both are subsidiaries of the same body corporate or each of them is *controlled* by the same person; and

(b) if two bodies corporate are affiliated with the same body corporate at the same time, they are deemed to be affiliated with each other.

The terms "subsidiary" and "controlled" have been italicized to draw attention to the fact that they are both terms that are also specifically defined in the CBCA:

(3) For the purposes of this Act, a body corporate is controlled by a person or by two or more bodies corporate if

(a) securities of the body corporate to which are attached more than fifty per cent of the votes that may be cast to elect directors of the body corporate are held, other than by way of security only, by or for the benefit of that person or by or for the benefit of those bodies corporate; and

(b) the votes attached to those securities are sufficient, if exercised, to elect a majority of the directors of the body corporate.

(4) A body corporate is the holding body corporate of another if that other body corporate is its subsidiary.

(5) A body corporate is a subsidiary of another body corporate if

(a) it is controlled by

(i) that other body corporate,

(ii) that other body corporate and one or more bodies corporate each of which is controlled by that other body corporate, or

---

61   As discussed in chapter 12, it is possible for a corporation to create preferred shares that, while equity for corporate law purposes, do not entitle the holder to any residual interest in the corporation's earnings or assets in the event of a liquidation or winding up.

(iii) two or more bodies corporate each of which is controlled by that other body corporate; or

(b) it is a subsidiary of a body corporate that is a subsidiary of that other body corporate.

Put in simpler terms, these statutory provisions mean that the "affiliates" of a hypothetical corporation, ABC Ltd., would include the following:

1. ABC Ltd.'s holding "body corporate." (That is, an entity that holds enough shares to control ABC Ltd. "Body corporate," under the CBCA, means any incorporated entity—whether incorporated under the CBCA or any other statute in any other jurisdiction.[62])

2. A subsidiary of ABC Ltd. (That is, a corporation of which ABC Ltd. holds sufficient shares to exercise control. Control, in this case, means "legal" rather than *de facto* control. The difference between these two concepts of control is important. As a practical matter, it is possible for a shareholder who owns far less than a majority share interest to control a corporation *as a matter of fact*; that is the reason, for example, that in most Canadian provincial securities statutes, a holder of 20 percent of a corporation's shares is usually said to be a control person,[63] and the acquisition of 20 percent of a corporation's shares is said to constitute a takeover bid for that corporation;[64] however, control of a corporation, for purposes of the CBCA (that is, legal control), means a holding of more than 50 percent of the voting shares, provided those shares entitle the holder to elect a majority of the members of the board of directors.)

3. Any "sister corporation" of ABC Ltd. (That is, any corporation that is a subsidiary of the same holding corporation as that of ABC Ltd. or that is controlled by the same person who controls ABC Ltd.)

4. Any corporation that is affiliated with any corporation to which ABC Ltd. is affiliated.

Shareholders of corporations affiliated with the "wronged" corporation have been accorded status as "complainants" under the CBCA in order to permit what the Dickerson committee described as "double derivative" actions.[65] "Double derivative" actions are especially important because many Canadian publicly traded corporations are, in fact, primarily holding corporations. Their chief business purpose is to hold the shares of other operating corporations rather than, or perhaps in addition to, carrying on active business activities themselves.

---

62   CBCA, s. 1(1), definition of "body corporate."

63   See, e.g., *Securities Act* (Ont.), supra footnote 54, s. 1(1)(c), definition of "distribution," and OSC rule 14-501 (1997), 20 OSCB 2690, definition of "control person." For a further discussion of this issue, see MacIntosh and Nicholls, supra footnote 45, at 178.

64   See, e.g., *Securities Act* (Ont.), supra footnote 54, s. 89(1), definition of "take-over bid."

65   Dickerson committee, supra footnote 3, at para. 481.

If the directors of one of the operating subsidiaries of such publicly traded holding corporations were to act in breach of their fiduciary obligations, the holding corporation—as the operating corporation's only (or largest) shareholder—would certainly have the right to seek leave to bring a derivative action. However, it is not unusual in the case of such related companies to find that there is partial (or significant) overlap in membership between the boards. Directors or officers of the holding corporation, in other words, might also be directors or officers of the operating subsidiaries. In such circumstances, the directors of the holding corporation might be understandably disinclined to cause the holding corporation to exercise its shareholder rights. These directors would, in other words, be in the position of deciding whether to authorize bringing a law suit against themselves. By permitting shareholders of the holding corporation to commence a derivative action in respect of wrongs done to any of the holding corporation's subsidiaries, this potential hurdle is overcome, and the policy underlying the existence of the derivative action is safely preserved.

CORPORATE DIRECTORS AND OFFICERS AND THE CBCA DIRECTOR

The categories of complainant described in paragraphs (b) and (c)—that is, present and former directors or officers and the Director[66]—are straightforward. Little will be said about these categories here, other than to note that the reference to the CBCA Director as an eligible complainant at first seems at odds with the Dickerson committee's avowed preference for self-enforcement of the CBCA. However, a clue to the inclusion of this language may be found in the committee's explanation of a similar provision included within the "investigation" section of the Act (discussed in chapter 14):

> [T]here is a public interest in the proper conduct of corporate affairs, and while the protection of the public interest may be a by-product of the protection of shareholder interests, we are not persuaded that it is a necessary by-product. Accordingly, [the investigation section] provides for an application by the Registrar.[67]

ANY OTHER "PROPER PERSON"

The final paragraph, (d), is of considerably greater interest. Paragraph (d) represents something of a catch-all or basket category that empowers the court to allow a derivative action (or indeed, an oppression action, as discussed below) to be commenced "by any other person who, in the discretion of a court, is a proper person to make an application."

Lord Atkin famously put to himself the question, "Who then in law is my neighbour?"[68] The corporate lawyer might similarly ask, "Who, then, in corporate law is a

---

66   The Ontario *Business Corporations Act* definition of complainant does not include language comparable to "Director" under the CBCA.

67   Dickerson committee, supra footnote 3, at para. 465. "Registrar" was the term used by the Dickerson committee to refer to the incorporating officer under the proposed CBCA. (Ibid., at para. 52.) The Dickerson committee preferred the term "Registrar" to the term "Director" (the term already used under the federal *Canada Corporations Act* that pre-dated the CBCA) because, in the committee's view, the term Director could be confused with the directors of the corporation. (Ibid., at para. 505.) Needless to say, this particular recommendation was not adopted; and so the CBCA retained the term Director.

68   *McAlister (or Donoghue) v. Stevenson*, [1932] AC 562 (HL), at 580.

'proper person'?" The question cannot be answered without some theory concerning the nature and purpose of the derivative action.

The purpose of the derivative action has been seen by some to transcend the mere safeguarding of the corporation's own economic interests. Writing in 1986, M.A. Maloney suggested that the derivative action ought to be used to protect a broad array of stakeholder interests:

> The changing face of capitalism and the role which corporations play in furthering its aims dictate the necessity of flexibility. As the notion of which interests the corporation is working towards changes, and becomes increasingly sophisticated, so must the pool of applicants [i.e., complainants entitled to commence derivative actions] change.[69]

Because the derivative action is intended to remedy wrongs committed against the corporation, a "proper person" to commence such an action must be someone who may be expected to advance the interests of the corporation, and not merely the complainant's own interests. So much is clear. However, this does not mean that only altruists may qualify as "proper persons." Few derivative actions would be sustained by "proper persons" if altruism were such a prerequisite. (Although human beings certainly are capable of performing altruistic acts, few find the practice habit forming.) Typically, an applicant seeking leave to commence a derivative action, on the basis that he or she is a "proper person" to do so, will be someone with some financial interest in the corporation, who seeks, on behalf of the corporation, to obtain financial compensation from a wrong-doer. If the corporation is successful in obtaining such compensation, then ultimately the value of the complainant's interest in the corporation, whatever it may be, will be enhanced.

It has been held that a creditor of a corporation may be a proper person, provided "he or it would nevertheless be a person who could reasonably be entrusted with the responsibility of advancing the interests of the corporation by seeking a remedy to right the wrong allegedly done to the corporation."[70] Indeed, it has been suggested that if a party satisfied this test, the party need not even be a creditor with an existing debt, but merely someone with a contingent liability.[71] The Supreme Court of Canada has recently suggested (albeit in a case that involved neither a derivative action nor an application for an oppression remedy) that the state of the corporation's financial health may be relevant to the court's determination of whether or not a creditor ought to be considered a "proper person" to bring a derivative (or oppression) action because, "creditors' interests increase in relevancy as a corporation's finances deteriorate."[72]

---

69   Maloney, supra footnote 33, at 319. This passage is one part of Maloney's article, which is quoted in *First Edmonton*, infra footnote 70, though not endorsed by the court.

70   *First Edmonton Place Ltd. v. 315888 Alberta Ltd.* (1988), 40 BLR 28, at 63 (Alta. QB). This decision was subsequently, in effect, overturned on appeal, (1989), 45 BLR 110 (CA), but the Court of Appeal did not express disagreement with this aspect of the lower court's reasons. Technically, the appeal itself was adjourned and the order appealed from was stayed. This may seem a bit confusing, but here is the rationale. The Court of Appeal determined that until the first action—an action that had been brought by the landlord against the numbered company itself—had been concluded, thus establishing the liability of the numbered company in the first place, "the basis for any right to bring that derivative action ... is speculative" (at 112).

71   Ibid., at 63.

72   *Peoples Department Stores Inc. v. Wise*, 2004 SCC 68, at para. 49.

A trade creditors' committee, established to represent the interests of the trade creditors of a corporation, was found to be a proper person to bring a derivative action on behalf of that corporation, notwithstanding that such an association would not, normally, be considered a "person" at law at all. The court, in this case, relied on the extended definition of person in the Ontario *Business Corporations Act*, and the fact that even that definition did not, by its terms, purport to be exhaustive.[73]

Some of the factors that the court might consider relevant in determining whether a party ought to be considered a "proper person" within the meaning of s. 238 were discussed by the Alberta Court of Queen's Bench in *First Edmonton Place Ltd. v. 315888 Alberta Limited*.[74]

In *First Edmonton Place*, the party seeking to bring a derivative action was the landlord of a building. A corporation had signed an agreement to lease this building for 10 years. It was the three directors of that corporation that the landlord wished to sue. The background to this dispute was, briefly, this. To induce the corporate tenant to enter into the 10-year lease, the landlord had offered a number of valuable incentives, including an 18-month rent-free period, an allowance for leasehold improvements, and an additional cash consideration. Once the corporation had entered into the lease with the landlord, the corporation's three directors had, in effect, sublet the office space from the corporate tenant. They used the space to carry on a law practice.

The three individuals occupied the premises for just 21 months (including the 18-month rent-free period). They then abandoned the building. Moreover, they had, evidently, caused the corporate tenant (over which they had complete control) to pay over to them personally the cash lease inducement that the corporation had originally received from the landlord. Accordingly, although the corporate tenant was, of course, still liable to honour the terms of the 10-year lease, the corporation had no funds or other assets, so it was unable to make any rental payments, and had no assets to satisfy any judgment the landlord might obtain against it. The corporation was, as such penniless parties are often called, "judgment proof." It was futile for the landlord to pursue its claim, unless some other parties could be found with the means to satisfy any eventual judgment.

The landlord's only contractual claim lay against the worthless corporate tenant; so the landlord sought to bring a derivative action—in the name of the corporate tenant—against the three individual directors. The goal was to obtain a judgment against these three individuals in favour of the corporation. The landlord would then sue the tenant corporation under the lease. If the corporation managed to win funds from the three directors in this derivative action, it would then have the means to satisfy, in whole or in part, the landlord's claim for breach of the lease agreement.

This strategy, however, depended on a finding by the court that the landlord was a "complainant" for purposes of the provision in the Alberta *Business Corporation Act* that is equivalent to CBCA s. 238.

As discussed above, the court rejected fairly summarily the landlord's argument that it ought to be considered a holder of a "security" of the corporation. A more extensive analysis was undertaken, however, with respect to whether or not the landlord was,

---

73   *Sammi Atlas Inc., Re* (1997), 36 BLR (2d) 318 (Ont. Ct. Gen. Div.).

74   Supra footnote 70.

nevertheless, a "proper person" to commence a derivative action. McDonald J suggested that in deciding if any particular applicant ought to be considered a "proper person," the purposes of the derivative action itself must be borne in mind. Those purposes he identified as minority shareholder protection and ensuring managerial accountability. More specifically, he reasoned:

> In the case of a creditor who claims to be a "proper person" to make a s. 232 application, in my view the criterion to be applied would be whether ... he or it would nevertheless be a person who could reasonably be entrusted with the responsibility of advancing the interests of the corporation by seeking a remedy to right the wrong allegedly done to the corporation.[75]

McDonald J's judgment certainly implies that creditors, and indeed even holders of mere contingent interests, might well be in a position to satisfy this test. It is equally clear, however, that the interests of creditors would not always, or even perhaps typically, be synonymous with the corporation's interests in a way that would justify permitting creditors, as a matter of course, to pursue a derivative action. In fact, it is enlightening to consider the policy questions raised when a creditor seeks leave to bring a derivative action within the broader context of the developing law of the duty of directors toward a corporation's creditors, as recently discussed by the Supreme Court of Canada in *Peoples Department Stores Inc. v. Wise*.[76] Some of the implications of this judgment were canvassed earlier in chapter 10. Here, one notes only the observation of the Supreme Court that "[t]he interests of shareholders, those of the creditors and those of the corporation may and will be consistent with each other if the corporation is profitable and well capitalized and has strong prospects. However, this can change if the corporation starts to struggle financially."[77] What is interesting about this statement is that it implies that creditors' interests are most likely to be consistent with those of the corporation when the corporation is financially healthy and it therefore seems that creditors should certainly qualify as proper persons to bring a derivative action under these circumstances. However, as noted earlier, the Supreme Court in that same case suggested that the interests of a corporation's creditors are *more* deserving of the protections of the derivative action and oppression remedy when the corporation is *not* financially healthy.[78] Thus, it appears that there is authority to support the proposition that creditors are most qualified to be considered "proper persons" when a corporation is thriving financially ... and when it is not.

Procedural Steps

LEAVE OF THE COURT

Even if a person clearly satisfies the "complainant" definition, this qualification alone does not guarantee that he or she will be permitted to pursue a derivative action. An important procedural hurdle remains. A complainant who wishes to launch a derivative action must seek the court's leave before doing so. The Dickerson committee, in its draft

---

75   Ibid.

76   *Peoples Department Stores*, supra footnote 72.

77   Ibid., at para. 44.

78   See text accompanying footnote 72, supra.

of the CBCA, modelled this leave process on an earlier provision in Ontario's corporate statute. The rationale for the specific procedure it proposed was, in the committee's view, that it would "circumvent most of the procedural barriers" then standing in the way of such actions, yet "incidentally" lower the risk of so-called strike suits. (The phrase "strike suits" refers to unmeritorious litigation that is commenced solely for the purpose of putting pressure on defendants with the hope that they will agree to pay some money to settle the action simply to end the nuisance.)[79]

The fear that facilitating access to the courts will lead to a proliferation of strike suits is frequently raised in the context of Canadian corporate and securities law reform.[80]

But are derivative actions especially likely to be abused in this way? Any disreputable plaintiff prepared to launch a meritless "strike suit" would hardly need to frame his or her action as a derivative action to begin with. And there is no general "leave" requirement imposed on those who wish to initiate (non-derivative) legal proceedings against corporations or their managers. Accordingly, it seems unlikely that avoiding strike suits is a particularly important rationale for the derivative action leave requirement.

Davis and Iacobucci have suggested that the leave requirement is intricately linked to the statutory provision that allows the court to order the corporation to pay the complainant's costs on an interim basis.[81] This is by no means an unreasonable argument. Davies has also noted this link in the comparable UK procedures.[82] However, this explanation is not quite complete. A court also has the power, for example, to order an interim cost award in the case of an oppression remedy, but no similar leave requirement is required for bringing an oppression application. Furthermore, leave is required in a derivative action whether or not a complainant is seeking such a cost order. So the link to costs, though certainly important, cannot fully account for the leave requirement.

In fact, a better explanation of the leave requirement is that it provides the means by which a non-director can assume what is otherwise the director's exclusive authority to act in the name of the corporation. In other words, the leave requirement is necessary in the case of a derivative action, but not for an oppression action, because the CBCA has bestowed managerial authority on the directors under s. 102, and it would thus be impossible (and undesirable) if every complainant could simply usurp that power by making allegations of impropriety against the directors. The leave requirement thus offers a sensible statutory solution to one of the rigidities created by *Foss v. Harbottle*. At the core of the

---

79 Dickerson committee, supra footnote 3, at para. 482.

80 See, e.g., TSE Committee on Corporate Disclosure, *Final Report: Responsible Corporate Disclosure—A Search for Balance* (Toronto: Toronto Stock Exchange, 1997) and *Five Year Review Committee Final Report—Reviewing the Securities Act (Ontario)* (Toronto: Queen's Printer, 2003), at 26.

81 Edward M. Iacobucci and Kevin E. Davis, "Reconciling Derivative Claims and the Oppression Remedy" (2000), 12 *Supreme Court Law Review* (2d) 87, at 105 ff. There are actually two provisions in the CBCA that deal with the subject of interim costs: s. 240(d), which applies only to applications to commence a derivative action, and s. 242(4), which applies to any applications made under part XX of the CBCA, which would include oppression applications as well as derivative actions.

82 Davies, supra footnote 31, at 455: "So the price of the possibility of the company's financial support for the [derivative] claim is a greater degree of supervision by the court over its conduct by the individual shareholder." However, the author goes on to point out that court approval is nevertheless required for *all* derivative actions, regardless of whether such an indemnity order is made.

second prong of *Foss v. Harbottle* is an assumption (accurate in the *Foss* case itself) that it is the shareholders of a corporation that have the power to cause a corporation to commence litigation. Indeed, the constitution of the corporation involved in the *Foss v. Harbottle* dispute made it clear that the shareholders—and only the shareholders— enjoyed this power. Under the CBCA, where the usual power to authorize a corporation's legal proceedings resides in the board of directors, rather than with the shareholders in general meeting, an application of the principles of *Foss v. Harbottle* could theoretically make derivative actions a virtual impossibility: a complainant would not be permitted to commence such an action unless and until that action was first approved by the body authorized to make that determination—namely, in the case of the CBCA, the board of directors. The leave requirement thus permits the court to intervene to override managerial control in those cases, but only in those cases, where it is appropriate to do so.

What are the overarching general principles to be taken into account by the court in deciding whether or not to grant leave to a complainant to bring a derivative action? In *Richardson Greenshields of Canada Ltd. v. Kalmacoff*,[83] the court explained that,

[i]n deciding whether leave should be granted, it should be borne in mind that a derivative action brought by an individual shareholder on behalf of a corporation serves a dual purpose. First, it ensures that a shareholder has a right to recover property or enforce rights for the corporation if the directors refuse to do so. Second, and more important for our present purposes, it helps to guarantee some degree of accountability and to ensure that control exists over the board of directors by allowing shareholders the right to bring an action against directors if they have breached their duty to the company.[84]

The leave application, it has been said, is fundamentally a matter between the complainant and the corporation and its directors, and so the court is reluctant in the context of such an application to grant status to third-party intervenors.[85]

NOTICE TO THE DIRECTORS

Before a derivative action may be pursued by a complainant under the CBCA, notice must be given to the directors of the corporation at least 14 days[86] before application is made for leave of the court to commence the derivative action. (Most provincial statutes require that "reasonable notice"[87] be given, rather than specify a particular minimum notice period.[88])

The purpose of the notice requirement is clear. Because a derivative action, by definition, is an action brought seeking a remedy for wrongs done to the corporation, the

---

83   Supra footnote 52.

84   Ibid., at 584.

85   *Lederer v. 372116 Ontario Ltd.* (2001), 53 OR (3d) 203 (CA).

86   Prior to the statutory amendments in 2001, the requirement was that directors be given "reasonable notice" of the impending action. The change to a specified 14-day notice period was said in a commentary issued at the time of the proposed amendments to be intended to provide "clarity and certainty."

87   See, e.g., *Corporations Act* (NL), s. 369(2)(a); *Business Corporations Act* (NB), s. 164(2)(a); *Companies Act* (NS), s. 4(2)(a); *The Corporations Act* (Man.), s. 232(2)(a); *The Business Corporations Act* (Sask.), s. 232(2)(a); and *Business Corporations Act* (Alta.), s. 240(2)(a).

88   The CBCA itself, prior to the amendments in 2001, also called for the provision of "reasonable notice." The Ontario *Business Corporations Act*, s. 246(2), like the CBCA, requires that reasonable notice be

corporation itself (through its directors) ought first to be given the opportunity to, as it were, "do the right thing" and take charge of the action.

It may be that, in certain cases, it is not practicable to provide notice to the directors. For example, the matter may be an urgent one. Providing notice might result in unacceptable delay. The court retains the authority to abridge or, indeed, to dispense with the notice requirement ("as otherwise ordered by the court") in appropriate circumstances.

Even in cases where there is no emergency, a court might be pressed to waive compliance with the notice requirement if it might reasonably be assumed that providing notice would be futile. For example, where a complainant proposes to commence a derivative action naming every member of the board of directors as a defendant, it seems improbable that the board would take steps to launch such an action itself. In the United States, jurisprudence has developed around the issue of when demand on directors by a complainant in cases such as this will be excused altogether by the courts.[89] No similar body of law appears to have been generated in Canada, although legislative reformers have raised the possibility of dispensing with the notice requirement when all directors of the corporation are named as defendants.[90] Cases such as *Gorner v. Martin*[91] and *Levi v. MacDougall*[92] have occasionally been cited as authority for the proposition that notice may be dispensed with in circumstances where it would clearly be futile.[93] However, it is doubtful that these cases support such a proposition in light of the specific statutory requirement to give notice contained in the CBCA. *Gorner v. Martin*, as a subsequent court correctly pointed out,[94] was decided before this explicit statutory notice requirement had been enacted, and this was true of *Levi v. MacDougall* as well.

One issue that has received attention in the American courts relates to the weight the court ought to give to the directors' own assessment of a proposed derivative action, particularly in cases where that assessment is made by an independent committee of the board composed entirely of directors who have not been named as defendants in the action. The decision whether or not to launch an action on behalf of the corporation requires the very sort of cost–benefit analysis required of other corporate decisions that are indisputably the responsibility of the board of directors. Provided the particular directors making the decision are not tainted by self-interest, then, why should the court override their business judgment on this issue any more than, say, on the question of whether to pursue a particular strategic acquisition?

---

given. Section 233(1)(A) of BC's *Business Corporations Act* contains a slightly different requirement—namely, that "the complainant has made reasonable efforts to cause the directors of the company to prosecute or defend the legal proceeding."

89 See, e.g., Robert C. Clark, *Corporate Law* (New York: Aspen Publishers, 1986), at 641ff.

90 Alberta Institute of Law Research and Reform, Report no. 36, *Proposals for a New Alberta Business Corporations Act* (Edmonton: Institute of Law Research and Reform, 1980), at 145.

91 (1985), 4 CPC (2d) 72 (Nfld. TD).

92 [1941] 2 DLR 171 (BCCA).

93 See, e.g., Harry Sutherland et al., *Fraser & Stewart Company Law of Canada*, 6th ed. (Toronto: Carswell, 1993), at 718, discussing *Gorner v. Martin* and Beck, supra footnote 29, at 566-67, referring to *Levi v. MacDougall*.

94 See *Pappas v. Alcan Windows* (1991), 2 BLR (2d) 180 (Nfld. TD).

Auerbach v. Bennett[95] is an especially well-known example of a case where this matter was considered. There, the New York Court of Appeal held that where a special litigation committee appointed to evaluate a shareholder's derivative action determined that the action should not be continued, the court should interfere with that finding only in one of two cases: (1) if there was evidence that the committee lacked independence, or (2) if the procedures adopted by the committee were inadequate or inappropriate. The substance of such a committee's decision would enjoy the protection of the business judgment rule (and would, therefore, be beyond the reach of the court) provided it was a decision reached by an independent committee engaging appropriate procedures. In summary, the three key determinants of judicial deference to a litigation committee's decision that emerge from the case are independence of the committee, good faith, and reasonable investigation.

A variant of this reasoning is found in *Zapata v. Maldonado*.[96] There, a shareholder had properly commenced a derivative action. He had not made any prior demand on the corporate board of directors because he had been excused from doing so. Later, however, an independent committee of the board of directors was struck to consider whether the action should be continued. That committee determined that it was not in the corporation's best interests that the action be continued. Although the facts were rather more complex than this brief summary suggests, the fundamental issue before the court was whether a decision taken by an independent litigation committee to *discontinue* a validly *commenced* derivative action was effective where the plaintiff had been excused from making a demand on the board of directors of the corporation to commence the litigation in the first place.

The court in *Zapata* reasoned that this situation was materially different from those cases in which demand is made on the board of directors, and a litigation committee is struck by the board to assess the litigation before it is commenced. In those "demand made" cases, they noted, provided the committee was independent, acted in good faith and conducted a reasonable investigation, its decision is to be respected. Where, however, the plaintiff was not required ever to make a prior demand on the board, and properly commenced the litigation without making such a demand, the matter was different. It would be wrong in those circumstances, the court reasoned, to say that the board might never thereafter be permitted to appoint a special independent committee to assess the litigation and to seek dismissal, if the best interests of the corporation warranted such an action. At the same time, it would be equally wrong to suggest that a litigation committee's decision ought to receive the same deference as in those cases where a demand was initially made on the board. In particular, the court was concerned about the prospects of unfair delay by the board in striking such a committee, as well as the inevitable concern that even ostensibly independent directors are likely to have empathy for their fellow directors.[97]

---

95   393 NE 2d 994 (NYCA 1979).

96   430 A 2d 779 (Del. 1981).

97   This latter concern is sometimes referred to as "structural bias." See e.g., James D. Cox and Harry L. Munsinger, "Bias in the Boardroom: Psychological Foundations and Legal Implications of Corporate Cohesion" (1985), 48 *Law and Contemporary Problems* 83.

Accordingly, the court opted for a "middle course." Specifically, it suggested a two-stage procedure. The first stage would require the court to assess whether the litigation committee was indeed independent, acting in good faith, and had performed a reasonable investigation. In stage two, it was suggested that the court should apply its "own independent business judgment" in determining whether derivative litigation previously commenced should be dismissed at the behest of the litigation committee.[98]

"ACTING IN GOOD FAITH"

Before granting leave to commence a derivative action, the court must be satisfied that the complainant is acting in good faith. The onus placed on an applicant to establish good faith is said to be high. The reason for imposing this requirement is to ensure that derivative actions are not undertaken lightly. After all, the effect of the derivative action is extreme. It upsets the normal "sovereignty" of a corporation's board of directors, and allows an outsider to compel corporate resources to be expended in litigation.[99]

The complainant's belief in the merits of the case, although not necessarily determinative of "good faith" for purposes of the leave requirement, necessarily has been found to be a "proper factor" for the court to consider and "cogent evidence" of good faith.[100] Certainly, it is not necessary for the complainant in seeking to establish good faith to show that he or she has a material financial interest in the outcome of the derivative action as, indeed, it is very much the purpose of the derivative action (as opposed to the oppression remedy) that a complainant be permitted to initiate litigation in circumstances where no personal remedy is available.[101]

ACTION "APPEARS TO BE IN THE INTERESTS OF THE CORPORATION"

Before a derivative action may be commenced, the court must be satisfied that bringing the action "appears to be in the interests of the corporation."

Courts have focused narrowly on this language, noting that it requires only that the court be satisfied that it *appears* to be in the interests of the corporation that the derivative action is brought. That is, it is not necessary that the court ultimately determine that bringing the action is, in fact, in the interests of the corporation.[102] Thus, it has been said that the word

---

98 A corollary to the principle that a truly independent committee may seek to have a derivative action dismissed is that such a committee must be given the time to undertake a reasonable investigation and that, accordingly, a previously commenced derivative action ought normally to be stayed to permit that investigation to proceed. (*Abbey v. Computer & Communications Technology Corp.*, 457 A 2d 368 (1983).) However, in the recent Delaware case *Bachand v. HealthSouth Corp.*, CA no. 19968-NC (Del. Ch. Ct. 2003), the Delaware court argued that there would be an exception to the normal rule that a stay be granted in such a case if the special litigation committee did not meet the *Zapata* standards of independence and, thus, would not be worthy of judicial deference even if it did ultimately conclude that the claim ought to be dismissed.

99 See, e.g., *McAskill v. Transatlantic Petroleum Corp.*, [2003] 5 WWR 178 (Alta. QB).

100 *Discovery Enterprises Inc. v. Ebco Industries Ltd.* (1998), 50 BCLR (3d) 196 (CA), leave to appeal to Supreme Court of Canada dismissed [1998] SCCA no. 406 (QL).

101 Ibid.

102 *Richardson Greenshields*, supra footnote 52.

"appears" signals that no certainty is required.[103] Rather, as the BC Court of Appeal has put it, "what is sufficient at this stage is that an arguable case be shown to subsist."[104]

EVIDENCE OF SHAREHOLDER APPROVAL NOT CONCLUSIVE

Subsection 242(1) of the CBCA provides that an action brought under part XX of the Act (a part that includes, for example, oppression applications as well as derivative actions) is not to be dismissed or stayed by the court

> by reason only that it is shown that an alleged breach of a right or duty owed to the corporation or its subsidiary has been or may be approved by the shareholders of such body corporate, but evidence of approval by the shareholders may be taken into account by the court in making an order under section 214, 240 or 241.

This provision, the Dickerson committee explained,

> abrogates that aspect of the rule in *Foss v. Harbottle* that bars a shareholder from complaining of alleged misconduct on the ground that the impugned act *might* be authorized or ratified at a meeting of shareholders, a concept that has been described as "... the major absurdity of the *Foss v. Harbottle* rule."[105]

COSTS

At the time of application for leave to commence a derivative action, the court is empowered to make an interim order of costs, to be paid by the corporation to the complainant for the purpose of funding the litigation. In England, the seminal case of *Wallersteiner v. Moir (No. 2)*[106] established the principle that a derivative action litigant could seek indemnity from the corporation, a principle that Davies notes is now embodied in the English *Civil Procedure Rules*.[107] In fact, however, the original rationale for ordering interim costs appears to be somewhat diminished in the context of a modern Canadian derivative action where the range of remedies, as discussed above, is no longer limited to an order in favour of the company itself.

Nevertheless, the CBCA explicitly empowers the court to make such a costs order. The challenge for the courts is to determine under what circumstances such an order ought to be made. In *Turner v. Mailhot*,[108] the Ontario High Court (as it was then called) determined that a complainant that had satisfied the statutory requirements for leave to bring a derivative action could be taken "to have established a *prima facie* right to indemnity."[109] The court considered many of the same factors that had been discussed by the English Court of Appeal in *Moir*, including the financial ability of the complainant to

---

103 *Acapulco Holdings Ltd. v. Jegen*, [1997] 4 WWR 601 (CA).

104 *Bellman v. Western Approaches Ltd.* (1981), 130 DLR (3d) 193, at 201 (BCCA) and *Discovery Enterprises*, supra footnote 100.

105 Dickerson committee, supra footnote 3, at para. 487, citing Gower, 3rd ed., at 586.

106 [1975] 1 All ER 849 (CA).

107 Davies, supra footnote 31, at 455.

108 (1985), 50 OR (2d) 561 (HC).

109 Ibid., at 567.

bring the action without a cost indemnity, and the plaintiff's personal monetary interest in the outcome of any eventual action. In the *Turner* case itself, the plaintiff did not claim that he would be financially unable to bring the action without an indemnity, and, in view of the facts of the case, it was evident that the plaintiff would in fact enjoy a substantial personal benefit were the action to succeed. Nevertheless, the court considered it appropriate to award a partial costs indemnity on an interim basis.

In the recent Ontario case of *Barry Estate v. Barry Estate*,[110] the court set out three factors to be taken into account when considering an application for an award of interim costs to a complainant:

- the strength of the applicant's case;
- whether the applicant's financial circumstances might, in the absence of an order, make it impossible for the claim to be pursued; and
- where the applicant lacks financial ability to pursue the action without an indemnity for costs, the critical existence of "some connection between the conduct complained of and the applicant's financial inability."[111] This connection, however, need not involve a "direct cause and effect relationship."[112]

More recently, the BC courts,[113] in particular, have expressed some wariness about the awarding of interim costs to a derivative action complainant. In *Discovery Enterprises Inc. v. Ebco Enterprises Ltd.*,[114] for example, the BC Court of Appeal warned that awarding costs at the leave stage of a derivative action offended the principle against granting one party an "adversarial advantage."[115] The court cited with approval the observation of Tysoe J in *International Precious Metals Inc. v. Cooke*[116] that cost considerations are normally relevant to litigators' decisions and, accordingly, "the person having conduct of a derivative action should make the decisions bearing in mind that they will not necessarily be reimbursed for the legal costs."[117]

Finally, although discussions of derivative actions understandably focus on the costs of the *complainant*, it is also perhaps worth noting here that under recent changes to the CBCA, effected in 2001, a CBCA corporation is now permitted, with court approval, to advance costs to an officer or a director who is a *defendant* in a derivative action.[118]

---

110 [2001] OJ no. 2991 (QL) (Sup. Ct.).

111 Ibid., at para. 3.

112 Ibid., at para. 7. Note that the applicant in *Barry Estate* had sought an award of interim costs not only against the corporation, but also against another defendant. The court noted that there was "not precedent for such an award" (ibid., at para. 12) of costs to be made against a party other than the corporation, and refused to make such an award in that case.

113 Kaplan and Elwood have indeed suggested that BC law on the interim award of costs now differs from that of Ontario. See William Kaplan and Bruce Elwood, "The Derivative Action: A Shareholder's 'Bleak House'?" (2003), 36 *University of British Columbia Law Review* 443.

114 (1999), 50 BLR (2d) 207 (BCCA).

115 Ibid., at 217.

116 (1993), 10 BLR (2d) 203 (BCSC).

117 Ibid., at 225.

118 CBCA, s. 124(4).

Scope of Available Remedies

A derivative action is brought to address wrongs done *to* a corporation. Traditionally, therefore, damages in a successful derivative action would be awarded only to the corporation itself. Such a limited remedy is consistent with the notion that a corporation is a separate legal entity, but rigid adherence to such a principle could lead to quite unfair results. For example, consider the facts in *Regal Hastings v. Gulliver*, a case discussed in chapter 11. The directors of a corporation were found to have seized an opportunity properly belonging to the corporation itself. But, all of the individuals who had owned shares in the corporation at the time of the directors' disputed acts had sold their shares before the lawsuit against the directors had been commenced. Thus, the only people who had actually been harmed (these former shareholders) gained nothing from the lawsuit; however, the new shareholders, who had purchased their shares in the corporation with full knowledge of the directors' actions, reaped a windfall.

The CBCA addresses the potential for that sort of unfairness by introducing greater flexibility into the range of orders a court is empowered to make in connection with a derivative action. Specifically, s. 240 of the CBCA empowers the court to "make any order it thinks fit" in connection with a derivative action. The section then goes on to provide a non-exhaustive list of possible orders, one of which expressly permits the court to order that any amounts payable by a defendant may be paid "in whole or in part, directly to former and present security holders of the corporation or its subsidiary instead of to the corporation or its subsidiary."[119]

Procedural Steps Mandatory When Action Is Derivative

When an action is clearly derivative in nature—that is, when the plaintiff has no basis on which to sue in his or her personal capacity—the procedural steps mandated by the statute for the launching of a derivative action cannot be avoided. This principle may seem both straightforward and non-controversial, except when it is recalled that in the untidy world of real-life disputes, personal and derivative claims may be hopelessly interwoven. In *NPV Management Ltd. v. Anthony*,[120] the Newfoundland and Labrador Court of Appeal endorsed the statement of Barry J in *Pappas v. Acan Windows Inc.*,[121] that where derivative and personal claims are inextricably linked, such that "it is not possible to clearly separate the personal and derivative claims, then ... both those claims should be discontinued, where no leave has been obtained, unless the derivative claims are merely incidental to and clearly of secondary importance to the personal claims."[122] Of course, it may not always be entirely clear whether a particular claim is merely derivative rather than personal in nature. The Dickerson committee was well aware of the potential of such hybrid disputes to arise. In their view, in "borderline" cases—involving actions that simultaneously constitute wrongs to the corporation and

---

119 CBCA, s. 240(c).

120 (2003), 231 DLR (4th) 681.

121 Supra footnote 94.

122 Ibid., at 216. Cited in *NPV Management,* supra footnote 120, at 693.

potential abuse of minority shareholders—the aggrieved party ought to be able to choose whatever remedy (derivative action or relief from oppression) was best suited to addressing the problem.[123]

THE OPPRESSION REMEDY

Framing the Issue

A corporation may be an artificial person, but its shareholders, directors, and officers are all too human. Their wills are bound, from time to time, to clash. Disputes are inevitable. The joint founders of a new business may begin their professional association in perfect harmony, unanimously (even cheerfully) agreeing about the direction and management of their new enterprise. But, over time, they may drift apart. Perhaps they may discover that their management styles and philosophies are not only different but incompatible. Perhaps they may come to have conflicting visions about the future growth of their common venture. Perhaps one founder may begin to believe that another is not carrying his or her fair share of the burdens of building the business. Or perhaps they may simply have a falling out that has its genesis in their personal relationship, but, as such disputes inevitably do, soon spills over into the workplace.

Whatever the reason, when business associates find themselves at loggerheads, the future of the business itself may soon be in jeopardy. Bickering supplants constructive debate and, in the worst cases, one party to the dispute may even try to lock out the other, either figuratively or literally.

Disputes like this can, of course, occur within partnerships as well as within corporations. But when a business is conducted through an incorporated entity, there is an additional wrinkle. If one shareholder owns a majority of the voting shares (either alone, or together with a group of like-minded friends), that controlling shareholder may exercise his or her power to effectively force out the members of a rival shareholding faction, making it impossible for those rivals to participate in the business in a meaningful way. If the rivals have always enjoyed seats on the board of directors, for example, the holders of the majority of the voting shares can use those votes to remove rivals from the board. If the rivals had served as officers of the company, the majority shareholders, after electing themselves (or their friends) to the board, can then dismiss those officers, and so on. The power of the holder of a minority share interest in a corporation—unless protected by the terms of a shareholders' agreement[124]—is very limited indeed.

Historically, the law offered little protection or even sympathy for minority shareholders of corporations. The traditional "hands off" view of the courts is nicely captured in the words of the Ontario Court of Appeal in a judgment from 1928:

> [A] minority shareholder … must endure the unpleasantness incident to that situation. If he chooses to risk his money by subscribing for shares, it is part of his bargain that he will

---

123 Dickerson committee, supra footnote 3, at para. 484.

124 Shareholders' agreements, including unanimous shareholder agreements, are discussed in chapter 4.

submit to the will of the majority. In the absence of fraud or transactions *ultra vires*, the majority must govern, and there should be no appeal to the Courts for redress.[125]

There were two branches to this old policy of judicial non-interference. The first, as Beck has noted, was that corporate arrangements were regarded as private matters, beyond the reach of the courts.[126] The majority—that is, those who held a majority of the voting shares—had the legal right to speak for the corporation. And the principle of majority rule usually made good practical sense. After all, a corporate decision authorized by anything less than unanimous shareholder approval would invariably leave at least one shareholder unhappy; but business could hardly be carried on at all if every embittered minority shareholder were able to trot off to court to complain about actions taken by the majority. Such was the nature of the "unpleasantness" to which the Court of Appeal referred: if one agrees to become a minority shareholder in a corporation, one must, in a spirit of corporate democracy, accept the will of the majority.

The second branch of the policy seemed to emerge from partnership (and "joint stock company") law. Beck suggested that

[t]he essence of partnership was, and is, mutual trust and confidence among all partners. Trust and confidence cannot be established by judicial decree and the Chancellor refused to interfere in the internal disputes of a partnership "except with a view to a dissolution."[127]

So it was that, even when the actions of the majority crossed the line of unfairness and so justified court intervention, disgruntled minority shareholders had available to them but a single remedy: apply to the court seeking to have the company wound up on "just and equitable" grounds. That quoted phrase still appears in the winding-up (or corporate dissolution) provisions of many modern Canadian corporate statutes.[128]

There is an obvious problem in providing only the extreme remedy of winding up. Rather like the deterrent to war supposedly provided by the threat of nuclear retaliation, it is either so drastic that aggressors may boldly assume that exploited minorities will hardly dare to invoke it or, if it is indeed granted, it will not sensibly remedy a problem at all. It will simply annihilate an otherwise viable business—perhaps with disastrous consequences for innocent employees, creditors, and others.

Concerns of this sort prompted the UK Parliament, in response to a recommendation made by the 1945 Cohen committee, to enact the forerunner to the modern statutory oppression remedy. The fundamental premise of that original UK statutory provision was straightforward—a shareholder could apply to the court claiming oppression at the hands of the

125 *Re Jury Gold Mine Dev. Co.*, [1928] 4 DLR 735, at 736 (Ont. CA). This passage was quoted by the Lawrence committee in their report on Ontario business corporations law. Following their reproduction of this passage, the committee posed the rhetorical question, "At what point does unpleasantness become oppression?" See Lawrence committee report, supra footnote 28, at para. 7.3.9.

126 Beck, supra footnote 29, at 548. The principle is perhaps most strongly expressed by Lord Davey in *Burland v. Earle*, [1902] AC 83, at 93 (PC): "It is an elementary principle of the law relating to joint stock companies that the Court will not interfere with the internal management of companies acting within their powers, and in fact has no jurisdiction to do so."

127 Beck, supra footnote 29, at 550.

128 See, e.g., CBCA, s. 214(b)(ii).

majority. If the court hearing the application was satisfied that facts existed that *would have* justified winding up the company on just and equitable grounds, some less drastic order could be made instead. That is, the court could, rather than bring an end *to the company*, order a less intrusive remedy "with a view to bringing to an end *the matters complained of*."[129]

This new remedy represented a significant reversal of traditional corporate law principles. In fact, the UK innovation was viewed by the Lawrence committee in 1967 as simply too radical a step at that time for Ontario. They strongly recommended against introducing any similar provision into the Ontario corporate statute, and soundly criticized the UK measure as one that

> raises as many problems as it lays to rest and, more importantly, is objectionable on the ground that it is a complete dereliction of the established principle of judicial non-interference in the management of companies.[130]

Such fears did not, apparently, dissuade the BC legislature. The BC *Companies Act* (as it was then called) very early on contained a provision initially modelled on the original oppression remedy found in s. 210 of the UK *Companies Act* of 1948. But for many years, the BC statutory oppression remedy was the only one of its kind in Canada.

As we shall see, Canadian corporate law has since moved far from its early reticence to permit court interference in a corporation's internal affairs. Modern Canadian corporate statutes typically contain "relief from oppression" provisions that invite courts to engage in creative, activist solutions to intracorporate disputes. It is not only the range of available remedies that has been expanded. The scope of eligible complainants has also been broadened. Although the paradigm oppression case involves disputes between shareholders of private corporations in which the majority shareholders are acting to the disadvantage of the minority shareholders, this is by no means the only sort of corporate dispute now embraced by Canadian statutory oppression remedies.

Statutory Oppression Remedy

The above introduction touched briefly on the history of the oppression remedy provisions now found in most Canadian corporate statutes. The forerunner to the modern oppression remedy, first introduced into the UK *Companies Act* following a recommendation of the Cohen committee in 1945, did not appear to have much impact in the United Kingdom. Few cases were launched under it. Iacobucci et al. wrote that, as of 1975 (that is, more than 25 years after the provision had been enacted), "section 210 had been successfully invoked only twice."[131]

A poorly designed tool is bound to rust unused, and the original UK remedy was a poor tool indeed. The various shortcomings of s. 210 of the old UK Act were identified in

129 *Companies Act*, 1948 (UK), 11 & 12 Geo. VI, c. 38, s. 210(2) (emphasis added).

130 Lawrence committee report, supra footnote 28, at para. 7.3.12.

131 Frank Iacobucci, Marilyn L. Pilkington, and J. Robert S. Prichard, *Canadian Business Corporations* (Toronto: Canada Law Book, 1977), at 202. Professor Welling abruptly concluded of the UK oppression remedy (prior to its material amendment in 1980), "that it never worked there." (See Bruce Welling, *Corporate Law in Canada: The Governing Principles*, 2nd ed. (Toronto: Butterworths, 1991), at 555.)

the 1962 *Report of the Company Law Committee of the Board of Trade*[132] (the Jenkins committee). When the Dickerson committee undertook its review of Canadian federal corporate law in the 1970s, it had the benefit of the prior work of the Jenkins committee. The Dickerson committee thus proposed a new form of oppression remedy that would address the specific weaknesses that had been identified in the English legislation.

The Dickerson committee's proposal for a new oppression remedy was adopted when the CBCA was first enacted in 1975, and was subsequently emulated by many other Canadian provincial statutes. At the heart of the Dickerson committee's proposal were the following modifications to the UK model:[133]

- A remedy ought to be available even in those circumstances where the actions complained of would not necessarily be dire enough to justify winding up the corporation on just and equitable grounds.
- A remedy ought to be available not only where there has been an oppressive course of conduct, but also in cases of isolated acts of "oppression."
- The grounds for relief should be expanded so that a complainant might seek redress in the case of acts that were wrongful, even if they were not actually illegal. Thus, the remedy should be available not only in cases of "oppression" (as that term had traditionally been defined[134]), but also in cases where corporate actions are taken that are "unfairly prejudicial or unfairly disregard the interest" of the complainant (or perhaps, as will be discussed below, of others).
- Although the oppression remedy was originally envisioned as a form of protection for minority shareholders, the remedy ought not to be so narrowly confined. A complainant should be afforded protection from oppression even if he or she has not, strictly speaking, been harmed in her or his capacity *as a shareholder*. Needless to say, in small, private corporations, in which shareholders are also usually directors, officers, and employees, a minority shareholder's interests *as a shareholder* might not be affected in the least by the heavy-handed actions of the majority. Nonetheless, he or she might have been the victim of substantial harm if, for example, he or she had lost his or her position as a director or officer.[135]

It is against this background that we now turn to consider the CBCA's "oppression remedy."[136] The remedy is delineated in s. 241:

---

132   *Report of the Company Law Committee* (Cmnd 1749) (London: Her Majesty's Stationery Office, 1962), at para. 200ff.

133   This list is based on the Dickerson committee report, supra footnote 3, at para. 485.

134   See, for example, *Scottish Co-operative Wholesale Society Ltd. v. Meyer*, [1959] AC 324 (HL), in which the term was interpreted to mean "burdensome, harsh or wrongful" (per Viscount Simonds, at 342) or perhaps exhibiting "lack of probity and fair dealing" (per Lord Keith, at 364).

135   The Dickerson committee referred to a discussion of this point in the then current edition of Gower's *Modern Principles of Company Law*. The point is dealt with in the current edition of this work as well. See Davies, supra footnote 31, at 516.

136   Although this discussion focuses on the CBCA's oppression remedy, most provincial statutes contain similar provisions. See, e.g., *Business Corporations Act* (Alta.), s. 242; *The Business Corporations Act* (Sask.), s. 234; *The Corporations Act* (Man.), s. 234; *Business Corporations Act* (Ont.), s. 248; *Business*

241(1) A complainant may apply to a court for an order under this section.

(2) If, on an application under subsection (1), the court is satisfied that in respect of a corporation or any of its affiliates

(a) any act or omission of the corporation or any of its affiliates effects a result,

(b) the business or affairs of the corporation or any of its affiliates are or have been carried on or conducted in a manner, or

(c) the powers of the directors of the corporation or any of its affiliates are or have been exercised in a manner

that is oppressive or unfairly prejudicial to or that unfairly disregards the interests of any security holder, creditor, director or officer, the court may make an order to rectify the matters complained of.

(3) In connection with an application under this section, the court may make any interim or final order it thinks fit including, without limiting the generality of the foregoing,

(a) an order restraining the conduct complained of;

(b) an order appointing a receiver or receiver-manager;

(c) an order to regulate a corporation's affairs by amending the articles or by-laws or creating or amending a unanimous shareholder agreement;

(d) an order directing an issue or exchange of securities;

(e) an order appointing directors in place of or in addition to all or any of the directors then in office;

(f) an order directing a corporation, subject to subsection (6), or any other person, to purchase securities of a security holder;

(g) an order directing a corporation, subject to subsection (6), or any other person, to pay a security holder any part of the monies that the security holder paid for securities;

(h) an order varying or setting aside a transaction or contract to which a corporation is a party and compensating the corporation or any other party to the transaction or contract;

(i) an order requiring a corporation, within a time specified by the court, to produce to the court or an interested person financial statements in the form required by section 155 or an accounting in such other form as the court may determine;

(j) an order compensating an aggrieved person;

(k) an order directing rectification of the registers or other records of a corporation under section 243;

(l) an order liquidating and dissolving the corporation;

(m) an order directing an investigation under Part XIX to be made; and

(n) an order requiring the trial of any issue.

(4) If an order made under this section directs amendment of the articles or by-laws of a corporation,

(a) the directors shall forthwith comply with subsection 191(4); and

(b) no other amendment to the articles or by-laws shall be made without the consent of the court, until a court otherwise orders.

Corporations Act (NB), s. 166; *Companies Act* (NS), Third Schedule, s. 5; and *Corporations Act* (NL), s. 371. The BC *Business Corporations Act* also contains an oppression remedy provision (s. 227). The BC provision, however, has some unique features. See, e.g., *supra* footnote 6.

(5) A shareholder is not entitled to dissent under section 190 if an amendment to the articles is effected under this section.

(6) A corporation shall not make a payment to a shareholder under paragraph (3)(f) or (g) if there are reasonable grounds for believing that

(a) the corporation is or would after that payment be unable to pay its liabilities as they become due; or

(b) the realizable value of the corporation's assets would thereby be less than the aggregate of its liabilities.

(7) An applicant under this section may apply in the alternative for an order under section 214.

This broad statutory language is the source of one of the most rapidly expanding areas of modern Canadian corporate litigation. In fact, more than perhaps any other branch of Canadian corporate law, the significance of the oppression remedy, as it has been developed in the courts, cannot be properly understood without first carefully reviewing the texts of the leading oppression remedy cases, old and new. What is more, the oppression remedy "canon" is expanding rapidly as litigants and the courts continue to test the boundaries of this remarkably flexible remedial tool. Yet, a review of the oppression jurisprudence must be undertaken with the understanding that these cases are highly fact specific and wholly fact dependent. As Carthy JA of the Ontario Court of Appeal has said,

> The point at which relief [under the oppression remedy] is justified and the extent of relief are both so dependent upon the facts of the particular case, that little guidance can be obtained from comparing one case to another.[137]

Consequently, it is with considerable trepidation that the following brief and tentative notes of introduction are offered below. These comments are offered principally in the hope of encouraging the reader to explore this developing area of law carefully on his or her own, rather than with a view toward attempting anything like an authoritative pronouncement. With these caveats always in mind, then, some of the more intriguing issues raised by the oppression remedy include:

- Who may initiate an oppression application? Can an oppression remedy properly be sought in respect of harm done to someone other than the complainant?
- What constitutes acts that are "oppressive, unfairly prejudicial or [that] unfairly disregard the interests" of a party? Put another way, what precisely are the interests that the oppression remedy may be said to protect?
- How broad are the court's remedial powers under the statute?

Who May Initiate an Application for an Oppression Remedy?

There is no doubt that the Dickerson committee conceived of the oppression remedy as a tool that would be most often used by minority shareholders of private corporations whose interests were being unfairly jeopardized by the actions of the majority share-

---

137 *Themadel Foundation v. Third Canadian General Investment Trust Ltd.* (1998), 38 OR (3d) 749 (CA).

holders.[138] However, the language they recommended was not limited to private corporations, nor restricted to wrongs done to shareholders. The framers of the legislation were well aware of the broad way in which the provision had been drafted, though even they might have been surprised by the volume of litigation it has subsequently generated.

Subsection 241(1) states that a "complainant" may apply for a remedy under that section. The word "complainant" is defined in s. 238. It is, of course, the same definition that applies in the case of derivative actions, as discussed at some length earlier in this chapter.

In addition to the comments made earlier, however, a few additional points about this word are worth noting here.

First, courts have permitted parties who are not yet shareholders, but who have a vested right to acquire shares, to be considered complainants.[139] But the courts have not been prepared to extend the scope of the complainant definition one step further so as to enable a person to seek an oppression remedy in cases where it is the impugned act itself on which the applicant, in effect, relies as conferring the status necessary to qualify the applicant as a complainant.[140]

Second, there is a growing body of authority supporting, in particular, the proposition that a creditor may be a "proper person" for purposes of seeking an oppression remedy. That conclusion might have seemed implicit from the wording of s. 241(2), which specifically includes reference to potential harm to creditors. However, recall that the term "complainant" does not explicitly include reference to creditors (other than holders of debt securities), and the drafters chose not to modify this aspect of the definition for purposes of the oppression remedy.[141] Even under the Alberta *Business Corporations Act*, which specifically includes "creditors" within the definition of "complainant" for purposes of the derivative action, for purposes of the oppression remedy, a "creditor" may only be a complainant if, in the discretion of the court, the creditor is a "proper person" to make an application seeking an oppression remedy.[142] The New Brunswick *Business Corporations Act*, however, includes creditors as complainants for purposes of both derivative actions and oppression remedies.[143]

---

138 Dickerson committee, supra footnote 3, at para. 484: "[The section] will be invoked most frequently—but not always—in respect of a corporation the shares of which are held by only a relatively small number of persons, a so-called 'close corporation,' since its usual object is to remedy any wrong done to minority shareholders."

139 See, e.g., *Vlasbom v. NetPCS Networks Inc.* (2003), 31 BLR (3d) 255, at para. 199ff. (Ont. SCJ).

140 See, e.g., *Trillium Computer Resources Inc. v. Taiwan Connection Inc.* (1992), 10 OR (3d) 249 (Gen. Div.) and *Joncas v. Spruce Falls Power & Paper Co.* (2000), 48 OR (3d) 179 (SCJ), aff'd. [2001] OJ no. 1505 (QC) (CA).

141 Note that under the Alberta *Business Corporations Act*, a creditor is automatically included within the definition of "complainant" for the purposes of bringing a derivative action, but is included as a complainant for purposes of commencing an oppression application only if the court finds that the creditor is a "proper person" to make the application. See *Business Corporations Act* (Alta.), s. 239, definition of "complainant."

142 *Business Corporations Act* (Alta.), s. 239(iii), definition of "complainant."

143 *Business Corporations Act* (NB), s. 163 (c).

Interestingly, there is some indication that the Dickerson committee's intention was not necessarily to make this remedy generally available to creditors who were not also shareholders. The Dickerson report suggested that the reason for including references to securityholders, creditors, directors, and officers in s. 241(2) was to permit a shareholder who was *also* a member of one of these groups to base his or her claim on the harm that he or she had suffered in his or her non-shareholder capacity.[144]

The courts, too, have been somewhat wary of too readily permitting creditors to launch oppression actions. Farley J, for example, of the Ontario Superior Court, has warned that "oppression cases should not be used by creditors to facilitate ordinary debt collections,"[145] and, in another earlier case,[146] cautioned against debt actions "routinely" being "turned into oppression actions."[147] In his view, a creditor ought not to be considered a complainant except where the creditor's complaints relate to circumstances "giving rise to the debt," and even then only where the creditor is "in a position analogous to that of a minority shareholder."[148]

Such judicial caution is well-advised. After all, it is almost invariably the case that creditors who seek to pursue an oppression remedy do so because they wish the court to find some party, other than their corporate debtor, liable for the debt. The oppression remedy, in other words, is frequently used by creditors who wish to have the court "pierce the corporate veil," but with the sanction of a statutory provision rather than in reliance on sometimes less flexible common law principles.[149] There is no doubt that the oppression remedy empowers a court to make an order against a corporation's shareholders, its directors, or anyone else for that matter.[150] But, unless judicial restraint is exercised, the oppression remedy could very well swallow up the law of contract and of tort, too, in any dispute involving a corporation.

Thus far, at any rate, it has only been in certain relatively rare circumstances that the courts have considered it appropriate for creditors of a corporation to be permitted to seek an oppression remedy. In particular, for example, it may well be appropriate to accord a creditor "complainant" status for purposes of pursuing an oppression remedy if some action has been taken that has prevented that creditor from taking steps to protect itself in more traditional ways, such as through measures to secure repayment of a loan obligation.[151]

---

144 Dickerson committee, supra footnote 3, at para. 485: "In addition [s. 241] is made applicable to all cases of conduct that are [oppressive, etc., to] any security holder, creditor, director or officer and not just to the narrow case where a shareholder is oppressed in his capacity as a shareholder."

145 *Olympia & York Developments Ltd. (Trustee of) v. Olympia & York Realty Corp.* (2001), 16 BLR (3d) 74 (Ont. Sup. Ct.).

146 *Royal Trust*, supra footnote 51.

147 Ibid., at para. 12.

148 Ibid.

149 See the discussion of "piercing the corporate veil" in chapter 7.

150 See CBCA, ss. 241(3)(f), (g), and (j); *Budd v. Gentra* (1998), 43 BLR (2d) 27 (Ont. CA); and *Re Sidaplex Plastic Suppliers Inc. v. The Elta Group Inc. et al.* (1998), 40 OR (3d) 563 (CA).

151 This rationale was suggested in *First Edmonton*, supra footnote 56: "Where the applicant is a creditor of the corporation, did the circumstances which gave rise to the granting of credit include some element which prevented the creditor from taking adequate steps when he or it entered into the

This rationale seems to explain, for example, the outcome in *Re Sidaplex-Plastic Suppliers, Inc. and The Elta Group Inc. et al.*[152] In that case, a creditor of a corporation was permitted to pursue an oppression remedy against the sole director and sole shareholder of that corporation. A letter of credit that secured the applicant's debt was thought, by creditor and debtor-corporation alike, to be in good standing. In fact, it had been allowed to lapse, shortly before the corporation sold all of its assets. The proceeds of that sale of assets were used to retire the corporation's bank debt, a debt that had been guaranteed by the corporation's sole shareholder and director. In other words, the sale personally benefited the corporation's sole shareholder by extinguishing any liabilities to which he might otherwise have been exposed pursuant to the guarantee he had given. But, once the corporation was stripped of its assets, needless to say, the creditor's claim against the corporation itself became worthless. In these circumstances, the court permitted the creditor to seek an oppression remedy against the corporation's sole shareholder and director.

Creditors with liquidated claims, then, have been considered complainants. But what of those with unliquidated claims or even contingent interests? At one time, doubts were raised as to whether holders of more contingent claims would have status to seek an oppression remedy. A series of recent cases, however, has suggested that an applicant with a contingent claim may well, in appropriate circumstances, be permitted to proceed with an oppression application.[153]

As well, it has been held that there is a more compelling case for permitting involuntary (as opposed to voluntary, contractual) creditors to have complainant status because, by definition, there is no way for involuntary creditors to seek to protect themselves by contract.[154] Finally, this discussion of a creditor's right to seek an oppression order cannot be concluded without some mention of recent statements of the Supreme Court of Canada that touch on this subject. In *Peoples Department Stores Inc. v. Wise*,[155] the Supreme Court seemed to offer special encouragement to creditors contemplating the mysteries of the CBCA oppression remedy. After suggesting that courts should be particularly disposed to consider creditors to be "proper persons" when a corporation is teetering financially,[156] the court states that "[s]ection 241 provides a possible mechanism for creditors to protect their interests from the prejudicial conduct of directors."[157] Indeed, so "broad" does the court find this remedy, that

---

agreement to protect his or its interests against the occurrence of which he or it now complains? Did the creditor entertain an expectation that, assuming fair dealing, its chances of repayment would not be frustrated by the kind of conduct which subsequently was engaged in by the management of the corporation?"

152 Supra footnote 150.

153 See, e.g., *R v. Sands Motor Hotel* (1984), 28 BLR 122 (Sask. QB); *Prime Computer Ltd. v. Jeffrey* (1991), 6 OR (3d) 133 (Gen. Div.); *A.E. Realisations*, supra footnote 53; and *Gestion Trans-Tek Inc. v. Shipment Systems Strategies Ltd.* (2001), 20 BLR (3d) 156 (Ont. SCJ).

154 *Levy-Russell Ltd. v. Shieldings Inc.* (1998), 41 OR (3d) 54 (Gen. Div.).

155 Supra footnote 7.

156 Ibid., at para. 49.

157 Ibid., at para. 51.

its availability, in the justices' view, "undermines any perceived need to extend the fiduciary duty imposed on directors by s. 122(1)(a) of the CBCA to include creditors."[158]

Although the Dickerson committee clearly envisioned the oppression remedy as a provision that would usually be used when disputes arose between the shareholders of small, private corporations,[159] the remedy is not limited on its terms to private corporations. Shareholders and creditors of public corporations have also sought to use the oppression remedy. One of the most intriguing uses made of the provision occurs in the context of hostile takeover bids.

A hostile takeover bid refers to an offer to acquire a controlling interest in the outstanding shares of a corporation without the agreement or endorsement of the directors of the company subject to the bid (the "target" company).[160] Directors and managers of a corporation that is subject to such an unsolicited hostile bid will often implement measures aimed at thwarting or at least delaying the bid in some way, generally to give the target company's board of directors more time within which to generate possible alternative transactions that may result in the shareholders receiving a higher price.[161]

A hostile bidder, needless to say, finds these sorts of defensive measures irritating, frustrating, and potentially expensive. A bidder would like to circumvent these tactics so that its offer can be put to the target company's shareholders and, as the bidder hopes, accepted by many or most of them. One strategy that hostile bidders have pursued in recent years when bedeviled by anti-takeover defences is to launch an oppression action against the target company and its board of directors. Note that the basis for such a claim is *not* that the bidder has been unduly prejudiced in its capacity as bidder.[162] Rather, the bidder will have typically acquired some shares in the corporation before formally launching its bid. Thus, the bidder will argue that the target's *shareholders* (of which the bidder itself is one) are being harmed by virtue of the fact that the directors have taken improper actions, which have deprived the shareholders of the opportunity to decide for themselves whether they wish to tender their shares to the bid.[163]

---

158 Ibid., at para. 51.

159 Dickerson committee, supra footnote 3, at para. 484.

160 For a detailed discussion of hostile takeover bids and the policy issues they raise, see Christopher C. Nicholls, *Corporate Finance and Canadian Law* (Toronto: Carswell, 2000), at 336ff. For additional detail concerning the securities law requirements surrounding takeover bids generally, see MacIntosh and Nicholls, supra footnote 45, at 295ff.

161 This explanation, in any event, is generally the reason given for implementing hostile takeover defences. For a discussion of other less admirable motives that have been suggested by commentators from time to time, see Nicholls, supra footnote 160.

162 Farley J, of the Ontario Court General Division (as it was then called), coined the colourful phrase "bitter bidder" to refer to a frustrated takeover bidder seeking to characterize itself somewhat disingenuously as an exploited minority shareholder in order to advance its hostile bid. See *Benson v. Third Canadian General Investment Trust Ltd.* (1993), 14 OR (3d) 493, at 511-12.

163 See, e.g., *347883 Alberta Ltd. v. Producers Pipeline Inc.* (1991), 92 Sask. R 81 (CA); *Rogers Communications Inc. v. MacLean Hunter Ltd.* (1994), 2 CCLS 233 (Ont. Gen. Div.); *CW Shareholdings Inc. v. WIC Western International Communications Ltd.* (1998), 39 OR (3d) 755 (Gen. Div.); and *Maple Leaf Foods Inc. v. Schneider* (1998), 42 OR (3d) 177 (CA).

In these cases, the courts have an especially delicate balancing act to perform. The oppression remedy certainly ought not to be used to permit courts to interfere without restraint in the management of corporations. However, at the same time, prudent judicial reluctance to interfere in a corporation's affairs cannot be mistaken for unwillingness to restrain improper conduct. As a result, these cases often focus on the principled basis on which directors of target companies may legitimately act to forestall a takeover bid, acting in the best interests of the target corporation and its shareholders. Although these cases are important and instructive, they are most usefully discussed within the broader context of Canadian takeover bid regulation and corporate governance standards, and so will not be discussed in detail in this chapter.

One final point on who may launch oppression proceedings: there is recent case authority to suggest that the injury complained of need not even have been suffered by the complainant himself or herself.[164]

What Interests Does the Oppression Remedy Protect?

Although, by convention, s. 241 of the CBCA (and its provincial counterparts) is commonly referred to as the "oppression remedy," the term "oppression" has gradually become something of a misnomer. Section 241, after all, permits a complainant to seek a remedy not only in cases where "oppressive" acts have been committed by or on behalf of the corporation, but also in cases where there has been conduct that falls short of "oppression," but that nevertheless is "unfairly prejudicial to or that unfairly disregards the interests" of a securityholder, creditor, officer, or director. Inclusion of these additional grounds invites the courts to fashion remedies even in cases where, strictly speaking, there has been no violation of the complainant's legal rights as such. The CBCA's oppression provisions do not speak expressly of permitting a complainant to seek a remedy in respect of *threatened* harm. However, that broader language does appear in certain provincial corporate statutes.[165]

The courts have made clear that the spirit of the oppression remedy, as the Dickerson committee itself had suggested, is to be found in the language of Lord Cooper in *Elder v. Elder and Watson Ltd.*, namely: "[T]he essence of the matter seems to be that the conduct complained of should at the lowest involve a visible departure from the standards of fair dealing, and a violation of the conditions of fair play on which every shareholder who entrusts his money to a company is entitled to rely."[166]

Legitimate/Reasonable Expectations

At about the same time as the Dickerson committee proposed the new version of the oppression remedy, the House of Lords rendered its influential decision in *Ebrahimi v. Westbourne Galleries Ltd.*[167] *Ebrahimi* had begun as, among other things, an oppression

---

164 *Joncas v. Spruce Falls Power and Paper Co.*, supra footnote 140.

165 See, e.g., *Business Corporations Act* (Ont.), s. 248(2) and *Business Corporations Act* (BC), s. 227(2)(b).

166 [1952] Scots Law Times 112, at 113, cited in Dickerson committee, supra footnote 3, at para. 485, and by the Jenkins committee, supra footnote 132, at para. 204.

167 [1973] AC 360 (HL).

action under what was then s. 210 of the UK *Companies Act*. But, in fact, the appellant, one of three shareholders of a private company who had been excluded from the board of directors by the other two, lost on the oppression aspect of his case (primarily because s. 210 required evidence of an oppressive course of conduct, which was not proved). The court did, however, order the company to be wound up on "just and equitable grounds," and it was this—and only this—aspect of the case that was before the House of Lords. The House of Lords in *Ebrahimi* famously declared that

> a limited company is more than a mere legal entity, with a personality in law of its own: that there is room in company law for recognition of the fact that behind it, or amongst it, there are individuals, with rights, expectations and obligations inter se which are not necessarily submerged in the company structure.[168]

The concept of "legitimate expectations" continued to evolve significantly in the United Kingdom, especially following the promulgation in 1980 of what is now s. 459 of the UK *Companies Act*, the "unfair prejudice" remedy (a provision that makes no mention of "oppression"). That development culminated (or perhaps it might be said, terminated) with the landmark 1999 decision of the House of Lords in *O'Neill v. Phillips*.[169] The significance of the *O'Neill* case to the development of UK company law, in general, and the notion of "legitimate expectations," in particular, has been the subject of considerable comment.[170] Note here, one brief extract from the speech of Lord Hoffman that may help to illustrate why the case has received so much attention from English lawyers with an interest in the notion of "legitimate expectations" in the context of what is now the "unfair prejudice" remedy in s. 459 of the *Companies Act*:

> In *Re Saul D Harrison & Sons plc* ... I used the term "legitimate expectation," borrowed from public law, as a label for the "correlative right" to which a relationship between company members may give rise in a case when, on equitable principles, it would be regarded as unfair for a majority to exercise a power conferred upon them by the articles to the prejudice of another member ... . It was probably a mistake to use this term, as it usually is when one introduces a new label to describe a concept which is already sufficiently defined in other terms. In saying that it was "correlative" to the equitable restraint, I meant that it could exist only when equitable principles of the kind I have been describing would make it unfair for a party to exercise rights under the articles. It is a consequence, not a cause, of the equitable restraint. The concept of a legitimate expectation should not be allowed to lead a life of its own, capable of giving rise to equitable restraints in circumstances to which traditional equitable principles have no application.[171]

In Canada, it has become recognized as a critical aspect of the oppression remedy that the section is aimed not merely (or even primarily) at protecting the *rights* of shareholders (or other complainants). It may also be invoked to protect their "expectations." Which

---

168 Ibid., at 379, per Lord Wilberforce.

169 [1999] 2 All ER 961 (HL).

170 For an enlightening general discussion of the significance of the decision, see Davies, supra footnote 31, at 518ff.

171 Supra footnote 169, at 970.

expectations? Not all expectations, it is clear. As one court put it, the remedy does not exist to protect each individual shareholder's subjective "wish list."[172] Rather, expectations are to be protected if they are "legitimate" (to use the term more often found in the English cases) or "reasonable" (to use the adjective that has become customary in the Canadian cases).

Indeed, the notion of "reasonable expectations," though not mentioned in the statute itself, has nevertheless come to be said to lie at the core of the Canadian oppression remedy, at least in the absence of evidence of the sort of "wrongful, harsh, and burdensome" conduct that has always constituted remediable oppression, even in the absence of the more easily satisfied standards of "unfair prejudice" and "unfair disregard of interest."

It was thought important that the oppression remedy be able to protect more than legal rights because, among other things, the paradigm oppression case—excluding a minority shareholder from the board of a private company—typically involved no violation of the excluded shareholder's legal rights. After all, majority shareholders, as a matter of law, are generally entitled to elect, or not elect, whomever they wish to the board of directors.

The very flexibility of the oppression remedy, however, soon led it to become many corporate litigators' weapon of first resort. As a result, the volume of oppression cases is large and growing at a rapid pace. No comprehensive summary of this mountain of jurisprudence is possible or, in this short chapter, even desirable. Accordingly, only a few of the principles that have emerged from the cases are noted below:

- The court in one recent case has suggested that, when considering an application for an oppression remedy, three key issues must be addressed: "(1) Was the impugned conduct outside the range of reasonable business judgment; (2) Was the impugned conduct inconsistent with the reasonable expectations of the complainants; and (3) Did the impugned conduct cause prejudice to the complainant?"[173]
- An oppression remedy is available, even if there is no evidence of "bad faith or want of probity";[174] indeed, a remedy may be pursued even where the impugned action was not intended to harm the complainant.[175]
- The "reasonable expectations" protected by the oppression remedy refer to "expectations raised in the mind of a party by the word or deed of the other, and which the first party ordinarily would realize it was encouraging by its words and deeds."[176]
- "Reasonable expectations" are not necessarily static; they can change over time.[177]
- "Reasonable expectations" "must be measured objectively within the four corners of the pact [the complainant] made with his [or her] partners."[178]
- Corporate law itself can be the basis for "reasonable expectations." That is, it is reasonable for a complainant to expect that directors and officers will comply with

172   See *82099 Ontario Inc. v. Harold E. Ballard* (1991), 3 BLR (3d) 113, at 186 (Ont. Ct. Gen. Div.).

173   *Main v. Delcan Group Inc.* (1999), 47 BLR (2d) 200, at para. 31.

174   *Brant Investments Ltd. v. Keep Rite Inc.* (1991), 80 DLR (4th) 161 (CA).

175   *Downtown Eatery (1993) Ontario Ltd. v. Ontario* (2001), 54 OR (3d) 161 (CA).

176   *Westfair Foods Ltd. v. Watt* (1991), 79 DLR (4th) 48, at 54 (Alta. CA).

177   *Aquino v. First Choice Capital Fund Group* (1996), 143 Sask. R 81 (QB) and *82099 Ontario Inc. v. Harold E. Ballard*, supra footnote 172.

178   *Krynen v. Bugg* (2003), 64 OR (3d) 393 (SCJ).

their corporate law duties.[179] This appears to suggest that there may sometimes be unavoidable overlap between the oppression remedy and the derivative action. Courts will frequently consider whether the allegedly oppressive actions of directors or officers have been taken in the best interests of the corporation. If they have not, this seems to be compelling evidence of oppression. Indeed, breach of fiduciary duties has been said to satisfy the test of oppression.[180] However, if the allegedly oppressive acts were found to have been taken in the best interests of the corporation, there is some uncertainty as to whether an oppression remedy is available. Some courts have suggested that acts taken honestly and in good faith with a view to the best interests of the shareholders cannot be viewed as oppressive, even to non-shareholder complainants.[181] Others, however, have said that actions may well be found to cause unfair prejudice or unfair disregard even if taken in the best interests of the corporation.[182]

- "Reasonable expectations" can be evidenced by agreements between the parties, such as the terms of a shareholders' agreement[183] or other documents.[184]
- In fact, even a draft agreement—though not creating contractual rights—may constitute evidence of "reasonable expectations."[185]
- Nevertheless, an oppression remedy may be available against one party to a shareholders' agreement even when the party is acting strictly in accordance with his or her rights thereunder.[186]
- In the case of a public corporation, "reasonable expectations" can be created by disclosure in public documents (such as information circulars or prospectuses)[187] and by public announcements.[188]
- Conversely, where a transaction document specifically contemplates the occurrence of some event, this can be evidence that such an event could not be considered outside a complainant's "reasonable expectations."[189]

---

179 See, e.g., *UPM-Kymmene Corp. v. UPM-Kymmene Miramichi Inc.* (2002), 214 DLR (4th) 496, at para. 201 (Ont. SCJ), aff'd. (2004), 42 BLR (3d) 34 (Ont. CA).

180 See, e.g., *Calmont v. Kredl* (1993), 42 AR 81 (QB), aff'd. (1995), 165 AR 343 (CA).

181 See, e.g., *Metropolitan Toronto Police Widows and Orphans Fund v. Telus* (2003), 30 BLR (3d) 288, at para. 78 (Ont. SCJ): "I further find that the actions of the directors were in the best interests of the corporation and its shareholders and accordingly, although to the disadvantage of the Bondholders, do not constitute oppressive conduct giving rise to any remedy pursuant to the provisions of the CBCA."

182 See, e.g., *Sabex Internationale Ltée* (1979), 6 BLR 65 (Que. SC).

183 *218125 Investments Ltd. v. Patel* (1995), 33 ALR (3d) 245 (QB) and *Armstrong v. Northern Eyes Inc.* (2000), 48 OR (3d) 442 (Div. Ct.), aff'd. [2001] OJ no. 1085 (QL) (CA).

184 *Metropolitan Toronto Police Widows and Orphans Fund*, supra footnote 181.

185 *Gordon Glaves Holdings Ltd. v. Care Corp of Canada* (2000), 48 OR (3d) 737 (CA), application for leave to appeal to Supreme Court of Canada dismissed [2000] SCCA no. 411 (QL).

186 *Bury v. Bell Guinlock* (1984), 48 OR (2d) 57 (HCJ), aff'd. (1985), 49 OR (2d) 91 (Div. Ct.).

187 *Themadel Foundation*, supra footnote 137 and *Deutsche Bank Canada v. Oxford Properties Group Inc.* (1998), 40 BLR (2d) 302 (Ont. Ct. Gen. Div.).

188 *Gazit (1997) Inc. v. Centrefund Realty Corp.* (2000), 8 BLR (3d) 81 (Ont. SCJ).

189 *Casurina Limited Partnership v. Rio Algom Ltd.*, [2004] OJ no. 177 (QL) (CA), application for leave to appeal to Supreme Court of Canada dismissed [2004] SCCA no. 105 (QL).

- Although the oppression remedy was clearly intended to protect minority share-holders from majority shareholders, it is evidently possible for a majority share-holder to seek an oppression remedy against a minority shareholder under appropriate circumstances.[190]

This short summary, the reader must be cautioned, is far from exhaustive. The scope of the statutory oppression remedy is continually being tested and refined within the crucible of the Canadian courts, and definitive statements about the limits of the remedy are liable to be as premature as they are misleading.

The Broadness of the Court's Remedial Powers

A court is empowered to make any interim or final order it sees fit in connection with an application for an oppression remedy. However, note that the purpose of the oppression remedy is to rectify oppressive conduct, not to impose punishment.[191] As Farley J has put it, "[t]he job for the court is to even up the balance, not to tip it in favour of the hurt party."[192]

It is fair to say that probably the remedy most frequently ordered in oppression cases is an order requiring the shares of one shareholder to be purchased by another share-holder, or perhaps by the corporation itself.[193] And, also note that one of the most important practical implications of the oppression remedy is that it can be used to impose personal liability on a corporation's shareholders, directors, or officers (or others) under circumstances where, as a matter of common law, no such personal liability would necessarily be imposed.[194]

However, what is truly noteworthy about the oppression remedy is the enormous flexibility it bestows on courts to craft creative remedies. Indeed, the legislature has provided in s. 241(3) a list of possible orders that is nothing short of remarkable. For example, a court may actually amend the corporation's articles or bylaws, or amend or even create a unanimous shareholder agreement for the parties.[195] The court may make an order appointing directors "in place of or in addition to" the directors in office.[196] The court may vary or set aside a contract or transaction to which a corporation is a party.[197] These rather extraordinary remedies, and others in s. 241, are in addition to what might be considered the more conventional powers of the court to order that the impugned

---

190 See, e.g., *Gillespie v. Overs*, [1987] OJ no. 747 (QL) (HCJ).

191 See, e.g., *Naneff v. Con-Crete Holdings Ltd.* (1995), 23 OR (3d) 481 (CA).

192 *Harold E. Ballard*, supra footnote 172, at 197.

193 Such a remedy is specifically contemplated by CBCA, s. 241(3)(f).

194 See, e.g., *Budd v. Gentra*, supra footnote 150; *Sidaplex v. Elta*, supra footnote 150; and *Piller Sausages & Delicatessens Ltd. v. Cobb International Corp.* (2003), 35 BLR (3d) 193 (Ont. SCJ), aff'd. [2003] OJ no. 5128 (QL) (CA).

195 CBCA, s. 241(3)(c).

196 CBCA, s. 241(3)(e).

197 CBCA, s. 241(3)(h).

conduct cease,[198] that compensation be paid,[199] that a receiver or receiver-manager be appointed,[200] or, in the most extreme cases, that the corporation be dissolved.[201]

Relationship Between Derivative Action and Oppression Remedy

Derivative and oppression applications—although often overlapping in real life, especially in the case of small, privately held corporations—are, in principle, quite distinct. The derivative action is available only in the case of harms alleged to have been committed against the corporation itself. Accordingly, a plaintiff not otherwise included in the specifically enumerated categories of the "complainant" definition ought only to be permitted to launch such an action if there is good reason to believe that the plaintiff is well positioned (and, one might add, well motivated) to champion the interests of the corporation and not merely the plaintiff's own interests. No such consideration applies in the case of the oppression action, which was intended, after all, to protect the interests of disenfranchised security holders and perhaps other corporate stakeholders.

In addition, the statutory language found in the oppression remedy provision specifically refers to situations where actions are alleged to have caused harm to, among others, creditors[202] of the corporation—a class of person not specifically mentioned in the categories of permitted "complainants" or in the derivative action provisions of the CBCA.[203]

As Professor MacIntosh has explained in some detail,[204] there are sound, understandable reasons that a complainant may feel compelled to commence both a derivative action and an oppression proceeding in respect of the same set of facts. Courts have been prepared to permit this way of proceeding,[205] but, as noted above, some courts have sounded important notes of caution.[206]

However, a curious issue is raised when a derivative action and oppression application are pursued simultaneously. Because the derivative action is, in principle, an action of the company itself, can the same counsel act for the complainant in both actions? After all, in the derivative action, the company is theoretically the plaintiff. In the oppression proceeding, based on the same set of facts, the corporation will be a defendant. Does this raise issues of conflict of interest or even concerns about privilege that make it impossible for the same lawyer to act in respect of both proceedings?

---

198 CBCA, s. 241(3)(a).

199 CBCA, s. 241(3)(j).

200 CBCA, s. 241(3)(b).

201 CBCA, s. 241(3)(l).

202 CBCA, s. 241(2)(c).

203 Recall, however, that the Alberta *Business Corporations Act* contains different wording. See footnote 141, supra, and text accompanying footnotes 142 and 143, supra.

204 Jeffrey G. MacIntosh, "The Oppression Remedy: Personal or Derivative?" (1991), 70 *Canadian Bar Review* 29.

205 See, e.g., *Acapulco Holdings Ltd. v. Jegen*, [1997] 4 WWR 601 (Alta. CA).

206 See text accompanying footnotes 120 to 123, supra.

This issue was dealt with squarely by the BC Court of Appeal in *Discovery Enterprises Inc. v. Ebco Industries Ltd.*[207] Newbury JA rejected the suggestion that the same lawyer was automatically precluded from acting in respect of both the derivative and oppression applications. She noted:

> I do not think that the relationship between [the applicant] and the [corporation] can at the same time be both "adversarial" and fiduciary. The fact that the company's name is used as plaintiff ... should not obscure the substance of the litigation.[208]

This analysis led her further to conclude that there was, in fact, no necessary conflict for the solicitor and, accordingly, no need for him to be prevented from acting in respect of both proceedings. She left open the possibility that if some real conflict did emerge in the course of the litigation, it could be dealt with at that time.

CONCLUSION

The derivative action and the oppression remedy are the two most important Canadian corporate statutory remedies. The oppression remedy, in particular, has become an especially flexible tool in the hands of creative lawyers representing the interests of aggrieved corporate stakeholders. The interplay of the derivative action and the oppression remedy helps to illustrate the essential tension in corporate law between respect for the notion of the corporation as a separate legal entity (seen, for example, in the formal justification for the derivative action procedures) and the recognition of the economic realities of the corporation, especially private corporations of the "incorporated partnership" variety.

As important as these two remedies are, however, remember that they are not the only distinctly corporate statutory remedies. Discussion of several of these other remedies is taken up in chapter 14.

---

207 (1998), 58 BCLR (3d) 105 (CA), application for leave to appeal to Supreme Court of Canada dismissed (1999), *SCC Bulletin*, at 1549.

208 Ibid., at para. 9.

CHAPTER FOURTEEN

Corporate Statutory Remedies: Dissent and Appraisal Rights, Compliance Orders, "Winding-Up" Orders, and Investigation Orders

DISSENT AND APPRAISAL RIGHTS

Framing the Issue

The principle of majority rule has long been considered the very cornerstone of corporate democracy. As discussed in chapter 13, at one time the courts so rigidly applied this principle that minority shareholders were often forced to endure rather heavy-handed treatment by the majority, treatment that today would no doubt form the basis of successful oppression applications.

But majority corporate rule—even absent oppression—may not always be appropriate. On occasion, a corporation's controlling shareholders may favour some important corporate changes—changes genuinely undertaken in the interests of the corporation as a whole and in no way motivated by any desire to harm the minority (or with any reasonable expectation that such harm will occur). Such changes may nevertheless be so fundamental that some minority shareholders may legitimately protest that the very nature of the corporation in which they had chosen to invest is being altered against their will.

Recall, for example, the imaginary corporation discussed in chapter 6—Nothing But Beer Brewing Inc. This corporation was created solely for the purpose of brewing beer. Its articles of incorporation contained an unusual restriction, forbidding the corporation from carrying on any other sort of business.

Suppose that shares in this company have been sold to investors. Some years have passed. The beer brewing industry has fallen on hard times. The managers of Nothing But Beer Brewing Inc.—with the best and most honourable of intentions—determine that the company's resources might be far more profitably employed in a very different line of business—manufacturing shoes. The majority of the shareholders of Nothing But Beer Brewing Inc. heartily endorse such a change. The prospects of financial success in the shoe manufacturing business are much brighter than in the moribund beer brewing industry. However, a very small group of shareholders—holding less than 1 percent of the total outstanding shares—are opposed to this dramatic shift in business focus. They have no interest in being shareholders in a shoe manufacturer. They had only ever intended to own shares in a beer brewing business. Indeed, they would never have purchased their shares in the first place if they had known such a radical change in the business might one day be undertaken.

The concerns of these small shareholders are no doubt legitimate. But, equally legitimate are the views of the majority shareholders who may well feel that it is both undemocratic and commercially unreasonable to give to every shareholder—no matter how small his or her investment in the company—a sort of perpetual veto over important corporate changes.

The law in such cases might well have rigidly adhered to the paramountcy of corporate majority rule. Minority shareholders might then have been required in every case to accept the will of the majority (at least in the absence of oppression) as the fair and inevitable consequence of their decision to invest in a capital-pooling vehicle such as a business corporation. Alternatively, the law might—with equal justification—have decreed that, while majority rule is appropriate for most corporate decisions, when the very essence of the corporation itself is to be undermined by a proposed transaction, nothing short of unanimous consent will suffice. Or, to put it differently, all shareholders might be said to enjoy a kind of "vested right" in their property that cannot be altered by majority vote.[1]

In fact, the CBCA—and those provincial statutes that emulate it—chose a third route that steers an intermediate course between these two equally rational, but inflexible, extremes.

The shareholder dissent right and appraisal remedy is the means by which the CBCA attempts to reconcile the competing values of majority rule and fair recognition of the legitimate concerns of minority investors when the fundamental nature of their investment is to be changed. The dissent and appraisal remedy, accordingly, permits the majority to make whatever fundamental changes to the business they deem appropriate, but accords to the minority in the case of certain fundamental changes a right that ordinary equity holders normally[2] do not enjoy—namely, the right to demand that their shares be repurchased by the company and their capital returned to them.[3]

---

1   See Robert W.V. Dickerson et al., *Proposals for a New Business Corporations Law for Canada*, vol. I, Commentary (Ottawa: Information Canada, 1971), at para. 344 (Dickerson committee).

2   Of course, corporations can create shares with so-called retraction rights—that is, features that would permit the shareholder, subject to certain conditions, to require the corporation to redeem his or her shares at a price fixed by the share conditions. But common or ordinary shares—as those terms are conventionally used—would not typically provide retraction rights. More important, however, the dissent and appraisal right permits shareholders to require the corporation to repurchase their shares notwithstanding that the shares themselves do not purport to grant the shareholders any such rights.

3   Dickerson committee, supra footnote 1, at para. 347.

Rationale Underlying the Appraisal Remedy

The rationale underlying the appraisal remedy has frequently been analyzed and critiqued. Robert Clark, for example, has suggested that two general sorts of arguments have traditionally been made in support of such remedies. These arguments he classifies as relating either to defeated shareholder expectations or to protection against certain kinds of unfairness that cannot adequately be protected against using other shareholder remedies, often because of the opaque nature of the harm.[4]

Clark finds the defeated expectations rationale, of which the beer brewery/shoe manufacturer example is an illustration, to be unsatisfactory. Among other things, he notes that expectations are fluid, not static. Moreover, as he puts it, "investors nowadays care only about the risks and expected return presented by their investments. They are not usually attached, out of sentiment or ideology, to a particular company or kind of company."[5]

Clark also questions the suggestion that the appraisal remedy provides protection to shareholders against potential unfairnesses that cannot be remedied by other means (such as the oppression remedy). If preventing unfairness is the rationale for the provision, he notes, then it is not clear why certain events trigger the appraisal remedy, while other transactions, that could have identical economic effects, do not.

There have been more sophisticated attempts to justify the appraisal remedy. Modern portfolio theory, after Markowitz,[6] and the capital asset pricing model that developed from it, suggest that investors do (or should) concern themselves only with the extent to which an investment affects the risk and expected return of their entire investment portfolio. In that respect, it is not a stock's unique risk that is critical, but rather its "beta"— that is, the measure of the extent to which the price of the stock varies with the market as a whole.[7] Peter Letsou has suggested that the appraisal remedy can thus be understood as a means by which shareholders are permitted to terminate their investment when transactions are undertaken that are likely to alter the market risk (or beta) of their shares.[8]

Indeed, the existence of an appraisal remedy in some circumstances is perhaps better viewed primarily as a provision that facilitates corporate finance (*ex ante*) rather than as an *ex post* remedy for abuse. In other words, the fact that changes to fundamental share conditions trigger an appraisal remedy provides assurance to prospective shareholders that they may invest with confidence because they will not later be forced to continue to hold shares on terms that differ materially from the shares in respect of which they have made their initial investment decision.

To understand this argument, imagine an alternative corporate law regime in which share rights could always be varied by majority vote. There would be no reason to suspect that such changes would be undertaken lightly or improperly because, after all, all members of the class would be affected by any change in the same way. It must surely

---

4   Robert Charles Clark, *Corporate Law* (New York: Aspen Publishers, 1986), at 444.

5   Ibid.

6   See, e.g., Harry M. Markowitz, "Portfolio Selection" (1952), 7 *Journal of Finance* 77.

7   For a discussion of portfolio theory, the capital asset pricing model, and beta, see Christopher C. Nicholls, *Corporate Finance and Canadian Law* (Toronto: Carswell, 2000), at 101ff.

8   Peter Letsou, "The Role of Appraisal in Corporate Law" (1998), 39 *British Columbia Law Review* 1121.

be presumed that those holding a majority of shares would not agree to changes detrimental to their own interests.[9] Of course, in some cases, the majority shareholders might be in a position of conflict. They might also have some additional interest in the corporation not shared by the objecting minority. So, for example, shareholders holding a bare majority of a corporation's Class A shares, might also hold 100 percent of a corporation's Class B shares. It might be feared that the majority could well be tempted to sacrifice their interests as holders of Class A shares in exchange for some special benefit they expect to receive as holders of Class B shares.[10] However, concerns of that sort could be addressed *ex post*, for example, through the oppression remedy.

Thus, when initially making their investment decision, prospective shareholders could be reasonably assured that their share rights would not be altered in future for improper or capricious reasons. However, without an appraisal remedy, they could not be satisfied that the specific features of the shares that enticed them to invest would never be altered against their will. The existence of the appraisal remedy provides a credible commitment to prospective shareholders about the nature of their proposed investment. Such a provision may enhance the value of share ownership itself and, potentially, reduce the issuing corporation's cost of capital.

Other explanations for the appraisal remedy have been offered. Of these, it may be that Bayless Manning's explanation—though unconventional—is among the most revealing. Manning observes that the rhetoric surrounding the appraisal remedy consistently characterizes it as a device intended to protect minority shareholders from exploitation by the majority. However, he suggests, to the contrary, that the real point of introducing the appraisal remedy was to give to the majority greater flexibility and, hence, greater power than they enjoyed under earlier corporate law regimes.[11]

---

9   One notes, for example, that debt instruments typically provide that the terms of the instrument may be varied if holders of a specified minimum amount of the outstanding instruments concur.

10   In this regard, it is interesting to note that there is old case law in support of the proposition that debentureholders must—when they vote on matters that will bind the minority—exercise their voting power bona fide for the benefit of the class as a whole. See *British American Nickel Corp., Ltd. v. O'Brien*, [1927] 1 DLR 1121 (PC). In that case, a large debentureholder agreed to vote in favour of a significant capital reorganization in exchange for a promise that he would receive a block of common stock in the corporation (no such offer being extended to any of the other, smaller bondholders). It is generally thought that no such constraint applies to shareholders; although the Privy Council in *British American Nickel* did, in fact, refer *both* to a "holder of shares or debentures" in those instances "where his vote is conferred on him as a member of a class" (at 1124), as opposed, evidently, to situations where the power to vote "arises not in connection with a class, but only under a general title which confers the vote as a right of property attaching to a share" (at 1123). There were suggestions in some older English cases, of which *Allen v. Gold Reefs, Ltd.*, [1900] 1 Ch. 656 was among the most well-known, that majority shareholders were also obliged to vote their shares "bona fide for the benefit of the company." That proposition does not appear to form part of Canadian corporate law, in particular since the development of the extensive array of legislative protection for minority shareholders. For further discussion of this point, see chapter 12, footnote 30.

11   Bayless Manning, "The Shareholder's Appraisal Remedy: An Essay for Frank Coker" (1962), 72 *Yale Law Journal* 223.

Potential Impact of the Appraisal Remedy

To take advantage of the appraisal remedy, shareholders need to be made aware of it. The CBCA therefore requires that when a shareholders' meeting is called to consider a transaction that may trigger appraisal rights, the material sent to shareholders concerning such a meeting must disclose the fact that the proposed transaction may trigger these rights. It is sometimes said that the existence of appraisal rights may well constrain business decision making. That is, an otherwise beneficial major transaction might become impossible if a significant number of dissenting shareholders threaten to exercise their appraisal rights. The corporation would thus be compelled to repurchase the dissidents' shares, resulting in an inordinate drain on the corporation's cash resources.

This risk is well understood. It was specifically referred to by the Dickerson committee in their report,[12] and is frequently mentioned by practitioners. However, it is not clear how significant an impediment to beneficial transactions the possibility of multiple dissenters actually poses. Robert Clark, for example, notes that, if a proposed transaction has genuine economic benefit for a corporation and these benefits are properly explained by a corporation's management, it seems difficult to understand why a significant number of shareholders would dissent. But, in any event, he reasons, even if large numbers of shareholders did dissent (perhaps on non-economic grounds), it is unclear why the corporation would not be able to raise sufficient financial resources to purchase the shares of the minority.[13] Perhaps, however, Professor Clark underestimates the occasional difficulty that firms of a certain size have in obtaining debt finance—especially when, by definition, the purpose of that financing would be to reduce the equity cushion that lenders would otherwise enjoy. Moreover, a corporation may be very reluctant to take on additional debt if, for example, market interest rates are particularly high.

CBCA Dissent and Appraisal Rules

The desire to balance the competing interests of majority rule and minority protection by providing dissent rights is easily explained and readily understood. But translating this goal into a detailed, workable statutory remedy, not surprisingly, has proven considerably more difficult.

At the time of the Dickerson committee's report in 1971, dissent and appraisal rights were a common feature of US corporate statutes.[14] The goals of the CBCA provisions are thus informed by previous US experience. The principal issues raised by the CBCA's appraisal remedy (and similar remedies found in various provincial corporate statutes) are the following:

- Which fundamental changes to the corporation will trigger the appraisal remedy?
- What specific procedures must be followed by dissenting shareholders in order to exercise their appraisal rights?

---

12   Dickerson committee, supra footnote 1, at para. 347.

13   Supra footnote 4, at 446.

14   Forty-nine of the 50 states, as well as the District of Columbia, Puerto Rico, and the Virgin Islands, had appraisal remedies in their corporate statutes. See Manning, supra footnote 11, at 226, note 4. See also, Dickerson committee, supra footnote 1, at para. 347.

- How are the shares of dissenting shareholders to be valued for purposes of determining the price at which the shares of these dissenting shareholders are repurchased?
- Should shareholders of widely held public corporations (who can readily dispose of their shares in the capital markets if they wish) enjoy dissent and appraisal rights?

Fundamental Changes That Trigger the Appraisal Remedy

Not every corporate change triggers the right of dissenting shareholders under the CBCA to demand that their shares be repurchased. Those corporate actions that do trigger these rights are often commonly referred to as "fundamental changes." However, although this phrase does appear as the title of part XV of the CBCA, it is neither a defined term under the CBCA nor otherwise a legal term of art.

The proposed changes that will trigger appraisal rights under the CBCA are specifically itemized in s. 190. The list includes:

- amendments to provisions of the corporation's articles relating to: (1) restrictions or constraints on the issue, transfer, or ownership of shares of the class owned by the dissenting shareholder,[15] (2) restrictions on the business(es) that the corporation may carry on,[16] and (3) the rights of holders of a class of shares, as described in s. 176;[17]
- amalgamations (other than so-called short-form amalgamations under s. 184 between a corporation and its wholly owned subsidiary);[18]
- continuance of the corporation into another jurisdiction;[19]
- a sale, lease, or exchange of all or substantially all of the corporation's property other than in the ordinary course of the corporation's business;[20]
- "going-private transactions" and "squeeze-out transactions" (as expressly defined in the CBCA);[21] and
- an arrangement under s. 192, if the court orders that shareholders are permitted to dissent in connection with the arrangement.[22]

A number of these triggering events are discussed in greater detail below.

---

15   CBCA, s. 190(1)(a).

16   CBCA, s. 190(1)(b).

17   CBCA, s. 190(2).

18   CBCA, s. 190(1)(c). The exception as it appears in s. 190 would also technically apply to another type of short-form amalgamation involving two corporations, both of which are wholly owned subsidiaries of the same parent corporation. However, by definition, there would never be dissenting shareholders in the case of such an amalgamation because the only shareholder of either amalgamating corporation would be the parent corporation, and, under the terms of s. 184, the directors of the parent corporation must have authorized the amalgamation in the first place.

19   CBCA, s. 190(1)(d).

20   CBCA, s. 190(1)(e).

21   CBCA, s. 190(1)(f).

22   CBCA, ss. 190(1) and 192(4)(d).

Alterations to Share Ownership, Business Restrictions, or Rights of Holders of a Class of Shares

Dissent and appraisal rights are triggered by some, but not all, amendments to the corporation's articles. Recall that the articles are a key part of a CBCA corporation's constitution, or constating documents. (The other constating documents are the corporation's bylaws, and—as the Supreme Court of Canada has recently ruled[23]—an existing unanimous shareholder agreement.) The articles are especially significant because, once provisions are included in the articles, they are subject to a more onerous "constitutional amending formula" than are the bylaws. Bylaws may initially be made by directors' resolution;[24] and although all such bylaws must subsequently be confirmed by vote of the shareholders, that confirmation may be by ordinary resolution (that is, by a simple majority vote).[25]

Any proposed amendments to the corporation's articles, however, must be approved by "special resolution"—that is, by at least two-thirds of the votes cast at a properly convened shareholders' meeting.[26] Certain matters, as discussed in chapter 2, are required to be included in the articles. But, in addition to those mandatory provisions, the CBCA provides that any item that is permitted to be included in a corporation's bylaws may, instead, be included within the corporation's articles.[27] Incorporators might want to ensure that matters they consider to be of especial importance are subject to the more onerous amending procedures of the articles.

---

23 *Duha Printers (Western) Ltd. v. Canada*, [1998] 1 SCR 795.

24 CBCA, s. 103(1).

25 CBCA, s. 103(2).

26 CBCA, s. 173(1) and the s. 2(1) definition of "special resolution." It is perhaps worth reiterating that a special resolution does *not* require the affirmative votes of two-thirds of *all* of a corporation's outstanding shares. Provided that a meeting is properly convened, it is only necessary that two-thirds of the votes cast in respect of the proposed amendment be voted in favour. Thus, for example, if a corporation has issued and outstanding a total of 1,000 shares, all of the same class, a special resolution need not necessarily require the affirmative vote of 667 shares. Suppose a quorum for a meeting of shareholders is a majority of the outstanding shares. Provided the meeting has been properly called—with adequate notice, including adequate disclosure of the matters to come before the meeting—shareholders holding just 501 of the outstanding shares would constitute a valid meeting. If every shareholder present chose to vote on a proposal to amend the articles, a special resolution would be passed on the votes of just 334 shareholders (that is, two-thirds of 501). Moreover, provided that the vote was conducted properly, if, say, 100 shareholders simply chose not to vote at all on the proposal to amend the articles, a special resolution would be passed on the votes of just 267 shareholders (that is, two-thirds of the 400 votes cast). Thus, in this example, a special resolution would be validly passed by the vote of 267 shares, though this number is far less than two-thirds, or, for that matter, even less than a simple majority of the total *outstanding* shares. If this result seems odd or unfair, recall that elections for those seeking public office in Canada are, similarly, decided based on a majority (indeed, more typically, a plurality) of the votes *cast*, not on a requirement that candidates receive votes equal to a majority of all eligible voters. An alternative rule that required resolutions to receive the approval of a majority (or two-thirds majority) of all outstanding shares would impose enormous practical problems, especially for large, publicly traded corporations. Resources would be needlessly squandered soliciting proxies from small shareholders all over the country who had little interest or incentive to vote in a considered way on matters to come before the meeting.

27 CBCA, s. 6(2).

It might be thought that the requirement that amendments to the articles must receive the approval of a two-thirds shareholder vote would provide adequate protection from capricious attempts to change the underlying nature of the corporation. In any event, it might be argued that minority shareholders who objected to such changes ought to be obliged to accept any amendments that enjoy such strong shareholder approval. Of course, for the most part, it is true that shareholders who are opposed to duly approved amendments to the articles have no recourse against the corporation. However, where those amendments touch on the objecting shareholders' share rights, or relate to restrictions on the corporation's business, different considerations apply. Such changes are thought to be so fundamental to the nature of the shareholders' investment that objecting (or "dissenting") shareholders may, if they wish, "withdraw" their investment from the corporation.

Changes to business restrictions contained in the articles of a CBCA corporation are roughly analogous to changes made to the "objects" clause of corporations incorporated under older forms of corporate legislation. Recall from chapter 6, that the objects clause in the memorandum of association of a corporation formed under the early UK *Companies Act, 1862* could not be amended under any circumstances—even with the unanimous consent of all of the shareholders of the corporation.[28]

The rigidity of this older law illustrates the profound significance once attached to the business objects through which a corporation defined itself. The CBCA no longer requires that a corporation either specify objects or impose restrictions on its business. However, when a corporation chooses to include business restrictions in its articles, it is an offence under the CBCA for that corporation to carry on any business contrary to those restrictions.[29] Furthermore, shareholders may reasonably be assumed to have based their investment decision on the presence of such restrictions contained in the corporation's articles.

As for amendments touching on certain share rights, the case for triggering an appraisal right is obvious enough. If changes are made to the share ownership or transfer restrictions attaching to the very class of shares owned by an objecting shareholder, that shareholder has good reason to end his or her investment in the corporation.

There are two other features of these CBCA appraisal-triggering events that deserve mention. First, s. 190(2) provides that holders of any class or series of shares entitled to vote under s. 176 will also have dissent rights if the articles are amended in any of the ways described in s. 176. Section 176 permits even those shareholders whose shares do not normally enjoy voting rights to vote in respect of certain proposed changes affecting their shares. There is something especially noteworthy about the list of changes set out in s. 176. It includes not only amendments to the articles that would *directly* affect the class of shares entitled to vote, but also certain amendments made to the share conditions of other classes or series of shares, having an indirect effect on the holders of the class entitled to vote.

The Dickerson committee recommended extending this protection to cases where amendments had this sort of indirect effect on a class of shares. They sought such a

---

28   The case usually cited as authority for this proposition is *Ashbury Railway Carriage & Iron Co. v. Riche* (1875), LR 7 (HL). However, as explained in chapter 6, this principle was not a judicial creation, but was, instead, embodied in the *Companies Act, 1862* itself.

29   CBCA, ss. 16(2) and 251. Recall from chapter 6, however, that acts undertaken by a corporation in violation of its articles are not, for that reason only, invalid (CBCA, s. 16(3)).

provision in the hopes that it would statutorily overrule a specific line of English cases.[30] To explain this point, consider the facts of one of the cases that the Dickerson committee had in mind: *White v. Bristol Aeroplane Co.*[31]

In *Bristol Aeroplane*, a corporation with two classes of shares—preference and ordinary—proposed to amend its constating documents to increase its authorized capital. It then intended to issue additional preference shares and additional ordinary shares to the current holders of the ordinary shares. The effect of this transaction would be this: the current holders of the ordinary shares would acquire sufficient voting power to ensure that they could always outvote the current holders of the preferences shares, whether at a meeting of all of the company's shareholders together, or at a meeting of preference shareholders only.

The preference shareholders were understandably concerned about this plan. They argued that they ought to be permitted to vote separately, as a class, on such a proposal, because, under the articles, they were to have a separate class vote in respect of any amendment that would "affect" their rights. The English Court of Appeal held that the increase in authorized capital, and the issue of additional shares, did not "affect" the rights of the preference shareholders. They were, therefore, not entitled to vote separately in respect of the change.

To similar effect was the judgment of the English Court of Appeal in *Greenhalgh v. Arderne Cinemas Ltd.*[32] There, the plaintiff sought to prevent a five-for-one subdivision (a stock split) of the corporation's shares. The shares to be subdivided in this way were not shares of the same class as those owned by the plaintiff. However, the effect of the stock split, for practical purposes, would be to convert the shares of that other class into shares of the same class as those held by the plaintiff. The final result of all of this was that the plaintiff's voting interest would be massively diluted. Essentially, the plaintiff would no longer have enough votes to control the corporation.

Lord Greene famously acknowledged that although the plaintiff's rights had been affected by this transaction "as a matter of business,"[33] they had not been affected as a matter of law because, as he saw it, the rights attached to the plaintiff's shares had not changed a whit.

The challenged transactions described in these two cases, if undertaken today by a CBCA corporation, would trigger both special class voting rights, and dissent and appraisal rights.[34] These rights, in other words, are no longer necessarily limited to changes made directly to shares of the class held by the dissenting shareholders.

---

30 Dickerson committee, supra footnote 1, at para. 358.

31 [1953] Ch. 65 (CA).

32 [1946] 1 All ER 512 (CA).

33 Ibid., at 518.

34 The increase in authorized capital undertaken in *White v. Bristol Aeroplane* would trigger special voting rights pursuant to s. 176(1)(a) and corresponding dissent rights under s. 190(2). (Of course, as a practical matter, it is no longer necessary for a CBCA corporation to limit the number of shares it is authorized to issue in its articles. It is possible, and very common, for a CBCA corporation simply to provide in the articles that the corporation is authorized to issue an unlimited number of shares.) The exchange or conversion of shares of one class into shares of another, as undertaken in *Greenhalgh v. Arderne Cinemas*, would trigger special voting rights under s. 176(1)(g) and corresponding dissent rights under s. 190(2).

One remaining ambiguity was eliminated by the addition to the CBCA in 2001 of s. 190(2.1). This short subsection provides that the dissent right described in s. 190(2) "applies even if there is only one class of shares."

There had been some case authority in support of the proposition that the s. 176 voting rights did not apply if a corporation had only one class of shares outstanding and that, accordingly, dissent rights were also unavailable in such cases.[35] To be sure, these cases were controversial. As Fruman J of the Alberta Court of Queen's Bench put it in 2001 (citing an Industry Canada report),

> in the 21 years since its pronouncement, the *McConnell* decision, which has been referred to politely as a "technical anomaly," has never been followed.[36]

The logic and the fairness of Fruman J's conclusion, and of the addition of s. 190(2.1), which now enshrines this reasoning in the CBCA, have much to commend them. One does note in passing, though, that if s. 176(2) had been intended, prior to the 2001 amendment, to apply even in cases where a corporation has only one class of shares, it is curious that the drafters of the CBCA saw it necessary to include s. 190(1)(a) in the statute. This paragraph expressly provides a dissent right when a corporation resolves to

> amend its articles under section 173 or 174 to add, change or remove any provisions restricting or constraining the issue, transfer or ownership of shares of that class.

Note that s. 176(1)(h) provides for a vote in the case of any proposal to amend the articles to "constrain the issue, transfer or ownership of the shares of such class." Thus, s. 190(1)(a) would appear to be entirely redundant in light of the combined effect of s. 176(1)(h) and s. 190(2) if, indeed, the s. 176 voting rights (and therefore the s. 190(2) dissent rights) had always been meant to apply where a corporation had only one class of shares. Nevertheless, with the recent addition of s. 190(2.1) this point has become moot.

Amalgamations

The CBCA permits two or more CBCA corporations to amalgamate into a single corporation. There are many reasons—relating to operational efficiencies, tax considerations, and other matters—that corporations might wish to amalgamate.[37] The business reasons for pursuing amalgamations are not, however, the concern here. The point is that when two corporations want to amalgamate, the shareholders of each must approve the amalgamation, and they must do so by special resolution.[38] Shareholders of either amalgamating

---

35   See *McConnell v. Newco Financial Corp.*, [1979] BCJ 612 (QL) (BCSC).

36   *LSI Logic Corp. of Canada, Inc. v. Logani*, [2001] AJ no. 1083, at para. 41 (QL) (QB).

37   At one time, for example, a corporation that had accumulated significant tax losses—which the *Income Tax Act* permits a corporation to "carry forward" and so deduct against future years' income—could join with another corporation that had significant income so that the loss carry forwards of the first company could be used to reduce the taxable income of the second. The Canada Revenue Agency has since taken steps to try to restrict this practice. Amalgamations are also a common method by which one corporation effectively acquires the business of another. For a discussion of amalgamation as an acquisition technique, see Nicholls, supra footnote 7, at 309ff.

38   CBCA, s. 183(5).

corporation who oppose the transaction are given dissent and appraisal rights. These rights recognize, once again, that, on amalgamation, the very essence of the corporation in which the shareholder originally invested may change. Thus, although the newly amalgamated corporation might very well constitute an investment with better financial prospects than its predecessors, it nevertheless may not accord with an individual investor's preferences. What is perhaps anomalous, however, is that while shareholders are permitted to vote on proposed amalgamations, they are permitted no such vote on major business acquisitions. In other words, if Company A wishes to amalgamate with Company B, the shareholders of Company A are entitled to vote on the matter. However, if Company A wishes to acquire all of the assets and undertaking of Company B in an asset sale, the shareholders of Company A enjoy no similar voting privileges.[39] The power to undertake such an acquisition is entirely within the control of Company A's board of directors. This is curious in that, as an economic matter, the end result of both transactions would, from the perspective of Company A, be essentially identical, particularly if Company A paid for the assets it was acquiring from Company B by issuing shares in Company A to Company B that were subsequently distributed as a dividend to Company B's shareholders.

Continuance

Background on Continuance

The CBCA, typical of most modern corporate statutes, permits a corporation, on satisfying specific procedures, to "export" itself to another jurisdiction. What this means is that the corporation will continue just as though it had been originally incorporated under that other jurisdiction. Such continuances (or reincorporations) are not uncommon in the United States. Many public corporations, in particular, have chosen to be continued under the corporate statute of Delaware, especially in anticipation of certain major transactions or reorganizations that it is thought can be most advantageously completed in that jurisdiction.

As discussed in chapter 1, no Canadian provincial corporate jurisdiction has ever emerged as an especial favourite of out-of-province corporations. Although the CBCA appears to attract a disproportionate number of Canadian public company incorporations,[40] it does not appear that this is due to the same factors that account for the Delaware phenomenon.[41] Nevertheless, there are a variety of reasons that corporations might have for choosing to continue from one Canadian corporate jurisdiction to

---

39 Of course, the shareholders of Company B would be entitled to vote in either case, because such a sale of assets by Company B would constitute a sale of "all or substantially all" of Company B's assets, as discussed below.

40 Wayne D. Gray states that "50% of the largest 500 non-financial corporations in Canada are incorporated under the CBCA." Wayne D. Gray, "Corporations as Winners Under CBCA Reform" (2003), 39 *Canadian Business Law Journal* 4, at 5.

41 In particular, the dominance of Delaware is thought, in no small measure, to be the result of the expertise of the Delaware courts—in particular the Delaware Chancery Court—in corporate law matters. Disputes under the CBCA are, of course, litigated before the same courts in every province that adjudicate disputes under provincial corporate statutes.

another.[42] Perhaps the most common reason is that continuance may be a necessary preliminary step to amalgamation. Most Canadian corporate statutes do not permit amalgamations between corporations from different jurisdictions.[43] Thus, if, for example, a corporation incorporated under the Ontario *Business Corporations Act* wishes to amalgamate with a corporation incorporated under the CBCA, it will first be necessary for the Ontario corporation to be continued under the CBCA, or for the CBCA corporation to be continued under the Ontario Act. Given the high degree of similarity between many Canadian corporate statutes, it has sometimes been suggested that amalgamations between Canadian corporations incorporated under different, but substantially similar, statutes ought to be more widely permitted.[44]

The statute under which a corporation is incorporated is very much a foundational issue. It is no surprise, then, that a proposal to, in effect, reincorporate in another jurisdiction triggers the right of shareholders to dissent and have their shares acquired at fair value. Occasionally, however, the purpose of the appraisal remedy in this context is misunderstood. One practitioner, for example, in an otherwise excellent article, has argued that dissent rights ought to be removed in cases where a corporation is continuing from one Canadian jurisdiction to another substantially similar jurisdiction, suggesting that

> [t]he appraisal remedy is justified if, but only if, the effect of the continuance is to materially adversely affect the rights of shareholders. Where the corporate statutes are substantially similar, *ex hypothesi* no such adverse effect occurs.[45]

With respect, this argument appears to misstate the point of the appraisal remedy. One must recall, first of all, that appraisal rights are triggered only in those cases where a majority of the shareholders have approved a transaction—a rather unlikely scenario in

---

42   The same technical differences between statutes that are relevant to the original incorporation decision would also be relevant to the continuance or reincorporation decision.

43   There are severals exceptions. The new BC *Business Corporations Act* not only permits a BC corporation to amalgamate with a "foreign corporation" and continue as one company under BC law (s. 269), but, also under specified circumstances, permits a BC company to amalgamate with a foreign corporation and continue as an amalgamated corporation in the foreign corporation's jurisdiction of incorporation (s. 283ff). Section 187 of the Alberta *Business Corporations Act* provides that an Alberta corporation (other than a professional corporation (s. 187(2)) may amalgamate with an extra-provincial corporation, and continue thereafter as an Alberta corporation, provided that one of the two corporations is the wholly owned subsidiary of the other (s. 187(1)(b)), and further provided that the extra-provincial corporation is similarly authorized under its own governing statute to undertake such an amalgamation (s. 187(1)(a)). The term "extra-provincial" corporation in the Alberta Act is not confined to corporations incorporated within a Canadian jurisdiction. Accordingly, this provision appears to permit an Alberta corporation to amalgamate with a corporation originally incorporated in, say, Delaware, where the general incorporation statute permits mergers and consolidations between Delaware corporations and corporations from foreign jurisdictions, notwithstanding that the corporation following the merger or consolidation is not to be a Delaware corporation. See, Delaware *General Corporation Law*, s. 252. The Northwest Territories *Business Corporations Act*, s. 189, also permits a corporation incorporated under that statute to amalgamate with an "extra-territorial corporation," provided that the extra-territorial corporation is permitted by its incorporating statute to do so, and further provided that one of the amalgamating corporations is a wholly owned subsidiary of the other.

44   See, e.g., Gray, supra footnote 40, at 30.

45   Ibid.

cases where the continuance will have a "materially adverse" effect. Thus, the existence of the appraisal remedy cannot be adequately explained on the basis that it is intended to be activated only in cases of such adverse effects.

Moreover, one observes that dissent rights are triggered in certain cases—most especially cases involving a sale of all or substantially all of the corporation's property—where it is the *qualitative* significance of the event, not any notion of material adversity, that is the governing factor. Corporate law has other remedies designed to protect shareholders from *objective* harm. The appraisal remedy serves a very different purpose. It exists to protect shareholders from fundamental *changes*—even where those changes, presumably, are not reasonably expected to result in any objective harm. Indeed, no such changes can be undertaken until two-thirds of the corporation's shareholders have approved of them.

There may indeed be valid policy reasons for arguing that continuance ought not to trigger the appraisal remedy. It might be said, for example, that continuance does not represent a fundamental enough change to warrant triggering such rights. Furthermore, the existence of dissent rights may lead to unfair opportunism on the part of some shareholders. However, the fact that a proposed continuance causes no material harm is not, of itself, adequate justification for removing it from the list of triggering events.

Sale of "All or Substantially All" of the Corporation's Property

If a sale by a CBCA corporation is considered to be a sale (or indeed a "lease or exchange") of all or substantially all of the corporation's property (other than in the ordinary course of business), two special sorts of protective provisions in the statute are triggered. First, s. 189 requires that such a transaction must be approved by the shareholders of the corporation. What's more, that approval must be by special resolution (that is, by a two-thirds majority) rather than by a simple majority.[46] Furthermore, all shareholders are entitled to a vote on this matter—even shareholders whose shares do not normally entitle them to a right to vote.[47] If one series or class of shares is specially affected, that series or class is also entitled to vote separately.[48] This means that, unless the holders of that class approve the sale by their own, separate two-thirds vote, the transaction cannot be undertaken. The second protective provision, of course, is that even if the requisite shareholder approval is obtained, shareholders who dissented are entitled to an appraisal remedy.

It has sometimes wrongly been suggested that the purpose of these protections is to safeguard shareholders from an improvident sale of the corporation's property—that is, a sale at an undervalue. That is surely not the purpose of the section. In the first place, the directors and officers of the corporation are under an overriding legal duty to protect the interests of the shareholders. A sale at an undervalue would expose them to personal liability. Moreover, it is unclear how the shareholders in the normal course would have the means to determine if a particular sale of assets was, or was not, for full value. It would certainly be unusual for shareholders to retain independent appraisers in order to permit them to cast an informed vote at a shareholders' meeting.

---

46 CBCA, s. 189(8).

47 CBCA, s. 189(6).

48 CBCA, s. 189(7).

In fact, shareholders are permitted to vote on a proposed sale of the corporation's undertaking because such a sale—even if the price obtained by the selling corporation is fair or even generous—would change the fundamental nature of the shareholders' investment. It is important to understand this fact to make sense of the discussion that occurs in the cases on this topic of the "qualitative" and "quantitative" tests for determining if a proposed transaction involves "substantially all" of a corporation's assets.

The Dickerson committee suggested that, at common law, the directors had power to dispose of the entire corporate undertaking without shareholder consent.[49] In the drafters' view, such unconstrained power was inappropriate at least in cases where the transaction was not in the ordinary course of the corporation's business.

If the drafters of the CBCA had limited the application of s. 189 to transactions involving "all" of the corporation's assets, the provision would have presented fewer interpretive difficulties. Of course, it would also have offered little protection to shareholders. Devious directors could have avoided putting a proposed sale of the corporation's business to a shareholder vote simply by ensuring that some immaterial part of the corporation's undertaking was not included in the sale. Accordingly, it is clear that, if shareholders are to enjoy meaningful rights under s. 189(3), the section must also apply to transactions involving the sale of something less than all of the corporation's assets. Nonetheless, the inclusion of the phrase "or substantially all" in s. 189(3) has led to some interpretive uncertainty.

Mark Gannage has produced a nice summary of many of the leading Canadian cases that have considered the question of when a sale of assets by a corporation does or does not constitute a sale of "all or substantially all" of the corporation's property.[50] The only point that will be noted here is that it is clear that the Canadian courts have, generally speaking, rejected the idea that the inquiry involves simple quantitative calculations. A mere quantitative test has been described by the Ontario Court of Appeal as

> formulaic, requiring a comparison of the proportion, or relative value, of the transferred property to the total property of the transferor.[51]

Such a test, without more, is not sufficient. As that same court noted, "the meaning of 'all or substantially all' is context-dependent, and does not lend itself to simple arithmetic calculations."[52]

This is not to say that quantitative analysis is irrelevant, only that it is not determinative. Drawing in part on American precedents, Canadian courts have affirmed that whether a particular transaction involves "substantially all" of a corporation's property requires a "qualitative" as well as a quantitative assessment. In *Canadian Broadcasting Corporation Pension Plan (Trustee of) v. BF Realty Holdings Ltd.*,[53] Cronk JA of the Ontario Court of Appeal expressed the issue in this way:

---

49   Dickerson committee, supra footnote 1, at para. 370.

50   See Mark Gannage, "Sale of Substantially All the Assets of a Corporation" (2000), 33 *Canadian Business Law Journal* 264.

51   *Canadian Broadcasting Corporation Pension Plan (Trustee of) v. BF Realty Holdings Ltd.* (2002), 214 DLR (4th) 121, at para. 45 (Ont. CA).

52   Ibid., at para. 48.

53   Ibid.

[A] qualitative analysis seeks to determine the nature of a transferor's core business activities, and the property involved in carrying out such activities. The purpose of the inquiry is to assess whether the transferred property is integral to the transferor's traditional business, such that its disposition or transfer strikes at the heart of the transferor's existence and primary corporate purpose.[54]

Many other Canadian cases have also referred to the significance of considering qualitative as well as quantitative factors in order to determine whether a particular transaction will trigger the shareholder voting rights of s. 189(3) and the corresponding dissent and appraisal rights.[55] Indeed, as one Ontario judge put it, "the qualitative test is to be preferred as the acid test."[56]

US cases have influenced the reasoning of Canadian courts on the question of when a transaction constitutes a sale of "all or substantially all" of a corporation's property. Accordingly, it is useful to consider a recent Delaware Court of Chancery case that has provided some useful insights into the relationship between the "qualitative" and "quantitative" aspects of the test. *Hollinger Inc. v. Hollinger International Inc.*[57] involved a dispute between Hollinger Inc., a Canadian corporation controlled by Conrad Black, and its US affiliate, Hollinger International Inc. ("International"). Hollinger Inc. owned 18 percent of the equity in International, but, more importantly, held a 68 percent voting interest. International had proposed selling its interest in The Telegraph Group Ltd., an English company that owned the prestigious English newspaper, the *Telegraph*. Hollinger Inc. argued that such a sale represented a sale of "substantially all" of International's assets and, therefore, required the sanction of International's shareholders pursuant to the provision in Delaware's *General Corporation Law* (s. 271) that is similar to CBCA s. 189(3).

The matter came before the court as a motion for a preliminary injunction. In fact, The Telegraph Group Ltd. was not held directly by International, and a technical defence had been raised on the basis that the protections of s. 271 should have no application to such indirect sales. Vice Chancellor Strine recognized that ruling that s. 271 had no application to such indirect sales "would, as a practical matter, render § 271 an illusory check on unilateral board power at most public companies."[58] However, he declined to rule on this issue, determining that his decision would favour International even if The Telegraph Group Ltd. were owned directly.

Specifically, Strine VC concluded that "the Telegraph Group does not come close to comprising 'substantially all' of International's assets."[59] Although acknowledging that

---

54   Ibid., at para. 46.

55   See, e.g., *85956 Holdings Ltd. v. Fayerman Brothers Ltd.* (1986), 46 Sask. R 75 (CA); *Martin v. F.P. Bourgault Industries Air Seeder Division Ltd.* (1987), 45 DLR (4th) 296 (Sask. CA); *Lindzon v. International Sterling Holdings Inc.* (1989), 45 BLR 57 (BCSC); *GATX v. Hawker Siddeley Canada Inc.* (1996), 27 BLR (2d) 251 (Ont. Ct. Gen. Div.); *Benson v. Third Canadian General Investments Trust Ltd.* (1993), 14 OR (3d) 493 (Gen. Div.); *Cogeco Cable Inc. v. CFCF Inc.* (1996), 136 DLR (4th) 243 (Que. CA); and *Hovsepian v. Westfair Foods Inc.* (2003), 37 BLR (3d) 78 (Alta. QB).

56   *Benson v. Third Canadian General Investments Trust Ltd.*, supra footnote 55, at 506.

57   CA no. 543-N (Del. Ch. Ct. 2004).

58   Ibid., at 6.

59   Ibid., at 7.

the proper test involves not only quantitative but also qualitative elements, Strine VC nevertheless characterized the test as one that "focuses on economic quality."[60] After noting that the history of s. 271 was not to provide shareholders with additional protection, but rather to reverse the common law rule that would require unanimous shareholder approval of a sale of all or substantially all of the corporation's assets."[61]

Applying the tests articulated in *Gimbel v. Signal Cos., Inc.*,[62] Strine VC determined, first, that The Telegraph Group Ltd. was not "quantitatively vital to the operations of International."[63] Then, noting that "the relationship of the qualitative element of the *Gimbel* test to the quantitative element is more than a tad unclear,"[64] Strine VC interpreted the qualitative test as one that is focused on "economic quality and, at most, on whether the transaction leaves the stockholders with an investment that in economic terms is qualitatively different than the one that they now possess."[65] And further, that "the qualitative element of the *Gimbel* test addresses the rational economic expectations of reasonable investors."[66]

A further issue occasionally mooted by Canadian corporate law practitioners is the question of whether or not a transfer of assets from a publicly held holding company to a wholly owned subsidiary should, or should not, trigger the shareholder voting requirements of s. 189. There is nothing in the CBCA that provides an exemption in such a case, although it is noteworthy that the new BC *Business Corporations Act* does provide such an exception.[67] There is a certain absurdity to requiring shareholder approval for a transaction that has no meaningful economic impact from the shareholders' perspective. Indeed, since financial statements are produced on a consolidated basis, the fact that assets were owned by a subsidiary rather than directly by the parent company would be unknown to most investors in any event. However, if no shareholder approval is required in the case of such an inter-company approval, it is not entirely clear what would prevent the subsidiary corporation from subsequently disposing of the transferred assets without the vote of shareholders of the parent corporation—the very loophole noted by Strine VC in the *Hollinger* case discussed above. If such a sale to a subsidiary may be said to have been made in the ordinary course of business, then no shareholder approval requirement would, in any event, be triggered. But the meaning of "ordinary course of business" is, itself, a nebulous concept, and hardly one on which corporate directors (or their legal counsel) might wish to depend. In the absence of judicial authority to the contrary, it seems that shareholder approval ought to be sought for such a sale to a subsidiary; but a more rational approach would be to provide—as the BC legislation does—for an exemption in the case of such a sale, along with an express recognition that when a sale is made by a subsidiary that, if made directly

60   Ibid., at 77.

61   Ibid., at 63. Note how this differs from the pre-CBCA history as recited by the Dickerson committee. See text accompanying footnote 49, supra.

62   316 A 2d 599 (Del. Ch. Ct.), aff'd. 316 A 2d 619 (Del. SC 1974).

63   Ibid., at 69.

64   Ibid., at 76.

65   Ibid., at 77.

66   Ibid., at 79.

67   *Business Corporations Act* (BC), s. 301(6)(c).

by the parent corporation would constitute a sale of all or substantially all of the parent company's assets, that sale will require the approval of the parent company's shareholders.

Going-Private Transactions and Squeeze-Out Transactions

Background

To business people, the term "going private" refers to the process by which a corporation is transformed from a publicly traded company to a private or closely held corporation. However, the term "going-private transaction" has acquired a somewhat more technical meaning under Canadian securities law.[68] For purposes of the CBCA, the term "going-private transaction" and the related concept "participating securities" are defined in the CBCA Regulations as follows:

> 3(1) For the purpose of the definition "going-private transaction" in subsection 2(1) of the Act, "going-private transaction" means an amalgamation, arrangement, consolidation or other transaction involving a distributing corporation, other than an acquisition of shares under section 206 of the Act, that results in the interest of a holder of participating securities of the corporation being terminated without the consent of the holder and without the substitution of an interest of equivalent value in participating securities of the corporation or of a body corporate that succeeds to the business of the corporation, which participating securities have rights and privileges that are equal to or greater than the affected participating securities.
>
> (2) For the purpose of subsection (1), "participating securities" means securities of a body corporate that give the holder of the securities a right to share in the earnings of the body corporate and after the liquidation, dissolution or winding up of the body corporate, a right to share in its assets.[69]

At the risk of oversimplification, then, a going-private transaction is a transaction involving a distributing corporation (a public corporation) that has the effect of eliminating the interest of minority shareholders.

---

68 See, e.g., OSC rule 61-501. Amendments to this rule (in force June 29, 2004), define a new term, "business combination," to replace the term "going-private transaction." This term is, however, deemed to be equivalent to the term "going-private transaction." (See paragraph 1.6 of rule 61-501.) For an explanation of the interplay between rule 61-501 and the Ontario *Business Corporations Act*, see Jeffrey G. MacIntosh and Christopher C. Nicholls, *Securities Law* (Toronto: Irwin, 2002), at 333ff.

69 *Canada Business Corporations Regulations, 2001*, at s. 3. The going-private and squeeze-out transaction provisions should not be confused with the "compulsory acquisition" rules in CBCA s. 206. The compulsory acquisition rules permit a person who has completed a takeover bid for the shares of a CBCA distributing corporation that has been accepted by the holders of at least 90 percent of the outstanding shares (other than those held by the bidder) to acquire the remaining outstanding shares of the corporation within 120 days after the bid. The price to be paid for these remaining shares must either be the takeover bid price or, if the dissenting shareholders so elect, the "fair value" of the shares determined in accordance with procedures set out in the statute. Following amendments to the CBCA in 2001, the Act also now provides a reciprocal right to dissenting shareholders in s. 206.1. That is, after a takeover bid in which a bidder acquires 90 percent of the corporation's remaining outstanding shares, any holder who did not tender to the bid may compel the bidder to acquire his or her shares on the same terms as the shares acquired under the bid. Dissenting shareholders are thus not obligated to hold onto a small, illiquid holding in a corporation that is now controlled by a new majority shareholder. The Ontario

At one time, some litigation lawyers had one view of the legality of "going-private transactions" under the CBCA, while most corporate and securities lawyers had quite another. After a see-saw battle of early legal actions,[70] CBCA policy statements, and provincial securities commission initiatives,[71] we have arrived at the current state of affairs. Simply put, the CBCA now expressly permits going-private transactions provided they are completed in compliance with any applicable provincial securities regulation,[72] such as a special rule promulgated by the Ontario Securities Commission, OSC rule 61-501.[73]

A "squeeze-out transaction," a new term added to the CBCA in 2001, is essentially the private corporation parallel to the going-private transaction. Like a going-private transaction, it is aimed at eliminating (or squeezing out) minority shareholders. However, it is not referred to as a going-private transaction for the simple reason that, by definition, it is a transaction undertaken by a corporation that is already private (that is, not by a public or distributing corporation).

More technically, "squeeze-out transaction" is defined in CBCA s. 2(1) as follows:

> "squeeze-out transaction" means a transaction by a corporation that is not a distributing corporation that would require an amendment to its articles and would, directly or indirectly, result in the interest of a holder of shares of a class of the corporation being terminated without the consent of the holder, and without substituting an interest of equivalent value in shares issued by the corporation, which shares have equal or greater rights and privileges than the shares of the affected class.

Because squeeze-out transactions do not involve public corporations (or "distributing corporations," as they are referred to in the CBCA), provincial securities laws do not

---

> *Business Corporations Act* has similar compulsory acquisition rules. (See Ontario *Business Corporations Act*, ss. 187-189.) However, under the Ontario Act rules, dissenting shareholders may elect to have the corporation acquire their shares at fair value when exercising their right to compel a takeover bidder to subsequently acquire those shares.

70   See, e.g., *Alexander v. Westeel-Rosco Ltd.* (1978), 22 OR (2d) 211 (HCJ) and *Carlton Realty Co. v. Maple Leaf Mills Ltd.* (1978), 22 OR (2d) 198 (HCJ).

71   See Nicholls, supra footnote 7, at 367; see also footnote 73, infra.

72   CBCA, s. 193.

73   These provisions had a rather complicated legislative history, as summarized in the following extract from the "briefing book" prepared by Industry Canada analyzing the 2001 CBCA amendments:

> There is a concern that the CBCA only sets out rules for one type of [going-private transaction (GPT)] (compulsory acquisitions) and that other forms of GPT may not be permitted. This uncertainty can cause CBCA corporations considering a GPT to continue into another jurisdiction in order to ensure that the desired transactions can legally be carried out. The amendment would define a GPT in the regulations and specify that such transactions are allowed to the extent that such transactions comply with the applicable provincial securities laws, if any.

> This provision was substantially changed as a result of an amendment introduced at the Senate Committee stage. Bill S-11 originally proposed to expressly allow GPTs and to incorporate by reference—in the regulations—standards of fairness for minority shareholders mandated by provincial securities regulators. The proposed amendment was predicated on Ontario and Quebec harmonizing their GPT requirements. Before the Bill went to print, Industry Canada was informed by both Ontario and Québec that they had agreed to harmonize their requirements. Bill S-11 was therefore tabled with a GPT regime that incorporated by reference a harmonized set of rules. It

apply to them. Accordingly, minority shareholders of such corporations do not enjoy the protection that those securities laws provide in the case of "going private transactions." The CBCA thus offers its own set of rules governing squeeze-out transactions, rules that rely on the protections of a separate class vote of the holders of affected securities, other than those affiliated with the corporation or those who will receive special consideration as a result of the proposed transaction. These protective features are similar to provisions contained in the going-private rules set out in OSC rule 61-501.[74]

Because a going-private or squeeze-out transaction will typically terminate the minority shareholders' interest in the corporation in any event, the chief advantage offered by the availability of the appraisal remedy in these cases is probably that it acts as an effective "floor price," to ensure that the terms at which the going-private or squeeze-out transaction is undertaken do not result in minority shareholders receiving less than fair value for their shares.

Statutory Arrangements

The statutory arrangement procedure in s. 192 of the CBCA has become a very important part of Canadian corporate law practice; but its significance will not become immediately apparent from a simple reading of the statutory language. The word "arrangement" itself may lead some to confuse this procedure (which is regularly used by healthy corporations to effect sophisticated transactions) with statutory measures to which only distressed corporations typically have recourse.[75]

Statutory arrangements can be used as a means of structuring business acquisitions and complex reorganizations such as spin offs. A detailed discussion of the specific reasons for pursuing arrangements and the advantages for doing so are well beyond the scope of this book.[76] The only point to be made here is that arrangements may involve

---

was later learned that although the Ontario rule and the Quebec policy are harmonized in substance, there are technical differences of application which make incorporation by reference difficult, if not impossible. As a result, under Bill S-11, a corporation would in practice be required to comply with inconsistent provincial requirements, which was not the intent of the provision and would cause great confusion in the marketplace.

Another issue is that the Québec requirements are contained in a policy statement rather than in legislation, regulations or rules. Policy statements do not have the force of law. It would therefore be inappropriate for federal legislation to mandate compliance with a provincial policy statement since this would have the effect of elevating its legal status beyond that intended by its province of origin. In order to avoid these problems, the incorporation by reference has been removed. The CBCA would now permit GPTs subject to compliance with applicable provincial securities legislation.

Available online at http://strategis.ic.gc.ca/epic/internet/incilp-pdci.nsf/en/cl00290e.html.

74 Supra footnote 68.

75 Referring, for example, to the arrangement procedures under s. 182 of the Ontario *Business Corporations Act* (the section corresponding to s. 192 of the CBCA), one law professor has suggested that "it is inherent in an arrangement that the corporation will be in dire circumstances before an arrangement is proposed with shareholders (or other security holders)." See Kevin Patrick McGuinness, *The Law and Practice of Canadian Business Corporations* (Toronto: Butterworths, 1999), at 1081.

76 For further discussion of arrangements, see Nicholls, supra footnote 7, at 316ff.

the same sort of fundamental change to a business or to a shareholders' interest as an amalgamation or amendment to the corporation's articles. However, the CBCA does not automatically accord dissent rights to a shareholder in the case of changes effected by arrangement. The court has a discretion under s. 190(4)(d) to grant (or indeed not to grant) such rights to dissenting shareholders. In *Re Electrohome Ltd.*,[77] Spence J, interpreting similar provisions of the Ontario *Business Corporations Act*, held that dissent rights would not be appropriate in the context of a particular transaction, and included with his reasons a memorandum, which provides useful insight into the sort of considerations that are relevant in such a case.

Procedure for Exercising Dissent Right

The detailed appraisal remedy procedures in the CBCA were evidently modelled on comparable provisions in New York's corporate statute.[78] There is no question that the rules are complex. The Dickerson committee, although acknowledging the unwieldy length of these provisions, nonetheless viewed them "necessary to render the substantive right to dissent meaningful."[79]

Some amount of procedural complexity is surely unavoidable. Shareholders must be told—specifically—how and when they are required to register their dissent. Corporations, similarly, must be given specific guidance as to how and when they are obliged to purchase shares from dissenters. If the Act did not specify dates by which certain events must take place, it would obviously be difficult for anyone to complain that actions had not been taken in time.

Furthermore, the matter of establishing the "fair value" at which dissenters' shares are to be purchased by the corporation is especially problematic. The appraisal procedures require the corporation to offer dissenting shareholders a price for their shares. If that price is accepted, the sale may be easily and swiftly concluded. But, if the dissenters are not satisfied with the corporation's offer, matters become much more complicated. The appraisal section must set out the procedures that will govern the ensuing process.

The complexities of the appraisal remedy procedures have caused commentators to fear that dissenting shareholders might inadvertently lose their appraisal rights as a result of failure to comply with the complex technical rules.[80] This concern is certainly worth noting. However, as Professor Welling has suggested, it is unlikely that courts would allow minor technical defaults to deprive dissenting shareholders of their appraisal rights.[81] There is some case authority that seems to support Professor Welling's sanguine view.[82]

---

77   (1998), 40 BLR (2d) 210 (Ont. Ct. Gen. Div.).

78   Dickerson committee, supra footnote 1, at para. 370.

79   Ibid., at para. 373.

80   See Jeffrey G. MacIntosh, "The Shareholder's Appraisal Right in Canada" (1986), 24 *Osgoode Hall Law Journal* 203.

81   Bruce L. Welling, *Corporate Law in Canada: The Governing Principles*, 2nd ed. (Toronto: Butterworths, 1991), at 576: "while the procedure must be followed, this cannot be interpreted as meaning that the corporation can expect to thwart the dissenting shareholder who fouls up in some minor, technical way."

82   See, e.g., *Jepson v. Canadian Salt Company*, [1979] 4 WWR 35 (Alta. SCTD).

Registered Shareholders/Beneficial Owners of Shares

The dissent and appraisal rights may be exercised by a "holder of shares." This language implies a "registered" holder, not a beneficial owner of shares. It is noteworthy that although certain other provisions of the CBCA were amended in 2001 to explicitly refer to beneficial owners, as well as registered shareholders, no such change was made to the dissent and appraisal section.

However, in *Lake & Co. v. Calex Resources Ltd.*,[83] the Alberta Court of Appeal did effectively permit non-registered shareholders to exercise appraisal rights. The court confirmed that the statute, by its terms, extended the protection of the appraisal remedy only to registered shareholders. Indeed, the court recognized that there were good policy reasons for limiting the remedy to registered holders.[84] This was not the end of the story, though. The corporation in *Calex* had sent an information circular to its shareholders in connection with the shareholders' meeting that had been called to approve the transaction in question. The court found that that information circular was misleading because it did not make clear that the corporation had taken the position that only registered shareholders would be entitled to dissent. Thus, the court ruled that the beneficial owners of shares who gave notice of their intention to dissent before the shareholders' meeting would, indeed, be entitled to an appraisal remedy.

At first blush, the Court of Appeal's conclusion may seem perplexing. After all, why should it be necessary for a corporation to state, explicitly, that "its position" is that only registered shareholders are entitled to exercise dissent rights when, as the Court of Appeal acknowledged, it is the corporate statute itself that imposes this limitation? The court was clearly influenced, however, by the fact that the circular, on its face, anticipated that it would come into the hands of beneficial owners of shares. In fact, the circular referred to the fact that many shares of the corporation were not registered in the names of the beneficial owners. (Recall from chapter 12 that many shares of Canadian public corporations are held through a depository; thus, smaller shareholders of public corporations almost invariably will be beneficial owners, not registered holders, of shares.) Thus, the circular appeared to have been written as though it were intended to be read by beneficial as well as registered shareholders. Yet, it did not, in the court's view, clearly indicate that only registered shareholders would be entitled to exercise appraisal rights. This omission was serious. Beneficial owners of shares would not necessarily be aware of what steps they would need to take to become registered holders so that they could exercise their appraisal rights. Thus, although the court in *Calex* did not base its decision on the principle of estoppel, the reasoning is very similar to an estoppel argument: the actions of the corporation were such that it would be unfair to permit the corporation to rely on what would otherwise be its legal right to limit the appraisal remedy to registered shareholders.

A somewhat more intriguing issue is whether a shareholder may buy shares in a corporation for the very purpose of exercising a dissent right. In *Silber v. Pointer Exploration Corp.*,[85] the Alberta Court of Queen's Bench suggested that this was permissible,

---

83   [1996] AJ no. 772 (QL) (CA).

84   Ibid., at para. 47.

85   [1998] AJ 903 (QL) (QB).

at least in a case where the information circular delivered in connection with the meeting
at which the fundamental change would be voted on did not specify that dissent rights
could be exercised only by shareholders of record as of the record date set for delivery of
notice of the meeting.

Determination and Payment of "Fair Value"

The appraisal remedy entitles a dissenting shareholder to receive "fair value" for his or
her shares. What, precisely, is "fair value"? And by whom is it calculated?

Valuation of any asset is difficult. Valuation of intangible assets, like shares, is especially challenging. The court will not necessarily be required to determine the fair value
of dissenting shareholders' shares. In the first instance, it is the obligation of the corporation to calculate the fair value of the shares to be purchased, and to make an offer to
purchase the dissenting shareholders' shares at that amount, including with the offer an
explanation of how the value was determined.[86] If the dissenting shareholders accept the
price offered by the corporation for their shares, that is the end of the matter.

However, things may not run quite so smoothly. The CBCA specifically permits either
the corporation[87] or the dissenting shareholders[88] to apply to the court to have the court
fix fair value. Courts, needless to say, are not valuation experts. The CBCA does authorize the court to appoint one or more appraisers "to assist the court"[89] in making the value
determination. But the Ontario Court of Appeal has made it clear, in interpreting equivalent language in the Ontario *Business Corporations Act*, that the court is not obliged to
appoint an appraiser.[90] Moreover, it is clear that, if an application is made to determine
fair value, neither the dissenter nor the corporation bears the burden of proof. It is for the
court to determine the value, based on "the evidence, the pleadings and in the exercise of
its judgment."[91] As the Court of Appeal put it in *Smeenk v. Dexleigh Corp.*,

> It is the judge's job to assess the value of the shares, but it is the duty of the parties to
> present evidence to assist him in his assessment.[92]

Accordingly, appraisal cases frequently include judicial discussion about the proper
valuation of corporate shares,[93] and the various methods that have been adopted by
valuers and the courts to this end.[94] For our purposes, it is sufficient to observe that the

---

86   CBCA, s. 190(12).

87   CBCA, s. 190(14).

88   CBCA, s. 190(15).

89   CBCA, s. 190(21).

90   *Smeenk v. Dexleigh Corp.* (1993), 15 OR (3d) 608 (CA).

91   *Ford Motor Company of Canada, Ltd. v. Ontario Municipal Employees Retirement Board* (1997), 36 OR
     (3d) 384 (CA).

92   Supra footnote 90, at 612.

93   See, e.g., *Re Wall & Redekop Corp. et al.*, [1975] 1 WWR 621 (BCSC) and *Canadian Gas and Energy
     Fund Ltd. et al. v. Sceptre Resources Ltd.* (1985), 61 AR 67 (QB).

94   For a discussion of the competing valuation methods, see Nicholls, supra footnote 7, at 345.

valuation exercise is not a straightforward one, and so adds a layer of uncertainty on top of the procedural complexities of the dissent and appraisal remedy.

It has been found, in a narrow set of circumstances, that while there is an ongoing dispute about the value of dissenters' shares, the dissenting shareholders may be permitted to obtain partial summary judgment where the corporation has made an admission of the *minimum* fair value of those shares.[95] However, merely making an offer to dissenting shareholders (as the corporation is, after all, required by statute to do) is not, in and of itself, such an admission of value.[96] This conclusion is sensible because it is, after all, possible that the fair value ultimately fixed by the court will actually be lower than the offer made by the corporation.[97] Moreover, as the courts have observed, construing a corporation's offer as an admission of this sort would create unfortunate incentives for corporations to make unreasonably initial low offers.[98]

An Exception for Public Company Shares?

In many American corporate statutes, the appraisal remedy is not available to shareholders of public companies whose shares trade on established securities exchanges.[99] The philosophy underlying this exemption is simple enough: if a shareholder of a publicly traded corporation objects to a fundamental change approved by the majority, he or she can easily end his investment in the corporation by selling his or her shares. The inclusion of such a "market exception" in some American statutes is said to have been influenced by a 1962 academic paper written by Bayless Manning.[100] The Dickerson committee regarded such an exception as inappropriate in the Canadian context, owing to two factors: the trading market for Canadian securities was thinner than in the United States; and in many corporations large blocks of shares might be held that could not be easily liquidated.[101]

---

95 *Roytor & Co. v. Skye Resources Ltd.*, [1986] OJ no. 25 (QL).

96 Supra footnote 91.

97 *Smeenk v. Dexleigh*, supra footnote 90 and *New Quebec Raglan Mines Ltd. v. Blok-Andersen* (1993), 9 BLR (2d) 93 (Ont. Gen. Div.). Both of these cases were cited by the Ontario Court of Appeal in *Ford Motor Company of Canada, Ltd. v. Ontario Municipal Employees Retirement Board*, supra footnote 91.

98 See, e.g., *Ford Motor Company*, ibid.

99 See, e.g., Delaware *General Corporation Law*, s. 262(b)(1):

> (1) Provided, however, that no appraisal rights under this section shall be available for the shares of any class or series of stock, which stock, or depository receipts in respect thereof, at the record date fixed to determine the stockholders entitled to receive notice of and to vote at the meeting of stockholders to act upon the agreement of merger or consolidation, were either (i) listed on a national securities exchange or designated as a national market system security on an interdealer quotation system by the National Association of Securities Dealers, Inc. or (ii) held of record by more than 2,000 holders; and further provided that no appraisal rights shall be available for any shares of stock of the constituent corporation surviving a merger if the merger did not require for its approval the vote of the stockholders of the surviving corporation as provided in subsection (f) of §251 of this title.

100 Manning, supra footnote 11. John Howard notes the significance of Manning's essay in the drafting of US provisions in "The Proposals for a New Business Corporations Act for Canada: Concepts and Policies," in *Special Lectures of the Law Society of Upper Canada 1972* (Toronto: Richard de Boo, 1972), 17, at 49.

101 Ibid.

COMPLIANCE ORDERS

When a shareholder acquires shares in a corporation, he or she expects that the corporation will abide by the rules it has set for itself—in its articles and its bylaws—as well as by the rules imposed on it by its governing statute and even, where relevant, by any unanimous shareholder agreement. To be sure, the provisions of the articles, bylaws, and shareholder agreements may be amended at any time if the proper procedures for amendment are followed. But unless and until such amendments are made, the corporation has no right to stray from the existing provisions.

What happens if a corporation does act in violation of its corporate instruments? We will say nothing here about the infamous *ultra vires* doctrine. More than enough has been said about that subject in chapter 6. Although, theoretically, a corporation might be prosecuted for acting in breach of the incorporating statute itself,[102] prosecutorial resources are limited, and the breach by corporations of their governing statutes is likely to rank very low on the priority list of government officials. Moreover, it is unlikely that shareholders would generally be pleased to see the corporation prosecuted. Any fines payable by a corporate scofflaw would simply detract from the value of the corporation itself and thus would decrease, not increase, the value of the shareholders' investment. It is not punishment that the shareholder looks for in such cases. It is simply compliance.

Traditionally, in memorandum jurisdictions—such as the United Kingdom—where the memorandum and articles of association are said to constitute a contract, members of the corporation were understood to have the right to bring an action for the enforcement of the corporate compact. Indeed, such a right was recognized by the Supreme Court of Canada in *The Theatre Amusement Co. v. Stone*.[103] But, as the Lawrence committee observed in their 1967 report, the status of shareholders of corporations in jurisdictions where corporate laws follow an alternative model of incorporation has been much less clear. Recognizing this ambiguity, the Lawrence committee recommended that a specific provision be added to Ontario's corporate statute providing to shareholders the right to enforce the corporation's "constitution."[104] This recommendation was accepted, and a compliance provision was added to Ontario's corporate statute. That provision subsequently became the basis for a similar provision in the CBCA,[105] which is now found in s. 247. The basic features of s. 247 are:

- *Status to seek order*: A compliance order may be sought by a "complainant" (the same defined term used for purposes of the derivative action and oppression remedy) *or* by a creditor of the corporation.

---

102 See, e.g., CBCA, s. 251: "Every person who, without reasonable cause, contravenes a provision of this Act or the regulations for which no punishment is provided is guilty of an offence punishable on summary conviction." CBCA s. 16(2) provides: "(2) A corporation shall not carry on any business or exercise any power that it is restricted by its articles from carrying on or exercising, nor shall the corporation exercise any of its powers in a manner contrary to its articles." Thus, failure by a corporation to act in accordance with its articles or the CBCA itself would constitute an offence under the Act.

103 (1915), 50 SCR 32, at 36-37.

104 *Interim Report of the Select Committee on Company Law* (Toronto: Province of Ontario Legislative Assembly, 1967), at para. 8.1.3 (Lawrence committee report).

105 See Dickerson committee, supra footnote 1, at para. 493.

- *Subjects of compliance order*: A complainant or creditor may apply to the court for an order to restrain the breach of any of the following: the CBCA; the articles of the corporation (a term that includes not only the articles of incorporation but also articles of amendment, articles of amalgamation, articles of continuance, articles of reorganization, articles of arrangement, articles of dissolution, and articles of revival[106]); the bylaws of the corporation; or a unanimous shareholder agreement.[107] Such an order may be sought against the corporation itself, or any director, officer, employee, agent, auditor, trustee, receiver, receiver-manager, or liquidator.

Some early Ontario case authorities suggested that a compliance order was available only to correct simple mechanical omissions, and only if the relief claimed was personal to the complainant, and not derivative in nature.[108] That authority was the subject of some criticism.[109] In a recent Alberta case, the court held that neither of these limitations should apply to the court's discretion to grant a compliance order.[110]

A shareholder, creditor, or other complainant seeking a compliance order and nothing else will not be entitled to monetary relief. Accordingly, although a compliance order may seem to offer some advantages to aggrieved shareholders in a limited range of circumstances,[111] it would be unusual for the incentive to seek such a remedy (at least in isolation) to outweigh the burdens of making such an application. However, under certain circumstances a compliance order may seem to offer an appropriate and reasonably convenient remedy.

"WINDING-UP" ORDERS

At one time, winding up the corporation was the only remedy available to minority shareholders of a private corporation seeking to extricate themselves from an unworkable business relationship. A disgruntled shareholder would have little choice under such circumstances but to apply to the court to have the corporation wound up (that is, liquidated and dissolved). If the court were satisfied that there were "just and equitable grounds" for granting such extreme relief, the order would be granted.

---

106 See CBCA, s. 2(1), definition of "articles."

107 A unanimous shareholder agreement, as discussed in chapter 4, is specifically defined in the CBCA to mean an agreement as described in s. 146(1), or a declaration as described in s. 146(2). See the definition of "unanimous shareholder agreement" in CBCA, s. 2(1). Unlike an ordinary shareholders' agreement, which is merely a contract between the parties, a unanimous shareholder agreement, as so defined, enjoys a status akin to that of the corporation's constating documents (i.e., its articles and bylaws). See supra footnote 23.

108 *Re Goldhar and Quebec Manitou Mines Ltd.* (1976), 61 DLR (3d) 612 (Ont. Div. Ct.).

109 See, e.g., Welling, supra footnote 81, at 59-60 and R.L. Campbell, "Summary Enforcement of Directors' Duties: *Re Goldhar and Quebec Manitou Mines Ltd.*" (1978), 2 *Canadian Business Law Journal* 92.

110 *Caleron Properties Ltd. v. 510207 Alberta Ltd.*, [2001] 3 WWR 323 (Alta. QB).

111 See, e.g., *Fidelity Management & Research Co. v. Gulf Canada Resources Ltd.* (1996), 27 BLR (2d) 135 (Ont. Ct. Gen. Div.).

The term "winding up" is of English origin. It is often used by Canadian corporate (as opposed to tax or insolvency) lawyers somewhat loosely and perhaps inaccurately.[112] The term "winding up" does not, in fact, appear in the CBCA. The term "winding up" is, however, used in other Canadian corporate statutes, including the Ontario *Business Corporations Act*, which still provides in s. 207(1)(b) that a corporation may be "wound up" if a court is satisfied that it is "just and equitable" to do so. And, of course, the term is still used in the federal *Winding-Up and Restructuring Act*,[113] a statute that is of particular importance to financial institutions. Accordingly, although caution is advised in the use of the term in Canada today, for the remainder of this section, the term "winding up" will be used, notwithstanding that—at least with respect to CBCA corporations—the term "liquidation and dissolution" is, strictly speaking, more accurate.

When a corporation is "wound up," all of the corporation's assets are sold. After the payment of its outstanding debts, any remaining proceeds from the asset sale may then be distributed to the shareholders in accordance with their relative share interests. When the orderly process of winding up (or perhaps winding down) the corporation's business is completed and its assets have been distributed, the corporation will be formally dissolved, and its artificial corporate "life" brought to an end.

Thanks to the expansion of alternative shareholders' remedies, especially the highly flexible oppression remedy discussed in chapter 13, the circumstances in which aggrieved shareholders feel obliged to seek (and courts are prepared to grant) a winding-up order have narrowed considerably. Indeed, although the CBCA, for example, still provides in s. 214 that a shareholder may apply for a winding-up order, this provision is now critically linked to the oppression remedy. That is, an aggrieved, and perhaps vindictive, shareholder—determined to force a winding up—cannot circumvent the more flexible provisions of the oppression remedy by choosing only to launch a winding-up application. Section 214 specifically states that when an application is initiated under that section, the court is free, nevertheless, to make an order under s. 241 (that is, the oppression remedy provision) if it sees fit.[114]

Similarly, note that one of the orders a court is specifically empowered to make under the oppression remedy provision is an order "liquidating and dissolving the corporation."[115] An applicant seeking an oppression remedy is permitted, under the oppression

112   Tax practitioners, in particular, note that the term is used in the *Income Tax Act*, but in a somewhat technical sense, and not as a synonym for liquidation and dissolution. The phrase appeared in the English *Joint Stock Companies Act* of 1844. It was also included in the title of a 19th century Canadian statute, *The Winding Up Act*, at a time when Canada had no bankruptcy legislation. Thus, as Wegenast notes, "up to 1920 the winding-up of companies for insolvency, as well as for other causes, took place under the Winding-up Act." F.W. Wegenast, *The Law of Canadian Companies*, reprinted with an introduction by Margaret P. Hyndman (Toronto: Carswell, 1979), at 100. The current version of the *Winding-Up Act* is now entitled the *Winding-Up and Restructuring Act*. See footnote 113, infra.

113   RSC 1985, c. W-11. For a brief discussion of this statute and its place within the framework of the Canadian insolvency regime, see The Insolvency Institute of Canada, *The Winding-Up and Restructuring Act: Recommendations for Reform*, A Report of the Insolvency Institute of Canada (June, 2000). Available online at http://www.insolvency.ca/papers/REPORT4.doc.

114   CBCA, s. 214 (2).

115   CBCA, s. 241(3)(l).

remedy section, to apply in the alternative for a winding-up (or, more correctly, "liquidation and dissolution") order under s. 214.[116] Moreover, the provisions of s. 242, which apply to applications made under the oppression remedy section (and other applications under part XX of the CBCA), are also specifically made applicable to applications for a winding-up order.[117]

Finally, the grounds on which a court may order that a corporation be wound up include grounds essentially identical to those on which an oppression remedy may be based.[118] These grounds were included following a recommendation of the Dickerson committee aimed at relieving the overly restrictive judicial gloss that had developed on the concept of winding up on just and equitable grounds, as discussed briefly below.[119]

Winding Up "On Just and Equitable Grounds"

In addition to the oppression-like grounds for winding up contained in s. 214(1)(a), there are two other bases set out in s. 214(1)(b) on which winding up may be ordered. The first confirms that a provision in a unanimous shareholder agreement that entitles a shareholder to call for a corporation to be dissolved when a triggering event occurs can, indeed, be the basis for a winding-up order.[120] The second is much broader in scope. It reads as follows:

> (b) if the court is satisfied that ...
>   (ii) it is just and equitable that the corporation should be liquidated and dissolved.[121]

As discussed above, historically, "just and equitable grounds" were the only basis on which winding-up orders were made. The Dickerson committee recommended retention of the "just and equitable" basis for the granting of a winding-up order as a "residual provision" that would ensure that "a useful fund of case law is not discarded."[122] Though they cited no specific examples, they suggested that this case law indicated two recurring situations of just and equitable grounds for dissolution: (1) shareholder deadlock (a perennial problem in two-shareholder corporations in which each shareholder holds exactly 50 percent of the voting shares) and (2) controlling-shareholder or director overreaching that borders on fraud.[123]

There are statutory provisions allowing for dissolution on just and equitable grounds in most provincial partnership statutes as well. There is little doubt that the English corporate law cases on the subject are heavily influenced by partnership-type considerations. A lengthy canvass of English and Canadian cases on the subject of winding up on

---

116 CBCA, s. 241(7).

117 CBCA, s. 214(3).

118 CBCA, s. 214(1)(a).

119 Dickerson committee, supra footnote 1, at paras. 453, 455.

120 CBCA, s. 214(1)(b)(i).

121 CBCA, s. 214(1)(b)(ii).

122 Dickerson committee, supra footnote 1, at para. 455.

123 Ibid.

just and equitable grounds was recently undertaken by MacDonald CJTD of the Prince Edward Island Supreme Court Trial Division in *Re Hillcrest Housing Ltd.*[124]

When Wegenast wrote his influential text on Canadian corporate law in 1931, he suggested that English cases on the "just and equitable" ground for winding up included instances where the shareholders were in deadlock, where the "substratum" of the corporation's business had gone, where the corporation was hopelessly unprofitable, where the majority shareholder had misappropriated profits, or where the directors had taken certain actions that caused the shareholders to lose confidence in them.[125] Curiously, though, he suggested that "the Ontario Courts, for reasons which it is difficult to assign, have failed to follow the English decisions."[126]

Section 214 Versus Voluntary Dissolution

One final point to be made here is that s. 214 is a remedial provision. It is not, however, the only provision in the CBCA that authorizes the dissolution of a corporation. A corporation may be dissolved voluntarily—not because of any irreconcilable dispute among its members, but simply because it is no longer thought to serve any useful purpose. Some cavalier solicitors in the past were rumoured to have counselled clients who no longer had need of a corporate entity simply to cause the corporation to dispose of all of its assets, have all officers and directors resign, and then, as the corporation defaulted on its filing and fee obligations, simply allow the government to wind up the unneeded entity and thus save the fees that must otherwise be paid to complete a voluntary liquidation. This rather untidy way of handling things seems to represent the corporate law equivalent of abandoning an unwanted vehicle at the side of the road for others to dispose of. For a host of reasons, this approach to voluntary winding up is ill-advised, if not reckless. The voluntary liquidation procedure for a small shell company is, in any event, quite simple and inexpensive.

INVESTIGATION ORDERS

An investigation order is not a remedy. However, the ability to obtain such an order provides a means by which prospective litigants who suspect wrongdoing by corporate insiders may acquire further information that would otherwise be exclusively within the possession of those very insiders. The investigation order is thus closely linked to the corporate remedies that have been discussed in this chapter and in chapter 13.

The CBCA's investigation order provisions are found in part XIX of the statute. The Dickerson committee considered that investigations would serve two purposes: to help protect shareholders against mismanagement of the corporation, and, more broadly, to protect the public interest.[127] The Dickerson committee envisioned that an investigation

---

124 [1998] PEIJ no. 57 (QL) (PEISCTD).

125 Wegenast, supra footnote 112, at 103.

126 Ibid.

127 Dickerson committee, supra footnote 1, at paras. 464-465. It was this latter public interest concern that prompted the Dickerson committee's recommendation that the Director be specifically permitted to apply to the court for an investigation order.

order could be an extremely useful tool for helping to uncover information about corporate mismanagement that, as they put it, "is, by its very nature, likely to be known by the suspected wrongdoers and unlikely to be known or voluntarily disclosed to those seeking to complain."[128]

The mechanics of seeking an investigation order are relatively straightforward. However, the courts have demonstrated some understandable wariness about granting this sort of order. Application for an investigation order may be made by a securityholder (that is, a shareholder or a holder of a debt security) or by the CBCA Director.[129] The Dickerson committee imagined that most investigation orders would, in fact, be sought by the Director. And, in any event, under the committee's original proposals, an investigation order could be sought by shareholders only if they held at least 5 percent of the issued shares of a class. Under the CBCA today, a shareholder seeking an investigation order (or, for that matter, any securityholder seeking such an order) is not required to hold any specified number or amount of the corporation's securities. Given that the court will order an investigation only where there actually appears to be impropriety, it seems proper that any shareholder, no matter how small his or her share interest, ought to be entitled to apply for such an order.

Once such an application has been made, the court may order an investigation of the corporation *or its affiliates* if it appears to the court that

(a) the business of the corporation or any of its affiliates is or has been carried on with intent to defraud any person,

(b) the business or affairs of the corporation or any of its affiliates are or have been carried on or conducted, or the powers of the directors are or have been exercised in a manner that is oppressive or unfairly prejudicial to or that unfairly disregards the interests of a security holder,

(c) the corporation or any of its affiliates was formed for a fraudulent or unlawful purpose or is to be dissolved for a fraudulent or unlawful purpose, or

(d) persons concerned with the formation, business or affairs of the corporation or any of its affiliates have in connection therewith acted fraudulently or dishonestly.[130]

One thus notes that an investigation order will not be made unless it appears to the court that some impropriety has occurred. Thus, as the Ontario Divisional Court stated in *Ferguson v. Imax*:[131]

[T]he section clearly requires the court to conclude that it appears that the business or affairs of the corporation have been conducted in a manner that is oppressive or unfairly prejudicial to or that unfairly disregards the interests of the applicant before an investigation may be ordered. It is not enough that there has been a complaint made by a security holder, or that there is some evidence of oppressive conduct. The court must examine the evidence and make a finding that it appears that there has been oppressive conduct. The court cannot

---

128 Dickerson committee, ibid., at para. 464.

129 CBCA, s. 1(1), definition of "security," and s. 234(1).

130 CBCA, s. 229(2).

131 (1984), 47 OR (2d) 225 (Div. Ct.).

direct that the investigation be made in order to assist the court in making such finding. The finding must be made before the investigation can be directed.[132]

If the court believes it appropriate to make an investigation order, an inspector will be appointed, and will exercise those powers determined by the court in the order. These powers can be very broad. They may include, for example, the power to conduct a hearing, including powers to compel witnesses to attend and give evidence under oath, as well as powers to compel production of documents and to enter premises, examine anything found there, and take copies of documents or records.[133]

One point should be emphasized: the purpose of an investigation order is to find facts, not to adjudicate legal issues. That purpose is implicit from the language of the statute, and has been reiterated by the courts.[134] Thus, courts have declined to make an investigation order where it is the legal implications of corporate conduct, and not the facts, that are under dispute. In such circumstances, the court has noted, it would be more appropriate for the applicant to launch a lawsuit seeking the desired remedy.

One obvious practical advantage of the investigation order procedure for aggrieved securityholders is that the court is empowered to order the corporation itself to pay the costs of such an investigation.[135]

The basis on which an investigation order may be granted was discussed in a recent Ontario decision, *Catalyst Fund General Partner I Inc. v. Hollinger Inc.*[136] In that case, shareholders of Hollinger Inc. sought an investigation order to obtain information concerning related-party transactions entered into between Hollinger Inc. and certain of its officers. Campbell J granted the investigation order, basing his decision on, among other things, "the legitimate expectations of all the minority shareholders of [Hollinger] Inc. ... to be satisfied that the matters of related-party payments will be not only investigated but reported on fully and promptly."[137] Contrasting the concept of reasonable expectations in the context of an oppression remedy to the concept in the context of an application for an investigation order, Campbell J noted:

> In the case of inspection relief, there must be at the very least an index of suspicion or appearance that reasonable shareholder expectations have not been met in viewing the actions or non-actions of management and directors.[138]

Campbell J did note, however, that inspection orders must not be made lightly, because they are both costly and intrusive,[139] and that the threshold test to be met by applicants "involves more than mere suspicion of impropriety."[140]

132 Ibid., at 232-33.
133 CBCA, ss. 230(1)(c)-(g).
134 See, e.g., *Re Royal Trustco Ltd. (No. 3)* (1981), 14 BLR 307 (Ont. HCJ).
135 CBCA, s. 230(1)(j).
136 [2004] OJ no. 3886 (QL) (SCJ).
137 Ibid., at para. 37.
138 Ibid., at para. 39.
139 Ibid., at para. 49.
140 Ibid., at para. 57.

CONCLUSION

Corporations are generally bound by the same legal rules to which natural persons are subject. When corporations do not honour their contracts, for example, they may be sued for breach of contract and they are subject to normal contract remedies. Similarly, when they commit torts, they may be sued in much the same way as natural persons. The special corporate law remedies discussed in chapter 13 and in this chapter are not meant to supplant those traditional forms of action. However, in certain instances where the corporate form itself might otherwise prove to be an obstacle to justice, Canadian corporate statutes provide an important range of special civil remedies. Though it is the corporation's shareholders for whom these remedies have primarily been designed, some, as we have seen, may also be available to other corporate stakeholders. The development of these remedies has increasingly come to define the balance of power between majority and minority shareholders, corporate "insiders," and third parties dealing with the corporation.

Index